Abolition

A History of Slavery and Antislavery

In one form or another, slavery has existed throughout the world for millennia. It helped to change the world, and the world transformed the institution. In the 1450s, when Europeans from the small corner of the globe least enmeshed in the institution first interacted with peoples of other continents, they created, in the Americas, the most dynamic, productive, and exploitative system of coerced labor in human history. Three centuries later, these same intercontinental actions produced a movement that successfully challenged the institution at the peak of its dynamism. Within another century, a new surge of European expansion constructed Old World empires under the banner of antislavery. However, twentieth-century Europe itself was inundated by a new system of slavery, larger and more deadly than its earlier system of New World slavery. This book examines these dramatic expansions and contractions of the institution of slavery and the impact of violence, economics, and civil society on the ebb and flow of slavery and antislavery during the last five centuries.

Seymour Drescher is University Professor of History and Sociology at the University of Pittsburgh. He has taught at Harvard University and was Distinguished Professor at the Graduate Center of the City University of New York. Dr. Drescher has also been a Fulbright Scholar, an NEH Fellow, and a Guggenheim Fellow, and he was both a Fellow and the inaugural Secretary of the European Program at the Woodrow Wilson International Center for Scholars. Among his many works on slavery and abolition are *Capitalism and Antislavery* (1986); *From Slavery to Freedom* (1999); and *The Mighty Experiment* (2002), which was awarded the Frederick Douglass Book Prize by the Gilder Lehrman Center for the Study of Slavery, Resistance, and Abolition in 2003. He has also co-edited a number of books, including *A Historical Guide to World Slavery* (1998) and *Slavery* (2001).

Abolition

A History of Slavery and Antislavery

SEYMOUR DRESCHER

University of Pittsburgh

CAMBRIDGE
UNIVERSITY PRESS

CAMBRIDGE UNIVERSITY PRESS
Cambridge, New York, Melbourne, Madrid, Cape Town, Singapore, São Paulo, Delhi

Cambridge University Press
32 Avenue of the Americas, New York, NY 10013-2473, USA

www.cambridge.org
Information on this title: www.cambridge.org/9780521600859

First published 2009

Printed in the United States of America

A catalog record for this publication is available from the British Library.

Library of Congress Cataloging in Publication data
Drescher, Seymour.
Abolition : a history of slavery and antislavery / Seymour Drescher. – 1st ed.
p. cm.
Includes bibliographical references and index.
ISBN 978-0-521-84102-3 (hardback) – ISBN 978-0-521-60085-9 (pbk.)
1. Slavery – History.   2. Antislavery movement – History.   I. Title.
HT861.D74   2009
306.3'6209 – dc22   2009006849

ISBN   978-0-521-84102-3 hardback
ISBN   978-0-521-60085-9 paperback

To Abiona, Samuel, and Jesse

Contents

Preface

As an institution of global proportions, slavery's fortunes rose and fell over the course of half a millennium. This book examines the intercontinental interaction of violence, economics, and civil society in accounting for the ebb and flow of slavery and antislavery. For thousands of years before the mid-fifteenth century, varieties of slavery existed throughout the world. It thrived in its economically and culturally developed regions.[1] The institution was considered indispensable for the continued functioning of the highest forms of political or religious existence. It set limits on how a social order could be imagined.

Beyond the organization of society, enslavement was often conceived as the model for the hierarchical structure of the physical universe and the divine order. From this perspective, in a duly arranged cosmos, the institution was ultimately beneficial to both the enslaved and their masters. Whatever moral scruples or rationalizations might be attached to one or another of its dimensions, slavery seemed to be part of the natural order. It was as deeply embedded in human relations as warfare and destitution.

By the sixteenth century, however, some northwestern Europeans began to recognize an anomaly in their own evolution. Jurists in the kingdoms of England and France noted that slavery had disappeared from their realms. They claimed that no native-born residents were subject to that status. Although slavery might be recognized elsewhere as one of the normal facts of social relations, their own laws had ceased to sanction it. A "freedom principle" was now operative, for both their own native-born residents and even foreign slaves who reached their legal jurisdictions ceased to be slaves.[2]

---

[1] For a lucid overview of these themes see David Brion Davis, *Slavery and Human Progress* (New York: Oxford University Press, 1984), Part One, and Davis, *Inhuman Bondage: The Rise and Fall of Slavery in the New World* (New York: Oxford University Press, 2006), ch. 2.

[2] For some summaries of the "freedom principle," see Sue Peabody, *There Are No Slaves in France: The Political Culture of Race and Slavery in the Ancien Régime* (New York:

The jurists of this freedom principle necessarily viewed their emancipatory enclave as a peculiar institution. Beyond their own "free air" or "free soil," slavery remained a recognized legal status. There was no question that if the subjects of their realms entered zones of enslavement, they might still be reduced to the status of chattel.

For more than three centuries after 1450, Europeans, Asians, and Africans helped to sustain and expand slavery. Western Europeans did so far beyond their own borders. By 1750, some of their imperial extensions were demographically dominated by slaves to a degree unprecedented anywhere on earth. Their colonies were sites of systematic exploitation unparalleled in their productivity and rates of expansion.

At the end of the eighteenth century, this robust transoceanic system entered a new era of challenge, spearheaded by the emergence of another northwestern formation – organized antislavery. On both sides of the Atlantic, residents of the world's most dynamic and efficient labor systems were also among those most committed to the extension and consolidation of the freedom principle. In the course of little more than a century, between the 1770s and the 1880s, that vast transoceanic extension of slavery created after 1450 was dismantled. The transatlantic slave trade that had once loaded more than 100,000 Africans per year was abolished. By the 1880s, the institution of slavery was abolished throughout the New World.

Then, in a second wave of European expansion from the 1880s to the 1930s, imperial dominion operated under the banner of antislavery, not slavery. By the early twentieth century, the institution's former quasi-universal status as a normal element of human existence had been revisioned as an institution fated for inexorable extinction. A world without slaves was now a casually accepted premise of human progress.

That was hardly the end of the story, however, during the second quarter of the twentieth century, slavery dramatically reappeared on the very continent that had prided itself as humanity's engine of emancipation against a "crime against humanity." For a brief moment, Europe housed the largest single slave empire in five centuries of modern history.

Viewing these centuries of slavery, this book poses a number of questions. How did societies with the least involvement in slavery "at home" manage to create overseas extensions with the highest percentages of human chattel in the history of the world? How did new civil and political formations within and beyond Europe turn the tide of human affairs against that slave system at the very peak of its performance? How did a second age of empire-building

Oxford University Press, 1996); and Seymour Drescher, *Capitalism and Antislavery: British Mobilization in Comparative Perspective* (New York: Oxford University Press, 1987), ch. 1, 2. For recent overviews of the *long durée* of slavery see *Women and Slavery*, 2 vols., Gwyn Campbell, Suzanne Miers, and Joseph C. Miller, eds. (Athens, OH: Ohio University Press, 2007–2008); and *Slave Systems Ancient and Modern*, Enrico dal Lago and Constantina Katsari, eds. (New York: Cambridge University Press, 2008).

in the Old World construct a more ambiguous emancipation strategy under the banner of imperial antislavery? And, how did antislavery's vanguard continent reconstruct slavery in the twentieth century?

The examination of any complex process over so vast a period of world history produces a pervasive awareness of any single historian's limitations. In this project, I have had to wander far beyond the line of my comfort zone and the major areas of my own previous research. It is nearly impossible to master the cascade of scholarship that has inundated the fields of slavery and abolition during the past half century of historiography.[3] I have been compelled to rely, as never before, on colleagues quite close to home. For their generous comments and caveats, I offer my deepest thanks to many members of that close-knit collective that is our History Department: Reid Andrews; William Chase; Alejandro de la Fuente; Christian Gerlach; Van Beck Hall and Patrick Manning, who read portions of this study in their areas of expertise. My dean, John Cooper, generously provided me with that invaluable ingredient at a critical moment – free time. My secretary, Patty Landon, efficiently moved the manuscript through the inevitable stages of fine tuning. A number of our graduate research students offered me substantial research and bibliographical assistance: Karsten Voss, Delmarshae Sledge, Bayete Henderson, and Jacob Pollock. Margaret Rencewicz helped to compile the index.

The footprints of those who aided this study are abundantly evident in the footnotes. I must, however, single out two individuals. As he invariably has done since the first draft of my first venture into the history of slavery, my dear friend and critic, Stanley Engerman of the University of Rochester, read the entire manuscript in its initial (and rough) draft. He was generously seconded by Frank Smith of Cambridge University Press on the final version of the manuscript.

Because I speak so frequently of fifty-year segments of historical change in this study, it seems appropriate to note that its publication marks half a century of scholarship. I take this opportunity to recall the departed who determined my trajectory toward and within the writing of history: Hans Kohn at the City College of New York; and George L. Mosse at the University of Wisconsin. Nor can I omit, among the living, David Brion Davis of Yale University, with whom I have remained in continuous dialogue for four decades.

Finally, I thank Ruth, as, and for, always.

---

[3] I have attended less to East Asian slavery in this study of the global rhythms of slavery and antislavery. China, Korea, and Japan all exhibited their own variants of the institution. For the most part, their institutions followed internal cycles, independent of developments beyond the region. Where I did find congruences, I attempted to incorporate them into this account.

PART ONE

EXTENSION

I

A Perennial Institution

In March 1844, an English traveler in Morocco presented himself to the governor of Magador. James Richardson announced that he was the agent of a "Society" for promoting "the Abolition of Slavery and the Slave Trade in Every Part of the World." His mission was to petition the Emperor of Morocco to join all men in all parts of the world in abolishing a traffic "contrary to the rights of Men and the Laws of God." The governor replied that Richardson's mission was "against our religion; I cannot entertain it, think of it or interfere with it in any way whatever." The purchase and sale of slaves was authorized by the Prophet himself. If the governor were even to accept the petition, he told Richardson, the Sultan, he claimed, would order the governor's "toungue to be cut from my mouth." Moreover, recorded the Englishman, were the Moroccan Emperor to agree with the Society and abolish the traffic in slavery throughout his dominions, all the people would rise in revolt against him and the Emperor would be the first to have his head cut off. The governor, he concluded, "politely declined to receive the petition."[1]

In March 1844, the governor of Magador was not alone in refusing to receive petitions requesting the abolition of the slave trade or slavery. In 1840, the U.S. House of Representatives, after years of vituperative debate, enacted a rule prohibiting that body "from receiving, much less considering, antislavery petitions."[2] In 1842, the Moroccan ruler himself had dismissed a far more modest request from the British Consul-General. The British government requested information on any measures that the Sultan had taken toward the abolition of the African slave trade. The Sultan responded that the traffic was a "matter on which all sects and nations have agreed from the time of Adam".... And, because "no sects and nations

---

[1] PRO Fo84 540 (Slave Trade) fols. 103–106.
[2] William W. Freehling, *The Reintegration of American History*, 199–200. This "gag rule" endured until the end of the 1844 session.

disagreed on the subject, its acceptability required 'no more demonstration than the light of day.'"[3] Nor could anyone dream, when James Richardson was conversing with the governor of Magador, that precisely a century later there would be more slaves toiling in his own civilized continent than in all the plantation societies of the Americas.

No one in the first half of the nineteenth century would have challenged the Sultan on the antiquity of slavery. In the 1850s, American Southern writers and politicians could accurately avow that free labor societies were still a "little experiment" emanating... from "a corner of Western Europe" and, thus far, a "cruel failure." As late as the 1790s, English abolitionists could still be dismissed in Parliament as quixotic dreamers for their effrontery in proposing to abolish trading in slaves along a large segment of the coast of Africa. One noble lord sarcastically dismissed the proponents of the prohibition as megalomaniac "emperors of the world" for imagining that sweeping lines of demarcation could be drawn on a map of the earth, prohibiting a trade as old as humanity.[4]

A few decades earlier this attitude was common even among enlightened reformers. Adam Smith cautioned his Scottish students not to mistake their society as exemplary in the matter of slavery. Their own small corner of the world was the only area from which slavery had slowly disappeared. Less than a millennium earlier, Europe itself had been a major supplier of slaves to the Muslim World. The men, women, and children who were led as captives across the Alps and the Mediterranean were then the most valuable commodities underdeveloped Europe could offer to Islamic Africa and Asia.

Modern scholarship has increasingly detailed the nuances, complexities, and variations of an institution in whose name communities acquired, maintained, and reproduced people deprived of the protections of kinship or legal status that were available to other members of the community. At the moment of acquisition, and often for the remainder of their lives, they were subordinate individuals with limited claims on the society in which they lived and died. Their bodies, their time, their service, and often their children were available to others, as sources of labor, pleasure, and management, or as objects of violence.

Historians have long recognized a large cluster of analogous institutions and relationships extending across the globe and over millennia as variations on a condition called slavery. The most crucial and frequently utilized aspect

---

[3] See Bernard Lewis, *Race and Slavery in the Middle East: An Historical Enquiry* (New York: Oxford University Press, 1992), 3.

[4] On Southerners, see Russell B. Nye, *Fettered Freedom: Civil Liberties and the Slavery Controversy 1830–1860* (1963), 304, 308, 309, quoted in Robert Fogel, *Without Consent or Contract* (1989), 343; and David Eltis, *Rise of African Slavery* (2000), 4. On the English dismissal of abolitionist pretentions at the end of the nineteenth century, see Seymour Drescher, *Capitalism and Antislavery: British Mobilization in Comparative perspective* (New York: Oxford University Press, 1987), 268 n.13.

of the condition is a communally recognized right by some individuals to possess, buy, sell, discipline, transport, liberate, or otherwise dispose of the bodies and behavior of other individuals. Within this definition would fall individuals who might be agents of supreme political power, such as eunuchs of an emperor's court. They might be incorporated into an elite band of warriors as the mainstay of imperial authority and military expansion. Their lives could be materially abundant or miserable. They might be pampered sexual servants of the wealthy. They might be short-term captives whose main value was as subjects of elaborate ritual sacrifice or as candidates for deadly medical experiments. They might be subject to rulers, corporate institutions, or individual members of a society. They might serve economic, military, sexual, reproductive, or religious ends. Such individuals were, at least initially, unprotected by ties to the community. Slaves were usually designated as outsiders, either by the fact of initial captivity, purchase, or inherited status.

Exit from the status of dependency might depend upon the choice of masters and be constrained by higher authority and communal sanctions. In small, relatively isolated societies, potential enslavability might be ascribed to almost any non-member.[5] Historians and social scientists may focus on any one of a number of criteria that were significant markers of the institution in their specific areas of interest. David Brion Davis, concerned with New World slavery, emphasizes the crucial status of slaves as chattel. Other scholars have highlighted aspects of slavery in which proprietary claims are less significant markers of the status. For comparative purposes, I will have occasion to look briefly at examples of bondage in which proprietary claims for coercive control of other individuals were absent. In the Soviet Gulag system, for example, lifetime servitude was not a component of submission to forced labor. Captives not condemned to death were allotted terms of imprisonment.[6]

---

[5] On the range of relationships see, inter alia, Orlando Patterson, *Slavery and Social Death: A Comparative Study* (Cambridge, MA: Harvard University Press, 1982); and *Freedom in the Making of Western Culture* (New York: Basic Books, 1991); David Brion Davis, *Inhuman: Bondage: The Rise and Fall of Slavery in the New World* (New York: Oxford University Press, 2006), esp. chapter 2; Stanley L. Engerman, *Slavery, Emancipation and Freedom: Comparative Perspectives* (Baton Rouge: Louisiana State University Press, 2007), part one, sec. III; *Slavery in Africa: Historical and Anthropological Perspectives*, Suzanne Miers and Igor Kopytoff, eds. (Madison: University of Wisconsin Press, 1977); Ehud F. Toledano, *As If Silent and Absent: Bonds of Enslavement in the Islamic Middle East* (New Haven: Yale University Press, 2007); and *Slave Systems: Ancient and Modern*, Enrico dal Lago and Constantina Katsari, eds. (Cambridge: Cambridge University Press, 2008), Part I, 1–102.

[6] See Oleg V. Klevniuk, *The History of the Gulag: From Collectivization to the Great Terror* (New Haven: Yale University Press, 2004), 290–291. I include the Gulag as exemplary of the great expansion of coercion in the Eastern hemisphere during the second quarter of the twentieth century.

Many historians of slavery have taken as their point of departure the distinction between *societies with slaves* and *slave societies* as crucial for understanding the emergence and evolution of slavery. These theoretical categories were developed over decades of research and interpretation into various types or stages of the institution. They have been applied to both its New and Old World variants. In this division of the institution, the phrase societies with slaves applied to societies where slaves were generally held in smaller aggregates, often in household units. The enslaved were marginal to the most value-adding economic activities. In societies with slaves, the distinction between slaves and other subordinate groups is portrayed as more porous and ambiguous than in slave societies. Slave societies are, therefore, deemed to have lower rates of exit from enslavement via individual manumission. In such societies, slaves would be less likely to be attached to households or to family units. The lower ratio of slaves to non-slaves would require less highly organized policing systems. And, in the more feminized domestic systems of slave societies, large-scale collective resistance would be less frequent.

In slave societies, the dominant social groups depended far more upon the wealth generated by slave labor. In their large-scale units of production, it was more difficult for enslaved individuals to achieve freedom, much less enter the slave-owning class. Above all, in slave societies, slavery became the normative model of social relationships at the center of economic production. For Moses Finley, who initially articulated the distinctive characteristics of slave societies, it was the dual *location* of slaves, at the centers of both production and power, that provided the key to understanding the emergence and maintenance of a slave society.[7] In Finley's initial perspective, apart from ancient Athens and Roman Italy, slave

---

[7] See Moses Finley, "Slavery," *International Encyclopedia of the Social Sciences* (New York, 1968); and *Ancient Slavery and Modern Ideology* (New York: Viking Press, 1980, expanded edition, 1998), (*quotes on pp. 80–82*); 79–82; for the extension of the dual model to the New World see Ira Berlin, *Many Thousands Gone: The First Two Centuries of Slavery in North America* (Cambridge, Mass: Harvard University Press, 1998), 8–9. Many regions of Africa, where slaves represented a quarter to half of the population, would clearly qualify for what Finley called slave societies. Those most engaged in commercial agriculture had proportions of slaves that equaled or exceeded those of ancient Roman Italy or the lower antebellum southern United States. Muslim societies in North Africa and Asia, where slaves might account for less than 10 percent of the inhabitants, experienced no internal pressure to abolish the institution before the mid-nineteenth century. For the most recent and thorough discussion of comparative approaches to slave systems in world-historical context, see Enrico Dal Lago and Constantina Katsari, "The Study of Ancient and Modern Slave Systems: Setting an Agenda for Comparison," in *Slave Systems: Ancient and Modern*, Dal Lago and Katsari, eds. (Cambridge: Cambridge University Press, 2008), 3–31. For a systematic comparative perspective on processes of individual and collective deliverance from slavery, see above all, Olivier Pétré-Grenouilleau, "Processes of Exiting the Slave Systems: A Typology," *ibid.*, 233–264.

societies were confined to certain parts of the Americas in the four centuries after 1500.

The chronology of slavery's successive expansions and abolitions might point us in another direction. For those interested in the expansion and pro-hibitions of the institution from a global perspective, both slavery and the long-distance slave trade endured longest and most uninterruptedly in parts of the world with presumably less impact from slavery than those usually designated as slave societies. Whether located in areas usually designated as slave societies or societies with slaves, the institution was entrenched in the Old World far longer than in its modern New World variants. Slavery was widely diffused throughout Africa, Asia, and the Mediterranean until the twentieth century. For a millennium after the collapse of the Western Roman Empire, states within its former orbit sanctioned slavery. The eighteenth-century sources of Old World abolitionism would arise chiefly in areas that were distinguished by not being centers of an otherwise ubiquitous institution.

In other words, the heuristic value of the distinction between slave soci-eties and societies with slaves may be more useful in examining relationships and behavior between zones of slavery than in accounting for the rise and fall of the institution itself. In every society with a system of slavery, one must devote equal attention to the processes of enslavement and reproduc-tion as well as the ease of exit from the institution by way of flight or armed resistance. A system with extremely high rates of manumission logically pre-scribes a high demand for fresh captives with all of the corresponding mor-tality, morbidity, family disintegration, individual psychological trauma, material deprivation, and insecurity entailed in that process. So, what may appear as relatively mild bondage for the enslaved within any society may look more like a plunge into disorientation, deprivation, and degradation for recruits from without. In this work, slave systems will be approached primarily in terms of the degree to which they retarded or facilitated the growth or destruction of the institution or its components.

Historically, three aspects of slavery stand out as starting points in any intercontinental account of slavery and abolition. The first is slavery's obvi-ous antiquity, ubiquity, and durability. Certain characteristics of the insti-tution endured in most areas of the world. They persisted despite short-term shifts – demographic and economic crises, or political, cultural, and social upheavals. Another important characteristic of slavery was that it was remarkably transferable across time and space. Roman slave law left its imprint wherever the major Mediterranean civilizations spread. It would be reconstituted in the colonial Americas, South Africa, the Indian Ocean world, and Eurasia. It would be regenerated in zones of devastating warfare, in busy port cities, or in booming agricultural frontiers. During the first mil-lennium of the Common Era, the institution of slavery was clearly a shared institution in all regions linked by cultural affiliation with the monotheistic tradition and Roman civil law. Like Judaism, Christianity and Islam viewed slavery as immutable as marriage and human warfare. These traditions, in turn, drew upon older traditions inherited from Mesopotamia and the Mediterranean. All of their successive heirs sanctioned enslavement arising from conflict, purchase, or birth. All sought to regulate and delimit its scope. All developed codes for recruitment, enforcement, and exit.

David Brion Davis has long since traced the network of beliefs and rationalizations about slavery inherited from the ancient Mediterranean and Near Eastern worlds. Aristotle furnished two millennia of statesmen and theologians with the philosophic justification of slavery. The Church fathers, especially St. Augustine, linked bondage to the inherited penalty for sin. What is most remarkable about the ancient world's surviving commentaries on slavery is their relative brevity and infrequency. Aristotle's is the only surviving ancient attempt at a formal justification of slavery. Whether or not human beings might be unjustly enslaved, there was only one condition on which Aristotle could imagine the institution's disappearance: masters could do without slaves when "each instrument could do its own work...as if a shuttle should weave of itself and a plectrum should do its own harp-playing."[8] Most commentaries were geared towards improving, mitigating, or even glorifying slavery. An outstanding example was the embedding or imbuing of religious doctrine with metaphors of slavery. Saint Paul and early Christian leaders drew upon Jewish and other Levantine traditions to designate themselves and their followers as slaves of God or Christ. Christians or Muslims could locate themselves in the same relationship of powerless subjection to the all-powerful deity as the slave to his owner. Because even highly positioned slaves were never exempt from both physical and symbolic degradation, reliance on the metaphor "bolstered the acceptability of slavery in the real world and increased the ammunition of those who wished to regard it as a natural human institution."[9]

Nowhere in Christianity, from Byzantium to Britain, was there a diminution of the salvational value allotted to spiritual enslavement to Christ

---

[8] See David Brion Davis, *The Problem of Slavery in Western Culture* (Ithaca: Cornell University Press, 1958), ch. 3. On the rarity of extended analysis of ancient slavery, see Finley, *Ancient Slavery*, 117–118. The quotation from Aristotle is from *The Politics of Aristotle* Ernest Barker, trans. (Oxford: Clarendon Press, 1948), 12.

[9] Keith Bradley, *Slavery and Society at Rome* (New York: Cambridge University Press, 1994), 153. The master-slave bond could signify a supremely loving relationship as well as a form of degradation. For Isaiah, slavery was biblically linked with his prophetic power: "This is my slave, whom I uphold, my chosen one, in whom I delight. I have put my spirit upon him." Isaiah 42:1, quoted in Catherine Hezser, *Jewish Slavery in Antiquity* (Oxford: Oxford University Press, 2005), 328. Slavery was a path to salvation. Christian bishops and Byzantine officials used the old Latin and Greek words *servus* or *doulos*, to refer to their exalted status in church and state. Although other terms, especially "prisoners" (*captives*) came to designate those who were newly enslaved as chattel in the traditional sense, there was no abandonment of the traditional terms from the honorific concept of slavery.

or to worldly slavery as a penance with salvational potential. Well after 1500, visitors to Russia still recorded inhabitants as describing themselves as servants and slaves. Muscovite magnates claimed the exclusive right to be called the sovereign's slaves. At the same time, the very real degradations of enslavement were "God's scourge." Of course, alongside the narratives of glorious enslavement ran parallel narratives of glorious liberation and freedom. Eighteenth-century Italians or Britons, "redeemed" from Muslim corsairs, were celebrities in elaborate public rituals that reenacted their salvation from social death to their restored status as free Christians.[10]

Earlier Roman laws' formulaic acknowledgment of man's natural liberty were likewise linked to later messages of physical and spiritual liberation drawn from biblical narratives. The *Qur'an's* analogous proclamation of freedom as man's natural status could be matched by Christian scholastic declamations, linking Gospel texts with natural law theory to demonstrate Christ's "perfect law of liberty" and the "natural liberty by which men are naturally free and not slaves." These extrapolations of both sacred slavery and holy freedom were clearly compatible with the continuation of slavery as an institution even where slavery had virtually vanished as a real social relationship. Medieval writers seemed "blind to the implications of their own Christian psychology when they related to problems of servitude and religious freedom." Even the English Common Law left open the question of captive slavery long after there were no longer any legally identifiable bondsmen in England.[11]

Western Europeans began to shift the locus of their self-perceptions to the libertarian side of the equation by the end of the Middle Ages. Throughout much of western Europe, rural populations gradually and sometimes violently established their freedom from customary and heritable bondage. Early modern European legal traditions shifted property rights in both goods and labor to the individual, recognized as an independent contractual agent. Rural peasants, as well as elites, eliminated the positive valuation of slavery and grounded their claims to liberation in Christian teachings and general assertions of human dignity, liberty, and equality. When fifteenth-century

[10] Bradley, *Slavery and Society at Rome*, 89; Richard Hellie, *Slavery in Russia 1450–1725* (Chicago: University of Chicago Press, 1982), passion; Marshall T. Poe, *"A People Born to Slavery": Russia in Early Modern European Ethnography* (Ithaca: Cornell University Press, 2000), 216–219; David A. Pelteret, *Slavery in Early Medieval England: From the Reign of Alfred until the Twelfth Century* (Rochester, NY: Boydell Press, 1995), 89; Robert C. Davis, *Christian Slaves, Muslim Masters: White Slavery in the Mediterranean, the Barbary Coast, and Italy, 1500–1800* (New York: Palgrave Macmillan, 2003), 176; Linda Colley, *Captives* (New York: Pantheon Books, 2002), 78–79.
[11] Brian Tierney, "Freedom and the Medieval Church," in *The Origins of Modern Freedom in the West*, R. W. Davis, ed. (Stanford: Stanford University Press, 1995), 94–95; and J. H. Baker, "Personal Liberty under the Common Law," in ibid, 190.

peasants in Catalonia mobilized to demand an end to the "bad customs" of bondage, their argument was grounded in a notion of Christian liberation. Christ's sacrifice did not just free humanity from original sin, but restored it to its original liberty. Using the Roman law analogy, naturally free human beings had not been enslaved by original sin, but by the law of nations. In Spain, bondage had been the outcome of a Christian holy war. During the reconquest of Spain, rulers purportedly inflicted servitude upon resisting Muslim inhabitants to induce them to convert. What had been only a temporary stimulus had abusively become, according to the peasant thesis, a sustained violation of natural law and of the divine precept that bound human freedom to Christianity.[12] Catalonian peasants thus offered a historical and Christian gloss to the famous abstract principle of Roman law: man was free by nature and slavery was legitimized only by the laws of nations. In such narratives, elaborated by elite scribes and invoked by late medieval peasants, Christianity was dissociated from servility.

Catalonian peasant claims for freedom grounded in natural and Christian liberty constituted no direct assault on the institution of slavery itself. The peasants' argument was embedded in the specific history of the Christian reconquest of Iberia. The conquest narrative actually sustained the idea of slavery as appropriate for infidels. Servitude was the consequence, not of sin in general, but of specific unbelief. For peasants, as well as for crusading warriors, the premise of a frontier with mutually enslaving enemies legitimized slavery and rationalized its reproduction through a "just war" conquest. The peasants made their bid in terms of inclusion with fellow believers in the status of liberty. Their lords acknowledged that their servile exactions were "bad customs," and finally accepted the premise that their Christian peasants were not slaves.

The general thrust of western European institutional and ideological development before 1500 was toward the recognition of the peasantry as part of the community of freemen. "Rustics, no matter how contemptible in the eyes of the elite could not be regarded consistently as alien in the same sense of infidels" or heretics. In this struggle to redefine the boundaries of servitude, the antagonists had neither motive nor need to proceed to more universal arguments. Their mutual narrative assented to the consensual premise that some are free and others slaves.[13]

Further to the north, in England, a similar consensus among native born inhabitants held that "contract lay at the heart of the relationship between

---

[12] Paul Freedman, *The Origins of Peasant Servitude in Medieval Catalonia*, (New York: Cambridge University Press, 1991), 191–192.

[13] Paul Freedman, *Servitude*, 217; Compare with Charles Verlinden, "Orthodoxie et esclavage au bas moyen age," *Melanges Eugène Tisserant* V (2) (Vatican: Biblioteca Apostolica Vaticana, 1964), 427–456.

the late medieval English servant and his or her employer." All service fell along a spectrum of constraint from slavery and serfdom to free agency. Within the contract, freedom could still entail penal sanctions. Bond servants were subject to the authority of the lord and could be punished for failure to fulfill services to which they had freely assented.[14]

The rash of fifteenth-century English statutes enacted to curtail wage levels, decrease labor mobility, and enforce contracts against employees may have made the end of serfdom a mixed blessing for the workers in the short run. Masters could invoke public sanction for non-fulfillment of service from the Statute of Labourers in 1349 to the repeal of the Masters and Servants Act in 1875.[15] "Unfree" labor, however, was not a form of slavery. Both slavery and serfdom in England were vacated, rather than abolished. The fact that slaves could no longer be identified in England by the end of the sixteenth century was to be more significant for the ending of Western slavery than the fact that masters continued to constrain freemen to labor.[16]

This overview of Mediterranean Islam and Western Christianity at the beginning of the era of European transoceanic exploration and expansion reveals already differentiated zones with regard to slavery. The general premise, on both sides of the religious line, was that the followers of Christ and Muhammed did not enslave their own believers. That principle, developed at an earlier point in Islamic law, had become roughly articulated through nearly a millennium of frontier conflict across and around the Mediterranean and the Black Sea. However, the religious frontier remained a porous one. The normative guidelines for the recruitment, maintaince, and manumission of slaves were frequently disobeyed.

In areas of Muslim rule, the principle of holy war (*jihād*) beyond the Islamicized line and non-enslavement within the line of Islamic domination both delimited and encouraged enslavement. Beyond the frontier of Dar al-Islam, non-Muslims were fair game for enslavement. Fulfillment of the Qur'anic admonition to open paths to manumission ensured a steady demand for fresh captives. On the other side of the religious line, analogous and similarly unevenly obeyed inhibitions had developed within

---

[14] See Robert J. Steinfeld, *The Invention of Free Labor: The Employment Relation in English and American Law and Culture, 1350–1870* (Chapel Hill: University of North Carolina Press, 1991). At the point of contract, servant and master stood in a position of voluntary assent. P. J. P. Goldberg, "What was a Servant," in *Concepts and Patterns of Service in the Later Middle Ages* (Boydell Press), 9–10.

[15] See Robert J. Steinfeld, *The Invention of Free Labor*, and Steinfeld, *Coercion, Contract, and Free Labor in the Nineteenth Century* (New York: Cambridge University Press, 2001).

[16] For a similar disappearance of slaves, except on galleys, in France before the mid-seventeenth century, see Sue Peabody, *"There Are No Slaves in France": The Political Culture of Race and Slavery in the Ancien Regime* (New York: Oxford University Press, 1996), ch. 1.

Christian-dominated areas. Centuries of conflict and reconquest intermittently sharpened the fault line.[17] Whether one looks upon them as slave societies or societies with slaves, the complex of slave laws, slave markets, and benefits accruing to slaveholders offered ample incitement for the perpetuation and extension of enslavement.

Muslims suffered enslavement to other Muslims in North Africa. Muslims were also offered by Muslims as slaves to Christians. In Iberia, the Valencian kingdom's legal code provided for enslavement as the penalty for free Mudejar (Muslims) found guilty of crimes ranging from attempts at unauthorized movement from the kingdom to failure to honor a civil contract for repayment of a debt. Muslims were allowed to pledge their own children as collateral, with obvious consequences for default. The presiding judge was often a Muslim *qādi* (judge). Those who violated the code of *shari'a* (holy law) through offenses that called for the death penalty could have their sentences commuted to slavery by the courts. Many convicts were redeemed by local co-religionists. Those enslaved for committing severe offenses against Mudejar mores, such as theft or adultery, were usually handed over for slavery.[18]

At the beginning of the early modern period, what most distinguished Iberia from northwestern Europe was the actual presence of slavery and a functioning slave law. In this respect, Spain more closely resembled other Mediterranean and later transatlantic slave societies than the Christian societies of northwestern Europe. Hispanic law, *Las Siete Partidas,* drawing from the Roman and Justinian slave codes, recognized birth, self-alienation, and especially war as valid grounds for enslavement. Like its predecessors, *Las Siete Partidas* recognized the natural freedom of human beings. In addition, it protected the marital bond, allowed appeals against abusers, and provided for punishing murderers of slaves and adjudicating slave appeals for a change of masters. It set general legal and moral boundaries for the institution and provided legal procedures for exiting from slavery via manumission. The Roman law principle that human beings were "naturally" free was interpreted by jurists to mean that, other things being equal, judges were to favor freedom.[19] The code's primary purpose, then, was to rationalize, not abolish, slavery. As elsewhere, high rates of manumission meant further incentives for the slave trade.

The pervasive impact of the institution may be gauged by two incidents. At the end of the fifteenth century, Europeans were still being enslaved by other Europeans. This situation lasted, with diminishing frequency, for two more

---

[17] Alphonse Quenum, *Les églises chrétiennes et la traite atlantique du xve au xixe siècle* (Paris: Karthala, 1993), 51.

[18] *Ibid.,* 59.

[19] Alejandro de La Fuente, "Slave Law," *Law and History Review* (2004), 22 (2): 356.

centuries. In terms of enslavability, Europe was not a single unit nor were its inhabitants a single unenslavable people. In 1370, at the heart of Latin Christianity, Pope Clement V proclaimed that captured enemy Venetians would be sold as slaves.

Further east, European slavers found alternatives whenever one or another source of captives dried up for religious or military reasons. When the enslavability of Orthodox Greeks by western Europeans became more uncertain, traders turned to Muslim Albanians, Bosnians, and Bogamils. Well into the seventeenth century, Christian Russians, Moscovites, Lithuanians, and Poles were still enslaving each other's war captives. Prisoner exchanges of Russians with Poles and Lithuanians became the rule only in the second quarter of the seventeenth century. Within the rapidly expanding empire of Muscovy, voluntary self-enslavement allowed masters to own and sell Orthodox Christians without endangering the souls of these slaves. Russian slavery shared some characteristics of its Muslim neighbors to the South and East. Slave soldiers on the Muslim model were recruited until the mid-sixteenth century.[20]

The concept that Eastern Orthodox Christians were more susceptible to servitude remained current among Europeans well into the period of transatlantic colonization. During the English occupation of Tangier in the 1670s, the Royal Navy captured a Moorish vessel. The commander sold the Negro captives on board and kept the Greeks for use as oarsmen in English galleys.[21] At the same moment, Jean-Baptiste Colbert was issuing instructions in the name of Louis XIV to transfer captured Greek galley slaves to French vessels. In the view of the French minister, the captives were schismatic subjects of the Ottoman ruler.

Within western Europe itself, the possibility of enslaving heretics was raised by the emergence of Protestantism. In response to the Dutch uprising against Phillip II, Balthasar de Ayala, jurist of international law, advocated placing the rebels beyond the pale of Christian liberty. In *De iure et offices bellicis,* published in the Netherlands in 1582, he invoked biblical injunctions to cast the rebels within the orbit of Holy War penalties. Heresy was to be allowed no quarter. Those who were not consumed in "fire and blood" could be deprived of their possessions and enslaved.[22]

Sixty years later, the English Civil War stimulated similar responses. The Earl of Stamford proposed that royalist military prisoners who refused to join the Parliamentary forces be sold to the Barbary pirates as slaves. Oliver Cromwell himself threatened Scots and Irishmen with enslavement

---

[20] Richard Hellie, *Slavery in Russia,* 39.
[21] Aylmer, "Slavery under Charles II," *English Historical Review* (1999), 114 (456): 378–388, p. 381.
[22] Cited in Geoffery Parker, *Success is Never Final* (Basic Books, 2002), 139–140.

if they continued their resistance.[23] Neither Phillip II nor Cromwell ever reduced their opponents to chattels, but the intermittent wartime discourse on enslavability suggests that western Europeans of the sixteenth and seventeenth centuries had by no means been converted to the notion that all fellow Europeans or fellow Christians were exempt.

In assessing the boundaries of early modern enslavement in Europe, the Jewish diaspora offers an interesting perspective on the cultural and geographical boundaries of the institution. Throughout the Mediterranean, Jews were at best tolerated minorities in a world defined primarily by religion. The most significant moment in the history of early modern European Jewry came near the end of the fifteenth century. In 1492, Spanish Jewry, comprising the largest single Jewish population in Europe, were offered a choice between conversion to Christianity, expulsion, and death. Significantly, the options considered by the Spanish rulers did not include enslavement. Ferdinand and Isabella certainly did not decide against enslavement on the grounds that Jews were fellow European residents. Muslims in Spain were still among the legally enslaved population within their domains. The Spanish monarchs did not opt for the forcible enslavement of Jews for the same basic reason that had made them decide in favor of expulsion. They feared that the large number of "Conversos," (Jews already converted to Christianity), would be tempted by the unconverted to retain their Jewish practices and affiliations. More enslavement might only exacerbate religious contamination and pollution of "the blood."

Mass enslavement, however, clearly remained within the policy range of Iberian monarchs at the end of the fifteenth century. This was demonstrated almost immediately after the Spanish expulsion of the Jews. The Portuguese king placed a price on each Jewish refugee fleeing from Spain. Large numbers of refugees, however, too poor to pay, illegally crossed the border. King Joao then declared the defaulting Jews to be his slaves. In neighboring Spanish Valencia, enslavement for such default was already an ongoing practice among non-Christians. The Portuguese king's enslavement of the Jewish migrants was not symbolic. Thousands of Jewish children were quickly seized from their parents and shipped off to create a new colony off the coast of Africa in Sao Tomé. Five years later, under Spanish pressure, the remaining refugees in Portugal were forcibly converted. Children were again seized en masse and used as hostages in the coercive process.

Jewish texts themselves tell us as much about the range and limits of Mediterranean slavery beyond Iberia. Early in the seventeenth century, Leone da Modena's book on Jewish religious practices, *Historia dei riti Ebraicé*, devoted a brief chapter to slavery. In the *"Levant* or *Barbary,"* he noted, Jews held and sold slaves, "according to the custom of the place

---

[23] Charles Carlton, *Going to the Wars: The Experience of the British Civil Wars* 1638–1651 (London: Routledge 1992), 253.

in which they live."[24] This was a traditional extension of the Halachic principle, that the "law of the land is the law" in all non-religious matters. He
made no mention of the institution among the small pockets of Jewry in
Europe.

Equally useful in this respect are the texts analyzed by Jonathan Schorsch
to describe the institutional practices of post-expulsion Sephardic Jewry
and of later "New Christians," as they made their way back into southern
Europe. In areas with a clearly functioning institution of slavery, Sephardic
Jews negotiated to retain the right to enter territories with their slaves and to
retain them. This was mainly because Italian slave codes contained restrictions against the ownership of slaves by Muslims or Jews.[25] The grants of
residency explicitly set aside their prohibitions on Jewish slave ownership.
Communal pacts with Ferrara, Florence, Savoy, Pisa, and Livorno contained
such exemptions.

North of the Alps, whether under Catholic or Protestant rule, some char-
ters issued to Jews mentioned their right to bring or own slaves. When
the English considered allowing Jewish reentry in the 1650s, however, the
rules on servants contained only a prohibition against hiring Christians as
domestic servants. In Northern Germany, the city of Glückstadt offered only
permission to hire free servants.[26]

Because nothing in seventeenth-century Jewish law prohibited the ownership of slaves, the regional variations are to be attributed to differences
in the dominant "law of the land." Jews were not allowed to sustain slave
ownership within any state where it no longer existed. The North/South
distinctions in slaveholding among Jews thus coincided with the actual presence or absence of slave law in a given European polity. By the time of the
Spanish expulsion at the end of the fifteenth century, the Mediterranean and
northwestern zones of Europe had clearly taken divergent paths.

During periods of violent crisis and revolution, even northwestern European rulers and jurists could still imagine enslavement as a potential threat
against rebels and enemies. In practice, however, they did not turn to the
expedient of reinstating hereditary slavery within their realms. Spain and
Portugal continued slavery at home, as well as overseas, for almost two
centuries before the beginning of northwestern European colonization. As
we shall see, this European division would become a source of tension when
overseas Christian masters brought their personal slaves across to Europe.
All colonizing metropoles that did not explicitly sanction slavery at home

---

[24] Leone da Modena, *History of the Present Jews Throughout the World* [*Historia dei riti
Ebraiċe*] (London, 1650). See also Jonathan Schorsch, *Jews and Blacks in the Early Modern
World* (New York: Cambridge University Press, 2004), 174–175.

[25] Steven Epstein, *Speaking of Slavery: Color, Ethnicity and Human Bondage in Italy* (Ithaca:
Cornell University Press, 2001), 157.

[26] Schorsch, *Jews and Blacks*, 53–63.

were to experience some tension in sustaining the distinction between slavery abroad and non-slavery at home.

This forecast the significance of the presence or absence of slave law, institutions, and enslaved people in the long term fate of the institution of slavery. Colonizing northern European states would have to adapt to new overseas variations of the institution. Along the Mediterranean lay the traditional counterparts of Christian-Muslim slavery. The doctrines of *jihād* and Holy War, with their unchallenged justifications of infidel enslavement, contributed to an unbroken institutional linkage of enslavability. In one respect, slavery was, therefore, more ubiquitously embedded in the fabric of Muslim societies than in northwestern European societies by the early sixteenth century.

Here, one can use Moses Finley's analytical emphasis on the critical location of slaves in a given society. Early modern Mediterranean slavery was more important to the centers of power and wealth in the Maghreb and the Ottoman Empires than to European rulers and elites. The sixteenth-century Ottoman Empire, like many of its predecessors, recruited soldiers, administrators, sexual partners, and heirs from among captive infidels. In the western Mediterranean, Muslim rulers and merchants relied upon slaves as principal sources of both wealth and power.[27] At the western edge of Islam, Christian captives played a vital role in the economies and societies of the North African states. Many of their enslaved population were obtained as military captives from sub-Saharan Africa or Eastern Europe. Others were victims of piracy and raids on the shores of lands inhabited by Europeans. Slaves thus contributed heavily to the labor and capital of the Maghrebian and Ottoman lands. Many were held for resale and ransom. Others were fit into varied niches of the local economy and domestic households. The rulers and upper layers of society on the Barbary coast appear to have been even more dependent upon slavery as a source of revenue than were their European and Ottoman counterparts.

As a wealth-and-power generating enterprise, corsair fleets of North Africa, like those of the later New World plantations, required continuous replenishment. Corsairs needed rowers to power their fleets, and captives to elicit ransoms from their captives' kin, communities, or rulers. As ransom payments became more important to the Maghrebian economy relative to the value of permanently retained slaves, their rulers were especially eager to exchange elite captives for ransom. Maghreb ports were culturally more cosmopolitan than those on the Mediterranean's northern shore. Algiers' 40 percent native Maghrebians were embedded in a larger cohort of slaves, refugee families, janissaries, renegades, and mixed offspring, which probably could not have been matched for diversity by any European port

[27] Y Hakan Erdem, *Slavery in the Ottoman Empire and its Demise* (New York: St. Martin's Press, 1996), ch. 1 and 2.

of the sixteenth and seventeenth centuries. Slaves in the Muslim world were drawn from all frontiers of Islam: sub-Saharan Africa; trans-Mediterranean Western Europe; the Balkans; the non-Muslim hinterlands beyond the Black Sea; the Caucasus region; and Central Asia. The proportion of slaves going to and coming from each area varied with the military situation of Islam relative to the *Dār al-Harb* – the abode of war. If one extrapolates from Ralph Austen's estimates of slave imports to Lybia and Egypt, the North African tier of Islam was probably receiving 6,000 Africans a year from across the Sahara in the early modern period. During periods of rapid expansion, like that of the Ottomans in the fifteenth and sixteenth centuries, conquest brought huge surges of captives directly into the slave markets of the empire. The sack of Mahon in Minorca in 1534 produced 6,000 slaves. After its fall, the entire population of Lipari, amounting to 12,000 souls, was boarded for the slave markets. Between such extraordinary flows, a steady stream of enslaved captives moved northward from sub-Saharan Africa.[28]

Whatever the relative proportions of slaves distributed among the wide range of Muslim occupations – domestics, artisans, agricultural laborers, concubines, soldiers, and eunuchs – it is apparent that slavery was as deeply embedded in Islam in 1500 as it had been three-quarters of a millennium before. However modulated the pronouncements on good treatment in the *Qur'an*, the enslavability of unbelievers, particularly "pagans" (*mushrikūn*), was an implicit assumption for most of the Islamic commentators.[29] Muslims were also frequently captured by other Muslims, and turned up in slave markets. Some of the most troubled thought in Islamic literature was stimulated by the frequent enslavement of fellow Muslims This perspective was not restricted to captives at Islam's frontiers. Although sixteenth-century slaves in Anatolia were usually Russians or Ukrainians, the chief legal counsel during the Ottoman-Iranian wars of Süleyman the Magnificent declared that heretical Shiites should not be regarded as Muslims. Those so denounced were frequently enslaved, and those who were enslaved were denounced as infidels at the time of capture.[30]

Of course, slaves could be and were much more than "property with a voice" (*mal-i-natik*). "A lowly government official who became a wazir

---

[28] Jacques Heirs, *The Barbary Corsairs* (2001), 196. Hunwick, "Black Slaves in the Mediterranean World," in *Slavery and Abolition*, 11.

[29] See Ralph Austen, "The Mediterranean Islamic Slave Trade out of Africa: A Tentative Census," in *Slavery and Abolition* 13:1 (1992), 214–248 and "The 19th Century Islamic Trade from East Africa (Swahili and Red Sea Coasts): A Tentative Census," in *Slavery and Abolition* 9:3 (1988), 21–44.

[30] William Gervase Clarence-Smith, *Islam and the Abolition of Slavery* (Oxford: Oxford University Press, 2006), 42–45; Humphrey J. Fisher, *Slavery in the History of Muslim Black Africa*, (New York: New York University Press, 2001), ch. 1, 29; and (Surauja Faroghi, *Subjects of the Sultan: Culture and Daily Life in the Ottoman Empire* (London: I. B. Taurus, 2000), 63.

narrated his metamorphosis in the passage of a single night's sleep from possessing nothing the day before freedom to awakening the owner of horses, mules, camels, property (māl), and slaves. (mamálik)."[31] But, in the social and legal world of Islam they all shared the vulnerability of a liminal condition. Unlike free residents who could appeal to networks of family, locality, or community, slaves had only the law to reinforce their claims. Freedmen who prospered as slaveowners inevitably perpetuated the institution that opened the path to their own mobility. In every major power center in Islam, the elite were the principal, but not the exclusive owners of the slaves in their midst.[32] Consensually, then, the institution was sanctioned by the the *sharī'a* of Islam, as well as by the Roman law of all nations. Wherever one places them along the spectrum of slave societies to societies with slaves, a society without slaves never emerged in the Muslim states before the mid-nineteenth century.[33]

In sub-Saharan Africa, the institution was distinctive in a different way. When the Europeans first entered into direct and continuous contact with sub-Saharan societies during the fifteenth-century, they immediately grasped the importance of slavery as an institution beyond the frontier of *Dár al - Islam*. Finley's characterization of slavery's place in Greco-Roman antiquity holds equally true for much of tropical Africa: "there was no action or belief or institution that was not affected by the possibility that someone involved might be a slave." John Thornton concludes that the distinctiveness of African legal traditions is crucial in analyzing Euro-African relations. In contrast to Europe, "slaves were the only form of private, revenue-producing property recognized in African law."[34] By contrast, in early modern Europe, the primary form of revenue-producing property was land.

Lauren Benton, in an extensive survey of world legal systems, has countered that Thornton exaggerates the differences and overlooks the similarities between the two legal systems. In her perspective, it "is not clear that the *concept* of ownership in many African kingdoms was radically different from what it was in *Las Siete Partidas* in Iberia." If African nobles ultimately derived their rights and wealth from positions in the state,

---

[31] Shaun E. Marmon, "Domestic Slavery," in *Slavery in the Islamic Middle East*, Shaun E. Marmon, ed. (Princeton: M. Wiener, 1999), 10.

[32] Seng, "A Liminal State," in *Slavery in the Islamic Middle East*, Shaun E. Marmon, ed. (1999), 25–42.

[33] Hunwick, "Black Slaves in the Mediterranean World: Introduction to a Neglected Aspect of the African Diaspora," in *Slavery and Abolition*, 13:1 (1992), 5–38. Lewis, *Race and Slavery*, ch. 8; and John R. Willis, ed., *Slaves and Slavery in Muslim Society*, 2 vols. (London: F. Cass, 1985), I, 27–46.

[34] Finley, *Ancient Slavery*, 65; and John Thornton, *Africa and the Africans in the Making of the Atlantic World* (New York: Cambridge University Press, 1992), 74.

"the holders of captaincies and *encomenderos* in the Atlantic islands and the Americas derived their powers over native laborers in the same way."[35]

Whether or not the concept of ownership was analogous, Benton's argument overlooks the fact that the *encomienda* system was introduced by the Spanish monarchy as an alternative to allowing European settlers to legally treat the natives of the New World as enslaved chattels. Thornton's argument, focusing on the relative value of African property in persons in relation to property in land, attempts to account for "the remarkable speed with which the continent began exporting slaves" as soon as the first seaborne contact occurred between Europeans and sub-Saharan Atlantic Africa. Europeans directly tapped into the long-standing trans-Saharan trade and diverted some of the internal African trade to the Atlantic.[36] The reverse certainly did not occur regularly. Despite the deportation of children to São Tomé in the 1490s and convicts to other overseas areas for four centuries thereafter, Europeans and North Africans did not replicate this pattern.

Thornton's fundamental point bears pondering. Slavery was rooted in the legal, institutional, and economic structure of many societies. In sub-Saharan Africa, however, slaves were the principal form of capital. Their enslavement and exchange were linked to the most dynamic segments of the African economy.[37] The possession of such captives was, as in many Muslim societies, an efficient way of increasing power and status. Slaves could be acquired in wars or raids without having to permanently occupy territory. Within Africa they were placed in all sectors of the economy: as agricultural laborers, recruits for the military, and carriers of other commodities on commercial routes. Warrior states relied heavily on enslaved armies and slave administrators to keep regional nobilities in check and to sustain revenue flows by creating kin-free loyalties centered on imperial thrones. As an institution, slavery may well have been as important in sub-Saharan political and economic systems as it was in the Muslim societies to the North.[38]

Benton, however, perceptively calls attention to institutional similarities of slavery in Africa and Mediterranean Europe. As indicated earlier, enslaving captives was an ordinary feature of Mediterranean cross-raiding for centuries before and after 1500. Whatever the differences in proportions of human and non-human sources of wealth and revenue, African and Iberian mechanisms of judicial enslavement co-existed through centuries of

---

[35] Compare Lauren Benton, *Law and Colonial Cultures: Legal Regimes in World History* (New York: Cambridge University Press, 2002), 49–52; and Thornton, *Africa*, 72–88.

[36] Thornton, *Africa*, 95–96.

[37] *Ibid.*, 74–86, and 107.

[38] *Ibid.*, 90, 108.

Euro-Mediterranean and Euro-African contact.[39] The magnitude and per-vasiveness of slavery as an institution that extended from Aragon to Angola, and from Madeira to Malacca was only enhanced in the European imagination by European global exploration.

Boundaries and Opportunities c. 1500

Generations of scholars have identified slavery as a loss of status and identity, not a loss of humanity. The loss always involved a dramatic removal of the protections afforded by family, kin, community, or nation.[40] Understanding the boundaries and limitations of enslavement, as David Eltis and others have shown, is crucial in analyzing the comparative evolution of early modern slavery. In every society with slaves, it was necessary to distinguish between those ordinarily eligible for enslavement from those who were not.[41] Even within Europe, resident "insiders" could be enslaved in 1500. Sixteenth-century Russian masters developed a myth of spurious difference between themselves and their slaves, but Russian law also clearly recognized that slaves within the Muscovite realm were resident members of the community of the Orthodox Christian faithful who had voluntarily entered the status. At the other end of Europe, in fifteenth-century Valencia, legitimizing an enslavement entailed a formal acknowledgement from the slaves that they had been obtained by capture or had voluntarily placed themselves in a situation of indebtedness, leaving themselves or their children exposed to enslavement. In South Asia, voluntary enslavement was also widespread. In some African societies, shared ethnicity and culture "might even mean an increased acceptability for enslavement given the focus on kin groups and their expansion through absorption of outsiders."[42]

Nevertheless, during the millennium before 1500, the trend towards the non-enslavability of ones own co-religionists tended to broaden along with the expansion of the Christian and Islamic worlds. Over time, religious goals with universalizing aspirations and claims of spiritual equality expanded the community of believers who could not be enslaved. In areas of greatest cultural and religious diversity, in central Eurasia and sub-Saharan Africa, there was no decrease in vulnerability to enslavement.

---

[39] Benton, *Law*, 58.

[40] *Slavery in Africa: Historical and Anthropological Perspectives*, Suzanne Miers and Igor Kopytoff, eds. (Madison: University of Wisconsin Press, 1977); Claude Meillassoux, *The Anthropology of Slavery: The Womb of Iron and Gold* (Chicago: University of Chicago Press, 1991) Miers & Kopytoff, 1977.

[41] David Eltis, *The Rise of African Slavery in the Americas* (New York: Cambridge University Press, 2000), 59.

[42] *Ibid.*, 89; see also the emphasis of Miers and Kopytoff, "African Slavery as an Institution of Marginality," in *Slavery in Africa*, ch. 1.

By 1500, most settled populations in northwestern Europe were no longer legitimately enslavable within their own region. Elsewhere, outsiders were at greater risk in situations of upheaval, conflict, or catastrophe. Even northwest European Christians living on their own coasts could still be transformed into slaves. Europeans abroad shared a condition of vulnerability with Afro-Asians. Ex-Christian Barbary corsairs ("renegades") even specialized in the enslavement of their own countrymen. Whether such renegades literally returned to the sites of their birth and kin, many of the most successful renegade *re'is* brought both their seafaring knowledge and familiarity with local geography to bear on their fellow Christians.

The fact that these corsairs spent their lives crossing the frontiers between culture and statuse demonstrates the incompleteness of the boundaries of enslavement in 1500. Escape from slavery through flight homeward or assimilation and manumission were only two points on a spectrum of reactions to the precipitous imposition of degraded status and extreme vulnerability. Some who began as enslaved freemen ended up as slavers. When renegade corsairs waged warfare on Christian ships, a portion of their able-bodied captives were recruited to join their captors. Instability of loyalties was a common cultural trait of Mediterranean seamen and corsairs. If one then fell back into the hands of Christian authorities, a recaptive might claim that he had converted only under duress. The stakes were high. Those who could not convince their judges (often the Inquisition) about the insincerity of their shift of loyalties to their former captors would most likely find themselves once again chained to the oars of a galley.

One should not make too much of these dramatic cultural transgressions and shifts in status. It is unlikely that more than a very small portion of those who were seized and enslaved were able to make double or triple border crossings between slavery and freedom. Using the estimates of Europeans taken into captivity in Barbary, the 3 to 4 percent rate of ransom and escape pales before the 17 percent mortality rate of those who died as slaves, even setting aside the fatalities entailed during violent capture. Among those captives who were launched further afield – across the Atlantic, the Sahara, or the Indian Ocean – only a minuscule number probably ever returned to their homes.[43]

In the Muslim world, black Africans who lived in the extensive border region between the abodes of peace and war were also at risk of enslavement or re-enslavement. Their fate frequently engaged the attention of *Shari'a* legal authorities. If a group was known to have converted to Islam, taking its members captive was explicitly forbidden. If, however, there were doubts about the legitimacy of enslavement, some interpreters gave the benefit to the

[43] Robert C. Davis, *Christian Slaves Muslim Masters: White Slavery in the Mediterranean, the Barbary Coast and Italy, 1500–1800* (New York, Palgrave Macmillan, 2003), 20–21.

dealer. Others insisted that the burden of proof lay upon the traders. Black Muslim rulers continued to complain about the misuse of *jihād* against their subjects. The problem persisted for nearly half a millennium after 1500.[44]

Northwestern Europe

Further north, on the shores of Christian Europe, "the illicit sale of black Muslims by white Muslims to Christians was a common practice on the Maghribean coast at the end of the fifteenth century."[45] By contrast, northwestern Europe was an anomaly. By the beginning of the sixteenth century, servile obligations that had succeeded slavery had yielded to contractual systems of labor. The presumption of personal rights was more clearly vested in European individuals.[46] Insofar as northwestern Europeans recognized the anomaly, however, they continued to think of their situation as peculiar to their own region. Although a mid–sixteenth-century English Parliament unsuccessfully attempted to legislate branding as punishment for vagrant laborers, there was widespread awareness among the English that hereditary bondage had been reduced to virtual non-existence.[47] Chattel slavery had largely disappeared within most of the region north and west of the Alps. By the middle of the sixteenth century, Sir Thomas Smith observed that even the villeins of England to "be so few that it is almost not worth the speaking." In 1593, William Harrison not only denied the existence of English bondsmen but claimed that "such is the *privilege* of our countrie by the *especiall* grace of God, and bountie of our princes, that if any come hither from other realms, so soone as they set foot on land they become so free of condition as their masters, whereby all note of servile bondage is utterlie removed from them."[48] Most writers who made similar observations merely

---

[44] Bernard Lewis, *Race and Slavery in the Middle East: An Historical Enquiry* (New York: Oxford University Press, 1990), 57–59; Mohammed Ennaji, *Serving the Master: Slavery and Society in Nineteenth-Century Morocco* (New York: St. Martin's Press, 1999), ch. 6, 7.

[45] Debra Gene Blumenthal, "Implements of Labor, Instruments of Honor: Muslim, Eastern and Black African Slaves in Fifteenth-Century Valencia" (PhD thesis, University of Toronto, 2000), 421, n. 951.

[46] Eltis, *Rise of African Slavery*, ch. 1 and pp. 61–83; and Eltis, "Europeans and the Rise and Fall of African Slavery in the Americas: an Interpretation," in *American Historical Review* 98 (1993), 1399–1423, esp. 1422–1423.

[47] C. S. L. Davies, "Slavery and Protector Somerset: The Vagrancy Act of 1547," in *Economic History Review* 1–3 (1966), 533–549.

[48] See *Origins of Modern Freedom*, Davis, ed. 13. To late Medieval English commentators, it was easy to imagine men as free in one place and slaves in another, or servile in relation to one person and free in relation to all others: "A man can be noble and non-noble at the same time...witness the case of English gentlemen taken in the kingdom of France, who while they are in the hands of the enemy are their slaves and captives; in England they remain free and noble as they were before." Upton, *De Officio Militari* E. Bysshe, ed. (London, 1654), 3–4.

noted it in passing. As late as the end of the eighteenth century, Adam Smith could only comment, "the time and manner, however, in which so important a revolution was brought about, is one of the most obscure points in modern history." This national "free soil" concept reverberated in English self-portraiture throughout the seventeenth and eighteenth centuries. It is juridically an extension to the countryside of a principle formulated by medieval communes whereby the "free air" of cities was declared incompatible with bondage.

Across the English Channel, the "freedom principle" was invoked by Continental jurists with equal pride.[49] Further south, islands of freedom might be designated even within kingdoms where slave laws were still enforced. According to the terms of certain thirteenth-century capitulations in Iberia, fugitive Muslim slaves of the Vall de Uxó (*moros de la Vall*) could not be held captive once they reached their native communities in Spain. Other Muslims in Spain fled southward to Granada before 1492 and, thereafter, with somewhat greater difficulty, to North Africa. For black non-Muslim African slaves in late fifteenth-century Spain, however, the favored direction of flight was toward the Pyrenees to France and Navarre. In 1495, a recaptured black slave told his captors that he had been convinced by other slaves that if he reached French territory, a few days of residence would confer freedom. He offered this testimony in a Spanish court because he had been informed that such freedom was irreversible, even if he returned to Spain.[50]

The northern Netherlands boasted similar legal traditions. When a Portuguese ship with 130 slaves aboard was brought into the Dutch harbor of Middleburg in 1596, the town council decided to prohibit sale of its cargo and to release the captives "into their natural liberty." Pieter Emmer speculates that this might not have done most of the freed slaves much good. They "would undoubtedly have been taken straight to the market in Antwerp" in the Spanish Netherlands a few miles south, where slaves were regularly bought and sold. Nevertheless, when another Dutch ship captured a Portuguese slaver ten years later, the captor sold its cargo to the vessel of another nation because it was impossible to sell slaves in the

---

[49] See *ibid.*, 191, and Seymour Drescher, *Capitalism and Antislavery: British Mobilization in Comparative Perspective* (New York: Oxford University Press, 1987), 15 and 172–173, n. 31). On the creation of a double spatiotemporal border between Europe and the rest of the world, see Kathleen Davis, "Sovereign Subjects, Feudal Law, and the Writing of History," *Journal of Medieval and Early Modern Studies* 36:2 (2006), 223–261. By the early eighteenth century, the Spanish Netherlands seemed to have aligned themselves with the "free principle" zone of their neighbors: "The Slaves which the *Spaniards* bring with them into *Flanders* are Free upon their arrival, as has been adjudged by the Grand Council of State at Mechlin." (Quoted in *Afer Baptizatus: or, the Negro Turn'd Christian* (London, 1702), p. 44.)

[50] P. C. Emmer, *The Dutch Slave Trade, 1500–1850*, Chris Emery, trans. (New York: Berghahn Books, 2006) and S. Drescher, *Capitalism and Antislavery* (New York: Oxford 1986), 172–173, n. 31. Blumenthal, "Implements," 42, 404–405.

Netherlands. The Dutch States-General seems to have agreed. It instructed all Dutch seamen who acquired Barbary Muslim captives to unload them in Mediterranean ports.[51]

By 1500, the French juridical tradition and the French courts had nationalized earlier urban freedom principles. France, too, could contain no slaves. The French jurist Jean Bodin treated it as a matter of historical record that when slaves reached his country, they were free. Bodin drew a theoretical regional line between slave and free soil. Slavery existed throughout the world "excepting certain countries in Europe." The border was historical as well as geographical. In Europe, he claimed, especially in France, slavery had once existed and then vanished. It was the sixteenth-century Portuguese and Spanish who threatened to erode the line and Europe's distinctiveness by expanding the institution both overseas and within Europe itself.[52]

Slavery was given slightly freer rein when reason of state dictated. To accommodate Muslim slaves on French galley ships, the free soil principle was shaved: "Any man who once touched the lands of the kingdom is free." wrote an official of the French King's Navy. Galley service, was exempt from the principle, however, "because they [slaves] are bought in foreign countries, where this kind of trade is practiced." Another official suggested to French minister Colbert a policy of purchasing a full assortment of Greeks, Albanians, and Russians at Istanbul. That was deemed permissible because Tartars beyond the Black Sea had sold them to the Turks.[53] Implicitly, slavery, although defunct in the metropolis, was not abolished at or beyond the shoreline where most galley slaves would spend the bulk of their lives, chained to the oars in a middle passage without end. Between the lines of these bureaucratic memos, one easily senses Northern Europeans trying to come to terms with an intruding world of slavery in which they were only occasionally involved.

In 1500, most of the world was still deeply invested in the institution of slavery, but all areas were not involved in the same way. Africa, Eurasia, and the Mediterranean, all harrowed by active agents of enslavement, were also all dependent upon slavery. If the brutality and degradation by slavers or the resistance of the enslaved had been the principal cause of antagonism to the institution, these very areas should have been the breeding grounds

51 See Peabody, *"There Are No Slaves,"* 4–5; Seymour Drescher, "The Long Goodbye: Dutch Capitalism and Antislavery in Comparative Perspective," in *From Slavery to Freedom: Comparative Studies in the Rise and Fall of Atlantic Slavery*, 196–224, esp. 204–205; and Allison Blakely, *Blacks in the Dutch World: The Evolution of Racial Imagery in a Modern Society* (Bloomington: Indiana University Press, 1993), 226. For links of popular antislavery to pre-modern developments in western European religious and civic struggles, see Robin Blackburn, *The Overthrow of Colonial Slavery 1776–1848* (London: Verso, 1988), 36–41.
52 Peabody, *"There Are No Slaves,"* ch. 1.
53 André Zysberg, *Les Galériens: vies et destinés de 60,000 forçats sur les galères de France, 1680–1748* (Paris: Editions du Seuil, 1987), 59.

for nascent antislavery. Yet, they were not. Rather, they were locked into an institutional system of raid and trade. Slaving ebbed and flowed in magnitude, but without any prospect of termination. The pervasiveness of the system delimited its residents' imaginations as well. Even in the European region, where it was no longer a fact of everyday life, the institution's absence registered itself as an exception to the rule. Especially for Europeans venturing beyond their frontiers and for rulers and merchants launching overseas adventures, the world beyond Europe seemed a predatory world exacerbated by interminable conflict.

2

Expanding Slavery

On the eve of the Reformation in 1516, the future father of the Baptist movement traveled through Italy. Like Martin Luther, Andreas Karlstadt was dismayed by much of what he saw. In Rome, he encountered one institution, however, that did not seem to catch the attention of his fellow German clergyman – the buying and selling of slaves:

Now hear how this kind of sale occurs. It used to be that people could sell one another, and allow their body to be owned by the buyer. And the buyer could again sell his bought servant to another, just like somebody who sells an ox allows the buyer to possess the body. Even nowadays this is not uncommon or strange in Naples or Rome. Such people are sold together with their children and are called servants.

Karlstadt's response to slave markets in 1516 was indicative of distance, as well as disapproval. He encountered an institution that was both existentially strange and biblically familiar. "Of such servants our text speaks," he mused. He invoked Deuteronomy, 15:11–12, calling upon sellers of humans to leave servants untrammeled and free. Nor were they at liberty to reclaim them later for servitude. "For then they anger God and besmirch the covenant and the name of God. . . . " Luther might well have responded to Karlstadt, as he did to the peasants' demands for freedom a decade later, by appealing to the example of the patriarchs or to other verses in Deuteronomy. Karlstadt himself would soon be swept up in Germany's religious and social upheavals. In any event, his observations reflect no awareness that slavery was already enjoying a vigorous expansion beyond Europe. Nor were Europeans themselves to remain insulated from the predatory repercussions of that renaissance.[1]

---

[1] Calvin Augustine Pater, *Karlstadt as the Father of the Baptist Movements: The Emergence of Lay Protestantism* (Toronto: University of Toronto Press, 1984), 73. Martin Luther himself would invoke St. Paul's injunction that slaves and masters must accept their stations so that the earthly kingdom should survive. Neither Luther nor John Calvin questioned

The Mediterranean: A Slaving Sea

For a century after 1500, it was still possible for northwest Europeans to treat slavery as insignificant for their own small corner of the world. It was even possible for the inhabitants of that region to boast about the absence of slavery within its confines. Nevertheless, it was equally clear to all members of these northwestern European societies that the principle did not apply even to themselves beyond the jurisdictions of their own legal and political systems. If anything, the vulnerability of western Europeans to enslavement increased during the centuries when they were institutionalizing new systems of slavery. For nearly two hundred years after 1500, Europeans' consciousness of slavery was framed more by conditions in the Mediterranean than the Atlantic, Pacific, or Indian Oceans.

Enslavement through "just war" expanded along with the increasing tempo of Christian-Muslim conflict during the sixteenth century. The Portuguese and Spanish extended their reconquest of Iberia into North Africa. Their acquisitions were more than matched by the rapid extension of Ottoman land and sea power in a great arc from Algeria to Russia. Accompanying the great campaigns of the sixteenth century, intermittent corsairing and mutual raiding intensified. The great reservoirs of enslavement in the sixteenth century were inhabitants and seafarers of the Mediterranean and Black Sea basins.

Karlstadt had barely glimpsed a residue of the violence and slave trade that never entirely ceased on either side of the Muslim-Christian frontiers. Just as northwestern Europeans began to intensify their commercial penetration of the Mediterranean at the end of the sixteenth century, the Barbary corsairs extended their own activities into the Atlantic. During the first half of the seventeenth century, corsairs raided the Atlantic coasts of Portugal, Spain, France, England, and Iceland. Occasionally, they roamed as far as Brazilian and North American coastal waters. Over the course of three centuries, Icelanders, Irish, Scottish, Welsh, English, French, German, and Scandinavian captives flowing from western Europe would be joined by Greeks, Albanians, Armenians, Hungarians, Poles, and Russians from the eastern parts of Europe.[2] Raiding and piracy were, of course, two-way streets. Inhabitants of Morocco, Algiers, Tunisia, Tripoli – both Arabic and Turkish speakers – would find themselves captives in the markets of the Christian-ruled islands and coastal cities of the northern Mediterranean or at the oars of galleys launched by Christians. Despite the free air/free soil traditions evolved before

the legitimacy of chattel slavery. See Davis, *Problem of Slavery in Western Culture*, 106; and Robin Blackburn, *The Overthrow of Colonial Slavery, 1776–1848* (London: Verso, 1988), 35.

[2] Bartolomé Bennassar and Lucille Bennassar, *Les Chrétiennes d'Allah: L'histoire extraordinaire des renégats XVIe et XVII siècles* (Paris: Perrin, 1957).

1500, the potential for enslavement extended over the entire continent of Europe and its colonial extensions. Those who lived near or sailed on the Mediterranean remained most vulnerable. Those who lived in areas more remote from Muslim power or who were subjects of the strongest state rulers in northern Europe experienced increasing, if not total, security from enslavement by the middle of the eighteenth century. At greatest risk were those with no powerful or wealthy state rulers or mobilized co-religionists to intervene for them. Although the Portuguese king claimed all defaulting Spanish Jews as slaves, others who fled to North Africa were taken captive and held for enslavement pending redemption by their North African co-religionists.[3]

Northwestern Europeans also became more vulnerable to enslavement in the first half of the seventeenth century. The peak of enslavement along the Mediterranean littoral coincided with the period in which most of the major slave colonies of the New World were established. For the western and central Mediterranean, Robert C. Davis estimates the number of Christians enslaved by Muslims at a million or more. The period in which Europeans were at greatest risk was the century between 1580 and 1680. An average of 7,000 Christian captives per year were enslaved in the Maghreb. This excludes the number of captives brought from eastern Europe into the heartland of the Ottoman Empire. During the peak century for enslavement of western Europeans, Richard Hellie calculates an annual average arrival of 4,000 enslaved Muscovites, and possibly a higher number of Polish captives entering the Ottoman realm. Hundreds of thousands from eastern Europe were captured and sold into the slave markets of Asia, the Crimea, and the circum-Mediterranean, and incorporated into the Muslim armies as slave soldiers or as galley slaves. It has been estimated that more than 10,000 slaves per year passed through the Crimean slave market in Kefe.[4]

From Atlantic Europe, at least 20,000 British and Irish were held as slaves in North Africa between 1600 and the middle of the eighteenth century. Eight thousand of these were seized in the first half of the seventeenth

---

[3] See Samuel Usque, *Consolation for the Tribulations of Israel*, Martin A. Cohen, trans. (Philadelphia: Jewish Publication Society of America, 1977), 200–201.

[4] Richard Hellie, *Slavery in Russia 1450–1725* (Chicago: University of Chicago Press, 1982), 23; *idem*. "Migration in Early Modern Russia, 1480s–1780s" in *Coerced and Free Migration: Global Perspectives*, David Eltis, ed. (Stanford: Stanford University Press, 2002), 307. Alan Fisher, in *A Precarious Balance: Conflict, Trade and Diplomacy on the Russian-Ottoman Frontier* (Istanbul: Isis Press, 1999), 31–34, offers a long list of estimates of captive Slavs between the late fifteenth and late seventeenth centuries. Cumulatively, they indicate totals in the high hundred thousands; Fisher, however, cautions that Ottoman records do not lend support to such high estimates. As late as the end of the seventeenth century, Ottoman captives were set to work in construction gangs in southern Germany. See János J. Varga, "Ransoming Ottoman Slaves from Munich (1688)," in *Ransom Slavery Along the Ottoman Borders: Early Fifteenth to Early Eighteenth Centuries*, Géza David and Pál Fodor, eds. (Leiden: Brill, 2007), 169–182.

century, just as England was launching its own venture into establishing overseas slave colonies. Precise numbers for some of these coerced migrations are elusive, but recent estimates offer us a rough estimate of relative magnitudes. While the Iberians were establishing their Atlantic colonies during the century after the Portuguese exploratory voyages along the sub-Saharan African coast (c. 1440–1540), more Europeans were enslaved in North Africa than were Africans in Europe, the Atlantic islands, and the Americas combined. Well into the early seventeenth century, the numbers of Africans landing in the Americas did not exceed the number of enslaved Europeans landed in Africa.[5]

When Europeans launched their vessels into the "slave world" beyond their own shores, one thing was clear. Seaborne Europeans "beyond the line" could have as easily ended up among the enslaved as the enslavers. There were far more British slaves in North Africa until the 1640s than there were Africans in the British colonies.[6] The 7,000 Frenchmen held in the Algerian, Tunisian, and Tripolitanian areas of North Africa certainly outnumbered African slaves in the French colonies, even into the late seventeenth century. It was only during the second half of that century that more African captives were shipped to the Americas than were European captives to Africa. In a broader perspective, throughout the seventeenth century there were probably more individuals enslaved and imported into the Muslim orbit than into its Christian counterpart. During that century, Europeans imported an average of 19,000 Africans each year into the Americas. During the same period, about 9,000 Africans were annually transported across the Sahara, Red Sea, and Indian Ocean into Muslim-dominated lands.[7] To these, one would have to add those retained in Muslim-dominated areas of Africa below the Sahara and in East Africa.[8]

---

[5] For comparative numbers, compare Davis, *Christian Slaves*, and David Eltis, et al., second edition of the *Transatlantic Slave Trade Database* (hereafter TSTD).

[6] Eltis, *Rise of African Slavery*, 57. See also Linda Colley, *Captives* (New York: Pantheon, 2002), 50–56.

[7] Compare TSTD with Paul E. Lovejoy, *Transformations in Slavery: A History of Slavery in Africa* (New York: Cambridge University Press, 1983), 60, Table 3.7. For a discussion of the "eastern" slave trade from Africa, see, above all, Olivier Pétré-Grenouilleau, *Les Traites négrières: Essai d'histoire globale* (Paris: Gaillimard, 2004), 144–149; and Ralph A. Austen, *African Economic History: Internal Development and External Dependency* (London: James Currey, 1987), 275.

[8] Patrick Manning suggests that two million Africans were exported from the Savanna and the Horn in the sixteenth and seventeenth centuries. *Slavery and African Life: Occidental, Oriental, and African Slave Trades*, (New York: Cambridge University Press, 1990), 84. Owners would have absorbed a considerable number of slaves who would have been detained en route in the course of the deportation. For nearly two centuries after the beginning of European expansion to the Americas (1500–1680), the combined flow of enslaved Europeans (3 million) and Africans (1 million) to Muslim North Africa and the Middle East was nearly triple that of the 1.5 million Africans carried to the New World. In one sense, the situation dramatically changed between the 1680s and the close of the eighteenth century. Europeans

Two other continents added substantially to the Muslim supply of slaves. Scattered Crimean figures suggest that about 10,000 captives a year were imported into Muslim areas during the seventeenth century. Warfare produced surges in enslavement and an unknown number of captives to the total. The Ottomans seized 80,000 people in the single campaign that culminated in the siege of Vienna in 1683. As many as 20,000 rebels were allegedly transported to Iran for sale in 1619–1620. At the eastern edge of the early modern Muslim world, South and Southeastern Asia were major sources of two million slaves in the two centuries after 1565. In Southeast Asia, Bali exported 100,000 Hindu slaves between 1620 and 1830. Even at the core of the Islamic world, the enslavement of Iranian "heretics" by Ottoman Sunni rulers was "a regular feature of the interminable Ottoman-Iranian wars." The virtues of mobility within the institution tended to exacerbate its predation. Islam's emphasis upon manumission through concubinage, marriage, and charity exerted upward pressure on the demand for fresh slaves, with its characteristic high mortality, brutality, and family dissolution.[9]

The habits of the hardened heart developed by slavers preclude meaningful regional differentiation in the brutality of the various trades. In the Mediterranean, after the mid-seventeenth century, captive western Europeans were far more likely than Africans to be redeemed by their fellow countrymen. In the transatlantic trade, western Europeans were less likely to be involved than their more eastern counterparts in the initial recruitment of the enslaved. They generally purchased people already enslaved or captured by Africans. European victims had some hope that they might return to their families. Their cargoes of African men, women, and children had virtually no hope of returning to their communities of origin.

Christians and Muslims in the Mediterranean engaged in symmetrical processes of violent seizure, transportation, and disposition. They occupied roles of both predators and victims. Their coastal areas were lands of mutual devastation. Mediterranean women and children on both sides were routinely subjected to the same casual sexual predation reserved primarily for Africans in the transatlantic system.

Nevertheless, there were some distinctions within the Mediterranean slave systems that may have had an impact upon their later receptivity to abolitionism. The political economy of the Maghreb appears to have been

---

imported five times as many slaves into their transatlantic colonies (7.2 million) as were delivered to the Muslim lands in North Africa and western Asia. Nevertheless, one must bear in mind that in comparing the New and Old Worlds, it was only in the rate of expansion that the eighteenth century Euro-Atlantic empires distinguished themselves. The slave populations and populations of the Eastern Hemisphere vastly overshadowed those of the Americas in magnitude. Even in West Africa, the labor reservoir of transatlantic slavery probably had more slaves within its own boundaries than in all of the Americas combined at the end of the eighteenth century. I have profited from consulting David Richardson's manuscript on "Involuntary Migration in the Early Modern World, 1500–1800."

9 See Clarence-Smith, *Islam,* 11–16; and Erdem, *Slavery,* 29–33.

more dependent upon slaving than was the Christian-dominated Mediterranean. In the "golden age" of cross-raiding (c. 1550–1660), the ports of the Maghreb were disproportionably dependent upon the profits generated by corsairing.[10] Both power and wealth flowed from a continuous influx of captives. The dependence of slaving galleys upon human propulsion demanded a constant reproduction of able-bodied adult male captives. In the Maghreb, the city-state ports could well be described as slave societies. Their economies rested more directly on the distribution of wealth generated from corsairing. The survival of the rulers also depended upon the receipts of their tenth or fifth shares of booty.[11] Maghrebian authorities had to tread a thin line. In contrast to the rulers of northern Europe, it was peace that most threatened the coffers of the state and the more fragile tenure of their non-hereditary rulers. When, under naval pressure, the Dey of Tripoli negotiated a simultaneous suspension of corsairing against both French and Dutch shipping, he was promptly overthrown. For Tripoli's corsairs, it was self-evident that their city could not afford to cease hostilities against all of the major European shipping powers. On the other hand, a simultaneous conflict with all the commercial powers threatened to cut off products vital to the corsairing process itself.[12]

Although Mediterranean corsairing played less of a role in the political economies of the wealthier and more diversified northern Europeans, it is important to note that for the two centuries following 1500, their rulers showed little hesitation about participating in slave activity when opportunities arose. Naval galleys needed rowers. They routinely used combinations of captive Muslims, North Africans, and Christians and, occasionally, even sub-Saharan Africans and Amerindians. When need for oarsmen abated, an admiral could instruct his officers to take any Turks, Moors, and Negroes captured aboard Maghrebian vessels and sell them at the best market in the western Mediterranean.[13]

If Europeans engaged in slaving as freely as Muslims, what were the legal and cultural limits to enslavement during two centuries of growth in Mediterranean slaving from the late fifteenth through the late seventeenth centuries? Religion both justified the expansion and shifted the boundaries of enslavability.[14] Although Moscovites ceased selling slaves into Islam after

[10] Bennassars, *Les Chrétiens d 'Allah*, 384–385.
[11] Davis, *Christian Slaves*, 58.
[12] C.R. Pennell, *Piracy and Diplomacy in Seventeenth-Century North Africa*, (Rutherford: Associated Presses, 1989).
[13] G.E. Aylmer, "Slavery Under Charles II: The Mediterranean and Tangier," *English Historical Review*, 144: 456 (1999), 378–388.
[14] Until the late fifteenth century, slaves were still being imported to western Europe from eastern Christian areas (See Blumenthal, *Implements*, 42); and from western Europe itself. Before the Spanish conquest of 1492, Christians were still seizing Moorish fishermen from Grenada. The Christian/Muslim rationales of just war and *jihād* enslavement were easily accommodated to private enterprise.

the mid-sixteenth century, Kazonis could still buy Russian girls in Novgorod in the early seventeenth century.[15] Once enslaved, the slave's legal status was still not altered by conversion. In the New World, the overwhelming majority of Africans transported was assumed to have been enslaved as heathens. In the Mediterranean, the situation was more complicated. Slaves returning to Christian jurisdiction could be renegade corsairs captured with arms in hand. They might be enslaved Christian rebels who seized their vessel and returned to Christendom with captives of their own in hand. Some slaves were recaptured more than once. All of these cases created complex problems about the status of considerable numbers of captives. In Catholic countries, such issues naturally invited the intrusion of the Inquisition. Things were equally complex from the slave's perspective. Captured female slaves sometimes refused to acknowledge their Christian origins, either out of fear of the whole Inquisitorial process or in hopes that their Muslim husbands would find and redeem them.[16]

Border crossing abounded. Well into the seventeenth century Christians born in Salonika, Hungary, Russia, Romania, Albania, and Ragusa were not routinely freed. When an English commander seized an Algerian ship with ninety-four Africans and twenty-four Greek captives aboard, he created a demarcation of his own. He reported having sold the Negroes (including the women and children) and kept the Greeks captive for galley service. The Royal Navy Board approved the action, but the Greeks' plea for freedom, on grounds of their Christianity, was rejected. The government relented only after the galley to which the captives were assigned was declared unfit for service. Throughout the proceedings, the Greeks' identity as Christians and Europeans was clearly not taken as *prima facie* evidence of entitlement to freedom.

Recaptured Catholics might have recourse to Papal adjudication. The knights of Malta, heavily engaged in corsair warfare, requested a formal opinion from the Congregation of the Supreme and Universal Inquisition created by Paul III in 1542. Its response was formal and measured. Renegades taken in arms were to remain slaves even after their reconciliation with the Church. Exceptions could be made for fear-induced conversions of the very young. The Iberian Inquisitors were apparently less forgiving than the Romans. Their tribunals limited their role to hearing confession, offering truth and reconciliation, and returning the prisoner to his bench on the galleys.[17]

It must be recalled that the early modern period was a moment of bitter, often mortal, sectarian dissension within western Europe. On the high seas, crews were tempted not to make too much of fellow-Christian or European identity. When a large Flemish vessel overpowered a Portuguese caravel,

[15] Blumenthal, *Implements*, 21; Hellie, *Slavery in Russia* 73.
[16] Bennassars, *Chrétiens*, 427.
[17] Bennassars, *Chrétiens*, 353-354.

it sold the ship's crew in Morocco. During the French-Catholic siege of French-Protestant La Rochelle in the early seventeenth century, English and Moorish ships combined to seize a French merchant vessel. The English took the boat and the Moors took the crew to Algiers.[18]

Intra-European rivalries often led Christians to work against their Christian enemies. In ransoming negotiations with North Africans, Catholic Mercedarians and Trinitarians favored one ethnic group over another. At times, they even sabotaged negotiations for others. The subjects of weaker or poorer European rulers were more often abandoned to their fates. The almost continuous state of war between European states from the mid-sixteenth to the early eighteenth centuries helped to perpetuate the Muslim corsairing. A peace treaty between a Maghreb port ruler and a European government guaranteed greater predation against other nationals and assured a flow of supplies to those Muslim rulers in amity with one or another European state.[19] No group demonstrates the fragility of faith-based inhibitions against Euro-Euro slaving than the fate of renegade corsairing captains. They were virulently hated for using their European skills in oceanic seamanship to facilitate extending Moorish predation into the Atlantic. Renegades familiar with the coastal areas added tens of thousands to the list of Christian captives. To skilled Christian captives, they demonstrated the opportunities for wealth and power awaiting potential converts who might become venture capitalists in slaving. Renegades had some analogues among the leading pirates of the Atlantic, but they had no peers in the political influence they exercised as role models in a slaving society. They also offer the clearest evidence of the fragility of "European" or "Christian" culture in creating inhibitions against enslaving "ones own." Indeed, it is precisely in the "take-off" period of the transatlantic slave trade, from the mid-sixteenth through the late seventeenth centuries, that barbary piracy was dominated by born and bred Christian renegades. From one-third to one-half of Maghreb corsairs were then of European origin.[20]

This Mediterranean zone of shifting fortunes had an impact upon victims as well as predators, who were sometimes both, by turns. Years at the oar, rather than turning them against slavery often inured them to the process of enslavement. Like their counterparts among the *ra'is* in the Maghreb, once restored to freedom, they might return as Christians to the only skill that they knew from the inside out – corsairing. Jean Bonnet, born near Marseille, went to sea as a youth and was captured by Barbary pirates. Four years later he and other Europeans, from the Netherlands to Greece, paddled from Tunisia to Malta in a stolen boat. Then, via Sicily and Italy, they made their way back to France. There Bonnet bought a vessel and went back to

---

[18] Davis, *Christian Slaves*, 112. Bennassars, *Chrétiens*, 171, 208.
[19] Davis, *Christian Slaves*, 47, 112.
[20] Robert Davis, "Counting European Slaves on the Barbary Coast," in *Past and Present* 172 (2001), 87–124, esp. 121.

sea, "to avenge the cruelties that I had suffered in my slavery."[21] Such skills
could also be directly transferred to the transatlantic slave trade from West
Africa.

A number of significant characteristics emerge from an overview of
Mediterranean slavery during the two centuries after 1500. The religious
foundations for ascertaining the boundaries of slavery on the European side
of the sea did not alter during the early modern period. Penalties for heresy
might be raised to the level of agonizing execution or lifetime servitude in
the galleys, but European rulers refrained from enslaving Europeans within
their own legal jurisdictions. However, the most salient feature of the corsairing system during those two centuries is that they coincided with the
founding years of Euro-Atlantic slavery. Europeans never felt more vulnerable to enslavement than when they were creating their novel variant of
the institution in the New World. Northwest Europeans in particular were
reintroduced into a wider world where enslavement was part of the normal
array of risks in traveling. Nothing could have more intensely reinforced the
idea that slavery was the prevailing system throughout most of the globe
than that they were its victims as well as its agents.

Down to the late eighteenth century, enslavability also remained enshrined in the religious worldviews of those who lived in this immense zone
of vulnerability. The very processes of ransoming and redemption were formulated in symbolic terms that accepted slavery as part of the divine order.
These rites of passage were increasingly formalized during the seventeenth
century. Robert Davis aptly calls his chapter on the liberation of ransomed
individuals "Celebrating Slavery."[22] Enslavement continued to be embedded in the notion that enslaved Christians were sinners, deserving of divine
punishment and tested by God. The more vulnerable the society, the more
elaborate the ritual of return. Significantly, in Italy, the reintegration process
was literally enacted as a series of stages: from slavery in Africa, across the
sea to Europe and, via overland processions, to a final site of church redemption. The redemptive religious orders often first rented and finally paid for
the ransomed. They purchased their captives like any slave dealer, sometimes bidding in the slave market against Muslim traders.[23] The context

[21] Antonini Galland, *Histoire de l'esclavage d'un marchand de la ville de Cassis, à Tunis*
(Paris: Editions de la Bibliothèque, 1993), 134–135; see also Gillian Weiss, "Back from
Barbary: Captivity, Redemption and French Identity in the Seventeenth and Eighteenth-
Century Mediterranean," Ph.D. thesis 2003, passim.

[22] Davis, *Christian Slaves*, ch. 6 Antiquity's legacy still "gave a certain moral dignity to slavery." See also, Davis *Problem of Slavery*, 85–90.

[23] Freeing slaves remained a form of charity: "to loosen one from the chains of slavery is
to feed the starving, give drink to the thirsty, dress the naked, cure the sick, console the
afflicted, aid one in danger, and is finally to return the Citizen to the Fatherland, the Subject
to the Prince, the Father to his Sons, the Son to his Parents, the Faithful to the Church."
(Davis, 185).

was clear. Slavery remained a fact of the cosmos, as permanent as hunger, illness, war, or poverty. It would remain so until some messianic moment in which it would disappear, along with all other forms of human suffering and injustice. Meanwhile, as in the scriptural admonitions studied by Muslim counterparts in the Maghreb, emancipation was a blessed deed of charity in a world of ills.

Here again, we have hints that things were already different in northern Europe. Mediterranean powers continued to have specific and partially symmetrical uses for captives on their own galleys into the eighteenth century. Even France, with its distinctively northwestern European "freedom principle," suspended that principle for galley slaves. Galley slaves remained slaves in the full legal sense and retained that status on French soil, as well as on board their vessels. The Dutch had neither need nor desire to accumulate Muslim captives in the Netherlands or overseas. The Dutch Republic ordered its naval forces to dispose of all captured corsairs in the Mediterranean, where there was a market for them.[24]

At the end of the sixteenth century, the English government, too, was more anxious to ban than to encourage servile immigration. It made strenuous efforts to expel the few blacks who had already been brought into the kingdom. When England began to take Maghrebian prisoners in retaliation, indications are that the corsairs were either sold in the Mediterranean or brought to England to stand trial as pirates. As in the Maghreb, some of the younger captives' lives were spared as potential recruits for Christianity, but they were not held as slaves.[25] England's initial acquisition of Tangier (1661–1684) briefly tempted its agents to follow the Mediterranean pattern. Tangier may have been the prototype in some respects for other British Mediterranean strongholds such as Gibraltar, Minorca, and Malta. These islands relied upon Islamic societies for supplies in Britain's conflicts with other European states. There is no indication, however, that those supplies ever included slaves. On the contrary, by the early eighteenth century, "London had become the locus for Māghariba traders" and Moroccans looked to England for redress from injuries inflicted by foreign ships.[26] By the last half of the eighteenth century, Islam was receding even in the British popular imagination as a zone of British enslavement.[27]

---

[24] See Corneluis van Bynkershoek, *Quaestionum Juris Publici, Libre Duo* 2 vols., translation of the 1737 ed. by Tenny Frank (Oxford, 1930), II, 28, and Drescher, *Capitalism and Antislavery*, 173.

[25] See Nabil Matar, "Muslims in Seventeenth-Century England," *Journal of Islamic Studies*, 8:1 (1997), 63–82.

[26] Nabil Matar, "The Last Moors: Māghariba in Early Eighteenth-Century England," *Journal of Islamic Studies*, 14:1 (2003), 37–58.

[27] The last substantial group of British writings about captivity in North Africa was provoked by an incident in 1756. (See Colley, *Captives*, 126).

The relationship between Europeans and the Muslim Mediterranean states as both predators and victims certainly did not encourage Europeans to associate slavery exclusively with race. Even at the end of the eighteenth century, the Mediterranean was a place where the institution was still firmly multireligious, multiethnic, and multicolored.

What was true of the Mediterranean was equally true of the earth as a whole. As geographies of the European world of the late eighteenth century casually noted, slaves still abundantly occupied every continent.[28] Moreover, in terms of abolition, the impulse toward abolitionism would not emerge from Mediterranean societies still implicated in the practice of enslavement. This Islamic-Christian borderland remained part and parcel of the normative old world of slavery, conceptually embedded in the traditions of the patriarchs, prophets, and lawgivers of the human race. Despite a gradual decline in the number of European prey during the eighteenth century, the sufferings of Mediterranean captives never suggested to its victims or redeemers, much less to their governments, that slavery itself was a condition to which no one should be subjected. That striking proposition would emerge outside the Euro-Muslim world of the inland sea.

Transoceanic Slavery

During the course of the fifteenth century, European navigators dramatically opened up sea lanes between the Atlantic, Indian, and Pacific Oceans. Toward the end of that century, inhabitants of five continents were unevenly brought into the first continuous contact with each other since the prehistoric dispersion of homo sapiens from Africa. Whereas the Muslim-dominated movement of slaves within and from Africa, Asia, and Europe continued unabated, interoceanic access opened the way for new dimensions of institutional development. During the next three centuries, Europeans moved nearly thirteen million enslaved Africans across the Atlantic to Europe, African coastal islands, the Indian Ocean basin, and, above all, the Americas. The overwhelming majority of the great new wave of migrants were Africans. For three and a half centuries after 1500, more than twelve million African slaves were transported across the Atlantic. They accounted for up to four of every five Atlantic migrants.[29] The expansion of economic activity that opened the way for the burst of transoceanic activity from the Old World toward the New World was, however, a slow incremental process.

---

[28] Drescher, *Capitalism and Antislavery*, 12–24.

[29] David Eltis, "Free and Coerced Migrations from the Old World to the New," in *Coerced and Free Migration: Global Perspectives*, 33–93, Table I; modified by Eltis, *Reassessment*, Table 4. To the transatlantic totals, I add the movements of Africans to the Atlantic Islands and Europe as in Philip D. Curtin, *The Atlantic Slave Trade: A Census* (Madison: University of Wisconsin Press, 1969), 116 and 119.

For almost two centuries after the Portuguese made direct contact with the peoples of the African Atlantic coast, sub-Saharan Africa was only one source of enslavement among many. As we have seen, only at the end of the seventeenth century did the Americas likely surpass the Euro-Muslim area as the major emporium for the world's newly enslaved people. Even within the Americas, there were probably far more Native Americans than Africans enslaved by Europeans during the century prior to the seventeenth-century.

The succession of seaward expansions along the African and American coasts routinely brought the Portuguese into contact with thinly populated lands in which the slave trade and slavery were logical short-term solutions to changing environments. They added up to a larger Atlantic plantation complex. The Canaries, the first offshore Archipelago encountered by Iberians, were inhabited by non-Christians. They provided ample opportunities for experimenting with combinations of trading and raiding for exportable items, including people. Slave raiding seems to have prevailed for almost half a century before the beginnings of colonization. In uninhabited island complexes, imported slaves, primarily from the Canaries, provided labor for profitable crops, especially sugar in Madeira.[30]

In the course of their island-hopping, the Portuguese clearly assumed that their maritime superiority over the local inhabitants would allow them to trade, raid, or otherwise settle areas as occasion allowed. But, as the Portuguese moved to mainland Senegal, they encountered conditions in which their own relative vulnerability pushed them decisively in the direction of acquiring slaves by negotiation rather than force. In 1441, just beyond Cape Bojador, they seized several Muslim Berbers along with a black slave. Two years later, they returned to the same area and were offered gold and ten more black slaves in exchange for two of their original Berber captives. Thereafter, more expeditions returned to Portugal with slaves acquired by trade.

Further south, the turn from raiding to purchasing was equally rapid. On land, the Portuguese expeditions were no match for the military power they encountered. All Europeans who followed the Portuguese to Africa found themselves in the same relative position, as they did in most of the populous zones of the Indian Ocean world. Onshore, they were guests trading at the sufferance of rulers to whom they could offer tribute and commodities. These commodities might include black slaves profitably transported from one area to another by their ocean-borne mode of transportation.

During the late fifteenth century, about a third of the Africans purchased by the Portuguese were retraded for gold, still the principal form of African wealth sought by Europeans. The other two-thirds were brought to the Atlantic islands or to Portugal itself. There, they were added to the assortment of slaves drawn from those islands of the Atlantic and the Mediterranean world.

---

[30] John Thornton, *Africa and the Africans*, 28–30.

As the Portuguese pushed further down the African coast, they simultaneously discovered a fine location for growing sugar and a deadly disease
environment for Europeans.[31] Nothing better illustrates the combination of
European advantage and vulnerability than the development of uninhabited
São Tomé at the end of the fifteenth century. São Tomé became a true human
and economic laboratory and slavery was the institution that facilitated its
development.[32] It was the first "white man's grave" in Africa. Its initial settlement in the early 1490s required the first large-scale coerced migration
of Europeans, as well as Africans. In addition to refugee Jewish children
from Spain, Portuguese convicts were dispatched to the island. To ensure
the next generation of settlers, a program of Euro-African procreation was
inaugurated. African slaves were transported from the continent and offered
as mates to the deported Europeans. Within two decades, the African partners and their offspring were emancipated. Further importations of slaves
ensured a continuously expanding labor force for sugar cultivation.

The learning curve could work both ways. By 1500, Africans on mainland
Senegambia were already employing slaves in a work regime identical to that
used by the Portuguese on São Tomé. Equally significant, São Tomé's slave
market was quickly extended southward to the kingdom of the Kongo. The
Portuguese king granted the São Tomé settlers privileges to engage in slave
trade from the moment of their settlement in 1493, just a few years after
the opening of Portuguese-Kongolese commercial relations.[33] Within little
more than a decade after 1493, there were 5,000 to 6,000 Africans, mainly
from central Africa, awaiting re-export on São Tomé, as well as 2,000 slaves
working on the island's sugar plantations. São Tomé had become the center
of an intercontinental network for the Atlantic trade that was to endure for
centuries.

Not only did each southward expansion of Portuguese exploration produce a new source of slaves but, within a generation of first European contact, central Africa was able to supply exports of slaves equal to all of West
Africa's combined. John Thornton concludes that from its very beginnings,
the Atlantic slave trade drew upon fully established slave systems along
the length of the African coast: Within Africa, the institution was legally,
socially, and politically prepared for "the capture purchase, transport, and
sale of slaves," even before the appearance of the Portuguese. African societies below the zone of Muslim domination and before the age of European
contact were available, on their own terms, for participation in the new

---

[31] Philip Curtin, "Epidemiology and the Slave Trade," *Political Science Quarterly*, 83 (1966),
190–216.
[32] A. Teixeira da Mota, *Some Aspects of Portuguese Colonisation and Sea Trade in West
Africa in the 15th and 16th Centuries* (Bloomington, IN: African Studies Program, 1978),
11.
[33] *Ibid.*, p. 12; and Thornton, *Africa*, 95–96.

extension of the Old World routes to slavery toward the end of the fifteenth century.[34]

As telling as the rapid development of the market is the apparent ease with which the institution, as separately understood by Christians, Muslims, and sub-Saharan Africans, became integrated at one level. Their legal and economic systems were sufficiently compatible to allow for the formation of a market of *long durée*. By the beginning of the seventeenth century, African rulers were aware of, and making ample use of, the fact that sovereignty was fragmented among Europeans as well as Africans. It would appear that already by the late 1500s the annual flow of African slaves into the Atlantic slave system equaled those flowing from the seven hundred year-old Saharan slave trade.[35]

European seamen initiated an even more unprecedented development in the history of slavery in the Americas. The fragility and failures of European transatlantic settlements during the centuries between Norse settlements and the Columbian voyages offer an indication of the significance of Europe's principal maritime advantage in the new "oceanic world." European mastery of wind and currents, which enabled Columbus to cross the Atlantic from Cádiz to the Caribbean and back, is further evidenced by independent European discoveries of new fisheries off the coast of Newfoundland and the encounter with Brazil of a Portuguese ship en route to India in 1500.

In America, however, Europeans initially did not encounter the serious epidemiological obstacle that severely limited their role in Africa. In Africa Europeans had quickly discovered a number of new vulnerabilities, especially in their susceptibility to tropical diseases. In the Americas, they encountered a different epidemiological enviornment. Europeans brought with them diseases that were as devastating to New World populations as "the white man's grave" was to Europeans in tropical Africa. Massive epidemics often preceded the first Europeans' arrival in a region, spread by the indigenous population.

---

[34] Thornton, *Africa*, ch. 3. For a general description of the functional compatibility of the slave trade with the prior institutional and economic structures of eastern, western, and sub-Saharan Africa, see also, Petré-Grenouilleau, *Traites negrières*, 18–184.

[35] Compare the Slave Trade Database annual figures with Paul Lovejoy, *Transformations in Slavery: A History of Slavery in Africa* (Cambridge, UK: Cambridge University Press, 2000), 59–60 and Petré-Grenouilleau's estimates for the 16th and 17th centuries "oriental trades," 148–149. Patrick Manning, *Slavery and African Life: Occidental, Ovental, and African Slave Trades* (New York: Cambridge University, Press, 1990), 18. Figure 1.1 indicates that transatlantic slaving did not exceed the oriental slave trade until the second half of the seventeenth century. See also the censuses of Ralph Austen, cited above in ch. 1, n. 29. These figures for the slave trade from Africa do not, of course, include the inflow of slaves to the Muslim world from Eurasia. The combined Afro-Eurasian slave trades far exceeded the magnitude of the transatlantic coerced during the first two centuries after Columbus' voyages.

Epidemics might initially ease the path to European domination. This was most strikingly illustrated in the conquests of the Aztec dominions in Mexico and the Inca Empire in South America. Over the longer term, however, the demographic devastation of indigenous populations by up to 80 or 90 percent of their precontact numbers, created an enormous dearth of labor. The combination of European domination of land and resources combined with high mortality in zones of conquest was to lead to a dramatic expansion of slavery and the slave trade.[36]

Enslavement of the Native Americans

In developing the institution of slavery in the Americas, Europeans proceeded as experimentally as they had on the coasts of Africa. New conditions presented problems of institutional development that were different from those encountered by the Portuguese in their movement along the Atlantic islands and the African coast. Because of the incremental pace of exploration over the course of a whole century, it had been possible for the Portuguese to selectively explore the whole array of traditional activities and rationalizations developed during encounters with Islam over the previous eight centuries. The repertoire of raiding, trading, and rescue, and of conversion, salvation, and civilization could be reconfigured over the course of the century to adjust to new opportunities and constraints. On the spot in Africa, it was sufficient to learn and manipulate the rules of the game to gather and exchange a steady stream of captives sufficient to extend to an ever-expanding range of markets in Mediterranean Europe, the Atlantic islands, Asia, and, ultimately to the Americas.

In the Americas, Europeans discovered indigenous social groups that were analogous to those whom Europeans encountered in Africa and Asia. One means of accumulating labor was to initially tap into those designated as bondsmen by native elites. Elsewhere, Europeans often cut through the existing network of social structures to identify enslavables, especially under the conditions of rapidly expanding political and military domination by the Europeans and even more rapidly descending native numbers.

There is no indication that Europeans everywhere favored slavery in the Mediterranean sense as the only, or even the best, mode of domination and labor control. The uprooting, natal alienation, and designation of individuals as chattel was not necessarily appropriate to people who, on initial

---

[36] *The Native Population of the Americas in 1492*, 2d ed., William N. Denevan, ed. (Madison: University of Wisconsin Press, 1992), x. There is considerable dispute over the estimates of the Native American population on the eve of the Columbian voyages. However, there appears to be a general consensus that a fairly precipitous decline occurred following the arrival of Columbus. This phenomenon must be incorporated into the analysis of the growth of slavery in the Americas. See David Henige, *Numbers From Nowhere: The American Indian Contact Population Debate* (Norman, OK: University of Oklahoma Press, 1998), 306.

contact, were perceived to be in a state of universal voluntary submission. The first Columbian expedition did not encounter the same deadly reception as had the Norsemen off the coast of North America centuries before. Nor did they have to learn the Portuguese lesson of the benefit of trading along the African coast. Columbus's *First Letter From America*, widely publicized by the Spanish monarchs, described the island as a source of great potential wealth. The gentle disposition of the natives and their unsophisticated weaponry ensured that minimal force would be necessary to keep their untold numbers in check. Moreover, Columbus described them as disposed to willingly accept both Spanish sovereignty and Christianity.

Finding on his return to Hispânola that the Europeans left behind had been killed by the native Taínos, Columbus reverted to the "just war" tradition of enslaving natives as rebellious enemies and savage cannibals. Unable to locate gold or wealthy societies with whom trade goods could be exchanged, he sent five hundred native captives back to Europe for sale. Although 40 percent died en route to Spain, the Catholic monarchs initially approved the sales. However, they also made the sale provisional, pending a determination of the legitimacy of enslaving people originally described by Columbus as gentle natives willing to convert. After a five year delay, they ruled that the Native Americans in Spain had to be released.[37]

Unlike the almost invariable acquisition of Africans as slaves, Native Americans were not routinely treated as slaves. In their own prior overseas expansion to the Canary Islands during the fifteenth century, Castilians had already established a different precedent. Following, conquest, the local inhabitants were divided up and given to prominent settlers (*encomienda*).[38]

This was also the major mode of labor distribution in Hispânola. Using the networks of local indigenous authority, the *encomendero* was given an inalienable grant of native labor. For all those areas designated as already conquered, the individuals held their authority over a cohort of laborers who were not slaves. The same system was subsequently favored in centers of accumulated populations in rapidly conquered Mexico and Peru.

In areas where the Indian populations were more dispersed or rapidly declining, a second system, called the congregation, was initiated. Indians were gathered closer together in urban-style units ("reduction") for more rapid assimilation to European cultural norms of religious conversion and labor. Parallel institutions (*aldeas*) were founded in Brazil. The monarchs deemed enslavement as unfitting for natives who had already become subjects of the crown, and who would more easily assimilate to European

---

[37] Helen Nader, "Desperate Men, Questionable Acts: The Moral Dilemma of Italian Merchants in the Spanish Slave Trade," in *Sixteenth Century Journal*, 33:2, 2002, 401–402.

[38] James Lockhart and Stuart B. Schwartz, *Early Latin America: A History of Colonial Spanish America and Brazil*, (New York: Cambridge University Press, 1983), 19–23; 71–72.

norms without the added traumas of family disorganization and physical displacement.[39]

These systems of organization were alternatives to the coexisting institution of slavery. The enslavement of Native Americans continued as integral to the arsenal of Iberian colonial labor control for 250 years. It remained quasi-legitimate until the very end of the colonial era. Although slaves and free Indians were both located in a hierarchy of dependency, slaves were full private property.[40] The enslavement of Indians, until constricted, was rationalized throughout the Americas under a number of traditional arguments: as punishment for alliances with enemies of the sovereign; as a mechanism of conversion; as a punishment for savagery; as a mode of rescue (*resgate*) and resettlement. As in the Mediterranean, the success of the process depended upon internal ethnic or tribal divisions among the "enslavable."[41]

As in Muslim North Africa, Indian enslavement was mainly a phenomenon of borderlands where imperial or colonial public authority was poorly enforced. It might precede, succeed, or coexist with other modes of controlling Indian labor and behavior, a constant problem for thinly settled elites.[42] Especially early in colonization, sharp drops in population resulted in dramatic experimental shifts between these institutions. In Santo Domingo, the initial encomienda system was rapidly undermined by the depletion of the native population. The Spanish monarch then sanctioned slave raiding in neighboring Caribbean islands. Santo Domingo colonists rounded up more than 10,000 slaves in five years.[43] This island soon absorbed the entire populations of surrounding islands. Such roundups simply added to the elimination of Caribbean native populations by disease. They were soon replaced by African slaves purchased from the Portuguese. Africans were more expensive to acquire than the early native captives, but less difficult to obtain than the Carib warriors of the lesser Antilles and coastal South America.[44]

---

[39] Lockhart and Schwartz, *Early Latin America*, 72–73, 196–197.

[40] Robin M. Wright and Manuela Carneiro da Cunha, "Southern, Coastal and Northern Brazil (1580–1890)," in *The Cambridge History of the Native Peoples of the Americas* (Cambridge, UK: Cambridge University Press, 1998), III, part 2, 302–312. See also the decree of the French Royal Council of 1745, quoted in Almon Lauber Wheeler, *Indian Slavery in Colonial Times* (New York: Columbia University Press, 1913), 64.

[41] For the history of enslavement in the South American borderlands, see the essay of Wright and Cunha, in *Cambridge History of (the Native Peoples of the Americas*, 3 vols. (Cambridge, UK: Cambridge University Press, 1996–2000), III, 2, 315 ff.

[42] Lockhart and Schwartz, *Early Latin America*, 68–72; 92–96.

[43] Genaro Rodriguez Morel, "The Sugar Economy of Espanola in the Sixteenth Century," in *Tropical Babylons: Sugar and the Making of the Atlantic World, 1450–1680*, Stuart B. Schwartz, ed. (Chapel Hill: University of North Carolina, 2004), 103.

[44] Kenneth F. Kiple and Kriemhild C. Evans, "After the Encounter: Disease and Demographics in the Lesser Antilles," in *The Lesser Antilles in the Age of European Expansion*, Robert

As the colonial frontier moved southward into Central America, the quest for labor for mines and porterage accelerated. The second quarter of the sixteenth century appears to have marked the apogee of Amerindian slavery. Nicaragua became a vast zone of enslavement. There, the spectre of total annihilation seems to have had more impact in eliciting final imperial constraint on enslavement than the pleas of Las Casas and other humanitarian voices. In 1533, the Governor of Nicaragua told the Spanish Crown that 6,000 Indians had died in a single epidemic of measles, that free Indians were fleeing illegal transportation by unlicensed vessels, and that the supply of natives could barely last four years at the current rate of attrition. Three years later, the trade was officially prohibited.[45]

Portuguese colonists also made Indians the primary targets of their enslavement efforts in the Americas for most of the century after 1492. What began in Brazil as a minor trade with the Native Americans for tropical items, such as logwood, was transformed by the discovery that coastal Brazil was an outstanding site for the production of sugar.[46] The native population resisted conversion to labor in the sugar fields and the colonists turned to enslavement to recruit sufficient labor for their plantations. Colonists began systematically to gather workers through raiding. Jesuit-organized missions also sought to congregate sufficient free labor as an alternative to coerced labor. In certain areas, Jesuit missionaries clashed with Portuguese slavers. In others, the Jesuits participated in the trade.[47]

Both systems of concentration proved demographically disastrous, stimulating both further raids and the colonists' switch to an African slave labor force. Despite this transition and increasing imperial Portugese legislative

---

L. Paquette and Stanley L. Engerman, eds. (Gainesville: University Press of Florida, 1996), 50–67.

[45] See David R. Radell, "The Indian Slave Trade and Population of Nicaragua during the Sixteenth Century," in *The Native Population of the Americas in 1492*, William M. Denevan, ed. (Madison: University of Wisconsin Press, 1976), 73–75. William L. Sherman, *Forced Native Labor in Sixteenth-Century Central America* (Lincoln: University of Nebraska Press, 1979), offers a much more conservative estimate of 50,000. With estimates of enslavement varying from 50,000 to 450,000, Murdo Macleod concludes that "a total of 200,000 Indians for the whole Nicaraguan slaving period appears to be conservative." Using Macleod's figure would probably rank Central America as the largest-scale slaving zone in the sixteenth-century world. Even Sherman's estimate would render Central America alone as almost equal in volume to the Atlantic slave trade before 1550. Murdo J. Macleod, *Spanish Central America: A Socioeconomic History, 1520–1720* (Berkeley: University of California Press, 1973), 52.

[46] See Stuart B. Schwartz, *Sugar Plantations in the formation of Brazilian Society: Bahia, 1550–1835* (Cambridge, UK: Cambridge University Press, 1985), and *Cambridge History*, III (2), 318–19; 363.

[47] See Anne Christine Taylor, "Amazonian Western Margins (1500–1800)," in *Cambridge History... Native Americans*, III, pt. 2, 215: on "the remarkable persistence" of the slave trade in the *montãna*: "This paltry slave economy generated very little wealth...."

constraints after 1550, the enslavement of Indians continued for two centuries. As along the Spanish frontier, enslavement in Brazil was tied to cycles
of conflict, economic growth and conversion rationalized by notions of just
war, salvation, and civilization. In Hispanic zones experiencing severe economic decline, it may have been the only institution that kept impoverished
masters from "going native." In Brazil, thousands of Indians were being
enslaved well into the eighteenth century, as successive Portuguese monarchs
alternatively constrained, abolished, and tolerated revivals of the institution.
At the headwaters of the northern Amazon, slaving reached its zenith only
during the middle of the eighteenth century.[48]

In North America, Indian slaves rarely played as significant a role in the
colonial economies as they did in parts of the Iberian-dominated Americas.
In the first phase of British colonization, the enslavement of Native Americans often preceded or coexisted with the establishment of African slavery.[49]
It is worth noting, however, that in 1775, Native Americans constituted the
overwhelming majority of slaves in Canada, Britain's most northern colony.
Indian slavery played a key role in at least one early British colonial settlement. In the 1670s and 1680s, Carolina's labor force consisted primarily
of European indentured servants. When the supply of indentured servants
declined and planters could not successfully compete for African slaves, the
colonists turned towards Native Americans. By 1710, Indian slaves made up
a quarter of the colony's bound laborers. Thereafter, the number of Indian
slaves and their share of the labor force declined.[50]

What most clearly emerges from an overview of early modern slavery in
the Americas is that Native Americans never disappeared from the roster
of those publicly recognized as slaves. With the slow consolidation of state
power and the end of large-scale resistance, the enslavement of Indians
slowly declined in the Iberian orbit. The Spanish Crown's prohibition of
enslavement in 1652 was largely observed except at contested frontiers.
In the Portuguese Amazon region, however, enslavement continued and
increased in some areas because the price of African slaves remained beyond

[48] *Ibid.*, 215.
[49] Betty Wood, *The Origins of American Slavery: Freedom and Bondage in the English
Colonies* (New York: Hill and Wang, 1997); Alan Gallay, *The Indian Slave Trade: The
Rise of the English Empire in the American South, 1670–1717* (New Haven: Yale Univer-
sity Press, 2002); and *Culture and Identities in Colonial British America*, Robert Olwell and
Alan Tully, eds. (Baltimore: John Hopkins University Press, 2006), esp. ch. 1, 2.
[50] In the case of French Canada, the late seventeenth century opened a market for Pawnees
enslaved by other Indians and sold to the French. Market conditions ensured that Native
American slaves played a larger role in the Canadian variant of the institution than did
Africans. See Marcel Trudel, *L'Esclavage au Canada français: histoire et conditions de
l'esclavage* (Quebec: Presses Universitaires, 1960) 41 ff., and David Brion Davis, *The Problem of Slavery in Western Culture* (Ithaca: Cornell University Press 1966; rev. ed. Oxford
University Press, 1988), 179.

the means of most Portuguese colonists along the Amazon and Orinoco watersheds.

Alternatives: Asians and Europeans

Colonial European enslavement of Native Americans during the centuries following the Columbian voyages illustrates a number of important points about the globalization of slavery during the early modern era. In the flurry of experimentation that followed the opening of the Atlantic, the Europeans' first recourse was to the coercion of people already settled close to their original habitats. European adventurers' appetite for labor experimentation extended everywhere around the world. Their institution building was as experimental and pragmatic as their opportunities. The appetites for employers of labor in the New World expanded still further in the wake of Magellan's arduous feat of circumnavigation early in the sixteenth-century.

As early as the late sixteenth century, the deep demographic crisis in Spanish America stimulated a search for movable labor from Asia. In 1573, Diego de Artieda proposed a slave traffic in Filipinos to meet the labor demands of New Spain. In 1601, mine owners in Mexico petitioned for "Chinese, Japanese, and Javanese" laborers via the Philippines.[51] Under the rubric of *chinos*, slaves from East Asia were imported via Manila

---

[51] Russell R. Menard and Stuart B. Schwartz, "Why African Slavery? Labor Force Transitions in Brazil, Mexico, and the Carolina Lowcountry," in *Slavery in the Americas*, Wolfgang Binder, ed. (Konigshausen and Neumann, 1993), 89–110. Colonizers in the Indian Ocean world had no difficulty adjusting themselves to the creation of new zones of slavery. The Portuguese slave trade to Spanish Manila included captives from China, Japan, India, Indonesia, and Africa. Their market extended to Spanish America and "Asians were a significant part of their slave cargoes. . . . " See Tatiana Seijas, "The Portuguese Slave Trade to Spanish Manila: 1580–1640," *Itinerario*, 32:1 (2008), 19–38. On the Dutch trade, see Marcus Vink, "'The World's Oldest Trade', Dutch Slavery and the Slave Trade in the Indian Ocean in the Seventeenth Century," *Journal of World History*, 14 (2) (2003), pp. 131–177. European slavers could become deeply entangled in the complexity of the boundaries of enslavement in East Asia. By the end of the sixteenth century, traders in Japanese slaves faced challenges on three fronts. Jesuits sought the help of imperial authority in restricting Portuguese slavers of Japanese because they interfered with the conversion process. Japanese Christians protested against the sale of the faithful to non-Christians. The Chinese authorities threatened Portuguese traders with decapitation if enslaved Japanese were imported into the seaport of Macão. Fearing the Japanese as a subversive threat, the Chinese urged the Portuguese to stick to their by-now traditional prey: "You are Westerners and so what use are Japanese to you when you [can] use blacks"? In unifying the fragmented Japanese polity, a Japanese Shogun also opposed the Portuguese exportation of Japanese, even while he undertook the enslavement of Koreans after invading neighboring Korea. See Nelson Thomas, "Slavery in Medieval Japan," *Monumenta Nipponica*, 59:4 (2004), 463–494. The Mughals of India also expelled Portuguese traders from a Bengali port when their activities threatened to contribute to the depletion of the cultivators in that region. See Sanjay Subrahmanyam, "Slaves and Tyrants: Dutch Tribulations in Seventeenth-Century Mrauk-U," *Journal of*

into Mexico. When the enslavement of Filipinos was prohibited (with the usual "just war" escape clause), slaves from China, India, Indonesia, and Madagascar were transferred to New Spain via Manila. With the movement of Indian Ocean and East Asian slaves across the ocean, the sun never set on Phillip II's slaving empire. The prohibition in 1700 on the further shipping of slaves from the Philippines coincided with a demographic revival in New Spain. The growth of Afro-Mexican and Mestizo free labor reduced the Spanish demand for both Asian and African slaves.

Even where slaves were still desired in large numbers, the cost of shipping labor eastward from the Indian Ocean and Pacific worlds could not compete with the transatlantic slave trade.[52] About two-thirds of the ten million Africans who survived their Atlantic crossing were landed in Europe's sugar colonies. From 1580 to 1820, between 60 and 85 percent of all transatlantic migrants were African slaves. From the late seventeenth century onwards, the European plantation complex clearly recruited slaves from Africa at a faster rate and in greater numbers than did the Muslim world. The number of European nations entering the system dramatically increased, reaching a peak around 1700. More than two-thirds of the Africans arriving in the New World during the existence of the transatlantic slave trade were delivered during the century and a half between the last of Louis XIV's wars and the aftermath of Napoleon Bonaparte's defeat.

Was this massive turn to African slave labor the only feasible alternative to the development of the Atlantic system? Until recently, the historiography of the rise of New World slavery focused on an explanation largely in terms of basic economic factors[53]: abundant land in America; an abundant labor supply in Africa; and capital, technology, and consumer demand in Europe. It is often assumed that Europe could not have supplied competitive labor for the plantations. Except for a brief period during the mid-seventeenth century, both free and indentured European laborers were relatively too costly to transport and too vulnerable to willingly sustain the harsh continuous labor required to produce the most profitable commodities in the Americas. Africa was exceptional in offering a wider, more stable, and more elastic source

---

Early Modern History, 1:3 (1997), 209. In Asia, as in Africa, European traders had to maneuver between powerful rulers.

[52] David Eltis, "Free and Coerced Transatlantic Migrations: Some Comparisons," *American Historical Review*, 88:2 (1983), 251–280; and Eltis, "Free and Coerced Migrations from the Old World to the New," in *Coerced and Free Migration: Global Perspectives*, David Eltis, ed. (Stanford: Stanford University Press, 2002)," 33–74, esp. figures 1 and 2, and table I.

[53] See, inter alia, Russell R. Menard, "From Servants to Slaves: The Transformation of the Chesapeake Labor System," *Southern Studies*, 16 (1977), 355–90; David W. Galenson, *White Servitude in Colonial America: An Economic Analysis* (Cambridge, UK: Cambridge University Press, 1984); Hilary McD. Beckles and Andrew Downes, "The Economics of Transition to the Black Labor System in Barbados, 1630–1680," *Journal of Interdisciplinary History*, 18 (1987).

of the most reliable lifelong captive labor in the Atlantic world. And, by the end of the seventeenth century, enslaved Africans had become the trade commodity of choice for European and African merchants on the Western coast of sub-Saharan Africa.

Some historians have emphasized that Africans were not, of course, the only potential source of Old World labor for settlement in the lowland New World. As David Eltis notes, western Europeans were at least as abundant and as available for transoceanic migration as were West Africans. Indentured servitude was briefly cost-effective for two colonizing states, England and France. Portugal, the initiator of the Atlantic slave trade, shipped off a large number of convicts in the initial stages of its overseas empire. In the mid-seventeenth century, a higher number and proportion of migrants left England than at any point between 1500 and 1800.[54] Moreover, Eltis states, hypothetical transatlantic shipments of Northern Europeans stowed aboard as tightly as were Africans, would have been quicker to arrive and cheaper to deliver because Euro-American voyages were shorter. Crew and passenger mortality would have been lower than in the African trades. Dockside loading costs of northwestern Europeans were always lower than were their West African counterparts. Convicts from much of Europe were already manning galley ships in the Mediterranean and military fortifications all over the world.[55]

A system for harvesting all European convicts, prisoners, and vagrants for labor in the New World "could easily have provided fifty thousand forced migrants a year without serious disruption to either international peace or existing social institutions that generated and supervised these potential European victims." That they did not, concludes Eltis, was because of an "almost intangible barrier," to an "inconceivable" policy. This cultural barrier, already unbreachable on the eve of transatlantic colonization, made it possible for Europeans to kill other Europeans in battle, burn them as witches and heretics, execute them as thieves, chain them to galley benches, ship them overseas as convicts, but never to transport them to lifetime of forced labor, much less as chattel.[56]

---

[54] For English migration estimates, see E. A. Wrigley and R. S. Schofield, *The Population History of England 1541–1871: A Reconstruction* (New York: Cambridge University Press, 1981), 528–529. Despite a net migration of 2.7 million, during the whole era of England's participation in the Atlantic slave system the country's population increased by 700 percent. See David Eltis, "Free and Coerced Migrations," 33–74 for a discussion of comparative African and European streams. Other historians who have considered Europeans as potential alternatives to Africans as the labor force are Robin Blackburn, *The Making of New World Slavery: From the Baroque to the Modern 1492–1800*, (London: Verso, 1997), 350–363; and Russell R. Menard, "Transitions to African Slavery in British America, 1630–1730: Barbados, Virginia and South Carolina," *Indian Historical Review*, 15 (1988–89), 33–49.

[55] Eltis, *Rise of African Slavery in the Americas*, 64–80.

[56] *Ibid.*, 70ff.

This hypothesis has important implications for any analysis of the emergence of abolitionism at the end of the eighteenth century. In fact, by 1500, the barriers against Euro-European lifetime servitude were high, but not insuperable. We have already seen that some Europeans in a position to do so sold other Europeans into enslavement, even to non-Europeans. European rulers, especially those who took the lead in transoceanic trade and colonization, publicly invoked their right to treat other Europeans as slaves within their own realms. Recall that, in 1493, the Portuguese king had no qualms about enslaving refugees from Spain to launch the colony of São Tomé. His Spanish counterparts, Ferdinand of Aragon and Isabella, even more casually enslaved fellow Europeans. Following the siege of Málaga in Granada between 1487 and 1502, Italian merchants, acting as royal slave brokers, accomplished the ransoms or sales of 450 Jews and 6,000 Muslims.[57] The traditional "just war" rationale still made it perfectly unobjectionable to dispose of their captives in the market. Western European rulers had more serious misgivings about enslaving other Christians, but within eastern Europe Christians continued to become slaves of Muslims into the eighteenth century.

Within western Europe, however, even the most despised European was spared degradation to chattel status, and the barrier against Euro-European enslavement generally held in the western European colonies.[58] Nevertheless, it was far from "inconceivable" that any of Europe's potential labor pool of convicts, prisoners of war, and vagrants could have been converted into chattel slaves or forced laborers for life. Recall the suggestion that English royalist military prisoners who refused to join the Parliamentary army be sold to the Barbary pirates as slaves. Cromwell himself threatened to ship "into slavery in Barbados all those captured in arms."[59]

---

[57] Helen Nader, "Desperate Men," *Sixteenth Century Journal*, 33:2 (2002), 401–422, esp. 407–408.

[58] Eltis, *Rise of African Slavery*, 70. See also Eltis, "Europeans and the Rise and Fall of African Slavery in the Americas: An Interpretation," *American Historical Review*, 98 (1993), 1399–1426, where Eltis aptly conflates chattel slavery and lifetime servitude for purposes of analyzing the potential substitution of European convicts for African slaves as the labor force of choice in the plantation Americas. Of the two differentiating criteria between convict and slave labor (lifetime service and status heritability), the first was obviously not affected by any cultural or psychological inhibition against the acceptability of chattel status. In terms of cost and productivity, it is not clear that a steady delivery of adult Europeans to the Americas at much lower rates of mortality than were incurred in the African slave trade would not, also, have been cheaper than raising slaves from infancy in the tropical colonies. See Seymour Drescher, "White Atlantic"? The Choice for African Slave Labor in the Plantation Americas," in *Slavery in the Development of the Americas*, David Eltis, Frank D. Lewis, and Kenneth L. Sokoloff, eds. (New York: Cambridge University Press, 2004), 31–69.

[59] Carleton, *Going to the Wars*, 327–28.

Even more significant, European governments reserved the penultimate penalty of lifetime servitude for Europeans assigned to the traditional site of European enslavement, the Mediterranean galleys. The classes of offenders so punished in France were military deserters and religious dissenters. Why were such potential laborers, already designated for service unto death, not sent westward to meet the endless demand for coerced labor? Let us begin with the Portuguese. The Portuguese first choice for coerced cash-crop laborers were always those on the spot. They required no long distance transportation. By the beginning of the sixteenth century, Africans had already become the labor force of choice for São Tomé. The epidemiological impact of pathogens in São Tomé was as decisive in the Portuguese choice as was the impact of Euro-African pathogens on the Amerindian populations of Brazil. It led the Portuguese planters in Brazil to switch from Native American to African slaves for the production of sugar. More striking, however, is that by the time of that switch, African slaves had been a source of labor supply for Portugal for a century. There simply was an insufficient pool of potential coerced labor at home, much less awaiting employment for intensive labor overseas. The Portuguese government had to recruit black slaves, not only for labor at home, but also on the high seas. African slaves met shortages of manpower in the Indian Ocean, and even on Portuguese slave ships. Given these simultaneous demands, the Portuguese ruler was hardly in a position to enter into conflict with its own landed elites to seize and deploy large numbers of his own subjects on deadly Atlantic islands or Brazilian plantations. Even criminals (*degredados*), exiled to various parts of the Portuguese empire, were immediately promoted from criminals to policing forces of order on departure from Europe.[60] The arrival of African slaves in the metropolis only made up for between one-third and one-half of the Portuguese laborers departing to man its seaborne empire. Only in the seventeenth century did the demand for slaves in the competitive Brazilian sugar economy slow down African imports into Europe.[61] Finally, imperial Old World priorities – on galleys, in North African fortress towns, and in enclaves along the coasts of the Atlantic and Indian Oceans – made it inconceivable that the Portuguese would ever be the coerced labor of choice for the development of Brazil's plantations.[62]

For the Portuguese, using foreign European prisoners of war instead of Africans was never available as an alternative to Africans for reasons that

---

[60] Timothy J. Coates, *Convicts and Orphans: Forced and State-Sponsored Colonizers in the Portuguese Empire 1550–1775* (Stanford, CA: Stanford University Press, 2001).

[61] See Vitorino Magalhães Godinho, "Portuguese Emigration," in *European Expansion and migration: Essays on the intercontinental migration Africa, Asia and Europe*, P.C. Emmer and M. Mörner, eds. (New York: Berg, 1992), 19.

[62] *Ibid.*, 24.

were not peculiarly "European." Expanding enslavability would have required an enormous reworking of the "just war" concept. One need not, however, consider only religious or pigmental obstacles to creating a European slave-labor stream to the Americas. Consider the vulnerability of all European colonizers themselves beyond the line. Within their own empires, the last thing that the Iberian monarchs could imagine was peopling its New World empire with expelled unbelievers. Even using newly minted "New Christian" or Protestant heretic slaves was militarily absurd. At the end of the fifteenth century, Iberian rulers had made strenuous efforts to cleanse their realms of Jews. When the Iberian Inquisition painstakingly identified individual descendants of Jewish converts ("New Christians") as "Judaizers," they were dispatched to the Mediterranean galleys, not to New World plantations. Catholic monarchs in France as well as Iberia made serious efforts to keep their overseas colonies religiously pure. In colonies such as sixteenth-century New Spain, where people of African descent in every major town outnumbered those of Europeans, it would have seemed the height of strategic folly to create an additional preponderance of new Protestant Christians over old Catholic Christians.

Portuguese imperial problems were not merely demographic and religious. They needed all of the capital they could spare, economic and human, to launch their transatlantic plantation complex.[63] They had to seek economic and human capital well beyond their own borders. Any attempt by Portugal, one of western Europe's smaller states, to attack other European states to obtain prisoners of war in lieu of enslaved Africans simply would have invited disastrous massive retaliation. It is difficult to conceive of any reasonable scenario that would have permitted even a much mightier European state to convert European prisoners of war into an annual forced migration stream of tens of thousands without serious disruption to its own international security.

Indeed, in the Portuguese case, we have an empirical demonstration, based upon power principles alone, of why Portugal could not undertake such a policy. Let us return to Portugal's pioneering decade, the year before Vasco da Gama rounded the Cape of Good Hope and opened the Indian Ocean to European trade, and two years before the Portuguese encountered Brazil. Recall that in 1497, King Manuel ordered the rounding up of all Jewish children whose parents refused to convert. Of this event, a Portuguese chronicler commented:

Now it appears that we might be regarded as neglectful if we did not state the reason why the king ordered the children of the Jews to be taken from them, but not those of the Moors, because they too left the kingdom because they did not wish to receive the water of baptism and believe what the Catholic Church believes. The reason was

---

[63] By the 1540s, the Crown was so concerned with the depletion of its population that departures from the kingdom had to be licensed. Coates, *Convicts*, 10.

that from the seizure of the Jews' children no harm could result for the Christians dispersed throughout the world, in which the Jews, because of their sins, do not have kingdoms or lordships, cities and towns, but rather, everywhere they live they are pilgrims and taxpayers, without having power or authority to carry out their wishes against the injuries and evils which are done to them. But for *our* sins and punishment, God allows the Moors to occupy the greater part of Asia and Africa and a great part of Europe, where they have empires and kingdoms and great lordships, in which many Christians are under tribute to them, as well as many whom they hold as captives. For all these [reasons], it would be very prejudicial to take the Moors' children way from them, because it is clear that they would not hesitate to avenge those to whom such an injury was done on the Christians living in the lands of other Moors, once they found out about it, and above all on the Portuguese, against whom they would have a particular grievance in this regard. And this was the reason why [the Muslims] were allowed to leave the kingdom with their children and the Jews were not, to all of whom God permitted through his mercy to know the way of truth, so that they might be saved in it.[64]

The starting point for any analysis of the creation of transatlantic slavery must also consider the role of slave resistance by Africans. The slave ship was an explosive container of brutality and desperation. The miasma of despair bred many forms of resistance – hunger strikes, suicide, and insurrection, the greatest threat to each voyage. We now know a great deal about the frequency and distribution of slave revolts. It is clear that one cannot speak simply of "African" resistance. Revolts were far more likely on slaves shipped from a particular region. More than 40 percent of all insurrections arose among slaves boarded in the Upper Guinea sector of the coast.

One must approach a possible Euro-European slave trade from the same perspective. Such an enterprise would have had to be created not by "Europeans," but by national and imperial states. For two centuries, the average number of exiled Portuguese convicts deported annually was 250, or less than 5 per cent of the number of African slaves transported to Brazil. These first two centuries of the transatlantic slave systems were also the most warlike in modern European history, whether calculated in terms of years of warfare, frequency, average duration, or in magnitude. By the time the Portuguese began substituting African for Indian slaves in the Americas (1580–1640), the oceans were no longer dominated by the united Iberian monarchy. Northern Europeans now posed a greater danger to the Spanish and the Portuguese overseas empires than did the Maghreb privateers. Even when Philip II concentrated on convoying the treasure fleet from the Americas to Spain, the Portuguese *carreira da India* and the Iberian Newfoundland fishing fleets were devastated.

---

[64] From Damião de Gois, "Cronica do felicissimo Rei Don Manuel," in *Damião de Gois*, Antonio Alvaro Doria, ed. (Lisbon 1944), 53–56, translated in *The Jews in Western Europe 1400–1600*, John Edwards, ed. (Manchester: Manchester University Press, 1994), 61–67.

Nor was the situation much better for the rising northern European seapowers. By 1650, they became equally menacing to each other. When they founded their seventeenth-century colonial empires, the Dutch, English, and French states were in rough naval equilibrium. At least two of the three were almost always at war with each other after 1650. In such a situation, the prospect of mutual enslavement of their nationals could only have added an additional layer of ferocity to their European naval battles. Even without Euro-European enslavement, privateering and African slave resistance disrupted the flow of African slaves.[65] To the brutality of ordinary naval encounters would have been added the prospect of European captives below decks rising to join their fellow countrymen and rescuers.

Even more significant than the costs of shipboard surveillance at sea would have been those entailed in policing slave settlements. Newly arrived Africans found themselves isolated from any possibility of rescue by friendly West African forces. The opposite would have occurred with Europeans as captives. Every slave island would have become a target of opportunity for foreign rescuers. The ever-shifting combinations of antagonists in Europe would have signaled unstable combinations of potential enemy liberators and enslavers. When an Anglo-French conflict broke out in 1666, the French seized the English part of the divided island of St. Christopher. They appropriated its 400 black slaves and deported its 5,000 white settlers. In a world of unlimited enslavement, the victors would have multiplied their human booty by more than 1,200 percent. The unparalleled ratios of eight or nine African slaves to every free white islander could never have been replicated under conditions in which every capitalist also had to consider himself as potential capital.

Finally, one must consider the implications of large-scale Euro-European enslavement on Europe itself. Establishing colonies had a far lower priority for metropolitans than did their own survival. As with the Portuguese, ordinary domestic criminals were far too few in number to provide sufficient numbers for all imperial schemes and military ventures. For the Iberians, the needs of the galley warfare in the Mediterranean, troops in North Africa, and seaborne empires in the East prevailed over those of the Atlantic through the first half of the seventeenth century.

A look at the behavior of later colonial powers demonstrates the same priorities. More than any other northwestern colonizing power, the Dutch needed sailors and soldiers in the Old World far more than it needed field

---

[65] See Eltis et al., Transatlantic Slave Trade Database; Drescher, "White Atlantic?", 56. For a detailed analysis of slave revolts, see Stephen D. Behrendt, David Eltis, and David Richardson, "The Costs of Coercion: African Agency in the Pre-modern Atlantic World," *Economic History Review*, 54:3 (2001), 454–476, esp. 457, fig. 1. For an arresting study of the slave ship as a site of resistance, see Marcus Rediker, *The Slave Ship: A Human History* (New York: John Murray, 2007), passim.

slaves in the New World. The Dutch East India Company mobilized a voluntary and heavily foreign overseas movement of up to one million Europeans. This amounted to double the number of Africans loaded by Dutch slavers. Equally vital for survival were the Republic's armies in Europe. At times, 60 percent of its soldiers were foreigners. During the century that it established colonies in Brazil and the Caribbean, the Netherlands was often fighting for its very existence against the most formidable land armies in Europe: the Spanish army of Flanders at the beginning of the seventeenth century and the French armies of Louis XIV at the end.

In France itself, the crimes for which those subjects of Louis XIV were sentenced to lifetime servitude amply demonstrate that monarch's priorities: recalcitrant Protestants were sent to the Mediterranean galleys, thus purifying Catholic France without religiously polluting New France and the Caribbean. The other equally harsh sentence was for military desertion. Louis XIV expanded his 20,000 man army in the 1660s to 300,000 by 1710, the largest army in Europe. It amounted to more than six times the total French migration to the New World during his long reign. In an era of unprecedented mobilizations of Frenchmen for military service, what could overseas ventures expect? As the first Intendant of New France wrote to his sovereign in 1666, there was a dearth of "supernumeraries and useless subjects in old France to people the new one."[66]

Demographically, England offered the best potential for a non-African alternative slave labor during the establishment of the European colonies. As late as the 1650s, only one out of three migrants to the English Americas was an African slave. Until well beyond mid-century, English labor, much of it involuntary, was still available for long-term hire, with sufficient credit and infrastructural facilities to deliver them to the colonies at a profit. More than any other colonizers, British investors originally founded their plantation economy with a mainly European workforce. The seventeenth-century exodus from England actually peaked just before the turn to African slave labor, with more than one hundred thousand people departing from England to the New World.[67]

---

[66] Leslie Choquette, *Frenchmen into Peasants: Modernity and Tradition in the Peopling of French Canada* (Cambridge, MA: Harvard University Press, 1997), 248. On the significance of religious exclusion, see *ibid.*, 282. As Peter Moogk concludes, "even if it were possible to find the notarial records of all the French ports serving the Americas, and even if each deed for a contract [i.e., indentured] worker represented a real departure the total number of contract workers thus delivered [to Canada] would not exceed thirty-five thousand . . . about half the number of eighteenth-century German migrants to Philadelphia before the American Revolution." (*La Nouvelle France: The Making of French Canada – a Cultural History* (East Lansing: Michigan State University Press, 2000), 104. By 1666, more than two-thirds of the king's *engages* had gone home.

[67] Eltis, *Rise of African Slavery*, 83.

In the 1640s and 1650s, England produced a wide range of other possible sources of bound and coerced labor: prisoners of war, convicts, social undesirables, prostitutes, sturdy beggars, and vagabonds. One must certainly agree with Eltis that, if convicts and prisoners of war had been condemned to lifetime service or chattel slavery, planters would have paid a high price for them, possibly competitive with what was being offered for Africans. At this premium, "the British government and merchants might have found ways to provide more convicts" – presumably enough ways to raise the numbers of lifetime bondsmen to the annual quota of 10,000 laborers demanded by colonial planters each year by the beginning of the eighteenth century. All could have been shipped more cheaply than the Africans actually landed in the English Americas. The English Civil Wars of the 1640s and 1650s also produced an initial surge of prisoners of war, both domestic and foreign, coinciding almost precisely with the peak of enforced migration to English America.

What restrained Englishmen from taking the extra step to creating a condition of lifetime servitude for many of the inhabitants of the British Isles? Given the temptations of war-induced captives and religion-induced hatred on the one hand, and surging planter demand for cultivators on the other, this poses a crucial question. Eltis locates the failure to take the final step in a powerful internalized European cultural barrier. The line to slavery was not crossed, he hypothesizes, because of a fundamentally psychological European inhibition to cross it or (*pace* the Earl of Stamford) to even contemplate crossing it.

The answer may lie elsewhere. The history of impressments for the English navy offers an inkling of just what might have occurred in the event of a political decision to form a large-scale system of coercive labor in the new colonies. Impressment was an extraordinary extension of a voluntary labor market. In the 1650s, very few volunteers in Cromwell's navy were willing to sign up for a major colonization campaign in the Caribbean once news about mortality rates there filtered back to England. Outside the capital city, the "press" faced enormous difficulties. Parish constables were often afraid to carry out their recruitment orders. When a government had to threaten recalcitrant constables with impressment for nonfulfillment of their quotas, one can glimpse the sharply rising cost of enforcement, even in a national war emergency. Had planters simply offered higher prices for coerced laborers at a time when royalists and parliamentarians were desperately competing for popular loyalty, could massive coercion conceivably have brought the private rate of return close to the social rate of return?

In many parts of England, impressment, in fact, faced near paralysis. Some magistrates deliberately failed to press a single man for Cromwell's navy. If the failure to enforce payment of ship money to Charles I had produced imprisoned martyrs for liberty, what would imprisonment for failure to produce mass convicts for Barbadian planters have generated?

Government press gangs arriving to pick up even legitimately convicted petty thieves, destined for sugar gangs, found their prey gone and themselves in flight under a hail of stones. It was precisely the enduring strength of local self-government, a distinctive characteristic of English administration, that would have made the conversion of England into a zone of enslavement for its own citizens more expensive than almost anywhere else in Europe.[68]

Warfare within the larger British Isles might have offered a more promising path to coerced transatlantic migration than imprisonment of Englishmen.[69] Battles generated prisoners. Perhaps as many as 12,000 Irish, English, and Scottish royalists were thus transported. This was not, however, an economically viable mode of recruitment. Armies raised in the Civil War were intended as short-term and expensive human mobilizations. Deportation was almost always used as a deterrence, or as a short-term terror tactic, not a long-term labor supply strategy. The threat of deportation accomplished the political aim of pacification as effectively as did its implementation. A long and expensive war of attrition in Scotland was brought to an end by just the threat to ship into "slavery in Barbados all those captured in arms." The war did generate a flow of prisoners to the West Indies. But, the benefits to the planters were hardly commensurate with the costs of accumulation. England lost a higher percentage of its population between 1640 and 1660 than in either of the twentieth century's two world wars. Scotland may well have lost 6 percent and Ireland 41 percent.[70]

The implications of the choice to use enslavement, not as a one-time threat to induce pacification but as an ongoing policy designed to ensure an adequate flow of prisoners to the Caribbean, seem clear. Ireland and Scotland would have become lands of marronage, perpetually awaiting, as they did in the aftermath of the English Revolution of 1689, the arrival of French armies and Stuart pretenders to stir insurrection on an ever more virulent scale. A turbulent countryside in Ireland ran counter to English landowners' needs for agricultural labor in a devastated and depopulated country. Would the needs of proximate Ireland have been subordinated to the needs of distant planters?

To these costs, we must add those of reproducing the coerced labor of Englishmen abroad. The problem of negative slave population growth in the Caribbean would have had to be addressed. The ratio of females to males in the actual transatlantic convict flow during the eighteenth century fell far short of that among enslaved Africans during the same period. The reproductive deficit of potential European bondsmen in the Caribbean

[68] See Wrigley and Schofield, *The Population History of England*, 528–529.
[69] Barnad Capp, *Cromwell's Navy* (Oxford: Clarendon Press, 1989), Ch. 8.
[70] Charles Carlton, *Going to the Wars* (London: Routledge, 1992), 327–342.

would, therefore, have been worse than that of the Africans. The most imaginable alternative, lifetime service, would have offered a zero reproduction rate, requiring still greater imports from the British Isles than was the case with Africans.

Therefore, one can presume that a much higher net flow of Europeans to the Americas would have been required to assure the same servile labor population in 1750 or 1800 than was achieved by its African counterpart. This would not have been the only cost to the European colonization in the Americas. English indentured servitude in America would almost certainly have been terminated and the redemption system for foreigners would have been stillborn. The most neglected variable in this counterfactual exercise has been the lack of attention to the distribution of political power in English civil society. In determining the barriers that made involuntary labor from England unavailable for the booming plantation system, one must, therefore, consider more than ideology and culture.

On the one hand, English rulers had two special incentives to push for large-scale coerced English labor in the Caribbean. More mid-seventeenth century Englishmen were able and willing to migrate overseas than were those of any other nation. Between 1640 and 1700, more Britons left for the Americas than did Spanish, Portuguese, French, and Dutch migrants combined. In terms of per capita migration, the disparity is still more impressive. Secondly, after 1650, the English West Indies experienced a surge of economic expansion and coerced-labor productivity that is almost "obscene" from a modern perspective.[71] In the face of this economic double incentive, English labor experienced no major interruption in its trajectory toward individual freedom and free labor. Indeed, "it was during the seventeenth century that the English tradition of invoking 'ancient native liberties' and 'rights of the freeborn' first became an important feature of the Anglo-American political landscape.... By century's end, the 'freeborn' Englishman had triumphed so completely in language that he began to define for the English what was unique about their culture."[72] All this was done without coming into conflict with the tradition of voluntary service at home. To incorporate the additional expenses of transatlantic transportation, labor contracts were extended. Time was money. But the bedrock of prior consent was not breached.

Therefore, although Europeans were, hypothetically, alternatives to Africans in the creation of the transatlantic plantation complex, two aspects of European and African development must be compared. The first concerns the fundamental distinction between the predominant basis of metropolitan European wealth compared with that of many other parts of the world in the

---

[71] Eltis, *Rise of African Slavery*, ch. 8.
[72] Steinfeld, *Invention of Free Labor*, 95.

centuries after 1500. People were the principal form of revenue-producing capital recognized in African law. In Africa, wars and raids for slaves were equivalent to wars of conquest. In European legal systems, land was the primary form of private revenue-producing wealth.[73] In Iberia, European slaves remained a minor form of legal property. Further north, slaves were not part of the prevailing metropolitan legal or property systems. Control over European labor was thus exercised through property rights in other factors of production, in land or fixed capital.

Despite the fact that warfare was endemic to the European continent throughout the sixteenth and seventeenth centuries, European rulers assumed that the benefits of conquest could best be reached by keeping peasants and artisans on site and doing business as usual. When Louis XIV, Europe's preeminent war lord of the second half of the seventeenth century, invaded the Dutch Republic in 1672, he distributed a message to all the communities he could reach: "His Majesty has been obliged, only with displeasure, to carry the War into the Lands possessed by the Dutch, and his design is only to punish those of the government, and not to ruin the populace...." His Majesty further promised "to pay his army punctually, to keep them in order, to have them feed themselves, to allow civilians and their goods free passage into towns, to provide towns with inexpensive protection against marauders."[74]

Viewed from the perspective of European economic institutional development, introducing either slave law or massive lifetime servitude into northwestern Europe would have been, for reasons of political economy and institutional efficiency, detrimental to development. The costs of enslavement did not begin in the barracoons of Benguela, and the costs of lifetime servitude would not have been confined to the servants' upkeep in Bristol barracoons.

For almost two centuries, western European rulers were able to dissociate their metropolitan and colonial trajectories. As long as the slave trade lasted, the plantation slave societies would remain among the wealthiest and most productive areas of the world. The consequence was that the most optimal division of labor led to the Africanization of the plantation in the Americas. The political and economic constraints on extending such an innovation into Europe itself were fairly clear. The international balance of power and retaliation acted as another deterrent to introducing bondage for Europeans, even in the plantation zones. No European power had sufficient omnipotence to be tempted to ignore the risks of creating zones of euroservitude in its own colonies. Thus, western European rulers of the seventeenth century made a very judicious economic decision by not converting either

[73] Thornton, *Africa and Africans*, 74.
[74] Drescher, "*White Atlantic?*," 63–64.

their home territories or those of other European states into reservoirs of involuntary servitude for colonial purposes. Establishing a zone of mass enslavement throughout western Europe would have raised transaction costs, disrupted law and order, reduced property rights in one's own person, and created a reign of terror for a significant minority, if not all, of western Europe's inhabitants.

Early northwestern European rulers preserved some legal distance between their European and colonial areas. The consequence was a formal and formidable division of labor in the Atlantic world. On the African side, the slave trade functioned with increasing efficiency. It depended, in the first instance, upon an African social system that was well adapted to deliver captives to the coast. Sub-Saharan Africa's cultural fragmentation enabled practices of internal enslavement that were readily transferable to the movement of captives to overseas destinations. Accelerating demand in the eighteenth century stimulated new trading networks to move interior slaves to the coast on a steadier basis. In Europe and its colonies, the organization of the slave trade was matched by the development of one of the most complex economic enterprises in the preindustrial world. The authority and resources of the state, which would have had to be deployed at enormous cost to develop European coerced systems of labor, were used to subsidize the establishment of a transatlantic slave trade from Africa to the Americas. The relatively modest costs of organization, initially funded by licensed monopoly companies, gradually gave way to systems permitting increasing numbers of national groups to participate in one or another aspect of trade and production.[75]

On the American side of the Atlantic, the figures of African slave labor for plantation agriculture for Europe and its settlers were even more dramatic. Caribbean exports accounted for two and one-half times more than exports from the North American mainland. Exports were £74 for each white resident in the Caribbean and only £1.6 per white resident on the mainland. Small wonder that an informed "political arithmetician" like Arthur Young used these figures to demonstrate Britain's relative advantage in deploying capital to buy Africans for the staple plantations rather than encouraging free farmers and tradesmen to settle in the northern continental colonies. All colonies, from Brazil to Jamaica, exported more per capita than those northern colonies with smaller percentages of slaves or growing staples other than sugar. In the Americas, generations of Europeans found their material existence improved by migration, and those with the highest incomes resided in the Caribbean, not on the North American continent.[76] From the

---

[75] See Klein, *The Atlantic Slave Trade* (Cambridge University Press, 1999), ch. 4.

[76] Eltis, "Introduction," in *Slavery in the Development of the Americas*, (New York: Cambridge University Press, 2004), 11–12; Arthur Young, *Political Essays Concerning the Present State of the British Empire* (London: W. Strahan & T. Cadell, 1772), 326 ff; and

perspective of their individual prosperity and collective economic development, many Europeans enjoyed, for a while, the best of all possible New Worlds.

T.R. Burnard, "Prodigious Riches: The Wealth of Jamaica before the American Revolution," *Economic History Review*, 54:3 (2001), 506–522.

3

Extension and Tension

A description of the first mass seaborne importation of African slaves into the Iberian Peninsula left a searing memory. The royal chronicler Gomes Eannes de Azurara described the deep discomfort caused by the division of the victims' families on arrival at Lagos:

But what human heart, no matter how hard, would not be stabbed by pious feelings when gazing upon such a company of people? For some had their heads held low and their faces bathed in tears, as they looked upon one another. Others were moaning most bitterly, gazing toward heaven, fixing their eyes upon it, as if they were asking for help from the father of nature. Others struck their faces with the palms of their hands, throwing themselves prostrate on the ground; others performed their lamentation in the form of a chant, according to the custom of their country, and, although our people could not understand the words of their language, they were fully appropriate to the level of their sorrow. But to increase their suffering even more, those responsible for dividing them up arrived on the scene and began to separate one from another, in order to make an equal division of fifths; from which arose the need to separate children from their parents, wives from their husbands, and brothers from their brothers. Neither friendship nor kinship was respected, but instead each one fell where fortune placed him!.... And so with great effort they finished the dividing up, because, aside from the trouble they had with the captives, the field was quite full of people, both from the town and from the surrounding villages and districts, who for that day were taking time off from their work, which was the source of their earnings, for the sole purpose of observing this novelty. And seeing these things, while some wept, others took part in the separating, and they made such a commotion that they greatly confused those who were in charge of dividing them up.[1]

Thereafter, the shock gave way to routinized indifference and business as usual.

[1] *Children of God's Fire: A Documentary History of Slavery in Brazil*, Robert Edgar Conrad, ed. (Princeton, NJ: Princeton University Press, 1983), 9–10.

Between the mid-fifteenth and the late eighteenth centuries, the institution of slavery expanded and intensified on every coast of the Atlantic. Over four centuries, rulers and merchants in every commercial center in Europe sought to enter into the new transoceanic system. The original mercantile and political innovators in the Iberian and Italian peninsulas in the fifteenth and sixteenth centuries were joined by northwestern, northern, and central Europeans in the next two centuries. At one point or another, every major and most minor states on the Atlantic littoral attempted to gain entrance into the Atlantic slave complex. Rulers and merchants in Africa also opened up new sources for European carriers. Along both coasts of the New World, slavery became an established institution in every European settlement from Canada to Rio de la Plata and from the Aleutian archipelago to Chile. The flow of Africans into the Muslim world also continued unabated.

Over the course of these four centuries, Europeans narrowed their experiments with various constituent groups for their labor needs. By the mid-eighteenth century, Africans and their descendants constituted the overwhelming majority of the New World's slaves. The average number of Africans loaded for the Atlantic "Middle Passage" reached nearly 30,000 a year in the late seventeenth century, 50,000 a year in the first half of the eighteenth century, and exceeded 75,000 a year in its second half.[2] This new expansion of the institution required the participation of individuals from all continents. Producers, transporters, traders, and consumers of slaves and slave products inhabited the Indian and Pacific ocean worlds as well as those of the Atlantic.

Iberia

The general enlargement of the Atlantic system required the participation of inhabitants from Scandinavia to Chile and from Canada to southern Africa and the Indian Ocean World. It was Europeans and their descendants, however, who were to play pioneering roles in globalizing both the expansion and abolition of the institution. Among the most accessible institutional vehicles for controlling labor were traditions of Roman slave law as modified by the centuries of intermittent struggle with Muslims. From the moment Europeans first moved along Africa's Atlantic coast, they encountered situations that made it necessary to alter the traditional rationalizations for acquiring and holding slaves. The initial encounters with sub-Saharan Africans in the 1440s entailed violence against Muslims south of Morocco. A royal chronicler of early Portuguese explorations recorded that by the end of that decade "deeds in those parts involved trade and mercantile dealings

[2] David Eltis, "The Transatlantic Slave Trade: A Reassessment Based on the Second Edition of the Transatlantic Slave Trade Database," my thanks to the author for allowing me to consult this manuscript (hereafter TSTD).

more than force of arms."[3] Nevertheless, the Portuguese chose to represent Portuguese-African relations as equal to a state of war. This served a number of purposes. A fundamental principle of Roman law held that captives in a just war offered a *prima facie* legal basis for enslavement. The continuation of conflicts between Christians and Muslims sustained the principle that a holy war allowed combatants to reduce infidel captives to perpetual servitude.

In 1452 the Portuguese requested a Papal Bull approving their right to acquire newly explored areas. They presented their actions as an extension of the Holy War against Islam. The Papal response, probably a virtual transcript of the original Portuguese request, gave them "full and free permission to invade, search out, capture and subjugate the Saracens and pagans and any other unbelievers and enemies of Christ wherever they may be, as well as their kingdoms, duchies, countries, principalities and other property... and to reduce their persons into perpetual slavery," to convert them.[4] A single sentence seamlessly linked pagans and religious enemies, lands and inhabitants, trade and conversion. The right to seize the inhabitants as slaves was conflated with sanction to acquire them by purchase. The Portuguese were more concerned at this juncture with establishing their rights of domination over new territories against their potential European rivals than obtaining the right to acquire slaves. Iberians had been enslaving Canary Islanders for more than a century without assuming the need for any prior religious sanction from Rome.[5] Two years later, Pope Nicholas V reconfirmed his sanctions. Acknowledging that Negro slaves had been obtained by both force and lawful barter and converted to the Catholic faith, he extended his sanction to all territories that might henceforth be acquired.[6]

Four decades later, as soon as Columbus reported his first success in 1493, Ferdinand and Isabella of Spain requested Pope Alexander VI to give them similar authority in any future transatlantic acquisitions. The Pope extended identical favor to the monarchs of Spain in the New World and to Portugal in Africa and points east. Both crowns received "full and free permission" to reduce the persons of "Saracen and pagan" lands to perpetual servitude. These papal Bulls were confirmed, in 1494, by the Treaty of Tordesillas. The treaty fixed a precise line of demarcation with each country receiving title to half of the unconverted globe. Along the longitude running 100 leagues to the west of the Canary Islands, the lands were assigned to Spain. Everything

---

[3] Cited in A.C. de C.M. Saunders, "The Depiction of Trade as War as a Reflection of Portuguese Ideology and Diplomatic Strategy in West Africa, 1441–1556," *Canadian Journal of History*, 17:2 (1982), 219–234; esp. 220.

[4] Maxwell, *Slavery and the Catholic Church*, 53.

[5] Thornton, *Africa and the Africans*, 28.

[6] Maxwell, *Slavery*, 54.

to the east of the line was to belong to the Portuguese. In 1506, Pope Julius II reaffirmed these terms of the treaty.

What was at stake in all of these negotiations and demarcations between sovereigns and popes were rights to occupy lands, not to enslave or purchase non-Christians.[7] The slave trade was approved as another acceptable means of bringing the infidels to Christ. Some Papal decrees approving commerce as worthy in itself also underwrote that activity as a rationale for acquiring slaves. Under the benign influence of commerce: "a wild and barbarous tribe, dedicated to lust and sloth, devoid of charity, and living like cattle, is at present beginning to shine forth in religion." In this respect, every trader was equivalent to a civilizing missionary.[8]

This rationalization could seamlessly be applied to Guinea and all points beyond the line of Muslim domination. In Africa, Portuguese arms could do little and commerce could do much. Indeed, during the following century Guinea was redesignated a "zone of peace," to aid a Portuguese empire increasingly threatened by conflicts with seaborne unbelievers. A Papal brief, in 1552, noted with satisfaction that profits from the Guinea trade were able to defray the cost of conflicts in Portuguese India, North Africa, and Brazil.[9] Moral justification was equally available at the national level. A Portuguese canonist, consulted by the King, concluded that where no cause of war existed merchants were only bound to trade in an equitable and legal manner. Lists of officially prohibited merchandise included commodities useful to enemies (metals and munitions), not slaves. Religious authorities were likewise more concerned about Portuguese merchants who sold slaves to infidels or heretics than about those who bought them for incorporation into the orbit of Catholicism.[10]

In the course of establishing relations with Africans, the Portuguese therefore developed an array of institutional mechanisms for dealing with both warlike and peaceful situations. These rationales were applicable to Portuguese colonial expansion into Brazil. The most extended debates over the

---

[7] Saunders, "Depiction," 229.

[8] Saunders, "Depiction," 227, 232.

[9] Saunders, "Depiction," 230.

[10] See Emilia Viotti da Costa, "The Portuguese African Slave Trade: A Lesson in Colonialism," *Latin American Perspectives*, 12:1 (Winter 1985), 41–61; 55. The Portuguese were embedded in the African end of the transatlantic slave trade far earlier and more deeply than their subsequent competitors. In Central Africa, the colony of Angola and the kingdom of the Congo developed a bilateral cultural exchange that included sharing Catholicism with local customs. From their base in Angola, Luso-Africans often played a direct role in the wars and slave raids that fed the Atlantic slave trade. Thousands sold into the trade were already Christians. The institution of slavery was therefore well integrated into all four continental components of the Portuguese empire. See Linda M. Heywood and John K. Thornton, *Central Africans, Atlantic Creoles, and the Foundations of the Americas, 1585–1660* (New York: Cambridge University Press, 2007), 60–79; 123–168.

"natural slavery" of Indians in the Iberian empires involved only one portion of the arguments used for enslavement. Most of those who argued against identification of Indians as natural slaves did not bother to question the justifications for African slavery. The few voices raised in favor of Africans were more likely to inveigh against horrific abuses inflicted upon the captives than the need to limit the institution or abolish the trade entirely. Even Bartolomé de las Casas in the Spanish colonies and Jean Baptiste du Tertre in the French accepted the idea that some peoples – specifically Africans – might be "natural" slaves."[11]

A number of conclusions may be drawn from the experience of the Portuguese pioneers in their transmission of Mediterranean and African variants of slavery across the Atlantic. Proposals for modification or even abolition of one form or aspect of the institution left intact the concept of the institution's generic legitimacy. The texts of Holy Scripture and Roman Law were treated with deference. Well beyond Iberia the weight of Canon law and Roman Civil Law traditions reinforced the millennial authority of scriptural passages and scholastic annotation. Slavery was literally woven into private law in most of Europe. It is hardly surprising that for two centuries after 1500, northern European civil law jurists, without any material or intellectual interest in overseas slavery, would routinely repeat the Roman juridical designation of slavery embedded in the *ius gentium* – the law of all peoples. These same civil law jurists living in the zone of Europe without slave law might casually, and even proudly, refer to the development of mutual non-enslavement between European combatants. For these scholars, slavery was hardly a problem in their culture. In retrospect, nothing is as striking in their works as their general indifference to the implications of the emerging transatlantic institution on their writings.[12]

A final conclusion to be drawn from the Iberian case is the rarity of Portuguese concerns with the novel aspects of the Atlantic slave trade. The Portuguese did not request specific papal approval of the modes of acquisition of slaves or the institutional forms of slavery they successively established on the Atlantic islands in sub-Saharan Africa, Asia, or Brazil. In 1593, the Spanish Jesuit theologian, Luis de Molina (1536–1600), observed that the Spanish monarchs had invited theological debates on the condition of the Amerindians. The Portuguese kings had not convened a similar discussion of the African slave trade.[13] Most Spanish theologians drew a distinction between "making" slaves of the Indians and "having" African

[11] Eltis, *Rise of African Slavery*, 15.
[12] José Eisenberg, "Cultural Encounters, Theoretical Adventures: The Jesuit Missions to the New World and the Justification of Voluntary Slavery," *History of Political Thought* vol. xxiv no. 3 (2003), 375–391 and Eltis, *The Rise of African Slavery*, 15.
[13] Alan Watson, "Seventeenth-Century Jurists, Roman Law, and the Law of Slavery," in *Slavery and the Law*, Paul Finkelman, ed. (Madison: Madison House, 1997), 367–377.

slaves arrive from a continent largely beyond their power. Within Africa, Africans were very rarely subjects of either crown. The suppression of Indian slavery might arguably accelerate mass conversion to Catholicism in America. Many transported Africans received baptism only after becoming the chattel of Europeans.[14]

What Molina did not note was that the Spanish monarchs also did not choose to expand the range of the theological debate to African enslavement when they initiated discussion of the Amerindians. Philip II of Spain consulted theologians concerning the moral lawfulness of a license (*asientos*) to transport 23,000 Africans to the Americas. His concern, however, was about the justice of a state monopoly and the rate of profit accruing to the slavers, not about the justice of sanctioning enslaved cargoes. Speaking on behalf of the Portuguese king, the Jesuits of West Africa and Brazil replied to a Spanish Jesuit critic that the Lisbon "Tribunal of Conscience" (*Mesa da Consciencia*) had sanctioned the trade, and continued to both sanction and to participate in it. Rare protests in unprinted manuscripts or in small printings for theological audiences were largely ignored.[15]

Perhaps the most significant of all the institutional restraints upon the development of a powerful and sustained Iberian collective movement against slavery was the persistence of slavery in the metropolis itself. It survived in real human terms, in legal codes, in religious and civil traditions, and in the founding mythos of the crusading *Reconquista*. Lisbon and Madrid legislated on the institution of slavery in Portugal and Spain as well as in every other corner of their extended empires. New laws, whether they constrained or encouraged slavery, were discussed within an empire-wide context and a seamless tradition.

Portuguese Royal decrees were appended to Visigothic and Roman law juridical principles. Spanish slave law, *Las Siete Partedas*, was the heir of the Roman *Corpus Juris Civilis*. It was regarded as the supreme legal achievement of the Spanish medieval kings. In the New World, *Siete Partidas* remained the default source of slave law whenever a relevant provision could not be found in later royal decrees. No comprehensive update was issued by the Spanish Crown until 1789, three centuries after Columbus's voyage.[16] It remained a source of imperial pride, a more humane code than the earlier provisions of Roman law or the harsher slave codes of some Northern European colonies. Well into the nineteenth century, *Siete Partidas* attracted the attention of English abolitionists as they sought to ameliorate

---

[14] A.J. Russell-Wood, "Iberian Expansion and the Issue of Black Slavery: Changing Portuguese Attitudes, 1440–1770," *American Historical Review*, 83:1 (1978), 16–42; 35.

[15] See Jesús Maria Garcia Añoveros, *El Pensamiento y Los Argumentos sobre las esclavitud en Europa en el siglo XVI y su Aplicación a los indios americanos y a los negros Africanos* (Madrid: consejo superior de investigaciones Científicas, 2000), 215–216. Maxwell, *Slavery*, 67.

[16] Russell-Wood, "Iberian Expansion," 36.

their own overseas slave system. Interwoven as it was with humanitarian, juridical, and religious constraints, the Iberian variant of slavery placed many rationalizing layers of pride between the antislavery imagination and antislavery mobilization.

Beyond the Line

North of Iberia, the institutional and existential basis of slavery had nearly vanished by the end of the fifteenth century. As we have seen, a Dutch slaver was unable to market his cargo in Middleburg. When a Norman merchant attempted to sell a shipload of slaves at Bordeaux in 1571, the *Parlement* of Guyenne freed them on the grounds that "France, the mother of liberty, doesn't permit any slaves."[17] Fugitive black slaves in Spain were apparently fully aware that they would not be returned if they successfully crossed the Pyrenees.

There is no indication that these decisions involved a prohibition either on slaveholding or slaving beyond the political boundaries of local jurisdictions or metropolitan courts. If the issue of large scale slaving seemed settled within northwest Europe, the practice and authorization of enslavement beyond the boundaries of the metropolis was resolved in the opposite direction. As with their Iberian predecessors, northern European political and religious authorities offered no sustained opposition to overseas slaving or slaveholding. French monarchs felt no obligation to seek papal sanction nor did the Vatican claim jurisdiction over the establishment of French overseas slavery. Even within the metropole, jurists and *parlements* reiterated the ideal of the freedom principle throughout the seventeenth century but French legal scholars long maintained a silence about the status of North Africans captured or purchased in Mediterranean slave markets. King Henry III reaffirmed the freedom principle by liberating some Turks from a Spanish galley that ran aground near Calais. A century later, however, Louis XIV suspended the principle for captives seized or purchased for galleys by the French navy. The argument for allowing the purchase of slaves was added to the older rationale of a just and holy war. A default strategy was simply to reiterate the inapplicability of the freedom principle to purchased slaves from Muslim lands. As a French naval administrator reasoned: "Every Man who has once touched the soil of the kingdom is free, [except in the case of] the Turks and Moors sent to Marseille for galley service, because before arriving there they are bought in foreign countries where this type of commerce is established."[18]

---

[17] Sue Peabody, "*There are no Slaves in France*," 29.
[18] Peabody, "*There Are No Slaves in France*," 144–145, n. 6. See also Gillian Lee Weiss, "Back From Barbary: Captivity, Redemption and French Identity in the Seventeenth and Eighteenth-century Mediterranean" (PhD Thesis, Stanford University, 2002), 28.

The freedom principle was even more easily disposed of in France's trans-oceanic possessions. In 1648, Louis XIII formally sanctioned the Atlantic trade by his subjects as long as slavers made arrangements to bring the slaves to Christianity.[19] As with Portugal, the French monarchy received its religious sanction from the Sorbonne's "Court of Conscience." In 1698, Germain Fromageau ruled that nothing in the Bible, Canon Law, or Roman law's *ius gentium* prohibited the ownership of slaves acquired by legitimate means. Christian combatants could not enslave their fellow Christian captives but they had every right to enslave non-Christians. French collections of "cases of conscience and legal commentaries" continued to reiterate this principle into the late eighteenth century.[20]

When slave laws were created for the French colonies, they were formulated as full blown *Black Codes* by the Royal Council. Unlike their Iberian predecessors, the codes were presumed to apply to the colonies alone, leaving the metropolitan freedom principle intact. The complications created by slaves who were brought to France from the colonies is discussed in the next chapter, but the general principle of separation between a metropole without slaves and overseas possessions governed by the *ius gentium* was firmly embedded in the French empire.

Not only Catholic France made its institutional peace with slavery beyond the line. When the slave trade came under sustained attack in Britain at the end of the eighteenth century, assiduous anti-abolitionists uncovered two decrees of Protestant Synods held at Rouen and at Alençon in 1637. Echoing the civil and canon jurists, they resolved that "slavery hath always been acknowledged to be consistent with the law of nations [*ius gentium*]; is not condemned by the word of God, neither has it been abolished by the manifestation of the gospel; but only by contrary practice, insensibly introduced."[21]

As northwestern Europeans introduced slaving practices abroad, they recognized their native free soil principles as exceptional. Even before the formation of the Dutch Republic, the first sizable contingent of Africans in the Habsburg Netherlands was the result of Antwerp's prominent position as an entrepot for early sixteenth-century Portuguese colonial commodities. Antwerp's municipal laws prohibited enslavement. They provided that imported slaves had to be freed if they petitioned the authorities. Otherwise, masters were not forced to free them. Some Moorish slaves seemed to have been freed after they were baptized, probably strengthening the widely diffused western European perception that baptism and manumission were somehow related to legal as well as spiritual assimilation. Whatever the

---

[19] Robin Blackburn, *The Making of New World Slavery* (London: Verso, 1997), 281.
[20] See Gillian "Back from Barbary," 30–31.
[21] G. Franklyn, *An Answer to the Reverend Mr. Clarkson's Essay* (London, 1789; rpt. Fisk University Library, 1969), xv–xvi.

tradition, slaves were manumitted only by will at the time of the master's death.[22]

In the northern Netherlands, the decentralized state structure and the lack of a transnational religious authority offered few institutional arenas for questioning the establishment of overseas slavery. Early in the seventeenth century, the States-General of the Dutch Republic authorized the creation of two autonomous trading companies to develop and coordinate Dutch activity in the East and West Indies. Their institutional bias in favor of pragmatic commercial policies virtually assured the acceptance of slavery within the jurisdictions of the United East India Company (VOC, est. 1602) and the West India Company (WIC, est. 1621). Voting power in these companies was weighted in favor of provinces with the greatest economic investments. The VOC apparently had no qualms about accepting slavery as a necessary condition of success in the Indian Ocean world. From the outset, the VOC considered the acquisition of slaves to be both feasible and desirable. Their early successes in the Indonesian archipelago reinforced this inclination. An early Director of the VOC was unequivocal: "we cannot exist without slaves." He coupled his exhortation with an oceanwide range of suggested sources of slaves from the east coast of Africa to India and the island of Ceylon.[23] The VOC practiced slaveholding wherever and whenever circumstances permitted.

At first, the WIC hesitated to enter the Atlantic slave trade. Once fully engaged, however, the WIC never turned back. Its major political venture was the coordinated seizure of a major Portuguese sugar plantation zone in Brazil as well as Portuguese slave factories on the African coast.[24] Before the conquest, the Dutch apparently did not envision the establishment of overseas colonies based upon African slavery. The merchant William Usselinx, born in Antwerp, an early advocate of the WIC, initially envisioned replication of the Portuguese achievement overseas without recourse to African

---

[22] Allison Blakely, *Blacks in the Dutch World: the Evolution of Racial Imagery in a Modern Society* (Bloomington: Indiana University Press, 1993), 226.

[23] See G. Masselman, *The Cradle of Colonialism* (New Haven: Yale University Press, 1963), 348–363.

[24] Above all, see *Fifty Years Later: Antislavery, Capitalism and Modernity in the Dutch Orbit*, Gert Oostendie, ed. (Pittsburgh: University of Pittsburgh Press, 1996); and Emmer, *Dutch Slave Trade*, 13–16. Neither Jelle C. Riemersma, *Religious Factors in Early Dutch Capitalism 1550–1650*, (The Hague: Mouton, 1967), nor a recent collection of Dutch scholarship, *Riches from Atlantic Commerce: Dutch Transatlantic Trade and Shipping 1585–1817*, Johannes Postma and Victor Enthoven, eds. (Leiden: Brill, 2003), make mention of slavery as a problem in Dutch culture or politics. The English governor of Jamaica wrote that the Dutch were ruled by the axiom that "Jesus Christ was good, but trade was better." Quoted in Cornelis Goslinga, *The Dutch in the Caribbean and on the Wild Coast 1580–1680* (Gainesville: University of Florida Press, 1971), 369; see also P.C. Emmer, "Jesus Christ Was Good but Trade was Better: An Overview of the Transit Trade in the Dutch Antilles, 1634–1795," in *The Lesser Antilles*, 206–222.

slaves. He wanted Dutch settlements to employ Indians to work the mines and fields of the tropical Americas as voluntary workers. His premise was that they could simply produce tropical commodities in exchange for European manufacturers.[25] As soon as the Dutch occupied Brazil, however, Governor Prince Maurice of Nassau dismissed as an idle fantasy any thought of foregoing slavery. He proceeded to encourage the transatlantic slave trade with the WIC's full support.

The merchant companies of the Netherlands were also unhindered by the equivalent of Protestant religious missions alongside their commercial enterprises. At home, some clergymen initially offered moral arguments against following the Portuguese model of colonization, but there was no parallel to the complaints of Catholic theologians about conditions of the trade or treatment of the enslaved in the new settlements. Dutch colonization came to be characterized by very minor outlays for the conversion of non-Christian peoples combined with an expansive policy towards the immigration of religious minorities. The Dutch overseas companies lacked significant numbers of Dutch citizens ready to undertake transoceanic voyages for settlement. The Netherlands required non-nationals to sustain both its metropolitan defense and overseas activities. Its reservoir of underemployed or unemployed was probably the smallest in the world, and its relief system for the poor was the best in the world. Forty percent of Dutch naval and merchant crews, and up to 60 percent of its soldiers, were foreigners. Almost a million Europeans were mobilized for the VOC's ventures alone. No wonder that a broad array of foreigners were necessary to man ventures not only to the tropical zones of Brazil and the Caribbean, but to settle the temperate New Netherlands in North America and the Cape Colony in South Africa.[26]

Emblematic of the disassociation of slavery from Dutch political and religious institutions was the relationship between overseas slaves and the metropolitan community of believers. In 1618, on the eve of colonization, the Dutch Republic sponsored the Synod of Dordrecht. It was the last united meeting of the Protestant Reformed Churches in Europe. That the Synod expressed no concern for the legitimacy of slavery is unsurprising. Protestant seafarers were only intermittently engaged in the slave trade, and Protestant rulers still possessed no overseas territories with slave populations. The Churches, therefore, addressed the question of slavery only in its old European frame of reference. The Synod forbade the sale of Christian slaves and declared that such bondsmen "ought to enjoy liberty with other Christians." Communicants were urged to baptize slaves born into Reformed households. Did baptism, however, entail manumission?

---

[25] J. Van Doal, and A. Heertje, *Economic Thought in the Netherlands: 1650–1950* (Aldershot, Avebury, 1992), 14–16.

[26] See Emmer "Jesus," 207–208; and Drescher, "White Atlantic," 54–56.

The Synod characteristically decentralized the decision-making process. It left the question of baptism's relation to freedom to be determined by the individual autonomous churches. As no political entity in the Christian or Islamic worlds recognized that a change in slaves' religious status automatically changed their legal status, Protestant legislation duly followed the Old World traditions.

Protestants certainly did not adopt the less ambiguous solution of the Portuguese pioneers. The Portuguese rulers rigorously foreclosed the possibility of linking the baptism of African slaves to freedom. Before being boarded in Africa, captives were assembled before customs officials. No captives could be boarded without a ticket certifying their incorporation of the Catholic faith. The application of baptismal water at a hog trough was inscribed by the application of hot irons to the arms and chests of the converted. Baptism simultaneously opened the door to spiritual freedom and foreclosed any legal claim to freedom.[27]

Both the Protestant Dutch WIC and the English colonists in the New World confirmed the tradition that baptism did not automatically emancipate slaves. The institutional separation of civil status and church membership remained intact. The polyglot Dutch colonies offer another important insight into the generic European response to the emergence of overseas slavery. The multiethnic divisions between Netherlanders, Frenchmen, Germans, and Englishmen in their colonies resulted in no major variations in the acceptability of the institution. Nor did the presence of a substantial Jewish presence create any tangible variation in the relation of a slave's legal status to his religious conversion. Whatever the relative religious tolerance of the Dutch WIC, it would no more tolerate questioning the institution of slavery than did its monarchical European counterparts elsewhere. No religious or ethnic group within the Dutch colonial sphere mobilized to accelerate manumissions of slaves, much less urge their members to withdraw from participation in the institution.[28]

The Dutch metropolitan legal system remained as disengaged from Atlantic slavery as did the Dutch Reformed Church. Civil Law traditions in the United Provinces differed in each province, but none had any slave law. Nor did the States-General create any for use overseas. In a decree of 1629, a casual reference by the WIC implied its right to apply Roman slave law in its jurisdiction. It simply made a defunct portion of an ancient body of law available for its overseas governors and colonial councils. In turn, overseas legal practice was virtually ignored by jurists in the Netherlands. Never was this New World institution further

---

[27] Joseph Calder Miller, *Way of Death: Merchant Capitalism and the Angolan Slave Trade, 1730–1830* (Madison, WI: University of Wisconsin Press, 1988).

[28] Schorsch, *Jews and Blacks*, 248–250; 287–291.

removed from western European imperial gaze than in the writings of seventeenth-century Dutch jurists.[29] In this inattention, Dutch jurists were not alone. As late as 1758, the Swiss jurist Emmerich de Vattel's survey of civil law led him back to the traditional justification of enslaving as the sparing of captives' lines. His response was rather to express disgust at such victims' acceptance of life at such a price:

If anyone counts life a favour when it is offered only with chains, let him enjoy it, let him accept the kindness, submit to its conditions, and fulfill his duties! But they are not what I shall teach him: he may find enough said of them in other authors: I shall dwell no longer on the subject, indeed this disgrace of mankind is happily extinct in Europe.[30]

Out of metropole, out of mind.

As with the Dutch, early English colonization planners were not particularly interested in African slaves as a source of labor. They envisioned various combinations of Native Americans and European indentured servants as their labor force. England's initial failures to recruit willing Indians were initially dismissed by critics as matters of bad management. Like the Dutch merchant Usselinx, an English prospectus for a colony on the South American coast assumed that the Indians in the Guiana would "worke a month or more for an axe of eighteen or twentie pence price." The prospectus contemptuously dismissed prior English failures as readily as Usselinx had dismissed the Portuguese experience. Only poor handling of relations with the natives had forced Virginians or New Englanders "to carry men over to doe their worke for them, least otherwise they be driven to worke themselves."[31]

In whatever ways plans for a Puritan holy community in New England differed from other early English ventures, a prohibition of slavery was

---

[29] Watson, "Seventeenth Century Jurists, Roman law, and the Law or Slavery," in *Slavery and the Law*, Paul Finkelman, ed. (Madison, WI: Madison House, 1997) 236–377. On the dearth of attention to overseas slavery among seventeenth-century philosophers, see also Jonathan I. Israel, *Radical Enlightenment: Philosophy and the Making of Modernity, 1650–1750* (New York: Oxford University Press, 2001), passim.

[30] Vattel, *Le Droit des gens, ou principles de la loi naturelle* 2 vols. (London, 1758), II section 152: Q: "Whether one can enslave prisoners of war." It would be worthwhile exploring the only abortive Dutch colonial venture in North America explicitly designed to exclude slaves from the new colony. Its constitution, drafted by Franciscus van den Enden, a former Jesuit, was intended as a venture in social equality. Its radical provisions included communal living and joint ownership of property, as well as the exclusion of slaves. Van den Enden's exclusions extended far beyond slaves. Catholics, Jews, Lutherans, Quakers, etc. were also to be banned. Slaves were only one of a host of outsiders to be banned from the community. See Israel, *Radical Enlightenment*, 179.

[31] *Publication of Guiana's Plantation . . . with an Answer to Objections of Feare of the Enemie* [i.e. Spain] (London, 1632), 15.

not among them. In the Puritan's Caribbean colony of Providence Island, servitude was the linchpin of their labor system. As soon as indentured labor fell short of expectations, the Company turned to African slaves. Their colony became the first English Settlement in the Americas to identify African slaves as its labor of choice. By the time the Spanish snuffed out the colony in 1641, slaves already formed a majority of its inhabitants. Barbados itself reached that condition two decades later. Puritan North America was no more fastidious. In 1640, the 150 African Americans in Massachusetts were equal in number and in proportion to those in Virginia.[32]

The founders of overseas colonies made due allowance for the activities of the merchants and colonizers who went to them. Their handbooks universally assumed that conditions were so far beyond the control of Europeans as to necessitate some form of bonded labor. By the mid-seventeenth century, this assumption was firmly embedded in Europe's geographical consciousness. Richard Blome's world geography axiomatically advised any youth embarking on a long-distance mercantile venture to put home rules in abeyance. Merchants were cautioned to practice circumspection; to observe others' religious practices, virtues, vices, and way of life; to engage in no religious disputes; "*to accede to the customs*, subsidies, tributes, and tolls of each foreign country and regarding *every commodity*." For these diasporas too, the law of the land was the law. Blome's geography slipped the buying of slaves quite simply into his enumeration of the goods traded by the English Royal African Company. The company carried "other good commodities, besides, with great quantities of *Negroes*, for the supply of this *Majesty's American Plantations* to the great advantage of the *Inhabitants*.... [and] 3,000 *Negroes* yearly to the Spaniards...."[33]

Of all the perspectives through which seventeenth-century Englishmen were encouraged to view the world beyond the ocean, the economic dominated. Undertaking new trades and settlements were expensive and risky ventures. Slaving and slaveholding made their ways into the mercantile consciousness only slowly and discretely. Lewes Roberts' book, *Merchant's Map of Commerce*, went through repeated editions between the 1630s and the beginning of the eighteenth century. The 1638 account of Africa did not even mention slaves among the exports of significance to his readers. The author focused only on the obligation to pay tolls as part of complex trade customs, and warned prospective traders that the Africans were as clever as the Europeans. His sole reference to the slave trade was to the 30,000

---

[32] Karen Ordahl Kupperman, *Providence Island, 1630–1641* (New York: Cambridge University Press, 1993), 151, 151–169; and *Historical Statistics of the United States of America* 2 vols. (Washington, DC: U.S. Bureau of the Census, 1976), II, Table Z 1–19.

[33] Richard Blome, *A Geographical Description of the Four Parts of the World, Taken from... the Famous Monsieur Sanson,* [originally published in 1645],... *also a Treatise of Travel* (London, 1670/1683).

slaves yearly sold to "the Portugal's," then carried to "Brasile to work in their *Silver Mines.*"[34]

Later works began to adjust to the growth of the English West Indian colonies. As the English migration rate fell to its lowest level in a century, the demographic advantages of using African slaves in the Caribbean were highlighted. Whereas metropolitan employers feared a brawn drain, every person with capital going abroad could employ eight or ten blacks for one white servant. With an African slave alternative, the demand for "provisions, clothes, household goods, sea-men and all others employed [in producing] materials for building, fitting and victualling, of ships, [meant that] every English-man in Barbadoes or Jamaica creates employment for four men at home."[35] This line of argument continued unabated in the late seventeenth century because the Caribbean islands had then become the most productive per capita economies in the world. Indeed, by the beginning of the eighteenth century, "the Caribbean region probably had a higher per capita income than Britain... and Britain probably had the highest income of any of the eighteenth-century colonial powers."[36]

A century and a half after the founding of Jamestown in 1607, slavery appeared to have emerged triumphant as the labor of choice in a broad swath of the Americas. Britain's only eighteenth-century attempt to establish an imperial colony without slaves seemed to clinch this argument. In the early 1730s, the sponsors of a colony in Georgia prohibited the importation of African slaves to make it less vulnerable to Spanish threats to the South. They also hoped that the colony would function primarily as an asylum to transform the unproductive classes of Britain and the refugees from Europe

---

[34] *The Merchants Mappe of Commerce* London, 1638), 79. The work was republished, as the *The Merchants Map of Commerce... The Natural and Artificial Commodities of all Countries...* in 1671, 1677 and 1700). A century after Blome's geography, in the wake of the British acquisitions of more islands in the Caribbean, the author of *Some Observations which may contribute to afford a just idea of the Nature, Importance and Settlement of our New West India Colonies* (London, 1764), lamented that "the better sort" in England still looked on America "as if in the Moon." Most of the English poor in his part of England dreaded overseas "adventures." The more impoverished areas of Ireland and Scotland would be a source for some recruits but "many will die." "For the poor the islands were not the promised land flowing with milk and honey." Experience showed that for the sake of successful development, volunteer tradesmen and slaves were suitable.

[35] See Sir Dalby Thomas, *An Historical Account of the Rise and Growth of the West-India Colonies and of the Great Advantages they are to England* (London, 1690).

[36] David Eltis, "The Slave Economies of the Caribbean: Structure, Performance, Evolution and Significance," in *General History of the Caribbean, III The Slave Societies of the Caribbean*, Franklin W. Knight, ed. (London: UNESCO Publishing, 1997), 105–137, esp. 123. For similar contemporary assessments, see Young, *Political Essays Concerning the British Empire* (London: 1772), 359–360. In regard to profitability, Adam Smith reached the same comparative conclusion regarding the relative profitability of growing corn, tobacco, and sugar in the New World. See *Wealth of Nations*, 173–174.

into yeoman farmer soldiers.[37] Within a few years, it was widely recognized that the Carolinian slaveholders could undersell the newly arrived Georgians growing rice and corn. The colony's very first report to the trustees in London noted that Carolinians had the advantage of working Negroes day and night and even on Sunday with miserable provision for maintenance. The reporter concluded that "a white man in these lands, if he cannot buy a slave, must work himself like a slave."

A group of German refugees opposed the introduction of slaves in the New World as threats to security, morality, and Christian life. Johann Martin Boltzius, the principal spokesman for the opponents of slavery, agreed with the proponents of legalization that the Negroes were "lazy, thieving and rebellious." He maintained, however, that such behavior was a result of enslavement, not an argument in favor of it. Despite this, Boltzius' economic argument was premised on the assertion that slave labor was too competitive. It would drive out free labor.[38]

If any issue impinged upon the wisdom of the Afro-Atlantic slave system from an economic perspective it arose from the perception of Africa's under-development as the western Atlantic developed prodigiously in the eighteenth century. Some observers were struck by the stark contrast between the enormous wealth generated by slave labor on a few tropical islands in the Americas and the economic underdevelopment of a vast continent representing "a quarter of the globe." Africa, after all, supplied the very slave labor being shipped from West Africa at high cost in time, money, and mortality. As early as 1728, Nathaniel Cutler's work, *Atlas Maritimus and Commercialis*, addressed the question at length. The list of tropical products planted at the English factories on the Gold Coast already covered the whole range of commodities shipped from the Americas. Why had these experimental crops that had "thriven to admiration," not transformed the continent? The *Atlas* could only blame the populations on the supply side. Whether or not they were of "the blasted race of old Cham and his Son Canaan" was immaterial; they were surely "a vile accursed race," the worst cultivators of the earth. Nor were North Africans, "all thieves," any different than the Negroes of the Western part. Their most civil nation, Egypt, was as "perfidious, thievish, and murdering race.... as can be

---

[37] See David Brion Davis, *Problem of Slavery in Western Culture*, 144–150, and Josiah Child, *A New Discourse of Trade* (London: John Everingham, 1698), 180–191. Child's *Discourse* was republished at least seven times between 1693 and 1800.

[38] George Fenwick Jones, *The Georgia Dutch from the Rhine and Danube to the Savannah*, 1733–1783 (Athens, GA: University of Georgia Press, 1992), 266, 324 n. 54. The early German opposition to slavery in both Georgia and Pennsylvania's Germantown (1688) was probably conditioned by the shock of first encounters with Africans slaves. A century later "Pennsylvania Germans," both Lutheran and Reformed, opposed the abolition of slavery. Owen S. Ireland, *"Germans Against Abolition: A Minority's View in Revolutionary Pennsylvania," Journal of Interdisciplinary History*, 3:4 (1973), 685–706.

expected from a mixture of *Saracens, Mamalukas, Turks, Jews, Negroes* and *Arabians.*"[39]

A generation later, Malachy Postlethwayt, writing from a very different perspective, reiterated the same frustration. Africa had not been improved by centuries of contact. Sweeping aside Africans' supposed savagery or indolence, he focused upon their equal potential: "Are not the rational faculties of the negro people in the general equal to those of the human species?" Postlethwayt seconded the *Atlas Maritimus's* observation that every product in Asia or the West Indies could be produced as readily and profitably in Africa as in the New World. However, he now faulted the slave trade, not the inhabitants, as the great obstacle to the civilizing process. Nevertheless, however deeply he mused on alternative possibilities, Postlethwayt was clear about the bottom line: "This [slave] trade, as it stands, is as *good* as any we have." Each edition of his *Dictionary*, between 1751 and 1774, echoed the same judgment.[40]

Finessing the Line: Law, Climate, and Race

In the establishment of the English colonial slave systems, the tension between the need for variance from the English legal system and the desire to appeal to that tradition was recognized early in the nation's transoceanic ventures. Discontinuities between what was appropriate to England and to overseas areas were axiomatically accepted. Queen Elizabeth's first patent for colonization to Sir Walter Raleigh in 1584, cited the colonies' location in "remote, Heathen and barbarous lands," as requiring rights to establish particular laws and statutes – with a caveat. Overseas laws were to be "agreeable to the laws of England, and be not contrary to the Christian Faith, and so as the said people remain subject to the Crown of England."[41] "Agreeability," of course, entailed neither parliamentary representation nor applied the common law freedom principle to every resident beyond the line.

A late seventeenth-century treatise on maritime law attempted to grapple with the issues that arose from trying to establish a "bondage principle" appropriate to the world beyond Europe. Like Postlethwayt, sizing up the world "as it stands," Charles Malloy still confidently assumed that slavery was a general if not a universal institution. So, under certain conditions, enslavement was not repugnant to "natural justice by covenant [voluntary

---

[39] *Atlas Maritimus and Commercialis, or, a general view of the world*... (London: James and John Knapton, 1728), 237–371.

[40] See Malachy Postlethwayt, *The Universal Dictionary of Trade and Commerce*, (London: 1751; 1766 and 1774); entry: "Africa." See also the "Introductions" to the 1766 and 1774 editions concentrating on prospects in the Caribbean. Reviewers reiterated the focus on "the trade, as it stands." *The Monthly Review* xvii, (October 1757), 311–312.

[41] The patent was issued in 1584.

surrender] or by *Transgression* [imposition]." Malloy duly noted that "slavery in Christendom is now become obsolete" to such an extent that the "minds of princes and states having, as it were, universally agreed to esteem the words *Slave, Bondsman* or *Villain* as barbarous. . . ." Prisoners of war could not be "subjected to servile things" unless, with a nod to the Mediterranean, they were "renegades."[42] In England itself, of course, slavery and bondage "were so discontinued" that "Trover was not maintainable" even for a "More or other Indian."

Having ventured thus far, Molloy then hedged on the inadmissibility of servility, even in England. All persons born there, as well as all their descendants born in Virginia, Jamaica, and so on, were freemen. Yet, English law did not explicitly exclude a "justifiable" servitude that might equal that of captives. Having conceded so much, Molloy footnoted his distaste to the institution as practiced overseas: "The *English* Merchants and others at the *Canaries* [Canary Islands] do here support this unnatural custom: So likewise at *Virginia* and other plantations." In England, there was at least no contract that could oblige hereditary service. Magistrates were even obliged to dissolve voluntary indentures and award damages against masters who punished with extraordinary rigor. Molloy's observations concerning the appropriateness of laws enforcing servitude were invariably inflected by tropes of fluidity and geography: "plain reason shows us that natural and mathematical laws have more certitude than civil. . . . " Human actions were "subjected to different circumstances" and latitudes.[43] In the British colonies, a startlingly new labor regime linked to a status repudiated at home was being enshrined in a passive, almost stealthy process of legal accommodation.

In contrast to other major European monarchies, the British crown never developed an imperial slave code. For lands under the king's sovereignty, but not Parliament's, the Crown permitted local practices that diverged from common law traditions. Within this framework, the institution of slavery evolved with maximum legal protection and minimal legal hurdles for slave-owners. Barbados inverted the common law principle *in favorum*

---

[42] Charles Molloy, *De Jure Maritimo it Navale: or, a Treatise of Affaires Maritime and of Commerce* (London, 1682). *De Jure Marimino* went through six editions between 1676 and 1769.

[43] *Ibid.*, 335–36 and chapter IX. To English jurists, their countrymen enjoyed a unique advantage over Continentals. The Roman slave law tradition had no standing in England. Even a devoted English student of the civil law happily dismissed it as irrelevant. On slavery, English municipal law and common law took precedence in conflicts between the two traditions. Slave law was particularly "incongruous, improper and not suiting with every nation so differing and, as I may say, directly opposite to the *Roman* Law." See Sir Robert Wiseman, *The Law of Laws, on the Excellency of the Civil Law above all other Humane Laws Whatever, showing of how great use and necessity the civil law is to this Nation* (London, 1686).

libertas. The colony decreed that "Negroes and Indians that came here to be sold, should serve for life, unless a contract was before made to the contrary."[44] As early as 1652, a Rhode Island statute casually referred, not to the common law, but to the "common course . . . practiced among English men to buy negars, to that end that they may have them for service or slaves forever." Colonial Carolina's *Fundamental Constitutions* more elaborately included (and later ignored) a provision against the enslavement of Indians. To entice European migration, it excluded idolatry or ignorance as grounds of enslavement. Most importantly, it guaranteed that "every Freeman of Carolina, shall have absolute power and authority over his Negro slaves of what opinion or religion so ever."[45]

The Carolina *Fundamental Constitutions* offer remarkable evidence of the casual acceptance of these distinctive provisions. Founding lawmakers were allowed extraordinary leeway to introduce the institution with minimal attention to explicit justification. Nothing exemplifies the disengagement of English juridical and political philosophy from the colonial setting as well as John Locke's *Two Treatises of Government* and his *Carolina Constitutions*. The *Treatises* themselves open with a ringing declaration: "Slavery is so vile and miserable an estate of man, and so directly opposite to the generous temper and courage of our nation; that it is hardly to be conceived that an *Englishman* much less a gentleman, should plead for it."[46] The same *Treatises* then casually refer to the legitimate power of a West Indian planter over slaves whom he bought with his own money.[47] This unambiguous declaration is a far cry from the *Treatises'* later description of slavery as "nothing else but the state *of War continued, between a lawful Conqueror, and a Captive.*"[48] Can one imagine any investor in the Royal African Company, including Locke himself, not preferring the more unambiguous authority conveyed by purchase in the *First Treatise*? The Company's Royal Charter authorized it to trade "with and *for* Negroes." The Crown simultaneously legitimized the buyers and the sellers of human commodities. Slaves were henceforth enumerated by cash value alone in the imperial customs ledgers.

---

[44] See Jonathan A. Bush, The British Constitution and the Creation of American Slavery" in *Slavery and the Law*, Paul Finkelman, ed. (Madison, WI: Madison House, 1997), 379–418.

[45] On Barbados, see Richard S. Dunn, *Sugar and Slaves: The Rise of the Planter Class in the English West Indies 1624–1714* (New York: W.W. Norton, 1972). On Rhode Island, see Jordan, *White over Black*, 70; on South Carolina, see David Armitage, "John Locke, Carolina, and the *Two Treatises of Government*," *Political Theory*, 35:5 (October, 2004), 602–627.

[46] Locke, *Two Treatises*, Hollis, ed. (1764); *The First Treatise*, chap. 1, sec. 1.

[47] *First Treatise*, chap. XI, sec. 130 and 131. The master's power over his slave in contrast to the master's own family members is absolute, "unto the power of life and death." (*Second Treatise*, chap. 6, sec. 86).

[48] *Second Treatise*, ch. 4: sec. 24.

Once more, however, the ledgers left an unexplained gap between their clear delineation of slaves as property overseas and their silence about their status in England itself. None of the customs regulations ever published in the metropolis levied duties on the entrance or exit of slaves, as they did in colonial ports.[49] For Locke, and for royal administrators, Africans and their descendants purchased overseas by slavers, Carolinians, or West Indians were slaves in the strictest sense of the law. The early draft of the relevant article of the *Fundamental Constitutions* had only stated: "Every Freemen of Carolina shall have absolute authority over his Negro slaves of what opinion or Religion whatever (Article 109)." In his own hand, Locke altered the article to read "absolute *power and* authority." Absolute power would define the full extent of the master's authority.[50]

Carolina's *Fundamental Constitution* was similarly quite latitudinarian regarding the religion of the masters. It welcomed adherents of any faith professing a belief in God, including Jews, heathens, and dissenters as members of the community. But, Locke's insertion brushed aside any appeal "whatever" by a slave to the shelter of faith against a master. The article effectively disclaimed any obligation on the part of masters to bring slaves into the community of the faithful.

The English-speaking world's discussion of the legal foundations of African slavery was also remarkably abbreviated. Practical problems of legal ownership, transfer, and policing demanded answers in every colony. Nowhere, however, in colonial statutes, Parliamentary Acts, or Crown decisions did there develop anything remotely like a jurisprudence of slavery. The institution was not discussed in treatises on the common law. It was elided in those on civil law. No imperial slave code developed to fill the gaps, nor did a large body of case law develop in the courts of England. In the century before the landmark case of Somerset v. Stewart in 1772, there were only a dozen decisions considering the implications of colonial slavery. Nor did "the common law ever meddle with, ratify, reject or otherwise directly address slavery in the colonies," other than to accept it, as in the Rhode Island declaration of 1652, as custom.[51] The result, as Jonathan Bush emphasizes, was that slavery's relation to freedom, especially in England itself, remained inconclusive and uncertain. The status of overseas slavery was secured by colonial statutes or constitutions.

English parliamentary statutes did assure and regulate the movement of slaves as commodities from Africa. But, the government directly interfered only with those aspects of the institution concerned with imperial trade and defense. It only indirectly sanctioned New World slavery as a wealth producing and social institution. Legal treatises, mostly written in England,

[49] Drescher, *Capitalism and Antislavery*, 27, 185 n. 8.
[50] Armitage, "John Locke," 609.
[51] Jonathan A. Bush, "The British Constitution," 388.

said almost nothing about slavery within the empire. Even that little writing referred to ancient or medieval precedents.

Insofar as English jurisprudence took cognizance of slavery in America, it affirmed that the institution lay beyond the line of Britain and its common law. At the end of the seventeenth century, Chief Justice Holt, rejecting a slave-owner's plea, famously stated that "the (common) law took no notice of a negro." But in the same decision he also advised the plaintiff that he should have declared "that the sale of the Negro was in Virginia, and, by the laws of that country Negroes are saleable; *for the laws of England do not extend to Virginia, being a conquered country the law is what the King pleases.*"[52] As long as Britain's rulers were content with this bifurcated situation, neither the English courts nor the British parliament had incentive or occasion to intervene.

Britons who crossed the ocean, of course, sought clarity about the status of their property and personal rights beyond the line. Free colonists, indentured servants, and metropolitans all sought to have the common law extended to English colonists abroad. As long as only the voices of freeborn Englishmen could be heard in judicial and parliamentary circles, European colonists, indentured servants, and convicts were all relative beneficiaries of the assurance that their lives would never be, in the words of James Knight, "as cheap as negroes." Habeas corpus was dearer to Englishmen in "remote" colonies, where their health and lives might be endangered by "imprisonment in a hot climate" before they could possibly obtain relief from a royal writ.[53]

James Knight's allusion to climate invoked another commonplace justification for slavery beyond the line. Climate clearly could not have been the sole rationalization for slavery during the early global expansion of European slavery. By the last quarter of the eighteenth century, slavery was established at every latitude in the Americas settled by Europeans. It could hardly have formed a major component of justifications for the institution by the pioneering Spaniards, whose monarchs sought to limit enslavement even in tropical areas fully under royal authority. Iberians owned slaves in the temperate zones of Europe, on the plateaus of Mexico, and in the highlands of Peru. Throughout the early modern period, western Europeans, especially Britons, viewed temperate eastern Europe as the abode of massive servility and slavery. One world geography after another informed its readers that Polish and Russian peasants were "mere slaves"; that Greek and Balkan Christians were routinely enslaved by the Turks. They casually mentioned the slave trading of Christian Caucasians, where "beautiful white females" and their children "were exposed like beasts to the highest

---

[52] Bush, "The British Constitution," 396.
[53] James Knight, *The State of the Island of Jamaica* (London, 1726), 35.

bidder to gratify avarice."[54] Nor were Europeans allowed to forget the Maghreb. In a world where Adam Smith relegated Africa, Asia, large parts of the Americas, and Europe (including the Scottish mines) to slavery, the institution was clearly not confined to one climatic zone or to the inhabitants of one continent. Europeans, Euro-Americans, North Africans, and Amerindians were not generally envisioned as "climatically" prone to servile status.

In the Caribbean, however, northwestern Europeans had to explain both the existence of Atlantic slavery and the respective roles of Europeans and Africans in this new social complex. Here, climate became a major alternative to capture as the justification for African enslavement.[55] Ironically, the earliest recognition of environmental impacts on Europeans was in recognition of Europeans' relative weakness. The deadly result of Europeans entering the disease environment of tropical Africa made it the "White Man's Grave." For early English migrants, the West Indies also achieved a reputation for deadliness. As news about the mortality rates filtered back to England in the 1650s, few volunteers in Cromwell's navy were willing to serve in the Caribbean. The first settlers in Barbados were also depicted as perishing in droves. Only the hope of great monetary gain prompted voluntary migrants to risk dying away in "those torrid vineyards."[56]

Most of the Caribbean islands began their rapid ascent in the production of sugar with a dramatic shift to an African slave labor force between 1650 and 1700. The unprecedented ratios of eight or nine Africans to every European on the islands soon elicited further environmental and racial explanations and justifications. Retrospectively, it was deemed a mistake to have even attempted to settle the islands using European field laborers. By the end of the Seven Years War in 1763, most of those seeking the development of the newly-acquired French islands axiomatically accepted the need for fresh importations of African slaves. One British writer even began his discussion by noting that France's first great mistake in the Caribbean had been to depend too much upon military recruits as laborers, instead of accumulating a sufficient number of Negroes.[57] The belief that only Africans could both work and survive in the tropical lowlands was broadly shared.

---

[54] Seymour Drescher, *Capitalism and Antislavery: British Mobilization in Comparative Perspective* (New York: Oxford University Press, 1987), 16–17; 175–177.

[55] See Roxanne Wheeler, *The Complexion of Race: Categories of Difference in Eighteenth-Century British Culture* (Philadelphia: University of Pennsylvania Press, 2000), 21–28; 179–181; 183–188.

[56] See B.S. Capp, *Cromwell's Navy: The Fleet and the English Revolution, 1648–1660* (New York, 1989), ch. 8. Cromwell's "Sons of Violence" were cut down by the unseen enemies of fluxes, fevers, and diseases. (*Ibid.*, 212–214). The West Indian expeditions at the end of the century were estimated to have cost the lives of 40,000 seamen.

[57] John Campbell, *Candid and Impartial Considerations on the Nature of the Sugar Trade* (London, 1763), 11.

Even writers quite hostile to slavery presumed a link between climate and labor. Montesquieu's famous chapter mocking the usual justifications for slavery in the *Spirit of the Laws* (1748) became a major source for anyone who wished to attack the institution. Significantly, however, the chapter was located in the section of his work on climate, not in ones related to trade or liberty. Montesquieu's one concession to the institution of slavery was his statement that the public good or economic production in the tropics required coerced labor. But tropical climate, as antislavery writers were to increasingly argue, did not justify brutalized slave labor. In 1772, an anonymously published essay offered "a concrete, if quixotic" emancipation experiment for colonizing Britain's newly acquired province of West Florida. It involved purchasing slaves on the African coast, training them in England, and transferring them to Florida as liberated slaves. The result could be the first free African colony in America, initiating the gradual elimination of the institution in the Americas.[58]

However, apart from disease, a tropical climate or, as Philip Curtin terms it, a tropical exuberance was easily framed as a curse rather than an incentive to free labor. As the Scottish economist James Steuart hypothesized in 1767: "If the soil be vastly rich, situated in a warm climate, and naturally watered, the productions of the earth will be almost spontaneous: this will make the inhabitants lazy. Laziness is the greatest of all obstacles to labour and industry." Along with the "curse" of tropical diseases for Europeans, the deployment of non-Europeans in tropical production appeared to be at worst a necessary evil combined with great benefits.[59] Climate trumped morality. Diderot's great *Encyclopédie* contained unyielding antislavery articles entitled "Slavery" and the "Slave Trade." Alongside these, however, an article, "Torride Zone," acknowledged that "the very sun seems to tyrannize this world of slaves."[60]

Adam Smith's famously censorious words on the inferiority of slave labor in *The Wealth of Nations* did not challenge the axiomatic inferiority of European labor in the tropics: "In all European colonies the culture of the sugar-cane is carried on by negro slaves. The constitution of those born in

[58] C.L. de Secondat de Montesquieu, *De l'Esprit des lois* (Paris, 1950–55), book 15, ch. 7–8, 222–223, and 416; and [Maurice Morgann], *Plan for the Abolition of Slavery in the West Indies* (London, 1772). Perhaps not coincidentally, Morgann's *Plan*, first drafted in 1763, was published at the same time as the widely publicized Sommerset Case. For an insightful contextualization of the *Plan*, see Christopher Leslie Brown, *Moral Capital: Foundations of British Abolitionism* (Chapel Hill: University of North Carolina Press, 2006), ch. 4.

[59] Philip Curtin, *The Image of Africa: British Ideas and Action, 1780–1850* (Madison, WI: University of Wisconsin Press, 1964), 61–62. For an analogous perspective on the climatological impact on labor, see David S. Landes, *The Wealth and Poverty of Nations: Why some are so rich and some so poor* (New York: W. W. Norton, 1998), ch. 1. Barker, *The African Link*, 165.

[60] Drescher, *Capitalism and Antislavery*, 179.

the temperate climate of Europe could not, it is supposed, support the labour
of digging the ground under the burning sun of the West Indies."[61] For his
own reasons, Anthony Benezet, the first effective activist against slavery and
the slave trade, affirmed the climatic suitability of Africans to the tropics,
even while he relentlessly attacked African slavery:

Although the extreme heat in many parts of Guiney is such as is neither agreeable
nor healthy to the *Europeans*, yet it is well suited to the constitution of the *Negroes*;
and it is to these heats that they are indebted for the fertility of their land, which in
most places so great, that with little labour grain and fruit will grow in the greatest
plenty.[62]

As the status of New World slavery approached its apogee of economic
inevitability late in the eighteenth century, German thinkers extended the
climatological argument to discussions of Jewish emancipation and integration into European civil society. In the late 1770s, a German journal
published a series of letters assessing the impact of sugar, now brought
"by the mountain" from the West Indies to Europeans. These insatiable
consumers "accustomed themselves to this seductive salt to such an extent
that they believe themselves unable to live without it." The problem for
Europeans remained that the part of the New World where it was grown
had so little similarity with the Old World. Its "cruel heat" created a climate for which "a German body is not made." Johann David Michaelis, a
German orientalist, proposed an ingenious pharaonic solution to Europe's
insatiable craving for sugar, and for Germany's "Jewish problem." Jews
could serve both Germany's dietary and imperial needs in a more direct way
than through civic integration and equalization of rights. Their transportation to the tropics would be a cheaper and quicker solution than "ten generations" of regeneration in Europe. Jews, thought Michaelis, could become
"even more useful if we had sugar islands which from time to time could
depopulate the European fatherland, sugar islands which, with the wealth
they produce, nevertheless have an unhealthy climate." Since Jews were "an
unmixed race of more southern people," they were well suited to grow cane
alongside African slaves.[63]

So, even at the peak of forced African migration to the Americas, Europeans still proposed to deploy other Europeans to the Caribbean for the
purpose of expanding cultivation by coerced gang labor. The cultural barriers to enslaving Europeans remained less absolute than some have imagined.

---

[61] Smith, *Wealth of Nations*, 586.

[62] See Anthony Benezet, *A Short Account of that Part of Africa Inhabited by the Negroes*
(Philadelphia: 1762), 12–13.

[63] Jonathan M. Hess, *Germans, Jews and the Claims of Modernity* (New Haven: Yale University Press, 2002), 81–84. The most famous proposal for integration came from Christian
Wilhelm Dohm, with his book, *On the Civic Improvement of the Jews* (1781).

The discussions opened up by the emerging mythos of tropical exuberance and tropical dangers brings us finally to the role of race in the emergence and maintenance of Atlantic slavery in the three centuries after 1450. By the mid-eighteenth century, it was clear to most Europeans living on both sides of the ocean that Africans and their descendants constituted the overwhelming majority of slaves in the Americas. As David Brion Davis accurately summarizes, African slaves had become an integral, intrinsic, and indispensable part of New World history. However, despite the congruence of Africans and slaves in the late eighteenth-century Americas, it is less clear that "slavery and blackness" were virtually synonymous in the minds of Europeans on the eastern side of the Atlantic.[64]

We have already noted that the institution still thrived, as it had for centuries, in all "Four Parts of the World." In one important sense, slavery within the Americas was becoming less synonymous with African descent in the late eighteenth century than it had been a century before. In Latin America, free Afro-Latin Americans outnumbered slaves by almost two to one. Only in Brazil and Cuba did the slave population exceed the free blacks. Even in these two areas, free blacks composed 40 percent or more of their Afro-Latin American populations. Those areas in which the identification between black and slave was most apparent were in the Northern European colonies.[65]

Europeans were still less likely to identify Africans as synonymous with slaves outside the Americas. In their accounts of West Africa, slave traders invariably detailed a variety of social, political, and cultural systems. Such traders necessarily had contact with Africans as rulers, merchants, and masters. On the coast of Africa, the relationship was not one of European masters and African subordination. European readers were repeatedly reminded of the economic acuity of African slave traders and the power of African rulers. The resulting image of Africans formed by Europeans was a composite of a wide range of situations in Africa, America, and Europe.

The fact that most slaves in the Atlantic were of African descent by no means exhausted the European vision of the world's slave population in the late eighteenth century. Nor was slavery synonymous with black Africans in the eyes of other Old World societies. Racial stereotyping, of course, was possible in a world of many shades of slaves. Centuries before the European oceanic ventures, Arabs had accumulated European, African, and Asian slaves in large numbers. They tagged blacks with characteristics

---

[64] Davis, *Inhuman Bondage*, ch. 4; and Anthony J. Barker, *The African Link: British Attitudes to the Negro in the Era of the Atlantic Slave Trade* (London: Frank Cass, 1978), 60.

[65] See George Reid Andrews, *Afro-Latin America 1800–2000* (New York: Oxford University Press, 2004), 41; Table 1.1; and Stanley L. Engerman and B. W. Higman, "The Demographic Structure of the Caribbean Slave Societies in the Eighteenth and Nineteenth Centuries," in *Slave Societies of the Caribbean*, Franklin W. Knight, ed. (London: Unesco, 1997), 405–104; Table 2.1 (1).

of inferiority and servility, and associated them with degrading forms of labor. This was especially true with regard to the so-called *Zanj*, a term encompassing Bantu speaking captives from East Africa.[66] In any event, both the Muslim and Christian-dominated areas having multiethnic or multipigmented groups as the sources of their slaves did not prevent Muslims, Christians, or Jews from forming analogous stereotypes ascribing inherent servility and incapacity to blacks. It is also likely that Iberians received a ready-made body of negative images through Muslim writings and culture.

Moreover, as we have seen, for three centuries after the development of large-scale flows of Africans across the Atlantic, rationalizations for slavery were primarily religious and legalistic rather than naturalistic and scientific.[67] The biblical story of the "curse of Ham" as a rationale for a divinely ordained black slavery did reverberate through centuries of intensive European contact with Africans after 1450. The curse, however, played a negligible role in sustaining either the slave trade or slavery. Despite its recent historiographical currency, the curse of Ham does not appear to have been of great significance in the formulation of legal and theological documents sanctioning the institution. Neither papal bulls, nor councils of conscience, royal courts, or colonial legislatures appealed to the curse to rationalize their resolutions or laws. That Africans were merchants, rulers, and infidels in Africa had greater relevance in expanding and sanctioning their acquisition as slaves and their status within Christendom. The curse of Ham played its most important belated role in shoring up the nineteenth-century pro-slavery argument in the U.S. South. It seems unlikely, of course, that the curse encouraged the acquisition of more Africans than would have otherwise been transported to the Americas or the Muslim world. Before the nineteenth century, institutionalized racism, whether in the form of Iberian regimes of *castas* or northern Euro-American denials of civic equality, was directed more at free nonwhites than slaves.[68] Although slavery was

[66] Davis, *Inhuman Bondage*, 62–64, see also Bernard Lewis, *Race and Color in Islam*, (New York: Harper and Row, 1971), pp. 15–18; and Lewis, *Race and Slavery in the Middle East* (New York: Oxford University Press, 1990), 59–61.

[67] Fredrickson, *Racism: A Short History*, 44–46. See also James H. Sweet, "The Iberian roots of American Racist Thought," *William and Mary Quarterly*, 54:1 (1997), 143–166. Emiliano Frutta, "Purity of Blood and Nobility in Colonial Mexico: the formation of a noble lore, 1571–1700" *Jahrbuch für Geschichte Lateinamerikas*, 39 (2002), 217–235; Maria Elena Martinez, "The Black Blood of New Spain: *Limpieza de Sangre*, Racial Violence, and Gendered Power in Early Colonial Mexico," *William and Mary Quarterly*, 51 (2004), 479–520. For a succinct summary, see Davis, *Inhuman Bondage*, ch. 3; for increasing British literary interest in race from the 1770s, see Wheeler, *Complexion of Race*, ch. 4 and 5.

[68] Strikingly, the first time in the history of Jewish, Christian, and Muslim iconography that Ham was depicted as a man with a distinctive color was in Albany, New York, in 1843. See Benjamine Braude, "Michelangelo and the Curse of Ham: From a Typology of Jew-Hatred to a Genealogy of Racism," in *Writing Race Across the Atlantic World*, Philip D.

virtually uncontested as a necessary institution, neither did the beneficiaries or the critics of slavery take more than passing note of the rising scientific interest in race.

From a global perspective, the earth's rulers appeared as committed to perpetuating bondage as they had when the Portuguese purchased their first slaves on the African coast three centuries earlier.[69]

In 1772, Arthur Young offered a bird's eye view of bondage throughout the globe. He made the zone of freedom appear narrow indeed. Filled with the century's new enthusiasm for numbers, Young estimated that of the earth's 775 million inhabitants, all but 33 million could be classified as unfree. If British readers could take pride in the statistic that one in three free people were subjects of his Britannic majesty, the proportions did not encourage optimism about the immediate prospects of humanity as a whole.[70] In the very year that Young was estimating the statistics of freedom and bondage, a landmark case in favor of freedom was being argued before Lord Mansfield, England's chief justice. Francis Hargrave, on behalf of a black servant, James Somerset, opened with a picture of the preponderance of people in bondage, identical to the view of Young. If the right of slavery, he warned the court and his countrymen,

is here recognized, domestic slavery with its horrid train of evils may be lawfully imported into this country.... It will come not only from our colonies and those of other European nations, but from Poland, Russia, Spain and Turkey, from the coast

Bender and Gary Taylor, eds. (London: Palgrave, 2005), 79–92. On the separate origins and different curses of slavery and blackness in scriptures, and their interpretations, see, *ibid.*; Ephraim Isaac, "Genesis, Judaism and the 'Sons of Ham,'" *Slavery and Abolition*, 1 (1980), 3–17; and David M. Goldenberg, *The Curse of Ham: Race and Slavery in Early Judaism, Christianity and Islam* (Princeton, NJ: Princeton University Press, 2003). The import of this scholarship is brilliantly summarized in David Brion Davis, "Blacks: Damned by the Bible," *New York Review of Books*, November 16, 2006, 37–40. On the comparative breadth and permeability of the system of *castas* in Ibero-America, see Magnus Mörner, *Race Mixture in the History of Latin America* (Boston: Little Brown, 1967); and Andrews, *Afro-Latin America*, 40–51.

[69] From a global perspective, an over-emphasis on the ideological discourse of the nineteenth-century U.S. South tends to distort the degree of identification between slavery and Africans. In the Indian Ocean world, even Portuguese conceptions and uses of enslavement diverged sharply from the nineteenth-century Western linkage of slaves with the "African race." In Portuguese Goa, slaves from India, China, and Malaysia, and of Afro-European, Afro-East Asian, Afro-Indian, and Afro-Indo-European heritage, served alongside East Africans. This did not mean that persons with such backgrounds had access to ruling Portuguese circles. It did mean, however, that the identification of enslavement with one continent or one color was still not paramount. See Timothy Walker, "Slaves or Soldiers? African Conscripts in Portuguese India, 1857–1860," in *Slavery and South Asian History*, Indrani Chatterjee and Richard M. Eaton, eds. (Bloomington: Indiana University Press, 2007), 234–261.

[70] Arthur Young, *Political Essays Concerning the Present State of the British Empire*, (London, 1772), 20–21.

of Barbary, from the western and eastern coasts of Africa, from every part of the world, where it still continues to torment and dishonour the human species.[71]

This was no fanciful estimate of the balance of power between slavery and freedom on the eve of the age of abolition.

Across the Channel, even detestation of slavery had to reckon with the sheer solidity of the institution. In 1770, the Abbé G.-T. Raynal's *History of the Two Indies* was published in Amsterdam. The *History*'s account of European global predation was infused with antislavery sentiments. For the deeply troubled Abbé, the world outside of Europe was developing completely counter to the civilizing process evident within Europe itself. One continent had gradually evolved toward freedom, combining material and economic progress. Yet, elsewhere, Europeans seemed to have transformed the gentle civilizing mechanism of commerce into avaricious brutality. A thirst for gold combined with a thirst for blood.

The contradiction seemed so bizarre that one could only grope for an explanation. Because slavery beyond the seas had pre-dated Europeans by centuries, Raynal fell back on Montesquieu's standby – climate. A tropical climate was an invincible seedbed of "the vices and virtues of slavery." In the tropical East, one encountered an ancient combination of political and civil slavery. To the depopulated Americas, the Europeans chose to bring Africans "accustomed to the yoke." Taking note of the large, free Afro-Latin American population in the Ibero-Americas, Raynal credited the Spanish for creating a system in which the African was at least alternatively slave or master.

Nevertheless, the vast, unfree world beyond the seas left Raynal frustrated by the tyranny of climate and distance. Commerce was degrading, not improving, the world. One could hardly look to the spirit of religion to reverse the rising tide of servitude. The *History* dismissed the tale of Christianity's liberating influence as a myth, even within Europe. One only had to glance eastward to Germany, Bohemia, and Poland where Catholic ecclesiastical principalities ruled estates worked by serfs without the least murmur from the Church.

The only hope for destroying the ever-expanding grip of slavery seemed to demand an appeal beyond Europe's mercantile and civil mechanisms. Raynal could envision only two possible sources of redemption – one from above and one from below. The first was an appeal to the great monarchs who ruled the world: "Kings of the earth, you alone can make this revolution." If the voice of humanity failed to move the mighty, humanity had but one other recourse. A new Spartacus would arise from the ranks of maroon fugitives constantly accruing in the slave islands. Raynal's range of potential agents

---

[71] *Howell's State Trials*, (London: T. C. Hansard, 1809–1828), vol. 20; Case of Somerset v. Stewart, (1772), col. 24.

of transformation reflected a deep sense of impotence and pessimism. As he wistfully wrote in a foreword to his survey of four centuries of European expansion: "Isn't the future splendor of these colonies a dream, and wouldn't the happiness of these regions be a still more amazing phenomenon than their original devastation?"[72]

The next fifty years would offer the world more splendor, more destruction, and more dreams of happiness than any reader of Raynal's *History* could have imagined. The next half century would witness both the age of revolution and the age of abolition.[73]

[72] On the paragraphs before, see Guillaume Thomas Raynal, *Histoire philosophique et politique des etablissements et du commerce des Européens dans les deux Indes*, 4 vols. (Geneva: Pellet, 1780), I, 14–15; 687–88 II, 3, 294, 358. Peter Jamack's introduction to a translated selection of Raynal's *History of the Two Indies* (Burlington, VT: Ashgate, 2006), xxv, points out that the *History's* default view "is clearly that the plantation colonies, and especially the sugar colonies, cannot prosper without black slaves."

[73] I am in accord with David Brion Davis, *The Problem of Slavery in the Age of Revolution* (Ithaca, NY: Cornell University Press, 1975), 21–22 in using "abolitionism" as a more activist expression of "antislavery," in the political sense. I also mean abolitionism to denote not just a variation of antipathy toward, or even resistance to, masters and slavery, which long preceded the rise of political hostility to the institution, but to refer to a collective mobilization to weaken or destroy slavery wherever that became a politically feasible project.

PART TWO

CRISIS

4

Border Skirmishes

Despite its apparent solidity and dynamism, the Atlantic system of slavery could not remain in equilibrium. Never had so many settlements been created in which from half to nine-tenths of the population were chattel. Never had enslavement been so rigorously confined to groups so physically distinguished from each other. Above all, never before had the asymmetry between the legitimacy of the institution in one part of an empire and its illegitimacy in another been so jarringly juxtaposed. In the Old World, the institution was not dominated by the demands for new mass-produced commodities. Male slaves in Afro-Asia also continued to perform political, military, and court duties as well as domestic functions. Beyond the household domains of rulers, slaves were devoted to demands for small-scale labor and for sexual and reproductive services. Women represented a far greater percentage of the total slave population than they did in the slave population of the New World. Throughout Afro-Asia, slaves remained deeply rooted in the legal and institutional structures of society. In sub-Saharan Africa, slaves were still the only form of private property recognized in law. In Moslem-dominated North Africa, the institution was consensually regarded as sanctioned by Islamic doctrine and tradition. Therefore, beyond the reach of European power and economic incentives, slavery did not exhibit the growing institutional disequilibrium of the Euro-Atlantic world.

Even in the New World, the potential threats to the institution's equilibrium were not all analogous in a hemisphere where slavery was a state-sanctioned institution from Alaska to the Hudson Bay and from Chile to Rio de la Plata. In the Americas, slave resistance in various forms was persistent throughout the duration of the institution. Its individual forms ranged from sabotage and theft to physical retaliation and suicide. Its collective forms included conspiracies and rebellions. More frequent than insurrections, however, was flight from bondage. The most serious took the form of permanent refuge in thinly inhabited forests or inaccessible terrain. In areas with such geographical advantages, maroon communities (*quilombos*) continued to exist as long as slavery endured. Such settlements often threatened the stability of neighboring local slave systems. Some of the most durable communities negotiated formal treaties with slaveholding regimes. These treaties guaranteed the freedom of Maroons and the autonomy of their communities. In exchange for their own freedom, the Maroons agreed to return future runaways from the plantations or populated slave areas. In such situations, firm ties of interdependence connected the plantation complex with maroon communities. In most instances the, long term survival of maroon communities depended upon skillful negotiation with the outside world. Some developed coercive labor institutions of their own.[1]

The major structural threats to the racialized slavery of the Americas remained latent, but always expanding. In the Iberian colonies, the major threat to the institution flowed primarily from the unintended consequences of free Afro-Latin American populations. In Iberia itself, the presence of slaves, and African slaves in particular, had long preceded the creation of their transatlantic colonies. There was no special zone of slavery in the Portuguese and Spanish empires. Their medieval slave codes were seamlessly transferred to their overseas possessions. The lines of difference and the trajectories of emancipation would only emerge belatedly during the half century conventionally called the "Age of Revolution," from the 1770s to the 1820s.

Future sources of tension within the Iberian orbit were almost literally American-born. Whereas free blacks and mulattoes amounted to 5 percent or less of the late eighteenth-century French, Dutch, and English colonial populations, they composed 20 to 50 percent of those populations in Latin America. Only in Portuguese Brazil and the Spanish Caribbean did the slave populations exceed that of free Afro-Latin Americans. In all of the Spanish mainland colonies, the free black populations were larger than their slave populations by 1770. In most of Spanish America, they also outnumbered the white population. In those parts of the Spanish mainland where they did not hold such an edge, the Mestizo and Indian populations also far

---

[1] On the complex relationships between maroon communities and resistance to slavery in neighboring societies, including Native Americans, see, inter alia, Eugene D. Genovese, *From Rebellion to Revolution: Afro-American Slave Revolts in the Making of the New World* (Baton Rouge: Louisiana State University Press, 1979); Michael Craton, *Testing the Chains: Resistance to Slavery in the British West Indies* (Ithaca: Cornell University Press, 1982); *Maroon Societies: Rebel Slave Communities in the Americas*, Richard Price, ed. (Baltimore: The Johns Hopkins University Press, 1996); Charles Beatty Medina, "Caught Between Rivals: The Spanish-American Maroon Competition for Captive Indian Labor in the Region of Esmeraldas During the late Sixteenth and Early Seventeenth Centuries," *Americas*, 63:1 (2006), 113–136; Alvin D. Thompson, *Flight to Freedom: African Runaways and Maroons in the Americas* (Kingston, Jamaica: University of West Indies Press, 2006), esp. ch. 10, "Maroons and Revolutionary Struggle." The main point in terms of challenges to the institution remains that "few, if any, Maroon Communities were in a position to wage a general anti-slavery or anti-colonial struggle. Only in from the late eighteenth century are their hints that some Maroons participated in a growing revolutionary consciousness."

outnumbered the whites.[2] Brazil had always been, and would remain, the single greatest importer of African slaves to Latin America. Along with Brazil, Cuba and Puerto Rico would become the heirs of the diminishing Caribbean slave systems of the Northern European empires during the age of revolution.

Afro-Latin Americans formed so large a part of the population of African descent because slaves had been freed at a higher rate than elsewhere in the Americas for centuries. Even in the most dynamic slave zones, Cuba and Brazil, the free blacks and mulattos composed 40 percent or more of the people of African descent. This meant that the boundary between legal freedom and slavery in Ibero-America ran within Afro-Latin America rather than between different geographic areas of the colonial empires: "While slaves were more likely to be Africans than Afro-Latin Americans, more likely to be black than racially mixed, and more likely to be male than female, the free colored population was the reverse: more American than African, more racially mixed than black, and with equal numbers of males and females." This balanced sex ratio, plus freedom, ensured the natural growth of free blacks. Ibero-American slaves, on the other hand, suffered a constant excess of deaths over births.[3]

African descent was not equivalent to slave status. Within the free population, the legal divisions of the *casta* regime were at once more abundant, less rigorous, more ambiguous, and more infuriating to the free Africans than that between free men and slaves. Moreover, toward the end of the eighteenth century, Spanish crown reforms began to offer greater opportunities for free blacks in crafts and business as well as in marital alliances, widening the racial fault lines within the free community. By the end of the century, those of African descent accounted for the largest black populations in the New World. In Latin America, the free non-whites would be decisive in dismantling the institution of slavery.

Although they experienced a far lower rate of manumission, slaves in colonies owned by northwestern European states stood some chance of exiting from slavery by crossing back over to Europe. Throughout the eighteenth century, an increasing flow of slaves to Europe demanded metropolitan attention to the anomaly of slaves on the "free soil" of Europe. Blacks who arrived in the metropole would raise serious questions about both their personal status and that of the institution of slavery itself. English, Dutch, and French legislation provided no clear guide to the outcome.[4] As indicated in chapter 2, the initial reaction to the arrival of slaves in the metropole

---

[2] Andrews, *Afro-Latin America*, (New York: Oxford University Press, 2004), 40.

[3] Ibid., *Afro-Latin America*, 40–51; quotation on p. 41.

[4] On the lack of seventeenth-century legislation in France, see Peabody, "*There are No Slaves in France,*" 11; On the Netherlands, see Seymour Drescher, "The Long Goodbye: Dutch Capitalism and Antislavery in Comparative Perspective, in *Fifty Years Later: Antislavery, Capitalism and Modernity in the Dutch Orbit* (Pittsburgh Press: 1996), 50 and note 47.

appeared to be liberation for the slaves. The number of slavers and colonists returning to Europe increased, creating serious social and economic problems over fleeing slaves who left their masters and refused to return.

In France, the courts were initially inclined to preserve the spatial and legal differences between the zone of slavery and the land of liberty. Provincial courts, finding no formal legislation on the subject, relied on local usage and routinely declared the slaves free. As increasing numbers of slaveholders returned to France with slave servants, the government attempted to provide an exemption to the "freedom principle." In 1716, a royal edict decreed that owners could retain their rights to return with their slaves, if there was a prior stipulation that the owner intended to keep their slaves only temporarily in France. Any failure to fulfill these regulations, however, gave slaves a legal right to challenge the master's claims. Since old-regime France was legally fragmented into twelve high courts (*Parlements*), the Parelement in any jurisdiction could register (or refuse to register) a royal decree within their own jurisdiction.[5] The largest Parlement (of Paris) declined to register the 1716 decree. It thereby opened a legal and geographical limbo that lasted almost until the French Revolution. On the one hand, the refusal to register the edict served to perpetuate the rhetorical tradition of France's free soil. Lawyers representing slave owners almost invariably paid homage to the general maxim that France's soil freed entering slaves. They asserted only that the royal edict created an exception to the rule. Those who wished to halt the flow of colonial slaves into France and limit "freedom" for racial reasons acknowledged that the ambiguity of the status of blacks arriving with colonists had to be clarified.[6]

Victories by colonial slaves in the French courts stimulated further royal attempts to close loopholes, but the hemorrhage continued. The question became caught up in the rising challenge to monarchical authority. Some Parlements claimed that slavery, once tolerated, would turn the French monarchy into despotism. The linkage of colonial slavery with metropolitan liberty also induced counter arguments linking the threats of uncontrolled liberty for blacks in France with racial inundation.[7] The conflict, therefore, aroused both political and racial anxieties. Some lawyers argued that blacks, once in France, "contracted habits and a spirit of independence" making them potential agents of insubordination. They echoed a growing anxiety on the other side of the Atlantic that a color line was a necessary reinforcement for a social system in which blacks outnumbered whites by ten to one. As in the Iberian colonies, new racial barriers were enacted for descendants of Africans who had escaped the status of slavery through manumission or by having a white parent. Even when they allowed temporary exceptions for

---

[5] Peabody, *ibid.*, 12–14.

[6] Pierre H. Boule, "Racial Purity or Legal Clarity? The Status of Black Residents in Eighteenth-Century France," *Journal of the Historical Society*, 6:1 (March, 2006), 19–46.

[7] Peabody, *"No Slaves,"* 97–105.

black residence in France, many officials routinely reiterated the principle that blacks should be destined for servitude and the cultivation of America.[8] Some metropolitan lawyers saw both slavery and blacks as contaminating France. A king's attorney feared the development of public markets in Paris where men would be bought and sold. On the colonial side of the Atlantic, planters were elaborating an ideology in which the color line was seen as an essential support of the social system. As in Latin American settlements, generations of interracial sexual intercourse was tangibly creating a class of individuals not envisaged by legal categories of the *Code Noir*.[9]

This perspective intensified toward the end of the eighteenth century. On the eve of the French Revolution, the share of free men of color in St. Domingue only amounted to 6 percent of the total population. This share was still quite small in comparison with the free population of color in the Latin American colonies. In a population that was nearly 90 percent African, this relatively small free colored population was approaching equality in numbers with its free white counterpart. In St. Domingue, the free population of color may have rivaled Brazil's free colored population in its share of slave ownership. In any metropolitan society, such a group would already have been considered potentially closer to the landowning elite than the laboring poor in its interests and outlook. Many French metropolitan officials, colonial governors, and members of the colored elite viewed their potential role in the slave system in this way.[10]

Most white planters, however, increasingly considered the equation of blackness with servility as essential to maintaining the overwhelming majority of the population in servitude. Significantly, the last major prerevolutionary legislation in 1777 concerning blacks resident in the metropole was entitled *Police des Noirs*. In France, the struggle of individual slaves for release from colonial ties had led to a hardening of the metropolitan color line by the closure of France to free blacks. The closure was based explicitly and exclusively on a color line rather than a legal line between slaves and free men. Unlike previous royal decrees, the *Police de Noirs* was registered by the *Parlement* of Paris, which attempted to close all future loopholes to freedom for blacks.[11] In the Caribbean, the struggle of free blacks and mulattos for civic equality had given birth to racially segregationist measures. Even those who rejected their full implementation favored a "moderate segregationism."

The *Police des Noirs* was explicitly formulated in favor of the colonial interests who controlled almost 100 black laborers overseas for each free black resident in France. The title of the decree of 1777 indicates the relative

---

[8] Boulle, "Racial Purity."
[9] Yvan Debbasch, *Couleur et Liberté: Le jeu du critère ethnique dans un ordre juridique esclavagiste* (Paris: Dalloz, 1967), ch. 2.
[10] See Debbasch, *Couleur et Liberté*, ch. 2 and 3.
[11] Peabody, *"No Slaves,"* 111–119.

ease with which *noirs* (blacks) could pass muster much more easily than
esclaves (slaves). Slave was a taboo term because it directly clashed with
the traditional freedom principle. Racial classifications did not. As Pierre
Boule argues, the absence of references to the slaves (henceforth, "people in
service") became the *sine qua non* for registration of the decree. Exclusion
was the means by which the purity of French soil could be reconciled with
the maintenance of the colonial system abroad. The color line could be as
effectively reaffirmed through exclusion abroad as liberation at home. A
French Commission investigating the problem of blacks in the metropole
concluded that "the race of negroes will be extinguished in the kingdom as
soon as the transport of them is forbidden."[12]

With the passage of the *Police des Noirs*, colonists arriving in France with
black slaves were obliged to "deposit" them in warehouses [*dépots*] pending
their return to the colonies. In this way, blacks from the colonies would
be treated much like other goods brought ashore solely for reexport. The
government carefully negotiated each word of the final draft decree to ensure
that there would be no final objections by the *Parlement* to its registration.
What followed its promulgation was uneven enforcement, endless appeals
by planters for exceptions, and more successful court suits by blacks for
liberation. It was clear by the 1780s, however, that "the notion of racial
purity was firmly entrenched in the minds of even the staunchest defenders
of liberty."[13]

News of the American Declaration of Independence in 1776 and subsequent French intervention in favor of the United States in its war of
independence had no impact on the legal status of blacks in France. The
French bureaucratic and legal elites agreed to sustain the line between freedom and slavery. It remained clear that these boundary conflicts raised by
movements of slaves were being fought out in French ports and on French
soil. The nation's policy toward the Atlantic slave trade and overseas slavery
remained unaltered. For each successful black petition for freedom accepted
by the Admiralty Court of Paris between 1777 and the outbreak of the Saint
Domingue Revolution in 1791, nearly 10,000 African slaves were loaded
on French ships for the French colonies. Each boarding was subsidized by
the French government. At the end of the old regime, slaveowning colonists
anticipated no threat to their social system.

The stresses produced by slaves crossing the line produced continuous
reaffirmations of the colonial/metropolitan divide, despite increasing antislavery publications in France. In the Dutch orbit, the transatlantic flow of
a few hundred slaves from the colonies produced even less of a ripple in the
Netherlands than in France. In 1776, only a tenth as many Africans resided
in the Dutch Republic as in France. Although the French monarchy

---

[12] *Ibid.*, 116–117.
[13] *Ibid.*, 135.

arduously negotiated the status of blacks with the *Parlement* of Paris, the Dutch States-General quietly decreed that slaveholders coming to the Netherlands could also secure their property by following procedures like those being suggested in France. The line was drawn even more unambiguously in Denmark. In 1802, Denmark's Upper Court ruled that the "free soil of the mother country did not confer freedom on the enslaved." This affirmation came at the precise moment that Denmark was putting its gradual abolition of the African Atlantic slave trade into effect. The Prussian monarchy offered another variant of boundary clarification. Prussia, which lacked overseas colonies, did not permit its citizens to own slaves. Resident foreigners in the kingdom, however, were allowed to exercise all rights over their slaves short of endangering their lives.[14] Isolated escapes at the individual level or even maroon victories at the communal level ended as Pyrrhic victories at the imperial level. Before the French Revolution, challenges to the boundaries of slavery by resident blacks or their lawyers largely ended in a modified reaffirmation of most slaveholders' rights in Europe.

In the Anglo-American zone, the contest took a different turn. In England, as in the Netherlands, the metropolitan core kept slavery at a distance by turning a blind common law eye toward the institution. The English government fully acknowledged property rights in persons on the Atlantic and the piecemeal construction of slave laws in each of their colonies. It avoided creating an imperial black code in the manner of the monarchs of Spain, Portugal, and France. The earliest, most famous, and most terse decision by English Chief Justice, John Holt, put the matter succinctly in a series of freedom suits in the early 1700s. The English common law he declared, took no "notice of Negroes being different from other men. By the common law no man can have a property in another, but [only] in special cases, as in a villein, but [not to kill him] so in captives took in war, but the taker may not kill him, but may sell them for ransom: there is no such thing as a slave by the law of England."[15]

Holt's decision seemed as definitive as the affirmation of the "freedom principle" across the Channel. There was no slave law in England. The common law did not recognize any special status for black Africans. Nor did they fall within the purview of laws applicable to ancient villeins, or modern indentured servants. On the other hand, under Virginia law, blacks could be securely held as property in Virginia. By Royal Charter, they could be purchased by English sea captains in Africa and sold in the Americas. The

---

[14] Seymour Drescher, "The Long Goodbye," 25–66, esp. 30 and note 13. On Denmark and Prussia, see Neville A. T. Hall, *Slave Society in the Danish West Indies: St. Thomas, St. John, St. Croix*, B. W. Higman, ed. (Baltimore: The Johns Hopkins University Press, 1992), 33–36.

[15] Steven M. Wise, *Though the Heavens May Fall: The Landmark Trial that Led to the End of Human Slavery* (2005), 29.

initially clear lines began to be blurred by migration. As slaves began to move across the Atlantic, they might arrive in England as a captain's "share" in a slaving voyage. They might come as servants of colonial officials, merchants, or planters. Young Africans might be purchased as exotic trophies for the wealthy. Their keepers routinely behaved as though blacks in their custody could be sold at will as domestic servants, or shipped overseas.

Slaveholders began practices familiar beyond the line: from advertising and displaying blacks for sale to arranging church baptisms that offered public recognition of their servant's freedom. Black servants too, made their own flight to freedom a public issue. Their actions became visible in newspaper advertisements offering rewards for their capture. If some masters, following a popular, if not legal, tradition, used baptism as public recognition of freedom, some slaves contended that baptism made them free. A baptismal font could become battlefield. An item in a London newspaper in 1760 captured the stakes:

Last week a Negro girl about nine years old, having eloped from her mistress on account of ill usage, was brought to a Church in Westminster by two housekeepers, to be baptized. But the mistress of the girl, getting intelligence of it, while the Minister was reading the churching service, seized upon her in the face of the congregation, and violently forced her out of the Church, regardless of her cries and tears; telling the people about her that she was her slave, and would use her as she pleased.... 'We should be glad to be informed,' 'first, whether, it is in the power of a master or mistress of a Negro slave to prevent her being baptized after her arrival in England? Secondly, whether in this free country such a Negro still continues a slave after baptism? Lastly, whether upon complaint of ill usage, it is not in the power of a Justice of the Peace to discharge such a Negro from her slavery?'[16]

Some anxious English slaveholders elicited an out-of-court legal opinion in 1729, that baptism did not alter a slaves' status, but this had no standing as a case law precedent. The tenuousness of a masters' hold on both the services and value of his servants was obvious in common practice. Most magistrates refused masters' requests against runaways on the simple grounds that no law had been broken. Nor did their flight constitute a breach of the peace. Masters turned to validating their claims by hiring private enforcers to drag runaways onto ships bound for departure to the colonies, where their slave status was ratified.[17]

By the early 1770s, the uncertainties and expenses of private enforcement placed a considerable amount of property in people at risk. Contemporaries vaguely estimated that 10,000 to 15,000 blacks resided in England in 1770 – more than twice the number then residing in France and up to

---

[16] Quoted in S. Drescher, "Manumission in a Society without Slave Law," *Slavery and Abolition*, 10:3 (1989), 85–101.

[17] For an overview of the literature, consult Christopher Brown, *Moral Capital: Foundations of British Abolitionism* (Chapel Hill, NC: University of North Carolina Press, 2006), 91–94.

twenty times their numbers in the Dutch republic. British masters claimed that each black servant represented a capital value of £50, collectively representing as much capital as was annually invested in the British Atlantic slave trade.

British slaveholders were unlikely to have mentioned that only a portion of these 10,000 or more blacks were actually claimed by anyone as property. From a database of 4,000 blacks in England over the period between 1660 and the abolition of the British slave trade in 1807, Kathy Charter has found only fifteen cases in which a black was identified as a slave. No instance has yet been discovered in which a slave status was inherited in England and Wales, as it was in the colonies. None of the distinctive property or penal rights claimed by masters overseas, such as pledging blacks as collateral or public scourging with a whip, appeared in accounts of metropolitan blacks in eighteenth-century England. Blacks did not routinely appear on lists of chattel, as they would overseas. I have seen no accounts of blacks in Britain where they were used as collateral for loans. Finally, the prohibition of public scourging had apparently been definitively decided long before in the case of a Russian master and his alleged slave.[18] Even deportation, the colonial legality of the masters' ultimate weapon, was at risk. Those who claimed this right over their black servants were unwilling to test its validity in the courts, preferring to spirit blacks aboard vessels bound for the Americas.

The issue came to a head in 1771, when a slave, James Somerset, was seized by his master and released on a writ of habeas corpus obtained by Granville Sharp, England's most active abolitionist. The case came before England's chief justice, Lord Mansfield. The hearings extended from January to June 1772. No one challenged the fact that Charles Steuart had legally purchased Somerset in Virginia. At risk was more than the status of slavery or Charles Steuart's potential loss of his chattel. The West India planters and merchants collectively covered Steuart's legal expenses. The case quickly became the most widely publicized and discussed court drama over slavery in English history. In addition to extensive news coverage, more essays were published in the wake of the trial than the country had ever seen. The essays produced a level of public discussion that would not again be equaled until the emergence of political abolitionism fifteen years later.

The contenders outlined two threats to English society. For supporters of Somerset, sanctioning slavery threatened to deposit a lethal ingredient

---

[18] It was extremely rare in England to find anyone documented as a slave. Of 4,000 entries on blacks only 15 were ever so designated. See Kathy Chater, "Black People in England, 1660–1807," in *The British Slave Trade: Abolition, Parliament and People*, Stephen Farrell, Melanie Unwin, and James Walvin, eds. (Edinburgh: Edinburgh University Press, 2007), 66–83; esp. p. 72. On the prohibition against whipping a Russian slave, see "Cartwright's Case," (Rushworth (1569)), reprinted in *Judicial Cases Concerning American Slavery and the Negro*, 5 vols., Helen Tunnicliff Catterall, ed. (Washington: Carnegie Institution of Washington, 1926–1937), I, 9.

into England's free institutions. Granville Sharp contended that a decision in favor of slavery might also tempt masters to transport masses of black slaves to England, impoverishing British servants. Slave owners countered with a more racially tinged threat. A clear decision in favor of liberation might lure so many blacks to Britain as to stain the complexion of Englishmen and debase their minds.

Faced with the same institutional and ideological challenge as the Dutch and the French, the English response was distinctive. The Dutch and French states opted for legal clarification, police surveillance, and racial recycling. The mythos of free soil was affirmed by the registration and retention of blacks at the border of the nation. On the Continent, decision making remained isolated from the public sphere offering maximum opportunities for the planter class to lobby in the more closed environment of bureaucratic and judicial institutions. Planter representatives had ample opportunity to register their concerns. In France, opposition to the *Police des Noirs* could be registered through bureaucratic channels, but the discussion proceeded behind closed doors. With only brief interludes of publicity, the history of blacks in eighteenth-century France could be read as a series of *intra*governmental struggles to "regulate the boundaries between blacks and whites." Of course, French enforcement, as with other old regime legislation, was uneven and fragmented. Slaves continued to initiate freedom suits. They continued to resurrect those precedents that had thwarted prior attempts to police and exclude them. They were also faced with the new racial stigma that had been added to the old panoply of restrictions on blacks, including limitations on the rights of nonwhites to travel to and France. Masters had to register their slaves on arrival. For free blacks, the obligation to register with the government persisted well into the early years of the French Revolution.[19]

By contrast, the *Somerset* case received extended attention in an open courtroom under common law adversarial proceedings. Never had an issue involving slavery triggered more widespread and ongoing newspaper coverage and correspondence. Wide ranging speculation on the case's impact in England and beyond the Atlantic elicited a flurry of polemics. This development was exactly what Lord Mansfield had feared. He showed every sign of seeking to narrow and defuse the issue. During the hearings he suggested that the West Indians should aim either at an out-of-court settlement, or parliamentary legislation in support of their proprietary claims.[20] The public correspondence overwhelmingly demanded that the chief justice proceed to a verdict. After six months of continuances, one "Emilius" unleashed his impatience and anger in a newspaper letter just before the verdict: "Mean spirited, pitiable old Man! How much you've dodged that

---

[19] Peabody, *"There Are No Slaves,"* p. 137; and Boule, "Racial Purity," 38–40.
[20] Wise, *Though the Heavens*, 161, 173.

[Justice] Holt would have gloried in.... Good God! Is this the language of an English Judge? *Fiat Justicia, ruat Coelum* [*Do Justice, Though the Heavens Fall*].... ! – Dastardly Braggard."[21]

Mansfield did dodge to the very end. His verdict eluded comprehensive judgment, but offered no judicial support for slaveholders' claims in England. Otherwise, it was a masterpiece of brevity. The most widely publicized version was less than 150 words long:

The power of a master over his slave has been different in different countries. The state of slavery is of such a nature that it is incapable of being introduced on any reasons, moral or political, but only positive law, which preserves its force long after the reasons, occasion, and time itself from which it was created, is erased from memory. It is so odious that nothing can be suffered to support it but positive law. Whatever inconveniences, therefore, may follow from a decision, I cannot say this case is allowed or approved by the law of England, and therefore the black must be discharged.[22]

The *Somerset* decision has generated an unending stream of brilliant historical commentary about the degree to which it did or did not end the slave status of enslaved individuals while residing in England. However, all of the reported variants of the original decision, and there were many, agree on a few common principles: English law did not allow a master residing in England to deport someone on the grounds that he was legally a slave in some other region. Slavery was a variety of domination that had to be specifically sanctioned within the laws of each legal jurisdiction. Charles Steuart was not permitted to forcibly detain James Somerset within England to transport him back to a place in which he was still recognized as a slave. No monetary or other considerations to slaveowners could override the absence of positive law allowing slavery.

Mansfield had concluded with another phrase, which settled a point totally distinct from the permissibility of the master to deport – "therefore the black must be discharged." Other versions were, "therefore let the man [or the negro] be discharged." Both versions were paraphrases of Holt's explicit pronouncement that the common law took no exceptional notice of a Negro in regard to liberty. The other aspect of the phrase was even more expansive: "*must be discharged*." Mansfield might have returned Somerset into the "ordinary service" of Charles Steuart. Mansfield's friend, William Blackstone, in the 1770 version of his famous *Commentaries,* had noted that, despite the slave's entitlement to freedom on English soil, "the master's right to his service may possibly continue."[23] Mansfield's decision omitted any inference to that possibility.

---

[21] *Public Advertiser* (London) June 13, 1772. For other similar judgments see Drescher, *Capitalism and Antislavery*, 193 n. 51.
[22] Wise, *Though the Heavens*, 182.
[23] Wise, *Though the Heavens*, 39.

More important to our purposes than Mansfield's intended minimalization of the implications of his decision, however, was the degree to which it was almost immediately interpreted far more broadly in popular discourse. Whatever their powers elsewhere, masters were entitled to no pecuniary claims to or penal powers over their servants in England. The reactions of the many blacks in the courtroom on the day that "the Negro obtained his freedom" made its way across Britain. "All of them, as soon as Lord Mansfield had delivered the opinion of the court, came forward, and bowed first to the Judges, then to the bar, with symptoms of the most extravagant joy. Who can help admiring the genius of that government which thus dispenses freedom all around it?"[24] The blacks then shook each other by the hand and "congratulated themselves upon the recovery of the rights of human nature, and their happy lot that permitted them to breathe the free air of England."[25]

The black community in Britain would, of course, have been especially sensitive to the persistence of any subsequent claims by masters for residual property rights in them or of obligations to involuntary service arising out of their status overseas. Thereafter, however, blacks wrote as axiomatically of the absence of slavery in England as did the most self-congratulatory white correspondents in the popular press. Ottobah Cugoano, a prominent black activist, hailed the Somerset case as having freed blacks from deportation and placed them beyond the reach of colonial slave law in England. Blacks might be furtively spirited out of England by sea captains sailing for the Americas, but only as long as an owner was willing to risk arrest for illegal deportation.[26]

A second British court decision, in Scotland, shows how quickly the *Somerset* case came to be received as full liberation within the United Kingdom. Even before the decisive *Knight* case was brought forward, the impossibility of slavery in Britain had been reaffirmed. Lord Advocate Henry Dundas, at a hearing before the Scottish judges in 1776, claimed that "there was not now a slave in Britain, nor could possibly be from its constitution."[27] Significantly, Dundas felt no obligation to refer to the *Somerset* case, but to the British constitution itself as the definitive source

---

[24] *New York Journal*, Sept. 9, 1772, quoted in Patricia Bradley, *Slavery, Propaganda and the American Revolution* (Jackson, MS: University Press of Mississippi, 1998), 74–75.

[25] *Morning Chronicle*, June 23, 1772, quoted in Vincent Carretta, *Equiano the African: Biography of a Self-Made Man* (Athens, GA: University of Georgia Press, 2005), 208.

[26] On the widespread belief that the Somerset case liberated black people outside of England, see W. Jeffrey Bolster, *Black Jacks: African American Seamen in the Age of Sail* (Cambridge, MA: Harvard University Press, 1997), pp. 19–21, 149; Chater, "Black People in England," p. 68. See Folarin Shyllon, *Black Slaves in Britain* (London: Oxford University Press, 1974) appendix 2, 209, 212, 267.

[27] Iain White, *Scotland and the Abolition of Black Slavery, 1756–1838* (Edinburgh: Edinburgh University Press, 2006), 32. Dundas was no abolitionist. During the next two decades, he was decisive in postponing the prohibition of the British Atlantic slave trade through the British Parliament.

of freedom. In 1778, Joseph Knight, an African-born slave who had been brought to Scotland, left his master's service. Knight was apprehended and sentenced to "continue as before." A series of appeals climaxed in a decision on "the dominion assumed over this Negro (Knight).... Being unjust [it] could not be supported in this country to any extent.... therefore the defendant had no right to the Negro's service for any space of time; nor to send him out of the country against his consent...."[28] Mansfield's three fundamental points: no legal support for slavery; no deportation; no residual service obligation, were reaffirmed.

To his last days, Mansfield spoke out in general against consulting "popular declamation" in deciding legal issues. However, two decades after his decision he privately acknowledged to his old nemesis, Granville Sharp, that English law had indeed undermined slavery in Britain.[29] The impact of Mansfield's decision as freeing slaves within England was explicitly acknowledged by West Indians even as they belittled the material value of freedom for most blacks who abandoned their masters. "Veritas," a West Indian writing in the *St. James's Chronicle* in 1788, asked how many hundreds of slaves had since come with masters, who "knew they were on *free* ground and returned."[30] One could also belittle the freeing of blacks in London while Britain still sanctioned trading them abroad in record numbers. Benjamin Franklin, on a mission in England at a time of increasing tension with the colonies, belittled The *Somerset* decision to devalue any accrual of British moral capital at the expense of slaveholding Americans. On the day before Mansfield's decision, he juxtaposed Anthony Benezet's tally of victims of the slave trade to the "setting free of a single negro," in Britain as that nation "piqued itself on its Virtue."[31] Even in discounting the decision as no great gain for blacks in the Atlantic system, however, Franklin echoed the public consensus on the implication of the *Somerset* case as a decision for liberation.

Mansfield's decision could have been received in North America simply as a reiteration of Holt's original rejection of the intrusion of overseas slavery into England. Patricia Bradley's survey of the American press finds that hostile patriot newspapers actually sought to constrict information about the *Somerset* case. They usually limited their reporting to Mansfield's brief message of liberation. *The Boston Gazette*, the colonies' premier organ of patriot propaganda, noted laconically: "A correspondent [in England]

---

[28] See *Slavery, Abolition and Emancipation*, Michael Craton, James Walvin, and David Wright, eds., (London: Longman, 1976), 171.

[29] See S. Drescher, *Capitalism and Antislavery*, 43 and 197 n. 60.

[30] See *St. James's Chronicle*, March 25–27, 1788, *ibid.*, February 9–12, 1788.

[31] George S. Brookes, *Friend Anthony Benezet* (London: Oxford University Press, 1937), 422, B. Franklin to Benezet, August 22, 1772. On Benezet's pioneering role in abolitionism, see above all, Maurice Jackson, *Let This Voice Be Heard: Anthony Benezet, Father of Atlantic Abolitionism* (Philadelphia: University of Pennsylvania Press, 2009).

observes that as Blacks are free now in this country, Gentlemen will not be so fond of bringing them here as they used to be, it being computed there are now 14,000 blacks in this country."[32] Even if the decision spoke to the 10,000 metropolitan or more blacks rather than to James Somerset alone, it need not have aroused the Anglo-American empire. By the summer of 1772, however, colonial newspapers throughout North America were commenting at considerable length on the long-range impact of the Mansfield decision. *The Virginia Gazette* reported cases of slaves seeking the promised land of England. The reports of this Southern newspaper led readers to come to a similar conclusion as had popular opinion in England. Mansfield had outlawed slavery. For the next two years, *Virginia Gazette* advertisements for the recovery of fugitives stated that runaways were under the impression that they could reach England. That the *Somerset* decision promised them freedom was "a notion now too prevalent among the Negroes." Some commentators expressed even deeper fears – that the libertarian principles prevailing in England would be extended to America.[33]

The most significant transatlantic aspect of the decision was that it stimulated discussion from one end of the Continental colonies to the other. Why did this decision, which so modestly, if clearly, affirmed the "freedom principle" within England alone, reverberate for generations beyond its initial pronouncement? Why did it not provoke similar affirmations of free soil elsewhere in Europe? In 1761, for example, Portugal's Marquis de Pombal introduced a series of reforms that prohibited the introduction of new slaves to Portugal and to some northern Atlantic islands. A second law, in 1773, provided for the emancipation of imported slaves and prohibited the entrance of free colored laborers.[34] However, these Portuguese laws, the second virtually coincidental with the *Somerset* decision, caused no public discussion whatever in Portugal, its African colonies, or Brazil. Portugal's legislation, like most others, appealed to slave owners as affirmations of the line in a way designed to sustain the institution and the slave trade. There was also a reassuring clarity in the simultaneous support offered to its colonial slave and racial systems.

In the Anglo-American world, the *Somerset* decision was asymmetrical on both sides of the Atlantic. In rendering his decision, Mansfield had clearly

---

[32] *Boston Gazette*, September 21, 1772, quoted in Patricia Bradley, *Slavery, Propaganda, and the American Revolution*, p. 68. Bradley aptly notes that even the laconic notice in the *Boston Gazette* indicated no other interpretation than that "Blacks are now free in this country (England)," 73.

[33] Vincent Carretta, *Equiano, The African: Biography of a Self-Made Man*, (Athens, GA: University of Georgia Press, 2005), 212–213.

[34] Davis, *Problem of Slavery in Western Culture*, 239 n. 20. See also C. R. Boxer, *Race Relations in the Portuguese Colonial Empire*, 1415–1825 (Oxford: Clarendon Press, 1963), 100.

sided with Somerset. In one popular version of the decision, several news-papers reported the chief justice as referring to "a case so odious as the condition of slaves...."[35] Mansfield dismissed, through silence, any claims to compensation for the property loss that would be entailed in the (greatly exaggerated) claim that as much as £800,000 was actually in question. When the West Indians finally pushed to have their colonial claims extended into England, they lost. The British made no attempt to fortify the line by creat-ing a metropolitan warehouse for incoming slaves. They made no gesture, as in France or Portugal, to erect a metropolitan racial barrier to the entry of Africans with or without their masters. A survey of letters to English newspapers in 1771–1773 shows how little attention was given to the West Indian evocation of blood pollution or racial inundation during or after in the *Somerset* hearings.

Whatever the weight of the West India interest in British politics, it did not extend to institutionalizing slavery in the metropole. During the hearings Mansfield made it clear that if the planters wanted legal enforcement of their claims in England such enforcement would have to come from national leg-islation. A West Indian sounding of support in parliament failed to arouse any response. The West Indians' sole consolation was that Mansfield left the institution intact abroad. That seemed to be sufficient. There was apparently less anxiety expressed about the *Somerset* decision in the West Indies than there was in North America. There is no indication that West Indians imag-ined that their imperial governors would ever contemplate an extension of the freedom principle to colonies valued solely for crops produced by slave labor. Colonials crossing the Atlantic were obliged to adjust to the clearly diminished status of their slave property in Britain. Seven years after his decision, Mansfield was personally informed of the consequences of *Somer-set* for masters crossing the line. Thomas Hutchinson, the former governor of Massachusetts and an exiled loyalist, informed the chief justice that all Americans who were bringing blacks to England, "had as far as I knew, relinquished their property in them, and rather agreed to give them wages, or suffered them to go free."[36]

The ramifications of Mansfield's decision went much further than its impact upon transatlantic voyagers. The discussion of the case quickly fed into the developing conflict between the Continental colonies and the impe-rial government. In some respects, Britain's North American colonies had already diverged farther from their Latin American and Caribbean counter-parts than had Britain from other imperial states. The *Somerset* case inten-sified northern public response toward slavery at a moment when it could easily be linked to other conflicts over the future of their communities.

[35] Wise, *Though the Heavens*, 186.
[36] Carretta, *Equiano*, 20.

From the founding of the northwest European colonies in the New World to the eve of the American Revolution, ten times as many Europeans departed for the British colonies as for the French. The Anglo-Dutch migration gap was even wider.[37] In 1770, however, the British Caribbean colonies closely resembled those of the other northwest European colonies in that their populations were up to 90 percent slave. Most of Britain's northern mainland colonies were similar to those in Spanish America in having colonies with nonslave majorities. In those North American colonies, however, the overwhelming majority of the free were also Euro-Americans.

Some English colonies were even more distinctive within the Western Hemisphere in having been founded during a generation when their own home country was wracked by profound civil conflict. Seventeenth-century nodules of resistance to the establishment of slavery briefly emerged in a number of British colonies.[38] One should not exaggerate this seventeenth-century development any more than the sixteenth century clerical protests against Latin American slavery. All colonies acceded sooner rather than later to the search for compliant and continuous labor in underpopulated and insecure new settlements. Even in the case of Rhode Island, there is no evidence that the restriction on perpetual servitude was enforced. Many transatlantic Anglo-Americans who established fairly radical extensions of English liberty in New England were swept up in enthusiasm for Cromwell's "Western Design," a scheme to acquire by force of arms Caribbean frontiers for a tropical English empire. The level of colonial susceptibility to the Western design is eloquent testimony to the continued fragility of antislavery sentiment even at moments when radical ideas of human equality and brotherhood intensified during the English Revolution. Only as the expedition faltered, did the colonials resign themselves to live with the "sufficiency afforded by New England rather than to lose their Englishness and possibly their lives in seeking the vaunted riches of the tropics."[39]

Against the fact that both Puritan and Quaker settlers quietly accepted the institution of slavery, it should be noted that they also provided the earliest public spheres in which antislavery made its first *political* inroads into the Atlantic slave system. In their precociousness, they actually preceded the conventional "age of colonial revolution" (1770s to 1820s). Their activities

---

[37] Eltis, "Free and Coerced Migrations," 62, Table 1.

[38] See John Donoghue, "Radical Republicanism in England, America, and the Imperial Atlantic, 1624–1661," PhD Thesis, University of Pittsburgh, 2005), ch. 2 and 3. For a comparative survey of attitudes toward slavery in early British colonial North America, see Davis, *Inhuman Bondage*, ch. 6.

[39] See Karen Ordahl Kupperman, "Errand to the Indies: Puritan Colonization from Providence Island to the Western Design," *William and Mary Quarterly*, 45:1 (1988), 94–96. Roger Williams, in particular, was ecstatic about Cromwell's venture.

offer evidence about the crucial importance of nonrevolutionary paths to abolition during this revolutionary age. The reaction to the *Somerset* case within Anglo-America was only one exploration of the feasibility of Euro-Atlantic societies without slavery "beyond the line."

Just as he emerged victorious from his long contest with Lord Mansfield in 1772, Granville Sharp was delighted to discover a counterpart on the other side of the Atlantic who had been at work on a much more ambitious project for almost twenty years. Anthony Benezet of Philadelphia had been patiently transforming his local Society of Friends into the first denomination to set a goal of withdrawing itself from connection with slavery. By 1772, he had expanded his mission to include the abolition of slavery and the slave trade throughout the British Empire. Benezet's search for a transatlantic counterpart reached Sharp on the very day that Mansfield delivered his decision.[40] The contact opened up a vast new avenue for both abolitionists. For all the overwhelming support in the press, Sharp feared that support for the decision might be too shallow and transitory. His personal appeal to two prominent members of the British cabinet, including Prime Minister Lord North, was ignored. Britain's first abolitionist was well aware that he was considered extravagant and quixotic. Nowhere else in the political class could he find leverage for further action. The slave and colonial trades were reaching record heights with no end in sight. Sharp feared that if the West India interest appealed for parliamentary relief against the *Somerset* decision, he might not find "fifty righteous men" in London willing to protest in a counter-petition.

So, Sharp was excited by Benezet's news that twenty to thirty thousand people from Maryland and Virginia might freely join to petition Parliament to suspend further slave imports. A petition issuing from the slave colonies in North America would surely "lay the foundations for a total prohibition of that most abominable branch of the African trade, the buying and selling of men."[41] Sharp's only word of caution was to urge Benezet to restrict the petition to the slave trade and to direct it to the King to avoid acknowledging the Parliament's authority over the colonies themselves.

In forming this innovative plan, Sharp was tapping into an old repertoire of collective action within civil societies on both sides of the Atlantic. British subjects regarded the right to petition as a fundamental right along with representative assemblies, strong local government, a plurality of religious communities, abundant voluntary associations, and newspapers. Petitioning constituted a weapon in the public sphere that Anglo-American abolitionism would use intensively during the century to follow.

[40] See York Minster Library, Granville Sharp Letterbook, Benezet to Sharp, May 14, 1772.
[41] *Ibid.*, Sharp to John Fothergill, October 27, 1772; Sharp to Benezet, August 21, 1772; and Brown, *Moral Capital*, 87–91; 99.

Benezet's letter to Sharp also hinted at a number of independent and overlapping strands of activity in America, which were emerging at the same moment. Benezet himself was a leader in American Quakerism's movement against slaveholding and slave trading. Benezet was a pioneer in transforming the movement's development from a position of denominational withdrawal into one with a broader transatlantic vision. Benezet's letter to Sharp also subtly alluded to a major caveat in this potentially potent political petition. The people of the Chesapeake slave colonies were convinced, he noted, "of the inexpediency, if not all of them of the iniquity of any further importation of negroes"....[42]

"Inexpediency" summed up the thrust of considerations that induced the Virginia House of Burgesses, completely independent of the Quakers, to repeatedly and ultimately unanimously demand the cessation of slave importations. Some stressed the considerations of security. Others emphasized the discouragement to a diversified economy caused by importations of slaves to whites, both skilled and unskilled. Others were disturbed by the difficulty that a large proportion of African slaves posed to the development of a community that wished to build itself in the image of free English societies on the other side of the Atlantic. All arguments converged on a point that would echo in Virginia throughout the age of revolution. There were already too many blacks in the colony. A ban on imports would help to diminish the black presence in the region. Many of those opposed to the slave trade carefully differentiated their expedient positions from any attack on property in persons.

Indeed, some similar prerevolutionary Northern colonial initiatives were tabled because their motions were not sufficiently clear in drawing a distinction between future and already vested rights in persons.

A third strand of antislavery emerged north of the Chesapeake, where slavery was significant as a demographic and economic component of the area's wealth or population. Prerevolutionary evangelical clergy and more secular luminaries from Boston to Philadelphia converted both the discourses of religion and political rights into petitions, sermons, and political action against the slave trade. Before 1774, the calls for political action against the trade necessarily demanded prohibiting the further importation of slaves into individual colonies. In New England, with the smallest black presence and the most highly developed networks of local government on the continent, colonists could direct their representatives to support antislavery initiatives in their respective assemblies. The Massachusetts legislators matched their Virginia counterparts in successive demands for bans on importation.

---

[42] See Jackson, *Let this Voice Be Heard*, 150–152; and Brookes, *Friend Anthony Benezet*, 292.

In New England, blacks for the first time collectively initiated a public campaign to abolish slavery. The significance of the Mansfield decision as a catalyst is all the more striking in that Somerset's victory appears to have stimulated the first petition against slavery. In the late 1760s, Somerset had lived as a slave in Boston while his master was Receiver-General of customs. There is no indication that New England afforded Somerset any encouragement to make a bid for freedom. In 1773, however, Massachusetts slaves took full advantage of their location in the region of America where their presence offered the least threat to the social order and gave them the easiest access to the means of political action. As soon as they saw an opening, they immediately employed all the mechanisms and ideas available to them: steering committees, petitions, and the ideology of liberty and natural rights.[43]

By 1774, imperial vetoes of slave trade restrictions were being added to the long list grievances against Britain. Action against slave imports was sufficiently consensual that the first Continental Congress could add it to the list of its economic sanctions against British trade. Moral condemnation of the slave trade was, however, sufficiently loaded with implications about the future of the entire institution that Jefferson's strong moral language condemning imperial encouragement of the slave trade was stricken from the list of tyrannies enumerated in the Declaration of Independence. As with Benezet's proposed petition two years earlier, the Continental Congress was given enough leeway, on grounds of expediency, to include African slaves on the boycott list of British imports. One dimension of this range of action was especially significant.

Cumulatively, what all of these prerevolutionary strands of antislavery activity amounted to was a fraying of the concept that had relegated the world beyond the Atlantic to a public tolerance of slavery. Anglo-America already contained actors who collectively moved toward seeking greater autonomy within the umbrella of British political and legal institutions. The movements against the slave trade betokened a political impulse to erase a major anomaly between the two sides of the Atlantic. In Britain, the *Somerset* and *Knight* decisions drew a definitive limit on the institution's potential expansion. On the North American mainland, the decision stimulated further action to limit the growth of slavery in a zone long penetrated by the institution.

What was the import of this ferment on both sides of the Anglo-American Atlantic in the period just before the Revolution? One might be tempted to emphasize its very limited achievement, signifying little more than a harbinger of an age of transformation. Perhaps without the revolutions that

---

[43] On Somerset in Massachusetts, see Wise, *Though the Heavens*, 4–5. See also Brown, *Moral Capital*, 105–107.

succeeded, this flurry of action would have amounted to little more than the intermittent effusions of outrage, like those of intellectuals like Las Casas.[44] They would probably have been even less threatening to the institution of slavery than the outbursts of revolt and the communities of runaway slaves (*quilombos* and *palenques*) from the palenques of sixteenth-century Brazil to the maroons of the eighteenth-century Caribbean. They would certainly have been less of a challenge than the slave revolt in Dutch Berbice in 1761.[45] For our purposes, it is heuristically worthwhile to pause and consider what

[44] It is worth noting that with few exceptions there were few expressions of fear of servile revolution in discussions of slavery before the French Revolution. Despite three centuries of intermittent conspiracies, both aboard slave ships and in plantation colonies, there is no indication that slaveholders' faith in the longevity of the system had been either shaken or corroded by the threat of insurrection. Some pro-slave trade writers, like the French elite, were lulled by the absence of recent massive slave uprisings in the Caribbean. At the outset of the first British national abolitionist campaign, one anti-abolitionist newspaper correspondent took it for granted that African slaves could never organize a durable uprising.

[45] For two hundred years, the historiography of abolition has largely followed Thomas Clarkson's 1808 assessment of the impact of the American Revolution: "As long as America was our own, there was no chance that a minister would attend the groans of the sons and daughters of Africa, however he might feel for their distress...." In this perspective, the split in the empire removed "an insuperable impediment to the relief of these unfortunate people." (Thomas Clarkson, an *Essay on the Impolicy of the African Slave Trade* (London: J. Phillips, 1788), 34). His conclusion was echoed by historians from Eric Williams, in his classic *Capitalism and Slavery* (1944) to Christopher Brown in *Moral Capital* (2006). Brown plays with an interesting counter-factual scenario. He imagines a narrowly averted revolution and a united Anglo-American empire. In that case, even had it emerged much later than it did, abolitionism and emancipation would have been associated with the threat of imperial disunion and British "authoritarian rule rather than with national unity, moral prestige and the advance of liberty." In this "alternative" history of the American Revolution, it is worth noting that Brown's line of argument enhances the short-term significance of events, contingency and agency in America, Africa, and Britain as the sine qua non of the abolitionist breakthrough. He correspondingly reduces the impact of structure and the *long durée* to a very modest role: economic development, changing patterns of communication and information, and sensibility toward brutality on both sides of the Atlantic. The violent shock of the American Revolution fortuitously opened up an opportunity for abolitionism in the 1780s that might otherwise have appeared only long afterwards, and perhaps never. In this scenario, had the unity of the British Empire postponed the emergence of abolitionism even by four years, say to 1791 instead of 1787, antislavery would have been associated only with bloody revolution in France and Saint Domingue rather than with British patriotism and Christianity. What, then, "would have been the fate of antislavery impulses around the Atlantic world during the nineteenth century without the ideological support provided by a well-established antislavery movement in the British Isles, without its reputation for moral excellence, and without its evidence of success?" (Brown, *Moral Capital*, 455–461). The opportunity for British, for Atlantic, for global antislavery was therefore fortuitous, fleeting, and fragile. David Brion Davis has also made a counterfactual foray into the history of antislavery without the American Revolution. He notes that in the aftermath of the Seven Years War, there was a relative decline in slave imports into North America and a consequent declining proportion of black slaves in the Northern Continental colonies. He notes that political impulses to constrain or end further importation of slaves drew upon both urban labor and colonial racism: "Even if South Carolina had allied with

the American Revolution interrupted, and, therefore, what might have happened had some reconciliation been effected by Anglo-American negotiation before the battle of Lexington. Compared with any prior period, the number of words and writings questioning the British Atlantic slave system burgeoned after 1770. Anglo-American expansion beyond the Proclamation Line of 1763 had been breached, but not massively. The conditions of future settlement of the frontiers certainly had not yet been determined. As shown by the behavior of many colonial legislatures, restriction of the African slave trade already had priority over maximizing the further importation of enslaved Africans for economic development. On the western side of the Anglo-American empire, the slave trade was already a highly politicized issue before the first shot was fired at Lexington. Some Americans took the lead in challenging the institution's status quo: clergymen and African Americans in New England, Quakers and radicals in the Middle Colonies, and aristocratic slaveholders in the Chesapeake. On the eastern side of the Atlantic, public action had been focused exclusively upon the black presence in the metropolis. With Sharp's aid, blacks had turned public attention to the status of colonial slaves on the island. But public interest in slavery remained higher than before the *Somerset* decision.

It was in North America that the slave trade first became a political issue. Benezet contacted Sharp in London in 1772 asking the Englishman to bring the issue of the slave trade before the British government. Sharp

---

Jamaica and other West Indian islands," Davis reasons, "British public opinion would have been incalculably strengthened by the division among slaveholding colonies." Moreover, the high rate of natural growth among the North American slave population would have enormously enhanced the arguments of British opponents of the Atlantic trade. (See David Brion Davis, "American Slavery and the American Revolution," in *Slavery and Freedom in the Age of Revolution*, Ira Berlin and Ronald Hoffman, eds. (Charlottesville, VA: University Press of Virginia, 1983), 262–282, esp. 266–67). Davis extends his counter-factual argument well into the nineteenth century. He incorporates subsequent British conquests in the Caribbean and beyond the Mississippi. Davis's scenario ends with a dual outcome. The first is a plausible surmise that continuing imperial unity would have *hastened* the international suppression of the African slave trade and retarded the westward expansion of slavery in the Americas. On the other hand, unity would have precluded British West Indian emancipation in 1833, eliminated the possibility of "free soil" zones after the model of the northwest Ordinance, and postponed emancipation for generations. This second prediction seems far less compelling. Absent the colonial union that did become the United States, Northerners might have become as, or more aggressive than Britons in agitating for the territorial confinement of slavery on the North American continent as well as in the Caribbean. In any event, temporal speculation about outcomes more than a generation beyond 1775 seem intrinsically perilous. If the American Revolutionary War had never occurred, what becomes of Brown's timing of the French Revolution or the subsequent outbreak of a slave revolution in St. Domingue – an upheaval as singular in its magnitude as its outcome? In this sense, both the Brown and Davis scenarios have one common conclusion. Without the American Revolution New World emancipation would have been delayed and would probably have taken place with even greater violence.

appealed directly, and in vain, to both the Prime Minister and the evangelical Secretary of State for the American Colonies. It was Benezet who also called, in vain, on his own transatlantic Quaker religious network to open up a metropolitan front against the slave trade. The English Friends dutifully reprinted a large quantity of Benezet's *Caution and Warning to Great Britain and her Colonies* and distributed them to each Member of Parliament and to merchants in London and Liverpool. They quietly dispatched a delegation to the English Board of Trade in support of the colonial petitions. But the English Friends, as Christopher Brown cogently notes, did not attempt to submit a separate petition against the slave trade during the years just before Lexington. The British Friends would not move for almost a decade.

In the exchange of correspondence between Benezet, Sharp, and the English Quakers, it is the Philadelphian who scoured the colonies for the public support which Sharp so vainly longed for. Sharp saw no means by which he might break the wall of indifference to the trade that seemed to pervade the English elite and government alike. It is equally important to note that Benezet did not look northward to New England in search for potential signatures. Rather he turned southward, where the opposition to the slave trade was emerging as much out of political opposition to importing more Africans as to importing more slaves. Thenceforth, antislavery in America was to tack relentlessly between antipathy to bondage as corrosive to a community based on individual liberty and antipathy to bondsmen as an alien threat to an imagined exclusive community of Euro-Americans.

For Britain, the American Revolution initially deepened the line between freedom and slavery in the British empire. British political abolitionism, when it emerged after the war, had lost what Sharp had so prized: the full weight of North American political support for curtailing the slave trade. Rather than being, as Clarkson imagined, a providential boon to British abolitionism, the loss of the Continental colonies after 1775 may well have been a loss to antislavery on both sides of the Atlantic. North Americans who opposed the slave trade lost the invaluable potential weight of a powerful "free state." The outbreak of hostilities dramatically subordinated the question of slavery to other priorities. Americans and their British allies focused on British hypocrisy in sanctioning the African trade. American loyalists and supporters of the British focused polemic attention upon the American confederation's hypocrisy in proclaiming liberty, but sanctioning slavery. In Britain, antislavery diminished dramatically as a salient issue during both the arrogant early war years and the despondent later war years.[46] Nor did antislavery make a rapid return to the public sphere with the signing of a treaty of peace.

---

[46] Brown, *Moral Capital*, 182–196.

This returns us to the structural foundations of abolitionism on both sides of the Atlantic. In accounting for the emergence of abolitionism at the end of the eighteenth century, it is important not to be fixated upon the dramatic clash of arms and ideas. The basis lay less in the circumstances afforded by opportunistic challenges than in divergences in the development of the coastal Americas from the fifteenth through the eighteenth centuries. By 1750, certain elements of coercion had been in decline for centuries in the northeastern quadrant of the Atlantic. Within northwestern Europe, associations had options for action against European rulers and elites that did not exist for most non-Europeans in the overseas world. These found expression in the general acceptance of an individual's property rights in his own labor. It meant that even where coercion of one's body and constraint of one's goods were socially and legally tolerated under certain circumstances, those constraints were regarded as originating in contract. The sense of contract extended to social and political relationships, including that between people and ruler. To be a full citizen in most of the eighteenth-century western European world meant that one had rights in oneself in relation to the market, the law, the family and the state.

Three developments triggered tension. Given the rapid growth of New World economies, populations, and secure societies, it was inevitable that European inhabitants of the Western Hemisphere began to contemplate their settlements, not just as exceptional outposts of Europe, but as communities that could autonomously govern their own futures. However, those who most wished to replicate, and even to fulfill and surpass, the norms of old world societies had to come to terms with what was for them a peculiarly brutal and cognitively dissonant institution. For the North American British colonies, imbued with the common law traditions that persisted before and beyond their wars of independence, it was inevitable that the *Somerset* decision would stimulate discussion among both citizens and slaves in the course of redefining their relationship to Europe.

Discussions of slavery and autonomy, of individual and political rights, which intensified before the revolution, would have remained on the table whether or not the relationship between England and New England in particular, and the Northern colonies in general, resolved their conflict as self-governing dominions without full independence. The Chesapeake colonies concern about the proportion and the future of blacks within their polities would have continued to raise unavoidable questions about the disposition of massive numbers of Africans living among them, with or without independence from Britain.

As for Britons, the question of the slave trade would probably have been thrust upon them by North Americans sooner rather than later. The war of American independence actually disrupted a growing transatlantic public discussion of slavery and of the moral obligations of empire in general.

As we shall see, the subsequent pattern of abolitionist and antiabolitionist responses throughout the Atlantic emerged in contexts that favored confrontations over the slave trade and slavery. The differential development of western Europe and the Western Hemisphere, kept at an equilibrium for almost three centuries after the Columbian voyages, could not forever remain impervious to the countervailing impulses to integration.

5

Age of the American Revolution, 1770s–1820s

The movement of black slaves to Europe illustrates just one of the ways in which longstanding expressions of antislavery sentiment began to coalesce at political and legal flashpoints. Developments on both side of the Atlantic demanded increasing attention to tensions inherent in a system that simultaneously subverted and sustained European overseas slavery. During the half century after 1775, the world changed in ways that had a fundamental impact on the future of slavery. A series of developments challenged the equilibrium required by the institution of slavery in the Americas.

The outstanding shift in the Atlantic world during the half century after 1775 was the successful overturning of the asymmetrical division of power between the New World and the Old World, of dominion on one side and dependency on the other. Throughout mainland of the Americas, most erstwhile colonies separated themselves from their original sources of protection and direction. In constituting themselves as independent nations, each new political formation had to raise fundamental questions about the boundaries of citizenship and individual liberty.[1] At both ends of the Atlantic, individuals explored opportunities for expanding the principles and practices of civil liberty and representative institutions.

Before 1770, most European populations had been relatively insulated from the governance of their nation's overseas settlements. Europeans who benefited most directly from the Atlantic slave system were those who also had the most privileged access to the attention of imperial rulers. The magnitude and dynamism of the institution of slavery had created substantial groups deeply interested in its maintenance: royal courts and colonial administrators; metropolitan merchants and slavers; plantation managers and planters; insurers, shippers, and processors of tropical goods. Slavery also elicited acquiescence from a broad swath of people on both sides of the

---

[1] Robin Blackburn, *The Overthrow of Colonial Slavery 1776–1848* (London: Verso, 1988). This re-examination was not confined to the New World.

Atlantic with reasons to hope for its continuation: those engaged in producing goods for slave-driven economic enterprises and those workers on land or sea who shipped goods or people across the ocean.

Finally, a widening network of tradesmen, artisans, seamen, and consumers welcomed the new opportunities and products that flowed into Europe, Africa, and the Americas. European rulers remained ideologically and economically embedded within a mercantilist complex that promised advantages for successful participation and disadvantages to those left out. As we have seen in the case of the Orientalist Johann David Michaelis, even German professors pursued projects of slave plantations in their dreams. For much less utopian imperial agents, colonies with slaves were deemed to be both seedbeds for further expansion and tangible assets that offset gains or losses at the end of frequent intra-European conflicts. During wartime, one or another power might encourage runaway slaves with promises of freedom. Large scale liberations of enemy slaves were unheard of before 1775.

The second major development affecting Atlantic slavery after 1775 was the intrusion of conflicts on the Atlantic and within the New World into the institution of slavery. In the Americas, this process developed along three important fault lines. What David Geggus concludes about the violence in the Caribbean between 1789 and 1815 may be applied to the Americas as a whole during the half century before 1825. Apart from campaigns launched by imperial powers, conflicts occurred primarily between and within three main social groups – "slaves seeking freedom, free coloreds fighting racial discrimination and whites seeking to sustain special status or to gain autonomy or independence."[2]

From the perspective of slave action, it is clear that resistance had begun centuries before the 1770s, and the rapid expansion of the Anglo-American press coincided with a rising frequency of revolts aboard slave ships during the eighteenth century. Indeed, scholars have estimated that African resistance on board slave ships reduced the potential magnitude of the slave trade by one million Africans over the course of more than three centuries.[3] Whatever its impact upon the Euro-American consciousness, however, slave resistance on the Middle Passage did not appreciably reduce the incentive for

[2] David Patrick Geggus, "Slavery, War and Revolution in the Greater Caribbean, 1789–1815," in *A Turbulent Time: The French Revolution and the Greater Caribbean*, David Barry Gaspar and David Patrick Geggus, eds. (Bloomington, IN: Indiana University Press, 1997), 1–50.

[3] See Stephen D. Behrendt, David Eltis, and David Richardson, "The Costs of Coercion: African Agency in the Pre-modern Atlantic World," *Economic History Review*, 54:3 (2001), 454–476 and David Richardson, "Shipboard Revolts, African Authority, and the Atlantic Slave Trade," *William and Mary Quarterly*, 3rd. ser. LXVIII (1) (2001), 69–92. On comparative slave resistance in the Indian Ocean world see Gwyn Campbell and Edward A. Alpers, "Introduction: Slavery, Forced Labour and Resistance in Indian Ocean Africa and Asia," Special issue, *Slavery and Resistance in Africa and Asia*, Edward A. Alpers, Gwyn Campbell, and Michael Salman, eds. *Slavery and Abolition*, 25:2 (August 2004), ix–xxvii.

slaving. Shipboard slave revolts, after peaking in the generation before 1775, fell steadily. By the first quarter of the nineteenth century, the rate of these revolts had dropped to their lowest level since the seventeenth century.[4] Even the peak period of relatively high shipboard resistance certainly did not impede the expansion of either the Atlantic slave trade or the plantation slave complex. Cross-race insurrection aboard slave ships was also virtually nonexistent before 1775 and would remain so during the following century.

In the prerevolutionary Americas, slave marronage and slave rebellions faced the same barrier to institutional impact. The most successful slave revolt in the Americas before the Franco-Caribbean revolutions of the 1790s illustrates this point. The slave uprising in Dutch Berbice in 1763 shook the very foundations of the colony. As in most revolts aboard slave ships, the leader's rebellion aimed at annihilation of the white enslavers. Although the Dutch were almost driven to the sea, time worked to their advantage. The colonists were resupplied from the Netherlands and neighboring colonial settlements. Aided by divisions within the insurgents' ranks and hostile Native Americans, the colonial authorities finally crushed the revolt. The brutality of both sides was extraordinary. Wives and children of the white planters were hacked to pieces before the planters' eyes. Defeated slaves were roasted alive. The horrific reciprocal pattern of giving no quarter probably reflected the limited expectations and maximal fears that each side held of the other.

Before 1775, the Caribbean sugar plantation zone partially replicated the slave ship in assuring the relative isolation of slaves from one colony to the next. A slave conspiracy or uprising in one island would usually be suppressed before it was widely known elsewhere. Europeans and allied free nonwhites could generally rely upon the threat of force or external succor,

---

[4] *Ibid.*, 467, Figure 2. This figure displays the "[r]elative distribution of voyages experiencing violent incidents and of all voyages over time." It appears that during the three generations before 1775 (1701–1775), when the incidence of revolt rose to its peak, 4.7 million Africans were being loaded for the Middle Passage. During the next three generations (1776–1850), the number of slave revolts steadily diminished with each generation while 5.7 million Africans were being boarded for the Middle Passage. In the generation after the "Age of Revolution," the rate of slave revolts per voyage declined to its lowest level in two centuries of slaving. Slave revolts demonstrably increased the cost of slaving. They significantly reduced the number of slaves who would otherwise have reached the New World. It seems unlikely, however, that they played a role in leading slavers to abandon the trade between 1775 and the ending of the trade in 1867. David Eltis places the peak of slave revolts in the period 1750–1794, but within that period he especially notes the twelve years from 1776 to 1777 as the peak of successful slave resistance (*Rise of African Slavery*, 232). Whether the peak should be set in 1766–1777 or more broadly between 1750 and 1794, there is a curious lessening of the insurrections early in the Age of Revolution. If shipboard revolts substantially increased the costs of the trade, the threat posed by insurrections decreased with the diminution of revolts toward the end of the eighteenth century. That drop accelerated in the nineteenth century.

to which slaves had no countervailing access. Racial similarities among the free and enslaved did not usually override divisions of status and ethnicity. The maroon communities of runaways rarely represented a major threat to the institution of slavery before 1775.

The British Imperial Perspective on Slavery, War and Revolution

The groundwork for the erosion of slavery in one part of the Anglo-American empire had already been laid before armed conflict erupted in 1775. As noted in chapter 4, Anglo-Americans shared a common civil and political legacy. On both sides of the Atlantic, they took pride in their representative political institutions and in the common law inheritance that protected the individual rights of freeborn subjects against arbitrary state coercion. With a relative abundance of newspapers, Anglo-Americans also shared the most widely diffused and least censored communications network in the world. They possessed an array of voluntary and religious networks that made them the frontrunners in an emerging associational world. In short, Anglo-Americans shared the most highly developed public sphere on the face of the earth.

However, with regard to slavery and the slave trade, the Anglo-American empire in 1770 presented a broad spectrum of involvement rather than a shared legacy.[5] At one extreme, the economies of the British West Indian colonies were almost completely reliant upon slavery. With populations more than five-sixths slave, these Caribbean islands contained the highest proportion of slaves to free individuals of any slave societies in human history. Because of a high mortality rate among slaves, the islands were also entirely dependent upon a continuous supply of fresh transcontinental captives to maintain and increase their sugar plantations. Only after the British slave trade had been suppressed in 1807 would the British slavers and planters show any political interest in the suppression of the Atlantic trade.

The North American continent also contained British-ruled economies that were heavily, if not as overwhelmingly, dependent upon the institution of slavery. In every colony from Maryland southward, at least one-third of the population was enslaved. In the southernmost Continental colonies, slaves accounted for up to half the residents (61 percent in South Carolina and 46 percent in Georgia). Invested as these colonies were in slavery, they differed from those in the Caribbean in an important demographic respect. Slaves born in North America made up only 22 percent of the enslaved population of the thirteen colonies. The institution's growth already depended more upon a natural increase in the slave population than on fresh captives

---

[5] I rely here and in the following on the census of John James McCusker, in "The Rum Trade and the Balance of Payments of the Thirteenth Continental Colonies, 1650–1775," PhD dissertation 1970, Appendix B, 548–716). See Brown, *Moral Capital*, 120–122.

from abroad. As early as 1740, native-born "Creole" slaves made up a majority of the slave population. On the eve of the revolution, they represented more than two-thirds of the slave population.[6]

In the British colonies north of the Chesapeake, slaves accounted for less than 10 percent of the 460,000 residents in the mainland colonies. The slaves' share of the populations in these colonies ranged from 11 percent in New York to 0.1 percent in New Hampshire. The New England colonies had the least impact from the presence of slaves. Nevertheless, they were heavily involved with slavery in the West Indies as suppliers of the plantation system and as carriers, processors, and consumers of colonial commodities.

Across the Atlantic, thousands of blacks resided in Britain by 1770. They amounted to 0.01 percent of the population, or one-tenth of the proportion in New Hampshire, the settlement with the lowest proportion of African Americans in the British colonies. On the other hand, Great Britain's metropolitan subjects dominated the empire's slave trade. In the generation before the American Revolution, British slavers were responsible for the transportation of 800,000 captives, or 90 percent of the Anglo-American share of the transatlantic traffic.[7] The overwhelming victory of the British in the Seven Years War had opened the door for conflict over governance and expansion within the rapidly growing Continental settlements. Of the three social groups affected by the development of antislavery in the Americas, free persons of color had the smallest presence in North America. Some free blacks would be incorporated into the fighting forces on both sides in the conflict but they played a relatively small role in affecting the future of the institution of slavery or the slave trade.

Debates over slavery varied in different parts of the empire. In Britain, the interest aroused by the *Somerset* case and colonial agitation for slave trade abolition after 1772 were adversely affected by the outbreak of hostilities. Those who sympathized with imperial suppression deprecated American patriots as hypocrites, demanding relief from British oppression to remain free to use the lash on their slaves. In the famous words of Samuel Johnson, American cries for freedom were "yelps for liberty" from "drivers of Negroes."[8] Anti-American polemicists avoided all mention of Britons at the highest echelons of society and politics who held abundant property in persons and had made the British Empire preeminent in both slaving and as slaveholders in the Atlantic world. Friends of America on the other hand, tended to avoid the issue of American slaveholding. Like advocates for autonomy in the Continental colonies, they particularly excoriated the

---

[6] See Robert W. Fogel, "Revised Estimates of the U.S. Slave Trade and the Native-Born Share of the Black Population," in Fogel et al., *Without Consent or Contract: Evidence and Methods* (New York: 1992), 53–58; table 4.3, 56–57.

[7] See Transatlantic Slave Trade Database.

[8] See Brown, *Moral Capital*, 120–122.

hypocrisy of Britons who mocked colonial appeals for liberty, whereas their fellow citizens conducted the world's largest slave trade.

As slave-related issues became embedded in political polemics, antislavery tracts virtually disappeared from the public sphere. American defiance of Britain, including a ban by the Continental Congress against the further purchase of British-borne slaves from Africa, elicited only one parliamentary suggestion aimed at taking advantage of the large slave populations in the colonies. In October 1775, William Lyettelton identified the South as a weak link among the revolting colonies "on account of the number of negroes in them." The former governor of South Carolina and Jamaica suggested that a few regiments would suffice to get the slaves to rise "and imbrue their hands in the blood of their masters." Parliament recoiled at the suggestion. Lyttelton's dramatic proposal was dismissed as "too horrid" and "too dangerous" to be experimented upon by either side.[9]

"Servile insurrection" was more vigorously invoked by those opposed to the British government's anticolonial policy. Well before the outbreak of hostilities, Edmund Burke warned against any temptation to counter the libertarian spirit of Virginia by declaring a general enfranchisement of its slaves. He noted that desperate British measures would call forth desperate countermeasures. American slave holders might attempt to match British emancipation proclamations with their own clarion calls in the West Indies.[10] As long as the rationale for suppressing the revolution aimed at restoring fellow Britons to the imperial fold, the government was embarrassed even by accusations that Hessian serfs were being used to enslave fellow Britons. Mass emancipation would have been equivalent to a scorched earth policy against one's own slave trade as well as against one's own brethren. Was it natural or necessary "to destroy America in order to obtain an honorable peace to this commercial country?" Would it be "sound policy to burn Liverpool and its fleet because of a mutinous crew?"[11]

Late in the revolutionary war, Burke returned to his attack, scorning Governor Dunmore's call to Virginia's slaves to desert their rebel masters in 1776. Burke thanked God that Virginia and Maryland had "providentially" put down that first initiative. He characterized any British military offensive in the South as an effort "to excite an insurrection of the negro-slaves of their masters." He appealed to the primal images of ancient servile insurrection familiar to all educated Britons: "the horrible consequences that might ensue from constituting 100,000 fierce barbarians to be both the judges and executioners of their masters"; and ending the "murders, rapes, and horrid

---

[9] *Cobbetts Parliamentary History* (London: Bagshaw, 1806), vol. 18 October 15, 1775, columns 733 and 747. Speeches of Governors Lytton and Johnstone.

[10] *Ibid.*, col. 502, March 22, 1775.

[11] *Ibid.*, col. 1177, Feb. 29, 1776, Temple Luttrell. Did Luttrell deliberately choose Liverpool, the slaving capital of Britain, to add a string to his analogy?

enormities" that were the objects "of all negroes who had meditated an insurrection."[12]

Even in the prolonged crisis of an extended war and its climax in a humiliating defeat, the British government never threatened to use slave insurgency as a strategy of British policy. The British opposition, too, embedded its rare attacks on the de facto use of black soldiers and appeals to American slaves within criticisms of the broader policy of imperial coercion or the military employment of Indians.

All this underlines the widespread presumption in the British political class that the conflict had to be a bounded one. It was limited by their acknowledgement of ties of consanguinity with their "American brethren"; of co-religiosity with fellow Protestants; and as co-heirs of a legal, political, and institutional tradition of common law and English liberty. The premise of distinctiveness between the zones of metropolitan freedom and overseas coercion had never included, nor was it meant to include, Britons beyond the line. Both in Parliament and out-of-doors, American sympathizers invoked kinship in opposing any policy that might encourage "savage" violence (i.e., by Indians or by Africans) against the descendants of freeborn Englishmen.

This claim set rhetorical boundaries to debates in Parliament. In its account of Dunmore's initiative, the *Annual Register* of 1776 unambiguously reported the episode as a "measure of emancipating the negroes." It further noted that the proclamation was "received with the greatest horror in all the colonies, and has been severely condemned elsewhere."[13] The swiftness of the counter-mobilization against Dunmore and virtual absence of support for the initiative indicated the reaction that any future offers of colonial emancipation might produce. There was, of course, another piece of the imperial mosaic that British legislators never lost sight of during the war in North America. In 1775, the British Caribbean contained about half the slaves in the British Atlantic empire. The assets of the institution were equally distributed between the British and the Americans.

There was a moment between 1775 and 1783 when Parliament was called upon to consider one element of the slave system relatively independent of its policy toward the United States. When the condition of the African slave trade came up for discussion in May 1777, the sole object of attention was on how to improve the mechanisms of the trade. The unchallenged premise of the discussion was that the African trade was not only essential to the West Indian economy, but had risen in importance in light of the "decline of our commerce with every other quarter of the globe."[14]

---

[12] *Ibid.*, vol. 19, cols. 698–699; 708 (February 16, 1778).

[13] See *Annual Register*, also quoted in Sylvia R. Frey, *Water From the Rock: Black Resistance in a Revolutionary Age* (Princeton, NJ: Princeton University Press, 1991), 71.

[14] *Ibid.*, vol. 19 col. 209, (May 28, 1777), Temple Lutrell. At the very moment that the question came forward, the British slave trade itself was falling to half its prewar volume.

When the question of the trade's morality was raised by MP David Hartley, another member paused to defend the enterprise. Cognizant of the fact that "some gentlemen may, indeed, object to the slave trade as inhuman and impious," his argument was a distillation of a century's commonplaces. The sugar colonies required cultivation. Cultivation required Africans. Without further imports, the laboring population would decline. Other powers stood ready to meet British needs, as well as their own. No one rose to challenge the rationale. Hartley's intervention was restricted to detailing the incredible cruelties of slavery. He simply urged the Board of Trade to find some means of mitigating it. The members proceeded to passage without a division.[15]

Given slavery's politicization in the early 1770s, even if simply in the guise of debating points, slavery received remarkably short shrift in public debates during the Anglo-American War. The moment might have been opportune.[16] Between 1778 and 1781, the volume of the British slave trade fell to its lowest point since the seventeenth century. By the time of the surrender at Yorktown, it was reduced to one-fifth of its prewar magnitude. Plantation profits also dropped to their lowest point in the eighteenth century. Privateers and enemy fleets threatened both the economic well-being and security of the British possessions from without, and left planters feeling inadequately protected. Whereas British military forces were dispersed for campaigns on the North American continent, francophone populations in the British conquered islands were important agents in the loss of Grenada, St. Vincent, and Dominica to the French. In other islands, maroon activities and rumors of slave conspiracies increased anxieties in the British Caribbean.[17]

---

[15] *Ibid.*, v. 19, cols. 305; 315, May 23, 28, 1777; (Temple Luttrell and David Hartley). There is no indication that, as late as the 1770s, the parliamentary committees on the African trade took any cognizance of the morality of the slave trade or the brutality of the slave ships. See Christopher L. Brown, "The British Government and the Slave Trade: Early Parliamentary Enquiries, 1713–1783," in *British Slave Trade: Abolition Parliament and People*, Stephen Farrell, Melanie Unwin, and James Walvin eds. (Edinburgh: Edinburgh University Press, 2007), 27–41.

[16] See Stephen Conway, *The British Isles and the War of American Independence* (Oxford, UK: Oxford University Press, 2000); Ian R. Christie, *Wilkes, Wyvell and Reform: The Parliamentary Reform Movement in British Politics, 1760–1785* (London: Macmillan, 1962); Eugene Black, *The Association: British Extraparliamentary Political Organization, 1769–1793*; (Cambridge, MA: Harvard University Press, 1963). Philip Harling, *The Waning of Old Corruption: The Politics of Economical Reform in Britain, 1779–1846* (Oxford, UK: Oxford University Press, 1996); and James Bradley, *Religion, Revolution and English Radicalism* (Cambridge: Cambridge University Press, 1990). Christopher Brown, *Moral Capital*, 182–195, hypothesizes 1778–1781 as the "ideal moment" for the emergence of abolitionism from the perspective of Britain's defeat and humiliation.

[17] See Andrew Jackson O'Shaughnessy, *An Empire Divided: The American Revolution and the British Caribbean* (Philadelphia: University of Pennsylvania Press, 2000), ch. 7; J.R. Ward, "The Profitability of Sugar Planting in the British West Indies, 1650–1834," *Economic*

Yet, at this nadir of British Caribbean and African fortunes, neither the British public nor the parliamentary opposition called for the investigation of any aspect of the system. The reason seems apparent. With the loss of the North American colonies, "the British West Indies stood as easily Britain's biggest overseas capital investment, no longer simply the jewel in the crown of the British empire, but now virtually the crown itself."[18] The West Indies remained Britain's single greatest source of extra-European imports and sugar remained the most valuable overseas commodity imported by Britain. With the end of the conflict in North America, Britain's strategic concerns refocused on the British West Indies. Its military vulnerability and economic value had both been revealed by the Anglo-American war. In the decade after hostilities, the Caribbean accounted for more than half of Britain's total expenditure for all colonial defenses.

In 1783, British planters lost the battle to have their old free trade connections maintained with North America, but neither their economic value to the empire nor their slave system came under severe scrutiny. On the eve of the American Revolution, the Caribbean elites were concerned with their security. A Jamaican slave plot of 1776 was a direct consequence of the conflict in America.[19] The slaves developed their conspiracy in tandem with the withdrawal of British troops to the mainland and the departure of warships to escort merchants past American privateers. The conspirators were aware that British military presence on the island was weaker "than at any other time in their memory."[20]

However, although desertion and marronage also increased wherever French military forces linked up with francophone planters and people of color in the Windward Islands, the events in Jamaica actually represented the last major slave uprising in the predominantly anglophone Caribbean colonies for the next forty years. Despite planter reluctance to see black troops under arms, the Caribbean military crisis led the governor and the colonial assembly of Jamaica to authorize free black regiments and the conscription of more than 5,000 slaves. Barbados armed slaves, and others were also shipped from North American and African sites for military

History Review, 31 (1978), 197–209; Selwyn H.H. Carrington, *The British Caribbean during the American Revolution* (Dordrecht: Foris Publication, 1988); and *The Sugar Industry and the Abolition of the Slave Trade, 1775–1810* (Gainesville, FL: University Press of Florida, 2002).

[18] See Michael Duffy, "The French Revolution and British Attitudes to the West Indian Colonies" in *A Turbulent Time: The French Revolution and the Greater Caribbean*, David Barry Gaspar, and David Patrick Geggus, eds. (Bloomington, IN: Indiana University Press, 1997), 78–101; Duffy, *Soldiers, Sugars and Sea-power: The British Expeditions to the West Indies and the War Against Revolutionary France* (Oxford: Clarendon Press, 1987), ch. 1; and Seymour Drescher, *Econocide: British Slavery in the Era of Abolition* (Pittsburgh: University of Pittsburgh Press, 1977), ch. 2.

[19] O'Shaugnessy, *An Empire Divided*, 151–154.

[20] *Ibid.*, 153.

service in the Caribbean.²¹ In short, whatever the difficulties that arose in the Caribbean, the British West Indies and their representatives in London remained united in loyal support of the British during the North American campaigns and contributed effectively to their own defense.

During the American Revolutionary war, the British had to consider the impact of any potential action on their insular possessions. A very vulnerable metropolitan government made preemptive political concessions to the islanders that their London agents had not even requested. In the immediate postwar years, the islands benefited from the imperial conclusion that British political interference in overseas colonial arrangements had led to the separation of its mainland Anglo-American colonies. News of the "saving" of the West Indies was received in Britain with general relief.²² The British decision to treat the Americans economically as a foreign power in 1783 did not imply any weakening of Britain's commitment to nurturing its slave empire. In short, there is no indication that either the still unfocused antislavery sentiment in Britain or slave resistance in the Caribbean was immediately strengthened by American independence.

North American Perspectives

What of North America, the third dimension of the British transatlantic empire? The ideology and culture of the revolution itself was elaborated in appeals to enlightenment, ideals of liberty and equality, Anglo-American religious revivals, and English institutions.²³ Just as the prerevolutionary libertarian agitation generated increased attention to the problems of slavery, the founding document of revolutionary British America explicitly espoused a universalized form of liberation ideology. The U.S. Declaration of Independence made no direct reference to African bondage. However, it unequivocally embraced principles of individual rights to equality and liberty that were implicitly subversive of the institution of slavery. Thomas Jefferson's initial draft of the Declaration incorporated the Virginian's long-standing perception that England was to blame for introducing slavery into the American colonies. It excoriated the British monarch for exacerbating the original curse by his unrelenting slave trade from Africa.

The king (George III), Jefferson wrote,

has waged cruel war against human nature itself, violating its most sacred rights of life and liberty in the persons of a distant people who never offended him, captivating

---

²¹ See O'Shaughnessy, *Empire Divided*, 172–181. Michael Craton, *Testing the Chains: Resistance to Slavery in the British West Indies* (Ithaca, N.Y.: Cornell University Press, 1982), ch. 14.

²² *Ibid.*, 237.

²³ See the magisterial overview of David Brion Davis, *The Problem of Slavery in Western Culture*, rev. ed. (New York: Oxford University Press, 1988), 291–493.

and carrying them into slavery in another hemisphere, or to incur miserable death in their transportation thither.... Determined to keep open a market where men should be bought and sold, he has prostituted his negative for suppressing every legislative attempt to prohibit or to restrain this execrable commerce.[24]

John Adams had been pleasantly surprised by Jefferson's indictment, but correctly anticipated that the Continental Congress would omit it from the final document. Because all of the colonies had already agreed to include the prohibition of further British slaves as an item of trade, it was the political and moral implications of Jefferson's article that accounted for its deletion. The deletion itself was a harbinger of the fate of the problem of slavery in America for half a century to come. For a generation after the Declaration, legislation concerning the slave trade was to remain exclusively within the domain of the individual states.

The conflict itself opened new doors to both free blacks and slaves. In 1775, they were a presence in the opening battles of the revolution at Lexington, Concord, and Bunker Hill. Initially, however, Southerners and George Washington himself forbade the recruitment of Negroes into the Continental Army. In November 1775, Lord Dunmore's offer of freedom to slaves willing to bear arms for the king caused Washington to reverse himself and to allow the reenlistment of free blacks in his own army out of fear of their desertion to the British.

The prolonged struggle for independence made black enlistment a recurring possibility. By 1778, the opportunities for freedom through service were widened by both sides in the conflict. Free blacks were entering the United States Army from Virginia northward. Slaves were being allowed into the U.S. army as substitutes for their masters. In the South, the Americans reacted to a major British campaign by authorizing the incorporation of blacks to provide sufficient manpower for their armies. The Congress offered payment to every owner who enlisted slaves and promised emancipation to the recruited soldiers at the end of the war, but most Southerners saw the plan as too radical a precedent to be allowed.

In the lower South, the British did recruit blacks into their campaign. Following Dunmore's precedent, General Henry Clinton welcomed deserters from the rebels into his lines. Those slaves who were captured while serving the rebels, however, were to be kept for sale as contraband of war. As Sylvia Frey observes, the British got more than they had bargained for. Thousands of slaves converted the proclamation into an exodus. Some slave owners staged a counter-exodus, fleeing northward with their slaves to escape the British forces. Loyalists tried to do the same in the opposite direction, moving with their slaves toward British lines. In a chaotic scramble, British

---

[24] See Don E. Fehrenbacher, *The Slaveholding Republic: An Account of the United States Government's Relation to Slavery*, completed and edited by Ward M. McAfee (New York: Oxford University Press, 2001), 17.

authorities attempted to sort out slaves of captured rebels from those desert-
ing their loyalist owners. Cassandra Pybus's careful calculations from the
existing records allow her to conservatively estimate that 20,000 runaway
slaves escaped into the British lines between 1775 and 1782. Of these, about
12,000 African Americans survived the conflict, and 8,000 to 10,000 left
the United States both free and slave. In addition, several thousand runaways may have escaped into freedom without leaving America. Despite the
defections the number of escapees was relatively small.[25]

The fate of slaves was as diverse as their individual situations. Some forced
the new American government to begin to formulate a national policy on
slaves. Of those who departed with the British forces and survived at the end
of the fighting, the most fortunate cohort found themselves in New York.
The preliminary peace terms required the British to withdraw their forces
"without causing any destruction or carrying away any Negroes or other
Property of the American inhabitants." In the treaty ending the war, the
new American government thus committed itself to treating slaves purely
as a form of property. The British commanding general, Sir Guy Carleton
had broad discretionary powers. Carleton informed the victorious General
Washington that the 2,700 liberated slaves under his protection, including
Washington's own, would not be returned. Having already been freed by
British proclamations before the end of hostilities, they could no longer be
considered property. Under the aegis of the British Crown, their destination
was to be Nova Scotia, beyond the legal jurisdiction of the United States.[26]

In standing behind their general's decision, the British government
ensured a diplomatic Anglo-American bone of contention that lasted for
another decade and was to be repeated in the second Anglo-American war
of 1812. In refusing to repatriate most of the black escapees, Carleton also
inadvertently contributed to the launching of a new zone of freedom in the
Old World. Some blacks who made their way directly to London at the war's
end constituted the first settlers in the "Province of Freedom," founded in
1787 on the shores of Sierra Leone. A second and larger wave of Americans
was to follow to Sierra Leone in 1792, after their sojourn in Nova Scotia.
A third wave, consisting of exiled rebel Jamaican maroons reached Sierra
Leone in the late 1790s. Finally, after the abolition of the British slave trade

---

[25] Compare Sylvia Frey, *Water from the Rock: Black Resistance in a Revolutionary Age* 87–
89, with Cassandra Pybus, "Jefferson's Faulty Math: The Question of Slave Defections
in the American Revolution," *William and Mary Quarterly*, 3rd ser. LXII:2 (April 2005),
243–264. On escapees who remained in the United States, see Ira Berlin, *Many Thousands
Gone: The First Two Centuries of Slavery in North America* (Cambridge, MA: Harvard
University Press, 1998), 263.

[26] See Cassandra Pybus, *Epic Journeys of Freedom: Runaway Slaves of the American Rev-
olution and Their Global Quest for Liberty* (Boston: Beacon Press, 2006), 66–71; Simon
Schama, *Rough Crossings: Britain, and the Slaves of the American Revolution* (New York:
Harper Collins, 2006), 127–132; and Brown, *Moral Capital*, 298–299.

in 1807, Sierra Leone became the major depot of recaptured Africans aboard slave ships.[27]

Despite the upheaval, the gains for antislavery at the national level were small. The war-time defections of the escapees represented only a small fraction of those who remained enslaved. America's uniquely high natural birthrate also ensured a rapid recovery of the numbers lost to both flight and death. The institutional arrangements for slavery, which had always been managed at the colonial level, continued to remain within the jurisdiction of each state. Only by consensus had the First Continental Congress pragmatically suspended the slave trade in 1774, and again in 1776.

With the return of peace and independence, control of the issue of slavery reverted to the will of the individual states, and the slave trade revived. Despite the bans enacted by every state but South Carolina, the United States imported far more new enslaved Africans between 1783 and 1808 than the estimated net loss of escaped and emancipated slaves during the revolutionary conflict. This does not include slaves added through territorial expansion (Louisiana) or through a natural increase in the birthrate, the most important source of slave population growth in the United States.[28]

The slaves who were shipped by the British at war's end to the Caribbean also went toward repairing the deficit created by the war-time diminution of the slave trade in the British West Indies. These enslaved exiles gave a boost to the expansion of the cotton culture in the 1780s. All in all, the net increase in Africans imported into both segments of Anglo-America between 1803 and 1807 appears to have exceeded all the losses resulting from flight, deportation, and private manumission in the American revolutionary generation.

However, significant sectional cracks quickly began to appear in the broad legal acceptance of slavery that existed before the American Revolution. In the wake of the American War of Independence, Vermont, New Hampshire, Massachusetts, Connecticut, and Rhode Island, the states with the lowest percentages of slaves, became pioneers in legislating the destruction of the institution either by constitutional articles or by judicial decisions based upon their new constitutions. In 1780, Pennsylvania became the first state in the world to abolish racial slavery by a duly deliberated legislative act

---

[27] See Philip D. Curtin, *The Image of Africa: British Ideas and Action, 1780–1850* (Madison: University of Wisconsin Press, 1964) ch. 4, 5; Pybus, *Epic Journeys*, ch. 5, 7, 9, 11; and Schama, *Rough Crossings*, ch. 7 ff.

[28] Frey, *Water from the Rock*, 170. Frey estimates the number of the "exiled" at one hundred thousand; Davis, *Inhuman Bondage*, 150, sets the net loss at eighty to one hundred thousand. Allan Kulikoff, "Uprooted Peoples: Black Migrants in the Age of the American Revolution 1790–1820," *in Slavery and Freedom in the Age of the American Revolution*, Ira Berlin and Ronald Hoffman, eds. (Charlottesville: University Press of Virginia, 1983) 143–171, esp. 144 estimates the number of fugitives at about 5 percent of all blacks in the southern colonies, or about 30,000 in 1780. Above all, see Pybus, "Jefferson's Faulty Math," 262–264.

following extended public discussion. Its legislation freed all slaves born after a certain date. New York and New Jersey followed suit more slowly in 1799 and 1804, respectively. Similar projects for gradual emancipation failed in Delaware and Maryland, establishing a latitudinal boundary to legislated emancipations until the American Civil War.[29]

Of all the northern states, New York offers the best glimpse of the concerns of Northerners in debates over the future of slavery in post-revolutionary America. There, the institution survived the impulse that had moved other states to immediate or gradual emancipation. Whatever their state's distinctive characteristics, New Yorkers shared with their neighbors a common revolutionary ideology. They also shared religious, legal, and institutional traditions with Anglo-Americans: representative institutions, a vigorous civil society, and a vibrant print culture. As elsewhere, newspapers were the main sites of political discussion outside the legislatures.[30] Although slavery was still expanding in absolute numbers into the 1780s, slaves constituted only 6 percent of the state's population in 1790.

Like most of their counterparts in the North, New York's modest anti-slavery organization considered itself to be intensely internationalist, constituents of a broad Atlantic movement. For American antislavery actors, Britain remained at the center of their political and cultural world, the hub of its information network. England's emergent abolitionism in the late 1780s helped to frame the debate in New York. They shared a strong respect for civil liberty and property, and an articulated distaste for the cruelty and arbitrary power of slaveholders. In all of the early founding committees on both sides of the Atlantic, the Society of Friends was heavily overrepresented. All were strategically committed to the conversion of public opinion and the orderly diminution and elimination of slavery.[31]

The movements also varied tactically in crucial ways. New York's Manumission Society, pursuing emancipation in a far longer battle than Pennsylvania or New England, found it necessary to rely more heavily on newspapers. The Society did not, however, attempt to undertake methods of mass mobilization and mass petitioning in the manner of its English counterpart. The

---

[29] Arthur Zilversmit, *The First Emancipation: The Abolition of Slavery in the North* (Chicago: University of Chicago Press, 1967). For a well researched analysis of the political forces that both stimulated and delimited the discussion of slavery in the United States, see Matthew Mason, *Slavery and Politics in the Early American Republic.* (Chapel Hill: University of North Carolina Press, 2006). See esp. 4, 25–27, 39, 80–82, and 148–149, and 214.

[30] David N. Gellman, *Emancipating New York: The Politics of Slavery and Freedom 1777–1827* (Baton Rouge: Louisiana State University Press, 2006). On emancipation in Pennsylvania, see Gary B. Nash and Jean R. Soderlund, *Freedom by Degrees: Emancipation in Pennsylvania and its aftermath* (New York: Oxford University Press, 1991), ch. 4., 123. In this and the following paragraphs, I follow Gellman's account.

[31] David Brion Davis, *The Problem of Slavery in the Age of Revolution* (Ithaca: Cornell University Press, 1975) ch. 5; Brown, *Moral Capital*, ch. 7.

Manumission Society was formed in the wake of a rejected bill for gradual abolition in 1785. The Society's subsequent activity was based on the perception that the state and its electorate were deeply divided by cross-cutting attitudes towards slavery, race, and citizenship.

In addition to the absence of both mass petitions and mass meetings, there was no attempt in New York to emulate the British abstentionist movement against slave-grown sugar in 1791–1792.[32] There were further differences between the antislavery movements on the two shores of the North Atlantic. In 1785, New York's first gradual emancipation bill failed because of a widespread preoccupation with its potential implications for race relations. The proposed emancipation legislation was quickly bogged down in stigmatizing amendments. In the New York legislature, the assembly refused to extend the franchise to free blacks or to remove stigmatizing amendments punishing cross-color marriages with heavy fines. The upper house ultimately vetoed the bill because its racially coded provisions would create a permanent "class of disfranchised and discontented citizens" who could jeopardize the republican political system. In 1799, racial inequality continued to be the price exacted by the legislature in exchange for passing New York's gradual emancipation act. The price was again reaffirmed by unequal terms of enfranchisement when the New York legislature voted to end slavery by 1827.[33]

There was a third important difference in what antislavery Britons and Americans had to face during the age of revolution. British abolitionists had to confront only two houses of legislative authority. Antislavery New Yorkers found themselves enmeshed in a complex federation in which most of the decisions about the institution were consciously placed beyond the constitutional competence of the national government.

From the moment of America's Declaration of Independence, there was universal agreement among the revolutionary leaders that individual states were to determine the status of slavery and regulate the slave trade within or into their jurisdictions. This assumption profoundly affected the way slavery was addressed in relation to the public finances of the government. Each state had one vote in both the Continental Congress (1774/1776) and under the Articles of Confederation (1781). As far as the American-Atlantic slave trade was concerned, the wartime constraints on imports were only a suspension rather than a termination of the slave trade. With the return of peace, the trade in African slaves was renewed by merchants on both

---

[32] Gellman, *Emancipating*, 85–91; and Seymour Drescher, *Econocide: British Slavery in the Era of Abolition* (Pittsburgh: University of Pittsburgh Press, 1977), 114–119. English abolitionists were hoping for a similar triumph of free labor sugar in their renewed colonization of Sierra Leone. See Drescher, *The Mighty Experiment: Free Labor versus Slavery in British Slave Emancipation* (New York: Oxford University Press, 2002), 90–94.

[33] Gellman, *Emancipating*, 50, and ch. 5, 6.

sides of the Atlantic. In America, New England once again provided most of the vessels. Georgia and Carolina again imported most of the slaves. In the United States, the Confederation Congress of the 1780s declined even to resolve that the individual states be called upon to pass laws prohibiting the trade. States that banned the importation of slaves during the mid-1780s were those whose citizens were neither principal carriers nor importers of slaves. The Georgia legislature made it quite clear in 1784 that the new Confederation's power over foreign trade did not "extend to prohibit the importation of Negroes."[34]

Slavery first became a significant financial issue in assessing the distribution of taxes to finance the national government. States with large slave populations were anxious to avoid having that one form of wealth counted disproportionately for purposes of tax assessment when all other forms were not counted. In the debates over the Articles of Confederation, John Adams of Massachusetts concluded that if workers were taken as the indicator of wealth, all workers were equally productive. A Virginia representative countered that slave labor was less productive, and that "two slaves should be counted as one freeman." Between these two estimates of productivity and wealth lay the germ of the famous three-fifths compromise that is, that a slave counted for three-fifths of a free man. These original estimates, of course, were only offered in another context.

The range of casual estimates shows how little the three-fifths debate had to do with the relative productivity of slave and free labor. It had even less to do with the race or the humanity of the slaves. For purposes of taxation, the most accessible data – numbers of people – was simply the most accessible index of state wealth. Slaves were a very unevenly distributed source of wealth. As long as states were represented as single voting units, slaves had more implications for the distribution of taxes than for the institution of slavery.[35]

When the Constitutional Convention of 1787 shifted the issue from taxation to representation, the stakes for the two sides suddenly became inverted. If slaves were treated as unrepresentable wealth, Virginia's delegation in the new House of Representatives would have been diminished by 30 percent. Because so much was at stake, Pierce Butler of South Carolina wanted to scrap the 5:3 tax ratio and simply count slaves fully as both persons and property. Butler thus reversed the Southern position and agreed with John Adams's original estimate of slave productivity. Slaves were equal to freemen as wealth producers. They should be so represented in a government

---

[34] Don E. Fehrenbacher, *The Slaveholder's Republic: An Account of the United States Government's Relations to Slavery*, Ward M. McAfee, ed. (New York: Oxford University Press, 2001), 18, 21–22, 25.

[35] See Robin L. Einhorn, *American Taxation American Slavery* (Chicago: University of Chicago Press, 2007), 120–199.

instituted "primarily for the protection of property." Governor Morris of Pennsylvania countered that any representation of slaves at all would be unacceptable to his constituency. When Morris suggested apportioning representation solely based on the free population, the motion failed by ten to one. Once slave representation was agreed to, there was no argument about the three-fifths ratio, the bargain having already been struck over taxation five years earlier.

By contrast, the discussion of the Atlantic slave trade demonstrated the national limits of tolerance for the institution. Delegates from the lower South argued for sectional limitations on congressional power to control foreign trade so as to prevent federal control over the slave trade. Significantly, positions on the issue continued to follow fault lines already developed before the revolution. The upper South aligned itself with states further north in hostility to the trade. It was a Maryland delegate, Martin Luther, who moved that to exempt the slave trade from national control was "inconsistent with the principles of the Revolution and dishonorable to the American character."[36] The Jeffersonian denunciation of the slave trade, tactfully deleted from the Declaration of Independence in 1776, had not been forgotten.

The Georgia and Carolina delegations made it clear that their states would not ratify a document that subjected the slave trade to national legislative authority. Once again, the high priority given to achieving a more complete, if not perfect, union allowed for a compromise: a twenty-year exemption clause from federal governance. Despite James Madison's closing echo of Luther's insistence that even a temporary exemption would stain the national character, the slave trade hiatus was accepted, along with another provision requiring the return of fugitive slaves crossing state lines. The national legislature was thus given power to both curtail and protect aspects of the institution beyond the boundaries of individual states. The Constitution here explicitly delimited one aspect of the *Somerset* principle: in the United States slaves might be legally pursued within the jurisdictions where their status was determined by positive law.

As Fehrenbacher cogently argues, discussions of slavery impinged on many of the deliberations of the Constitutional Convention but, beyond the slave trade debates, delegates made no concerted effort to affect the future of the institution itself. With slavery still a legal presence in most states, antislavery remained a diffuse sentiment among scattered groups, most of whom just wished to ensure its future diminution. Slavery's defenders were far more concerned than those who opposed its existence, and mobilized to guarantee the security of the institution. The omission of the word "slave" from the Constitution represented a major symbolic concession to antislavery sentiment. Otherwise, apart from the slave trade clause permitting

[36] Fehrenbacher, *Slaveholding*, 32–34.

eventual action against the slave trade, every clause implicitly addressing slavery seemed to favor the institution.

At least as important as that omission was the lack of publicity that enveloped the slavery debate. All of the Convention's discussions occurred behind closed doors. The delegates avoided any explicit national commitment to or against the institution, except to oblige the return of fugitive slaves from one state jurisdiction to another. Avoidance of the issue extended even to those who belonged to abolition societies. In 1787, the Pennsylvania Abolition Society requested its president, Benjamin Franklin, to deliver a memorial to the Convention, to which he was also a delegate. The memorial urged the Convention to consider abolishing the African slave trade. Franklin neither presented the memorial nor did he make any recorded speech on slavery during the proceedings. Antislavery sentiment was too diffuse and the priority of the union too strong to engender a sustained majority for immediate federal power over the foreign slave trade.

Developments at the state level indicate why the immediate abolition of the slave trade was taken off the national agenda by widespread consent. In the ratification process, the slave trade clause was used by both supporters *and* opponents of ratification. In the interim, alternatives were available. The legislative responses by individual states indicates that the majority of voters in most states was willing to move toward formal abolition. Between 1787 and 1789, the slave trade was either prohibited or partially shut down in seven more states. Outside the state legislative bodies, however, there were only very hesitant initiatives from civil society to raise the issue at the national level.

The earliest intervention by abolitionist petitioners at the national level revealed both the potential explosiveness of the question and the reluctance of almost all legislators to pursue issues related to slavery. In the first federal Congress in 1790, the Society of Friends from Pennsylvania and New York, supported by another appeal from the Pennsylvania Abolition Society (signed by Benjamin Franklin), petitioned Congress to curb the slave trade and to consider the condition of those in perpetual bondage. The reaction of the Southern states was so virulent that the Quakers were put on the defensive. The lower Southern states treated the petitions as invitations to civil war. Above all, they reacted against the implication that slavery itself was morally wrong. Equally telling, no prominent Northern representative came to the petitioners' defense. Congressional reaction clearly discouraged the presentation of such petitions. Congress offered no response to further petitions to curb the slave trade in 1791 and 1792. In 1793, the Pennsylvania Society of Friends decided to suspend further petitioning to the legislature until they could be assured of a better reception.

In America, an ultra-cautious initiative succeeded in making some nominal legal advances against the one part of the slave trade constitutionally within the purview of national legislature. In 1794, a new American Abolitionist Convention decided to ask Congress for a law prohibiting American citizens from participating in the slave trade between Africa and foreign nations. To obviate another debacle from hostile congressmen, the abolitionists did not venture another petition until they were assured that it would be fully considered. That assurance entailed an explicit promise by abolitionists to abstain from activity that might have an impact on the institution or "the rights of private property" within the United States.[37]

The American abolitionists thus successfully targeted the one aspect of the slave trade that was unacceptable to the entire country. Thereafter, American abotionist activity fell off sharply. Even the antislavery political literature within the various state societies declined. The American Abolitionist Convention made no further attempt to lobby Congress during the rest of the 1790s. Northerners continued to be more divided than Southerners about the intent of the constitution with regard to slavery.

The sequence of decisions from Philadelphia in 1787 to the legislative debates of the first Congress indicates that the highest priority of the founders was the creation of a strong national government designed to maintain a consensus among all of the states that had participated in the American Revolution. Nevertheless, the Constitution's antislavery potential was greater than that of the original Articles of Confederation. The new federal government still seemed dedicated to self-government and the most egalitarian political ideology in the world. It also seemed poised to eventually contain one of the most rapidly expanding slave systems in the world.

At the international level, the nation's leading diplomatic agents – John Adams, Gouverneur Morris, John Jay, and Thomas Jefferson – all articulated antislavery sentiments, but pursued slaveholders' property claims in the international arena. At the end of two wars with Britain, John Adams and John Quincy Adams, the only Northerners to hold the presidency between 1789 and 1830, vigorously affirmed to the British government that their nations slaves' status as property trumped their status as human beings. Four decades after the Declaration of Independence, John Quincy Adams had to endure a lecture by Lord Liverpool, to the effect that those who had been offered their freedom could not "in good conscience" be handed back into slavery.[38]

The United States Constitution created a new boundary within Anglo-America. English and American law now directly clashed when slaves fled overland to Canada. In 1819, John Quincy Adams, now as Secretary of State, continued to press slaveholders' property claims to recover their fugitives.

---

[37] Howard A. Ohline, *"Politics and Slavery: The Issue of Slavery in National Politics,"* PhD Thesis, University of Missouri, 1969, 241–242.
[38] Fehrenbacher, *Slaveholding*, 94.

The British reply reiterated and expanded the reach of the *Somerset* decision:

The legislature of... Upper Canada having adopted the Law of England as the Rule of decision in all questions relative to property and civil rights, the Negroes have, by their residence in Canada, become free... and should any attempt be made to infringe upon the right of freedom... the executive government could in no manner restrain or direct the judges in the exercise of their duty.[39]

The ruling plagued all future American attempts to recover fugitives or their progeny until the American Civil War. Despite the persistence of slavery in their own tropical colonies until 1833, British officials upheld the extension of the British freedom principle within any colony that had adopted the premise of the Mansfield decision against involuntary deportation. Before the end of the age of revolution, the *Somerset* decision encroached the legitimacy of slavery in North America just as it had in England.[40]

While the national legislature ineffectively prohibited American citizens from participating in the transatlantic slave trade to foreign countries, the United States even more dramatically expanded its slave frontier in the years prior to 1807. In 1804, the nation acquired 826,000 square miles of new territory from the French, known as the Louisiana Purchase. In this vast underdeveloped area, slavery was already established between the Gulf of Mexico and the Missouri River. American concerns about the implications of this acquisition were dominated by two priorities. Just before the Louisiana Purchase, the federal government demonstrated as much determination to restrict the expansion of the black presence in the United States as to enforce any legislation against foreign slave trade. In 1802–1803, during Napoleon's final struggle to reenslave the blacks of the French Caribbean colonies, a wave of fear swept through parts of the South. Congress reacted with a bill prohibiting any ship's captain from bringing any "Negro, mulatto or other person into any port or place of the United States" where a state had already prohibited such importations. The implicit national and racialist consensus against further migrants of African descent, whether slave or free, appears to have been accepted without dissent.

The only objection to the original bill's blanket prohibition of African importation came from a representative of northern shipping. He successfully opposed extending the ban to black Americans, who worked as sailors in the coastal shipping trade. In 1803, this seemed to have effectively abolished the transatlantic slave trade to America. By early 1803, all states had prohibited the further introduction of Negro slaves. Abolition was thus being folded into a law against all foreign blacks. For many legislators, this

---

[39] *Ibid.*, 102.
[40] Wiecek, William M., "*Somerset*: Lord Mansfield and the Legitimacy of Slavery in the Anglo-American World," *University of Chicago Law Review*, 42 (1974), 86–146, esp. 88.

would remain their prime reason for passing the U.S. Slave Trade Abolition Act of 1807.[41]

Instead, federal agents attempts at enforcement of the Abolition Act in Charleston in 1803 prompted South Carolina to reopen its slave trade. The acquisition of Louisiana the next year added a new market to the U.S. demand for slaves, which briefly overrode the legislation excluding foreign blacks. The threat of impending federal enforcement actually stimulated fresh importations on an unprecedented scale. In 1807, the number of slaves that disembarked in the United States exceeded those unloaded in the British Caribbean for the first time in the history of the Atlantic trade.

At the same time, the Jefferson administration was committed to closing the African slave trade into the new Louisiana territory. Local popular pressure to retain the institution carried the day to different degrees in both the organization of the lower (Orleans) and upper (Missouri) settled segments of the new territory. Despite Jefferson's prohibition against the entry of Africans directly into Louisiana itself, the flow of both African and African-American slaves from the older states ensured the continued growth of slavery within the Louisiana territory. A single petition from the American Abolitionist Convention requesting the prohibition of all further importation of slaves into Louisiana was ignored by Congress.

The residents of Louisiana successfully lobbied Congress not to inhibit slavery in the territory. The governor, a strong supporter of race-based exclusion, unsuccessfully sought to block the trade. In the spirit of the 1803 law of exclusion, he did not want to see "another of that wretched Race, set his foot on the shores of America." By mid-1804, almost every ship reaching New Orleans had slaves aboard. A final compromise closed the new territory to direct imports of foreign slaves, but left domestic importation unimpeded. Even foreign-born slaves continued to enter the territory legally, via Charleston, and illegally through other Gulf ports.[42]

In terms of popular mobilization, the final passage and significance of the British and American Acts of 1807 differed considerably. In the U.S. Congress, the debate over the Slave Trade Abolition Act was framed in a far from consensual moral context. During the previous generation, there had been no general debate on the morality of the slave trade or slavery itself, either in the public sphere or in the national legislature. During the debate over the Abolition Act, a South Carolina representative put the matter

---

[41] Ohline, *Politics*, 343–348.

[42] *Ibid.*, 382–390. As Congress discussed the future of slavery in Louisiana, the Senate considered a project for the gradual emancipation of every slave carried into the territory. It was defeated with the assent of Northern Federalists Timothy Pickering and John Quincy Adams of Massachusetts, and Republican John Smith of Ohio. John Craig Hammond, *Slavery, Freedom and Expansion in the Early American West* (Charlottesville: University Press of Virginia, 2007), 39. Once again, it would appear that these senators were free to act without extensive abolitionist pressure from their constituents.

bluntly. Many Southerners did not hold slavery to be criminal at all: "I will tell the truth. A large majority of people in the Southern States do not consider slavery as even an evil." He warned that African captives, released on Southern soil, would not be allowed to survive: "We must either get rid of them or they of us.... Not one of them would be left alive in a year."[43]

One dimension of slavery seemed amenable to joint Anglo-American coordination in the half century following the American Revolution – the ending of the African slave trade. As noted, many colonies had been at the forefront of agitation against further importation before the War of Independence. In December 1806, thirty years after his ringing denunciation of the transatlantic slave trade was stricken from the Declaration of Independence, President Jefferson announced to Congress that the United States could now withdraw its citizens "from all further participation in those violations of human rights which have so long continued on the unoffending inhabitants of Africa."[44]

The lopsided vote in favor of slave trade abolition demonstrated that the nation at large was overwhelmingly opposed to further importations of Africans. Even here, however, where there was near unanimity, any amendment or discussion of the trade that tended to imply a moral condemnation of the institution elicited a new outburst of threats of disunion from the lower Southern States. The racially exclusionary implications of the Abolition Act elicited no protest from the national legislators.

American civil society was similarly subdued both before and after the passage of the Abolition Act. Some state governments encouraged early congressional action in preparation for the legislation, but there appears to have been almost no pressure from antislavery societies or the press. The meeting of the American Abolition Convention, early in 1806, encouraged its locals to propagandize and solicit petitions throughout the states. Congress, however, outlawed the importation of Africans before any petition campaign, if one was planned, ever got underway. Despite prolonged disputes over enforcement details, there was no attempt during the extended legislative debates to apply popular pressure on the nation's representatives. The Senate's deliberations, as usual, were not published.

Nor was there much celebration following the passage of an Abolition Act that had been anticipated for twenty years. Many congressmen were unsure about what the federal legislation had actually achieved. Some hardly mentioned it to their constituents. Antislavery organizations evoked only moderate degrees of enthusiasm. The American Abolitionist Convention donated to Congress a copy of Clarkson's two volume *History of the Abolition of the British Slave Trade* (1808). No contemporary account of American slave trade abolition would ever be published. The gift of Clarkson's work, which

---

[43] Davis, *Problem of Slavery in the Age of Revolution*, 135–136.
[44] Fehrenbacher, *Slaveholding Republic*, 144.

emphasized British abolition as a moral crusade, was accepted by Congress over the objection of sixteen representatives.[45]

African-American communities manifested the most visible public reaction to the passage of the act. Significantly, their responses tended to link the American and British legislation. African-American commemorations were pointedly muted by white abolitionist anxiety that African Americans should not read too much into the Abolition Act. In the wake of its celebration of Abolition Act's passage in New York, the state abolition society warned the free black community that their "method of celebrating the abolition was improper, [tending to injure] themselves and harming the reputation of the New York Society."[46]

The message to the Boston black celebrants in 1808 was even more pointed. Although African Americans took the initiative, the ceremony was permitted only after the Governor and the city's Selectmen gave their approval. The sermon, delivered by Calvinist minister Jedediah Morse, focused upon caution rather than hope. The celebrants were warned that the doctrine of equality was not to be so construed as to subvert order and subordination; that they were not to think that African slavery was worse than moral sin; that the slave trade had benefited "multitudes.... brought from the darkness of paganism, to a Christian land," and that they were not to expect a change in the domestic institution in the South.[47] Caution, minimal expectations, and subdued gratitude were the watchwords for black civil society. The wall against foreign imports of slaves was strengthened, whereas the path to American participation in slavery's internal expansion widened. After the return of peacetime commerce in 1815, the American government was chiefly concerned with preventing slave smuggling from the West Indies into the coastal areas of the Gulf of Mexico. Florida, another potential American slave zone, was a center for smuggling Africans into the United States.[48]

American policy makers were now simultaneously concerned with prohibiting further importations of African slaves and resisting British pressure to become part of a multinational system to shut down the transatlantic slave trade. In 1818, the U.S. Congress moved to reduce the penalties against

---

[45] As Matthew Mason sums up the salience of the public discussion of abolition, "what impresses the reader of the newspaper coverage of the 1806–1807 slave trade bill is its relative paucity." "Slavery Overshadowed: Congress Debates Prohibiting the Atlantic Slave Trade to the United States, 1806–1807," *Journal of the Early Republic*, 20:1 (2000), 59–81. Quotation is on p. 77. See also Ohline, *Politics*, 410–411, 429–430. "Failure to record antagonistic debates about slavery since 1790 had been a major way of hiding the political issue of slavery." *Ibid.*, 425.

[46] *Ibid.*, 432–433.

[47] *Ibid.*, 432–435.

[48] Rafe Blaufarb, "The Geopolitics of Latin American Independence," *American Historical Review*, 112:3 (2007), 742–763.

American slavers in hopes of ensuring enforcement. Once again, there were the telltale characteristics of U.S. abolitionism – no evidence of pressure from outside the legislature and no record of congressional debate preceding the law's passage. The following year, a Southern-sponsored revision of the Abolition Act required the federal government to create a naval patrol and to arrange for the return of slaves aboard any captured vessels returning to Africa.

By the 1820s, successive legislative acts made American penalties against importing Africans amongst the harshest in the world. The Senate refused to enter into any treaty agreement that would subject American vessels to a mutual right of search with the British. So, British ministers rejected slave extradition from Canada on grounds of British public opinion. President Adams retorted that the "universal repugnance" of American public opinion would not allow considering a treaty that allowed a foreign naval officer to search an American vessel for slaves "under any circumstances whatever." As the British moved from attacking the slave trade to promising slave emancipation in the mid-1820s, American legislation became wary of further cooperation. In the U.S. Senate, British proposals for joint ventures against the slave trade aroused too much suspicion of being wedges against slavery itself.[49]

The United States itself was increasingly delimited into zones of slave and free states. On the eve of the Constitutional Convention in 1787, the old Confederation Congress quietly incorporated an antislavery article into an ordinance for organizing the Northwest Territory, the undeveloped frontier north of the Ohio River. Although the finality of the prohibition was to be challenged in Illinois as late as 1824, by the end of the age of revolution, slavery was definitively excluded in states lying north of the Ohio River. Correspondingly when the territory south of the Ohio was created in 1790, no ban on slavery was included. As a result, states west of the Appalachians were, therefore, also divided into slave and free states.

The Louisiana Purchase in 1804 opened up the trans-Mississippi territory for development under the auspices of the United States. As noted, slavery was not excluded from any area involved in the Purchase. By default, the ordinance excluding slaves from the Northwest Territory became the exception rather than the rule in the unorganized lands controlled by the federal government. The extended discussions over the organization of Louisiana stimulated neither a sharp polarization in the national legislature nor a popular movement to reserve a territorial line of free soil westward from the Ohio River. Even the largest slave revolt in United States history, near New Orleans in 1811, raised no deterrent to continuing the institution in the Louisiana territory. In 1812, the southernmost portion of the territory beyond the Mississippi entered the union as the slave

---

[49] Fehrenbacher, *Slaveholding Republic*, 150–158.

state of Louisiana. Regarding the Missouri territory north of Louisiana, a motion to prohibit the further admission of slaves was routinely defeated in Congress.[50]

Dramatic changes in the Atlantic world in the four decades after the ratification of the United States Constitution ended in a tacit balance between slave and nonslave areas in the expanding United States. Neither foreign wars, external slave revolutions nor slave resistance in Louisiana triggered the first great post-revolutionary crisis over slavery in America. Instead, it was the peaceful pattern of settlement along the Missouri River in 1819 that aroused the most passionate explosion of rhetoric in the national legislature since the Southern reaction to initial Quaker petition during the first federal Congress. When Missouri applied for entry into the union as a slave state in 1819, its northerly location seemed to violate the latitudinal division between slave and free zones traced by the Ohio River. It would become the second slave state created west of the Mississippi, with another slave territory being organized (Arkansas) and not one free territory within the Louisiana Purchase yet in sight. Moreover, the fate of Illinois's antislavery constitution of 1818 was still in question.[51]

Congress divided bitterly over an amendment, proposed by James Tallmadge, to make Missouri's admission to statehood provisional on the prohibition of further introduction of slaves and the gradual abolition of the institution through the operation of the free womb principle. Southern congressmen again exploded with threats of disunion. Tallmadge's amendment sparked weeks of debate and deadlock in the legislature. For the first time, a slavery-related issue stimulated a national mobilization outside of Congress. Northern congressmen, who had opposed the Tallmadge amendment, found themselves under the pressure of public mass meetings from Boston to Philadelphia. The mobilizers evoked the imagined "future character of our nation and the future weight and influence of the free states if now lost – it is lost forever." State legislatures in the Northeast responded by instructing their congressional representatives to bar the entry of future slave states. Never had the North appeared so aroused. There was widespread fear that the slave region, "already dominant in the executive," would "forever remain our masters."[52]

In response to this sectionalized attack some surviving Southern Founding Fathers intervened to emphasize that the Constitutional Convention had not authorized congressional control over slavery. Jefferson adopted the argument that a diffusion of slaves to the West would not increase their number and would ease eventual emancipation. The Missouri crisis deeply

[50] *Ibid.*, 260–261.
[51] Robert Pierce Forbes, *The Missouri Compromise and its Aftermath: Slavery and the Meaning of America* (Chapel Hill: University of North Carolina Press, 2007), ch. 2.
[52] Forbes, *Missouri Compromise*, 56 ff.

frightened political leaders interested in the survival of the union. Eventually, threats from Southerners drove enough Northerners to accept a division of the Louisiana Purchase at the 36° 30′ latitude, prohibiting slavery in all of the lands west and north of Missouri. In 1820, the immediate question of political balance was preserved by the admission of both Missouri and Maine to statehood. With the decision to set a boundary to the future expansion of slavery along the line of 36° 30′ latitude, overt Northern attacks on slavery ebbed in the national legislature.[53]

The crisis reinforced the prior hesitation of political leaders to address the problem of slavery at the national level. It hardly closed discussion in various parts of the South on the institution's future. The furor over the Denmark Vesey conspiracy in South Carolina inspired representatives to declare that the national legislature had no authority to discuss or to interfere with slavery in the remaining federal territories. Among Northerners, antislavery arguments continued to reverberate, but Northern Congressmen seemed to tacitly subscribe to a new Southern understanding that the Declaration of Independence had created neither a legislative nor moral imperative regarding the institution of slavery or the status of free blacks. In another legislative move, Missouri aligned itself with a national, not a sectional, trend. On admission to the Union, Missouri barred the entry of free blacks into the state. As far as the national government was concerned, human rights of liberty and civil equality applied to whites alone.[54]

The immediate outcome of the Missouri compromise appeared to reaffirm the long-term trend. Constricting slavery was no more embedded in the American national agenda when Jefferson died on July 4, 1826, then when he had drafted the Declaration of Independence fifty years before. Half a century after 1775, the process of abolition in the United States had apparently reached an impasse. North of the Chesapeake and Ohio, the states' political representatives had begun to refer themselves as "free" states. Fifty years after the American Revolution, Americans on both sides of the Mason-Dixon Line still seemed to be overwhelmingly united in preventing a further influx of slaves into the nation. The dream of a "whitened" New World was not unique to North Americans, but the United States was distinctive in producing a long-term collective movement favoring the reversal of the flow of Africans into the New World. The American Colonization Society (ACS), founded in 1817, was dedicated to sending blacks back to Africa,

---

53 *Ibid.*, 260–261.
54 Fehrenbacher, *Slaveholding* Republic, 264–265. William W. Freehling has shown how deeply divided the South was in discussing the possibility of ending slavery. Among the crosscurrents of resolutions, irresolution ruled. (See Freehling, *Road to Disunion*, ch. 9–11). During the Missouri crisis, Thomas Jefferson foresaw that the hardening of a "geographical line, coinciding with a marked principle, moral and political, once conceived and held up to the angry passions of men, will never be obliterated, and every new irritation will mark it deeper and deeper." (Freehling, *Road to Disunion*, 155).

above all those who were already free and those who might have freedom made contingent upon their departure.[55]

The ACS hoped to elicit the financial support from both the federal government and individual states. Their plans were also linked to the United States' commitment to suppressing American-Atlantic slaving. In 1819, the day after the passage of an act authorizing cruisers along the coast of African, the ACS requested that Congress's $100,000 appropriation to fund the patrol also be used to establish an African colony. The settlement would be for voluntary black migrants from the United States. As with its British colonial predecessor in Sierra Leone, the colony could serve as the destination of return for contraband slaves captured at sea. The ACS, with a substantial number of slaveholders as prominent sponsors, called for the voluntary expatriation of free and freed blacks.

In its early years, the ACS elicited the largest mobilization of the free African-American population before the emergence of radical abolitionism. From the very founding of the ACS in Washington, however, many free blacks felt deeply threatened. The overwhelming majority of free blacks in the Americas offered free passage out of their country refused to migrate to Africa or the Caribbean. African Americans thereby thwarted the most important project envisioning their elimination from the United States.

By the time the ACS was ready to establish a national cohort of local chapters, most of Philadelphia's free blacks were prepared to react. James Forten, one of the wealthiest African Americans in the new republic, actively mobilized protests against the ACS. Its opponents were acutely aware of the possibility that planters might free and deport their most intractable slaves and use colonization as a terrifying threat to their remaining slaves. In January 1817, 3,000 blacks convened at Mother Bethel Church in Philadelphia, exceeding the largest recorded mobilization of Northern whites (over the Missouri crisis) two years later. They resolved that they would not be uprooted from their country, and insisted on their inseparability from their enslaved brethren. This mobilization was decisive in the later abolitionist rejection of colonization as a solution to the problem of slavery.[56]

By the mid-1820s, the boundaries of North American slavery had been reconfigured in ways that had not existed fifty years before. The battle

---

[55] On the American Colonization Society, see Eric Burin, *Slavery and the Peculiar Solution: A History of the American Colonization Society* (Gainesville: University Press of Florida, 2005); and Allan E. Yarema, *America Colonization Society: An Avenue to Freedom?* (Lanham, MD: University Press of America, 2006).

[56] Julie Winch, *A Gentleman of Color: The Life of James Forten*, ch. 8–10. The ACS continued to attract enough black support to hold a large scale interracial meeting in Philadelphia as late as 1833. Forten was obliged to mobilize a counter-gathering featuring eyewitness testimony of disillusioned repatriates form Liberia. The debate for the sympathy of African Americans attracted the intervention of William Lloyd Garrison with *Thoughts on African Colonization* (1832).

against further transatlantic imports seemed closed. If the Constitutional provision for retrieving fugitive slaves also appeared to prohibit even Northern "free states" from becoming "free soil" areas consonant with the *Somerset* precedent, the number of new-born slaves in those states was now zero. The proportion of slaves in the Northern states was already minuscule. The overwhelming majority of articulate citizens in the Northern states regarded slavery as an institution that would inexorably disappear within their jurisdictions.

In the upper South, a burst of statutes in the 1780s, combined with accelerated private manumissions, opened up a vista of gradual abolition of slavery. By the 1820s, however, that trend had halted. New slave states, extending over a larger geographic area than their free counterparts, had entered the union after 1790. The stirrings towards racial inclusiveness opened up by the transatlantic religious revival of the 1780s and 1790s had failed. The vision of a slow death for slavery had stalled. Westward expansion and census returns showed that far more people were enslaved over a far wider area at the end of the age of revolution than at the beginning.[57]

For African Americans, slavery and racism were expanding more rapidly than freedom. The American slave trade's last surge between 1783 and 1807, plus the acquisition of Louisiana, added more new slaves to the United States than had been freed through state-sponsored gradual emancipation laws and individual manumissions combined. For the Founding Fathers, aspirations toward ending slavery had been marginalized in favor of the complex task of building a large republic. Few of their heirs after half a century were prepared to risk the destruction of the union. Some sought to disperse black slaves westward into the new territories, others to disperse African Americans eastward to Africa or southward into the Caribbean.

The most significant political outcome of the Missouri compromise after 1820, was a new party system dedicated to channeling conflict away from direct sectional confrontations over slavery. In civil society, even the denominations that had once raised disturbing questions about slaveholding among

---

[57] Alexis de Tocqueville returned from his journey to America with a grim prognosis. The principle of abolition would extend into the upper South in the course of time. Slavery would remain more deeply rooted further South, with an oppressive racism everywhere. The result would be struggles entailing collective annihilations. See Alexis de Tocqueville, *De la démocratie en Amérique* (Paris: Gallimard, Pléiade edition 1992), 1030, note on 414. In his notes, Tocqueville concluded more grimly: "We have already seen the *whites* destroyed in the West Indies [Haiti]. Our children will see the *blacks destroyed* throughout most of the United States ... at the end of the successive retreat of the Negroes towards the south." Tocqueville felt obliged to confide to himself that of all the means by which the conflict between the two races in the South could be accelerated, the most powerful catalyst would be the abolition of slavery. John C. Calhoun would not hesitate to reach the same conclusion and to pose the issue not as a choice between racial domination and annihilation, but slavery and freedom.

their own congregants muted their critical stance. Antislavery societies devoted much of their energies toward removing white anxieties about the behavior of free blacks. They looked to temper racial attitudes by demonstrating that education and religion would help free blacks demonstrate their potential for respectability.

In the absence of large-scale radical abolitionism, the ACS could maintain its plausibility as a Janus-faced agency favoring both gradual slave emancipation and gradual black removal. Within this frame of reference more antislavery societies flourished in the South than in the North.[58] This reflected a widespread view that the problem of slavery would have to be resolved by the slave states themselves. More radical voices intruded, but at the national level the problem of slavery was still only indistinctly comprehended and left largely to Southern gentlemen.

From the African-American perspective, the half century after the American Revolution seemed to invite discouragement and desperation rather than hope for even incremental liberation. Suddenly, in 1829, David Walker's *Appeal to the Coloured Citizens of the World* [and]... *especially to those of the United States* was published in Boston. It shocked Northern white abolitionists and alarmed Southern slaveholders, alike. Its promise of divine vengeance and apocalyptic destruction was treated in Charleston as a tocsin for slave insurrection. Walker's most immediate target, however was the free blacks of the North. He needed first to dispel his own community's acceptance of their degradation. In its scripture-drenched rhetoric and its denunciation of an unfulfilled Declaration of Independence, Walker's *Appeal* was equally scathing of blacks who collaborated in oppressing their own brethren, inspirational white ministers who called for reforming every sin, but slavery and racism, and colonizationists whose synonym for emancipation was deportation.[59]

For all of its virulence, Walker's call to action was embedded in the same broader currents of American society from which "gentlemen of color," like

---

[58] Merton Dillon, *Slavery Attacked: Southern Slaves and their Allies* (Baton Rouge: Louisiana State University Press, 1990), 114, and Elizabeth Fox-Genovese and Eugene D. Genovese, *The Mind of the Master Class: History and Faith in the Southern Worldview* (New York: Cambridge University Press, 2005), 231–234.

[59] David Walker's *Appeal... to the Coloured Citizens of the World, but in particular, and very expressly, to those of the United States of America*, Sean Wilentz, ed. (New York: Hill and Wang, rev. ed. 1999), esp. art. 3 and 4. South Carolinans were especially aroused when they discovered a copy of Walker's polemic on the person of a visiting sailor. The most serious slave conspiracy in the United States had been uncovered in Charleston earlier in the decade. On the Denmark Vesey conspiracy see Robert L. Paquette and Douglas R, Egerton "Of Facts and Fables: New Light on the Denmark Vesey Affair," *The South Carolina Historical Journal*, 105:1 (2004), 25–26; Fehrenbacher, *Slaveholding*, 116; and David Robertson, *Denmark Vesey* (New York: Alfred A. Knopf, 1999). On political attitudes in general toward slavery in the wake of the Missouri Compromise, see Forbes, *Missouri Compromise*, ch. 4 and Fehrenbacher, *Slaveholding*, 265–266.

James Forten, launched his more polite and less confrontational mobilization. The *Appeal* closely followed the appearance of *Freedom's Journal*, the first African American newspaper. It was of a piece with the establishment of the Massachusetts General Colored Association. Walker's speech to that Association, just before the publication of the *Appeal*, shows why few of its members would have understood the *Appeal* as a call for insurrection of slaves or free blacks. There, he exulted in their mutual emergence from an "unorganized condition." He saw the Association as the nucleus of a national movement, society, legally "forming societies, opening, extending and keeping correspondence."[60] In short, Walker was catching the associational wind that was already sweeping through American society and would soon lift abolitionism as well.

In 1829, Walker also knew that African Americans were no longer as isolated in the wider world. Besides their brethren in Haiti, he hailed an English nation on the move towards emancipation. Fifty years after the Declaration of Independence, it was clear to Walker that a major shift had occurred in the geography of Anglo-American slavery. The Atlantic no longer separated a western colonial zone, where chattel slavery was ubiquitous from an eastern metropolis where abolition had no political salience. The boundary of slavery had shifted within North America itself. *Somerset* ruled just north of the United States border. In the northern half of the United States, the institution of slavery was consigned to the remnants of an ever-diminishing cohort. Just south of the Mason-Dixon Line, in the border states, what William Freehling calls "conditional antislavery" – eventual, delayed, and, at best, gradual emancipation – remained the dominant orientation.[61]

Along the Gulf states, slavery retained its hold. Staple growing southerners, with South Carolina in the vanguard, fought every initiative, even colonization, that would implicitly devalue the indefinite prospects of their ever-expanding institution. From the lower South came an intensifying counterpoint of vociferous dissent arising from the existential fact that slavery was now a problem in search of practical resolution almost everywhere in Western civilization.[62]

---

[60] *Ibid.*, Appendix I, 79–83, "Address Delivered before the General Colored Association at Boston," first published in *Freedom's Journal*, December 19, 1828. On the development of African American associations and their link to political activism, see James Oliver Horton and Lois E. Horton, *In Hope of Liberty: Culture, Community, and Protest Among Northern Free Blacks, 1700–1860* (New York: Oxford University Press, 1997), esp. ch. 7 and 8. On the significance of the Anglo-American connection, see Van Gosse, "'As a Nation, the English Are Our Friends': The Emergence of African American Politics in the British Atlantic World, 1772–1861," *American Historical Review*, 113:4 (2008), 1003–1028

[61] William W. Freehling, "The Founding Fathers and Conditional Antislavery," in Freehling, *The Reintegration of American History* (New York: Oxford University Press, 1994), ch. 1.

[62] David Brion Davis, *Slavery and Human Progress* (1984), part II, ch. 4.

Despite the vibrancy of slavery below the Ohio River and beyond the Mississippi, and the firewalls of constitutional noninterference, a new gap was emerging in Western perceptions of the institution's temporality. Even European conservatives in post-Napoleonic Europe were reconfiguring the history of Europe to demonstrate that the great expansion of European overseas slavery was an anomaly, an aberration within the long durée of Christianity.[63] The increasing currency in the South of references to their "domestic institution" reflected a paradigmatic shift. In civil law tradition, slavery was axiomatically held contrary to the law of nature, but conventional in the law of nations. Its position within the laws of "civilized nations" was now under siege.

[63] On the perspective of Anglo-American Protestantism see Davis, *Slavery and Human Progress*, Part II, ch. 3. For post-Napoleonic France, see Elodie Le Garrec, "Le Debat sur l'abolition de la traite des Noirs en France (1814–1831): Un reflet de l'evolution politique, economique et culturelle de la France." (Memoire de Maîtrise d'Histoire contemporaine, Université Bretagne-Sud, 2002–03), 139–142. Tocqueville treated the progressive framework as consensual in 1843: "Christianity had destroyed servitude; the Christians of the sixteenth century had reinstated it. They never accepted it, however, as anything more than an exception to their social system and they were careful to restrict it to only one of the races of man." *Democracy in America*, 393; and Tocqueville, "On the Emancipation of Slaves" (1843), in Seymour Drescher, ed. and trans. *Tocqueville and Beaumont on Social Reform* (New York: Harper and Row, 1968), 148. For the French intellectual establishment, "Christianity was the key." M. I. Finley, *Ancient Slavery and Modern Ideology*, 12–35.

6

Franco-American Revolutions, 1780s–1820s

Interrevolution, 1783–1791

Neither the American Declaration of Independence nor the achievement of independence itself caused any change of course among the slavers, colonists, or rulers of Europe. Not since the mid-seventeenth century had there been such a flurry of new projects designed to gain entry into the booming Atlantic system. The institution of slavery continued to enhance the wealth of those who controlled it and the affluence of those who purchased or sold its output. Given the comparatively high productivity of slave labor in New World agriculture, slave and slaving systems remained competitive and expansive.[1]

All of the major and many of the minor Atlantic players assumed that slavery was, or could be, a significant component of their wealth and power. The shared impulse for encouraging the expansion of slavery was not confined only to those nations and merchants that were still the century's biggest players – the British, the French, and the Portuguese. The attractiveness of the plantation complex was evidenced by a surge of newcomers. The seventeenth-century opening of the North Atlantic slave trade had encouraged a rush of small states from the Baltic: Denmark, Sweden, Brandenburg, Hanau, and Courland. A second rush got underway in the 1780s. Ostend merchants in the Austrian Netherlands (now Belgium) took advantage of the sharp wartime drop in the British and French slave trades. As the transatlantic slave trade reached its absolute peak in the decade after 1783, merchants from the Austrian Netherlands to Italy sought permission to deliver slaves and invest their capital into the booming sugar colonies. Like their

---

[1] See R. W. Fogel and S. L. Engerman, *Time on the Cross* (Boston, MA: Little Brown, 1974), 247–257; Fogel, *Without Consent or Contract* (New York: W.W. Norton, 1989), 84–89; and David Eltis, "The Slave Economies of the Caribbean," 123.

seventeenth-century predecessors, the Ostend merchants also lobbied their Habsburg ruler to acquire a Caribbean island or a foothold in Guiana for use as a slave entrepôt. The booming eighties also stimulated Tuscan merchants to plan a direct trade from the West Indies to an Italian port.[2] Further north, the Swedish monarch chartered a new merchant company to the West Indies via the island of Saint Bartholomew, acquired from France. The Spanish monarchy abandoned their three century-old policy of contracting mono-poly rights to deliver slaves. Their major effort of liberalization of their slave trading system was meant to encourage the plantation development of Cuba and Trinidad. By 1800, more Africans were arriving in Spanish and Portuguese America than ever before.[3]

Of all the jostling participants in the post–American Revolutionary War boom, the French were the frontrunners. Between 1785 and 1790, more slaves were brought into French colonial seaports than those of any imperial power, not even counting the French islands of the Indian Ocean. In contrast to the prewar pattern, most of the Africans now arrived in French vessels, every ton subsidized by the French treasury to the tune of 2 million livres per year. The 55,000 slaves unloaded in 1790 were far more than had ever been shipped under any national flag. The slavers fed a plantation system that more than doubled its output of sugar and nearly tripled its export of coffee in the generation before 1789.[4]

The most valuable of all the French slave colonies was Saint Domingue. By 1790, 500,000 slaves worked on 8,000 plantations. They accounted for a third of the sugar sold in the Atlantic and an even greater share of the coffee market. At the outbreak of the American Revolution, the French Caribbean already exported nine times as much coffee for the European market as did their British counterpart. In the decade after the return of peace, St. Domingue further increased the gap. This "Pearl of the Antilles"

---

[2] On the above see, Drescher, *Econocide: British Slavery in the Era of Abolition* (Pittsburgh: University of Pittsburgh Press, 1977), 170–171, and Drescher, "Jews and New Christians in the Atlantic Slave Trade" in *The Jews and the Expansion of Europe to the West, 1450–1800*, Paolo Bernardini and Norman Fiering, eds. (New York: Berghahn Books, 2001), 439–484; Drescher, *Capitalism and Antislavery: British Mobilization in Comparative Perspective* (New York: Oxford University Press, 1987), 171–172; and E. Ekman, "Sweden, the Slave Trade and Slavery 1784–1847," *Revue Francaise d'histoire d'outre-mer*, 62: 226–227 (1975), 221–231.

[3] See George Reid Andrews, *Afro-Latin America 1800–2000* (New York: Oxford University Press, 2004), 19–20.

[4] For slave trade figures, see Eltis et al., "Reassessment," and Robert Louis Stein, *The French Slave Trade in the Eighteenth Century An Old Regime Business* (Madison: University of Wisconsin Press, 1979), 41–42. For French Colonial exports, see Jean Tarrade, *Le Commerce Colonial de la France à la fin de l'Ancien Regime: L'Evolution du régime de l'Exclusif de 1763 à 1789*, 2 vols. (Paris: Presses Universitaires de France, 1972) I, 34.

alone accounted for two-fifths of France's overseas trade. Two-thirds of French overseas investments went to that colony.[5]

Saint Domingue stood out not only in relation to its plantation counterparts but also to its own metropolis. Economically, the metropole and its slave colonies had grown increasingly interdependent. While the colony was undergoing its surge of wealth, metropolitan France was sinking into crisis. The bankrupt monarchy had reached a point of fiscal collapse, political paralysis, and violent resistance. It would be well into the destruction of the old regime in France before a similar collapse – later, longer, and stronger – occurred in the Caribbean colonies.

On April 30, 1789, George Washington was inaugurated as America's first president. A week later, Louis XVI convened the Estates-General of France, inaugurating a revolution that was to shatter the social order of France. In its age of revolution, the Franco-American slave empire was to undergo a more volatile series of transformations than any other system of the Atlantic world. In 1789, the French Declaration of the Rights of Man and Citizen declared liberty to be a universal right. Even more consequentially, five years later in February 1794, (16 Pluviôse an II of the revolutionary calendar) the republic decreed the abolition of slavery throughout all parts of its French empire. If fully implemented, three-quarters of a million slaves would have been liberated and raised to full citizenship in a single day. The reverberations of this decree were to be felt far beyond the boundaries of the empire.

Yet, the French abolitionist moment was as fragile as it was dramatic. During the age of revolution, slaves, in some of its colonial areas (St. Domingue-Haiti) would be liberated after years of struggle. In others (Martinique and the Mascarines), slaves would never experience a single year of freedom. In still others (St. Lucia, Guadeloupe, Guyana) the liberation of 1794 would be reversed. During the age of revolution, France therefore had the distinction of being the only Western colonial power that ever reestablished its slave system. In the course of three decades, it also resurrected its overseas slave trade twice more and abolished it twice more. Only in Haiti, where French military power and the French demographic presence was utterly destroyed, was slavery definitively brought to an end. In no area of the revolutionary age was the institution's fate sealed and unsealed with so much blood.

Certain striking differences between the Anglo-American and Franco-American empires affected both the course and the outcome of antislavery in the two areas. In most of the Anglo-American colonies that achieved independence, whites constituted the dominant population demographically,

[5] David Patrick Geggus, *Haitian Revolutionary Studies* (Bloomington, IN: Indiana University Press, 2002), 5–6. Olivier Petré Grenouilleau, *Les Négoces maritimes francois* (Paris: Berlin, 1997), 124.

politically, and economically. In the portion of the British empire that most closely resembled the French tropical empire, the dominant white group made no effort to overthrow British authority nor did the slaves challenge the slave system for most of the half century after 1776.

As in the Anglo-Caribbean colonies, the slaves of the French colonial system typically constituted 80 or 90 percent of the population. St. Domingue's slave population of 500,000, however, was the largest in the Caribbean, exceeding the total in all of the British colonies combined. Its free people of color (*gens de couleur*) nearly equaled the colony's 40,000 whites and far exceeded in number and proportion those anywhere else in the British or French West Indies.[6] Moreover, taken as a whole, the colony's 30,000 free people of color constituted the wealthiest such group in the richest and most productive colony in the Americas. In St. Domingue's West and South, the *gens de couleur* outnumbered the whites. A small elite, the rich colored planters were usually educated like their white counterparts, and some moved freely between the colony and Paris.[7]

The combined demographic and economic affluence of this nonwhite sector both intensified calls for more racial restrictions from whites and deepened embitterment among the colored elite. Colonial whites attempted to erect barriers to political, social, and military mobility based upon color and genealogy.[8] The psychological tensions produced by this segregationist system upon groups who were individually economic or cultural peers were exacerbated by the less hostile reception that educated men of color met with in the metropolis. Unlike slaves, the free black population of the islands had family and social ties in France. In contrast to their counterparts in the British empire, the *gens de couleur* were poised to play a more pivotal catalytic role in the opportunities opened up by the collapse of the old regime both in France and the Caribbean.[9]

Overseas slavery remained an emerging, but still marginal presence in prerevolutionary French political discourse. As in Great Britain and British

---

[6] Carolyn E. Fick, "The French Revolution in Saint Domingue: a Triumph or a Failure?" *A Turbulent Time: The French Revolution and the Caribbean* ed. David Barry Gaspar and David Patrick Geggus, eds. (Bloomington: Indiana University Press, 1997), 56.

[7] Geggus, *Haitian Revolutionary Studies*, 79. Fick estimates the number of slaves held by Saint Domingue's free colored slaveholders to be more than 100,000 (p. 56). This would have made them the largest nonwhite group of slaveholders in the Americas.

[8] On the racialization of colonial society in response to the emergence of free people of color, see inter alia, Yvan Debbasch, *Couleur et liberté*, vol. 1, ch. 2.

[9] See David Geggus, *Haitian Revolutionary Studies* (Bloomington: Indiana University Press, 2002). John D. Garrigus finds that in the South province of Saint Domingue, the free people of color were clearly outperforming their white neighbors. In the 1760s, the free colored class participated in 41 percent of transactions in slaves. In the 1780s, they accounted for nearly 57 percent of slave marketing activities and 49 percent of slave leases. *Before Haiti: Race and Citizenship in French Saint-Domingue* (New York: Palgrave Macmillan, 2006), 177.

America before the American Revolution, there were almost no avowed defenders of slavery and the slave trade on moral grounds. Abbé Raynal's vibrant *Histoire des deux Indes* and a few projects for gradual abolition focused attention broadly on slavery as a problem. In the wake of his own participation in the American Revolutionary War, the Marquis de Lafayette initiated an unpublicized emancipation experiment on the Guyana coast of South America. France's small contingent of political economists were at one with their major British counterparts in morally condemning slavery. Some agreed with Adam Smith that, "in the end," free labor was cheaper and more efficient than slave labor. The most politically influential economist offered an important caveat to this prognosis. Anne-Robert Turgot, for a time the principal advisor to Louis XVI, maintained that slavery did serve the accumulation of wealth and commerce. To the very end, French officials viewed the Caribbean colonies as an invaluable source of revenue and foreign exchange in a regime sliding precipitously towards default. Prerevolutionary French economists, too, were "very hesitant indeed" when they turned their attention to slavery.[10] As in Britain, moral judgments were counterbalanced by the widespread assumption that economic progress was linked to a general civilizing process. Only rarely was the violence and brutality of the institution of slavery made the centerpiece of a study, as in Condorcet's *Reflections on Negro Slavery* (1781).

Even while acknowledging colonial economic benefits, old regime colonial administrators showed awareness of the tension between metropolitan norms and transatlantic practices. In the 1780s, royal ordinances began to focus on the management of slaves on the plantations of absentee owners. There were continuous ministerial discussions about security problems from the imbalance between whites, free people of color, and the overwhelming slave majority. Two contrary solutions were proposed. The one favored by most white colonists was based upon the premise that the

---

[10] See David Brion Davis, *Problem of Slavery in Western Culture* (New York, Oxford University Press, rev. ed. 1988), ch. 13, 14; Philippe Steiner, "Slavery and French Economists, 1750–1830," in *The Abolitions of Slavery from L. F. Sonthonax to Victor Schoelcher, 1793, 1794, 1848*, Marcel Dorigny, ed. (New York: Berghahn Books, 2003), 133–143, esp. 141. The message of the *Encyclopédie*, the collective monument of the French Enlightenment, was a mixture of indifference, unease, and hostility. (See Jean Ehrard, "Slavery before the Moral Conscience of the French Enlightenment: Indifference, Unease, Revolt" in Dorigny, *Abolitions*, 111–120. The problem of slavery was relatively marginal to the Encyclopedists. (Ibid., p. 111). In its 72,000 articles, Jean Ehrard could find only thirty-three explicit references to the slave trade and slavery. In the small segment of fifty articles that might logically have elicited comments on racial slavery, fifteen failed to even mention the subject and twenty addressed it neutrally. Of the remainder, only ten condemned it and three extenuated it. For the persistence of the assumption that non-Europeans had to be at the disposition of Europeans as laborers in the tropics, see William H. Sewell, *A Rhetoric of Bourgeois Revolution: The Abbé Sieyès and What is the Third Estate?* (Durham, NC: Duke University Press, 1994).

maintenance of white supremacy was essential to the survival and prosperity of the plantation colonies. From this perspective, frequent manumissions were an ever-growing threat to the colonial system.

A second alternative was based upon the premise that in a society with a population that was 90 percent slave, free people of color were absolutely essential to maintaining order. This necessary barrier to slave resistance required an amelioration, and perhaps even a termination, of the racial contempt and institutional disabilities that had humiliated and angered nearly half of the free population. The model lay very close at hand in the colony with whom the French shared the island of Hispāniola, the mixing of races in the Spanish-ruled Santo Domingo. Royal administrators, fully aware of what from their perspective was both an "unjust prejudice" and an "infinitely delicate" problem, endlessly recycled ministerial memoranda for a generation. The stalemate reached behind bureaucratic closed doors at the end of the old regime would be repeated in the public sphere in 1789.[11]

One innovation introduced on the very eve of the revolution was the emergence of a new association, the *Société des Amis des Noirs* (Society of Friends of the Blacks), in February 1788. The *Amis des Noirs* was constituted in Paris in response to an appeal from Britain. The English Society for Effecting the Abolition of the Slave Trade was formed in London in 1787. The *Amis des Noirs* began its work under the still effective control of the monarchy. Against the pressure of an alarmed colonial lobby, it could not hope to freely publicize its ideas. Composed of an elite with good connections, the *Amis des Noirs* were allowed to establish an unofficial *journal*. The government restricted its publications to translations of information about British activities under the innocuous heading, *Analyse des papiers anglais* (Analysis of English Newspapers). The translations included the London Committee's initial appeal for a French counterpart. This Anglocentric beginning was fraught with consequences. Thomas Clarkson, the most active member of the London Committee in Britain, provided much of the empirical information and rhetorical strategies employed by *Amis des Noirs*.[12] Nevertheless, the *Analysis* became the means by which the *Amis's* own activities were made know to the larger public.

From the beginning, the *Amis des Noirs* was far more ambitious in its aims. Abolition of the slave trade was the exclusive target of the London Committee. The British strategy, which envisioned a natural decline of slavery as the consequence of ending transatlantic imports, was deemed too slow and passive. The *Amis* insisted on identifying slaveholding itself as a

[11] David Patrick Geggus "Racial Equality, Slavery, and Colonial Secession during the Constituent Assembly," *American Historical Review*, 94: (5) (1989), 1290–1308, esp. 1293).

[12] See Thomas Clarkson's *Essai sur les désavantages politiques de la traite des nègres en deuz parties. . . . Precede de l'Extrait de l'Essai sur le commerce de l'espèce humaine, du meme autheur, traduit de l'Anglais par M. Gramagnac* (Neufchâtel, 1789).

crime and not a legitimate form of property. As a consequence, it called for the gradual abolition of the institution itself by direct metropolitan intervention.[13]

This politicizing of slavery, combined with the more volatile revolutionary situation in France, induced abolitionists on both sides of the Channel to imagine that France might take the lead in ending the slave trade. The calling of the Estates-General in 1789 was accompanied by a vast collection of demands for change (*cahiers de doléances*) from all over France. The three legal estates and every parish in France drew up lists of their grievances. The *Amis des Noirs* viewed the *cahiers* as an excellent vehicle for inserting slavery onto the agenda for national regeneration. In response to their call, nearly fifty of the six hundred "general *cahiers*" reaching the Estates-General at Versailles made some demand for action on slavery, often accompanied, however, by reminders about the need to preserve the "public interest." In his opening speech to the Estates-General in 1789, the king's chief minister, Jacques Necker, included a reference to the need to turn France's attention to the plight of black slaves.[14]

From the outset, however, the *Amis de Noirs* and their project suffered from a number of serious disabilities. The *Amis* had a very restricted membership. It remained an elite organization in Paris with a few hundred members at its peak of membership. It functioned principally as a lobby to fellow members of the political elite. Even at the peak of its influence, in 1789, its power to generate nationwide support for abolitionist initiatives was meager. The year before, in Britain, the first wave of abolitionist petitions specifically requested the termination of the slave trade. They accounted for more than half of all public petitions delivered to Parliament that year. In France, a year later, demands for some action on slavery appeared in 10 percent of the general *cahiers* but were buried among dozens of other requests for reform on every document. All told, the *cahiers* of the nobility and the third estate devoted about as much attention to the slave trade and slavery combined as they did to the much more minuscule institution of convicts on the French galleys in the Mediterranean. In no collection of *cahiers* did any of the class actors place overseas slavery as high as 400th on their lists of grievances calling for national reform. A more accurate indicator of slavery's priority was the frequency of its appearance on the tens of thousands of other *cahiers* drafted for the peasants, nobles, clergy, and members of the third estate. In all *cahiers* of the French Third Estate, the combined total of demands for "attention" to slavery and the slave trade amounted to between

---

[13] Marcel Dorigny, "Mirabeau and the Societé des Amis des Noirs: Which Way to Abolish Slavery?" in Dorigny, *Abolitions*, ch. 10.

[14] Yves Benot, *La Révolution Française et la fin des colonies* (Paris: La Découver 1998), 107–108.

one-tenth or one-fifth as many as those calling for action on serfdom. At the parish level, slavery simply did not register at all as a cause for concern. It ranked only 419th on the list of Noble demands and 533rd on those of the Third Estate.[15]

Equally significant was the disposition of slavery at the very peak of revolutionary enthusiasm in the summer of 1789. On the tumultuous night of August 4–5, 1789, the first two estates of the National Assembly dramatically renounced their legal privileges one after another. During the course of the proceedings, the duc de La Rochefoucauld-Liancourt proposed extending the emancipation of French serfs to overseas colonial slaves. Ominously, even on that "eternally celebrated night of August 4," slavery was one of the few proposals that aroused vocal disapproval from the privileged notables. The motion was quietly dropped from the final decree. A few weeks later, the discussion of the founding document of the new order missed a second opportunity for the National Assembly to address the glaring anomalies of slave trading and ownership. As with the American Declaration of Independence, slavery was not addressed in the French Declaration of the Rights of Man and Citizen.[16]

During the same volatile summer, Thomas Clarkson, England's indefatigable abolitionist organizer, was dispatched to France. His mission was to encourage the French abolitionists to take full advantage of their revolutionary situation. On arrival, he was utterly surprised by the plans of the *Amis des Noir* plans for popular pressure. They wanted Clarkson to request his own British colleagues to launch a second mass petition in England, as they had done in the previous year. This time, however, the *Amis* wanted its countrymen to call for the abolition of the slave trade by France. Clarkson diplomatically pointed out that the British legislature was not in the habit of receiving petitions from other nations. Such an intrusion into the French public sphere might have a very counterproductive effect on the French public. Although the *Amis* assured him that the French would glory in such an expression of sentiment, the English abolitionist unequivocally rejected the idea.

For Clarkson, the expression of such dependency upon the English was a harbinger of later French abolitionist subordination to foreigners. In Paris, Clarkson himself was quickly identified by antiabolitionists as an English

[15] See Gilbert Shapiro and John Markoff, *Revolutionary Demands: A Content Analysis of the Cahiers de Doleances of 1789* (Stanford, CA: Stanford University Press, 1998), Appendix I, Subject Codes. For comparisons of slavery with other grievances, see S. Drescher, *Capitalism and Antislavery: British Mobilization in Comparative Perspective* (New York, Oxford University Press, 1986), 54; and Drescher, "Women's Mobilization in the Era of Slave Emancipation: Some Comparisons," in *Women's Rights and Transatlantic Antislavery in the Era of Emancipation* (New Haven: Yale University Press, 2007), 98–120, Table 5.1.

[16] See John Markoff, *The Abolition of Feudalism* (University Park: Pennsylvania State University Press, 1996), 431 n. 12

government spy or a radical refugee from England, one whose abolitionist ideas were so wild that he had been ejected from the London Committee. His life was threatened. Clarkson's careful canvass of potential French support in the French National Assembly confirmed his suspicions and falling expectations. Without England's prior initiative to abolish the trade, only one quarter of the National Assembly would consider supporting abolition. The white colonists were gaining influence with the passing of each week.[17]

As significant as the erosion of support for abolition in the French legislature was the absence among the *Amis* of any ability to launch a popular mobilization in France like that which had already induced the British legislature to consider a parliamentary inquiry into the possible abolition of the British slave trade. The French abolitionists were evidently so distracted by the upheaval at home that they could only rarely appear at their society's meetings much less formulate plans to popularize initiatives for overseas change. They lacked the provincial cadres who organized the popular petition and subscription drives in Britain beginning in 1788. Brissot de Warville, founder of the *Amis des Noirs*, might have been dubbed "the Quaker," but he had no access in France to an analogue of the Quaker or other religious and business networks and skills that made such a critical contribution to both the London and provincial committees that mobilized petitioning at the grass-roots level across the Channel.[18]

Moreover, the first notice of the *Amis'* intention to request consideration of the question of slavery before the National Assembly was met by a preemptive counter-mobilization of colonial planters, metropolitan merchants, and seaport notables, which the French abolitionists were never remotely able to match.[19] Weighing its options, the *Amis* acknowledged that securing the revolution in France might require holding back on the slave trade for

---

[17] Thomas Clarkson, *History of the Rise, Progress, and Accomplishment of the Abolition of the African Slave-Trade by the British Parliament*, 2 vols. (London: Longman, Hurst, Ress and Orme, 1808), II, 126–127.

[18] See J. R. Oldfield, *Popular Politics and British Anti-Slavery: The Mobilization of Public Opinion Against the Slave Trade, 1787–1807* (Manchester, UK: Manchester University Press, 1995), esp. ch. 5; and Judith Jennings, *The Business of Abolishing the British Slave Trade 1803–1807* (London: Frank Cass, 1997), ch. 3–5.

[19] See, inter alia, Valerie Quinney, "The Committee on Colonies of the French Constituent Assembly, 1789–1791," PhD dissertation, University of Wisconsin, 1967; Quinney, "Decisions on Slavery the Slave-Trade and Civil Rights for Negroes in the Early French Revolution," *Journal of Negro History*, 55: 2 (1970), 117–130; and Gabriel Debien, *Les colons de Saint-Domingue et la Révolution Française: Essai sur le Club Massiac (août 1789–août 1792)*, (Paris: A. Colin, 1953). The slaveholders were successful in stifling radical criticism in the Parisian public sphere. Early in 1790, they forced the closing of Olympe de Gouge's play, *L'Esclavage de Nègres*. See David Geggus, "Racial Equality, Slavery and Colonial Secession during the Constituent Assembly," *American Historical Review*, 94:5 (1989), 1290–1308, esp. 1294–1295.

fear of alienating the now mobilized French Atlantic ports. France's slave system was now larger than Britain's, its colonial wealth far greater, and its contribution to France's precarious finances far more significant than that of the British slave economy. In this context even a mutually negotiated Anglo-French treaty to prohibit their slave trades could be attacked as an asymmetrical sacrifice, with France as the big loser.

From the very outset of the French Revolution, British abolitionism had been inverted into a Machiavellian conspiracy against France's more dynamic overseas institution. This conspiracy theory was to far outlast the Age of Revolution. In 1789 and 1790, the pro-slave lobby in Paris, despite divisions between merchants and planters, achieved an almost unbroken series of victories against potential antislavery motions. However, in 1789–1790, some of the slave interest's is victories increased their vulnerability. It was the colonists of Saint Domingue who first breached the line between metropolis and colonies that had served to buffer their distinctive institution for more than a century. Even before the Estates-General became the National Assembly, delegates selected by Saint Domingue's white elite arrived at Versailles demanding seats as representatives of their colony. They asserted their claim on the grounds that Saint Domingue was an integral part of France, "one of the greatest provinces of the empire one of the most powerful and without doubt the most productive."[20]

The colonists believed that in the Estates-General, they could effectively defend themselves against potential antislavery attacks. They wished to solidify both their citizen's rights to representation and retain their overseas privilege of property in persons. The colonists thereby put themselves into the same vulnerable position at Versailles in which a North American state might have found itself had it been the only slave society to join the Philadelphia Convention in 1787. As in the debates over the U.S. Constitution, a discussion of colonial representation made it impossible to avoid the question of how many representatives each constituent territory should have. At Versailles, deputy Jean-Denis Lanjuinais "raised his voice against the slavery of the negroes." Like some American Northerners two years earlier, he wanted to count only Saint Domingue's minuscule 40,000 whites, pending any change in the status of slaves.[21]

Count Mirabeau also posed an objection that had been raised against slave state representatives in America. If human property was to be the basis of overseas representation why should metropolitan wealth be denied representation in the French legislature? The occasion also provided an opening for raising a second major anomaly of colonial societies beyond

[20] As Malick W. Ghachem observes, this was the assimilationist idea in a nutshell. "The Trap of Representation: Sovereignty, Slavery, and the Road to the Haitian Revolution," *Historical Reflections Reflexions Historiques*, 29:1 (2003), 123–144, quote on 127.
[21] *Ibid.*, 132.

the line. What of the *gens de couleur,* free citizens nearly equal to whites in number, but entirely unrepresented among the colonial delegates who had arrived at Versailles?

Whereas the white colonists struggled to maximize their interests, non-whites were completely unrepresented in the colonial delegation at Versailles in 1789–1790. The demands of the free colored citizens directly contradicted white colonial insistence that only a racial mystique, institutionalized by rigid legal barriers, assured the stability of overseas slavery and the plantations. The free *gens de couleur* in Paris, wealthy, organized, and vocal, constituted a direct threat to the emerging Franco-colonial compromise. Their lobby, the *Société des Colons Américains* (Society of American Colonists), immediately appealed as citizens to the Declaration's principles and demanded equality, at least for mulattoes. Some were ready to sustain slavery in exchange for renegotiating the color line of those living in freedom.

Initially claiming to be fortifiers, not subverters, of the institution of slavery, the free colored citizens denied that they endangered the colonial order. Nevertheless, the deep tensions between the racially divided slaveowners opened bitter fractures that spilled over into discussions of slavery. At one point, the *Colons Américains* "went out of their way to condemn the institution of slavery." One of the club's leaders, Vincent Ogé, declared to the rival white *Club Massiac* that they would have to prepare for the end of slavery. Like Clarkson, Ogé became a marked man in Paris. The project of deracializing citizenship suffered the same stalemate as the movement to dismantle the slave trade and slavery.[22]

At the same moment that the first United States Congress in 1790 put the nation on notice that the institution of slavery was off-limits to both federal legislation and discussion, the new French Constituent Assembly reaffirmed the old line between metropolitan and colonial institutions. Its Declaration of the Rights of Man would not extend overseas. France's small antislavery movement was overridden by the slave interest. Their lobbying, backed by petitions and addresses from mercantile port cities, cut the ground from under projected interventions by *Amis* like the Abbé Gregoire and Count Mirabeau. Like its U.S. counterpart, the National Assembly refused to hear further antislavery motions.

By the spring of 1790, the Constituent Assembly, now creating the nation's new constitution, again removed its overseas colonies from the inclusive potential of the Declaration of the Rights of Man. After months of political contention, the French legislators also decided to immunize themselves and their colonies from the other issue that might threaten the tranquility of the plantation system. They opted for silence on the subject of racial inequality as well as slavery. The National Assembly avoided electing

[22] Yves Debbasch, *Couleur et Liberté,* 144–146; 160–166; and Geggus, *"Racial Equality,* 1300–1301.

abolitionists to its Colonial Committee. The most important decree on the new constitutional status of the colonies was passed on March 8, 1790. The decree avoided using the term slaves, but overseas slaves were secured to their masters as colonial property. Slaveholders were further reassured that the metropole would respect "local customs" and not interfere with any branch of commerce. The decree criminalized any attempt to incite disorder in the colonies. The nation not only assigned complete authority over the institution of slavery to the colonies, but assured them against any interference in the transatlantic slave trade. The old regime's bounties for slaves delivered to the colonies remained intact.[23]

The decree of March 8, 1790, thus reaffirmed French slavery at its apogee. At the moment of the Saint Domingue slave uprising, 55,000 Africans were being landed in the French colonies, a number exceeding the annual imports of any nation from the beginning of the transatlantic slave trade. Throughout the Atlantic more than 100,000 slaves were landed in the French colonies in the triennium 1790–1792.[24]

The National Assembly however, was denied any respite. Both racial groups among the colonists were left unsatisfied by the compromise of 1790. The compromise over internal colonial autonomy began to collapse almost as soon as it was promulgated. From the outset, some white colonists claimed to have an associative rather than a dependent relationship with the metropolitan government. As noted, in the turmoil of the fall and winter of 1789, colonial deputies reiterated that France needed its overseas planters more than they needed France. Metropolitan deputies, of course, regarded the preservation of the plantation complex as essential only if it securely belonged to France.

It was in the Caribbean that the colonial settlement unraveled. If slave production loomed large in the calculations of French legislators, slaveholders were but a tiny cluster of whites in a sea of black slaves. The free colored population constituted a substantial proportion of the forces of order. In the west and south of Saint Domingue, they were a majority of the free inhabitants. At least a portion of the colonial whites declared themselves quasi-independent of Parisian legislative intrusion. Vincent Ogé returned to the colonies after receiving funds from abolitionists in England and purchasing arms in the United States. Quickly establishing himself in one part of Saint Domingue, he demanded the extension of the suffrage to all free males of color, limited only by metropolitan property qualifications.

---

[23] See Marcel Dorigny, "Mirabeau and the Société des Amis des Noirs: Which Way to Abolish Slavery?," in *The Abolitions of Slavery: from Santhonax to Victor Schoelcher, 1793, 1794, 1848* (New York: Berghahn Books, 2003), 121–132 and Florence Gauthier, *Triomphe et mort du droit naturel en Révolution 1789–1795–1802* (Paris: Presses Univerritaires de France, 1992), 170–171.

[24] Slave Trade Data Base.

Ogé's challenge was an isolated affair, quickly suppressed. Even in revolt, he continued to support slavery and refused to recruit slaves to support his armed defiance of white colonial rule. As in many violent uprisings to come, its impact owed more to its suppressors than to its instigators. Ogé and his co-leader, Jean-Baptiste Chavannes, were tortured, broken on a wheel, executed, decapitated, and impaled upon a pike. The horrific executions provoked a small petition campaign from some provincial metropolitan Jacobins. The Legislative Assembly, alarmed by this act of desperation and aware that the public was horrified by the brutality of its outcome, finally attempted to make a concession to the free population of color. In May 1791, a new colonial decree was designed to reassure free men of color that they could gradually progress toward full citizenship. The decree also reiterated to the planters that Paris would pass "no law on the state of slavery in the colonies of the Americas."[25] After a protest by Robespierre echoing the old regime's reticence to import the word "slave" into metropolitan law, the word slave was replaced by the euphemism "unfree person."

The debate on the extension of voting rights marked a decisive break with the taboo on discussions of colonial problems. It extended over an unprecedented five full days. It demonstrated the consensus that slavery was still considered essential to the value of the plantation colonies. All the major spokesmen for lowering the racial barrier insisted that the question was not about weakening slavery, but about avoiding instability that might disrupt cultivation. The Abbé Gregoire, Lanjuinais, and Pétion all emphasized that slavery would be more secure with the active support of the institution by free colored citizens. Robespierre, too, insisted that the subordination of the slaves would be reinforced by a class of citizens who were only asked to be allowed the right to command. Conversely, security would be threatened by further racial strife within the free population.[26]

The combination of white threats of independence and Ogé's revolt had broken the wall of silence imposed for two years by the Constituent Assembly. Even the minimalist compromise, offering the suffrage only to nonwhites born of free parents, was under attack from the moment it was passed. The *Amis* denounced its more explicit affirmation of slavery in the new constitution. On the other side, a large portion of the colony's white colonists openly refused to implement the compromise. The Constituent Assembly then retreated again in the fall of 1791. Having constitutionalized slavery, the Assembly now constitutionalized racial exclusion from the colonial assemblies. The Declaration of the Rights of Man did not apply to French overseas possessions. In yet another shift, the colonists were able to have the decree rescinded, preserving freedom only for nonwhites in France. Two

---

[25] Laurent Dubois, *Avengers of the New World*, 87–88.
[26] Florence Gautier, *Triomphe et mort du droit naturel*.

years after enshrining the Declaration of the Rights of Man, French colonial slavery and racial hierarchy remained intact.[27]

From the calling of the Estates-General to the eve of the Saint Domingue slave revolution in July 1791, both slavery and antislavery remained beyond the interest of most politically active provincials. As late as September 1791, the revocation of the suffrage for colonial nonwhites was greeted with a "gallic shrug of the shoulders" by the Jacobins. David Geggus's skepticism regarding the growth of large-scale popular solidarity with colonial nonwhites seems warranted. As of the summer of 1791, French Revolutionary ideology had created some openings for antislavery agitation in France and a potent vocabulary for conflict in the colonies, but little real change. It was from the Caribbean, and from the slaves themselves, that revolutionary action was to have its greatest impact on the progress of emancipation.[28]

For two years after the fall of the Bastille, the slave colonies still appeared to be islands of manageable slave resistance against a metropolis teeming with revolutionary aftershocks. In the summer of 1789 alone, the French peasantry initiated more than 1,000 separate contentious events.[29] During the same year, David Geggus describes only one major slave revolt in the French islands. Unfolding on the outskirts of the town of St. Pierre, Martinique, the uprising was probably stimulated by newspaper reports of the activity of the *Amis* in Paris. The slaves may have believed that their supporters in France had persuaded the king to free them. In anticipating such a liberation, their demands may have marked a striking innovation in French Afro-American resistance.[30] The revolt in St. Pierre, however, was not a response to revolutionary events in Versailles or Paris. The slaves' demands incorporated a strong tradition in European peasant revolts. The insurgents of 1789 still enjoined the sanction of royal liberation. They showed little sign of acting on the inspiration of the universalist libertarian rhetoric of the metropolitan revolution. As indicated earlier, inhabitants of the Caribbean had no indication that France's new political representatives included them within the purview of the Declaration of the Rights of Man. Although unrest increased in Saint Domingue and Cuba after 1789, there were fewer than two dozen instances of slave conspiracies and active resistance in the

---

[27] Davis, *Problem of Slavery in the age of revolution*, 137–148; Geggus, *Haitian Revolutionary Studies*, 13.

[28] See Michael Kennedy, *The Jacobin Club*, 209; Geggus, "Racial Equality," 1304–1305.

[29] Markoff, *Abolition of Feudalism*, 271, fig. 6.1.

[30] David Geggus, "The Slaves and Free Coloreds of Martineque During the Age of the French and Haitian Revolutions: Three Moments of Resistance," in *The Lesser Antilles in the Age of European Expansion*, Robert L. Paquette and Stanley L. Engerman, eds. (Gainesville: University Press of Florida, 1996), 282–284.

Caribbean.[31] All of them quickly failed. As with most previous slave con-spiracies in the Americas, they had either been uncovered at the planning stage, suppressed within a few days, or resolved by treaties with runaway collective communities.

The great Saint Domingue uprising of 1791 was extraordinary in the extent of the conspiracy, the massiveness of the uprising, the rapidity of its extension and, above all, in its resiliency. Compared to previous nonslave initiatives to abolish the slave trade or slavery undertaken in North America and Great Britain in the 1770s and 1780s, the insurrection on the northern plain of the colony in August 1791 began in secrecy amongst the slaves themselves. On August 14, a meeting of the slave elite, including drivers and coachmen from 100 plantations, was held on a sugar plantation in the Plaine du Nord parish. Far smaller conspiracies had been exposed by fellow slaves and quickly suppressed into fragmented uprisings or resolved by treaties with runaway communities. The plans of this large conspiracy also began to leak out and the insurrection was launched by some of the leaders to prevent the project from being compromised. Despite the lack of complete coordination, the outbreak quickly spread from plantation to plantation from night to night by slaves armed with machetes and beating drums. Within a little more than a month, more than 1,000 plantations had been seized and burned. Hundreds of whites had been summarily killed. Even greater numbers of slaves had been killed in brutal reprisals without daunting the rebels. Thus, even at the outset, the cost on both sides was virtually unprecedented.[32]

The initial guiding goals of the rebels seemed more multivalent than the effectiveness of their organization. Some invoked a royal emancipation withheld by whites bearing the revolutionary tricolor. The record number of recent African arrivals may have been bonded through religious voudou and other cultural symbols. In any event, the fact that participants from a hundred plantations had been able to conspire and combine was probably unprecedented. Through a combination of destruction and brutality, the rebels were able to inspire panic in a large portion of the colonial elite.

---

[31] *Ibid.*, 282, and David Geggus, "Slavery, War, and Revolution in the Greater Caribbean, 1789–1815," in *A Turbulent Time: The French Revolution and the Greater Caribbean* (Bloomington: Indiana University Press, 1997), 1–50; esp. list of Slave Rebellions and Con-spiracies, 1789–1815, 46–48. See also Yves Bénot, "The Chain of Slave Insurrections in the Caribbean, 1789–1791" in Dorigny, *Abolitions*, 147–154.

[32] On the outbreak, see above all, David Geggus, *Haitian Revolutionary Studies*, ch. 6; Lau-rent Dubois, *Avengers of the New World*; and Carolyn Fick, *The Making of Haiti: The Saint Domingue Revolution from Below* (Knoxville: University of Tennessee Press, 1990), Dubois's lengthy narrative of the prerevolutionary meetings follows John Thornton in giv-ing particular emphasis to African religious and cultural traditions in the consolidation of the communities formed by the prospective insurgents. See Dubois, *Avengers of the New World*, 99–102; and John Thornton, "African Soldiers in the Haitian Revolution," *Journal of Caribbean History*, 25: 1 and 2 (1991), 58–80.

The uncoordinated response varied from negotiations for freedom for rebel leaders to attempts to crush the insurgency through atrocity and terrorism.

The subsequent history of the long slave revolution was fraught with sudden reversals of position on all sides. In some places, the *gens de couleur* fought alongside slaves immediately after Paris's revocation of their rights, then switched again after the French reversal of the revocation. In the multiple conflicts over liberation, race, and separatism, slaveowners began to arm slaves to fight other slaves or to shift the balance of power against other free factions. Soon after the initial uprising in the north of the colony in the summer of 1791, blacks were fighting blacks as well as whites and free coloreds. By April 1792, a desperate French legislature, in yet another reversal, offered full citizenship to the entire free colored population.

Time after time, the situation was momentarily stabilized only to be reconfigured by new developments within the Caribbean, Europe, or the Atlantic world at large.[33] For two years after the outbreak, the stabilizing of France's largest slave system remained the government's highest overseas priority. This was true even for most radicals in the metropolis. In the French legislature, members of the *Amis* were denounced by Jacobins for having played a role in precipitating the disastrous uprising. As late as 1793, Léger-Felicité Sonthonax and Etienne Polverel, two radical Civil Commissioners dispatched by the new French Convention, were entirely committed to the maintenance of slavery. Until the end of 1793, royalist slave insurgents were routinely identified with the counter-revolutionary peasants of the Vendée.[34] By 1793, the national government remained committed to one major change. As agents of the French government, they were determined to crush anyone on the social spectrum from colonial and royalist separatists to Jacobin radicals who refused to acquiesce in the full equality now accorded to free colored citizens in defense of restoring order.

The rulers of France showed no sign of abandoning the institution of slavery. The Atlantic slave trade to the French islands remained intact, and 10,000 slaves were delivered even to the turbulent French colonies as late as 1793. The implicit decision to save slavery by yielding on racial equality appeared to be working and, at the end of 1792, Commissioner Sonthonax emphasized his commitment to the continuation of slavery to free coloreds as a lynchpin of governmental strategy.[35]

At the beginning of 1793, French troops had subdued the first site of the rebellion in the northern plain. Thousands of slaves who had fought

---

[33] Here, I largely follow the succinct account of David Geggus in *Haitian Revolutionary Studies* (Part One: Overview).

[34] Yves Bénot, *La Revolution Française et la fin des Colonies* (Paris: La Découverte, 1989), 136–173.

[35] Geggus, *Haitian Revolutionary Studies*, 13.

under the initial rebel leaders, Jean-François Papillon and Georges Biassou, emerged from the mountains and surrendered. Without any further outside intervention, the institution might well have survived, allowing for some combination of negotiated freedom for armed black soldiers fighting for France and a maroon community at the edge of a somewhat truncated plantation society.

The expansion of a continental Franco-European war into a Franco-Atlantic war transformed the pace and scope of the abolitionist process in the French Caribbean. Once France was at war with both Britain and Spain in the winter of 1793, both republican France and monarchical Spain began bidding for black rebels with offers of personal freedom and remuneration. Whites in St. Domingue could look to an Anglo-Spanish invasion to save them from the dual threat to slavery and racial equality. In turn, the Commissioners of the French Republic cast their lot with the nonwhites successively massacring or driving the whites from all parts of the colony, except where they were protected by foreign arms. More than ten thousand whites fled, becoming the largest white diaspora in the history of the Caribbean. From that point, the colony's internal history became a struggle between "the emergent power of the black masses and the predominantly brown-skinned middle class."[36]

Each turn in the war served to enhance the recruitment of armed slaves. The discipline of those remaining on the plantations broke down, especially among those who had experienced the full rigors of gang labor on the sugar plantations. The fortunes of war accelerated France's move toward the broadening emancipation. The threat of British invasion contributed to Sonthonax's emancipation decree in Saint Domingue in August 1793. Even then Paris hesitated either to ratify or to reject its Commissioner's initiative. As late as October, fomenting the slave uprising in the Caribbean was among the charges of counter-revolution brought against Brissot de Warville, a leading member of the now scattered remnants of the *Amis des Noirs*.

The threat of a general British sweep of France's Caribbean colonies was a powerful catalyst in hastening the Parisian decree of colonial slave emancipation in February 1794. On 16 Pluviôse Year II of the Revolutionary calendar, freedom was extended to all slaves under French sovereignty. The law was never enforced in France's Indian Ocean colonies or in Martinique, which fell into British hands after being conquered by British forces. Nevertheless, for the first time, a northwestern European imperial power legally erased the boundary between its free soil metropolis and its overseas slave colonies. Where French arms prevailed, the decree briefly presented slaves with a choice between the republican freedom and a monarchical status quo. In Saint Domingue, the British and Spanish forces, far too small and

[36] *Ibid.*, p. 14.

constantly depleted by disease, were also forced to recruit and arm thousands of blacks as soldiers. Toussaint Louverture, the insurgents' most brilliant general, moved decisively at a critical moment. In the spring of 1794, he renounced his ties to the Spanish monarchy, ceased to negotiate with the invading British, and brought most of his forces over to the republic. His decision became the turning point in the slave revolution.

During six more years of almost continuous fighting, Toussaint successively expelled the British, conquered the Spanish portion of the island, and defeated the colored general Rigaud, his major rival for control of the colony. The victorious general had thereby gained virtual independence from the French republic as well. Internally, his regime guaranteed freedom for all ex-slaves, racial equality for the colored population, and security of life and property for the remnant of former masters who remained or returned to the island to revive the plantations.

The war with Britain also dramatically expanded the strategic impact of France's general emancipation beyond Saint Domingue. In the wake of its emancipation decree, the French government dispatched a military expedition to the Caribbean under Victor Hugues in April 1794. Although the British held on to Martinique, Hugues quickly recaptured Guadeloupe. During 1794–1795, the radical republic also extended emancipation to two more of its retained colonies, St. Lucia and Cayenne. In the eastern Caribbean, slave liberation flowed from the combined military power of France and the recruitment of free men of color and slaves for military and naval warfare. With the arrival of Victor Hugues, inhabitants of the liberated islands became colonies of citizens, their freedom defined in French republican terms.[37] The French Revolution also offered the new citizens of the eastern Caribbean opportunities to take to the seas as privateers against the British and to invade the British-ruled islands of Dominica, Grenada, and St. Vincent – all colonies with large non-Anglophone populations.

Within two years, however, the threat of revolutionary warfare receded. In the lesser Antilles, British reinforcements from Europe and newly recruited slave regiments suppressed insurgencies launched by invading French forces. Indeed, for the British, the slave trade now became a major source of military recruitment for newly created West Indian regiments. Although the regiments were developed too late for the British to use effectively in Saint Domingue, their control of territory suitable for tropical plantation labor, as we shall see, more than doubled by the end of the Anglo-French conflict. The purchase of Africans for military purposes reached its peak in the decade between the British evacuation of Saint Domingue and the abolition of the British slave trade in 1807. For nearly two decades, all British expeditions

---

[37] Laurent Dubois, *A Colony of Citizens: Revolution and Slave Emancipation in the Slave Caribbean 1787–1804* (Chapel Hill, University of North Carolina Press, 2004), ch. 5 and 6.

in the circum-Caribbean from the coast of South America to New Orleans were dependent upon these West Indian regiments.[38]

The zone of freedom in the Caribbean stabilized by 1798 and then contracted because of unresolved conflicts within France itself. The prospect of the total loss of its colonies had been an important consideration in the decree of 16 Pluviôse. Many French revolutionaries never abandoned the idea that the tropical colonies should remain a source of wealth and power as well as military bases for the empire. Given British naval superiority and French continental priorities it was necessary for the French Caribbean to be largely self-sustaining in manpower. Thousands of former slaves, eager to abandon the regimen of the plantation were recruited as corsairs and soldiers. Those remaining on the land, however, had to supply both the food for internal sustenance and for exports exchangeable for vital manufactures and war supplies.

The one constant principle shared by British, Spanish, French, and Caribbean elites alike was that the Caribbean territories had to be retained as plantation systems. If British and Spanish authorities in Saint Domingue offered freedom in exchange for taking up arms, they never wavered in their commitment to sustain and restore slave labor. The French offered legal freedom, but linked it to compulsory labor. When Sonthonax decreed the abolition of slavery in Saint-Domingue, he and Polverel intended to retain nonmilitary slaves as agricultural workers tied to their plantations like contemporary European serfs. They were to work under conditions of compulsory remuneration. Victor Hugues introduced the same system in Guadeloupe. Emancipation was given with strings attached. It entailed a debt to the liberators. Ex-slaves could discharge that debt only by military or agricultural service. Former slaves were not redesignated simply as citizens, but as "cultivators." In Guadeloupe, anyone who refused assigned work was to be punished as a counter-revolutionary.

Freedom did not entitle ex-slaves to wages or to equal remuneration. In Guadeloupe, military costs were too high to permit the payment of wages. The revolution, which abolished the legal status of slavery in Guadeloupe, preserved a hierarchy of social distinctions based upon social utility. It increased the feminization of the plantation economy. In Saint Domingue, too, the workforce was feminized by military recruitment. Women were rewarded less than men. The outcome was a series of struggles over conditions of labor and leisure. French colonial policy was unable to "reconcile the promise of freedom with the economic exigencies deemed necessary for the survival of empire." Liberation remained configured by hierarchies, gender, and age. In Guadeloupe, Victor Hugues took great pride in having avoided the disintegration and indiscipline of more chaotic Saint Domingue.

---

[38] See Roger Norman Buckley, *Slaves in Red Coats: The British West India Regiments, 1795–1815* (New Haven: Yale University Press), ch. 5.

Coercion was necessary to counteract the laziness and ferocity induced by the climate, deserters from the military, and vagabonds from the plantations. Both the costs of conducting the war and the wages of civil and military services were met with local resources.[39]

The necessity of preserving the plantation system was not just a priority for revolutionary Europeans acting independently or on behalf of the French government. Toussaint Louverture, Saint Domingue's effective ruler after 1798, felt impelled to revive the staple export economy to maintain his 20,000 to 40,000 man army. Like Hugues in Guadeloupe, he used his military to impose a labor system disciplined by corporal punishment. He even sought to revive the importation of African slaves to replenish the huge deficit of labor that had resulted from the ten year struggle. David Geggus speculates that slave deaths in revolutionary Saint Domingue possibly reached 170,000 or one-third of the colony's slave population of half a million in 1791. That would have been roughly equal to the losses of all the European armies (British, French, and Spanish) in the Caribbean.[40] To revive the colony's economy, Toussaint even promoted the return of white planters from exile to manage the plantations. In other cases, estates were leased out to the army officers who remained the essential base of power in the new order.

Toussaint ultimately paid a high price for resisting the former slaves' strong preferences for their own small landholdings. The revival of coerced gang labor on the sugar plantations was deeply resented. The presence of white planters probably exacerbated the former slaves' suspicions. The economic outcome reflected the latent struggle between the rulers searching for saleable and taxable commodities and the ex-slaves searching for permanent release from plantation discipline. With the return of internal peace in 1800–1801, coffee production reached two-thirds of its 1789 level. Sugar,

---

[39] For the paragraphs above, I rely on Dubois, *A Colony of Citizens*, 343; 436;194–217; 284–288, and Frédéric Régent, *Esclavage, Métissage, Liberté: La Révolution française en Guadeloupe 1789–1802* (Paris: Bernard Grasset, 2004, 339–344.

[40] Geggus, in "Slavery, War and Revolution," estimates European military deaths at 180,000, (24–25). In a personal estimate of the loss of male slaves, David Geggus cautiously supplied me with a range of estimates. I have not included in these figures the tens of thousands of white and colored free civilians, and the upwards of 75,000 enslaved women lost to the colony through death and exile. Laurent Dubois estimates a corresponding population loss in Guadeloupe at 40,000. I have seen no estimates for the smaller French colonies between 1794 and 1802. The brutality of war was not bound by a simple black and white dichotomy. When Jean-Jacque Dessalines defeated André Rigaud to make Toussaint Louverture master of the entire colony, his troops executed thousands of southerners in reprisals after the fighting. Garrigus, *Before Haiti*, 305. In the aftermath of restoration, the reprisals against the ex-slaves were as bloody as Dessalines's executions of whites at the end of the war with Napoleon. Thousands of the nonwhite population may have been killed or deported by the French in reimposing slavery in Guadeloupe. Dubois, *Colony of Citizens*, 404.

the most important prerevolutionary cash output crop, fared much worse. Raw sugar production was down 80 percent. The output of more processed "clayed" or semirefined sugar had virtually vanished. In 1799, Guadeloupe coffee production under Victor Hugues was nearly two-thirds of what it had been in 1790, but sugar production had dropped by two-thirds.[41]

Toussaint's revival of the plantation system raised sufficient discontent that one of his best commanders, General Moïse, rose against the regime and paid with his life. Across the Atlantic, a victorious Napoleon Bonaparte decided to restore full French authority in the Caribbean colonies. As soon as peace briefly returned to Europe in 1801, the French reinvaded the island. Some of Toussaint's generals surrendered to the French to protect the property gains they had made during the previous decade. Toussaint himself was captured and deported. Another branch of the French military rapidly reconquered Guadeloupe. Its commanding general was ordered to restore slavery. A final uprising was led by the free colored men, Joseph Ignace and Louis Delgrès, but failed to rouse the mass of black cultivators. The latter mistrusted a group that had repeatedly suppressed their own insurrectional movements.[42]

French repression in Guadeloupe and the reopening of the slave trade had the effect of reunifying and galvanizing both the black and free colored populations of Saint Domingue against the French forces. Massive insurrection now replaced fragmented resistance. A French campaign of terror aroused more desperation than fear. With the resumption of war in Europe in 1803, the British navy cut off all possibility of large-scale French reinforcements reaching the island. The desperate brutality of the French army, now devastated by disease, was matched by the ferocity of the revolutionaries.

In its final battle for independence, Haiti became the scene of the most transformative event of the age of revolution. The old master class disappeared along with the institution of chattel slavery. In the end, it was the new Haitian victors who were to carry the conflict to its nearly genocidal climax, massacring most of the French who had not reached the blockading British warships and surrendered. The legacy of the plantation complex, which had impacted the economic policies of Sonthonax, Hugues, Toussaint, and Napoleon Bonaparte alike, continued to attract their Haitian successors. Dessalines (1804–1806) like Toussaint, attempted to negotiate a large-scale reopening of the African labor supply. His successors also tried to revive the plantations and forced labor. Haiti's *Rural Code* was grist for British planter propaganda in the debates over emancipation in the 1820s. Only in the 1830s, did Haitian rulers abandon the policy of coerced labor.

---

[41] On Guadeloupe, see Dubois, *A Colony of Citizens*, 214, 217; James Stephen, *Crisis of the Sugar Colonies* (London: J. Hatchard, 1802), 17. On Haiti, see Geggus, *Haitian Revolutionary Studies*, 23.

[42] Régent, *Esclavage Métissage*, 436–437, Dubois, *A Colony*, 387–401.

With regard to the surrounding Caribbean, the tenuousness of France's commitment to emancipation had become evident well before Napoleon's full restoration of slavery. When the French conquered the Netherlands in 1795, they initiated a revolutionary Batavian Republic but made no effort to induce their satellite to adopt colonial emancipation. On the contrary, at that time emancipation had not even been implemented in the French half of the island of St. Martin, where implementation of the decree of 16 Pluviôse had been forestalled by Dutch military occupation. A year later, French forces in the eastern Caribbean again made no effort to support a slave rebellion in Dutch Curaçao. When the French later attempted to occupy the island, they declared themselves in support of the status quo.[43] In neighboring Spanish dominated Santo Domingo, the French revolutionaries were hardly more active. After Spain's cession of the colony to France in 1795, some republican officials distributed copies of the emancipation decree, but the Spanish administrator resisted its implementation, denying that emancipation had been part of the treaty. Spanish slave law remained in full force. Nor did the rebel armies of French Saint Domingue intervene. Overt slave resistance was confined to one plantation uprising in 1796.[44] The institution would not be abolished until Toussaint invaded the eastern part of the island and apparently introduced abolition in 1801.

In France itself, the decree of 16 Pluviôse and its extension of freedom to the colonial empire was defended in the national legislature after the fall of the Jacobins and supported by a revived *Amis des Noirs*. However, the principle of general freedom remained under constant public assault by repatriated white Caribbean refugees and their allies. Their axiom of the essential difference between the tropical colonies and the metropole was also generally affirmed by French colonial agents. They also emphasized the limitations of freedom when applied to uncivilized Africans in tropical climates. The repeated failure of the French republic to implement its emancipation decree in its Indian Ocean colonies remained a constant reminder of the limited concern of Paris to impose abolition when not forced to do so by overwhelming slave resistance or the threat of imminent foreign conquest.

Even before Bonaparte's restoration of colonial slavery, his first constitution signaled the restoration of the principle of fundamental difference between European France and the overseas tropics. The decree reviving the institution of slavery in 1802 reduced the diversity of labor regimes that had emerged from the events of the 1790s. The principles of civil liberty and equality were affirmed for inhabitants of France. Chattel slavery and racial

---

[43] Cornelius Ch. Goslinga, the Dutch in the Caribbean and Surinam, 1791/5–1942 (Assen: Van Gorcum, 1990) 1–20.

[44] David Geggus, "Slave Resistance in the Spanish Caribbean in the mid-1790s," in *A Turbulent Time: The French Revolution and the Greater Caribbean* ed. David Barry Gaspar and David Patrick Geggus, eds. (Bloomington: Indiana University Press, 1997, 131–155.

hierarchy were restored in the colonies. Indeed, the differentiation between metropolis and colonies was standardized more rigorously than ever before. Blacks were officially prohibited from residing in continental France. For citizens of France, the revolutionary land settlement was sustained. In the colonies, the gains of the free colored population were negated. Only in Haiti, beyond the reach of Napoleonic power, was the right to property in persons constitutionally abolished.

The impact of the French Caribbean revolutions extended well beyond the boundaries of the empire. The revolutions shattered the enormous psychological weight of a system of slavery that had seemed inexorable despite intermittent black resistance from the coast of Africa to the plantations and towns of the Americas. For New World slaves in particular, the creation of a state peopled by citizens of African descent affirmed the possibility of freedom from both slavery and racial inferiority. Historians have increasingly detailed the reverberations of French slave revolutions across the Caribbean and through mainland North and South America. Many have emphasized the role of these revolutions in inspiring hope among slaves and fear and paranoia among the master class.[45]

As we shall see, however, many abolitionists, black as well as white, preferred not to dwell upon heroic slave violence that was so intimately entangled with atrocities. They were able to insist that violence was the inevitable consequence of the institution of slavery, not the nature of the enslaved. Toward the end of the age of revolution, some Europeans furthest removed from the bloodshed portrayed postrevolutionary Haiti in a very hopeful light.[46] If historians have sometimes exaggerated the heritage of Saint Domingue in individual conspiracies or revolts, its independence continually served as a generic inspiration throughout the age of revolution. Haiti more rarely served as a direct source of aid. Haitian governments were usually far more concerned with their own nation's survival than

---

[45] See, inter alia, *The Impact of the Haitian Revolution in the Atlantic World*, David P. Geggus, ed. (Columbia, SC: University of South Carolina Press, 2001); Alfred N. Hunt, *Haiti's Influence on Antebellum America: Slumbering Volcano in the Caribbean* (Baton Rouge: Louisiana State University Press, 1988); and Eugene D. Genovese, *From Rebellion to Revolution: Afro-American Slave Revolts in the Making of the New World* (Baton Rouge: Louisiana State University Press, 1981).

[46] See Karin Schüller, "From Liberalism to Racism: German Historians, Journalists, and the Haitian Revolution from the Late Eighteenth to the Early Twentieth Centuries," in *The Impact of the Haitian Revolution in the Atlantic World*, David Geggus, ed. (Columbia, S.C. University of South Carolina Press, 2001), 23–43; David Geggus, "British Opinion and the Emergence of Haiti, 1791–1805," in *Slavery and British Society*, James Walvin, ed. (London: Macmillan, 1982) 123–149; Geggus, "Haiti and the Abolitionists: Opinion, Propaganda and International Politics in Britain and France, 1804–1838," in *Abolition and its Aftermath: The Historical Context 1790–1916*, David Richardson, ed. (London: Frank Cass, 1985), 113–140 and Geggus, "Epilogue," in *Impact of the Haitian Revolution*, 247–252.

with its revolutionary potential. Postrevolutionary Haitian rulers needed to assure outlets for trade and protect their independence. From Toussaint's first disclosure of a revolutionary expedition to Jamaica in 1798 through Henri Christophe's careful cultivation of relations with sympathetic Britons, Haitian rulers were anxious to enter the world of sovereign nations rather than commit their resources toward ending the institution of slavery abroad.

Franco-Caribbean Revolutionary Impact

The Haitian Revolution had its strongest impact at the southern end of the greater Caribbean. Its direct role in stimulating the abolition of slave trade and the general emancipation of slaves elsewhere was meager. In the three decades following the outbreak of the Haitian Revolution, no European empire was inspired by its example to take definitive steps toward ending overseas slavery. Every one of the continental states that sustained the institution of slavery in 1804 remained officially committed to the maintenance of their slave colonies. Indeed, on the eve of the abolition of the British slave trade, Russia's government became the last European power to explore the possibility of acquiring a French colony in the Caribbean. Britain and the United States, the two major slave importing states that prohibited further slaving before Napoleon's defeat in 1814, clearly did not act under the immediate impact of the Haitian or French Revolutions. In 1792, Denmark was the first European power to enact a gradual abolition decree. The only important external consideration in Denmark's deliberations arose from its erroneous estimate that Britain was also on the verge of enacting abolition. Denmark's abolition law of 1792 allowed its possessions a decade to fully stock up on imported slaves.[47] The result was that during the whole period of the Saint Domingue revolt, record numbers of Africans were disembarked in the Danish Caribbean. Neither the Danish government nor the colonial planters seem to have been particularly concerned about the danger of slave rebellion. The significance of this record-breaking pace of Danish slaving during the decade of massive French slave resistance has usually been overlooked.[48]

The French and Saint Domingue revolutions probably contributed more to delaying than accelerating the passage of British abolition in 1806–1807. When the 1806 bill finally passed the British Parliament, both the threat from Haiti and the threat of slave insurgency in the British islands were at a low ebb. At the climax of the parliamentary debate in the House of Commons, the Cabinet member who opened the debate minimized the danger of slave

---

[47] See Sven E. Green-Pedersen, "Denmark's Ophaevelse af Negerslavhandelen" [Denmark's Abolition of the Slave Trade] *Arkiv*, 3:1 (1969), 19–37. The importation of Africans into the Danish Caribbean did not cease until after Britain captured the islands in 1807.

[48] See, Eltis, et al., Slave Trade Database.

insurrection. When Foreign Secretary Lord Howick opened the major debate on the British Abolition Bill in February 1807, he casually noted, "Look at the state of [our] islands for the last 20 years and say, is it not notorious that there never were so few insurrections among the negroes, as a the very time they knew that such an abolition of this infamous traffic was under discussion?" In a packed House of Commons, not a single MP rose to challenge his observation.[49]

In the Caribbean, Jamaica was the principal British colonial beneficiary of the Haitian revolution before 1807. Jamaica's exports of sugar increased by 35,000 tons from 1786–1790 to 1801–1805. That quantity was more than three and a half times greater than Cuba's increase. During the first decade of the nineteenth century, Jamaica led the world in exports of both sugar and coffee. So, rather than fearing the "seeds of destruction," Jamaican planters led the West Indian attack on abolition as being ruinous to its own future growth and competitiveness. Whatever the "fear factor" was elsewhere, David Geggus has drawn attention to Jamaica's enigmatic status as an island of stability in the revolutionary Caribbean of the 1790s. Still more striking then, was Jamaica's relative freedom from slave uprisings throughout the entire age of revolution. One of the most turbulent British colonies prior to the last quarter of the eighteenth century, Jamaica experienced no major uprising between Tacky's revolt in 1760 and the great "Baptist War" in 1831.[50]

In none of its major abolitionist decisions did the British government act on the premise that the danger of accumulating slaves outweighed the risks of expansion. In 1806, the most proabolitionist ministry to come into office during the twenty-year debate over slave trade abolition made a firm decision to retain the portion of conquered Dutch Guiana (Demerara), which had a higher percentage of newly imported Africans in Guiana than any of those in Britain's long-established colonies. Moreover, if Britain restored the rest of Guiana (Suriname) to its former Dutch rulers, the British government was

---

49 Hansard's *Parliamentary Debates* (henceforth (*P.D.*) VIII (1806–07), col. 952. In his account of slave resistance during the era of British Caribbean slavery, Michael Craton finds that "nowhere in the British West Indies did slaves rise up unaided on French revolutionary principles," and, "as planters were quick to point out, far more British West Indian slaves rallied to the aid of the imperial regime than actually rebelled... The white Frenchmen threatening invasion were accompanied by francophone blacks – foreigners all." Craton, *Testing the Chains: Resistance to Slavery in the British West Indies* (Ithaca: Cornell University Press, 1982), 165–168. In Parliament, the abolitionists asserted that the victims of the slave trade were future seeds of destruction, but their opponents consistently maintained that abolitionist propaganda, not slaves, was the principal stimulus to insurrections.

50 David Geggus, "The Enigma of Jamaica in the 1790s: New Light on the Causes of Slave Rebellions," *William and Mary Quarterly*, 44: 2 (April 1987), 274–279. The Jamaica maroons did revolt in 1795–1796, but were not joined by significant numbers of slaves. See also Craton, *Testing the Chains*, ch. 13, 14, and 17.

prepared to ask for nothing less than Cuba in compensation. Cuba had just become the largest single importer of slaves in the Caribbean. Beyond the Caribbean, in Africa, the British navy had just added the slave-importing Dutch Cape Colony to its roster of conquests in 1806. In South America, a British expeditionary force captured Buenos Aires, the slave-importing capital of Rio de la Plata. Thus, on the eve of abolition, the British empire increased its potential as a slave empire more than ten-fold.[51]

During 1806, British government purchases of African slaves for West Indian regiments also reached their all time peak.[52] For any government primarily concerned about the risks of slave revolts, especially in colonies worked by newly landed Africans, multiplying such risks in three separate areas of the globe would have been a policy bordering on insanity. Indeed, British Ministers, like British planters, made the same assessment about the high value of the slave trade to foreign colonies. In fact, so did the abolitionists. In 1805 and 1806, it was the parliamentary abolitionists who led the charge in demanding that British slave traders be prohibited from carrying Africans to foreign or conquered colonies. Interdicting the slave trade would hobble the economy of the enemy. So, the abolitionist rationale for passing foreign trade prohibition a few months before the Act of 1807 was that fresh slaves were "seeds of production" not "seeds of destruction." It was no accident that Abolitionist James Stephen was the author of Britain's most important polemic in favor of interdiction, and, in 1806, he drafted the Foreign Abolition Bill for the government.[53]

Even abolitionist propaganda downplayed Saint Domingue at the beginning of 1807. William Wilberforce's *Letter on the Abolition of the Slave Trade* was by far the longest abolitionist tract ever to appear against the slave trade. For the first 320 pages of its 350 page text, Africans were unrelentingly portrayed as helpless enslaved victims of brutality, racism, degradation, and neglect. Finally, on page 320, Wilberforce announced that he had to "mention two or three additional considerations," but he promised that he would "not dwell long on them." Among them was the "danger

[51] Seymour Drescher, *Econocide: British Slavery in the Era of Abolition* (Pittsburgh: University of Pittsburgh Press, 1977), 102–103; and Davis Geggus, "The Enigma of Jamaica in the 1790s: New Light on the Causes of Slave Rebellions," *William and Mary Quarterly*, 44:2 (1987), 274–299.

[52] Buckley, *Slaves in Red Coats*, 55, Table 1. Even the rate of resistance aboard slave ships appears to have dropped during the decade before 1807. The nineteen recorded incidents during the decade 1797–1806 were little more than one-third of the fifty-three recorded in 1783–1792. This earlier decade was the last one of peace before abolition as well as the apogée of the entire transatlantic slave trade. My thanks to David Eltis for his help in cruising the database.

[53] Roger Anstey, *The Atlantic Slave Trade and British Abolition 1760–1810* (Atlantic Highlands, NJ: Humanities Press, 1975), 368; and Seymour Drescher, "Civilizing Insurgency: Two Variants of Slave Revolts," in *Who Abolished Slavery? Slave Revolts and Abolition*, Seymour Drescher and P.C. Emmer, eds. (forthcoming).

of insurrections." Why the understatement? For Wilberforce in 1807, Haiti still represented "the wild licentiousness of a neighboring kingdom," enjoying none of the blessings of "true liberty" under the British Constitution. The danger arising from slave imports might ultimately be inevitable. At the moment, however, Britain was enjoying "a happy interval" in which she might "providentially . . . avert the gathering storm."[54]

In 1807, then, the Haitian Revolution played more of a role in limiting demands for antislavery reform to the prohibition of the transatlantic trade. Immediate emancipation, warned Howick, would only produce "horrors similar to those at St. Domingo." If colonial slaves were human and brethren they were still largely African and savage: "It must be remembered," noted another abolitionist MP, that "Dessalines himself was an imported African."[55] Both pre- and postrevolutionary Haiti were models to be avoided, not emulated.

In the decade following independence, Haiti itself had more reason to feel threatened than threatening. Its rulers had every reason to look to Britain and its command of the seas for protection against any renewal of French designs. In the United States, the slave revolution and Haitian independence evoked a greater sense of alarm, intermixed with interludes of potential business opportunity.[56] Beginning with Jefferson's administration, nonrecognition of Haiti became a cornerstone of United States foreign policy for sixty years. Haiti's very existence was regarded by Southern politicians, including most of America's presidents, as a potential threat to the tranquility of the union. The new black nation also remained an indelible presence in the minds of both slave conspirators and their suppressors.

In the Caribbean area, the decline in French staple production after Haitian independence seems on the whole to have been a stronger incentive for planters to continue slave imports from Africa than were fears of the trade's danger to the institution of slavery. Jamaica and Cuba, the islands closest to Haiti, continued or accelerated their importations of Africans during the most turbulent dozen years between the Saint Domingue uprising and the debacle of Napoleon's army. Moreover, it is unlikely that any substantial body of planters in any major slave zone bordering the Gulf of Mexico or the

---

[54] Wilberforce, *Letter*, 258–259; 320–324.
[55] *P.D.* ser. 1, vol. 8 (1806–1807), cols. 952, 955, 970, 975.
[56] At the end of the 1790s, both Anglo-American governments looked upon Napoleon as a far more threatening than Toussaint L'Ouverture. Toussaint was equally disposed to bolster his semi-independent status through American and British mercantile connections. See *The Life and Correspondence of Rufus King*, Charles R. King, ed. (New York: 1895–96) II, 474 ff. Rufus King to Lord Grenville, Dec. 1, 1798; King to U. S. Secretary of State, Dec. 7, 1798; King to Henry Dundas, Dec. 8, 1798; Dundas to King Dec. 9, 1798. After Haitian independence, however, Thomas Jefferson's administration launched a campaign to bar interaction with the new state.

Caribbean petitioned their imperial decision makers to end the transatlantic slave trade. At most, states temporarily restricted the inflow of slaves out of fear of rebellious contagion. Most reopened their doors to "fresh" Africans by the early nineteenth century, including North America, via Charleston and New Orleans.

The fact that every slave system, but the Franco-Dutch alliance, was moving record numbers of slaves from Africa during the years of maximum slave resistance (1792–1804) should tell us something about the relative impact of revolutionary resistance upon buyers and carriers of slaves in the Atlantic system during those dramatic years. Notoriously, South Carolina, demographically the most preponderantly slave state in the American union, raised United States' imports from Africa to their all time peak in the years between the crushing of Napoleon's army in Haiti and the passage of the U.S. prohibition of further importation on slavery. Imports of slaves into British, Spanish, and Brazilian ports were all higher during the fifteen years after the outbreak of the Saint Domingue slave insurgency than they had been in the fifteen years before. Iberian imports would increase still more dramatically after the Anglo-American abolitions.[57]

No country better illustrates the ambiguous impact of history's most successful slave uprising in the age of revolution than France. At the outbreak of the French Revolution, its antislavery movement was ideologically robust and institutionally weak. French abolitionists insisted on linking abolition of the slave trade to a legislative commitment to ending the institution of slavery as well. This bold commitment probably added to the early unification of interests opposed to the *Amis des Noirs*. The opponents were quite successful in that tactic. There is no evidence whatever of a large-scale nationwide campaign to open the question of abolition in the two years before or after the mass slave uprising. The broadest popular antislavery manifestations in France came only in the wake of the abolition of slavery on 16 Pluviôse – a total of nineteen or twenty celebrations. Thereafter, commemorations on the anniversary of emancipation became more sporadic and appear to have disappeared before Napoleon's restoration of slavery and the slave trade in 30 Floréal Year X (May 20, 1802). A month later (June 30th) the law excluding blacks and people of color from metropolitan France passed in its entirety without visable popular protest. Indeed, when Napoleon in his memoirs retrospectively sought to exculpate himself from the disaster that followed his colonial venture, he pointed to the colonial,

---

[57] See, for example, Paul Lachance, "Repercussions of the Haitian Revolution in Louisiana," in Geggus, *Impact*, 209–230. After 1802, Louisiana even reversed its exclusion of French refugees from Haiti. More than a thousand were admitted from Jamaica in 1803 and more than ten thousand from Cuba in 1809. (*Ibid.*, 213). The second migration required the suspension of America's abolition act of 1807.

merchant, and refugee clamor that led him to undertake the reconquest of Saint Domingue.[58]

More than anything else, the aftermath of Haitian independence indicates some of the limited effects of even the most successful slave uprising in history. Before abolishing its own transatlantic slave trade in 1807, British governments offered to negotiate a bilateral abolition with France. The first offer, in 1801, came as Napoleon was negotiating the retrieval and expansion of France's transatlantic territories as part of the short-term peace of Amiens. The second offer came in 1806, during a new round of peace negotiations between Britain and France. Napoleon rejected such proposals both before and after his catastrophic defeat by the Haitians. Even after both Haiti and Louisiana were irretrievably lost, the French ruler made no effort to recruit liberated slaves in an attempt to undermine the British slave colonies. A decade after France's unprecedented defeat in the Caribbean, the same imperial nation that had lost most of its slave system during the New World revolutions still refused to accept or even envision the triumphant self-emancipation of Haiti as an irreversible achievement. Initially, disasterous defeat led only to deeper denial. The statistical yearbook for France and its colonies in the year of Haitian independence still offered its readers Saint Domingue's trade and production statistics for the year 1788. A thick veil of censoring silence was thrown over the intervening events.

The French capitulation and Haitian independence were both treated as reversable episodes in an ongoing Caribbean conflict. Even brief news accounts of the details of horrific losses were buried beneath accounts of French triumphs in Europe. The small French military remnant in eastern Santo Domingo fed the illusion that the continuing internecine conflicts between successive Haitian leaders (Dessalines, Henri Christophe, and Pétion) would lead to the victorious return of the French. When stalled "progress" was occasionally noted, the blame was thrown upon the British navy. Even in retrospect, Haitian agency was given no quarter. The nation's existence and endurance was ascribed to the cursed memory of the *Amis des Noirs*. The only aspects of Haitian events allowed to appear in the heavily censored Napoleonic press were descriptions of the savage ferocity and appetite for booty among the rebels, and the interracial conflicts between blacks and browns. News of the general massacre of the French who remained in Haiti in 1804, was circulated in newspaper accounts of babies impaled or slaughtered on their mother's bosoms. French atrocities were never recounted. Descriptions of Emperor Dessalines's wife focused upon her "hair, or rather her wool," adorned with pearls and flowers. The

[58] See Jean-Claude Halpern, "The Revolutionary Festivals and the Abolition of Slavery in Year II," in Dorigny, *Abolitions*, 155–165; and "The Restoration of Slavery by Bonaparte," in *ibid.*, 229–236.

final capitulation of the French garrison in eastern Santo Domingo was attributed to disease and the English.[59]

Throughout the years of Napoleon's ever-decreasing colonial empire and the absence of any tangible commercial benefits to France tenure, the emperor showed no sign of deviating from his policy of restoring the prerevolutionary social structure and economy of the colonies. At the beginning of his reign, French officials briefly toyed with the idea of using the ex-slaves as warriors for French expansion rather than as plantation captives. Napoleon was more attracted by the possibility of restoring France's slave empire in Saint Domingue and expanding it into Louisiana.[60]

In the wake of its two momentous revolutions, France, therefore, had the distinction of being the only European nation ever to restore both slavery and the slave trade. The number of French citizens enslaved by their own government in 1802 probably far exceeded the number of Africans seized by French traders under force of arms during the whole era of the Atlantic slave trade. After the resumption of hostilities with France in 1803, the British fleet again shut down the French African trade and slowly conquered what was left of France's slave empire in the Indian Ocean and the Caribbean.

With the return of peace in 1814, France was again free to reenter the overseas world with a clean slate. The restored Bourbon monarchy fulfilled its reputation for having learned nothing and forgotten nothing. It aimed at an even more complete erasure of the age of revolution in its former colonies than in France itself. Louis XVIII's foreign ministry successfully negotiated for the return of most of its slave colonies. Although the British had abolished their transatlantic slave trade five years earlier, Talleyrand, the French Foreign Minister, argued that the British slave colonies had several years notice to stock up on Africans, with nearly 700,000 slaves imported between 1791 and 1807. The French negotiated the right to reassert its sovereignty over all former colonies lost during the long wars with England. Haiti's commercial potential was still measured by the vanished values of Saint Domingue in 1791. France's refusal to accept Haitian independence makes it evident why all of Haiti's rulers carefully avoided any attempt to export their revolution and cultivated British amity from the moment Toussaint achieved de facto autonomy from 1798. In response to news from

---

[59] See André Cabanis and Michel L. Martin, "L'Independence d'Haiti devant l'opinion publique française sous le consulat èt l'empire: ignorance et malentendus," *Mourir pour les Antilles: independence nègre ou l'esclavage, 1802–1804*, Michel L. Martin and Alain Yacou, eds. (Paris: Editions Caribéennes 1991).

[60] Robert L. Paquette, "Revolutionary Saint-Domingue in the Making of Territorial Louisiana," in Gaspar and Geggus, *Turbulent*, 204–220. Neither before nor after the expedition's failure was Napoleon responsive to any diminution of France's slave system. On the contrary, looking toward both the recovery of Saint Domingue and the acquisition of Louisiana from the Spanish, Napolean's "Western Design" envisioned only an expansion of slavery.

France, King Henri Christophe immediately began to plan a repetition of Haiti's scorched earth tactics of 1802–03 to render any reinvasion valueless to the French.

The British reaction will be dealt with in another chapter, but French public opinion was again dominated by the lobbying activities of the merchants and colonial refugees resident in France. In the wake of the "miracle" of the restored Bourbon dynasty's return, the old colonial interests saw another miraculous possibility in a restored Saint Domingue.[61] The port merchants had vigorously supported the return of the Bourbons. The King was fearful of any negative impact that immediate French abolition might produce on a loyal group in a restive France. A large number of ex-colonists were awarded lifetime tenures in the newly created upper legislative house, the Chamber of Peers. "No colony," concludes Paul Kielstra, "not even Algeria, was more intimately linked [than Saint Domingue] to the deep fibres of French life."[62]

In the wake of Napoleon's defeat at Waterloo, the memory of Haiti combined with British abolitionist pressure encouraged a French identification of antislavery with antipatriotism. Returning to Paris in 1814 for the first time since 1789, Thomas Clarkson was deeply disappointed by the disarray of the abolitionists in Paris. They had "not one Shilling" for propaganda, and again had to rely on the London Committee – this time even for funds.[63] Against mobilized hostility, French abolitionists were hopelessly weak. Of the surviving *Amis de Noirs*, the Abbé Gregoire was identified not only with the Caribbean slave revolution, but the execution of Louis XVI in Paris. Moderate liberal intellectuals were few in number and suspect to the incoming regime. French opposition to further steps to abolition at the public level became increasingly apparent in the fall of 1814. Both legislative houses of the new government strongly opposed any further concessions to Britain. The French government requested an anxious English government to wait for public opinion to subside. Only news of Haiti's deadly serious determination to fight another invasion to the death dampened French enthusiasm.

The volatility of the situation was illustrated only a few months later. In the spring of 1815, Napoleon triumphantly returned to France. The Bourbons fled. The emperor decreed the abolition of the French slave trade, although his edict was violated in French ports within a week. When Waterloo once more opened the door to the return to power of the Bourbon

---

[61] On the range and influence of pressure groups in post-Napoleonic France, see the comprehensive study of Paul Michael Kielstra, *The Politics of Slave Trade Suppression in Britain and France, 1814–1848* (London: Macmillan Press, 2000), 15–21. Olivier Pétré-Grenouilleau points out that in 1815 the *mentalité* of the mercantile class was still profoundly affected by the memory of their prerevolutionary prosperity. The first post-war reflex was a return to the past: See *Les Négoces maritimes français xviie–xxe siècle* (Paris: Belin, 1997), 161–165.

[62] Kielstra, *Politics* 19.

[63] Ellen Gibson Wilson, *Thomas Clarkson: A Biography* (London: Macmillan, 1989), 228, n. 55.

monarch, the king could no longer resist the demands of his British saviors. The British made retention of Napoleon's decree of abolition an implicit condition for Louis XVIII's uncontested return to his throne.

Enforcement of the decree was another matter. For the remaining years of the dynasty, the French legislature wrangled over the lax enforcement of the officially abolished French slave trade.[64] In the decade after Waterloo, the (now illicit) French slave trade climbed to levels rivaling those reached by French slavers in the 1770s. After Waterloo, no one in the French Chambers openly defended the (now illegal) African slave trade. Enforcement of a semi-coerced law invited an attitude of laxity in the whole chain of officialdom. To an elite in postrevolutionary shock, the Saint Domingue (never called the Haitian) uprising, was mentioned only rarely and obliquely in legislative debates. Slave revolution was treated as an event so savage as to need no elaboration. "Massacre" was omnipresent as a synonym for Saint Domingue. The "first disasters" had left France with "too many ruins" either to mention or forget. The very name of the former colony, able "to awaken revolt and massacre," had to be banished. Only once in the Chamber of Deputies was there an outburst of emotion over the subject. In 1821, a moderate abolitionist announced that the real ending of the French slave trade would also end the vicious elements of colonial "discipline" – death, disabling, and whipping. The reaction to his intervention would not have been unfamiliar to U.S. congressmen of the same era. The French abolitionist was immediately shouted down with accusations that his words would lead to assassination and massacre, just as they had thirty years before.[65]

When Haiti finally achieved formal recognition from the French monarchy in 1825, it would be at the cost of agreeing to pay an indemnity of 150 million francs in gold to compensate the families of the former plantation owners. The new nation was thus thrown deeply into debt to finance the schedule of payments. From the metropolitan perspective, the government wished to vindicate the legitimacy of colonial property as well as to aid former Saint Domingue landowners. Just as France was the only European imperial power to reinstate the institution after formal emancipation, so Haiti became the only ex-slave society in which the children of the fiercest resistors in the New World were forced to pay compensation to the descendants of their masters. The very nation whose slaves had first abolished an institution upheld by three of Europe's major colonial powers also paid the

[64] Kielstra, *Politics*, 61–137.
[65] See Elodie Le Garrec, "Le débat sur l'abolition de la traite des Noirs en France (1814–1831): Un reflet de l'évolution politique, economique et culturelle de la France. Thesis Université Britagne Sud, 2002–2003; 202–206. Of course, it was easier to conjure up the image of African or servile savagery if one never in the same breath evoked the Euro-European massacres of the Vendée, Spain, Calabria, etc. of the French revolutionary and Napoleonic decades. See David A. Bell, *The First Total War: Napoleon's Europe and the Birth of Warfare as We Know It* (Boston: Houghton Mifflin, 2007), ch. 5–8.

heaviest price in long-term costs: militarization, a truncated civil society, and poor economic development. It would be almost two centuries, and four French Republics later, before this injustice was officially recognized by a French legislature.[66]

Recognition of Haitian independence in 1825 hardly improved the status of antislavery in France. The combined effects of the French and Caribbean revolutions made it impossible to reorganize a formal abolitionist movement even at the elite level. Even leading antislavery political liberals such as the duc de Broglie, Benjamin Constant, and Auguste de Staël, did not want to be openly associated with the Abbé Grégoire. Nothing better summed up the situation of French abolitionism in the four decades after the outbreak of the slave revolt in Saint Domingue. The Abbé lived in frozen political isolation, stigmatized as the incendiary of two worlds. His very existence inhibited the reformation of an abolitionist society in France.[67]

The one extra-parliamentary organization pressing for strict suppression of illegal slave trading was a subcommittee of a society dedicated to collecting information on issues of social and international morality – the *Société de la Morale Chrétienne* (Society of Christian Morality). The subcommittee's very composition exposed members to charges of being "Unfrench." Five of the sixteen were foreigners. Its research was supplied chiefly by British abolitionists.[68] The quiet activity of this minuscule antislave trade group was emblematic of the larger and longer French context. The legacy of a generation of upheavals had left French civil society severely truncated in the name of order. All associational activity was restricted by law and subject to close scrutiny by police spies. The prerevolutionary *police des noirs* had been superceded by the policing of everyone. Newspapers, the lifeblood of the public sphere, were subject to close censorship. It was this comparative dearth of associational activity in his own country that most struck Tocqueville when he began to travel through America in 1831. He was now aware of the relative apathy of localities back in France, "an apathy so invincible that society seems to vegetate rather than thrive."[69]

---

[66] See Eugène Itayienne, "La Normalisation des relations Franco-Hatiennes (1825–1838)," *Outre-Mers; Revue d'Histoire*, 90:(2) (2003), 139–154, Jochim Benoit "L'Indemnité coloniale de Saint-Domingue et la question des repatries," *Revue Historique*, 246: (2) (1971), 359–376.

[67] See Lawrence C. Jennings, *French Anti-Slavery The Movement for the Abolition of Slavery in France, 1802–1848* (New York: Cambridge University Press, 2000), 7–8; and Seymour Drescher, "Two Variants of anti-slavery: religious organization and social mobilization in Britain and France, 1780–1870," in *Anti-Slavery, Religion, and Reform* (Folkestone U.K. and Hamden CT: Dawson/Archon, 1980), 43–63.

[68] Serge Daget, "A Model of the French Abolitionist Movement and its Variations" in Bolt, *Anti-Slavery*, 64–79.

[69] Alexis de Tocqueville *Democracy in America*, trans. Arthur Goldhammer (New York: Library of America, 2004), 104 n. 51.

Out of this context two sharply contrasting models of British and Continental variants of abolitionism had emerged by the end of the age of revolution. The distinguishing characteristic of the British abolitionists variant was what we have come to think of as prototypical social movements. They attempted to bring public pressure to bear on hostile economic interests and reluctant or indifferent agencies of governments. At critical moments, they used a wide repertoire of tactics – mass propaganda, petitions, public meetings, lawsuits, and boycotts – presenting antislavery as a moral and political imperative. Organizationally, they were rooted in local communities. They aimed at recruiting participation of groups otherwise excluded by religion, gender, and race. Continental variants were usually confined to small self-selected groups. They were generally reluctant, or unable by law, to seek mass recruitment and collective action. They therefore attempted to act as brokers between governments and economic interest groups.

The two variants were not absolutely fixed. There were times when British abolitionist elites confined themselves to quiet lobbying. There were also moments when Continental movements broke out of their self- or governmentally imposed shells. This was especially true in moments of heightened public interest in large scale reform or a broadening of the public sphere.[70] This characteristic of antislavery activity was to be closely linked to expansions and contractions of civil society in Continental Europe for most of the century after 1775. The legacy of hyper-associational life in France during the Great Revolution served more to convince authoritarian regimes that associations were also breeding grounds for subversion and violence.

Across the Atlantic, the devastated new nation that emerged from the brutal and brutalizing struggle for freedom and independence was an enduring symbol of self-emancipation. But, postrevolutionary Haiti was as ill-prepared to play a leading role in expanding antislavery as was postrevolutionary France. Militarism became an enduring feature of Haitian politics throughout the nineteenth century. Authoritarian government was combined with popular alienation in social classes below the military-political elite. A revolution of unparalleled ferocity left the new nation with a truncated civil society. Even in domestic affairs, the inability of the populace to

---

[70] See "Two Variants of Anti-Slavery: Religious Organization and Social Mobilization in Britain and France, 1780–1870," in Drescher, *From Slavery to Freedom*, ch. 2; Sidney Tarrow, *Power in Movement: Social Movements Collective Action and Politics* (New York: Cambridge University Press, 1994), ch. 1; and Charles Tilly, "Social Movements and National Politics," in C. Bright and S. Harding, eds., *Statemaking and Social Movements: Essays in History and Theory* (Ann Arbor: University of Michigan Press, 1984), 297–317. For an overview of important national variants of the relationship between abolitionism and democratization on the European continent in the late eighteenth and nineteenth centuries, see *Abolir l'esclavage: Un réformisme à l'epreuve France, Portugal, Suisse, xviiie–xixe siècles*, Olivier Petrè-Grenouilleau, ed. (Rennes: Presses Universitaries de Rennes, 2008), esp. Petré-Grenouilleau, "Abolitionisme et democratization," 7–23.

make public claims to which the government would respond nonviolently made any Haitian collective movement to agitate against the institution of slavery beyond its own boundaries equally improbable.[71] Haiti's impact during the age of revolution would be felt primarily outside the French imperial orbit. For slaves and oppressed free blacks, its independence would evoke the possibility of radically transforming a world that denied them a share in a universalized liberty and equality.

The Saint Domingue revolution did not, however, radically alter the balance of power in the Atlantic world or beyond.[72] For opponents of antislavery, Haiti became a metaphor for dispossession and racial annihilation. Even for governments and less threatened elites, Haiti's postrevolutionary history offered cautionary evidence on the viability of commercial economies in postslave societies. Nevertheless, the age of revolution had undermined some eighteenth century axiomatic assumptions. Fifty years after the Declaration of Independence, the institution of Western slavery was no longer so consensually divided by oceans or climatic zones.

---

[71] David Nicholls, *From Dessalines to Duvalier: Race, Colour and National Independence in Haiti* (New Brunswick, NJ: Rutgers University Press, 1996), 245–252; Mimi Sheller, *Democracy after Slavery: Black Publics and Peasant Radicalism in Haiti and Jamaica* (Gainesville: University Press of Florida, 2000); Michel S. Laguerre *Military and Society in Haiti* (Knoxville: University of Tennessee Press, 1993).

[72] David Geggus's edition of *The Impact of the Haitian Revolution in the Atlantic World* appropriately focuses upon the reverberations of the Haitian revolution in North America, the Caribbean, and Europe. Evidence of its immediate impact in Brazil is meager and is still more so in sub-Saharan or northern Africa.

7

Latin American Revolutions, 1810s–1820s

The Spanish Empire, c. 1775–1825

Latin Americans entered the revolutionary process decades later than their Anglo-American and Franco-American counterparts. Different areas and different social segments had a range of predecessors from which to draw. The white elites who began the quest for greater autonomy in the colonies of mainland Spanish America envisioned a North American model and outcome. Events in France and Haiti had different meanings for observers on both sides of the Atlantic.[1] In Latin America, the revolutionary process began with elites seeking local autonomy within a society that they envisioned as retaining the social hierarchies of the colonial regime. One of their greatest fears, however, was that the outcome might take a Franco-American turn toward conflict over racial equality or, even more radically, toward slave liberation. They were unable to avoid a drift toward both of these shoals. The initial insurgents encountered divisions first among themselves and then within the free colored and slave populations. These conflicts would occasionally replicate the terror and economic devastation of the Franco-Caribbean revolutions. The Spanish-American variant would ultimately resemble neither the Anglo-American nor the Franco-Caribbean revolutions in most respects, but would have a similarly ambivalent result for the fate of slavery.

The structure of Latin American society profoundly affected the process of its revolutions. At the outset, South America was neither overwhelmingly white and free like North America nor overwhelmingly black and slave like the French overseas colonies. In mainland Spanish America, slaves usually represented less than 10 percent of the population, with a demographic

---

[1] This and following paragraphs are greatly indebted to the first chapter of George Reid Andrews, *Afro-Latin America, 1800–2000* (New York: Oxford University Press, 2004).

weight analogous to the United States north of the Chesapeake.[2] Only Cuba and Brazil had proportions of slaves resembling those of the American South. Nowhere in the Spanish mainland of the Americas did the proportion of slaves approach those of the British, French, and Dutch sugar islands. The most heavily settled regions of mainland Spanish America were also distinguished from both the North American and Franco-American zones of revolution in having free populations numerically dominated by nonwhites. As in Saint Domingue, in the event of a sustained challenge to imperial political authority, the problem of equality for the free nonwhite majority, black, mestizo, mulatto, and Indian, would have to be addressed.

In comparison with both prerevolutionary Anglo-America and Franco-America, slavery was a problem of relatively low priority in the years immediately before the Hispanic revolutions. As in North America, those areas in Latin America with the longest and deepest investment in slavery were those that would be most determined to maintain slavery.

Well into the second half of the age of revolution, the institutions under the sovereignty of the Iberian monarchs were located in an area where they had been least challenged by ideological or political movements. Ibero-American societies were also those in which New World slaves and their descendants had developed the most varied adjustments to and exits from bondage. Slaves were distributed throughout the urban and rural sectors. They had cultural and welfare institutions with a degree of autonomy unparalleled in the northwestern European colonies. They had better developed legal paths to individual manumission. Their flight to autonomy in communities beyond direct colonial control were paralleled by a variegated mosaic of social ranks and occupations in the great urban centers of imperial power. Slaves challenged and mitigated the constraints of their status even if they did not subvert the foundations of the institution of slavery. The inhabitants of Ibero-America were aware of the challenges posed by the independence movements and slave revolts in North America and the Caribbean. In Ibero-America, however, it was initially less apparent that a political crisis over political autonomy or independence would imperil the social order. In some respects, the structure of Latin American slavery, including the safety valves of flight at the frontiers and cultural space within, may have marginalized fears about slaves as crucial actors in an imperial-Creole confrontation.

Some historians of Iberian slavery emphasize the degree to which the French and Haitian revolutions haunted the imagination of Ibero-Atlantic elites during the first generation of the age of revolution (1775–1800). In comparative terms, I am struck by the absence of the most important single

---

[2] The slave share of the population in Venezuela in 1800 most closely resembled that of New York state in 1775. However, Venezuela's nonwhite share of the total amounted to nearly 80 percent (including 49 percent free blacks and 18 percent Indians). The proportion of nonwhites had no counterpart in continental North America. (See Andrews, *Afro-Latin America*, 41, Table 1.1; Latin American population c. 1800).

indicator of such unease. In Anglo-America, the decade before 1775 was characterized by sustained attempts in many colonies to halt the flow of African slaves to the colonies. In Latin America, there seems to have been no parallel public or collective movement whatever to prohibit or even to curtail that flow. During the 1780s, the Iberian monarchies made a determined effort to accelerate their acquisition of African slave labor. The imperial government promulgated a new *Black Code* in 1789. Historians often interpret the Code as evidence of an imperial desire to shore up the material and legal privileges of slaves, obligating owners to guarantee their welfare as human beings. Indeed, slaveholder protests secured the suspension of the Code's enforcement. What such interpretations overlook is the fact that the Code of 1789 was introduced in conjunction with a policy to maximize the flow of new African slaves into Spain's dominions.

At the beginning of this study, we emphasized that one can not judge the mildness or the amelioration of the institution by transformations within slavery, but ignore the impact of modes of recruitment on its sustenance and growth. The central aim of the legislation in this instance was quite explicit. For the first time, the monarchy undertook measures to convert slaving from monopoly contracts to a free trade. The imperial government correctly anticipated that a large surge of African slaves might increase problems of slave discipline. The Code's amelioration was more preemptive than ameliorative. The planters were unimpressed by the potential danger of the surge or and by the government's proposed solution. At the very moment when emancipation was being proclaimed in both Saint Domingue and Paris, the ameliorative portions of the Code were suspended in response to slaveholder protest.

The imperial perspective on expansion remained unchanged by the victories of Toussaint Louverture in 1800 and of Dessalines in 1803. Permission for free trade in African slaves was periodically renewed, the last time in April 1804. Actions spoke as loud as words. While the great slave revolution raged in neighboring Saint Domingue in the 1790s, Cuba imported twice as many slaves as it had before the French Revolution. During the following two decades, in the wake of Haiti's victory over Napoleon, the annual average of slave imports nearly quintupled over the rate of imports, before the publication of the Code of 1789. The low point for Cuban imports coincided not with the high points of the Haitian revolution and wars of independence, but with the immediate aftermath of the Anglo-American Abolition Acts of 1807. The fact that the trade was expanded in the year of the French Revolution and renewed in the wake of the final victory of the Haitian war of independence offers an annotated commentary on the relative impact of the events in Haiti on Spanish royal policy. In the face of those events, more African slaves were arriving in Spanish America than ever before. What was true for Spanish America was equally true for Portuguese America. The European and Saint Domingue revolutions set off a frenzy for the expansion of the slave trade and tropical staple production.

Merchant capitalism in Latin America may have teetered on a "knife edge" between free trade in slaves and the fear of slave uprisings, but the bottom line (before the Napoleonic-induced crises) of Iberian sovereignty in 1808 was continually resolved in favor of ever more slavery.[3]

What was true for the Ibero-American mainland was even more apparent in the Spanish Caribbean islands. Fifteen thousand Africans arrived in Puerto Rico between 1775 and 1807, three times the number landed during the previous two centuries. Seven of every eight slave ships arriving in the Rio de la Plata between 1742 and 1806 did so after 1790. The rate of slaves imported into Venezuela increased by more than two-thirds, from 600 to 1,000 per year between 1774 and 1807. At the northern rim of Spain's American empire in Florida, the slave population rose from 29 percent of the total in 1784 to 53 percent in 1814. By 1800, more Africans were arriving in Spanish America than ever before. Protests came from colonies that were failing to obtain slaves. Whatever the residual threats posed by the events in the French Caribbean, they were seen more as opportunities than as dangers from beginning to end. In 1804, a former governor of New Granada, Narváez, complained that due to a ban on slave importation during hostilities between Spain and Britain, "not a single *bozal* [African-born] slave has entered in seven years, to the detriment of the region's agriculture."[4]

During the height of the Franco-Caribbean revolutions (1790–1802), nearly 5,000 slaves per year reached Peru. The region's slave population continued to grow, "perhaps by as much as 25 percent between 1795 and 1826."[5] Despite the massive slave rebellion in the French Caribbean in 1791, the government not only extended free trade in slaves to Cuba, Santo Domingo, Puerto Rico, and Venezuela, but opened it to gain maximum benefit from the opportunity. Caracas was free to purchase slaves from foreigners with only a brief suspension in 1803–1805. Whatever its pragmatic mobilization of slaves to defend the empire, during the peak years of the struggle over South American independence Spain remained committed to continued domination and to slavery between the 1780s and the 1820s.[6]

---

[3] On the Code, see Manuel Lucena Salmoral, *Los Codigos negros de la America Española* (Madrid: Alcalá de Henares, 1996). On slavery in Ibero-America in the generation before the struggle for independence, see Jeremy Adelman, *Sovereignty and Revolution in the Iberian Atlantic* (Princeton: Princeton University Press, 2006), 56–100.

[4] Quoted in Helg, *Liberty and Equality*, 56). See also Andrews, *Afro-Latin America*, 19–20. On Florida, see Jane Landers, *Black Society in Spanish Florida* (Urbana: University of Illinois Press, 1999), 161.

[5] Peter Blanchard, *Slavery and Abolition in Early Republican Peru* (Wilmington: Scholarly Resources, 1992), 3. Blanchard notes that the Peruvian figures are in dispute (*Ibid.*, 16, n. 5).

[6] See Aline Helg, *Liberty and Equality in Caribbean Colombia, 1770–1835* (Chapel Hill: University of North Carolina Press, 2004), 55; P. Michael McKinley, *Pre-Revolutionary Caracas: Politics, Economy and Society 1777–1811* (Cambridge: Cambridge University Press, 1985), 45; and David R. Murray, *Odious Commerce: Britain, Spain and the Abolition of the Cuban Slave Trade* (Cambridge, Cambridge University Press, 1980), ch. 1–3).

Whatever the private and public discussions of slavery and abolition during the period, the imperial government never altered its policy of expanding the Spanish slave trade and encouraging slavery during the age of revolution. The result was that what was left of Spanish America made the period after 1800 the most dynamic and massive in the four-hundred year history of Spanish New World slavery. Spain was to have the distinction of being the first and last European power to import African slaves into the Americas over the course of three and a half centuries.

The upward trend in all of these figures on the Spanish American slave trade has been used to support a more general hypothesis that this surge dialectically weakened the system of slavery in the New World by increasing the waves of resistance. Its plausibility is heightened by the fact that the massive surge of imports into Saint Domingue in the 1780s clearly increased the reservoirs of armed resistance once the slave revolution erupted. However, one must be cautious in linking rising numbers to a rising tide of resistance to slavery. Even in Saint Domingue, with its unprecedented influx of Africans in the 1780s, "organized violent resistance in Saint Domingue was relatively slight" in comparison to the British or Dutch colonies. One must be cautious about assuming a direct correlation between the magnitude of migration and the intensification of resistance.[7]

In this regard it may be significant to observe that Cuba registered more conspiracies and revolts between 1789 and 1815 than any colony in the Caribbean. Yet, slaves in Cuba stood less chance of acquiring their freedom than in any part of Spanish America, and more African slaves were brought into the colony between 1789 and 1808 than in any colony but Jamaica. In the latter colony, no revolts whatsoever broke out.[8] The four possible conspiracies were aborted by the authorities. What one can conclude, of course, is that wherever slave numbers increased they increased the potential pool of slaves available for resistance. In this sense, slaves were less the seeds of destruction than fuel for action usually for, but sometimes against, the institution in which they were held.

In conjuncture with calls to arms, revolutions, and uprisings in France, Saint Domingue and the eastern Caribbean, newly imported young African males became an important cause of increased slave rebelliousness on the Spanish mainland. From the 1770s to the 1790s, the formation of autonomous slave communities increased in Colombia and Venezuela on the

---

[7] Geggus, *Haitian Revolutionary Studies*, 7.

[8] See Eltis, *Economic Growth and the Ending of the Transatlantic Slave Trade* (New York: Oxford University Press, 1987), Table A 2, 245; and Laird W. Bergad, et al., *The Cuban Slave Market, 1790–1880* (New York: Cambridge University Press, 1995), 27, Fig. 3:1, Slave imports to Cuba, 1790–1866. Geggus, *Slavery, War, and Revolution in the "Greater Caribbean, 1789–1815,"* in *A Turbulent Time*, David Barry Gaspar and David Patirck Geggus, eds. (Bloomington: Indiana University Press, 1997), 46–50.

southern coastal regions of the circum-Caribbean.[9] During the 1790s, slave conspiracies and revolts in the Spanish Caribbean were more than twice as numerous in the Spanish circum-Caribbean (including Louisiana, New Grenada, and Venezuela) as in the British and Dutch colonies combined.[10] Fear of revolutionary agitators coming from the French colonies led local authorities to prohibit the landing of Creole slaves and to restrict importations of slaves to *bozales* (slaves imported directly from Africa). These restrictions were often applied as much to fleeing free refugees as to their slaves. In the wake of the Saint Domingue uprising, the imperial government prohibited the entry of slaves not born in Africa to prevent revolutionary "contamination" in Spanish American ports.

Following his reimposition of slavery, Napoleon deported black resisters from Guadeloupe to New Granada, as well as to the United States. The Viceroy of New Grenada ordered their expulsion, despite the colony's need for fresh labor.[11] On the other hand, slave uprisings in the Spanish Caribbean dramatically decreased between Haiti's defeat of Napoleon in 1802 and the beginning of the movement for Spanish independence. There was no spike of slave resistance from 1804 through 1810 as there had been at the height of the revolutionary uprising for emancipation during the previous decade. Before 1810, there is little evidence that two decades of profound challenges to the institution of slavery elsewhere received more than scattered discussion on the mainland. In the eyes of their masters and governors, slaves still belonged to a "well-defined social group whose rights and duties had been established by almost three centuries of Spanish colonial practice and legislation." Prior to the moves towards independence, abolition was a "non-starter" anywhere in Latin America.[12] Early moves towards the abolition of the slave trade soon after the stirrings of Creole autonomists' rebellions against Spain came without much prior discussion or any extended moral crisis.

Chile, as in northern U.S. states with very small slave populations, quickly moved to abolish the slave trade. Even Venezuela's quite conservative first Junta prohibited the slave trade in 1810.[13] Further south, in Buenos Aires, the first governing Junta, formed in 1810, restricted the slave trade. In 1813,

[9] Peter Blanchard, *Slavery and Abolition*, 39–40.

[10] Geggus, "Slavery, War," in *Turbulent Time*, 46–49 (Slave Rebellions and Conspiracies, 1789–1815).

[11] Aline Helg, "A Fragmented Majority: Free 'Of all Colors'... in Caribbean Colombia during the Haitian Revolution," in Geggus, *The Impact of the Haitian Revolution*, ch. 11, 160–161.

[12] John V. Lombardi, *The Decline and Abolition of Negro Slavery in Venezuela 1820–1854* (Westport: Greenwood, 1971, 35, and Adelman, *Sovereignty and Revolution*, 98. Blanchard, *Slavery*, 3–5 emphasizes challenges by both the imperial government (*the Black Code*), and the Tupac Amaru Indian rebellion (1780–1781) as well as older traditions of resistance and accommodation.

[13] McKinley, *Pre-Revolutionary Caracas*, 159.

the revolutionaries decreed the liberation of any slave entering the country from abroad. Slavery itself was to be gradually abolished without attacking the sacred right of property by liberating, at their age of majority, those born of slaves. The slave trade, however, continued despite further legislation in 1823 and a treaty with Great Britain in 1825 calling on the new nation to suppress the trade. Only in the 1830s, under persistent British pressure, did the slave trade wind down, culminating in a second Anglo-Argentine treaty in 1840.[14]

By the mid-1820s, every mainland country in Spanish America had prohibited further imports of slaves from Africa. As in North America, some territories continued to allow intracontinental imports on a small scale. There was little prior debate over the issue in the public press before the enactment of slave trade abolition. It is difficult to identify any articulated motives by the new legislators.[15] It seems plausible that the early revolutionaries wished to integrate their societies into the Euro-American orbit of civil equality, individual liberty, and citizenship that were integral to the political ideology of the American French and Caribbean revolutions. Moreover, the British government, with the world's most powerful navy, placed slave trade abolition high on its diplomatic agenda.

At the outbreak of the Spanish American struggle, Britain was an ally of Spain, already urging its government to move in the direction of abolishing the Atlantic slave trade. As soon as the Caracas Junta in Venezuela abolished its provincial slave trade, official agents were sent to the British West Indies, Britain, and the United States, informing them of the legislation, adopting free trade, and attempting to secure arms. The British connection would loom even larger after Napoleon's defeat. British support was then crucial to both sides in the struggle over Spanish American independence. Spain, seeking British financial aid in 1817, signed a treaty abolishing the Spanish slave trade as of 1820. This, at least, legally committed the Spanish authorities to the prohibition of the trade to all its remaining colonies.[16]

As indicated above, neither increased internal slave resistance nor the French Caribbean upheaval appear to have precipitated the series of emancipations in revolutionary Spanish America. Nevertheless, once the conflicts reached serious proportions and year followed year without a clear-cut victor, the slaves often played a vital role. Areas where large numbers of fresh arrivals were concentrated were also prone to recurring flight and increased incidents of slave resistance. They were also areas in which autonomous slave conspiracies and disruptive uprisings were most frequent. Along the

---

[14] Andrews, *Afro-Argentines in Buenos Aires, 1800–1900* (Madison: University of Wisconsin Press, 1980), 48–49; 56–57 and Andrews *Afro-Latin America*, 56–57.

[15] Andrews, *Afro-Latin America*, 57, table 2.1.

[16] See Rafe Blaufarb, "The Western Question: The Geopolitics of Latin American Independence," *American Historical Review*, 112:3 (2007), 742–763.

Caribbean coast of South America, where shipments were more sporadic, slave rebellion was exceptional. Only one open slave rebellion occurred in Caracas during the period coinciding with the Franco-Caribbean revolutions. In New Grenada, incidents of slave rebellion were few and disconnected despite the fact that most haciendas were geographically isolated, lacked security forces, and contained more slave than free inhabitants. By contrast, in the Spanish possessions the main importers of African slave imports, Cuba and Puerto Rico, were also the most frequent sites of slave rebellions in the twenty years ending with the defeat of France in 1814. They were also the colonies in which slavery remained most firmly entrenched, expanded most rapidly, and where the free population as a whole remained faithful to the crown.[17]

The issue of slavery's future was only incidentally introduced into the great political crisis of the Spanish empire in 1810. What set mainland Spanish America on the path to abolition was not the revolutionary model of Haiti, but Napoleon Bonaparte, the restorer of slavery in the French empire. Napoleon's deposition of the Spanish monarch in 1808 produced a crisis of monarchical legitimacy and a fragmentation of political hierarchies from Mexico to Chile. As in the French Revolution, the first issue requiring resolution was the relation of the overseas colonies to authority in the metropolis. In the wake of a Spanish rebellion against Bonaparte's coup, a constituent assembly (*Cortes*) was convened in Cádiz, in 1810. As in prior American and French constituent assemblies, the relative weight of regions and the boundaries of citizenship became critical questions. In these deliberations, slaves by consensus lay outside the boundaries of citizenship. The political weight to be accorded to the half-million slaves in Spanish America was of less moment to almost all the delegates than determining representation of its more than ten million free inhabitants.

The most critical conflicts arose over the representation of free nonwhites in the polity. The Cortes split deeply over the questions of racial equality and access to full citizenship. In a final, ominous compromise, political rights were accorded to all Europeans and to white, Indian, and Mestizo Americans. Free descendants of Africans were clearly excluded, with the support of the American delegates. The only sop for the *pardos* (mulattos) was a promise of citizenship to those who displayed "special merit." Into this narrow opening, events would soon pour all of the mainland's free Afro-Latin Americans and a large proportion of its slaves. Arguing in terms of racial harmony, a delegate from New Granada argued that stopping the flow of Africans could increase the uniformity of "the Spanish family."

---

[17] See McKinley *Pre-Revolutionary Caracas*, 124; Helg, "A Fragmented Majority," 169; and Geggus, "Slavery, War," in *Turbulent Time*, 48–49.

In contrast to the issue of racial equality, the abolition of slavery received short shrift at Cádiz.[18] A delegate from Mexico, home to the smallest proportion of slaves in Ibero-America, proposed the institution's gradual abolition. Less than a decade after Haiti's ex-slaves had shattered Napoleon's dream of restoring slavery, all of the representatives from the Caribbean basin opposed ending slavery. A Spanish anglophile liberal, Augustin Argüelles, sought consideration of bringing the slave trade to an end. Five years after the Anglo-American Acts of Abolition, the Cortes also rejected that motion. In the Spanish empire, each region resolved the questions in its own way. From New Grenada came the suggestion that the recent English example showed that abolition of the Atlantic slave trade would avoid a repetition of France's bloody slave liberation, whose consequences were already proverbial.[19]

In the imperial Cortes, the American delegates almost unanimously favored full political rights for the *castas* (mixed race peoples). Back in Spanish America, the question of legal disabilities for the colored *castas* was both urgently and positively addressed. In contrast to French whites in the French Caribbean, Spanish whites made no attempt to preserve the *casta* system. There was certainly no overwhelmingly powerful Spanish metropole in 1810 to veto the initiative. Both Spaniards and Creoles were profoundly aware of the relative proportion of free Afro-Latins to whites and of the need for their support in controlling their political future. As early as December 1810, Cartagena invited all races to vote on equal terms and to establish a Patriot Junta.

In other areas of Spanish America, it was loyalists who took the initiative. In 1813–1814, when Bolivar successfully executed European residents in Venezuela as part of his revolutionary program, the surviving royalists formed an alliance with *pardos* in the interior to overthrow the republic. The royalist strategy paid off. A major pardo and slave uprising near Caracas forced the republicans to surrender. As in Saint Domingue, slaves as well as free *castas* were drawn into the maelstrom and emerged armed and politicized. In Venezuela, as in Saint Domingue, the ebb and flow of success between both sides always impelled the more desperate group to dig more deeply into the social structure.[20]

Wars of attrition disrupted the plantation system as well. Slaves might flee the plantations to join one or another military formation or to escape both

---

[18] See Marie Laure Rieu-Millan, *Los Diputados Americanos en Las Cortes de Cadiz (igualdad o independencia)* (Madrid: CSIC, 1990), 169–172, and Murray, *Odious Commerce*, 40–43; and Jaime E. Rodríguez O., *The Independence of Spanish America* (New York: Cambridge University Press, 1998), 84–86.

[19] Marixa Lasso, "Race War and Nation in Caribbean Gran Colombia, Cartagena, 1810–1832," *American Historical Review*, 111: (2) (2006), 336–361; esp. 347.

[20] Lasso, "Race War," 345–346; Rodriguez, *Independence*, 8. and McKenley, *Pre-Revolutionary Caracas*, 171–173.

slavery and conscription. In Spanish America, as in the French Caribbean, armed conflict inverted the gender profile. In peacetime, manumission usually favored females. It should be borne in mind, however, that all too often entrance into the military was an accelerated pathway to displacement or death, as well as liberation. The ratio of black males to females in Montevideo in 1805 (119 to 100) became a severe deficit by 1819 (78 to 100).[21] The cessation of the slave trade, breakdown of order, and attrition of warfare all reduced the number of slaves. As the American Revolution reminds us, however, declarations of independence did not subvert the institution of slavery itself. The escalation of appeals to the slave population at large led to the numerical erosion of its base toward the mainland at the end of the wars of independence.

One must not look for consistency along an ideological or political spectrum in a period of such vertiginous shifts of fortune. At one point Bolivar, Venezuela's premier revolutionary, followed many American Founding Fathers in noting the contradiction between fighting for national liberation and maintaining slavery. One can hardly take this as a guide to the trajectory of Bolivar's policy on slavery. In 1813, the patriots attempted to enlist British armed intervention to suppress rebel slaves allied with the loyalists. The next year, in Jamaica, Bolivar, now a refugee, reassured the island's slave owners. It was the Spanish royalists who had forced slaves into armed service. British intervention in favor of the insurgents, he concluded, would not produce another Haiti. Two years later, Bolivar, relying upon Haitian assistance for new expeditions to Venezuela, definitively shifted towards abolitionism.[22] Thereafter, Bolivar not only supported gradual abolition, but extended the policy to Colombia and to all areas in which anti-Spanish armies were victorious. By 1821, "free womb" liberation became the dominant mode of abolition for most new nations of Spanish South America.

By the mid-1820s, the institution's future was clear. Without further transatlantic slave imports, a generation of rearguard efforts to tighten work discipline, revive the interregional slave trade, and extend the labor obligations of freeborn children (*libertos*) amounted to shuffling an ever-diminishing deck. With variations, free womb emancipation assured an endpoint in abolition with the working life of those remaining enslaved. Further internecine conflicts within Spanish America ensured that, in most new nations, slavery came to an end well before the natural death of the last slave. In most cases, slavery was terminated by the repeated aftershocks of Spanish American independence. These interminable political and military mobilizations forced liberals and conservatives to bid for support with further abolitionist gestures.[23]

[21] Andrews, *Afro-Latin America*, 64.
[22] Lombardi, *Decline*, 12–13.
[23] Andrews, *Afro-Latin America*, 64–67.

In Spain, although Napoleon's occupation opened the door to discussing slave trade abolition in the Cortes of Cádiz, the combined effect of Spanish South America's bids for independence bound the imperial government ever more closely to the expansion of slavery and the transatlantic slave trade. Even at the highpoint of Hispanic hopes for the retention and renewal of a united Spanish empire, the representatives of all the principal slaveholding regions in the circum-Caribbean and Peru opposed constricting slavery.[24]

Various potential paths to abolition were briefly raised at the Cortes, including slave trade abolition and the free womb strategy later adopted by most new mainland governments. The Cortes followed the precedent of the early French Revolution. All questions related to slavery were quickly shunted into the hands of a commission. Relaying the questions between various bureaucratic bodies quietly buried the issues.

The brief moment of Spanish debate affords a unique view of the conflicting pressures at work. In 1810, the British had been the principal source of financial and military support for the Spanish forces fighting the French occupation. Even before it abolished its own slave trade, in 1807, the British government had made it clear to Parliament that blocking the foreign slave trade was an integral element of the closure of imports to its own colonies. After 1808, British diplomacy was reinforced by naval power and the seizure of Cuban slave ships.

In the Spanish Caribbean, the very mention of an abolitionist project at the Spanish *Cortes* provoked violent reactions from slave owners. In 1810 Cuba was, after Jamaica, already the second largest slave colony in the Caribbean and well on its way to becoming the second largest sugar exporting colony in the world. The precarious imperial situation of Spain itself did not permit its rulers to add the hostility of the most faithful and profitable of her Atlantic colonies to their challenges. The Cortes began a tradition (reflected in its constitution) that was to characterize Iberian policy toward the problem of slavery that endured for the next half century. It adopted a policy of prudent silence while it tried to bridge the abyss between adopting a general principle in favor of ultimate freedom and a policy of minimal movement in implementing that principle.[25]

During the 1810s and 1820s, the crosscurrents of British pressure and economic incentive continued to have different outcomes in various parts of the old Spanish Empire. The newly independent nations of South America quickly signed treaties with Great Britain guaranteeing their withdrawal from the Atlantic slave trade and eventually denying the use of their flags to cover transoceanic slaving. After the 1820s, only the ports in the Rio de la Plata were briefly reopened to African captives.[26] The newly

---

[24] Rodriguez, *Independence*, 87.
[25] Rieu-Millan, *Los Diputados*, 172–173.
[26] Eltis, *Economic Growth*, 249, table A. 8.

independent nations moved slowly toward abolition via the free womb. The three mainland states that first enacted final emancipation by 1825 (Chile [1823], Central America [1824] and Uruguay [1825]) were South American nations with very small proportions of slaves and blacks. The first Spanish Caribbean area to achieve total abolition was Santo Domingo, the direct result of conquest by neighboring Haiti (1821).[27] This liberation was also the greatest and most direct emancipatory achievement of the postrevolutionary Haitian government. In some post-emancipation societies, the myth of racial equality and harmony superseded the threat of black vengeance. Fears of a race war occasionally arose in the wake of gradual emancipation but none of the putative conspiracies came to fruition. The colonies that remained under Spanish sovereignty took a different path. In Puerto Rico, slave imports rose steadily after 1810, reaching a peak in the 1820s and 1830s. From 1811 to 1830, slave imports into Cuba rose 175 percent above the corresponding period in prerevolutionary Spanish America (1791–1810).[28]

All told, in the whole area ruled by Spain in 1810, far more slaves were imported from Africa between 1810 and 1825 than were liberated by the new republics. By 1825, slavery had been condemned primarily where slaves in 1800 had composed ten percent or less of the population as a whole. In a general sense, by 1825 Spanish imperial slavery had been contracted and condemned where it was peripheral and consolidated and expanded at its lowland tropical core. There were also far more slaves living within the prerevolutionary boundaries of the Spanish Empire in 1825 than there had been in 1810. The geographic area in which the free womb principle prevailed by 1825 was far vaster than those which remained fully under unmodified slave law.

As in Anglo-America, dependence upon slave labor had been increased by a shift towards the gang labor cultivation of sugar. For those slaves living on the sugar plantations of Spanish America, the legal, social, cultural, and familial protections that had alleviated the harshness of the chattel status were weakened. For most slaves entering the Spanish imperial orbit after 1800, conditions could therefore "only be described as hellish."[29] The characteristic underfeeding and overwork of sugar harvest workdays of 16 to 20 hours, was now the fate of a greater proportion of the slave force than ever before in the history of Spanish-American slavery. Even more than in the Anglo-American and Franco-Caribbean cases, conditions for blacks had polarized.

On the European side of Spanish America, the monarchy devoted itself to a steady rearguard action to sustain the slave system in the face of

---

[27] Andrews, *Afro-Latin America*, 57.
[28] Eltis, *Economic Growth*, 249, table A. 8 and Bergad, et al., *Cuban Slave Market*, 27; and Lasso, "Race War," 359.
[29] Andrews, *Afro-Latin America*, 23–24.

increasing post-war British pressure. After attempting to influence the Cortes in 1811, the British government refrained from any further initiative over the issue of slavery itself. For the British, sustaining Spanish independence in the larger conflict against Napoleon took priority over issues arising beyond Europe. British power intervened only in the Cuban slave trade, seizing at least forty-three ships between 1809 and 1819.[30] The combination of Napoleon's defeat and a resurgence of British public agitation (to be discussed later) raised pressure against Spain to a new level in 1814. The British effort to prevent a revival of the French slave trade was closely linked to a wider effort to shut down the transatlantic slave trade. The British had one major weapon to wield in the negotiations. The Spanish court was desperately in debt and needed more funds to sustain its campaign against the revolutionaries in South America. As the tide turned against Spanish forces in 1817, Britain was able to elicit a treaty that offered a subsidy to the Spanish government for ending the slave trade. The British also gained a right to board any suspect vessels flying the flag of Spain. The Cuban planters and merchants bitterly opposed the treaty of 1817. The treaty also provided that the Spanish transatlantic slave trade would cease by 1820. As with similar bilateral treaties negotiated between Britain and other European states, "mutual rights of search" and "mixed commissions" treaties of adjudication for seized ships and slaves were signed with dozens of governments. These pioneer supranational judicial bodies were to expand dramatically in the twentieth century.

At the end of the age of revolution, however, it was clear that the treaty of 1817 was still a dead letter.[31] Although the Spanish government claimed that it had agreed to the prohibition of slaves on humanitarian grounds, planters, merchants, and bureaucrats argued that the treaty had been forced upon Spain by Britain only to protect her own slave colonies. Between 1820 and 1824, the British navy did not succeed in capturing a single Spanish slaver in the Caribbean. Cuban officialdom colluded in smuggling captives onto the island.[32] The evasion extended far beyond the Spanish noncompliance. The long years of warfare between 1792 and 1814 spawned a vast subterfuge as neutral flags were widely used as cover for slavers. In less than a decade after 1815, there was a nearly complete turnover of the ownership of ships in the slave trade to the Spanish Caribbean. The indirect supply of slaving capital and goods could no longer be controlled by British patrols in the same manner as ships sailing under covered by search treaties flags. In anticipation of the date set for closure, slave imports into Cuba between 1817 and 1819 reached an all-time high. In those years Cuban imports

---

[30] Eltis, *Economic Growth*, 109.
[31] Murray, *Odious Commerce*, 71.
[32] Murray, *Odious Commerce*, 78. With one warship, the *Wilberforce*, the Haitians were able to capture slavers and land the liberated captives on Haitian soil.

equaled two-thirds of those entering the far larger territories of Brazil.[33] In the Hispano-American, as in the Franco-American, Atlantic, uneven steps toward emancipation occurred in situations of severe political disorganization and extreme violence. In both Iberia and Spanish America, there was little leeway before 1810 to formulate critiques of the institution of slavery in the public sphere. As in the French case, the undermining of the Spanish monarchy precipitated a crisis in political legitimacy and violent rebellion on both sides of the Atlantic. Civil society disintegrated into civil and imperial war. Where the economic and military stakes in the institution of slavery were relatively minor, free womb legislation could be initiated early in the war for independence as an incentive to recruitment (Chile, 1811). Final abolition too could be enacted and enforced early (Chile, 1823). Where slaves were more important, both economically and demographically (Venezuela, Colombia, Peru, Ecuador), liberation might be restricted to slaves in arms and free womb legislation imposed only at the end of the conflict, allowing the institution of slavery to persist. As in most instances of military-led emancipations, those who remained enslaved at the end of the conflicts were disproportionately female.[34]

In these areas, especially, slaves significantly influenced the outcome as soldiers and runaways shared in the brutalities of a civil war not directly related to their particular status. Again, as in the French Caribbean, slaves were often engaged in deadly combat with each other sharing, on a smaller scale the brutality and mortality of Saint Domingue. Many left their slave status through death rather than liberation.

The Portuguese Empire, c. 1775–1825

The Luso-Brazilian world offers a hint of what might have happened had the Portuguese monarchy been undermined by revolutionary action, as in the case of France, or military deposition, as in the case of Spain. Both upheavals set off a chain of unprecedented civil violence and decision making by force of arms. Both led to the loss of major parts of their respective empires and their slave systems. In the Portuguese case, however, the age of revolution cost the metropole its most valuable colony without any weakening of the institution of slavery in either part of the two surviving fragments of the empire.

Even more intensively than its Spanish counterpart, the Portuguese empire intensified its commitment to slavery in the last quarter of the eighteenth century. "By 1790 South Atlantic merchant capitalism reached a fever pitch." Portuguese constraints over the slave trade from Africa were also

---

[33] Eltis, *Economic Growth*, 57–59.
[34] Andrews, *Afro-Latin America*, 41, 57, 64–65; and Peter Blanchard, *Under the Flags of Freedom: Slave Soldiers and the Wars of Independence in Latin America* (Pittsburgh: University of Pittsburgh Press, 2008), 168–169.

relaxed by 1800.[35] For half a century before 1775, Portuguese slavers landed an average of 20,000 African slaves per year in Brazil. In the 1780s, the annual average rose above 25,000, and, in the 1800s, it rose again to over 35,000.

In the 1820s, the average annual toll of enslaved Africans unloaded in Brazil exceeded 50,000. No other slave system had ever sustained such a level of slaving. At the other end of the Atlantic, the Luso-Brazilian slave system was faring equally well. In the two decades between 1810 and 1829, more than a million captives were boarded on Luso-Brazilian carriers – again a total unmatched in the annals of the transatlantic slave trade. West Central Africa, the hub of Portuguese slaving activity, posted record numbers of loadings. In Southeast Africa, Portuguese Mozambique became a major slaving supplier for the transatlantic slave trade in the generation after 1775. Its volume of deportations nearly trebled. The age of revolution found few echoes in South African quadrant of the Atlantic. The Luso- Brazilian slave system was thus the greatest beneficiary of the French and Spanish imperial revolutions and the Anglo-American slave trade abolitions.

In one respect, the scale of this South Atlantic slave trade poses a paradox for those historians who identify slave resistance as the principal agency of the process of abolition during the age of revolution. Brazil's imports of slaves far exceeded those imported into the French slave system in the 1780s and those imported into the Spanish slave system between the 1790s and the 1820s. To the end of the age of revolution the Luso-Brazilian trade kept its institution intact. It remained with greater potential territory for expansion than any other surviving system in the Americas. Despite the enormous growth in the demand for Africans, the price of Angolan slaves remained relatively stable during the first quarter of the nineteenth century. It also appears that the period was one of unprecedented prosperity for Angolan traders. It seems reasonable to assume that the prosperity experienced by slave exporters in Angola, in the 1820s, remained largely unaffected by British abolition. This was not the end of a favorable outlook for slavers. On the Middle Passage, the rate of slave resistance aboard slave ships fell to its lowest level since the end of the seventeenth century.[36]

Whatever the level of resistance to slavery in Portuguese Africa or on Portuguese slave ships, the robustness of Brazilian slavery was certainly not

[35] Jeremy Adelman, *Sovereignty and Revolution*, 83–90; 121–123.
[36] In the decade following the landing of the Portuguese court in Brazil, more than 450,000 Africans were landed in Brazil (See Eltis, *Reassessment*, and David Eltis, Frank D. Lewis, and David Richardson, "Slave Prices, the African Slave Trade, and Productivity in the Caribbean 1674–1807," *Economic History Review*, 58:(4) (2005), 673–700. Stephen D. Behrendt, David Eltis, and David Richardson, "The Costs of Coercion: African Agency in the Pre-Modern Atlantic," *Economic History Review*, 54:3 (2001), 454–476, Fig. 1457 and Fig. 2,467. For slave movements, see Slave Trade Database, D. Eltis, "The Transatlantic Slave Trade: A Reassessment Based on the Second Edition of the Transatlantic Slave Trade Database," Manuscript kindly provided by the author.

from any dearth of African slave resistance on the western side of the Portuguese Atlantic. On the contrary, the level of Brazilian resistance after 1800 appears to reinforce the findings of historians who emphasize a linkage between surging African imports and insurgency. Stuart Schwartz aptly describes one Brazilian cycle of slave resistance in the early nineteenth century as "the war against Bahian slavery."[37] During the era of the Franco-Caribbean revolutions and subsequent wars (1792–1814), that province alone imported as many slaves as did Cuba. In Bahia, the great wave of slave revolts began in 1809. It lasted for an entire generation, culminating in an uprising of Salvador's Muslim Africans in 1835.[38]

In most respects the Bahian slave uprisings were, at best, loosely linked to the ideological or political events of the age of revolution. Their beginning and end did not coincide with the crisis in the Caribbean world.[39] However, another aspect of Brazilian resistance is striking. At its peak, insurrection in Brazil was more continuous than in any other contemporary New World regime. Brazilian slaves were not acting in isolation from each other. The insurgencies in Bahia often occurred in tandem with rebellions in other parts of Brazil. Slaves were equally aggressive in the plantation regions further to the south. By the 1820s, the number of actual outbreaks exceeded those in any imperial or national jurisdiction during the generation between the American and Brazilian declarations of independence.[40]

This suggests an aspect of the Saint Domingue uprising, which may be analogous to, but not existentially linked with, Brazilian slave insurrections. Although Saint Domingue loomed large in the imaginations of Brazilian planters and Creoles slaves' African cultural inheritance and local networks appear to have played a greater role in the formation of slave resistance than in most other colonial systems.[41] In the early nineteenth century, Bahia's capital city, Salvador, was surrounded by *quilombos* (free black communities). "If destroyed in one place they reappeared elsewhere, nourished . . . by the uninterrupted stream of slaves arriving from Africa."[42] African ethnic

---

[37] Stuart B. Schwartz, *Sugar Plantations in the Formation of Brazilian Society: Bahia, 1550–1835* (Cambridge: Cambridge University Press, 1985), 479–488. On the African nexus of the Saint Domingue revolution, see John Thornton, "African Soldiers in the Haitian Revolution," *Journal of Caribbean History* 25 (1991): 58–80; and Thornton, "'I am the Subject of the King of Congo': African Political Ideology in the Haitian Revolution," *Journal of World History,* 4 (1993), 181–214.

[38] For the Mâle uprising see João José Reis, *Slave Rebellion in Brazil: The Muslim Uprising of 1835 in Bahia* (Baltimore: Johns Hopkins University Press, 1993).

[39] The omission of essays on both Brazil and Africa from the excellent collective assessment in *The Impact of the Haitian Revolution in the Atlantic World;* David Geggus, ed. (2001) implicitly is consistent with the existential distance between the Afro-Brazilian and Hispano-Caribbean worlds of slavery in the age of revolution.

[40] Andrews, *Afro-Latin America,* 77–78.

[41] Andrews, *Afro-Latin America,* 67–68.

[42] Reis, *Slave Rebellion,* 41.

identities appear to have played the role of an alternative civil society in allowing the organization of resistance. Although captives were brought to Brazil in record numbers, strengthening both African ties and nodes of rebellion, the rapid Africanization process itself formed a barrier to the extension of resistance into the Creole segments of the population. Cultural differences separated slaves, not only from Brazilian whites, but from free blacks and Creole slaves.

Salvador's climactic *Malê* rebellion in 1835 appears to have been more oriented toward Islamic culture in West Africa than toward the Franco-Caribbean revolutions. The language of their insurgency was closer to visions of a Muslim caliphate than a New World republic. One of the most interesting facets of this uprising was the insurgents' plan to enslave mulattos whom they captured.[43] To the extent that they remained within the Muslim orbit, unbelievers could be enslaved according to holy law. Thus, the rebellion had as much in common with the world of the Maghreb and the Sudan as the Caribbean and the Americas.

We may never know how seriously the rebels intended to invert the relationship between the enslaved and the free in Bahia. What does seem clear is that the Malês perceived the mass of free blacks as indifferent or hostile to their own project. The free Creoles of color amounted to one-third of Brazil's population, and were not disposed to align themselves with African-bred slaves. Well into the second quarter of the nineteenth century, the zone of Ibero-America that contained the most frequent incidents of slave resistance may have been less of an immediate threat to the institution than those with closer ties to European abolitionists or New World republicans.

Europeans, like Africans, intervened in the fate of the Portuguese empire. In November 1807, a few months after the passage of British slave trade abolition, Napoleon's army invaded Portugal and occupied Lisbon. James Stephen, the principal architect of the abolitionist victory, welcomed Napoleon's policy as another act of providence. With both Iberian powers forced into belligerency against Britain, the Royal Navy could wipe the ocean clean of every last slave ship launched from the African continent. Providence, the British government, and the Portuguese king had other plans. Averting captivity like the king of Spain, the Portuguese royal family were transported to Brazil on British warships. Portugal, with its capital shifted to Rio de Janeiro, escaped the crisis of legitimacy that engulfed the Spanish American empire.

The British government's top priority was resistance to Napoleon, but it quickly made it clear to the Portuguese that the price of their support included at least a pledge to curtail the Luso-Brazilian slave trade. By a treaty in 1810, Portugal promised to consider measures for the gradual abolition of its slave trade. As a first step, the Portuguese government also

---

[43] *Ibid.*, 121 ff, and Schwartz, *Sugar Plantations*, 42.

agreed to prohibit its ships from slaving on any part of the African coast not under Portuguese control nor from any factory abandoned by belligerent enemy powers. Portugal became the first continental European nation to place a part of Africa off-limits to its nationals. As was the case with similar agreements over the next half century, the Anglo-Portuguese treaty acknowledged, at least in principle, the "injustice and disutility" of the slave trade, as well as the security risk posed by the introduction of a "foreign and factious" population into Brazil.[44]

Africans and Britons were not the Portuguese king's only, or even chief, concern. Well before the end of the eighteenth century, the population of Brazil nearly equaled that of its metropole and was growing much faster. Portugal depended far more on its colony than the colony did on the mother country. Brazil's exports accounted for 80 percent of Portugal's colonial imports and 60 percent of its exports. Portuguese imperial rule in the Americas was also far weaker than that of Spain. The Portuguese Crown governed Brazil through its locally dominant elites. Brazilian Creoles were deeply involved in the implementation of colonial policy. They already ranked among the Crown's magistrates in Brazil and Africa. Most significantly, at the beginning of the nineteenth century Brazil was more dependent upon slave labor than any other colony in Spanish America. Slaves even constituted a greater proportion of the colony's total population (37 percent) than they did in the Spanish West Indies.[45] As for the slave trade, when the Portuguese monarch arrived in Rio de Janeiro, Brazil was importing twice as many Africans as were landed in all of Spanish America during the previous decade.

The coincidence of Portugal's political and economic dependence upon an abolitionist Britain, combined with Portugal's fiscal dependence upon Luso-Brazilian slaving, Brazil's dependence upon a nonreproducing slave labor force, and the British consumers ever-expanding appetite for plantation produce created a Pandora's box of conundrums for the governments of Brazil, Britain, and Portugal. In the short run, the Portuguese empire reaped the windfall of Anglo-American abolitions and Britain's assault on every vessel in a France-dominated Europe. Brazil received nine of every ten slaves arriving in the Americas between 1810 and 1814. Its share of the Atlantic sugar market had doubled since 1789. In Africa, slave prices on Portuguese-dominated coastal areas remained stable or fell.[46] Luso-Brazilian merchants and planters took advantage of the revolutions and wars that diminished

---

[44] Leslie Bethell, *The Abolition of the Brazilian Slave Trade: Britain, Brazil and the Slave Trade Question 1807–1869* (Cambridge: Cambridge University Press, 1970), 8.

[45] Andrews, *Afro-Latin America*, 41, Table 1.1.

[46] Paul E. Lovejoy and David Richardson, "British Abolition and its Impact on Slave Prices along the Atlantic Coast of Africa, 1783–1850," *Journal of Economic History*, 55:1 (1995), 98–119, esp. Table 3, 113.

the production of slave-grown commodities and hindered the flow of trade across the Atlantic for more than two decades after the outbreak of the Haitian revolution.

Peace in 1814 opened up new pressures on Portugal – from Britain with demands for containment and abolition of the trade, and from Brazil for autonomy and independence. The political actors within the empire managed to avoid the pattern of war, domestic upheaval, occupation, and civic disintegration that embroiled much of Euro-America between 1775 and 1825. As late as 1800, there had been only two significant conspiracies by free classes in Brazil against Portuguese authority and no major challenges to the Portuguese imperium within Africa. The incentives for the colonial elite to risk the dangers of violently challenging Portuguese domination were eased by the Portuguese Crown's flight to Brazil. The center of the Portuguese empire was effectively transferred from Lisbon to Rio de Janeiro.[47]

The full measure of the shift became evident at the end of the Napoleonic wars. King Dom João of Portugal decided to remain in Brazil. The colony was raised to the status of a kingdom. Brazil's next step towards independence was precipitated in Lisbon. The diminished Portuguese elite was unable to stop the inexorable reversal of roles between colony and metropole. In the New World's least violent transition to independence, the monarchy solomonically divided itself. After the king returned to Lisbon at the demand of the Portuguese, his son remained in Brazil and became its emperor in 1824.[48]

At the nation's inception, some Brazilian leaders suggested that slavery was inefficient as well as immoral. José Bonifácio de Andrada e Silva, one of the founding fathers of Brazilian independence, asked how a free people could sanction the right to steal "another man's freedom, and even worse, to steal the freedom of his children and his children's children." On the eve of independence, he suggested inaugurating the new order with a gradual abolition plan. The contradiction between political liberalism and slavery did not, however, bother most Brazilian politicians. The overwhelming majority of those who formed the new government were unequivocally in favor of maintaining the institution. A Manifesto of Independence, addressed by regent Dom Pedro to the Brazilian people in 1822, began by accusing the Portuguese *Côrtes* of having plotted to emancipate and arm Brazil's slaves.[49]

---

[47] Leslie Bethell, *Brazil, Empire and Republic, 1822–1930* (Cambridge: Cambridge University Press, 1989), 12, 17.

[48] Bethell, *Brazil*, 33.

[49] Emilia Viotti da Costa, *The Brazilian Empire: Myths and Histories* (Chicago: Dorsey, 1985), 57, 126–127; Portugal's acquiescence in a new Anglo-Portuguese slave trade treaty in 1817 was, for many Brazilians, evidence that the Portuguese had "sold out a vital Brazilian interest." (See Bethell, *Brazil*, 24; Andrews, *Afro-Latin America*, 56; Eltis, *Economic Growth*, 242–243, Table A.1, and below). Lisbon had actually only agreed to abandon the right to trade in Africans north of the equator and to create commissions to adjudicate capture

In defiance of such a putative project, the 1820s marked a new peak in the importation of Africans into Brazil: 430,000 African captives were added to the nation's population. This was a greater number of African slaves than had ever entered any other new world colony in a comparable period in the history of the institution. It was nearly equal to the number of slaves in the colony of Saint Domingue on the eve of its revolution.[50] At Brazil's Constituent Assembly in 1823, the landowners who favored a new and independent monarchy made it clear that the danger of losing their source of fresh labor outweighed any potential risks arising from either British nonrecognition or from slave resistance.

Brazil's elites were apparently far more worried by another major cohort in their society. They were acutely aware of the role played by the free men of color in the French Caribbean and Spanish American revolutions. Control of Brazil's slave system and its rapidly growing segment of African captives required that the free population form a united front against the threat of slave insurrections. But rare insurgencies of the free population were not to be tolerated. One revolt by mulatto soldiers and artisans, demanding racial equality in Bahia, was brutally repressed. It remained the exception not the harbinger of widespread revolt.

As Stuart Schwartz suggests, the wide distribution of slave ownership in Brazilian society meant that it was not the planter elite alone who wished to see the institution continued. For free blacks and mulattoes in Brazil, as in Spanish America, "the fight for independence was first of all a battle against whites and their privileges," not against slavery. Had slaveholding been restricted to planter and commercial elites, the example of Saint Domingue might have led to success for the rebellious slaves. Slavery in Brazil, however, "was not the exclusive interest of any one group; in that lay its strength." Nor did slaves' resistance find resonance in the writings of the free population, whether black or white.[51]

As in so many other cases, slaves always posed a latent threat in any transference of sovereignty. In Brazil, slave resistance received too little encouragement from the social world that surrounded them. Brazilian authorities appeared to find it more difficult to resist pressures from without than below. Its government faced unrelenting diplomatic pressure from the British to sign an antislave trade treaty. That pressure was backed by the implicit threat that Britain might otherwise withdraw its support for recognition of Brazil's independence. This could easily be followed by British naval action against

of slave ships. The Brazilian negotiator repeatedly insisted to the British government that Brazilians wished the slave trade to continue and that there would be "popular resistance" to a real measure of abolition. In Rio de Janeiro, Bonifáco reiterated to the British *chargé d'affaires* that any attempt by Brazilian governments to institute immediate abolition would be political suicide.

50 Bethell, *Abolition*, 33–45.
51 See Schwartz, *Sugar*, 467; Adelman, *Sovereignty and Revolution*, 98. Costa *Brazilian Empire*, 10; and Andrews, *Afro-Latin America*, 89.

the slave trade, undertaken with Portuguese acquiescence. After long negotiations, an Anglo-Brazilian treaty was ratified in November 1826. It engaged Brazil to abolish its slave importations by 1830. Slaving was thereafter to be punished as piracy. With that treaty, the principal market for Africans slaves in what William Wilberforce called "the very child and champion of the slave trade," was designated for closure.[52]

On the European side of the Atlantic, the impact of Britain's victory over Napoleon's ascendancy was felt even more quickly. The Portuguese slave system had been less negatively impacted by two generations of revolutionary and military upheavals than any other nation of Atlantic Europe. João Pedro Marques finds no evidence suggesting even a potential concern with a "problem of slavery" in Portugal. The Portuguese embassy closely observed the emergence of abolitionism in Britain from 1788 to 1792, but, thereafter, rarely took note of the subject until the passage of slave trade abolition in 1807. When British cruisers began to capture and drive away Portuguese slavers after 1808, the Portuguese response was to demand damages for illegal seizures.[53]

After the defeat of Napoleon, Britain pursued its more active antislave trade diplomacy. The Portuguese government, like that of France and Spain, signed the treaty but eluded its enforcement, step by step. In 1815, a second Anglo-Portuguese treaty restricted Portuguese slavers from trading in Africa north of the equator. The government in Brazil thereupon revoked a prior law that had placed limits on the number of slaves that could be loaded on slave ships.[54] The net result was an increased flow of slaves from further south in Africa, which was already the mainstay of supply for Brazilians. The British government refused to relent. It threatened to withhold subsidies previously offered for past treaties. The British navy seized Bahian ships venturing north of the equator in violation of the treaty of 1815. The looming threat of Brazilian independence and the mobilization of Spanish troops against Luso-Brazilian claims to the region that was to become Uruguay, overrode Portuguese reluctance to give way the slave trade.

The Portuguese thereafter pursued the pattern of French and Spanish responses to British pressure. The Portuguese were, of course, more dependent upon Britain both politically and financially than was France. The Luso-Brazilian public had been almost totally immune to the abolitionist discourse circulating through the Atlantic from the late 1780s. It is not coincidental that Portugal's last traditional defense of the slave trade was published the year after the Anglo-American abolitions. Its author was Azeredo Coutinho, bishop of Pernambuco in Brazil, and later of Elvas in Portugal. His premises were clear: the slave trade was time-honored and indispensable for Brazilian

---

[52] Bethell, *Abolition*, 60.
[53] João Pedro Marques, *The Sounds of Silence: Nineteenth-Century Portugal and the Abolition of the Slave Trade* (New York: Berghahn Books, 2006), 11; and Eltis, *Economic Growth*.
[54] Eltis, *Economic Growth*, Table A.1.

and Portuguese prosperity; African souls were rescued from African barbarity for salvation and civilization; events in Saint Domingue and France demonstrated the dangers of slave revolution and the necessity of Napoleon's revival of slavery. As Jeremy Adelman demonstrates, "abolitionism was a non-starter in both the Spanish and Portuguese empires." On neither side of the Atlantic did such a movement arise out of endogenous developments of civil society. Only deep internal political crises or continuous exogenous pressure from the British could impose conditions that would overcome the countervailing demands of protected economies and Iberian state treasuries heavily dependent upon the slave trade and slave labor.[55]

With the defeat of Napoleon and the persistence of British suppression, the Portuguese political elite abandoned such a straightforward defense of the slave trade. Apologetic literature registered a retreat to gradualism. Acknowledging the moral reprehensibility of the slave trade and the institution of slavery, the Portuguese pressed for some negotiated time period of tolerance, and refused to discuss any time frame at all on the ending of slavery. Plenty of ideological space was allowed to accommodate both clandestine slavers and nominally antislavery liberals. Abolitionist voices were virtually absent from the small Portuguese political class. There were no emotional appeals to the horrors of the slave trade.[56]

Portuguese legislators in the post-Napoleonic period followed the logical path laid out by their predecessors in the American Continental Congress, the early French Constituent Assembly in 1790, and the Spanish imperial Cortes of 1810. Portuguese legislators tried to say as little as possible about, and to make as few waves as politically feasible, over, slavery. It was an institution whose continued existence promised economic rewards and whose dismantling promised predictable divisions among the elite and unpredictable social, economic, and imperial risks. When the issue of abolition of the slave trade was briefly raised in the Portuguese constitutional Côrtes after the Liberal Revolution of 1821–22, it was quickly consigned to the limbo of a study committee. It remained there until the 1830s. Like their Spanish counterparts, Portuguese parliaments liberally borrowed Britain's epithet, "odious commerce," while expanding the commerce.

Perhaps the most distinctive characteristic of Luso-Brazilian policies on slavery was their governments' dependency upon "the primordial need to preserve Britain's support." Open defiance on the slave trade had to take second place to this consideration. When the foreign minister of newly

---

55 Adelman, *Sovereignty and Revolution*, 98–99. Marques, *Sounds of Silence*, 20–22, summarizes D. José Joaquim Azerdo Coutinho's *Analyse sobre a justiça do commercio do Resgate dos Escravos da Costa de Africa . . .* (Lisbon, 1808). For a good comparative perspective on slave resistance in the three major slave zones of the nineteenth-century Americas see Laird W. Bergad, *The Comparative Histories of Slavery in Brazil, Cuba, and the United States* (New York: Cambridge University Press, 2007), ch. 7.

56 *Ibid.*, 41–54.

independent Brazil presented the Anglo-Brazilian treaty to his Chamber of Deputies in June 1827, he noted that his government "had been forced to sign the treaty . . . *entirely against their will.*" Most deputies agreed with him that they were acting under compulsion in concluding a degrading treaty. Brazilian legislators could denounce the abolition treaty with Britain without daring to abolish it. They could and did petition the legislature to repeal the "hated abolition of the slave trade."[57] But no gesture towards abrogation was ever successful.

Portugal's vulnerability to British pressure made it the earliest European nation to surrender a portion of its sovereignty to the Royal Navy. For domestic consumption, Portuguese writers deployed arguments, which would remain staples of antiabolitionism everywhere in the Atlantic world for the next four decades. Within Britain, abolitionism was a diversion of attention from ills closer to home. Beyond Britain, it was a ploy to rescue the British slave colonies from inevitable decline and ruin. On the high seas, the British navy was actually a device to "recruit blacks . . . at no cost and little convenience" for the colony of Sierra Leone.[58]

Until Brazil declared its independence, Portugal defensively argued that its political economy was utterly dependent upon African slaves, pending the location of an alternative source of labor. After Brazil's separation, it became clear that Portugal continued to draw major fiscal benefits from its African colonies and from the transatlantic slave trade. Indeed, the loss of Brazil shifted planning back to the future of Portugal's African islands, São Tomé Príncipe and Cape Verde. The sites that formed the original nursery of Portugal's Atlantic slave empire reemerged in the 1820s as islands of hope. Within Africa itself, Angola became the imagined economy of a "new Brazil." It too required the slave trade.[59] Beyond Brazilian independence, "Africanization" of Portugal's ideal empire sustained the rationale for the slaving enterprise, which continued to depend on the Brazilian market. Portuguese slavers in the 1820s were carrying nearly three times as many captives to Brazil after the formal recognition of its independence than they had two generations before. In short, the political economy of the Portuguese elite looked as longingly toward slavery at the close of the age of revolution as it had at the start.

Ideologically, "tolerationism" continued to be the widespread response to Portugal's problem of slavery. In the 1820s, all works distributed in Portugal on abolition were funded by British-inspired, and probably Quaker-funded sources. As almost everywhere else in the Ibero-American orbit, no

[57] Marques, *Sounds of Silence*, 41–54; Jeffrey D. Needell, *The Party of Order: The Conservatives, the State, and Slavery in the Brazilian Monarchy, 1831–1871* (Stanford, Stanford University Press, 2006), 62; Bethell, *Abolition*, 62–65.

[58] Quoted in *Ibid.*, 69.

[59] Marques, *Sounds of Silence*, 78–83.

sustained antislavery movement had emerged after half a century of transatlantic revolutions. In the Americas, victories over the institution were collateral fruits of the struggles of Creoles for independence and of free persons of color for legal equality. In specific areas, one should not underestimate the benefits that accrued to slaves. The struggles offered openings, some very wide indeed, for slaves to assert and insert their freedom, through service, flight, and the intensification of all the traditional forms of resistance.[60]

In Europe, the postrevolutionary tendency towards nonenforcement was indebted to more than the lack of an indigenous abolitionist movement. Portugal shared in Continental Europe's general repression of civil society. One should not, however, ascribe the absence of antislavery discourse only to newspaper censorship, antiassociation laws, and police surveillance. In Spain and Portugal, as in France, there was no black presence, nor any large audience to demand continuous attention to the inconsistency between enacting the cruelties of the slave trade and acknowledging the trade's violation of civilized norms. By the 1820s, Portugal's exclusion from control over Brazil further diminished internal pressures to discuss the contradictions between metropolitan freedom and overseas slavery. In Portuguese Africa, there was no disturbing cycle of slave uprisings to match the "cycle of rebellion" in Bahia or to disrupt distant workings of the slave trade from the supply side.[61] Only a small portion of Africa, north of the equator, had been legally denied to Portuguese slavers by agreement with Britain. Although Portuguese slaving to Brazil was set to end by 1830, the portents were already clear that the traffic might not cease. The closer the moment of closure, the greater became the volume of imports. Brazilian slave trade reached record heights in 1829.

By 1830, primacy in the importation of Africans to the New World had long since shifted back from the northwestern European domination to Ibero-American. As many slaves were being delivered to Brazil and Cuba in the 1820s as had been freed by the Franco-Caribbean revolutions in the 1790s. There were more slaves in Latin America than there had been half a century before. If the planter and merchant elites acknowledged that the extinction of the slave trade was inevitable, the rising tide of captive African bodies landed each year seemed to extend the date of termination into an indefinite future.

---

[60] *Ibid.*, 87.

[61] According to Joseph Miller, the only attempted slave revolt known in the history of Luanda occurred in the 1740s, long before the Atlantic revolutions. *Way of Death: Merchant Capitalism and the Angolan Slave Trade, 1730–1830* (Madison: University of Wisconsin Press, 1988), 272.

8

Abolitionism without Revolution

Great Britain, 1770s–1820s

As we have seen in the cases of North America, the Caribbean, Latin America, and Continental Europe, the boundaries between slavery and antislavery in most of the Atlantic world appeared to shift as a result of unforeseen and unintended outcomes of violent struggles fought for other purposes. Within one nation, however, the boundaries shifted in a deliberative process matched only in one corner of the northern United States. Britain also experienced enormous vicissitudes in dealing with its overseas slave systems during the two generations after 1775. In the first decade of that period (1775–1783), the imperial power with the world's largest and most productive slave system lost control of half of it. In the middle decades of that period (1794–1814), the Caribbean remainder of that slave system was first threatened and then enlarged. On the eve of the post-war peace settlement with Europe, the British Empire again ruled over more slaves than it had at the outset of the American Revolution.

In 1814, Patrick Colquhoun estimated Britain's imperial slave population at 1.15 million, consisting of 634,000 in the British West Indies, 372,000 in conquered Caribbean colonies and 108,000 in conquered Asian colonies and dependencies. Even setting aside India, the British institution encompassed a slave population equal to those of the United States and more than those in Brazil. The trajectory of Britain's policy toward slavery was not primarily dictated either by the loss of its North American slave sector or the later dramatic threats to some Caribbean islands in the mid-1790s. As we have seen, during the decade preceding British abolition of the slave trade in 1807, the British empire had discovered a cheaper solution to the defense of the institution in the Caribbean, which had cost its military 80,000 men in the 1790s. Once it became the largest single purchaser of African slaves as recruits, the British military easily extended its empire to include all the colonies of its enemies. Ironically,

British colonial slaveholding reached its zenith in the wake of slave trade abolition.[1]

Even after returning some colonies to former belligerents in 1814, the areas most appropriate for slave settlement exceeded those controlled by the monarchies of Spain, France, and the Netherlands. In addition to its acquisition of Old World areas in which the institution was well established – the Cape Colony, Mauritius and Ceylon – Britain extended its slave frontier in the greater Caribbean alone more than tenfold in the half century after 1775. That rate of expansion exceeded even that of the United States of America.[2] Until British policies began to inhibit slavery's growth, the British transatlantic slave trade also reached its all time peak. By the end of the eighteenth century, British slavers were landing 50,000 slaves per year in the Americas and moving nearly 60 percent of the total number of captives shipped across the ocean.[3]

Thereafter, British slavery did not decline because of any major shift in the institution's contribution to the British economy. Nor did British slave production diminish as a proportion of Atlantic slave output during the last quarter of the eighteenth century. In 1807, British-controlled territories produced well over half of the sugar reaching Europe, up from less than one-third in 1775.

In response to this demonstrated robustness of Britain's colonial slave system and Britain's sustained commercial involvement in the Atlantic slave system, there has been an attempt to fit British slave trade abolition into the framework of the age of revolution. In this perspective, the abolition of the British slave trade (1788–1807) is interpreted as a response to a succession of crises: a post-war crisis of self-confidence in the wake of the war with America or a counter-revolutionary response to a protorevolutionary crisis in 1806–1807. Alternatively, the triumph of abolitionism in 1806–1807 is

---

[1] Roger Norman Buckley, *Slaves in Red Coats: The British West India Regiments 1795–1815* (New Haven: Yale University Press, 1979); and P. Colquhoun, *Treatise on the Wealth, Power and Resources of the British Empire* (London: J. Mawman, 1815), 46–47. The peak years of the British acquisition of slaves for Caribbean service between 1795 and 1815 was 1805 and 1806. See *ibid.*, 55 (Table 1) and 132 (Table 5). This tally includes legally freed recaptives from foreign slavers after 1808 who were "induced" to accept military service in the West India regiments. In respect to regimental numbers, abolition was not costless reform. It resulted in "a permanent reduction of the overall strength of the West Regiment from 1807 until the end of the war." (Ibid., 130). According to Buckley, West India blacks accounted for less than 7 percent of the 75,000 British military deaths in the West Indies between 1793 and 1815. They accounted for 17 percent of the total 424,000 casualties.

[2] Compare Colquhoun, *A Treatise on the Wealth*, 7 on the British Empire and *Historical Statistics of the United States*; for Brazil, Leslie Bethell and José Murello de Caravalho, "Brazil from Independence to the Middle of the Nineteenth Century," in *The Cambridge History of Latin America* vol. 3, *From Independence to c. 1870*, Leslie Bethell, ed. (Cambridge: Cambridge University Press, 1985), 679, 747.

[3] Eltis, et al., Slave Trade Database, 1799–1800.

framed as an ideological displacement of the rising discontent aroused by the industrial revolution.[4]

That there had to be some kind of reassessment of the British slave trade before 1807 is, of course, a truism. The slave interest was no longer able to maintain the status quo by 1806–07. This first major defeat of the British slave system in 1807 was the unmistakable marker of the political decline of the British slave system. Combined with the negative rate of slave reproduction in the British colonies, the elimination of the transatlantic trade signaled the proximate decline of the institution of slavery itself.[5]

---

[4] See above all, Davis, *Problem of Slavery in the Age of Revolution*, ch. 8, 9; and Blackburn, *Overthrow*, ch. 8. Davis sees the abolition of the slave trade as a displacement of ills closer to home. Robin Blackburn sees the process of slave trade abolition as occurring "at a time of exceptional national danger," derivative of a "radical revival" and a "shakeup within the ruling oligarchy." Apart from the vast literature on the "economic decline thesis" consult David Brion Davis, *Problem of Slavery in the Age of Revolution* (New York: Oxford University Press, 1999), ch. 8–9; and Robin Blackburn, *Overthrow*, ch. 2, 8: In this volume, Davis examines abolition before the 1820s as the elite's unconscious displacement of ills closer to home. Blackburn is especially focused upon abolition as a response to "a time of exceptional danger," itself deriving from a radical domestic revival and a "shakeup" within the ruling oligarchy. On an alternative view see, Seymour Drescher, "Whose Abolition?: Popular Pressure and the Ending of the British Slave Trade," *Past and Present*, 143 (May, 1994), 136–166; and Seymour Drescher, *Capitalism and Antislavery: British Mobilization in Comparative Perspective* (New York: Oxford University Press, 1987), ch. 4, 5; Eltis, *Economic Growth*, ch. 1; Eltis, *Rise of African Slavery*, 80–81. On the role of slave resistance, see the literature, comprehensively discussed, in Brown, *Moral Capital*, 21–22 n. 20. Some other recent studies have also revisited the impact of moral factors. Chrester Petley documents the cultural and political decline of the planters' sense of their unquestioned position in an imperial nexus after 1763. See "A Madness Overrunning the Whole World: Reactions to Abolitionism and the Decline of the British Planter Class" (manuscript kindly provided by the author). In a much more magisterial investigation, Christopher Brown has recounted the long march of protoabolitionists to moral mobilization between the Seven Years War and the political breakthrough in 1788. Brown references the reaction of the abolitionists' call to arms in 1787 as almost self-evident: "To a people who wished to think of themselves as Christian, moral, and free, the abolitionists presented an opportunity to express their reverence for 'liberty, justice, and humanity,' and at little cost to themselves. Who besides those with a personal stake in the slave system could object to that?" (*Moral Capital*, 450). However, it did require take twenty more years to carry abolition through Parliament. Perhaps the answer lies in the fact that the abolitionists were forced to address not the triad, "liberty, justice, and humanity," but "justice, humanity and sound policy."

[5] Seymour Drescher, *Econocide: British Slavery in the Era of Abolition* (Pittsburgh: University of Pittsburgh Press, 1977) 78, Table 17, "Shares of Sugar Exports to the North Atlantic, 1805–1806." These figures do not include the exports of slave-grown produce imported from the United States, especially cotton, the bulk of which was shipped to Britain during the period of the French Wars. Joseph Inikori estimates that British America accounted for 31 percent of the total value of New World export production in 1761–1780. In the following two decades, the former British-American share rose to 50 percent. The Caribbean share of British-American exports rose steadily from 55 percent on the eve of the American Revolution (1768–72) to 60 percent on the eve of slave trade abolition (1804–1806) to 67 percent by the end of the Napoleonic wars (1814–1816). See Joseph Inikori, *Africans and the Industrial*

A comparative perspective on British abolition illuminates what was to be the most distinctive, durable, and consequential development in the demise of New World slavery. Recall the shared civil and political context in which Anglo-American abolition emerged. In the last third of the eighteenth century, both Britons and Americans participated in representative political institutions and in a common law tradition guaranteeing individual rights against arbitrary state action or imprisonment. With a relative abundance of newspapers, they shared the most widely diffused communications network in the world. They also possessed an array of voluntary associations, which made them the frontrunners of an associational world.[6] In other words, during the age of revolution some Anglo-American societies possessed the most highly developed public sphere on the face of the earth.

What, then, was the distinguishing feature of British abolitionism? Before the end of the American War of Independence, the possibility of abolishing Britain's Atlantic slave trade had never been debated in Parliament. By the end of the French Wars three decades later, Parliament had entirely shut down Britain's own slave trade. Its government had begun the process of

---

Revolution (New York: Cambridge University Press, 2002), 202 (Table 4.8), 176 (Table 4.2); and Ralph Davis, *The Industrial Revolution and British Overseas Trade* (Leicester: Leicester University Press, 1979), 112–117, Tables 58–60 (imports by area, 1784–1816). From the British imperial perspective, this period was characterized by sharp initial war-induced reduction in its slave system at the beginning of the period, followed by a remarkable war-induced resurgence between the late 1780s and the 1810s. S.H.H. Carrington argues that there was a continuous decline in the profitability and prosperity of the British slave system after 1775. See *The Sugar Industry and the Abolition of the Slave Trade, 1775–1810* (Gainesville: University Press of Florida, 2002). David Rydan more recently argues that a short term decline before 1807 is an important component of the decision to abolish slavery. See *West Indian Slavery and British Abolition, 1783–1807* (New York: Cambridge University Press, 2009). For a recent assessment of the economic context of abolition, see David Richardson, "The Ending of the British Slave Trade in 1807: The Economic Context," in *The British Slave Trade: Abolition, Parliament and People*, Stephen Farrell, Melanie Unwin, and James Walvin, eds. (Edinburgh: Edinburgh University Press, 2007), 127–140. The crisis theory of British abolition certainly does not exhaust the variety of broad interpretations of its rise and success. Of the most stimulating hypotheses were generated by Eric Williams *Capitalism and Slavery* (Chapel Hill, NC: University of North Carolina Press, 1944) and David Brion Davis, *The Problem of Slavery in the Age of Revolution*, and have both generated extensive debates. On the former see Eltis *Economic Growth*, ch. 1; and Seymour Drescher, "Capitalism and Slavery After Fifty Years," *Slavery and Abolition*, 18 (3) (1997), 212–227. On the latter, see *The Antislavery Debate: Capitalism and Abolition as a Problem in Historical Interpretation*, Thomas Bender, ed. (Berkeley, CA: University of California Press, 1992). (See also note 19, below).

6 Peter Clark, *British Clubs and Societies, 1580–1800* (Oxford: Clarendon Press, 2002). On the long-term linkage between voluntarism and moral reformation in the eighteenth-century Anglo-American orbit, see Joel Bernard, "Original Themes of Voluntary Moralism: The Anglo-American Reformation of Manners," in *Moral Problems in American Life: New Perspectives in Cultural History*, Karen Halttunen and Lewis Perry eds. (Ithaca: Cornell University Press, 1998), 15–39.

internationalizing abolition. This dramatic change was embedded in a far larger transformation in British political culture and practice.[7] Parliamentary debates and governmental initiatives were now the daily grist of provincial newspaper readers. When legislative debates extended over weeks and months, newspapers, associations, libraries, debating societies, and public meetings offered parallel venues for ongoing discussions and petitions to the national legislature.[8]

Within this broader process, abolitionism came to occupy a distinctively innovative position. It combined new techniques of propaganda, petitioning, and association with the organizational techniques of mercantile and manufacturing lobbyists. Between its emergence as a national political movement in 1787 and the internationalization of transatlantic abolition at the end of the Napoleonic wars, political abolitionism became a pioneering organization in mobilizing hitherto untapped groups as actors for philanthropic and social reform. The movement's fortunes in Parliament during those three decades were also emblematic of the difficulties entailed in converting public pressure into law and policy.[9]

Antislavery Sentiment before Mobilization

One of the distinctive qualities of British political abolitionism was its emergence in conjunction with a massive wave of popular support in 1787–1788. Christopher Brown has meticulously traced the long history of abolition's protohistory down to the eve of popular mobilization. Two themes stand out in this story. The first is the steady stream of articulated distaste and revulsion that the overseas slave system continually evoked in eighteenth-century writings. Few travel accounts, imperial histories, or geographical compendia failed to mention its striking brutality and its deviance from metropolitan behavioral, legal, and religious norms. Some commented upon the ease with which most participants accepted the indifference to human suffering entailed in slavery's perpetuation.

Eighteenth-century culture was, therefore, already saturated with casual references to the violence done to social norms by the slave trade. By the

---

[7] Brown, *Moral Capital*, Parts III and IV.

[8] See Joanna Innes, "Legislation and Public Participation 1760–1830's," in *The British and their Laws in the Eighteenth Century*, David Lemmings, ed. (Woodbridge: Boydell Press, 2005), ch. 5. For an analysis of Britain's distinctive path to new forms of mass politics and popular relationships to the state, see Charles Tilly, *Popular Contention in Great Britain 1758–1834* (Cambridge, MA: Harvard University Press, 1995).

[9] See Seymour Drescher, *Capitalism and Antislavery: British Mobilization in Comparative Perspective* (New York: Oxford University Press, 1986), ch. 4; J.R. Oldfield, *Popular Politics and British Anti-Slavery: The Mobilization of Public Opinion Against the Slave Trade, 1787–1807*; and Judith Jennings, *The Business of Abolishing the Slave Trade 1783–1807* (London: Frank Cass, 1997).

mid-1780s, apologists for the slave trade would have found most lines of
defensive rationalization closed except those grounded on the sanctity of
private property, the economic value of slave labor, and the national interest
in sustaining valuable Atlantic trades and products.[10] The bad news for
pioneer abolitionists was that these reasons, all linked to the need for African
labor to produce staple agriculture in the tropics, were precisely those that
had easily sustained the slavery system against sporadic hostility for nearly
a century.

At the end of the American War of Independence, the British national
legislature still appeared to be unresponsive to abolitionist appeals. In June
1783, Quakers submitted the first public petition to Parliament against the
slave trade. Lord North, the British Prime Minister, complimented the petitioners on their generous feelings. He politely added that, unfortunately,
all of the European maritime powers had to make use of the African trade.
Many of the future legislative luminaries of abolition debates were present in
that session. None of them took issue with the prime minister's assessment.
The bill that had occasioned the Quaker petition, regulating the African
slave trade, passed through Parliament without further discussion.[11]

The following year, a Quaker abolitionist committee obtained an audience with the new ministry, led by the young William Pitt. Once again, there
was praise for the principle, but the committee was told that "the time was
not yet come to bring the affair to maturity."[12] The Quakers continued
to canvass the commercial and imperial elites, subsidize pamphlets, about
abolition, and place notices on the subject in the London and provincial
press. They were not encouraged by the parliamentary response. By 1785,
their distribution of 11,000 copies of Benezet's principal pamphlet to all
M.P.s, justices of the peace, and clergy had resulted in "an approbation of
our benevolence ... but little prospect of success."[13]

[10] Brown, *Moral Capital*, 369. On changing moral perceptions, see also David Brion Davis,
The Problem of Slavery in Western Culture, rev. ed. (New York: Oxford University Press,
1988), Part III and S. Drescher, "Moral Issues," in *A Historical Guide to World Slavery*,
S. Drescher and Stanley L. Engerman, eds. (New York: Oxford University Press, 1998),
282–290. For an extended argument on the causes of shifting moral imperatives, consult
the essays in Bender, ed. *The Antislavery Debate*, esp. Part 2. The security of the slave trade
was frequently verified even in its casual condemnations. Just ten years before the emergence
of abolitionism, the author of *The Present State of the West Indies* (London, 1778) (11),
noted, in passing, "this [Negro] trade, to the disgrace of the age, has so deeply taken root,
it is become so *necessary* to the present state of affairs, and our wants have justified it in
a manner so absolute that it is almost common-place to cry out the barbarity and cruelty
of it."
[11] Drescher, *Capitalism and Antislavery*, 62–63, and Brown, *Moral Capital*, 422–424.
[12] Brown, *Moral Capital*, 425.
[13] Drescher, *Capitalism and Antislavery*, 63 and 206 n. 42. As late as 1785, an item in
the *Public Advertiser* of London, on 21 January 1785, warned that to expect any relief
from Parliament was to expect the impossible, "till Negroes, by having boroughs for their

During the four years that followed the Quakers' (never repeated) petition to Parliament, the most voracious reader of the press would have been hard put to conclude that the Quakers had stimulated a rising tide of discussion about abolition, much less an expectation of political agitation.[14] Other evidence points in the same direction. Until 1786, the handful of active British abolitionists were still working in virtual isolation from each other. Writing his prize essay against slavery at Cambridge University in 1785, young Thomas Clarkson was completely unaware of Granville Sharp's decades of activity. Only on reaching London, early in 1786, did Clarkson discover that a Quaker antislave trade committee had been functioning for three years. The broader significance of the Quaker organization would become most apparent when they furnished cadres for the provincial, informational, and financial networks of the initial abolitionist movement. The small band of Evangelicals who were also to play a large role in the abolitionist process had furnished only one writer, James Ramsay, to the abolitionist cause.[15]

As late as the winter of 1787, neither the public nor the slave traders appeared to have been particularly impressed by abolition's political potential. The colonial agent for Jamaica in London counted William Pitt as "a great favorite" with the West India interest.[16] William Wilberforce's adhesion to abolitionism in 1787 came with a priceless bonus, his close friendship with Prime Minister William Pitt. In 1787, Pitt had clearly become sympathetic to politicizing the abolition issue. Pitt not only urged Wilberforce to take on the slave trade, but warned his friend that someone else might otherwise seize the initiative.[17]

property and loans at their disposal, shall have a party in the House of Commons at their command." (January 21, 1785). The most important antislavery tracts published between 1783 and 1787 were the writings of James Ramsay. Ramsay's detailed attack provoked a series of polemical exchanges in a correspondence that kept the issue of slavery before the reading public.

[14] As late as the thirty-three months between January 1785 and September 1787, the *Times* contained only four reports with antislavery overtones, an average of one every four months. By comparison, during the twenty-seven months between October 1787 and December 1789, the newspaper printed 210 such reports, or twice as many per month as in the entire prior thirty-three. See Drescher, *Capitalism and Antislavery*, 208.

[15] See Thomas Clarkson, *The History of the Rise, Progress, and Accomplishment of the Abolition of the Slave Trade by the British Parliament*, 2 vols. (London, 1808), I, ch. 7.

[16] Duke University Library, Fuller Letterbook I, 20, February 20, 1788.

[17] Robin Furneaux, *William Wilberforce* (London, 1974), 72. It is not unimaginable that Pitt perceived the slave trade question as an excellent counterweight to another *cause célebre*, the emerging impeachment of Warren Hastings. The Ministry's responsibility for Britain's imperial behavior in India was implicitly under scrutiny. In launching a simultaneous demonstration of humanitarian concern in Britain's Western empire, the government reduced any moral capital that the opposition might have hoped to reap from the East. Michael Duffy considers Pitt to have been "the first Prime Minister to bring public pressure on Parliament by means of petitions demanding reform...." for which he acted as "spokesman." One

The Breakthrough, 1787–1788

As noted, British abolitionism did not emerge at a crisis moment of chastened anxiety or national humiliation arising from the loss of the North American colonies. It was neither an attempt to resuscitate Britain's threatened image as the torchbearer of liberty in comparison with the new American republic nor a direct response to heightened internal class conflict or the devaluation of the British slave system in relation to the empire or the economy.[18] To the extent that moral self-scrutiny became an aspect of the post-war imperial discourse, it did so in the context of revived national self-confidence. By almost every empirical measure, popular abolitionism emerged at one of the most benign conjunctures of British history in the century between the Seven Years War and the American Civil War. A survey of London's newspapers in 1786–1787 shows a nation reveling in its prosperity, security, and power. From Cornwall to Aberdeen came reports that indicated the most abundant harvest in a decade and, in some places, in living memory. Industry was thriving and the cotton industry in particular was expanding at an unprecedented rate. Labor disputes had diminished in the coal mines and artisanal friendly societies were congratulated on their performances. Pitt was given full credit for the administration's successful financial planning and for anticipating a budgetary surplus.[19]

Prospects beyond the seas seemed equally bright. British goods were winning out everywhere. A commercial treaty with France in 1786 threw open a new market for British manufactures. British trade dominated entrepots from Canton to America. The West Indies was sending a fine crop of sugar. The French Islands were producing cotton and wool for English industry,

---

of Duffy's two examples is Pitt's motion against the slave trade. See Michael Duffy, *The Younger Pitt* (New York: Longman, 2000), 143.

[18] The most forcefully argued case for this perspective is Robin Blackburn's *The Overthrow of Colonial Slavery*, ch. 4. This does not, of course, mean that class conflict did not impinge upon public opinion and the parliamentary response to abolitionism during the twenty-year struggle that followed.

[19] Quantitative indicators reinforce the qualitative commentaries in the press. During the 1780s net migration rates from England fell to their lowest level in the more than three centuries between 1541 and 1871. See E. A. Wrigley, and R. S. Schofield, *The Population History of England: A Reconstruction* (Cambridge: Cambridge University Press, 1989), Table A3.3, 531–35. Further indicators of economic growth in output of commentaries, transportation and public finance may be found in S. R. Mitchell, *British Historical Statistics* (Cambridge: Cambridge University Press, 1988). The classic statement of the economic decline thesis and slave trade abolition is Eric Williams's *Capitalism and Slavery* (Chapel Hill: NC, University of North Carolina Press, 1944/1994), ch. 6. For recent overviews of the debate over the Williams thesis and its opponents, see David Brion Davis, *Inhuman Bondage: The Rise and Fall of Slavery in the New World* (New York, 2006) chapter 12; and David Richardson, "The Ending of the British Slave Trade in 1807: The Economic Context."

and expanding British West Indian output promised future imperial self-sufficiency.

What the press found most exhilarating was Britain's transformed international position. Plagued by aristocratic revolt and popular rioting, France was verging on bankruptcy and military impotence. The Netherlands was descending into revolution. The Dutch East and West Indian companies were both foundering. Britons were most fascinated by unfolding developments in the new American republic. In 1786 and 1787, newspapers offered an unending flow of bad news from New England to Georgia: the Confederation itself seemed to be disintegrating. When Lord Grenville presented a new bill on rules to govern trade between the United States and the British West Indies, he emphasized that the provisions had to be temporary because it was difficult to decide whether Americans were "under one government or no government at all."[20]

For Britain's fledgling abolitionists in 1787–1788, there was some good news from America: the ending of the slave trade by Rhode Island and other New England states and the Pennsylvania Abolitionist Society's memorial to the Constitutional Convention in Philadelphia, requesting a national abolition of the slave trade. The bad news was that the new U.S. Constitution placed a twenty-year prohibition on any implementation of abolition. Britain was hardly threatened by moral comparison with America. Slavery seemed secure within the United States. Although some American seamen were again sailing to West Africa to load slaves for the West Indies, others were themselves being enslaved by the corsairs of North Africa. The London press smugly listed the high prices demanded for Americans in Algiers alongside accounts of the Dey's brutal punishment of any corsair who dared to capture Britons in violation of Anglo-Algerian treaties. Never since Yorktown had British self-satisfaction been so spiced with *Schadenfreude*.[21]

Whatever the zeitgeist may have contributed to transforming abolitionism from a popular sentiment to a political movement in 1787, it was not any widespread notion that the British needed to snatch the role of liberty's torchbearer back from the United States. Popular abolitionism proceeded from a different premise: how could the world's most secure, free, religious, just, prosperous, and moral nation allow itself to remain the premier perpetrator of the world's most deadly, brutal, unjust, immoral offenses to humanity? How could its people, once fully informed of slavery's inhumanity, hope to continue to be blessed with peace, prosperity, and power?

Organized abolitionism began in May 1787, with the formation in London of the Society for Effecting the Abolition of the Slave Trade (the London Committee). As J.R. Oldfield has demonstrated, the London Committee

---

[20] See Drescher, *Capitalism and Antislavery*, 140–142; 247–248, for this and the following paragraph.

[21] *Ibid.*, 141–142.

would thereafter remain the nation's headquarters and coordinating center for popular mobilization. From the Quakers, who formed its original majority, the London Committee inherited experience in business organization, sources of funding, and a publishing and distribution network for books, pamphlets, official reports, and letters. Its members hoped that their provincial contacts would support an anticipated parliamentary intervention through local communications and petitions to representatives.[22] The London Committee's first priority was to gather first-hand evidence for an anticipated parliamentary inquiry. Thomas Clarkson was dispatched on a journey to Bristol and Liverpool, two slave-trading towns that were least likely to take the lead in furnishing abolitionist pressure on their MPs.[23]

On his way back to London, Clarkson was surprised and delighted to find that the town of Manchester had already formed its own abolitionist committee and intended to submit a mass petition to Parliament. From the outset, organized religious dissenters also rallied to the movement – Unitarians, Congregationalists, Baptists, Methodists, and evangelical Anglicans added their support to the Quaker cadres on grounds of morality, justice, and religion. For the first wave, however, Manchester's adhesion was particularly valuable to the London Committee. It undercut the traditional morality/policy dualism in British political culture that had discouraged or undermined earlier appeals against the Anglo-Atlantic slave system. Manchester was the epitome of a booming hard-nosed manufacturing town. Although not dominated by the Afro-Caribbean slave trades, some of its inhabitants had a tangible stake in them, larger perhaps than that of any other inland city in Britain. Although some of Manchester's leading cotton manufacturers, like the Peels, would be able to muster smaller-scale petitions against the abolitionists, they were never to come close to matching the 10,600 signatures supporting Manchester's abolition petition, much less the larger ones that followed.[24]

These ten thousand names, the largest of the 1787–1788 campaign, also offered striking evidence that Manchester's workers were also aligned with the abolitionist cause. This caught the slave interest by surprise.[25] Manchester's abolitionist signers represented about two-thirds of its eligible adult males. That forestalled any argument that abolitionism lacked a mass base. Along with Birmingham's later petition, Manchester was given pride of

---

[22] Oldfield, *Popular Politics*, ch. 3.

[23] For Clarkson's account, see *History* ch. 15–19. The London Committee does not seem to have taken a coordinating role in the wording of the first petitions. Oldfield, in *Popular Politics*, 47–48, correctly notes that the London Committee, from the outset, envisioned petitions as integral to their general quest for the support of public opinion. On the Quaker background to the mobilization, see especially Jennings, *The Business of Abolishing the Slave Trade*, ch. 2 and 3; and Brown, *Moral Capital*, ch. 7.

[24] Drescher, *Capitalism and Antislavery*, 67–75.

[25] See "Trebor Tnappilo's letter, 'A Friend to the African Trade,'" in the *Public Advertiser*, July 7, 1787.

place in affirming that a broad popular and economically informed portion of the nation had opted for abolition. Manchester's petition did not concern itself with the policy or economic aspects of the abolitionist case. Petitioners focused first and foremost on the need for political action against an offense to humanity, justice, and sound policy. Subsequent generations of petitions against the slave trade also stressed moral grounds for reform under the same triad of 'humanity, religion and justice.' Less than 5 percent of those petitions to come added any promise of economic advantage.[26]

The Manchester petition of December 1787 was innovative in another major respect. Newspapers were especially significant in the first national mobilization. There is no evidence that the local petitioning committees were in direct contact with each other during the initial campaign. Based upon Manchester's prior efforts at mobilization on economic issues, its abolitionists reprinted their petition in every major newspaper in England, calling for similar petitions. This summons probably helped to ensure that petitions for abolition composed more than half the total of petitions sent to Parliament in the 1787–1788 sessions. At a conservative estimate, at least 60,000 individuals signed the abolition petitions of 1788.[27]

The first abolition campaign caught allies of the slave interest by surprise. They were stunned by the speed and breadth of the national mobilization. The slave interest was as dismayed by the adhesion of prelates, universities, and other corporate communities as by the large popular base. The shock to Liverpool's merchants was especially severe. They appealed to the Home Office to take account of how far the people had been perverted and inflamed by abolitionists, increasing the danger of flames of rebellion and the torch of civil contest.[28]

Disoriented opponents of the abolition movement searched for historical perspective. One writer was reminded ominously of 1772, the year of the *Somerset* case in England and of Virginia's demand for ending the slave trade to the colony. More general were the terms thereafter applied to popular supporters' abolitionism by distressed defenders of the trade: "general clamour," "popular emotion," "phrenzy," "fanaticism," and so forth. All these terms implicitly recognized that the appeal for action was both widely and

[26] Drescher, "People and Parliament: The Rhetoric of the British Slave Trade," *Journal of Interdisciplinary History*, 20:4 (Spring, 1990), 561–580.

[27] One contemporary source claimed 100,000 signatories. (See Drescher, *Capitalism and Antislavery*, 82). This number equals or exceeds those estimated for other major petition campaigns during the previous two decades: those related to the Wilkes Affair in 1769–1770; to the American colonies in the mid-1770s; and to the dismissal of the Fox/North coalition in 1784. See James E. Bradley in *Religion, Revolution and English Radicalism: Nonconformity in Eighteenth Century Politics and Society* (New York: Cambridge University Press, 1990, 319–321).

[28] See Gilbert Franklyn, *Observations Occasioned by the Attempts made in England to Effect the Abolition of the Slave Trade....* (London, 1789) 21, and PRO, H.O. 42/13 25 May 1788. On opposition in London, see James A. Rawley, "London's Defense of the Slave Trade 1787–1807," *Slavery and Abolition*, 14:2 (1993), 48–69.

emotionally shared. Published appeals against the new abolition movement almost always acknowledged that their own "side has scarce found a single defender."[29]

The first wave of petitioning lifted the slave trade onto the political agenda. In February 1788, the prime minister, invoking intense popular interest, launched an inquiry of the Privy Council committee for trade and plantations into the slave trade. Its very mission marked a paradigmatic break with more than a century of governmental attention to the African slave trade. Instead of seeking ways to protect and enhance the trade, this investigation signaled a fundamental shift in the relationship between the metropolis and its overseas slave system. For the first time, the British political system was asked to treat Africans as fellow human beings in a foreign land rather than as factors of trade and production.[30]

In May 1788, the issue of abolition was formally introduced into the House of Commons as part of an implicit dialogue between Parliament and the people. Standing in for the ill Wilberforce, the prime minister framed his motion as a necessary response to "the great number and variety of petitions" that bespoke an engaged public. Pitt was powerfully seconded by other luminaries, such as Charles James Fox and Edmund Burke. Pointing to the petitions, Fox noted that he himself would have moved for consideration of abolition had Wilberforce not come forward. Burke rhetorically outbid the two previous orators. If the House "neglected the petitions of its constituents it must be abolished...."[31]

During the next eighteen years, bills for the abolition of the British slave trade would be moved twelve more times in Parliament, but always as an open question and not a government measure. Twice before 1807, abolition bills would succeed in the Commons only to be stymied in the upper house. Before 1806, two partial bills for eliminating British slaving to foreign colonies or from certain parts of the African coast would suffer similar fates in the House of Lords. Stephen Fuller, the Colonial Agent for Jamaica, had anticipated the situation: "The stream of popularity runs against us," he wrote as early as January 1788, "but I trust nevertheless that common-sense is with us, and that wicked as we are when compared with the abolishers, the wisdom and policy of this country will protect us." "Common" sense was institutionalized in the House of Lords. Until 1806, the peers would invoke their prerogative of independent examination to prevent the general abolition bills approved by the House of Commons from moving on to a definitive vote. Almost twenty years later, abolitionists had to develop

---

[29] *Morning Chronicle*, 5 February 1788.

[30] Drescher, *Capitalism and Antislavery*, 87–88.

[31] *Cobbett's Parliamentary History*, vol. 27 (1788–1789), May 9, 1788, cols. 495–505; and John Ehrman, *The Younger Pitt: The Years of Acclaim* (New York: E.P. Dutton 1969), 393.

a two-sessions, two-bills, two-Houses strategy to achieve total victory in Parliament.[32]

During the three years following the 1788 campaign, the London abolitionists focused their energies on procuring witnesses and evidence to be laid before a Commons Select Committee on the slave trade obtained by Wilberforce in 1789. The propaganda and the organization of the movement had to be sustained. In addition to its official seal with a kneeling slave, the Committee circulated the famous print of the slave ship Brookes. As a cheap, mass-produced product, it endured for a generation as the most widely disseminated image of the slave trade. The provincial committee system remained "the heart of organized anti-slavery." It was the network through which popular mobilization was organized.[33]

One should not lose sight of the distinctive ways in which abolitionism progressively deepened its base and intensified its appeal far beyond the affluent and educated urbanites who always constituted the majority of local committees. Abolitionism continually opened up new horizons for participation in the national movement. During Thomas Clarkson's first venture out of London on behalf of the Abolition Committee in the summer of 1787, he turned to common sailors for the bulk of his information. Although no African slaves were called to give evidence before the Commons Select Committee, the brutality and mortality suffered by the crews of slave ships became an effective abolitionist argument. Clarkson's informants included a black sailor, John Dean, who had been abused aboard a slaver. When one of Clarkson's informants was called to the House of Commons hearings, an observer wrote that the "whole committee was in a laugh." Wilberforce was asked, "Will you bring your ship-keepers, ship-sweepers, and deck cleaners in competition with our admirals and men of honor?"[34]

Clarkson's initial expansion of informants in the movement foreshadowed a broader pattern. Although female signatures on petitions were regarded as delegitimizing petitions for decades after 1787, their purses, voices, and pens penetrated the public sphere. Women appeared on the first publicized list of abolitionist subscribers in Manchester, in 1787, constituting 68 of a total of 302. Another list in London, in 1788, included the names of more than 200 women, about 10 percent of the total. Their participation was singled out for newspaper comment. As Claire Midgley observes, such lists affirmed the legitimacy of women's role in the public sphere. Another legitimizing link was provided by the slave trade's assault on the family. As

---

[32] See Roger Anstey, *Atlantic Slave Trade*, 288–89, 315–320, 330–332, and 364–402. See also Michael W. McCahill, *Order and Equipoise: The Peerage and the House of Lords, 1783–1806* (London: Royal Historical Society, 1978), 210.

[33] Oldfield, *Popular Politics*, ch. 5; Jennings, *Business*, ch. 3; David Turley, *The Culture of English Antislavery, 1780–1860* (London, 1991), ch. 5, esp. 118–121.

[34] Quoted in Marcus Rediker, *The Slave Ship: A Human History* (New York: Viking Press, 2007), 329. See also ch. 10. See also Clarkson, *History*, I, ch. 14–18.

the sustainers of the home, women were welcomed to add their voices and pens to the abolitionist cause. Women responded dramatically as poets and public speakers. As early as February 1788, abolition was discussed in "a ladies only" meeting in London. Newspapers commented upon the astonishing talent of one speaker, who won the decision in favor of abolition. Within a few weeks, the *Monthly Review* casually noted the appearance of an antislave trade work as that of another antislavery woman "joining the benevolent band."[35]

The press was equally impressed by the appearance of "a native of Africa" in another public debate on the slave trade. Before the late-1780s, the black presence had made itself felt in England chiefly through freedom cases in England or in accounts of anonymous victims: those thrown overboard to save water on the Atlantic voyage; those brutalized or executed in a horrific manner in the colonies; those freed during the American Revolution; those rescued by charity on the streets of London; or those boarded to found a new settlement in Sierra Leone. Published writers like Phyllis Wheatley and Ignatius Sancho might tangentially attack the slave trade, but they served primarily as celebrated evidence of Africans' potential for moral uplift and cultural achievement.

The advent of political abolitionism opened up new public space for Africans. In quick succession, Ottobah Cugoano and Olaudah Equiano became shapers of opinion rather than voiceless victims. To the themes of brutality published by Ramsay, Clarkson, and the Quakers, Cugoano's *Thoughts and Sentiments on the Evil of Slavery* (1787) boldly added a prescient argument for the creation of a maritime blockade against slavers. Two years later, the *Interesting Narrative of the Life of Olaudah Equiano, or Gustavus Vassa, the African written by himself,* made its author the most widely known African in Britain. Equiano's best-selling book and nationwide lecture tours provided most Britons with the most personalized experience of the Atlantic slave system they were to receive. Equiano epitomized an astonishing journey from captivity to freedom, conversion, and celebrity.[36]

---

[35] Claire Midgley, *Women Against Slavery: The British Campaigns, 1780–1870* (London: Routledge, 1992), 18–35; and Oldfield, *Popular Politics,* 135–141 and Moira Ferguson, *Subject to Others: British Women Writers and Colonial Slavery, 1670–1834* (New York: Routledge, 1992).

[36] On Cugoano, *Unchained Voices: An Anthology of Black Authors in the English-Speaking World of the Eighteenth Century,* Vincent Carretta, ed. (Lexington: University Press of Kentucky, 1996), 145–184, esp. 170–171. See Vincent Carretta, *Equiano the African: Biography of a Self-Made Man* (Athens, GA: University of Georgia Press, 2005); and James Walvin, *An African's Life: The Life and Times of Olaudah Equiano, 1745–1797* (London: Cassell, 1998). For a detailed analysis of the role of blacks in the emergence of British abolitionism, see Brown, *Moral Capital,* 282–298. In view of the public's focus on the African slave trade, Equiano may have altered his childhood narrative to maximize its impact by

The Second Wave, (1791–1792): The Triumphs and Perils of Popular Mobilization

The first wave of abolitionism enlarged the opportunities for new actors in the public sphere. The second wave expanded the public sphere still further. Three years of parliamentary hearings and maneuvering from 1788 to 1791 revealed the parliamentary influence of the mobilized slave interest. As early as July 1788, after the first petition wave, Wilberforce advised the London Committee to "avoid giving any possible offense to the legislature by forced or unnecessary associations."[37] There was no further collective intervention before Wilberforce's motion on abolition finally came in April 1791. Pitt, Fox, and Burke again fully supported the bill. From the beginning, the parliamentary abolitionists attempted to minimize the potential impact of abolition on the West Indies. They focused attention on the £600,000 to £900,000 annually invested in the slave trade itself. Their opponents took the opposite tack. They linked abolition to the fate of all West Indian capital, maximizing the risk nearly a hundredfold. At the end of the debate a backbencher concisely summed up the situation: "The leaders, it was true were for the abolition; but the minor orators, the pygmies, would, he trusted, carry this day the question against them. The property of the West Indians was at stake." Abolition was defeated by a vote 163 to 88. Whatever the merits of their argument, Roger Anstey concluded, the abolitionists lost resoundingly.[38]

The London Committee resolved that the time had come to renew its appeal to the nation for what was denied by Parliament. This time the mobilization was not left to the hazards of local initiatives. Clarkson systematically toured England. Another agent, William Dickson, covered Scotland. The emissaries were no longer seeking, but were dispensing evidence in the form of a carefully selected abstract of the testimony before the Select

claiming an African rather than an American childhood. See also James Sidbury, "Early Slave Narratives and the Culture of the Atlantic Market," in *Empire and Nation: The American Revolution in the Atlantic World*, Eliga H. Gould and Peter S. Onuf, eds. (Baltimore: Johns Hopkins University Press, 2005), 260–274, and 364 n. 7. On the subsequent historiographical controversy see "Olaudah Equiano, The South Carolinian? A Forum," Vincent Carretta, Paul E. Lovejoy, Trevor Burnard and Jon Sensbach, *Historically Speaking* vol. VII: No. 3 (January/February 2006), 2–16.

[37] British Library, Add Mss, 21255, Minutes of July 29, 1788 and July 1, 15, and 29, 1788, and *The Life of William Wilberforce*, Robert Isaac and Samuel Wilberforce, eds., 5 vols. (London, 1838), I, 183–84.

[38] *Cobbett's Parliamentary History*, vol. 29, col. 358, (April 19, 1791); and Anstey, *Atlantic Slave Trade*, 273. Slave arrivals in the British colonies were clearly peaking, slave, and sugar prices were rising, and productivity remained high. See David Eltis, Frank D. Lewis, and David Richardson, "Slave Prices, the African Slave Trade, and Productivity in the Caribbean, 1674–1807," *Economic History Review*, 58:4 (2005), 673–700.

Parliamentary Committee. They also orchestrated the timing of petition meetings to "excite the flame," but delay its "flaring forth" until the mass of petitions could simultaneously arrive in Parliament.[39]

The results far exceeded the Committee's expectations. Even two decades later, Clarkson's sober *History* allowed itself a moment of awe:

> Of the enthusiasm of the nation at this time none can form an opinion but they who witnessed it. There never was perhaps a season when so much virtuous feeling pervaded all ranks.... The current ran with such strength and rapidity that it was impossible to stem it.... [No petitions] were ever more numerous, as far as we have any record of such transactions.... The account stood thus. For regulation there was one; against all abolition there were four; and for the total abolition of the trade five hundred and nineteen.

Upward of 400,000 names flowed into London just in time for the opening of Wilberforce's second motion. These were probably the largest numbers of both petitions and signatures ever simultaneously reaching Parliament on a single subject. In some parts of the country, between a quarter and a third of the adult male population petitioned for abolition, with Manchester's proportion reaching nearly 50 percent.[40]

Geographically, the London Committee received positive responses from one end of the country to the other. No boundaries were drawn between backwaters and large towns or between principal and general inhabitants. Clerical assemblies, universities, and chambers of commerce took their places modestly beside trade organizations and worker friendly societies. The London Committee emphasized that it favoured popular petitions. The popular response to the great campaign of 1791–1792 indicates that the abolitionists received almost unlimited support within the contemporary boundaries of legitimate signers.

The organizers were clearly less worried about too little popular enthusiasm for abolition than too much. Their most important concern was actually the danger to their own popular mobilization from linkage with other or more radical programs. Most members of the London Committee also feared that other political issues might impinge on the abolitionist mobilization. Clarkson, who was himself very sympathetic to the French Revolution, was explicitly warned by Wilberforce to steer clear of discussing it for fear of damaging the abolition cause. Clarkson's own warning to William Dickson, en route to Scotland, was to urge him that it was "impossible to be too earnest in professing the distinction between emancipation and abolition." Dickson was also warned to steer the potential petition

---

39 British Library, Add Mss 21 256, Minutes of May 27, 1791; and Friends House Library, London, Temp. Mss Box 10/14, William Dixon, Diary of a Visit to Scotland, January 5th–March 19th, 1792.

40 Clarkson, History, II, 352–355; Drescher, *Capitalism and Antislavery*, 80; and Oldfield, *Popular Politics*, 114, 123 n. 83 and 84.

committees away from any discussion of policy except the most general idea that "what is unjust must be impolitick." Dickson also found that opponents of abolition were making some efforts to use the Saint Domingue slave uprising of 1791 against the petitioning. The outcome of the uprising was too uncertain, however, to have significantly affected the parliamentary debate.[41]

The London Committee also approached another mass antislavery mobilization with caution. Following the parliamentary defeat of abolition in 1791, a new abolitionist strategy emerged outside the orbit of the London Committee. A nationwide campaign was launched to abstain from the consumption of slave-grown sugar. This "antisaccharite" movement was more than just a symbolic means of pollution avoidance. It was meant to be an instrument of direct economic coercion against the whole slave interest and it dramatically broadened the public sphere. Special appeals were directed toward women, as managers of the household budget. They stressed women's special sensitivity to family separations and offered the boycott as a means of compensating for their exclusion from the petition campaign. Children, too, were also urged, and volunteered, to become part of this national consumer mobilization. On his speaking tours, Equiano distributed pamphlets against consuming slave sugar. Again, the bolder Clarkson privately favored the antisaccharite agitation in hopes of increasing the turnout for petitions, but Wilberforce feared abstention as likely to alienate moderates.[42]

Thus, alongside the carefully crafted and targeted appeal of the London Committee, appeared a parallel movement involving hundreds of thousands of other participants. Although we have no breakdown of the abstainers by age or gender, women and children, the majority members of most families, clearly lay outside the boundaries envisioned by most of provincial petition committees. Some abstentionist polemics explicitly identified the British legislature, as constituted, as an institution that was unlikely to abolish the slave trade. Because Parliament had failed to heed the express will of the people, the people had to "manifest to Europe and the World that public spirit, that virtuous *abhorrence* of SLAVERY, to which a British SENATE is unable – or unwilling to aspire."[43]

---

[41] William Dickson, "Diary of a Visit to Scotland, Instruction #1;" *Ibid.* February 5th and 14th, 1792. For the reception of the Saint Domingue revolution in Britain in the winter of 1791–1792, See David Geggus, "British Opinion and the Emergence of Haiti, 1791–1805," in *Slavery and British Society 1776–1846*, James Walvin, ed. (London: Macmillan, 1982), 123–149.

[42] Clarkson, *History*, II, 349–50; Wilberforces, *Life of Wilberforce* I, 338–339.

[43] See Drescher *Capitalism and Antislavery*, 56–60; Caretta, *Equiano*, 355; *Considerations addressed to Professors of Christianity* (London, 1792), 2; and W[illiam] A[llen], *The Duty of Abstaining from.... West India Produce.... January 12, 1792* (London, 1792) p. iii, "advertisement."

The language of this radical voice of abolitionism resonated with other voices calling for fundamental political reform in Britain. In the winter of 1792, the antisaccharite movement appeared to be but one more symptom of many radical challenges sweeping across the Atlantic world. Every British radical political organization hailed the surge of abolitionist petitions as the harbinger of still greater transformations. They happily incorporated "the end of the slave trade" into their toasts and resolutions. The Society for Constitutional Information and the London Corresponding Society found a natural affinity in the plight of enslaved Africans and oppressed Britons. The British press noted the French National Assembly's award of honorary citizenship to Wilberforce. As the flow of abolition petitions peaked early in 1792, the counterabolitionist strategy broadened to conflate abolitionism, not only with slave emancipation, but with every potential threat to public order, foreign and domestic. Antiabolitionists widely advertised publications detailing the horrors of the revolution in Saint Domingue. Clarkson felt impelled to publish a denial of membership in the Jacobin club of Paris. The London Committee also published his refutation of the West India Committee's accusation that the British abolitionist movement was responsible for the Saint Domingue uprising.[44]

During the extended parliamentary debates on abolition in April 1792, the news coverage of abolition reached a crescendo. The House of Commons spent much of the month of April analyzing the petitions and their significance. Fox reiterated the premise of 1788 – a table loaded with petitions indicated that the whole people of England felt a legitimate grievance. The unprecedented pile of sheets on the table in 1792 now emboldened some abolitionist MPs to welcome the charge that school-boys and people of the lowest status had signed on: "What did this prove but that individuals of all sorts, conditions and ages, young and old, master and scholar, high and low, rich and poor, the risen and the rising generation, had unanimously set every nerve on stretch for the overthrow of the... abominable and the indefensible?"[45]

For a few weeks, the new wave of public opinion seemed to have succeeded in reversing the defeat of 1791. The House of Commons voted for gradual abolition by a vote of 230 to 85, and for an immediate end to the

---

44 Thomas Clarkson, *The True State of the Case, Respecting the Insurrection at St. Domingo* (Ipswich: J. Bush, 1792); and Ellen Gibson, *Thomas Clarkson: A Biography* (Houndmills: Macmillan, 1989), 75.

45 *The Diary* (a London newspaper), April 14, April 24, May 4, 1792. In moments of major conflict with abolitionists, the colonists in the West Indies also petitioned Parliament, but in far smaller numbers. They later shifted their pleas toward the Crown, reflecting the "increasingly unpopular nature of the proslavery cause." See David Lambert, "The Counter-Revolutionary Atlantic: White West Indian petitions and Proslavery Networks," *Social and Cultural Geography*, 6 (June, 2005), 405–420.

British slave trade to foreign colonies. By a far smaller margin, the House of Commons voted to set the date of total abolition at 1796. Yet, within months, the abolitionist tide receded both in Parliament and in the country. In 1788, the House of Lords had barely assented to the Dolben regulatory measure. The House of Lord insisted upon hearing its own evidence and put off beginning the hearings until the following session. By then, the political window for agitation had closed. Fear of domestic radicalism was compounded by the twin threat of revolutionary slave emancipation in the Caribbean and still more by French revolutionary expansion in Europe. Early in 1793, as Britain went to war with France, "odium had fallen on collective applications" to Parliament for any reform.[46]

Nothing resembling the great popular agitation of 1792 was repeated before the passage of slave trade abolition acts in 1806–1807. Some historians have seen Parliamentary abolition as having occurred within a long lull in popular participation, stretching from 1792 until the 1820s.[47] If one looks beyond mass petitioning, however, the role of public opinion in 1806–1807 is abundant. In accounting for its changed form, one must bear in mind both the magnitude of the reactionary culture of the 1790s and abolition's relatively rapid reappearance as the first successful reform movement after the French Revolutionary decade. Even in the 1790s, for all of the innuendos about Wilberforce and Jacobinsim, the House of Commons never refused to consider his annual motions for abolition. By 1804, fears of popular radicalism had subsided. The British Volunteer Movement had demonstrated, in the view of Prime Minister Henry Addington, that "the people," continually assembled and armed, had indicated a collective determination to defend British independence that "transcended the divisions between social classes."[48] In these large associations, regularly gathered together, slave trade abolition was deemed quite compatible with the broader struggle for national liberty. Preachers told the volunteers that they were fighting to decide whether there should be any more freedom on earth and made an explicit connection with the moral imperative to welcome abolition.

A decade after the great mass petition of 1791–1792, abolition remained on the British policy agenda. In opening preliminary discussions for the Peace of Amiens (1802), Pitt's antiabolitionist successor, Henry Addington, felt impelled to propose negotiations for a mutual Anglo-French termination of the transatlantic slave trade to the Caribbean. Napoleon, already envisioning

---

[46] *Life of Wilberforce*, II, p. 18.
[47] See inter alia, James Walvin, "Abolishing the Slave Trade: Anti-Slavery and Popular Radicalism, 1776–1807," in Clive Emsley and James Walvin, eds. *Artisans, Peasants and Proletarians, 1760–1860* (London: Croom, Helm, 1985), 32–56. David Turley, *The Culture of English Antislavery* (1991); and Oldfield, *Popular Politics*, 186.
[48] Linda Colley, *Britons* (New Haven: Yale University Press, 1992), 309, 319.

a massive expansion of France's overseas empire, did not respond.[49] Britain was faced with a unilateral decision of considerable import for its slave empire. During the decade before British abolition, the empire acquired ten times more undeveloped territory suitable for slavery than it had occupied during the whole previous century in Trinidad, Guiana, and South Africa. Both sides realized that millions more captives were put at potential risk in Africa. Nevertheless, abolitionists managed to shut one door after another to restrain slave importation to these undeveloped lands until the general prohibition of 1807.[50]

Looking at the opening years of the nineteenth century, it is important to see the contrasts between the French, American, and British policies towards their potential slave frontiers. By 1801, Napoleon intended to dramatically expand France's commitment to the institution. His western design entailed France's retention and reconquest of the former French Caribbean colonies and expansion into the Louisiana territory, restored by the Spanish king to French sovereignty. Within two years, his disastrous defeat in Haiti delimited his Caribbean project. The resumption of hostilities with Britain and its naval supremacy doomed the rest of his colonial plans. The combined impact of Napoleon's break with revolutionary legacy and British sea power not only shattered his western policy, but disposed of his dreams of undermining Britain's domination of India and Australia as well.[51]

As previously noted, the United States' acquisition of Louisiana, in 1803, converted a Napoleonic developmental project into an American one. Even if we include only the areas reserved for slave development on the west bank of the Mississippi between New Orleans and St. Louis, by the 1820s, more arable land was available for the expansion of slavery in the United States than in the British Caribbean. From 1804 to 1808, there was a surge in the importation of African slaves into the new territory. This was supplemented by thousands of slaves already residing in the new territory, Franco-African slaves from Cuba in 1809–1810, and a continuous stream of African-American slaves into the southern tier of states carved out from the original Louisiana Purchase.[52]

British policy took a different turn. The development of Trinidad, conquered in 1797, and definitively transferred to Britain, was indefinitely curtailed. This was not due to any diminution of the potential supply of African slave labor or the lack of abundant land for development. Between the French emancipation decree in 1794 and the consolidation of Haitian

[49] Yves Benot, "Bonaparte et la Démence Coloniale (1799–1804)," in *Mourir pour les Antilles: Indépendance nègre ou l'esclavage (1802–1804)*, Michel L. Martin and Alain Yacou, eds. (Paris: Editions Caribéenes, 1991), 20–21.

[50] Drescher, *Econocide*, ch. 6.

[51] Thierry Lentz, "Bonaparte, Haiti et l'echec colonial du régime consulaire," *Outre-Mers*, 90:2 (2003), 41–60.

[52] Fehrenbacher, *Slaveholding Republic*, 150, 386 n. 71.

national liberation a decade later, the British were transporting more than 46 percent of Africans arriving in the New World, a higher share than they had ever before attained. During the same period their Anglo-French enemies delivered only 5 percent of the total. In 1805–1806, however, imports of African slaves to conquered Dutch Guiana were reduced. After 1808, all further importations of slaves from Africa was prohibited. The intercolonial transfer of slaves from the developed to the frontier plantations was also extinguished by the late 1820s. The impact of British and American abolition policies may be observed in the slave migration figures. In the generation between the Anglo-American abolitions of 1808 and British slave emancipation in 1833, the importing states of the American union received twenty times more new slaves than the frontier colonies of Trinidad and Guiana. Thus, British policy as early as 1802 already moved along a different trajectory than that of America.[53]

The dissociation between British abolition and French radicalism was also eased by Napoleon's reimposition of slavery in 1802. When Anglo-French hostilities resumed the following year, the French ruler became the potential enslaver of two worlds. Toussaint Louverture "torn like a felon from Domingo's plain" and shipped to Europe to die in captivity, suffered a fate that loomed over Britons too. The invasion scare of 1803–1804 stimulated speculations that French conquest would result in able-bodied Englishmen being "turned out in gangs, like galley slaves," or turned into factory and mining slaves.[54]

Correspondingly, the struggle of ex-slaves against France shifted the role of Saint Domingue's revolutionary masses to a potential ally against a common enemy. With each passing year after 1804, Haiti's turn to British merchants for vital trade links made the new regime appear less threatening to both British colonial and metropolitan interests. This shift was ultimately to be reflected in parliamentary debates. By 1807, Haiti was no longer an existential threat to the British colonies. It was now used primarily by abolitionists, not antiabolitionists, to warn of a precedent that might inspire fresh captives in the colonies at some future point. The absence of any indigenous their own colonies uprising in prompted the British government to

---

[53] S. Drescher, "The Fragmentation of Atlantic Slavery and the British Intercolonial Slave Trade, in *"The Chattel Principle" Internal Slave Trades in the Americas*, Walter Johnson, ed. (New Haven: Yale University Press, 2004), ch. 10, 237; Table 10.1.

[54] Austin Gee, *The British Volunteer Movement 1794–1814* (Oxford: Clarendon Press, 2003), 186; and Stuart Semmel, *Napoleon and the British* (New Haven: Yale University Press, 2004), 46, 57, 112. Haiti's impact on British opinion is detailed in David Geggus "British Opinion and the emergence of Haiti, 1791–1805," in *Slavery and British Society 1776–1846*, James Walvin, ed. (London, 1982), 123–149. On Haiti's diminishing role as a military threat before 1807, see Drescher and Drescher, "Civilizing Insurgency," in *Who Abolished Slavery? Slave Revolts and Abolitionism*, Seymour Drescher and Pieter Emmer, eds. (New York: Berghan Books, forthcoming).

dismiss the possibility of abolitionist-inspired revolts as a bugaboo conjured up by *anti*abolitionists.[55]

The decoupling of abolition from such exogenous threats did not, of course, suffice to insure abolition's success in Parliament. In 1804, Pitt's return to office and the uncertainty about the impact of newly independent Haiti on the British islands encouraged Wilberforce to reintroduce his abolition motion. The bill successfully passed through the House of Commons late in June, only to falter at the old hurdle. The House of Lords, quite untroubled by any sense of emergency, repeated their earlier insistence on hearing new evidence. The friends of abolition in the upper House advised postponement until the following year.

Relying solely on crying "Haiti" or on quietly lobbying Parliament was not enough. In 1805, Wilberforce saw the previous year's majority in the Commons melt into an unexpected minority. As Roger Anstey concluded, the victory of 1804 had been deceptive. "Enemies had only to exert themselves more, and friends less, and the day was lost."[56] Regrouping after the unexpected setback, the London Committee decided that renewed popular pressure was essential to break the stalemate. Given the potential pitfalls of a national mobilization, the London Committee confined its tactics to localized mobilizations, but they began to have a serious effect. As early as 1805, the slave interest protested that the "violent" propaganda being worked up in Yorkshire, Lancashire, and London by their antagonists was becoming a serious deterrent to the flow of capital to the Caribbean. The West India Committee had to revive its dormant propaganda movement.

As noted in chapter 6, with the formation of the Fox-Grenville Ministry early in 1806, the government and the abolitionists returned to the partial abolition tactic that had twice failed to gain traction in the House of Lords. After the passage of the foreign slave trade act in May 1806, attention immediately turned to the question of total abolition. Grenville, working with the abolitionist leaders, was aware that the Foreign Bill had passed on the grounds that it would help the British colonies keep a wartime edge over their belligerent competitors. The British government therefore made a final unsuccessful effort to negotiate with France a bilateral abolition agreement. Even after the military debacle in Haiti and his loss of Louisiana, Napoleon remained uninterested in the proposal. Total abolition in 1807 would have to rely primarily on the original abolitionist arguments grounded

---

[55] Lord Howick introduced the debate in the House of Commons on February 24, 1807; *Cobbett's Parliamentary Debates*, [hereafter P.D. (41 vols, 1804–20), VII, cols. 952] 952. See also, Drescher, *Econocide*, 169 and 256 n. 11.

[56] Anstey, *Atlantic Slave Trade*, 346; see also Clarkson, *History* II, 502-03; Drescher, "Whose Abolition? Popular Pressure and the Ending of the British Slave Trade," *Past and Present*, 143 (May 1994), 136–166; and Peter F. Dixon, "The Politics of Emancipation: The Movement for the Abolition of Slavery in the British West Indies, 1807–1833," Oxford University, D. Phil. Thesis, 1971, 119–132.

on "justice sound policy, and humanity." This required another appeal to society. Stephen urged Grenville to delay the final motion until after a general election, so that M.P.s might be *"instructed by large bodies of their constituents* to vote for an abolition of the slave trade." Grenville agreed, feeling that an increase in pro-abolitionist sentiment would also help to strengthen the ministry's position in parliament. The strategy worked.[57] In the crucial debate in the House of Commons on February 23, 1807, the actual margin of victory was 283 in favor and only 16 opposed – the same relative margin by which the Congress had passed the United State's Abolition Bill ten days earlier.[58]

The overwhelmed opponents of abolition were quite sure about what had created the abolitionists' unprecedented margin of victory. General Gascoyne of Liverpool, representing Britain's major slaving port, complained that every measure that invention or art could devise to create a popular clamor had been brought to bear:

The Church, the theatre, the press, had laboured to create a prejudice against the slave trade.... The attempts to make a popular clamour against the trade were never so conspicuous as during the last election, when the public newspapers teemed with abuse of the trade, and when promises were required from different candidates that they would oppose its continuance. There has never been any question agitated since that of Parliamentary reform, in which so much industry had been exerted to raise a popular clamour and to make the trade an object of universal detestation. In every manufacturing town and borough in the kingdom all those arts had been tried.[59]

It would be difficult to identify a more anguished register of the weight of public opinion in favor of abolition in the winter of 1807. It is crucial to note, however, that abolition did not become a symbol of national solidarity in 1807. The role played by Wilberforce in the passage of the abolition

57 Anstey, *Atlantic Slave Trade*, 395, 401–402; Drescher, *Econocide*, 218; Peter Jupp, *Lord Grenville 1759–1834* (Oxford, 1985), 388–89; and, Drescher, "Whose Abolition," 145. See also *P.D. VIII*, 718–719. On Sidmouth's opposition to the "popular cause," see also George Pellew, *The Life and Correspondence of Henry Addington, Viscount Sidmouth*, 3 vols. (London, 1847), II, 427–448. In his thorough analysis of abolition in 1807, Roger Anstey concludes that the "immediate explanation" for its passage "lies in systematic abolitionist lobbying." He notes, however, that without exception, the abolitionists were astonished that the negative position was so poorly supported by the opposition, despite their "unusual exertions" to procure votes, and what Wilberforce described as a "terrific list of doubtfuls." (*Atlantic Slave Trade*, 396–400) (my emphasis). The outcome conflicts with Anstey's logic for the abolitionist's parliamentary defeat in the previous balloting on abolition in 1805.

58 See Stephen Farrel, *Contrary to the principles of justice, humanity and sound policy*, in "The Slave Trade, Parliamentary Politics and the Abolition Act of 1807," in *The British Slave Trade: Abolition, Parliament and People*, Stephen Farrell, Melanie Unwin and James Walvin eds. (Edinburgh: Edinburgh University Press, 2007), 141–171.

59 *P.D. VIII*, 718–19. On Sidmouth's opposition to the "popular cause," see also George Pellew, *The Life and Correspondence of Henry Addington, Viscount Sidmouth*, 3 vols. (London, 1847), II, 427–448.

bill only increased the suspicions of radicals like William Cobbett, always hostile to "negrophile" altruism. Other radicals argued, ex post facto, that the Grenville government had acted only to relieve the West Indian planters. Jamaican planters vehemently disagreed. They were masters in the leading sugar and coffee colony in the world. Their assembly railed against the damage abolition had done to their future. Closer to home, Liverpool rioters took out their anger on their own member of Parliament. William Roscoe, who had voted in favor of abolition, was terrorized into withdrawing from his campaign for reelection in 1807. Within three months of the Act's passage, even Wilberforce came close to losing his Yorkshire seat because of a rumored campaign alliance with the very West Indian whom he had forced to withdraw from the 1806 election.[60]

Peace and Internationalization

The whole period, between the Peace of Amiens in 1802 and the Congress of Vienna in 1815, marked a turning point in the history of British and world slavery. France, America, and Great Britain were all poised for dramatic imperial expansions of their slave systems. In 1802, Napoleon hoped to link his reconquered French slave colonies in the Caribbean and his acquisition of Louisiana into a grand western design for becoming a preponderant imperial presence on both sides of the Atlantic. In 1804, the United States inherited the major segment of this vast frontier in Louisiana and promptly expanded its empire of slavery beyond the Mississippi. As noted, between 1802 and 1806, the British occupied and determined to retain the undeveloped territories of Trinidad and Demerara. In diplomatic negotiations in 1801, and again in 1806, the British government tried in vain to introduce the question of a bilateral prohibition of further slave imports from Africa. Between 1802 and 1806, the British took unilateral action to curtail African slave imports into their newly acquired major Caribbean acquisitions. By 1808, they began to exercise naval and diplomatic pressure to curtail the foreign slave trades. The wartime expedients expanded into a systematic international crusade before the Congress of Vienna. The only extra-European article to emerge from the Congress of Vienna was an international condemnation of the slave trade.

British public opinion did not approach a truly national consensus on internationalization until the summer of 1814. Foreign Minister Castlereagh's entrance into the House of Commons, with the victorious Treaty of Paris in hand, should have been his moment of supreme triumph.

---

[60] Drescher, "Whose Abolition," 149–152; Peter Spence, *The Birth of Romantic Radicalism: War, Popular Politics and English Radical Reformism, 1800–1815* (Aldershot, 1996), 36–37; Marcus Wood, *Slavery, Empathy, and Pornography* (Oxford: Oxford University Press, 2002), ch. 3; and F. E. Sanderson, 'The Liverpool Abolitionists,' in *Liverpool, the African Slave Trade, and Abolition*, Roger Anstey and P.E.H. Hair, eds. (Historic Society of Lancashire and Cheshire/Occasional Series, 1976), 126–156; Drescher, "Whose Abolition," 149–152.

According to the staid *Hansard* record, he was received with loud cheers. Then Wilberforce rose to speak. He denounced the treaty as the death warrant for a multitude of innocent victims – men, women, and children. The treaty's "Additional Article" reopened the French slave trade, with British sanction, for five full years. Other members were not backward in reminding the House of Commons that members of the government, including the Foreign Minister, notoriously had been among the diehard opponents of abolition seven years earlier.[61]

The London Committee quickly determined to launch another petition campaign, while tactically avoiding a challenge to the government. They condemned the treaty's slave trade article and gave Castlereagh credit for having done everything he thought possible. But the message was clearly aimed at the slave trade of France. For the fourth time in twenty-seven years, the public was called in against the Atlantic slave trade. The national response was resounding.

In many ways, it was the most impressive campaign of the entire struggle. Ultimately, a total of 1,370 petitions reached Parliament, well above the average annual number of all other petitions submitted between 1811 and 1815. At one point, abolitionists estimated that 750,000 people had signed up. Paul Kielstra has recently raised the final total to 1,375,000, although this figure may include petitions sent up to both Houses. In any event, for a nation with no more than 4 million males over the age of 16 years, between a fifth and a third of all those eligible to sign had added their names to the appeal.[62]

Castlereagh's own evaluation of the abolition campaign was concise: "the nation is bent upon this object. I believe that there is hardly a village that has not met and petitioned." The Duke of Wellington registered a similar impression on his way back to France to renegotiate the slave trade article: "I was not aware till I had been some time here [London] of the degree of frenzy existing here about the slave trade. People in general appear to think that it would suit the policy of this nation to go to war to put an end to that *abominable* traffic."[63] The Duke had absorbed the adjective if not the advocacy of the abolitionists.

With this great surge of petitioning, abolitionism moved beyond mearly registering a protest against an article in a peace treaty. It definitively launched Britain into a long-term international, moral, and political

---

[61] *P.D. XXVIII*, 274, 332, 352, 443.

[62] Paul Michael Kielstra, *Politics*, 7–15, 23–33; and Drescher, "Whose Abolition," 160–162. In 1814, just seven years after registering their fury over abolition, the citizens of Liverpool were among the most signed-up petitioners in Britain against the foreign slave trade. John Gladstone, a major West Indian investor, was responsible for raising the city's total number of signers from 2,000 to 30,000. Drescher, "The Slaving Capital of the World: Liverpool and National Opinion in the Age of Revolution," *Slavery and Abolition*, 9:2 (September 1988), 128–143, esp. 139–140.

[63] Drescher, "Whose Abolition?," 164.

campaign against the transatlantic slave trade. It was a pioneering development in the link being forged between the terms of public discourse and the mobilization of public opinion. In the course of a single generation, abolitionism had evolved from a program of an innovative public contender into a settled fixture of national policy. The first great reform movement to revive after the general eclipse of the 1790s, the power of abolition was successively ratified in legislative victories and governmental policy. By 1814, the abolitionism movement had spawned the first human rights organization and altered much of the Western world's perspective on the future of slavery as an institution.[64] The end of European hostilities in 1814 was also a major turning point in the history of slavery. The great popular mobilization of 1814 shocked the British government into making abolitionism a foreign policy priority.

Foreign Minister Castlereagh insisted on an end to Iberian inertia. Britain also pressed for joint action by the great European powers assembled at the peace Congress of Vienna. The other rulers' reactions ranged from deeply hostile to abolition mildly sympathetic, more or less in proportion to their distance from, and interest in, the Atlantic system. All were wary about giving the world's only super sea power more power at sea. In the end, Castlereagh got only moral support. The Congress of Vienna issued a joint declaration that the slave trade "desolated Africa, degraded Europe and afflicted humanity" and should be ended. The British understood the limits of the resolution. Because Britain had already begun to negotiate agreements that considered monetary compensation for withdrawal from the trade, nothing would "be done which Great Britain does not pay for."[65] On the other hand, the resolution annexed to the *Final Act* of the Congress of Vienna was the only item in the massive treaty that looked at the world beyond Europe. Its only comment upon world that was to condemn the slave trade as an offense to natural and religious laws.

British abolitionism's post-Napoleonic policy reflected the trajectory of Britain's internal and external development in the generation between 1788 and 1814. It emerged in the context of the "British miracle" of the late 1780s. The act of 1806-1807 came in the wake of Trafalgar and Britain's supremacy on the ocean lanes between Europe, Africa, and the Americas. Its breakthrough to global ambitions in 1814 reflected its unchallenged maritime hegemony and economic primacy at the end of the Napoleonic wars. In that year, the *Edinburgh Review* anointed England as "the public"

---

64 See Drescher, *Capitalism and Antislavery*, 67; and "Whose Abolition?," 162–166. For the effect of British policy on the transatlantic slave trade after British abolition, see David Eltis, *Economic Growth and the Ending of the Transatlantic Slave Trade* (New York: 1987). For the long-term impact of the abolitionist process on liberalism and Western culture in general, see David Brion Davis, *Slavery and Human Progress*, Part two, ch. 1; part three, ch. 3; and his *Inhuman Bondage*, 238–239.

65 Kielstra, *Politics*, 52; Bethell, *Abolition*, 14.

of Europe, "before whose tribunal the conduct of courts and nations is best canvassed." The same Thomas Clarkson who, in 1787, had trembled outside the port of Bristol at the immensity of the task before him now exulted, "Let the voice of the British nation once declare itself and the African slave trade *must universally cease.*"[66]

British abolitionism just as faithfully followed the depths as well as the heights of civil society's self-confidence. Abolitionism was a reform for good seasons. Even before Waterloo, abolitionists could threaten to call forth the booming public voice of the nation at will. By 1819, the same abolitionist voice was not even a whisper in the wake of Peterloo. Abolitionists dared not even think of popular agitation when crowds seemed ominously synonymous with riots and repression.

A more distant popular mobilization further dampened abolitionist initiatives after 1816. In 1815, James Stephen sought to capitalize on the momentum generated by the abolitionists' victorious petition. Parliament agreed to forward a suggestion for a permanent central registration of British colonial slaves. Thinly disguised as a means of tracing illegally imported Africans, Wilberforce conceived of it as a first small step in establishing state supervision for ameliorating and monitoring the condition of the colonial slaves. For West Indian slaveholders, it represented the first direct assault on their proprietary rights. It crossed the tacit line that the metropolitan government had promised the West Indians it would observe during the American Revolution. The planters openly denounced Wilberforce for opening the door to slave emancipation.

The slaves listened. In Jamaica, a song circulated among them: "Oh me good friend Mr. Wilberforce make we free.... " And ended, "Take force with force! Take force with force!" In Barbados, the slaves did turn to force. An uprising, known in folk tradition as Bussa's Rebellion, began on Easter Sunday, April 14, 1816. The site of the rebellion was especially shocking to West Indian masters. The Barbadian planters had long considered their slaves to be the most Creolized and content. Except for a minor uprising in 1702, no Barbadian slave resistance since had succeeded in reaching open rebellion. The island had the largest proportion of whites in any British Caribbean colony, making it in theory the least likely place for an attempted uprising.[67]

News of the debate on Wilberforce's registration bill prompted a number of slaves to believe that the Barbadian planters had thwarted a metropolitan emancipation plan. Some favored a nonviolent work stoppage. A major uprising on Easter Sunday was sufficiently coordinated and sustained to

---

[66] Quoted in Kielstra, *Politics*, 28.

[67] Hilary McD. Beckles, "Emancipation by Law or War? Wilberforce and the 1816 Barbados Slave Rebellion," in *Abolition and its Aftermath*, David Richardson, ed. (London: Frank Cass, 1985), 80–104, quote on p. 80.

destroy seventy of the largest plantations on the island. One-fifth of the year's sugar crop was burned. The slaves were defeated largely by loyal colored militia and the same black West India regiments that had played so active a role during the French wars.[68] Many historians have stressed the catalytic importance of "rumors" of outside support in slave insurrections. Barbados was no exception. In two other respects, Bussa's Rebellion also resembled similar episodes in Saint Domingue. The insurgents burned the fields. The revolt's suppression also evoked the authorities' resemblance to the more serious slave uprisings of the past. The leading rebels were executed and decapitated. Their remains were exposed to the public.

There were some important novelties in an uprising of this magnitude. Only one white civilian and one black British soldier were killed by the rebels. Barbadian slaves were no longer circulating the traditional rumor that the monarch's intention to liberate them was being thwarted by his advisors. Instead, they echoed the planters' words that registration was a step to emancipation. Furthermore, the conspirators were divided between those who preferred a "nonviolent strike with limited property damage," and others who insisted that freedom could only be won by following the Haitian precedent of destruction and extirpation. The revolt itself was something of a hybrid – widespread burning of the canefields, but virtually no bloodshed by the slaves. As we shall see, the restraint of the slaves points to a trait that would become the distinctive trait of late British colonial slave uprisings until their emancipation in the early 1830s.[69]

More immediately, however, the Barbados uprising undermined the abolitionists' standing argument that abolitionist motions in the British Parliament did not lead to violence overseas. The thoroughly Creole Barbadian slaves added a disconcertingly destructive echo to metropolitan mobilization for the reform of the institution of slavery. It momentarily depressed further metropolitan mobilization. For the first time, antiabolitionist accounts of the uprising predominated in the British press. The Registration Bill was identified as having stimulated a slave uprising on Britain's most stable Caribbean colony, an island that had been free of such an events for more than a century.

Wilberforce cogently argued that the violent planter reaction had actually stimulated the rebellion. Nevertheless, the Tory government persuaded him to withdraw his registry initiative in favor of requesting colonial legislatures to establish their own registration systems, whereas retaining their "own

---

[68] See Michael Craton, *Testing the Chains*, 259–265.

[69] Michael Craton, *Testing the Chains*, 260–262; H. McD. Beckles, "Emancipation by Law or War? Wilberforce and the 1816 Barbados Slave Rebellion," in *Abolition and its Aftermath: The Historical Context*, David Richardson, ed. (London: Frank Cass., 1985), 80–104. On the new pattern of slave rebellions, see Davis, *Inhuman Bondage*, 212–221, and in Chapter 9, this volume.

property." In the immediate wake of the uprising, Wilberforce could only defensively fall back on his earlier position of 1807 that the Registration Bill was merely an extension of his concern with the outlawed slave trade.[70]

Seven more years passed before abolitionists undertook another initiative in favor of the colonial slaves. In the meantime, British abolitionist policy focused on the slave trade. The government attempted to seal one legal loophole after another that prevented the Royal Navy from shutting down the transatlantic slave trade. After the passage of the Abolition Act in 1807, the unique advantage of British abolitionists was in being nested at the center of the world's sea power. Their own sense of moral priority enabled them to view with equanimity captures of slave ships that stretched and overstepped the boundaries of international law. So internalized was abolition after 1808, that Royal Navy enforcers faced little opposition at home when engaging in wartime seizures of foreign slave ships. With the return of peace, the British government necessarily had to turn to "soft power," bilateral treaties, and binational commissions to implement its policy.[71]

The moral premise that had dominated British abolitionist discourse was endlessly reiterated by the British government. This inevitably elicited a more cynical interpretation of a policy that persisted until the ending of the transatlantic slave trade. Conspiracy theories flourished even in the diplomatic discourse of foreign ministers and ambassadors. Humanitarian and economic motives clearly overlapped once the British had abolished their own slave trade. After 1815, foreign governments were quite aware of the relative decline of the British sugar colonies. In their perspective, Britain needed international abolition either to protect its own planters or, still more deviously, to shift the center of tropical production from the Atlantic to its Asian dominion in India. In this counterhistory, the moral argument was merely a humanitarian ploy to compensate for what the British discovered was an economically irrational policy. Such arguments, of course, ignored the fact that the British could have dispensed with the costs of abolition to both their taxpayers and planters. By simply suspending their own act in 1814, pending international agreement, their new tropical colonies in both hemispheres could easily have sustained and improved the British Empire's position in the slave plantation complex.[72]

Of course, the British government's theoretical option to use, or even threaten to use, such an alternative was foreclosed by British civil society. Popular mobilizations sometimes forced reluctant governments to express their slave trade policies in moral terms. As late as 1828, the Duke of

---

[70] Davis, *Slavery and Human Progress*, 176-177; and Gelien Matthews, *Caribbean Slave Revolts and the British Abolitionist Movement* (Baton Rouge: Louisiana State University Press, 2006), 34–30.

[71] David Eltis, *Economic Growth and the Ending of the Transatlantic Slave Trade*, ch. 6.

[72] Drescher, *Econocide*, 148–161; Eltis, *Economic Growth*, 3–16.

Wellington, the very architect of Britain's post-war preeminence, privately sneered at British slave trade diplomacy and enforcement as a fool's errand. A policy of chasing slavers from one national flag to another amounted to no more than a charade. It fooled only gullible moralistic Britons, not profit-seeking foreigners. The whole question, now Prime Minister Wellington told Foreign Minister Lord Aberdeen, "is one of impression. We shall never succeed in abolishing the foreign slave trade. But we must take care to avoid to take any step (sic) which may induce the people of England to believe that we do not do everything in our power to discourage and put it down as soon as possible."[73]

The bill for sustaining the moral project hardly remained hidden to British taxpayers. Every member of the reading public was aware of the budgetary costs incurred in sustaining naval patrols on the Atlantic, adjudicating and paying compensation for seized foreign ships, resettling "recaptives" from seized ships, subsidizing the colony of Sierra Leone, funding large subsidies for treaties signed by reluctant governments, and raising the price commodities grown by less-competitive British colonial planters. From the Congress of Vienna to the end of the Atlantic slave trade fifty years later, every British initiative on grounds of humanity and morality also exposed its governments abroad and its abolitionists to a question that has echoed down the centuries. There was an ever-expanding list of other inhuman conditions at home and abroad that should be addressed.

When one claims the moral high road, no good deed goes unquestioned. The odor of sanctity always raises suspicions of the scent of hypocrisy. Beginning at the Congress of Vienna, the Portuguese and the Spaniards demanded to know why English philanthropy only concerned itself with Africa's black slaves. What had Europe's premier naval power done to abolish white slavery in Mediterranean North Africa? Such a rhetorical challenge resonated with the moralistic Czar Alexander of Russia: "[It] is only by making the Slave Trade and the question of the Barbary Powers go *pari passu*," wrote Britain's ambassador at St. Petersburg, "that we can fully meet the wishes of the Emperor [the czar] and the other powers who press the point as one of universal interest." The British campaign at Vienna to define the slave trade as piracy strengthened the case for linking the two slaveries. Unlike its situation in 1787, however, Britain was now the standard-bearer of abolitionism. Some abolitionist MPs chided the government for its inaction, but it was an Englishman outside the abolitionist movement who publicized the horrors of white enslavement in North Africa. Britain had treaties with the Algerians exempting its citizens from corsair captivity. British seafarers drew commercial benefits from corsair depredations against unprotected travelers such as Americans and citizens of weaker Mediterranean states.

---

[73] September 4, 1828, quoted in Bethell, *Abolition*, 66.

Britons might fume at a German newspaper that threw the onus for the continuation of white slavery in Africa entirely on Britain, but all Europeans
who were eager to resume the Atlantic slave trade could use the corsairs'
impunity in holding enslaved Europeans as a test of British credibility. Possessing the world's most powerful navy entailed responsibility to undertake
a mission of liberation.

The British government found itself in a situation where its new moral
position impelled it into an operation against slavery on the North African
coast to sustain its credibility to other Europeans and Americans purchasing
slaves on the West African coast. As noted, the call for action in 1816 had no
defensive rationale. No Britons were being held in captivity. After a decade
of naval supremacy, Britain hardly needed a naval action to enhance its
reputation as mistress of the seas. There was neither glory nor booty to be
gained by victory over a relatively poor city of a lesser naval power. The
nation that had accumulated two decades of war deficits financing Europe's
armies against France hardly had further incentive to add either to its fiscal
debt or its casualty lists.

The day-long bombardment of Algiers on August 27, 1816, by the
Anglo-Dutch expedition was no flippant exercise in gunboat diplomacy.
The Anglo-Dutch expedition cost the British 128 dead and 690 wounded,
and the Dutch 13 dead and 52 wounded. No other naval action in the sixty
years of the British enforcement against African slavers inflicted a fraction
of the casualties on Britons as did this single day's antislave trade action.
Indeed, Algiers stands as the sole case in the sixty years of British slave
trade suppression in which a large number of British lives were lost in actual
combat.[74]

To evaluate this "act of British aggression" in terms of its success or failure
in terminating white slavery is to miss the main point of the expedition. It
was neither designed to demonstrate power, accumulate glory, nor wipe
out corsairing. It was to free thousands of enslaved Europeans – mostly
Neapolitans, Sardinians, and Romans – and to rescue British abolitionist
policy from the charge of hypocrisy. Moreover, the dissociation from the
abolitionists, both in means and ends, was almost complete. The leaders of
the abolition movement showed little interest in white slavery, either before
or after the action in North Africa. With their deep Quaker linkage, they
certainly had no interest in a massive bombardment.

A little noted aspect of the expedition is that it did not emancipate the
victims of the trans-Saharan slave trade. To do that might have led to a new

---

[74] Lord Cathcart to Castlereagh, May 28th, 1816; by Oded Löwenheim, "'Do Ourselves
Credit and Render a Lasting Service to Mankind': British Moral Prestige, Humanitarian
Intervention, and the Barbary Pirates," in *International Studies Quarterly* (2003) 47, 23–
48, quote on p. 40. The significance of the British intervention in the equation of moral
policy is elegantly analyzed by Oded Löwenstein.

charge of hypocrisy by the European powers, who were the real audience for the action in Algiers. Had the British demanded the liberation of thousands of African slaves in the Maghreb, but retained hundreds of thousands of slaves in their colonies, it would only have led to more charges of hypocrisy from another direction.[75] The point of the expedition was, of course, no more to free all of Algeria's slaves than it was to accumulate Algerian territory to enhance "legitimate" trade or to dramatize British naval power to the Europeans or Muslims. Its priority was to undercut the rationale of European governments for resisting British pressure to shut down the Atlantic slave trade. Whatever its relative cost in lives and wealth on both sides, the expedition succeeded in one major aim. During the flurry of bilateral negotiations following the raid in Algiers, none of the nations engaged in negotiations with Britain could invoke the "corsair defense" for further delay concerning the Atlantic slave trade. Moreover, because of its historic associations, the British expedition indirectly strengthened the rationale for linking African slaving to piracy.

The issue of moral credibility, of course, was now tied to a world view that the British way to civilization could and should be reproduced elsewhere. On the eve of British slave emancipation, Colonial Secretary Goodrich declared that his country's aim abroad was to "transfer to distant regions the greatest possible amount both of the spirit of civil liberty and of the forms of social order to which Great Britain is chiefly indebted for the rank she holds among the civilized nations." Precisely because of Britain's economic, political, and naval preeminence, counterabolitionists, whether conservative or radical, continued to detect deep Machiavellian schemes beneath generations of appeals to moral priorities. From 1814 onward, French statesmen never ceased to discover hidden levels of *realpolitik,* arrogance, and hypocrisy in British abolitionist initiatives. "Do you English mean to bind the world?" asked France's first Minister of Marine and Colonies under the restored Bourbons.[76] This perspective also reverberated through Iberia and much of the Americas. It has thrived for nearly two centuries in various strands of historiography.

For a generation after 1815, Castlereagh and his successors tried in vain to negotiate collective international treaties to implement the moral condemnation of the Congress of Vienna. The best that they could achieve was

---

[75] Haitians alone might have made the charge, but they were not represented at the Congress of Vienna nor even recognized as a state by any of the Conference's participants. Neither the slave and serfholding powers of Europe nor of North and sub-Saharan Africa were in a position to demand the abolition of slavery whether they were invited to the great diplomatic waltz in Vienna or not.

[76] The British Colonial Secretary is quoted in J.J. Eddy, *Britain and the Australian Colonies, 1818–1831: The Technique of Government* (Oxford: Clarendon Press, 1969), xiii. The French Minister is quoted in Reginald Coupland, *Wilberforce: A Narrative* (London: Colline, 1945), 396–397. See also, Kielstra, *Politics,* passim.

to negotiate a series of bilateral treaties creating two new tools for attacking the slave trade. Both entailed unprecedented surrenders of peacetime sovereignty. The first was a mutual "right of search." It allowed the ships of one nation to be boarded by another to look for African captives. Effectively, this gave the right of search to British ships. The Royal Navy constituted the principal fleet patrolling the sea lanes between Africa and the Americas. The second tool was the creation of bilateral "mixed commissions" on both sides of the Atlantic to adjudicate the validity of shipboard seizures. For the first time in Western history, supranational courts were empowered to bypass the rights of a subject to be tried solely by magistrates of his own state for acts committed on the high seas. These judicial bodies were quiet pioneers of an international court system that was to blossom during the twentieth century.

No signatory to such treaties was unaware that the commissions were also expressions of nineteenth-century "Pax Britannica." The British commissioners, however, did not always win. Weaker colonial states in a world of great powers now had an international tribunal of appeal against arbitrary seizures. Of course, the strongest states with slaves were the last to sign up. This left holes in the treaty network large enough to sail hundreds of thousands of Africans to the Americas. Monarchical France and republican United States both refused to fall into line. For the French, abolition was still too closely tied to the French Revolution, regicide, its Haitian humiliation, and British hegemony at sea to allow any French regime to concede a right of search long after the last slave ship had crossed the Atlantic from Africa. For the United States, memories of British impressments of Americans were compounded by the implication of British resolutions on gradual emancipation in 1823. Southern senators feared that expanding joint obligations for the suppression of the slave trade might effectively move the institution down the slippery slope toward slave emancipation. In other respects, abolitionists in Britain were able to leverage the economic, diplomatic, and naval power of their nation to globalize abolition by the 1820s. In South Africa, British conquest closed the Cape Colony to the slave trade in 1807. In Southeast Asia, Britain abolished the slave trade to Dutch Java in the Indian Ocean. Slave imports to British Mauritius (captured in 1810) were effectively shut down after 1827. In West Africa, the first "free soil" settlement was established under British sovereignty. Its status as the receiving depot for captured slave ships and freed captives was long compromised by coerced military recruitment and long-term apprenticeships. Nevertheless, Sierra Leone remained the primary refuge for those who would otherwise have been destined to be hereditary chattel on American plantations.[77]

---

[77] See Paul Michael Kielstra, *Politics*, for France; Fehrenbacher, *Slaveholding Republic*, 160, for the United States; and Richard B. Allen, "Licentious and Unbridled Proceedings: The

In the Americas, British recognition of national independence was usually first tied to formal abolition of the slave trade. Whereas Haiti remained a refuge for escaped slaves within the British Caribbean, Britain made Canada an asylum for American fugitive slaves. In the British metropolis and on all its warships at sea, the freedom principle prevailed by 1825. Because the law did not recognize the existence of slavery in Britain itself, the compensated emancipation law did not extend to black servants already resident in the United Kingdom. Elsewhere, the American defenders of the institution now stood more openly on the defensive. Most remaining slaveholding elites explicitly recognized that "European civilization," with which they strongly identified themselves, required the ultimate abolition of slavery. Even U.S. southern slaveholders, who elaborated a more positive pro-slavery defense of the institution, explicitly spoke of their human property as existing within discrete boundaries – a "domestic" and exceptional institution.[78]

On the other side of the ledger remained the enduring evidence of slavery's resiliency. Sub-Saharan Africans continued to furnish captives within its boundaries as well as shipping them northward and eastward to the Maghreb, the Ottoman and Persian empires, India, Zanzibar, Madagascar, and the Mascarenes. The transatlantic slave trade continued unabated.[79] In the Atlantic world, the British and American exits from the slave trade in 1808 merely allowed the Luso-Brazilian slavers to resume their premier position, which they had held before the eighteenth century. After half a century of revolutions, more African slaves were still landing in the Americas than were free European migrants. The network of diplomatic treaties and "rights-of-search" of slave ships negotiated between the British and other Atlantic politics in the decade after Waterloo remained porous.

Within the Americas as well, the institution encompassed far more human chattel in the 1820s than it had in the 1770s. In 1825, more slaves still lived within the boundaries of the remainder of the Spanish empire than had resided there at the beginning of the century. In Spanish- as in Anglo-America, slavery had been, or was being, gradually abolished only where slaves comprised 10 percent or less of the population. The institution was dramatically expanding in the Caribbean. The Brazilian empire remained

Illegal Slave Trade to Mauritius and the Seychelles During the Early Nineteenth Century," *Journal of African History*, 42 (2001), 91–116, esp. 100, Table 2, for Mauritius.

78 Compare David Brion Davis's chapter on "The Idea of Progress and the Limits of Moral Responsibility," in *Slavery and Human Progress*, 154–168 with Stanley L. Engerman's *Slavery, Emancipation and Freedom* (Baton Rouge: Louisiana State University Press, 2007), ch. 1.

79 See Eltis, Database, and the essays by Clarence-Smith and Ralph Austen in *The Economics of the Indian Ocean Trade in the Nineteenth Century*, ch. 1 and 2.

the chief beneficiary of the Anglo-American slave trade abolitions but, even without major imports, the United States slave population was growing more rapidly than that of Brazil, the major recipient of African captives in the Americas.

Slave production had increased even more rapidly than slave population growth. World sugar production was expanding at a more rapid rate in the 1810s and 1820s than in any of the three previous generations. The diversification of tropical production was also increasing apace. Slave cotton and coffee production expanded even more rapidly than sugar cultivation. It was precisely in the mid-1820s that cotton surpassed sugar as Britain's most important slave-grown import.[80]

In the same year as the signing of the Declaration of Independence, Adam Smith's *Wealth of Nation's* had confidently assured the Western world "that the work done by freemen comes cheaper in the end than that performed by slaves."[81] Fifty years later, the evidence for the superiority of free labor in the plantation societies of the New World was still spectacularly absent.[82] By the end of the French Revolutionary decade, knowledgeable abolitionists already recognized the competitive disadvantage of tropical plantation societies without slaves.

Across the Atlantic, the new colony of Sierra Leone had also totally disappointed the economic expectations of its founders three decades earlier. It had failed to enter into competition with slave colonies in any major cash crop. By the mid-1820s, its existence was justified in Britain solely as a humanitarian refuge for victims of the Middle Passage. By 1800, none of the former French colonies maintained more than a fraction of their prerevolutionary output even in the forced labor regimes of Saint Domingue under Toussaint, or Guadeloupe under Victor Hugues. After two more decades of independence, Haiti's sugar exports had declined still further than they stood under Toussaint. To other plantation regimes, Haiti's continued recourse to penal labor codes, in the 1820s, offered still further grounds for pessimism about the possibilities of its potential as a producer of commodities or wealth in comparison with neighboring slave economies. Even free Haiti, whose history epitomized the aspirations to mass emancipation and the destruction of the institution of slavery, had to remain more concerned with self-preservation than with expanding emancipation beyond its shores. In 1816, Haiti's ruler provided crucial aid to Simon Bolivar in his struggle for Venezuelan independence, but both Haiti's ambitions and its power to

---

[80] See Ralph Davis, *The Industrial Revolution*, 118–119 Table 61: "Imports 1824–1826."

[81] Adam Smith, *An Inquiry into the Nature and Causes of the Wealth of Nations* (Indianapolis: Liberty Fund, 1981), 98–99.

[82] Drescher, *The Mighty Experiment*, ch. 6 and 7.

affect the destinies of the institution of slavery were severely limited, even with regard to its own citizens.[83]

Other experiments in free or quasi-free labor in the Atlantic world and beyond still offered little evidence of sustained competitiveness with the slave colonies in staple export production. By the late 1820s, Caribbean slave colonies without further access to Africans were severely limited in their potential to expand. British frontier colonies could increase sugar production only by shifting their diminishing numbers of slave laborers from other crops within each colony. By 1825, it was nearly impossible for planters to move large units of field slaves from one colony to another.[84]

As for abolitionism, continental Europe, Latin America, and Africa all remained areas of dormancy. In France, abolitionism had made no progress at all during the first quarter of the nineteenth century. Cautious elites did not form associations dedicated to the cause of abolition. Launching a mass appeal was beyond the range of both possibility. Abbé Gregoire, the most famous veteran of the *Amis des Noirs*, lived in internal exile, the embodiments of the incendiary revolutionary. A small subcommittee of the *Society of Christian Morality* published data on the illegal French slave trade. The Prefect of Paris summed up its standing in official eyes: "Its principles and its aims are as congenial to every Protestant sect as they must be repugnant to every true Catholic."[85] The major concern of the U.S. federal government in acquiring Florida was to resist public pressure to seize the territory by force. As of the mid 1820s, every major acquisition after the War of Independence had expanded the range of the institution of slavery. In the New World society, with the largest number of slaves, the situation (for all the furor over Missouri) was propitious to the institution. By the mid-1820s, no area acquired by the United States after 1783 had yet been organized as a free territory. Between 1810 and 1830, the expansion of slavery in the United States outpaced the growth of "free soil" in the

---

[83] On Haitian slaving, see Rafe Blaufarb, "The Western Question: The Geopolitics of Latin America Independence," *American Historical Review*, 112:3 (2007), 742–763, esp. 752–753.

[84] Drescher, "The Fragmentation of Atlantic Slavery and the British Intercolonial Slave Trade," in *The Chattel Principle: Internal Slave Trades in the Americas*, Walter Johnson, ed. (New Haven: Yale University Press, 2004), 234–255.

[85] On France Lawrence Jennings, *French Anti-Slavery: The Movement for the Abolition of Slavery in France, 1802–1848* (New York: Cambridge University Press, 2000), ch. 1; Serge Daget, "A Model of the French Abolitionist Movement and its Variations," in *Anti-Slavery, Religion and Reform*, 64–79, quote on 71; and Seymour Drescher, "Two Variants of Anti-Slavery.... 1780–1870," in *ibid.*, 42–63. With minor exceptions, beyond France there was the sound of silence. For the Netherlands, see *Fifty Years Later*, passim; for Portugal, see João Pedro Marques, *Sounds of Silence*. See also *Abolir l'esclavage: Un réformisme à l'epreuve (France, Portugal, Suisse, xviiie-xixe siècles*, Olivier Pétré-Grenouilleau, ed. (Rennes: Presses Universitaires de Rennes, 2008).

developed territories west of the Mississippi. In one northern state, free-soil Illinois, the legalization of slavery remained a contested possibility into the 1820s.

For all of the constraints imposed upon the institution by 1825, plantation slavery had expanded in area and numbers. The African slave trade was under threat, but had not been substantially diminished. Both those who relied on or tolerated slavery and those who looked forward to its demise foresaw no rapid disintegration of the institution. The next great step in its demolition would come on both sides of the British Atlantic.

PART THREE

CONTRACTION

9

British Emancipation

By the beginning of the second quarter of the nineteenth century, "free soil" no longer stopped at the Atlantic edge of Europe. The world's most powerful economic and naval power had launched a policy to interdict the Old World supply of slave labor. The great powers of Europe and their newly separated states had all assented, if often insincerely, to prohibiting slave trading from or to their shores. A partial network of treaties provided the basis for the seizure of slave ships and the disposition of the captives in various enclaves in Africa and the Americas.

Despite all this, antiabolitionist skeptics still appeared to have correctly assessed the limits of the project. The volume of the transatlantic slave trade between 1826 and 1850 diminished by only 5 percent. In the New World the institution appeared never to be more vibrant. By 1850, there were probably five and a half million slaves in the Americas, more than at any point in the history of the Americas. In the world of Afro-Asia, there were probably more than three times that number of slaves, not counting varieties of bound laborers in Eastern Europe and concubines, who were still more numerous in parts of the Eastern hemisphere.

In terms of tropical production, the combined impact of British abolitionism on the Atlantic slave trade, revolutionary emancipation in the French colonies, and legislated emancipation in the British colonies, altered the distribution of slave-produced cash crops in the West Indies. The Anglo-French colonies had produced 89 percent of the value of Caribbean exports in 1770, compared with 1 percent for the Spanish colonies. By 1850, the now free labor Anglo-French colonies' share of output had decreased to 35 percent. The Spanish share had risen to 57 percent. Brazil and the United States added their weight to the share of slave-grown exports in the Americas. Brazil's share of world output of coffee increased from 18 to 40 percent in the 1840s, and American cotton's share of Britain's cotton imports rose from 30 percent in 1814–1816, to 62 percent in 1824–1826, to 82 percent in 1854–1856. The West Indian share correspondingly fell from 22 percent in

1814–1816, to 4 percent in 1824–1826, to less than 1 percent in 1854–1856.[1]

The core areas of mainland slavery in the Americas therefore had emerged relatively unscathed by the half century of revolutions. There, slavery continued its relentless spatial expansion. By 1860, according to Robert Fogel and Stanley Engerman, 835,000 slaves in the United States had been moved from the older states to the newer importing states. The latter states had 60 percent more of the slave population that they would have had at natural rates of growth. Brazil showed similar effects in its importations from Africa: 760,000 imported slaves, representing three quarters of Africans arriving in the Americas between 1826 and 1850 were delivered to the most dynamic zone of Brazil. During the second quarter of the nineteenth century, the flow of Africans to Brazil probably exceeded the number of slaves reaching the importing states of the United States. Following the abolition of the Brazilian transatlantic trade in 1850, Robert Slenes finds that comparing the

---

[1] In 1850, there were 3 million slaves in the United States, up to 2 millions in Brazil, and 400,000 in Cuba and Puerto Rico. For the United States, see Preliminary Report on the Eighth Census (Washington, D.C. 1862), 7; and for Brazil, see Leslie Bethell and José Murillo de Caravalho, "Brazil from Independence to the Middle of the Nineteenth Century" in *The Cambridge History of Latin America* vol. 3, *From Independence to c. 1870*, L. Bethell ed. (Cambridge: Cambridge University Press, 1985), 679, 747; for the Spanish Caribbean, see Christopher Schmidt-Nowara, *Empire and Antislavery* (Pittsburgh: Pittsburgh University Press, 1999), 16, 38. If only 10 percent of the African population about 1850 were slaves, they would have totaled up to 8 million in the mid-nineteenth century. (My total population estimate is derived from Angus Maddison, *The World Economy: A Millennial Perspective* (Paris: OECD, 1991), 222, Table A.4; average between estimates for 1820 (7.2M) and 1880 (90.5M). Patrick Manning estimates the slave percentage of the total population at about 10 percent. *Slavery and African Life: Occidental, Oriental and African Slave Trades* (New York: Cambridge University Press, 1990), 84. If the Muslim zone of Asia had a similar percentage of slaves, the total slave population would have amounted to well over the African total. (Based upon Maddison, *World Economy*, 213, Table A.3) The ratio of ten percent is likely to be a low end estimate. David Feeny sets the slave proportion of the Thai population in 1850 at one-fourth to one-third. See David Feeny, "The Demise of Corvée and Slavery in Thailand, 1782–1913" in *Breaking the Chains: Slavery, Bondage, and Emancipation*, Martin Klein, ed. (Madison: University of Wisconsin Press, 1993), 83–111. For late nineteenth-century estimates of slaves in Africa, see Martin Klein, *Slavery and Colonial Rule in French West Africa* (Cambridge: Cambridge University Press, 1998), 252–257. Klein estimates the French West African slave population at between 3 and 3.5 million. Paul E. Lovejoy and Jan S. Hogendorn estimate for the Sokoto Califate, a slave population of between 1 and 2.5 million; see *A Slow Death for Slavery: The Course of Abolition in Northern Nigeria, 1897–1936* (Cambridge: Cambridge University Press, 1993), 1. Near the mid-nineteenth century, Portuguese Angola had 87,000 slaves. (Communication from João Pedro Marques of the Instituto de Investigaçao Cientifica Tropical (Lisbon), November 3, 2006). In the second quarter of the century, transatlantic slave prices were high, encouraging an inward expansion of slavery. See P.E. Lovejoy and David Richardson, "The Initial 'Crisis of Adaptation': the impact of British abolition on the Atlantic slave trade in West Africa 1808–1820," in Robin Law, ed. *From Slave Trade to Legitimate Commerce: Commercial Transition in Nineteenth-Century West Africa* (Cambridge: Cambridge University Press,

slave population of the U.S. South and Brazil, the two "domestic" forced migration streams were of about the same magnitude.

Cuba, the last frontier of the transatlantic trade, experienced a similar dynamic growth. In their final phase, between the 1840s and 1860s, Cuban slave prices increased more rapidly than they had at any other comparable period. When prices rose sufficiently Cubans added indentured Asians to their sources of labor. The Asians may well have been worked as hard and treated as harshly as their African counterparts. But, even with prices for Africans soaring in the 1850s, Cuban planters purchased two African slaves for every Asian indentured laborer.[2] Viewing the combined impact of slave imports and natural growth of the slave population in the mid-nineteenth

---

1995), 52. The jihād wars in the Sokoto Caliphate supplied a huge market for servile labor. See P. E. Lovejoy, *Transformations in Slavery*, ch. 8; and Femi James Kolapo, "Military Turbulence, Population Displacement on a Slaving Frontier of the Sokoto Caliphate: Nupe c. 1810–1857" (PhD dissertation, York University, 1999). In northeastern Africa, Mehemmet Ali's modernizing in response to economic opportunities and threats resembled those of Continental Europe to British industrialization, save that he intensified slave raids to the south in search of his labor supply. For Asia, because of both definitional problems and empirical knowledge, estimates of British India's slaves around 1840 varied between 1 and 8 million. The highest estimate, by Sir Bartle Frere, was 16 million including the princely territories. See Howard Temperley, "The Delegalization of Slavery in British India," in *After Slavery: Emancipation and its Discontents*, H. Temperly, ed. (London: Frank Cass, 2000), 169–187, esp. 177. For my estimates of shares of Caribbean output, I have relied upon David Eltis, "The Slave Economies of the Caribbean: Structures, performance, evolution and significance," 113–119 (Tables 3.1 and 3.2); for Brazil's relative performance in coffee production, Eltis, *Economic Growth*, 294 n 6; for America's share of the British cotton market, Ralph Davis, *The Industrial Revolution and British Overseas Trade* (Leicester: Leicester University Press, 1978), 117–124, Tables 60–63.

[2] On the three American frontiers, see Fogel and Engerman, *Time on the Cross: The Economics of Negro Slavery*, 2nd ed. (New York: Norton 1989), 47; David Eltis, "A Reassessment of the Supply of African Slaves to the Americas," paper presented to the American Historical Association, Philadelphia, 2006, on Brazil, see Dale Graden, *From Slavery to Freedom in Brazil*, 2, Table 1.1; Robert W. Slenes, The Demography and Economics of Brazilian Slavery, 1850–1888 (PhD dissertation, 1975) 145 ff; Rebecca Scott, *Slave Emancipation in Cuba*, 1860–1899 (Princeton: Princeton University Press, 1985). In the Indian Ocean world, the planters of British Mauritius, who had access to both the African and Indian markets for laborers until the mid-1820s, preferred African slaves to any alternative sources as long as that market was open. Later, they consistently chose maximum compulsion of their laborers as long as they could obtain it. In the West Indies, Cuban planters exhibited the same propensity. British naval pressure resulted in a tripling of the price of slaves reaching Cuba between the early 1820s and the late 1850s. See Eltis, *Economic Development*, 193, and 263, table C.1. On the Cuban preference for African slaves to indentured Chinese, see *Mighty Experiment*, 193. On American interstate slave migration, see also Michael Tadman, "The Interregional Slave Trade in the History and Myth-Making of the U.S. South," in *The Chattel Principle*, Walter Johnson, ed. (New Haven: Yale University Press), 117–142, Table 6.1, 120. Michael Tadman's estimate of nearly 700,000 slaves in the United States interregional slave trade between 1820 and 1849 means that the flow of Africans into Brazil was greater than the number who moved into the developing territories of the American Southwest in the same period.

century, an abolitionist might well have reiterated James Stephen's bitter observation at the moment of Haiti's independence half a century before: "The monster, [slavery] instead of being cut off as the first burst of honest indignation promised, has been more fondly nourished than before; and fattened with fuller meals of misery and murder into far more than his pristine dimensions." Wilberforce's estimate of slavery's potential seemed to be borne out. Unimpeded, the institution could endure as "long as there remained cultivatable land in the Western hemisphere."[3]

Expanding Abolitionism

Against this background, a second front was opened against British slavery in the 1820s. Popular abolitionism was again its catalyst. In many respects, it resembled the earlier assault on the British slave trade. The pattern of agitation was familiar – a call for local organization, a flurry of publications, and a national petition campaign. In Parliament, Thomas Fowell Buxton accepted leadership from an aging Wilberforce. By the mid-1820s British popular influence over the Atlantic slave trade had reached its limit. The British West Indies was tightly closed against fresh major African imports. The intracolonial transfer of slaves was virtually at a standstill. The government was pursuing an ever-expanding bilateral treaty network to close the slave system on both sides of the Atlantic. Until the treaties could be completed and effectively enforced, the slave trade seemed destined to continue.

British abolitionists, therefore, turned their complete attention to dismantling colonial slavery. The institution was still susceptible to direct metropolitan public pressure. In 1823, a new organization modestly called itself a "Society for Mitigation and Gradual Abolition of British Colonial Slavery." Within seven years, it sharpened its policy into a single demand for immediate slave emancipation. By 1833, it successfully completed its popular campaign for the formal ending of the institution of slavery. Five years later, another popular campaign aborted the apprenticeship system that had been established for former slaves as a transitional stage to full freedom. By 1838, all special restraints on labor relations for ex-slaves were terminated. In most respects, the pattern of abolitionist contentious action was already quite familiar: propaganda and popular petition campaigns followed by abolitionist motions in Parliament, which elicited governmental responses mediating between abolitionist demands and the colonial masters' protests of hardship. The cycle would commence with another round of popular agitation. The emancipation cycle lasted fifteen years (1823–1838) compared with the twenty-year cycle that had led to the abolition of the slave trade in 1807.

---

[3] James Stephen, *The Opportunity, or Reasons for an immediate alliance with St. Domingo*, (London: Hatchard, 1804), 137. See also Wilberforce, *Letter on the Abolition*, 290.

There were, however, striking new domestic elements in the second cycle. After 1825, women emerged as an independent organizational component of the British antislavery movement. Once again, British civil society afforded opportunities for collective action against slavery that were not yet available elsewhere in the world. In Britain, women wishing to enter the public sphere could now do so. Women joined the national petitioning for parliamentary reform between 1830 and 1832. Although the legitimacy of their signatures was still challenged, they easily turned the ideology of "separate spheres" to their advantage on the question of slavery. The perceived attributions of femininity were used to rationalize women's self-assertion. The institution of slavery notoriously resulted in the destruction of families through captivity and sale. Secondly, the institution subjected women's bodies to a degree of private exploitation and public disciplinary degradation unmatched in Britain. The combination of metropolitan and overseas conditions resulted in a collective participation of women in antislavery mobilization unmatched in western Europe during the nineteenth century.[4]

Women's ideological influence was felt in the first British call for a shift from British abolitionism's initial gradualist stance in 1823. As early as 1824, Elizabeth Heyrick, a Quaker, published a pamphlet entitled *Immediate, Not Gradual Abolition*. There she attacked the government for acting as a buffer for colonial slaveholders. Reviving the radical campaign of 1791–1992, she also called for a massive consumer boycott to force immediate and unconditional emancipation.[5] Although the women's network was quickly launched, it took six years for the British Antislavery Society to accept the immediatist policy and four more for the government to fully implement it. As in the headiest days of popular mobilization against the slave trade, abolitionists appealed for abstention from slave-produced products as a means of withdrawing from complicity in the institution. This time, in contrast to 1791, some women extended the boycott even to cotton.[6]

---

[4] See inter alia, Linda Colley, *Britons: Forging the Nation 1707–1837* (New Haven: Yale University Press, 1992), 278–279; Alex Tyrell, "Women's mission and pressure group politics in Britain (1825–60)," *Bulletin of the John Rylands University Library* 60 (1980–81), 205; S. Drescher, "Women's Mobilization in the Era of Slave Emancipation: Some Anglo-French Comparisons," in *Sisterhood and Slavery* ed. Kathryn Kish Sklar and James Brewer Stewart, eds. (New Haven: Yale University Press, 2006), 98–120; and Drescher, "Public Opinion and Parliament in the Abolition of the Slave Trade," in *The British Slave Trade: Abolition, Parliament and People*, Stephen Farrell, Melanie Unwin and James Walvin, eds. (Edinburgh: Edinburgh University Press: 2007), 42–65; and note 6, on this page.

[5] Davis, *Human Progress*, 183.

[6] Claire Midgley, *Women Against Slavery* (London: Routledge, 1992), 60–62. The movement to abstain from slave-grown cotton had no significant impact upon the market for cotton textiles. As Clarkson had noted in 1791, cotton manufacturing towns could hardly be expected to join massively in undermining the sale of their own principal source of employment. Midgley estimates that the number of families who joined the abstention movement probably exceeded the campaign of 1791–1792.

The best evidence for the salience of women's participation lies in their takeover of British antislavery's most effective weapon – signatures on petitions. Until 1823, the abolitionist signers had been almost exclusively male. Thereafter, the direct participation of women became massive and decisive. The final breakthrough came in 1830, when the national Baptist and Methodist organizations began to welcome, and soon to plead for, women's petitions. Separate signings obviated charges of illegitimacy previously raised against mixed-gender petitions. As in the attack against the slave trade, petitioning remained the gold standard of abolitionist mobilization. As they had done from 1788 to 1814, British abolitionists continued to set the standard for what constituted the "weight" of mass opinion in 1823, 1831, 1833, and 1837–1838. They continued to set the records in terms of numbers of petitions, signatures and, above all, in their ability to overwhelm counterpetitions. The nation's newspapers universally acknowledged that public opinion had spoken definitively at each stage in the dismantling process.

Women also innovated brilliantly in the presentation of petitions by maximizing the visual impact of their signatures. In May 1833, on the day scheduled for the introduction of the Emancipation Bill to the House of Commons, the largest single antislavery petition in British history arrived at the doors of Parliament – "a huge featherbed of a petition." It was "hauled into the House by four members amidst shouts of applause and laughter." It bore 187,000 signatures, "one vast and universal expression of feeling from all the females of the United Kingdom."

As with the establishment of women's local societies, the proportion of women's signatures increased with each successive antislavery campaign. Probably 30 percent (approximately 400,000) of the 1.3 million signers of the 1833 petitions for immediate emancipation were women. In 1837–1838, the 700,000 female signatures "addressed" to the Queen amounted to more than two-thirds of the 1.1 million signatures reaching the House of Commons. The female "Address" from England and Wales, carrying 400,000 signatures, was again the most broadly signed address ever sent up from the country. By the climax of the antiapprenticeship campaign, the new Hibernian Anti-Slavery Society added 75,000 Irish women's signatures to the harvest.[7]

Even in Britain, the road to acceptance of emancipation was long. As late as 1829, a British Peer, introducing a petition signed by "a great many ladies," had the petition instantly ridiculed by another noble Lord, asking "whether the petition expressed the sentiments of young or old ladies." Four years later, with the massive antislavery women's petitions lying on the table of the House of Commons, Daniel O'Connell, could cleverly call upon those

---

[7] On the paragraphs above, see Midgley, *Women Against Slavery*; 62–66; Drescher, *From Slavery to Freedom*, 44–46, 57–55; and Nini Rodgers, *Ireland, Slavery and Anti-Slavery: 1612–1865* (New York: Palgrave Macmillan, 2007), 276.

old habits of mockery and the new ideology of separate spheres to shame opponents into respectful silence:

He [O'Connell] would say – and he cared not who the person was of whom he said it – he would that that person had had the audacity to taunt the maids and matrons of England with the offence of demanding that their fellow-subjects in another clime should be emancipated. He would say nothing of the bad taste and the bad feeling which such a taunt betrayed – he would merely confine himself to the expression of an opinion, in which he was sure that every Member of that House would concur with him, namely, that if ever females had a right to interfere, it was upon that occasion. Assuredly, the crying grievance of slavery must have sunk deep into the hearts, and strongly excited the feelings of the British nation, before the females of this country could have laid aside the retiredness of their character to come forward and interfere in political matters... and, he hesitated not to say, that the man, whoever he might be, who had taunted the females of Great Britain with having petitioned Parliament – the man who could do that, was almost as great a ruffian as the wielder of the cart-whip.[8]

No Member of Parliament was prepared to risk responding with either humor or disapproval. Even those, like William Cobbett, who deeply resented the interference of "187,000 ladies" almost as much as he detested abolitionists and blacks, had to await a more convenient and less solemn moment to scold the ladies for their foolish abuse of political power.[9]

As with the boycott of sugar, efforts were made to extend the consciousness of slavery down to the children. At the climax of fifty years of agitation, preparations were made in Birmingham to emphasize the unfinished business of abolitionism both in the West Indies and America. A great celebration was organized in Birmingham to celebrate the ending of the last preparatory stage to full freedom from slavery on August 1, 1838. The day began with an amassed chorus of 3,000 children singing hymns in front of the Town Hall, followed by a procession to new school buildings to be known as Negro Emancipation Schools.[10] And, half a century after the launching of the antislavery movement, an aging citizen could recall, in 1838, how his own sense of justice was first aroused by a print of the slave ship Brookes hanging on the wall of his home.

In this emancipation phase, initiatives from outside London became even more significant than they had been during the previous generation. Already, in 1821, James Cropper of Liverpool launched a personal, if unsuccessful, crusade to use equalization of sugar duties between West Indian and ("free grown") East Indian sugar as a means of attacking slavery. Birmingham was the site of the first women's antislavery society founded in 1825. Joseph

---

[8] Linda Colley, *Britons: Forging the Nation 1707–1837* (New Haven: Yale University Press, 1992), 279–280.
[9] Drescher, *Capitalism and Antislavery*, 145.
[10] Temperley, *British Anti-Slavery*, 63.

Sturge of that city played a leading role in the attack on the "apprentice-ship" system created by the Act of 1833. Instead of awaiting calls for peti-tions to the parliamentary leadership to launch public meetings in favor of emancipation, a new organization, an "Agency Committee" formed in 1831, divided the country into target districts. Like religious revivalists, Committee members moved from town to town urging audiences to circulate petitions, organize auxiliaries, and prepare for national elections. George Stephen, son of the abolitionist James Stephen, claimed that there were 1,200 locals in Britain by 1832.[11]

The antislavery movement of the 1820s and 1830s also became more reli-giously organized than its predecessor. The earlier campaigns had their locus of meetings and petitions in town halls. The Society of Friends disproportion-ately constituted the initial core of abolitionist committees, but made no such effort to emphasize the collective effort as their offspring. During the late 1820s, the petitioning effort became more articulated along denominational lines. British antislavery and evangelical nonconformity peaked together in the first four decades of the nineteenth century. The most dynamic period of nonconformist growth coincided almost exactly with that of antislavery. This provided abolitionists not only with a large pool of signatories, but also with networks for gathering individuals together for public lectures and financial aid. At the climax of the antislavery efforts in the 1830s, denomi-national venues rivaled other public gathering places as locations of petition meetings.

The drift towards denominationalism became apparent in the first great petition for "immediate" emancipation in 1830–1831, when the Methodists and Baptists organized the drives for signatures within their own congrega-tional units. The total number of petitions, mostly smaller than those of great town meetings, represented more than a quadrupling of the antislave peti-tions of 1814. Seventy percent of the 5,500 documents reaching Parliament originated in nonconformist congregations. Abolitionists quietly allowed the petitions to be laid on the table in deference to parliamentary reform. The Reform Act of 1832 had to pass safely through the legislature before slave emancipation could proceed.[12] In the petition of 1833, religious dissent, like the activation of women, also came into its own. Methodists signed up ninety percent of their membership. In doing so, they alone accounted for nearly 18 percent of the 1.3 million citizens who signed up.[13] Indeed, so great

---

[11] See Sir George Stephen, *Anti-Slavery Recollections: In A Series of Letters Addressed to Mrs. Beecher Stowe* (London, 1853); Temperley, *British Anti-Slavery*, 12–13.

[12] Drescher, "Public Opinion," in Walvin, *Slavery*, 40–41. Numbers of petitions alone did not guarantee victory. Abolitionists produced more than three times as many petitions in 1831 as ever before without any immediate impact in Parliament, and Chartism produced two mammoth petitions during the following decade to no avail.

[13] Drescher, *Capitalism and Antislavery*, 127–131.

was the role of dissent that Anglican abolitionists feared that the movement had been taken out of the hands of the "Saints," such as Wilberforce and Stephen, and captured by a nonconformist/radical alliance.

Because of the prominent role played by religious mobilization in the process of Anglo-American abolitionism, Protestant Christianity has often been retrospectively assigned a unique role in bringing the institution of slavery to an end. One must bear in mind, however, the differential responses to slavery by even its major Evangelical variants. The last quarter of the eighteenth century witnessed a broad recognition of slavery as a moral problem among Evangelicals in Anglo-America. In England itself, Methodists and Baptists responded almost immediately to the initial abolitionist call to action in 1788. In the 1780s and 1790s, Methodists and Baptists attempted to extend critical attitudes toward slavery to the Americas. In the West Indies, Evangelicals were quickly faced with stiff opposition by most planters to their initial mission. Over the next generation, they made their peace with the planters. This entailed rendering the institution of slavery unto Caesar and accommodating the planters' desire for a Christian message emphasizing obedience of bondsmen to masters. As late as the eve of emancipation's passage, British missionaries residing in the Caribbean ventured no overt condemnation of the planters or the institution.

In North America, south of the Chesapeake, the accommodation to emancipation was slower, but the clerical accommodation was virtually complete by the 1820s. Even further north, most Evangelical congregations never committed themselves to an English-style call for immediate emancipation. After British emancipation, some Northern church members began to align themselves with popular mobilizations designed to limit, if not abolish, the institution's expansion. Only in the 1850s did this containment policy become a mass movement in some parts of the North against a Southern "slave power." In most of the South, the churches continued to back away from modest attempts to erode the institution. The churches increasingly acknowledged slavery's permanence and finally moved toward an unapologetic defense on scriptural grounds. On the eve of secession, they largely confined the moral dimension of their advocacy to ameliorations within the framework of the institution.

The most significant innovation provided by religious activity beyond Britain was the public space opened up by missionary activity among slaves. And, the most striking new intruders into the abolitionist public sphere were the colonial slaves themselves. British nonconformist activities in the West Indies began in the 1780s, but it was not until the second decade of the nineteenth century that the conditions became more favorable for mission work in line with the imperial government's policy of "amelioration" and religious instruction for the slaves. The slaves, of course, used the religious assemblies to further both their own autonomous interpretations of religion and to prepare for liberation as well as salvation.[14]

The right to attend religious services inevitably created space for slaves to congregate and discuss news of abolitionist activities in Britain. Every major publicized parliamentary debate and pronouncement of governmental policy increased planter fears of chapels as networks of subversion.

In the metropolitan campaigns against the slave trade, Afro-Britons had played a role largely as outstanding individuals and anonymous victims. Bloody uprisings on ships had little place in abolitionist propaganda. With the launching of the colonial emancipation campaign, West Indian slaves themselves emerged as interlocutors. Before the 1820s, slave uprisings usually placed British abolitionists very much on the defensive. Their primary reflex was to exculpate themselves from association with violence. In its immediate aftermath, the Saint Domingue slave revolution produced widespread anxiety among the friends of abolition for a number of years. Although some insisted that insurgent slaves were reacting to lifelong inhumane treatment and only vindicating their human rights. Wilberforce was convinced that scenes of brutal revenge "operated to the injury of our cause." Even the sympathetic Clarkson was concerned that the Saint Domingue rebellion was detrimental to abolitionism in England.[15] Antiabolitionists incessantly conflated the revolutionary threat in the Caribbean with the more formidable threat at home from belligerent France.

Until the Barbadian slave revolt in 1816, abolitionists reflexively invoked the absence of major uprisings in the British Caribbean as proof that issues related to slavery could be freely discussed in Britain without fear of overseas repercussions. The Barbados revolt subverted the assumptions of both sides in debates about slaving and the relative security of even the most Creolized and assimilated slave colonies. Into the early 1820s, fear of more "servile war" delayed Buxton's acceptance of a leadership role in opening the parliamentary discussion of emancipation. Buxton was even more careful to avoid any reference to the Barbados uprising six years earlier. Only to himself did he confess his concern about the potential for another colonial revolt: "If a servile war should break out, and 50,000 perish, how should I like that?" His hesitancy was not unusual. When Buxton finally moved for consideration of slave emancipation in May 1823, he was careful to refer again to the long hiatus of violent slave resistance that had been the keynote of Lord Howick's "security argument" in 1807.[16]

---

[14] Turner, *Slaves and Missionaries*, ch. 3; Emilia Viotti da Costa, *Crowns of Glory, Tears of Blood: The Demerara Slave Rebellion of 1823* (New York: Oxford University Press, 1997) ch. 3.

[15] See Anstey, *Atlantic Slave Trade*, 276 n. 98; and Ellen Gibson Wilson, *Thomas Clarkson: A Biography*, 74–76.

[16] See Matthews, *Caribbean Slave Revolts*, 36–37; and Stephen, *Anti-Slavery*, 60.

A few months later, the slaves of Demerara rose in another rebellion. Initially, news of the outbreak promised to deliver another setback to abolition. In the end, of all the large-scale slave revolts in the British Caribbean, abolitionists lavished most attention on the Demerara uprising.[17] The Demerara revolt subverted many theories, abolitionist and antiabolitionist alike, about the causes of slave revolts. The uprising deserves careful scrutiny because the comparative behaviors of slaves and masters contributed crucially to a shift in metropolitan opinion about emancipation. Demerara, in 1823, was still the most "African" of the British Caribbean colonies. Its slaves, however, were clearly as attuned to Parliament's unprecedented discussion of emancipation as those of any other British colony. The government had immediately displaced Buxton's resolution by an alternative plan for amelioration instead of emancipation.

The slave outbreak itself was not based, as were so many prior events, on rumors of a nonexistent document or a decree in favor of liberation. The slaves' conspiracy was a direct result of the failure of Demerara's governor, under planter pressure, to publicize a very modest metropolitan list of amelioration measures. After the revolt's suppression, abolitionists were able to demonstrate that the immediate publication of the same document in neighboring Berbice had resulted in no disturbances whatsoever. Concealment from above fueled conspiracy from below. The range of rebel demands reflected both their aspirations for full freedom and their wish to get whatever advantages might be hidden in the document. Postrebellion investigations revealed that the insurgents had devoted an enormous amount of time and energy into trying to learn the actual contents of the reforms contained in the government's document. For weeks they hesitated to turn to action. Both in planning and in action the rebels talked of presenting their grievances to the governor.[18]

The second novel aspect of the revolt in Demerara arose out of some of the conspirators' positions in a missionary chapel. The chapel became the site of discussion of plans for collective action. Denied other autonomous space outside the plantation, the slave leaders used their minimal allotment of religious freedom and their status as deacons within the chapel of missionary John Smith to communicate freely with each other.

Once the uprising broke out, its leaders clearly revealed that they did not intend to overthrow British authority. They warned participants to disarm the captive managers and to hold them, but not kill them. Plantations were

---

[17] Matthews, *Caribbean Slave Revolts*, 107. On the historiography of slave resistance, see Eugene D. Genovese, *From Rebellion to Revolution: Afro-American Slave Revolts in the Making of the New World* (Baton Rouge: Louisiana State University Press, 1979) ch. 3; and Michael Craton, *Testing the Chains: Resistance to Slavery in the British West Indies* ch. 19.

[18] For details of the Demerara revolt, I rely upon the rich account of Emilia Viotti da Costa, *Crowns of Glory, Tears of Blood*, (New York: Oxford University Press, 1994).

seized. Masters and their families were incarcerated. The rebels sometimes inflicted humiliation on their captives. There was, however, no repetition of the atrocities of the Berbice revolt in 1763, much less those in the Saint Domingue uprising in 1791. In Demerara, where the 77,000 slaves and 10,000 to 12,000 insurgents vastly outnumbered the colony's 5,000 whites and free blacks, only 2 or 3 whites died in hostile action. Above all, the leaders attempted to impose self-discipline on their fellow insurgents and negotiate with the British governor, but rewrite the rules of slave contention. The slaves adhered to the general order not to kill their captives, and the governor and military officers engaged in negotiations with the mobilized slaves.

The exemplary moment of the Demerara uprising was most evident at the crisis point of confrontation. Five hundred advancing British troops and mobilized auxiliaries came face to face with, and were surrounded by, 3,000 to 4,000 slaves. They were asked by the commanding officer about their grievances. The responses ranged from demands for time off to attend Sunday services to clarification about rumours that they had been freed. Jack Gladstone, one of the slave organizers, handed the British colonel a document signed by captured managers and masters, testifying to their good treatment. Colonel Leahy responded by reading the governor's formal declaration of martial law. He ordered the rebels to lay down their arms and return to work. After a long, silent standoff, the British troops opened fire. Their disciplined barrage broke the deadlock. Then began the process of suppression. On-site round ups of slave leaders and summary executions were followed by formal, but equally summary trials and, in later stages, by more formal trials of the slave leadership.

The outstanding result of the revolt was its transformation into a cause célèbre in Britain. This process was certainly accelerated by the colonial government's indictment of the missionary whose chapel had been the major site of the conspiracy. Reverend John Smith of the London Missionary Society was indicted, convicted, and condemned to death, on the basis of slave testimony obtained under duress and later recanted. Smith died in confinement.

When news of the Demerara uprising first reached Britain, Thomas Clarkson had to interrupt a provincial organizing tour. The planters were preempting him. They were circulating publications throughout the nation's libraries, reading rooms, and coffee houses, accusing antislavery campaigners of being "traitors of our country." The traditional trope of "servile insurrections" produced a reflexive metropolitan response. Clarkson had to break off his tour to compose a pamphlet refuting planter accusations.[19] This

---

[19] Matthews, *Caribbean Slave Revolts*, 49–50, citing Clarkson's manuscript essay "Account of Efforts to Abolish Slavery 1807–1824," 33.

time, however, the negative effects of the uprising were quickly dissipated. The suppression involved some of the traditional methods of enacting rituals of punishment so terrifying "that no slave would ever dare try it again." This included exemplary executions of individuals chosen at random, decapitating them, and placing their heads on poles along the roads. The planters also reacted not only by executing slaves, but also by attacking white missionaries. Even the established Anglican Church in Demerara was vandalized and its minister pressured into giving up his position.[20]

Although some colonial assemblies in the islands also reacted to the Demerara rebellion and Reverend Smith's trial by expressing hostility to the missionaries, Smith's trial and death stimulated a counterattack by religious societies within the metropolis. Some historians are inclined to emphasize the fact that the one casualty of the Demerara uprising who was selected as its iconic martyr was a white missionary rather than any of the hundreds of executed black workers. In other words, the missionary "stole the martyr's crown." This overlooks the fact that the death of this freeborn native Englishman was converted into decisive evidence that the brutal suppression of the rebellion had been an assault on native-born Christian Britons as well as overseas Christian West Indians. Missionary Smith was the abolitionists' Archimedian fulcrum, which enabled them to raise popular contention in the New World to the level of the Old World. His death allowed the rebels to be identified not just as fellow men and brothers, but as fellow freedom-loving Christians. The Demerarans had reacted to their unnatural deprivation as would any freeborn Briton.

In response to Smith's death, hundreds of petitions were sent to Parliament by dissenting congregations. No previous suppression had ever induced such a mass metropolitan mobilization. British nonconformist chapels became a mainstay of future antislavery petition campaigns. They also were the driving organizational force in the radicalization of abolitionist demands for emancipation. The parliamentary general election of 1826 became the first, since 1806, in which slavery was an electoral campaign issue.

Thus, the most important step in the "Anglicization" of the slaves and the detoxification of slave insurgencies occurred within the cycle of the Demerara revolt. The leaders' membership in chapels linked their enslavement to their Christianization. Their actions were reconfigured in the emerging English class-relations model as a general strike against intolerable working conditions. Colonel Leahy, the commanding British officer in the climactic confrontation, inadvertently emphasized that he had been dealing with men who knew how to participate in an orderly negotiation. He acknowledged that he had made a list of the insurgents' demands, but had destroyed it

[20] Viotti da Costa, *Crowns of Glory*, 225–226; 274–276.

as useless. "For abolitionists, the dialogue between slaves and authorities justified their comparison of the conduct of the rebels in Demerara and that of workers at home."[21]

The rebel leaders did not, I must emphasize, undertake their action in the belief that a measured challenge to imperial authority was tantamount to suicidal martyrdom. They gambled on reconfiguring the rules of contention and aimed at aligning their situations as closely as possible with those of Britons. The slaves were fully aware that the language of contention that they articulated was framed within the religious, moral, and legal constructs of powerful agents of change in the metropolis.

The number of petitions to Parliament in favor of emancipation rose from 225 before the revolt in 1823 to 600 within 6 months after Smith's death. By 1826, some urban petitioners were signing in numbers equaling or exceeding their 1814 towns' totals: 72,000 from London; 38,000 from Glasgow; 17,000 from Edinburgh; 38,000 from Norfolk; and so forth. Elizabeth Heyrick's call for immediate abolition was published immediately in the wake of the suppression in 1824. It was only one of a cascade of publications. The revolt elicited the most British abolitionist commentary in the history of British colonial slave revolts. Equally striking was its stimulus to the timing of women's mobilization. It not only stirred the first revival of mass abstention from West Indian sugar, but stimulated the formation of women's antislavery societies, beginning with the city of Birmingham in 1825.[22] The attacks on missionaries thus added an important dimensions to the national abolition movement. It enabled abolitionists to emphasize parallels between events overseas and the nonconformists' struggle for an end to religious disabilities at home.

The slaves' own language of liberation in the name of human rights also resonated across the Atlantic. Abolitionists used the testimony of the authorities themselves to make the slaves speak the language of British labor. The insurgents downed tools rather than killing their masters, brutalizing women, or burning all the plantations. Slaves were workers who withheld their labor, not savages. In Demerara, as the *Edinburgh Review* phrased

---

[21] Matthews, *Caribbean Slave Revolts*, 76.

[22] See P.F. Dixon, "The Politics of Emancipation: The Movement for the Abolition of Slavery," (D. Phil, Oxford University, 215); Midgely, *Women Against Slavery*, 43 ff. 103–113; Matthews, *Caribbean Slave Revolts*, 107–110. In terms of religious mobilization after Demerara, it is noteworthy that as a percentage of antislavery petitions submitted to Parliament, those sent from dissenting congregations rose from 6 percent in 1824 to 72 percent in 1831. The number of petitions in 1831 was the highest ever recorded in half a century of the popular antislavery movement, the first to call for immediate emancipation, and the indirect catalyst to the Jamaica uprising. It is equally significant that "The Baptist War" of 1831–1832, the largest slave uprising in British colonial history, caused the least interruption in antislavery mobilization of all three slave revolts. In 1832, the exiled missionaries moved directly from the ships that exiled them back to Britain to the lecture circuit and parliamentary committees. See Drescher, *From Slavery to Freedom*, 39, Table 2.1.

it, "a *slight commotion* was occasioned among the Negroes...far more resembling a combination of European workmen to strike for wages for time or other indulgence than a rebellion of African slaves. Even an officer active in the repression duly testified that: some wanted three days and Sunday for church...."[23]

The slaves did not engage in a massacre because their uprising was designed to compel a dialogue between slaves and colonial political authorities who had withheld information about what the imperial government had intended for them. *The Christian Observer*, a publication of the established Church's Evangelical wing, said of the rebellion, "Let us suppose that the miners of Cornwall, or the iron-workers of Wales, or the keel men of the Tyne, or the weavers of Lancashire had conceived themselves whether justly or not to have been aggrieved by their masters...had struck work...and...had even gone the length of threatening violence...Would it be tolerated that these men should be forthwith attacked by a military force, killed in cold blood by hundreds, hunted down like wild beasts, tried and executed by scores as traitors?"[24] Who indeed, were the savages?

In conflating colonial slaves and British free laborers, the abolitionists were, of course, taking a risk. Colonial propagandists had been comparing the material conditions of their slaves to various British groups since the first campaign against slavery.[25] For fifty years, they argued that Irish or Scottish peasants, English workers, military conscripts, and a host of others lived less well than residents on their plantations. Colonial masters consistently asked why humanity should not begin at home. Their refrain was echoed for half a century by foreign slaveholders and their governments, British conservatives and working class radicals.

In 1824, however, it was the abolitionists who insisted on the comparison between British laborers at home and slaves abroad. The discourse between slaves and masters could be extrapolated into a dialogue between slaves and Britons. At least for the next dozen years, as the abolitionist movement peaked and triumphed, the abolitionists carried the day. Their priorities held, not only in the middle class constituency from which most of the activists were recruited but also among large segments of the working class itself. The Demerara slave revolt and repression actually allowed slavery to become an issue in the general elections in 1826, for the first time since 1807. Even

---

[23] Quoted in Matthews, *Caribbean Slave Revolts* 75–76, and 83. The language of labor in the Demerara revolt was part of a broader development within the slave colonies. Although not at liberty to fully enter civil society of the colony, the slaves used their capacity as laborers and worshippers to enter into contentious dialogue with their owners and governors. See *From Chattel Slaves to Wage Slaves. The Dynamics of Labour Bargaining in the Americas*, Mary Turner, ed. (Bloomington, IN: 1995); and Mary Turner, *Slaves and Missionaries: The Disintegration of Slave Society, 1787–1834* (Urbana IL: University of Illinois Press, 1982.

[24] Quoted in Viotti da Costa, *Crowns of Glory*, 282.

[25] Davis, *Age of Revolution*, 463–468.

William Cobbett, England's most notorious populist antiabolitionist and antiblack radical, deferred to working class sentiments in 1832. Running for a parliamentary seat, he pledged himself to support immediate emancipation.

Nine years after Demerara, on the eve of emancipation, the injustice of colonial slavery had been so deeply domesticated that the prestige and rhetoric of abolitionism were successfully deployed in the campaign to limit child labor in factories. By 1832, it was almost impossible to find a meeting, petition, or tract in favor of protecting British children that did not also demand "the immediate abolition of slavery both at home and abroad." By becoming fellow Christians and fellow workers, slaves were already perceived as individuals who loved and yearned for freedom in its civilized (and British) sense.[26]

Before these metropolitan denouements, however, another major slave revolt intervened. In the last rebellion before emancipation, it was the slaves who set the agenda. The Jamaica slave uprising of 1831–1832, also linked to religious networks, was known as "the Baptist War." By 1831, the cautious parliamentary-dominated Antislavery Society was being pressured from without to adopt immediate emancipation as its program. The nonconformists had taken the lead in a record mass petitioning in 1830–1831. More than 5,000 petitions were sent to the legislature. Women signed en masse. A radical "Agency Committee" unleashed a national lecture campaign. In the elections of 1830, the campaign for parliamentary reform became more enlivened than ever before by discussions of slave emancipation. As a result, many MPs pledged their support for emancipation. The West India interest's representation was reduced. Only the parliamentary reform crisis put emancipation temporarily on the back burner. For the first time in the history of the abolition movement, antislavery MPs refrained from using their massive accumulation of signatures to insist on a debate over immediate emancipation.[27]

In return for abolitionist forbearance, the government passed an "Order-in-Council" in November 1831, offering detailed protection for every aspect of the slaves' lives. Its most unanticipated consequence occurred in Jamaica on December 27, 1831. Slaves in the western part of the island launched the most well-organized and greatest slave insurrection in British colonial history. So many estates were consumed by fire that "the sky became a sheet

---

[26] See S. Drescher, "Cart Whip and Billy Roller: Antislavery and Reform Symbolism in Industrializing Britain," *Journal of Social History*, 15 (1981), 1–24, esp. 7. Cobbett had apparently learned his lesson by the general election of 1832. In the wake of the Demerara rebellion, Cobbett lost a bid to represent Preston in 1826. Opponents successfully turned his denunciation of the Missionary Smith as a "canting caitiff" against him. Cobbett also described blacks as "degraded brutes." He finished last among the candidates in the poll. See Peter F. Dixon, "The Politics of Emancipation: The Movement for the Abolition of Slavery in the British West Indies, 1807–1833," D. Phil, Oxford University, 1971, 229–230.

[27] Dixon, "Politics," 273–284.

of flame, as if the whole country had become a vast furnace." Nearly a fifth of Jamaica's slave population, up to 60,000 strong, joined the uprising. As in Barbados and Demerara, the insurgents were quite aware that metropolitan pressure for immediate emancipation was rising in Britain. They were still more aware that the colonial planters were reacting to the new Order-in-Council with unprecedented ferocity and defiance. Some Jamaicans openly spoke of secession from the empire and adhesion to the United States.[28]

As in the Demerara uprising, the plot was long in the making. Church affiliation again provided a means of organization. Plans were debated within a group headed by Samuel Sharpe, a chief deacon in the Baptist church. Armed with a license to practice and preach, he moved freely through a large portion of northwestern Jamaica. The final decision for the outbreak was held after a prayer meeting. The slave rebellion was not only the largest but the longest in British colonial history. Confrontations would last from December 27, 1831 through the end of January 1832. Only in the following month did the island's governor feel confident enough to proclaim the end of martial law.

In 1831, Deacon Sharpe envisioned the uprising as a work stoppage, backed by the threat of force in self-defense. Whites encountered on the estates were to be spared. His vision of an orderly work stoppage was shattered by the geographical breadth of the decentralized insurgency. Slaves burned plantations, and the damage to property was immense. The official estimate of lost property plus the cost of suppression amounted to more than £1.3 million pounds. Just like the rebels, the forces of order were scattered over a large area. This made it difficult for authorities to coordinate militia operations and behavior. Their on-site executions brought death to more than 200 slaves.

In one important respect, the Demerara precedent held good. As one Baptist preacher noted "amid the wild excitement of the night, not one freeman's life was taken, not one freewomen molested by the insurgent slaves."[29] Fourteen whites were killed in the course of the struggle. As David Brion Davis perceptively notes, 770 times as many slaves were involved in the Jamaican Baptist War as in Nat Turner's rebellion in Southampton Virginia the same year. Yet "Turner's men killed at least 3.5 times as many whites as the *combined* total in the infinitely larger Barbadian, Demeraran, and Jamaican insurrections."[30]

This pattern of slave behavior in the British colonies suggests that the looters and burners were aware that a metropolitan public that had massively petitioned in favor of immediate abolition a few months earlier would

---

[28] Michael Craton, *Testing the Chains: Resistance to Slavery in the British West Indies* (Ithaca: Cornell University Press, 1982), 294–296.
[29] *Ibid.*, 303, 312.
[30] Davis, *Inhuman Bondage*, 220.

weigh any massacre of whites into the equation of the slaves' "readiness" for freedom. An insurrection of Haitian proportions might well have delayed the emancipation process. Once more, as in Demerara, the most decisive aspect of the slave uprising was its aftermath. Once again the rebels were far exceeded in brutality by their suppressors. More than 300 slaves were summarily tried and executed. Planter assaults on the missionaries also escalated to new heights. Although there was no direct evidence of missionary complicity in the rebellion, a wave of violence swept through the western parishes. Nonconformist chapels were destroyed. The planters did not risk making more dead martyrs, but prominent Baptist missionaries were put on trial. Wesleyans and Baptists, especially, were forced to flee the island.[31]

Inadvertently, the planters not only remobilized British nonconformity but actually sent the slaves' representatives back to the metropolis. The refugee reverends returned at a critical moment. The passage of parliamentary reform immediately reopened the political agenda to slave emancipation. For the first time, a parliamentary Select Committee was appointed to consider the feasibility of emancipation. Buxton was able to make the motion for the committee in terms of its compatibility "with the safety of all classes in the colonies." The missionaries, in particular, William Knibb, offered dramatic eyewitness testimony to the Committee. He recounted the daily violence toward slaves as well as those killed in the hundreds by summary executions and hasty courts-martial. Knibb went before the public as well as Parliament, becoming one of the Agency Committee's strongest attractions. The crowds he attracted in his tour of Britain led Buxton to offer thanks to Providence for turning planter behavior into a means of slavery's own destruction.[32]

A comparative perspective indicates how important the behavior of slaves in revolt helped abolitionists to fray the line between colonial slaves and metropolitan freemen. The Baptist War did not play the same role in the abolition of British slavery as had the Saint Domingue revolution in French emancipation four decades earlier. Britain's slave colonies were not immediately imperiled by either external or internal threats in 1833. The colonial militia and 1,700 regulars had sufficed to suppress even a formidable Jamaican uprising of tens of thousands. The abolitionists, however, could now invoke the whole "cycle of violence" to emphasize the need for immediate resolution. Fifteen years before, the Barbados rebellion had halted a small wedge of imperial antislavery legislation in its tracks. The violence

---

[31] Turner, *Slaves and Missionaries*, 164. For an analysis of the conflicting languages of representation in Britain following the Jamaica uprising, see Catherine Hall, *Civilising Subjects: Colony and Metropole in the English Imagination, 1830–1867* (Chicago: University of Chicago Press, 2002), 107–115. On the abolitionist use of Jamaica to stress the urgency of emancipation, see Matthews, *Caribbean Slave Revolts*, 164–170.

[32] *Ibid.*, 172.

helped to deter further abolitionist mobilization for seven years. By 1832, however, British public opinion was so primed for continuous agitation that abolitionists could turn planter vengeance into fuel for liberation.

The final stage of the British emancipation process followed the path outlined for half a century. Popular mobilization was the catalyst with slave resistance added to metropolitan contention in the final decade of the attack on the institution. By 1832, the fate of slavery had become closely linked to the political movement that enacted parliamentary reform and to the most dynamic moment in expanding British nonconformity.[33] In the first general election campaign under the new Reform Act, the Anti-Slavery Agency Committee succeeded in getting hundreds of candidates to pledge support for immediate emancipation. Never had antislavery been so broadly debated. Upwards of 200 pledged candidates were elected, about 95 percent of them liberals. Even with this show of strength it required a final wave of 1.3 million petitioners to induce the government to introduce a motion in favor of emancipation.[34] Hammered out over four long months in 1833, the Emancipation Act was the combined result of the pressures brought to bear by the abolitionists and the West India lobby. The government had sufficient authority on both sides of the Atlantic to end an institution that could no longer be sustained without continuous agitation at home and abroad.

In this larger political process, the threat of further slave violence was less prominent than the forces that had traditionally driven abolitionist legislation. The potential for further slave resistance was, of course, now constantly more on the minds of Colonial Secretaries. Yet, when emancipation became a major issue in the British general election of December 1832, the threat of slave rebellion was not the most prominent rationale for immediate action. The king's opening speech to the new Parliament did not mention either the uprising nor emancipation. During the ensuing parliamentary session, the highest priority of the abolitionists was to ensure passage of an act for immediate emancipation. As soon as a majority voted for emancipation in principle, the abolitionists' task was to eliminate the government's apprenticeship stage, wherein slaves were to spend a number of years in a condition of partially unpaid servitude. It was at this point, late in the proceedings, that the abolitionists reintroduced the threat of bloody servile insurrection. Buxton and others moved to reduce the transition period of indenture to a single year. Otherwise, he warned, insurrection would again come to Jamaica in 1834 as surely as it had come before.[35]

---

[33] S. Drescher, *From Slavery to Freedom*, 37–40, esp. Figure 2.1.

[34] Roger Anstey, "The Pattern of British Abolitionism in the Eighteenth and Nineteenth Centuries," in Bolt and Drescher, *Anti-Slavery, Religion and Reform*, Christine Bolt and Seymour Drescher, eds. (Folkstone: Dawson, 1980), 19–42; and S. Drescher, *From Slavery to Freedom*, 46–48. On the role of emancipation in the parliamentary elections of 1832, see Drescher, "Public Opinion," in Walvin, *Slavery*, 36–39.

[35] Hansard's *Parliamentary Debates*, 3rd ser. vol.19, col. 1190 (July 24, 1833).

Parliament thought otherwise. Buxton's motion was overwhelmingly defeated. The slaves were probably equally aware of the limits of their potential power. A year later, and much to the relief of the abolitionists themselves, apprenticeship was initiated without an uprising in any of the eighteen colonies in which it was introduced. Four years later, apprenticeship itself was prematurely terminated by another popular mobilization in the United Kingdom, seconded by nonviolent agitation in the colonies.

The ending of British slavery was a more orderly transition than all previous mass emancipations in the plantation zones of the Americas, from Haiti to Spanish South America. The British government faced the same problem encountered by revolutionaries in the French Caribbean and mainland Spanish America: how to sustain the production of goods that had depended upon the institution of slavery. In introducing the Emancipation Bill in May 1833, Lord Stanley characterized it as "a mighty experiment." It would not only free 800,000 slaves, but it might exercise immense influence on the future of millions of foreign slaves. It would hopefully demonstrate the ability of free labor to sustain and even increase the production of tropical commercial staples.[36]

The final Emancipation Act combined four mutually interlocking principles. All slaves would be simultaneously freed without any provisions for special racial constraints. A new status as Apprentices would bind them to work for their ex-masters for a fixed portion of each working day, and for four to six years. Masters would receive financial compensation amounting to about 40 percent of the calculated market value of their slaves. The compensation fund was set at £20 million, an enormous sum of money for a government that had campaigned on a platform of austerity. The revenue to ensure that a compensation fund was to come from higher sugar duties and a virtual monopoly for British colonial sugar in Britain. In other words, civil liberty was to come at the expense of limited free labor for the ex-slaves, increased prices for consumers, and higher taxes for metropolitans.

Five years after passage of the British Emancipation Act, abolitionists launched a final popular campaign to hasten the end of the apprenticeship system. By the spring of 1838, ex-slaves again added their own mobilization to metropolitan signatures. The model of a work stoppage was revived. British immediatists continually referred to expectations of "the whole body of the apprentice population for immediate freedom." Pressured from both sides of the Atlantic, the colonial legislatures again gave way. By August 1, 1838, apprenticeship was abolished.[37]

[36] S. Drescher, *The Mighty Experiment: Free Labor versus Slavery in British Emancipation* (New York: Oxford University Press, 2002), ch. 8; William A. Green, *British Slave Emancipation: The Sugar Colonies and the Great Experiment, 1830–1865* (Oxford: Oxford University Press, 1976) ch. 4.

[37] Alex Tyrell, "The 'Moral Radical Party and the Anglo-Jamaican campaign for the abolition of the Negro apprenticeship system," *English Historical Review*, 99: (392) (1984), 481–502,

In its immediate impact, British emancipation became a beacon for all foreign abolitionists who wanted to see the institution of slavery dismantled without recourse to extreme violence – a counterexample to Haitian or Latin American scenarios. In America, William Lloyd Garrison was to hail "the instantaneous transformation of almost a million chattels into rational and immortal beings" as "the greatest moral miracle of the age."[38] Ten years later, Alexis de Tocqueville could only regard Britain's road to the abolition of the slave trade and colonial slavery as the ideal model of democracy in action. He asked his countrymen to consider what had taken place across the Channel: "Had the principal colonial and maritime nation on the face of the globe declared, sixty years ago, that slavery was going to disappear from its vast domains, what cries of surprise and admiration would have issued form all sides... How many fears and hopes would have filled every heart."

Emanipation was also an act without precedent in history. On a single day in 1834, 800,000 slaves had been called from social death to life. Neither at the announcement of coming freedom nor at the moment of implimentation had it produced "a *single* insurrection," nor had it "cost the life of a *single* man."[39] Turbulence there was, but it was the modern kind of contention – downed tools and strikes. Tocqueville was already echoing a new master narrative and withdrawal from labor. Emancipation was a peaceful reform generated from below and pursued for half a century. It was the act of a nation and not of its rulers. English governments struggled as long as they could against the adoption of every major step toward emancipation, from the abolition of the slave trade to the abolition of slavery.

Henceforth, as far as the world was concerned, Britain and her former Atlantic slave colonies were a zone of free soil and free labor. They had been made so by the ordinary legislative processes of the West's most stable polity for nearly three generations, beginning with the *Somerset* decision in 1772. The postemancipation British colonies were long to be deemed islands of relative tranquility in an empire of stability in a world beset by revolutions and civil wars. Among those for whom the ending of chattel slavery was the central issue of their lives, Britain now loomed as the model of effective popular mobilization. As Frederick Douglass praised British abolitionist

esp. 495–497; and Gad Heuman, "Riots and Resistance in the Caribbean at the Moment of Freedom," in Temperley, *After Slavery*, 135–149; Green, *Slave Emancipation*, ch. 5. Before 1865, even substantial riots seemed to result in relatively few deaths. See Mimi Sheller, "Quasheba, Mother, Queen, Black Women's Public Leadership and Political Protest in Post-emancipation Jamaica, 1834–1865," *Slavery and Abolition* 19:3 (December 1998), 90–117.

[38] Garrison, in *The Liberator*, 20 August 1841.

[39] Tocqueville, "On the Emancipation of Slaves" (1843) in *Tocqueville and Beaumont on Social Reform*, S. Drescher, ed. and trans. (New York: Harper and Row, 1968), 137–173, esp. 138, 150–154.

audiances: "We have discovered in the progress of the [British] anti-slavery movement, and in your other noble reforms, that there is a power even stronger – a power more potent than the bullet-box and cartridge-box."[40]

The impression of the British process remained very potent. Even the heady days of the revolutions of 1848 and their British echo in the Chartist's mass challenge to restricted British suffrage did not cause Douglass to lose sight of the cumulative power of peaceful agitation. As he reminded an American audience celebrating the fifteenth anniversary of British slave emancipation on August 1, 1848, "We have discovered in the progress of the anti-slavery movement that England's passage to freedom is not through rivers of blood. . . . What is bloody revolution in France, is peaceful reformation in England. The Friends and enemies of freedom, meet not at the barricades thrown up in the streets of London; but on the broad platform of Exeter Hall. . . . Their ramparts are right and reason. . . . Their Hotel de Ville is the House of Commons. Their fraternity is the unanimous sympathy of the oppressed and hungry millions."[41] For a brief moment, it did seem as though the British empire might provide both the impetus and model for the rapid erosion of chattel slavery throughout the world.

[40] *The Frederick Douglass Papers. Speeches, Debates and Interviews*, 5 vols., John W. Blassingame, ed. (New Haven: Yale University Press, 1979–1992), I, 373, delivered on (September 1, 1846).
[41] Ibid., II, 141–142, A Speech delivered at Rochester, New York on August 1, 1848.

From Colonial Emancipation to Global Abolition

In many respects, British anti-slavery reached its zenith in the decades of the 1830s and 1840s. British abolitionists mobilized five times to petition Parliament or to elect representatives favorable to their cause. The antislavery movement continued to set records for the numbers of petitions and addresses sent to London. In Parliament, a radical abolitionist could, with the confidence of an Inca ruler, threaten to cover the floor of the House of Commons with petitions until it responded favorably to public opinion. Antislavery ambitions increased in proportion to the magnitude of its seemingly unending power. With the end of slave apprenticeship in the summer of 1838, some abolitionists formed a "society to aid in the universal abolition of slavery." The following year this vision was institutionalized in the *British and Foreign Anti-slavery Society* (BFASS). It was to prove the most enduring of all antislavery organizations and, under a different name, remains the most durable human rights organization in human history. The BFASS at once became the clearing house for information about slavery and antislavery throughout the world.[1]

Exhilarated by the British victory over slavery, an American abolitionist suggested a London gathering of antislavery philanthropists from all civilized nations. In June 1840, the first World Antislavery Convention was convened with Thomas Clarkson delivering the opening address and five thousand spectators in attendance. The British delegation, led by London abolitionists and 250 representatives from provincial locals, was supplemented with representatives of missions from Canada to Mauritius in the Indian Ocean. The largest foreign contingent, fifty individuals strong, arrived from the United States. It included women, whose bid to be seated as delegates was defeated. Altogether, thirty-nine countries were represented, including Sierra Leone and Haiti.

---

[1] See Temperley, *British Antislavery*, esp. 62–84, and Suzanne Miers, *Slavery in the Twentieth Century: The Evolution of a Global Problem* (New York: Rowman & Littlefield, 2003).

Successive reports informed the delegates of the varieties of world slavery, from Native Americans in Canada through the Muslim world, India, and sub-Saharan Africa. There was the usual grim report on the Ibero-Atlantic slave trades, still conveying captives at near record heights. There were, of course, extensive and usually upbeat accounts of the progress of the "great experiment," as selectively evidenced in rising Barbadian land prices. The World Antislavery Convention concluded its proceeding with hopes: for the rapid demonstration of the superiority of free labor over slave labor in the British West Indies; for the impending victory of India's free-grown cotton over U.S. Southern slave-grown cotton; and of British Caribbean sugar over Cuban and Brazilian production. The Convention learned of plans for British antislavery projects in the Niger River.[2]

For the first time, British abolitionists seriously turned their attention to slaves who lay within the reach of British imperial power in Asia. The World Antislavery Convention marked the first serious survey of slavery in India. Throughout the half century between 1788–1838, the subcontinent was of marginal concern in debates over abolitionist initiatives within Britain. Abolitionist attention to Indian Ocean slaves in the late 1820s entailed only those on colonial plantation islands.[3]

British abolitionism had grown out of a rising concern with British tolerance, encouragement, and participation in the Atlantic slave system. In India, slavery was not related to the production of any major product exported to Britain. Although a small-scale slave trade existed from Africa to India, slave recruitment in India was not comparable to the massive uprooting of Africans. The institution itself was embedded in complex systems of religion and obligation that had preceded British conquest and were regarded by Indian elites as organic elements of their society and culture. Their systems of bondage seemed to be at odds with both the institutions of civil liberty as they had emerged in the Atlantic world and with the rigorous classification of slaves as chattel property further to the west.

Until the ending of British plantation slavery, abolitionists were wary of slavery in India for other reasons as well. West Indian slaveholders attempted to defend their own institution by conflating it with bondage in the East. Abolitionists countered by emphasizing the differences in recruitment, in the wholesale uprooting of families, the imbalance of genders, the divergent systems of labor discipline, and the capitalist ethos that sustained western

---

[2] Drescher, *Mighty Experiment*, 86–90; 152–154.
[3] Anthony J. Barker, *Slavery and Antislavery in Mauritius, 1810–1833: The Conflict between Economic expansion and humanitarian reform under British rule*. (New York: St. Martin's Press, 1996). Before 1840, the problem of antislavery had been a problem in and for *Western* culture. (See the focus of David Brion Davis's four magisterial studies on *The Problem of Slavery in Western Culture* (1966); *The Problem of Slavery in the Age of Revolution* (1975); *Slavery and Human Progress* (1984); and *Inhuman Bondage* (2006).

slavery. In 1833, liberating 800,000 slaves of African descent with compensation seemed a formidable enough challenge.

Finally, to have added the untold numbers of bondsmen to the price of compensated emancipation for the 800,000 slaves to be emancipated in 1833 would have been to offer the opponents of change a golden argument for inaction. Moreover, before their victory in the traditional slave colonies, British abolitionists preferred to distance East Indian slavery as far as possible from West Indian slavery. The East Indian interest was usually wary of any analogy between East and West. It was in the West Indian interest to conflate the two. They could thereby subvert appeals to substitute "free" Indian sugar from the West Indian variety. They could also deflate preemancipation abolitionist arguments in favor of equalizing the duties on East and West Indian sugar to allow competition between free and slave labor.[4]

Bewildered by the variety of servile statuses in India with its regional variations, multiple schools of laws, texts, customs, and social practices, and its complex interweaving of caste and servitude, both the East India Company and its parliamentary spokesmen were easily able to dispose of a casual attempt to link the emancipation bill of 1833 to Indian bondage.[5] It entered the proceedings during a discussion of the renewal of the East India Company Charter in June 1833. Without discussion or provision for compensation, the first version of the amended Charter provided that slavery in India would end even before the end of the West Indian system of slave apprenticeship, on April 12, 1837.

Practical objections were successfully raised in both Houses of Parliament. The East India Company's spokesmen warned that its authority and British rule itself depended on the support of India's elite and the passive acquiescence of India's overwhelmingly nonslave masses. The entire British presence amounted to a miniscule minority of the population. The upholders of the status quo in India raised the specter of an insurrection by the very Indian masters on whose support British rule depended. Any attempt to interfere with the religiously based bondage, especially the harems and zenanas of the Muslims, would "throw the whole country into a flame."

Parliament was hardly in a mood to launch two mighty overseas experiments at once. Acknowledging its own incompetence to choose an informed policy, the British legislators, with the consent of the abolitionists, assigned the entire problem of Indian slavery to the discretion of the Government of India.[6] By the time of the World Convention, seven years later, no further

---

[4] Davis, *Slavery and Human Progress*, 179–181.
[5] See Dharma Kumar, "Colonialism, Bondage, and Caste in British India," in *Breaking the Chains: Slavery, Bondage, and Emancipation in Modern Africa and Asia*, Martin A. Klein, ed. (Madison: University of Visconsin Press, 1993), 112–130.
[6] Temperley, "The Delegalization of Slavery in British India," in *After Slavery*, 169–187. Without further public agitation, the question lay dormant for the rest of the decade.

steps had been taken in India and no report published. Only when the BFASS threatened in 1839 to begin another public mobilization at the next general election, did the East India Company announce governmental policy on Indian Slavery.

The first British law against slavery in India was finally promulgated ten years after the Slave Emancipation Act of 1833. The relative significance of the two may be judged by the title of the second law: "Act V." Nevertheless, it marked the first British attempt to address the future of the institution itself on a large portion of continental Asia. Act V's crucial provision stated that the courts would no longer recognize or enforce claims arising out of slave status.[7] Act V was expanded by the Indian Penal Code in 1860, which made it a criminal offense to keep, capture, or transport captives for purposes of sale. The religious and economic contexts of bondage in India ensured that the path to free labor was drawn out over a century and more.

Historians have accurately described Act V and its successors as a "slow death for slavery." It initially required individual and collective initiative to be taken by slaves themselves. This "Indian model" or "delegalization" of slavery was to become the dominant mode of emancipation in the Old World. It contrasted with the statutory legislation that was characteristic of the ending of slavery in the Western Hemisphere. Afro-Asian slave emancipation clearly involved the imposition of a European frame of reference on non-European institutions. They extended capitalist labor relations of production and European legal precepts to imperialized societies.[8]

However, the early commitment of Europeans to generalizing a "free labor ideology" for their overseas colonies before the last third of the nineteenth century is often misleadingly overstated. In the mid-nineteenth century, coerced labor was still regarded as the workforce of choice by Dutch speaking masters in Java, Surinam, and the Transvaal; by Portuguese speaking masters in Brazil, Angola, and Mozambique; by English, Spanish, and French speaking planters in the Caribbean; and by English-speaking masters in the U.S. South. In Britain, penal labor laws were enforced for half a century after the abolitionists launched their first campaign for slave emancipation in 1823. In the same parliamentary session, English penal laws for agricultural laborers were reinscribed in a renewed "Masters and Servants Act." Under the Act's terms, employers could have their workmen sent to the house of correction and held at hard labor for three months for breaches of their labor agreements.

---

[7] Temperley, *British Antislavery*, 107; idem "The Delegalization of Slavery in British India" in *After Slavery*, 169–187, Kumar, *Colonialism*, 121–123.

[8] See Suzanne Miers, "Slavery to Freedom in Sub-Saharan Africa: Expectations and Realities," in *After Abolition*, 237–264. For a summary of Afro-Asian emancipation processes, see the collection edited by Martin A. Klein in *Breaking the Chains*, especially the editors' "Introduction: Modern European Expansion and Traditional Servitude in Africa and Asia," 3–36.

It is hardly surprising that the Act became the model for post-emancipation laborers in India, South Africa, and the Caribbean. It is more noteworthy, perhaps, that, in 1838, at the height of popular abolitionism, the British Colonial office (briefly) ruled that vagrancy and contract laws had to be *more* lenient for the newly emancipated slaves than for British laborers in the mother country.[9] British legislators' attitudes towards domestic free labor did not, therefore, change dramatically during the century of Atlantic slave trade abolitions and slave emancipations (1770s to 1880s). As noted, the fundamental distinction between contracted and involuntary labor had been regarded as the central difference between slavery and other forms of labor and noncriminal servitude, and had already been "hegemonic" in England for centuries before the *Somerset* decision. This remained the situation during the century that followed as well. Many free laborers within and beyond Britain were still liable to pay with their bodies for violating contracts, whether their rewards were in wages or in other forms of remuneration. Indeed, the Western society in which penal laws for laborers disappeared most rapidly in the generation after 1825 was the nation that was emerging with the largest slave labor force in the Western world.[10]

There is one more structural link between the emancipation processes in the East and West. In legal terms, the withdrawal of legal sanctions for slavery has been historically identified as the Indian model of emancipation. Yet, it became the template for subsequent antislavery processes throughout much of the Old World. Its historical precedent really lay in the first articulation of emancipation in the Anglo-American world – the *Somerset* decision of 1772. Whatever Mansfield's words may have left in ambiguity, no version of his decision omitted his conclusion. The power claimed over James Somerset as a slave was not allowed or approved by the law of England. Before that declaration, Mansfield had delivered a wish that the master/slave relationship should lay outside or beneath the law. He would have had it that masters believed their black servants were free, and the servants believed that they were slaves.[11] And so, slavery first died on the Indian model in Britain itself. Long before the Emancipation Act of 1833, no one identified any servant residing in Britain as a slave.

In this sense, the delegalization of Indian slavery was less an invention of the early 1840s, than a resuscitation of the old *Somerset* strategy under new pressure. Without the intervention of the abolitionist movement, the British bureaucracy would not have been moved to initiate action against the institution of slavery in the Indian Ocean world. That world also provided the setting for a new post-emancipation labor force. From the onset of the

---

[9] Green, *British Slave Emancipation*, 165.

[10] See Robert J. Steinfeld, *Coercion, Contract, and Free Labor in the Nineteenth Century* (Cambridge, UK: Cambridge University Press, 2001.) ch. 2.

[11] Wise, *Though the Heavens*, 182.

system of apprenticeship in 1834, most British plantation colonies began to experience labor shortages. Mauritius, located closest to India, turned to the subcontinent as an alternative to Africa. "Coolie" laborers were hired by the thousands. They were required to sign multiyear contracts as plantation laborers. Between 1834 and the end of apprenticeship in 1839, Mauritius planters imported an adult male workforce nearly equal in size to its ex-slave population. Their fixed wages and vulnerability to penal coercion for noncompliance made them less costly labor than African freedmen, even during apprenticeship. They could legally be forced to work far more hours per day than was legally obtainable from apprentices. More concerned with the prospect of a mass expulsion of Africans than the flight of ex-apprentices from the estates, the imperial government suspended indentured migration to Mauritius in 1838.

The abolitionists attempted to have the government expand the ban against indentured migration to all former slave colonies. John Gladstone, a Liverpool merchant with Caribbean plantations, attempted to follow the Mauritian precedent to render himself independent, "as far as possible [of] our negro population." After a disastrous mortality rate among 400 servants on the initial voyage, the abolitionists seized the opportunity to brand the experiment as "tantamount to a revival of the slave trade." Further official permission to secure Indian labor for the Caribbean was denied for years. Although not opposed to voluntarily contracted indentures in principle, abolitionists had sufficient political influence in the 1830s to make the government wary of the ease with which long distance transportation from India could slide into abuses. At the peak of its influence, in 1840, the BFASS was able to inform the World Convention that they had successfully defeated a proposal to lift the ban on migration to Mauritius.[12]

Just as new forms of unfree labor emerged to fill the void left by the ending of the slave trade, so did old forms of servile labor expand just beyond the free soil frontier of British power. South Africa became an area in which both apprenticeship and slavery persisted for generations beyond August 1, 1838. During the apprenticeship period, thousands of Afrikaans-speaking colonists (*Voortrekkers*) moved beyond the British sovereignty accompanied by their apprentices. The Boer migrants did not legally revive the institution of slavery, but perpetuated the legal status of apprentices. They ascribed the status to Africans, whom they captured in warfare and raids, much as

---

[12] See Marina Carter, *Servants, Sidars and Settlers: Indians in Mauritius, 1834–1874* (New York: Oxford University Press, 1995), ch. 1, Richard B. Allen, *Slaves, Freedmen and Indentured Servants in Colonial Mauritius* (Cambridge: Cambridge University Press, 1999), Madhavi Kale, *Fragments of Empire: Capital, Slavery and Indian Indentured Migration in the British Caribbean* (Philadelphia: University of Pennsylvania Press, 1988) and P. C. Emmer, "The Great Escape: The Migration of Female Indentured Servants from British India to Surinam, 1873–1916," in *Abolition and its Aftermath*, David Richardson, ed. (London: Frank Cass, 1985), 245–266.

did the non-Boer Africans around them. The practice of seizing children for service continued. Beyond the line of British sovereignty, its former Cape Colony subjects could retain marketable bondsmen with indefinite durations of service. Like their contemporaries in northern Africa, the Boers of South Africa continued to tap directly into the African source of servile labor already denied to their northwestern European contemporaries in the Atlantic world.

Abolitionists likewise extended their protective net over schemes to secure a massive African indentured labor force. Here, their argument was strengthened by the limits of British power in Africa.[13] Unlike India, the British government could not oversee the recruitment process from beginning to end. The alternative of recruiting those rescued from slave ships bound for West Indian plantations was politically even more difficult. Slaveholders throughout the Americas were ever ready to characterize any recruitment of African recaptives whatsoever as the slave trade in disguise. Because they were under continuous scrutiny by abolitionists and the metropolitan government, British colonial authorities had to be scrupulous in overseeing the treatment of indentured servants from India and the transfer of Africans recaptured from slave ships or recruited from British possessions. A whole complex of regulations had to be established, which had not been required in the recruitment of slaves.[14]

Suppression of the seaborne slave trade was the aspect of the institution of slavery over which abolitionists could exercise most influence. Into the last quarter of the nineteenth century, Britain remained the only European power that had both the means and the political will to constrain the slave trade. During the half century after the defeat of Napoleon, successive British ministries varied over how aggressively they wished to pursue antislave trade policies. All, however, professed a desire to suppress the slave trade "in every part of the world," and all foreign governments were informed that abolition was the goal "of Her Majesty's Government and the British Nation."[15]

The cumulative mass agitations of the 1830s only intensified the abolitionists' global project. The 1830s and early 1840s witnessed a cascade of

---

[13] See Elizabeth A. Eldredge, "Slave Raiding Across the Cape Frontier," in *Slavery in South Africa: Captive Labor on the Dutch Frontier*, Elizabeth A. Eldredge and Fred Morton, eds. (Boulder: Westview Press, 1994), 93–126; Fred Morton, "Captive Labor in the Western Transvaal After the Sand," 167–186, and other essays in this informative collection. See also Charles Swaisland, "The Aborigines Protection Society, 1837–1909," in Temperley, *After Abolition*, 265–280.

[14] See Rosanne Marion Adderley, *"New Negroes from Africa": Slave Trade Abolition and Free African Settlement in the Nineteenth-Century Caribbean* (Bloomington: Indiana University Press, 2006) ch. 2, and Johnson U. J. Asiegbu, *Slavery and the Politics of Liberation, 1787–1861: A Study of Liberated African Emigration and British Anti-Slavery Policy* (New York: Africana Publishing Corporation, 1969), 42–43, 69–71, 136–190.

[15] See Erdem Y. Hakam, *Slavery in the Ottoman Empire and its Demise, 1800–1909* (London: Macmillan, 1996), 70–77.

new treaties and additional "rights of search." Sweden, Norway, and Spain signed up to strengthen enforcement of the patrol against the slave trade in 1835; Argentina, Uruguay, Bolivia, Chile, and Ecuador fell into line between 1839 and 1843. Denmark, Sardinia, the German Hanse towns, Tuscany, the Two Sicilies, Haiti, Venezuela, Texas, Mexico, and Belgium had all signed up before 1850.[16] The Vatican was reluctant to appear to be reacting at the request of a Protestant power, especially one exerting pressure on Catholic Portugal. But, in 1839, Pope Gregory XVI was induced to issue an apostolic letter, *In supreme apostolatus*, condemning the slave trade and prohibiting any Catholic from defending the traffic in blacks.[17]

British efforts in multinational diplomacy reached their climax in the months following the world Antislavery Convention of 1840. Foreign Minister Lord Palmerston completed multilateral negotiations for what he told parliament would be a "Christian league against the slave trade." A preliminary treaty, signed by the five leading powers of Europe (Austria, Britain, France, Prussia, and Russia) was among "the most ambitious multinational initiatives prior to the League of Nations." It declared the slave trade to be piracy and entrenched British search and seizure policies into a pan-European convention, leaving America potentially exposed to censure as the major maritime power blocking the termination of the transatlantic slave trade. The treaty foundered on Franco-American opposition. The American ambassador in Paris launched a public relations campaign to break the ratification process at its weakest link. He was immeasurable aided by a French legislature still smarting over a British diplomatic humiliation of France in the Middle East. The multilateral treaty was aborted by the French legislature, and the treaty's failure marked the last major effort by Britain to close the American gap by a multinational treaty.[18]

British pressure on the southern European Catholic powers also increased in the 1830s. In December 1836, under intense British pressure, Portugal signed a new treaty with Palmerston, prohibiting the export of slaves from all the Portuguese dominions. At the same time, the liberal Portuguese Foreign Minister, Bernardo de Sá Nogueira de Figueiredo, tried to diminish the

---

[16] Eltis, *Economic Development*, 86–87.

[17] Kielstra, *Politics*, 198–199.

[18] Steven Heath Mitton, "The Free World Confronted: The Problem of Slavery and Progress in American Foreign Relations, 1833–1844," Ph.D. Thesis, Louisiana State University, 2005, 57. See Mitton's fine discussion of the convention, and Kielstra, *Politics* 202–206, on details of the diplomatic negotiations. It called for mutual recognition of the right of search within a zone extending from 80° east longitude to the coast of the Americas from 32° north, a point south of Casablanca encircling Africa, Sri Lanka, and all points westward in the Indian Ocean to the entire Atlantic Ocean from 700 miles south of Buenos Aires, northward to Savannah, Georgia. It included the U.S. coastlines of Georgia, Florida, and the Gulf of Mexico, including the American intercoastal slave trade. On the French background, see Jennings, *French Anti-Slavery*, 149–192, and Kielstra, *Politics*, 202–246. A new French government signed the treaty in December 1841, but opposition in the French legislature doomed its parliamentary confirmation.

geographical scope of Britain's right of search of slave ships and to end the mixed commissions instituted by the treaty of 1817. The Portuguese wanted to be allowed to continue slavery in Africa to offset their anticipated revenue losses from abolition of the slave trade to Brazil. The Portuguese government also feared the domestic consequences entailed in continually subjecting Portuguese national honor to a British ultimatum.[19]

As had happened with stronger powers (i.e., the United States and France), internal hostility to enforcement of slave-trade suppression led to tolerated nonenforcement. In July of 1839, Palmerston retaliated by obtaining a new Act authorizing the Royal Navy to apprehend any slaving ships flying the Portuguese flag, and to dispose of them in British courts. Palmerston promised to accept no time limit on this extraordinary exercise of power until slavery was eradicated from the face of the earth. A new treaty in 1842 declared that Portugal was bound in perpetuity to the British treaty, and declared slaving to be equivalent to piracy.[20] Thereafter, until the ending of the slave trade to Brazil, the major concern of every Portuguese government was to agree to British abolition policy while sustaining Portuguese sovereignty at the supply sources in Africa and the areas of slave cultivation in the Atlantic islands. Portuguese slaving continued. At the end of the 1840s, the volume of the slave trade to Brazil returned to its highest point in two decades.[21]

The years just before and after the World Antislavery Convention of 1840 witnessed an acceleration of British diplomatic efforts to close down the slave trade. By the early 1840s, British diplomatic initiatives against the slave trade were also extended broadly through areas of the Muslim world where slaving was widely practiced, including the Mediterranean, the Indian Ocean, and the Black Sea. As in Christendom, the brutality involved in fueling the institution had elicited considerable discussion in Islam for a millennium. Nevertheless, Muslim unease had never coalesced into an abolitionist movement before the 1840s. As long as the overwhelming majority of articulate Muslims professed a belief in the divine sanction of the institution, the suppression of slavery proved to be "a labour of Sisyphus."[22]

Slavery in the Muslim world, particularly the Ottoman Empire, was also discussed at the 1840 World Antislavery Convention. In a letter to Lord Palmerston, signed by Clarkson, the Convention requested the British foreign minister to obtain a condemnation of slavery by the Ottoman ruler. It was hoped that this would quickly lead to the suppression of slavery in areas under his authority and pave the way for its abolition elsewhere in the Muslim world. Palmerston transmitted Clarkson's letter to the British

---

[19] Marques, *Sounds of Silence*, 104.
[20] *Ibid.*, 124–125; and Bethell, *Abolition*, 156–166.
[21] Transatlantic Slave Trade Database. See also Bethell, *Abolition*, 142–152; and Marques, *Sounds of Silence* 101–123.
[22] William Gervase Clarence-Smith, *Islam and the Abolition of Slavery*, passim.

Ambassador in Istanbul on the same day that it was presented to him. Acting as culture brokers, British diplomats tred cautiously in formulating their message. Palmerston restricted his appeal to requesting only the mitigation and diminution of the slave trade. British diplomats approached slavery in the Ottoman realms as an institution that did not offend Muslims. Any sudden abolition decree in response to foreign and *Christian* pressure might encourage resistance and hostility, hinder the growth of antislavery sentiment, and retard the ending of the slave trade and slavery in the Ottoman Empire. This fear was confirmed by a rebellion within the Arabian province of Hejaz in 1855–1856, following partial prohibitions of the slave trade elsewhere in the empire.

The British also dealt separately with rulers at the periphery of the Ottoman Empire. They negotiated local agreements with the Imam of Musqat to constrict the slave trade to western India as early as 1841. British diplomacy had its earliest success with the Bey of Tunis. The British had particular leverage with its ruler. French colonial expansion in Algeria during the 1830s and 1840s made the Bey anxious to cultivate British diplomatic support. The British made it equally clear that good relations would be eased by a bold antislavery policy. In 1846, the Bey officially decreed the end of both the slave trade and slavery. However, the policy sparked a revolt against the reform on the grounds that abolition was not sanctioned by Islam. Although the Bey signed another treaty with Britain in 1875 promising to more fully implement the decree, the continued presence of slaves in Tunis allowed France to make the persistence of slavery one of its justifications for establishing a protectorate over the country in 1881.[23]

In 1847, the Ottoman Sultan acquiesced on the British suppression of the Persian Gulf slave trade on condition that the British would not publicize the treaty. Even the secret document officially justified the measure only as an action against the slave trade to America. The Shah of Iran also initially refused to negotiate a treaty, insisting that slavery was not only lawful but also promoted conversion. The British seizure of Iranian slaving vessels elicited an Anglo-Persian treaty restricting the slave trade. Other Muslim

---

[23] Gervase-Smith, *Islam*, 102, David Zisking, *Emancipation Acts: Quintessential Labor Laws* (Los Angeles: Litlaw Foundation, 1993), 421. Thereafter, abolitionists in France began to taunt their own regime for allowing a Muslim ruler to steal a march on christianity with his abolition of slavery before any Catholic monarch, had done so. In the Muslim orbit slaves were able to use British and other consular sites as free soil havens. In Tunisia, during the first four years after the Bey published the first restrictions on slavery, nearly a thousand slaves were confirmed in their liberation by the British Consul. See Montana, "Transaharan Slave Trade," 149. For similar patterns of slave flight to freedom, see Ennaji, *Serving the Master: Slavery and Society in Nineteenth-Century Morocco* (New York: St. Martin's Press, 1999), 43–46; Ehud Toledano, *As if Silent and Absent; Bonds of Enslavement in the Islamic Middle East* (New Haven: Yale University Press, 2007); and Y. Hakan Erdem, *Slavery in the Ottoman Empire and its Demise, 1800–1909* (New York: St. Martin's Press, 1996), 152–184.

states were incrementally drawn into the orbit of abolitionism. On its own initiative, the Ottoman government abolished Istanbul's public slave market in 1847, three years before a similar measure was legislated for Washington, DC.

When the British were drawn into the Black Sea and the Crimean War (1853–1856), their abolitionist aims expanded to include the prohibition of the Georgian slave trade in 1854–1855. The Ottoman's dependence upon Anglo-French naval support against the Russians invited those navies to suppress the slave trade and to help the Sultan to secure a crucial supply of Georgian soldiers for the Ottoman imperial army. The limits of such compliance were revealed, as noted, when the Ottomans were faced with the violent rebellion against abolition in the Holy Cities of the Hejaz.[24] Indeed, news of the Ottoman prohibition of the slave trade on the Black Sea and in North Africa led authorities in the Hejaz to believe that the decree might be extended to Arabia. They charged the Turks with anti-Islamic actions and apostasy. Although putting down the revolt, the Ottoman government branded such allegations as lies. The trade to the Hejaz was allowed to resume without constraint. British officials themselves identified the Hejaz as the heartland of Islam and as the site where "domestic Slavery has been an institution from the time of Mohammed."[25] They noted that some Turks were quite willing to see slavery brought to an end, but did not detect any group "who look upon it with the feelings of repugnance that it must excite in every European mind."[26] The author of fine distinctions in the minds of some Muslims and not others was obviously less inclined to see a similar range of attitudes in Christendom.

The Waning of Abolitionist Activism

The decade after 1833 marked a high water mark for British abolitionist successes within and beyond the empire. The victories gained were primarily against the slave trade, but occasionally against slavery as well. By the mid-1840s, however, many of the initiatives seemed to founder. The antislavery tide visibly receded in the metropolis. The great petitions of 1837–1838 proved to be the last in which antislavery could draw upon unified mass support. During the 1840s, Chartist and the Anti-Corn Law movements

---

[24] Ehud R. Toledano, *The Ottoman Slave Trade and its Suppression: 1840–1890* (Princeton: Princeton University Press, 1982) ch. 4, and 115–123.

[25] Consul Wylde of Jidda to Foreign Secretary Derby, February 17, 1877; quoted in Erdem, *Slavery*, 86 and Toledano, *Ottoman State*, 129–135.

[26] *Ibid.*, 87. For an analysis of the gap between Ottoman and European discourses on slavery, see Ehud R. Toledano, "Ottoman Concepts of Slavery in the Period of Reform, 1830s–1880s" in *Breaking the Chains*, 37–63. For an extended analysis of the broad spectrum of Muslim views of slavery during and after the abolition of Muslim slavery, see Clarence-Smith, *Islam*, Part II.

matched and exceeded the abolitionist's harvest of signatures. Scattered working class protests during the last rallies against slave apprenticeship in 1838 were harbingers of worse to come. Chartists invaded antislavery meetings at the end of 1840. Even where they were not attacked, new initiatives could gain no popular traction. By December of 1840. Buxton tellingly complained that "we dare not hold meetings thro' the country and we are bankrupts without them."[27]

Working class hostility was exacerbated by three convergent developments. The British economy moved into deep recession ("the hungry forties"). To the costs of the naval patrol off the coast of Africa, taxpayers had to fund the interest on the compensation package extended to the slaveholders. Consumers had to absorb the high cost of sugar as a consequence of protective duties in favor of British colonial sugar. In 1841, the abolitionists still retained enough residual strength in Parliament to help to defeat a Whig government that attempted to lower the protective duties. They could not, however, prevent the government from adopting a preemancipation argument of the planters – the comparative living standards of British and Caribbean workers. Less than ten years after sponsoring emancipation, the Whig government compared the liberated slaves, living in comfort on artificially high wages, to hungry British workers no longer able to purchase sugar or coffee at prices within their reach.

Abolitionists were now caught in a dilemma of their own making. For two years after the end of apprenticeship, they had widely publicized news on the high standard of living among the newly freed laborers in the British tropical colonies. Just before the Chartist's disrupted antislavery meetings, the BFASS journal had published a glowing report from a traveler to Jamaica: "Where else, in the whole wide world, is there a peasantry that with so little toil has such a command over the good things of this life? . . . They do not work hard, they live well, they send their children to school . . . build chapels at their own expense and support many of the missionaries."[28] Where else, indeed, demanded the Chartists? Not in Britain. Official reports from the West Indies corroborated antislavery reports.

Whatever the relative standards of living on either side of the Atlantic, trends appeared to be moving in opposite directions in the early 1840s. The legal statuses of British and West Indian workers had now converged. The abolitionists appeared to be favoring the idle poor abroad over the idled poor at home. Many industrialists in Britain sided with their workers. They too

[27] Patricia Hollis, "Anti-Slavery and British Working-Class Radicalism in the Years of Reform," in Bolt, *Anti-Slavery*, 294–315; Howard Temperley, *White Dreams Black Africa: The Antislavery Expedition to the Niger* (New Haven: Yale University Press, 1991), 57, 63. On the complex convergence and tension between Chartist and antislavery mobilizations from 1838 through the early 1840s, see Betty Fladeland, "Our Cause Being One and the Same: Abolitionists and Chartists," in James Walvin ed., *Slavery and British Society*, 69–99.

[28] Temperley, British *Antislavery*, 148–149.

felt betrayed by the realignment of the BFASS leadership against free trade. Sugar production in the British West Indies had fallen by nearly 30 percent since the end of apprenticeship, and by more than 35 percent since emancipation. Protecting colonies with falling or stagnant output made far less sense than trading with dynamic customers like Brazil and Cuba. These countries continued to thrive and grow with slave labor and slave trade imports. By the time the second (and last) World Antislavery Convention convened in London, in 1843, a majority or near majority of the old antislavery constituency had broken with the London Society's support of protective duties. The split over indefinite protection for post-emancipation British sugar resulted in a sharply divided movement three years before colonial protectionism was abandoned. The 1843 Convention could no longer agree to support the 1840 resolution exempting free labor sugar from slave labor competition. One by one, over the following year, abolitionists in Parliament and in the government were forced to concede and even to insist upon the fact that most British West Indian plantations could not compete with the slave-importing sugar and coffee producers of Brazil and Cuba.[29] As a "mighty experiment" in free labor competitiveness, emancipation had clearly faltered. Slave owners and their political supporters were certainly not convinced to follow the British example. In the generation following the Act of 1833, not a single major slaveholding government, including the slave states of the United States, decided to abolish the institution of slavery without the catalysts of civil war, revolution, civil mobilization, or military pressure.

Internal abolitionist divisions over sugar duties was, but one sign of the receding power of metropolitan abolitionism. The early 1840s also marked a recession in the fortunes of British antislavery all around the Atlantic basin. In 1840, Fowell Buxton organized another branch of antislavery, the African Civilization Society, to stem the slave trade at its source. The most elite organization in the history of British abolitionism, it was launched in June 1840, at the same time as the first World Antislavery Convention. Prince Albert, Queen Victoria's Consort, offered the inaugural speech before an audience filled with the cream of the aristocracy, the Established Church, and Parliament. This final ascendancy of antislavery to social preeminence proposed to transform the entire African Continent into an antislave trading and free labor zone.[30]

Under its auspices and in deference to the heightened political power and social standing of abolitionism, the British government dispatched an expedition to establish a free-labor settlement far up the Niger River. A successful settlement based upon free labor, it was believed, would lead Africans to abandon the trade in slaves. Plagued by malaria, the effort ended in complete disaster. In 1843, a psychologically broken Buxton announced

---

[29] Drescher, *Mighty Experiment*, 173–191.
[30] Temperley, *White Dreams*, ch. 1.

to the World Convention that the Niger expedition and the prior Sierra Leone experiment both proved that Providence itself had "erected a wall of malaria around it [Africa] which we cannot break through."[31] The abolitionist movement was now not only internally split over fiscal policy towards the ex-slave colonies, but was branded as a group of quixotic dreamers, willing to sacrifice British naval officers to devastating diseases in pursuit of utopian fantasies.

Except for France, the great powers of Europe posed no obstacles to Britain's Atlantic project. Smaller northern European governments were equally compliant. Denmark had withdrawn from the African trade to its Caribbean colonies as early as 1802, and its intercolonial slave trade had ceased after British reoccupation in 1807. At the end of the French wars, the British made reversion of the Danish, Swedish, and Dutch possessions contingent upon their renunciation of the slave trade. All three European states adjusted to the British diplomatic project, including the mutual right of search of slave ships. With small plantation colonies and an aging slave population, Sweden and Denmark initiated emancipations in 1846–1847. Popular mobilization in the two Baltic states was nonexistent and unnecessary. So unproblematic was slavery in the small Swedish colony of St. Bartholomew that Sweden's ambassador to France claimed to be simply unaware of the slaves' existence when British abolitionists approached him in the early 1840s. The Swedish Abolition Society subsequently rejected any public petitioning on the subject in favor of a private appeal to the king. When emancipation was enacted in 1846, the Swedish Diet's allocation was insufficient to pay compensation for the colony's 523 slaves. The king moved other national funds to effect emancipation. The Danish West Indies also constituted a small plantation complex. Its sugar production dropped steadily from the 1820s. Under pressure to follow British emancipation in the 1830s, the Danish government instituted ameliorative legislation as a step towards abolition. Following the British model, gradual emancipation with an intermediate transition was introduced in 1847. As in the British colonies, the transition was aborted by a popular mobilization. Unlike the British case, however, the pressure from below was entirely the result of slave action. In July 1848, in the wake of emancipation in the French colonies, 8,000 slaves assembled before the Governor General's headquarters. Once more, the process more closely resembled the Jamaican and Demeraran precedent rather than the Haitian revolt. Almost a century earlier, the slaves in Danish St. John had risen and annihilated almost every white resident on the island. In 1848, the slaves destroyed property rather than persons. The governor issued an order of immediate emancipation.[32]

---

[31] Quoted in Drescher, *Mighty Experiment*, 168.
[32] Neville A. T. Hall, *Slave Society in the Danish West Indies: St. Thomas, St. John, and St. Croix* B. W. Higman, ed. (Baltimore: Johns Hopkins University Press, 1992), 280.

French society demonstrated somewhat more mobilization towards abolition than the Baltic states, but it required yet another metropolitan revolution to put an end to France's second slavery. In response to the implementation of British emancipation, the French Society for the Abolition of Slavery was founded in 1834. Another burst of parliamentary activity was elicited in the wake of the end of British system of apprenticeship in 1838. Even more than its predecessor, the *Amis des Noirs,* the Society remained the preserve of a small elite dominated by members of the French Parliament. Although admiring the model of British mass agitation, members of the Society made no attempt to stimulate a popular movement or a nationwide organization in France. The French Abolitionist Society was inaugurated at the very moment when its government placed severe new restrictions on the formation of any associational activity. An Anglo-French war scare in 1840 made French abolitionists even more hesitant to be aggressively affiliated with a policy identified for more than a generation as an "English" cause. The war scare generated such a powerful anti-British backlash that the government prohibited even a small Anglo-French antislavery meeting in Paris in 1842.

Throughout the 1840s, the French abolitionist leadership moved cautiously. In 1844 and 1847, two modest petition campaigns attracted only 10,000 signatures each. The British mobilization of both 1814 and 1833 probably harvested the signatures of more than one in every five or six adults. The French attempt at a popular antislavery mobilization of 1844 was launched from outside the ranks of the elite. It attracted less than one potential French signatory in a thousand. French women played a modest role in the working class petition of 1844. They had virtually no presence at all in the second, more middle-class, petition of 1847. French Protestants, encouraged by their ties with the English, were always overrepresented in the small world of the French antislavery movement. As in most other European and Latin American countries, the Catholic hierarchy hesitated to affiliate itself with abolitionist agitation. On the eve of another revolution in 1848, there was some hint in one French Catholic newspaper that it was prepared to consider encouraging mass petitioning for emancipation. Relative to its British counterparts, however, French civil society put very little antislavery pressure on the French monarchy.[33]

It took yet another revolution in Paris, in 1848, and a warning about the possibility of a preemptive slave uprising, to induce a change. Within a week after the February 1848 Revolution in Paris, the new provisional government put immediate slave emancipation on their agenda. An emancipation decree was published just before the new republic's convocation of the National Constituent Assembly. The new government's principal abolitionist, Victor

---

[33] Larry Jennings, *French Anti-Slavery*, ch. 7–9; Drescher, *From Slavery to Freedom*, ch. 6; Drescher, "Women's Mobilization," 113; and Drescher, "Public Opinion," 26–29.

Schoelcher, feared that the Assembly might postpone liberation of the slaves pending the establishment of a compensation package on the British model. Schoelcher's assessment of national priorities was justified. There was no national anticipation or celebration of emancipation in the metropolis. The French Antislavery Society virtually ceased to function even before the emancipation decree in April 1848. Ex-slaves in the French colonies became the first with a right to vote for deputies to the French national legislature. However, in ending the second French Republic, Louis Napoleon Bonaparte again deprived the overseas colonies from representation in the metropolitan legislature.

The interim between the emancipation decree's promulgation in Paris and its arrival in the Caribbean saw a final wave of slave protests. The bloodiest episode occurred in Martinique between May 20th and 23rd, 1848. After more than thirty deaths and many wounded, the governors of both Martinique and Guadeloupe proclaimed immediate emancipation two weeks before the official notice reached the islands.[34] The French National Assembly later modestly compensated the ex-masters. The institution of slavery itself was never revived but, after Louis Napoleon Bonaparte's *coup d'etat* in 1851, the African transatlantic slave trade to the French sugar islands was revived under a system of long-term apprenticeships called *engagement à temps*.[35]

With the exception of the jointly occupied Franco-Dutch island of St. Martin, the Dutch colonies remained the last northern European state sanctioning slavery after 1848. Despite their pioneering role in the development of European capitalism and northern European slave colonies, there was little sign of abolitionism in the Netherlands either during or after the age of revolution. For a generation, British abolitionists unsuccessfully attempted to stimulate an abolitionist movement in the Netherlands. A steadily rising rate of slave unrest in Suriname did no better. When the Dutch finally began to dismantle their slavery system in 1863, they took full advantage of lessons learned from prior emancipations. They proved to be the most assiduous followers of the British model. They avoided some of the policies that made the "mighty experiment" unpalatable to planters throughout the Americas. They began in the East Indies in 1860. There, the number of slaves had already dwindled to about 7,000. For commercial agriculture, the Dutch already relied on a cultivation system. Agricultural laborers grew cash crops of coffee and sugar as a means of fulfilling their tax obligations to the Dutch. Compensation was paid to slave owners.

The Dutch West Indian slaves were freed three years later in 1863. The compensation package to slave owners was relatively generous, because the costs were covered by profits from the compulsory labor of the East

---

[34] Jennings, *French Anti-Slavery*, 283–284.
[35] Philip D. Curtin, *The Atlantic Slave Trade: A Census* (Madison: University of Wisconsin Press, 1969), 250; and Blackburn, *Overthrow of Colonial Slavery*, 507.

Indian plantations. As Pieter Emmer notes, in comparison with Britain, the Dutch emancipated its colonial slaves at a bargain price for metropolitan taxpayers.[36] The Dutch, like the Danes, adapted the British apprenticeship system, but extended it to ten years, from 1863 until 1873.

Finally, there was no delay between the ending of the slave apprenticeship system and the introduction of Asian indentured laborers. Within a decade after the ending of apprenticeship, East Indian migrants already outnumbered ex-slaves working on Suriname's plantations. Through all of these stages, the Dutch government was free to stick to its timetable. There was no metropolitan mobilization to accelerate or curtail the transition. In this respect, Dutch emancipation was smoother than its English predecessor. But, even with all the advantages of prior experiments, Dutch Suriname was not able to avoid a decline in post-apprenticeship sugar production. Metropolitan civil society had played a minimal role in emancipation. No nationwide celebrations marked the endings of slavery or apprenticeship. The only system that attracted less parliamentary attention before emancipation than Dutch slavery was the Javan cultivation system.

The Ibero-American Orbit

As might be imagined, the areas that constituted the greatest impediments to the British abolitionist project after 1840 were the two most dynamic slave importing systems of all. The European-controlled slave systems in Cuba and Brazil remained the most elusive holdouts against British diplomatic pressure to end the slave trade. Enslaved Africans continued to flow into Cuba for half a century after the first Anglo-Spanish agreement in 1817 to end the Spanish Caribbean slave trade by 1820.

The number of slaves disembarked in the Spanish Caribbean reached new heights during the very decade that British abolitionist mobilization reached its peak. More slaves were imported into Cuba and Puerto Rico in 1831–1840 than in any other decade in the history of the Spanish Caribbean. Spanish governments found the treaties useful as weapons to block further British attempts to expand the Anglo-Spanish mixed commission in Havana. African *emancipados*, rescued from slavers, were routinely dispatched to plantations as replacements for deceased slaves or distributed among people otherwise too poor to afford slaves. This Spanish form of apprenticeship (*emancipados*) became a lifelong servitude. In the eyes of the governors of Cuba, the captives were simply an addition to the servile labor supply.[37]

The three decades after 1830 also marked the "Cuban moment" in the long history of slave-grown sugar in the Americas. David Eltis estimates that Cuba must have then ranked among the top half-dozen countries of

---

[36] Emmer, *The Dutch*, 128.
[37] Eltis, *Economic Growth*, 249, Table A.8; Slave Trade Database, 1830–1839; and David Murray, *Odious Commerce*, 282–283.

the mid-nineteenth century world in per capita output of sugar.[38] At least until the late 1850s, the chief threat to the institution of slaves did not come from metropolitan civil society. There was no antislavery society in Spain during the half century after Waterloo. A Spanish government heavily dependent upon the revenues of Cuban plantations identified foreign sources as the principal threat to the institution of slavery. Some Cubans, on the other hand, also identified the unprecedented level of incoming slaves as the greatest threat to the island's future. After 1833, abolitionist ranks, black or white, could be fueled from Haiti, Jamaica, or even North America. Moreover, they were "supported by a large party in Europe whose aim was the triumph of Africans over Europeans."[39] These words, penned by a Spanish Captain-General of Cuba in 1835, were echoed by white Cubans who wished to put a stop to the slave trade. In terms of racial proportions of their populations, Cuba and Puerto Rico in the 1830s were more analogous to Virginia and Maryland than the other Caribbean islands. For men like José Antonio Saco of Santiago de Cuba, the imagined destiny of the island was to be a "whitened" community. The politics of whitening might include either loyalty to a future reformed Spanish empire or incorporation into the United States of America.[40]

Into this potentially explosive mixture of imperial politics – increasing numbers of Cuban slaves, marginalized free blacks, and Creole whites – British abolitionists managed to insert a firebrand at the end of the 1830s. David Turnbull, an ex-correspondent of the *London Times*, traveled to the British West Indies and Cuba just as the British campaign against apprenticeship reached its climax. In 1840, he authored a plan to allow illegally imported Africans to claim freedom before the Anglo-Spanish mixed courts created by the treaty of 1817. The planters' property in these persons would be radically delegalized and slaving would be quickly terminated. When a delegation of the BFASS met with Foreign Secretary Palmerston to present the final resolutions of the World Antislavery Convention, they also persuaded him to appoint David Turnbull as consul to Havana.[41]

Turnbull quickly became the most interventionist official in the British diplomatic core operating in a foreign country. Neither the Foreign Office nor the British Antislavery Society encouraged the new consul to incite an uprising. Turnbull, however, considered himself the point man of British humanitarianism in Cuba. From the moment that he arrived in the island, he clashed with the Captain-General, and created panic among the planters.

[38] Eltis, "Slave Economies of the Caribbean," in *General History of the Caribbean*, 123.
[39] Murray, *Odious Commerce*, 116.
[40] Christopher Schmidt-Nowara, *Empire and Antislavery: Spain, Cuba and Puerto Rico, 1833–1874* (Pittsburgh: University of Pittsburgh Press, 1999), ch. 1 and 2; and Robert L. Paquette, *Sugar Is Made with Blood: The Conspiracy of La Escalera and the Conflict between Empires over Slavery in Cuba* (Middletown: Wesleyan University Press, 1988) ch. 7.
[41] Murray, *Odious Commerce*, 136.

By assuming the role of protector of the Africans and publicizing his plan, he also became involved in conflicts with other British officials and alienated a British mercantile community anxious to avoid being identified with fomenting disorder. By openly defending free blacks, Turnbull frightened even anti–slave trade Creoles who feared that his aims led far beyond the abolition of the slave trade.

Turnbull's residency also coincided with the dramatic downturn in British Caribbean sugar production and with reports of British plans to transfer large numbers of liberated Africans from Sierra Leone to Jamaica. Cubans compounded this development by describing it as an imperial plan to ruin Cuban labor recruitment to save Jamaica. All reports of slave disturbances were tied to British abolitionist activity.[42] The British government attempted to rein in Turnbull. It first withdrew his right to act as guardian of *emancipados*, and then it removed him from Havana. Despite his departure, Turnbull's tumultuous tenure was enough to link his activities to an accusation of British involvement in the Escalera conspiracy in 1844. A score of British subjects were arrested, and the fate of free-born and enslaved Cubans caught up in the conspiracy was far worse. The round-up expanded to include thousands of suspects. One-third of those captured were sentenced to long prison terms or execution.[43]

The importation of African slaves fell for a few years after the reign of fear and terror unleashed by Cuban officials. By 1846, however, Cubans celebrated news of the end of British protection for free-grown sugar as a national holiday. Prices of slaves, land, and sugar all rose by 15 percent. The price of slaves rose to record heights. In 1856–1860, the average price of slaves was more than 250 percent higher than it had been in 1841–1845. The consequent expansion of the Cuban market helped to give the sugar trade a new life. From a low point of 3,400 African slaves per year disembarked in Cuba during the two years after La Escalera, slave imports rose again to more than 30,000 per year on the eve of the American Civil War.[44]

By the mid–1850s, the British threat to the institution of slavery in Cuba appeared to have receded. The BFASS ceased to have any major impact on British government policy. Spain was able to offset British pressure against the slave trade with countervailing U.S. diplomacy. American southerners and some Cuban planters agitated to have the United States annex the island. The threat of American reaction limited British policy. An outright antislave trade naval blockade by Britain might also provoke annexation by the United States. Spain's evasion of its slave trade treaties also hindered

---

[42] See Paquette, *Sugar*, 139–157; and Murray, *Odious Commerce*, 146–148.
[43] Paquette, *Sugar*, 229.
[44] Eltis, *Economic Growth*, 263, Table C.2. The price of slaves after 1850 was generally lower on most parts of the African coast than it had been before. See also Slave Trade Database for slave imports.

Britain from signing a treaty guaranteeing to protect Cuba for Spain. Thus stalemated, British pressure on Spain to enforce its treaty obligations against the slave trade ceased by the mid–1850s.[45] Seventy-five years after it became the first area in the Americas to prohibit the importation of Africans, the United States had become the last best hope of Atlantic slavers against British pressure. On the eve of the secession of the U.S. South, the slave trade was flourishing in Cuba. In 1859, Cuba imported the second highest number of slaves in the island's history.

Further south, British abolitionism also seemed to be in recession on both sides of the Atlantic from the early 1840s. In Africa, the Niger venture reinforced a generation of experience that no matter how many loopholes were closed by treaties, traffickers always managed to contrive alternative means to prevent a permanent diminution of the supply of African slaves. The economic structures of the societies on both sides of the southern Atlantic seemed to preclude rapid closure of the slave trade. The scene in Brazil was the worst, where three of four Africans delivered to the New World were landed during the 1840s. Here, too, Americans dogged the British. When Cuban slave imports briefly sagged after the Escalera conspiracy, North Americans helped Brazil pick up the slack. "The slave trade is almost entirely carried on under our flag and in American built vessels," complained the United States minister to Brazil in 1844. His successors were equally appalled by the fact that American consignees, factors, and agents abroad in pursuit of the slave trade "were immune from prosecution."[46]

Less visibly, British economic policy now turned a blind eye toward the distinction between slave and free-grown produce. The British swing toward free trade unleashed a flood of goods in both directions between Brazil and Britain. In 1846, the British *chargé d'affaires* in Rio de Janeiro wearily wrote to Palmerston, "*Brazil lives upon slave labour.* The government is carried on by the daily receipts of the Customs Houses...." "There are only three ways of making a fortune in Brazil – either by the slave trade, or by slaving, or by a coffee commission house," echoed the British ambassador two years later. British naval attempts to seize slavers and bring captives ashore might provoke attempts at recapture. "The ports of Brazil to a certain extent," he wrote, "are not the ports of a friendly but a hostile power." The Brazilian foreign minister frankly confessed that he could not see how any Brazilian government could enforce either existing or proposed legislation to suppress the slave trade. "I know of none who could or would attempt it, and when

---

45 Murray, *Odious Commerce*, 240, 298–299; 309–315.
46 *Fehrenbacher, Slaveholding Republic*, 176–177. If the American flag covered the movements of many slavers, British capital was also indirectly invested in the Brazilian slave trade. See Warren S. Howard, *American Slavers and the Federal Law, 1837–1862* (Berkeley: University of California Press, 1963), 282, and Craig M. Simpson's *A Good Southerner: The Life of Henry A. Wise of Virginia* (Chapel Hill: University of North Carolina Press, 1985), 62–69.

99 men in every hundred are engaged in it, how is it to be done?... In the streets, I would be stoned. I cannot consent to be *The* Man in Brazil from whom all his countrymen would turn away with contempt and aversion. *I will not Bell the Cat.*"[47]

The obstacles to suppression of the slave trade were echoed on the other side of the Atlantic by leading members of the Britain abolitionist movement itself. In March 1845, an eighty-five year old Thomas Clarkson presented a memorial to the government reflecting the Antislavery Society's views on a generation of efforts to suppress the slave trade. Naval patrols had failed and would continue to fail. As United States opposition to abolition showed, the treaty system would never be complete. In the absence of real commitment, abolition would always encounter bad faith among foreign powers, and cunning, fraud, or audacity among the slave dealers. The Antislavery Society's pacifist principles could only succeed where "a sense of humanity and moral rectitude" prevailed and where the demands of the slaveholders in the Americas would cease to exist. The Society therefore petitioned Parliament to seek an alternative policy.[48]

The moral economy of the abolitionists was powerfully seconded by the political economy of some free trade MPs. In 1845, William Hutt used the abolitionists' documentation on the slave trade to move the suspension of the naval patrol system on economic grounds. The policy, declared Hutt, had already cost the taxpayer double the £20 million allotted to emancipate Britain's colonial slaves. The great flaw in the interception system was that it violated the fundamental law of supply and demand. The flawed patrols produced higher profits for smugglers, less concern for the lives of captives, greater European hostility against British naval hegemony, and a patriotic backlash from societies participating in the slave trade. The basic policy error lay in seeking to limit transatlantic migration in the first place. Partial suppression might even have prolonged the "natural" ending of the slave trade by artificially suppressing supply. To extinguish the slave trade, Hutt concluded, "We should leave it alone." Despite being appalled at the callousness of his conclusion, the Antislavery Society concurred "to a certain extent with Mr. Hutt in his view of the facts," differing only with the "animus" of his motion.[49]

The debate over the African patrol reached its climax early in 1850. Hutt introduced a parliamentary resolution urging to the British government withdraw from any treaty that required the use of force to put down the slave trade. Although contemporaries lacked complete data on the world's sources of tropical exports, it was clear that abolitionism had wrought a

[47] Quoted in Bethell, *Abolition*, 272, 288, 290.

[48] Bethell, *Abolition*, 296–297; Temperley, *British Antislavery*, 176, 177–178; Drescher, *Mighty Experiment*, 187–188.

[49] Temperley, *British Antislavery*, 177–178; Drescher, *Mighty Experiment*, 187–188.

profound change in the distribution of sugar production toward the slave importing economies.[50] For the first time, a prime minister of the British government openly acknowledged that slave labor might well be able to undersell colonial free labor. Removing the British naval patrol, however, might well be the last straw in the collapse of the British plantations. They were, he warned Parliament, on the verge of succumbing to slave-importing Cuba and Brazil. Invoking party discipline, the prime minister managed to rally enough votes to beat back Hutt's motion.

The vote of 1850 would later be recognized by historians as "the last important stand of humanitarian politics" against the slave trade. Nevertheless, the handwriting was on the wall. Unless the naval policy began to succeed, the pressure to abandon it would grow more convincing with each passing year. The press was equally emphatic. The naval policy was failing, its logic was flawed, and public support was vanishing. A prime minister (Russell), and a foreign secretary (Palmerston) who had to threaten to resign to keep their party in line could not go back to that well too often.[51]

Far more than a British administration was now at stake. Everyone agreed on the notorious ability of slave-importing Cuba and Brazil to feed the world's ever-growing demand for plantation products. In Brazil alone, "3 to 4 million square miles" awaited cultivation. Fowell Buxton's son, Charles, estimated that to bring Brazil to the population density where free labor would be competitive with slavery would require the transportation of 240 million additional African slaves or twenty times as many captives as those who had been boarded from Africa during the previous 350 years.[52] The only alternative appeared to be a policy that defied both the pacifist moral principles of the Antislavery Society and the market principles of the economists. The man for the task was already in place. Palmerston had already shown his willingness to resort to gunboat diplomacy to force Portugal to sign a slave trade treaty. British cruisers seizing slavers and even legitimate ships at random had already brought down a Portuguese government and assured the speedy signing of an Anglo-Portuguese treaty in 1842.[53] It was now time to try the other side of the Atlantic.

Already, in January 1850, Russell told Palmerston that the day must come when Brazil would be treated "as the government of 1816 treated Algiers." Until 1850, Palmerston's desire for more ships on the Brazilian coast had always been trumped by other priorities. Treaty obligations required Britain to keep a certain number of ships off the African coast or to engage Argentina in the Rio de la Plata. Britain finally settled its differences with Argentina

[50] Eltis, *Slave Economies*, 113–119, Tables 3.1 and 3.2; Drescher, *Mighty Experiment*, 189, Table 11.1.
[51] *Ibid.*, 190–191.
[52] *Ibid.*, 192.
[53] Marques, *Sounds*, 125.

in 1849. British ships began to redeploy to the Brazilian coast. Still earlier in 1848, the British minister in Rio had detected "a very satisfactory change . . . taking place in the mind of the Brazilian government *and public* on the importation of slaves . . . more rapidly than I dared hope or could . . . have believed possible." Even at the end of 1849, however, "only a tiny, essentially urban minority of Brazilians had been converted to abolition". . . . Even in retrospective "there is little evidence for thinking that in the years 1849–50 the landed interest . . . was demanding the abolition of the slave trade."[54]

The situation in Brazil was dramatically transformed by another act of naval aggression. As political pressure mounted against the naval patrol in Britain, the government increased seizures of slavers. Within a few weeks of the House of Commons' vote on Hutt's motion, the Foreign Office advised the British admiralty that there were no further limits to British searches and seizures of suspected slaving ships "*at any place within Brazilian waters* as well as on the high seas." By June, a reinforced British fleet was not only capturing suspected vessels but conducting on-shore raids in the largest and most successful antislaving naval action since the bombardment of Algiers in 1816.[55]

The Brazilian government found itself hovering on the verge of a major disaster. Armed Anglo-Brazilian hostilities were occurring in Brazilian territorial waters, which might quickly escalate into a full blockade of Brazilian trade. Any prospect of wider armed resistance had to encompass the lessons of the age of revolution. Elsewhere, the interventions of polarized mass conflict had led to the destruction of the social and political order in Latin America. In Bahia, where memories of the Mâlé uprising reverberated, potential slave mobilization compounded the shock of British intervention.[56] The elite's first reflex was to have as confined a public sphere as possible. The crucial legislative debate on the slave trade, in September 1850, was held in secret session. Unlike Cuba, Brazil was relatively isolated from the great European power conflicts. The French minister to Rio was unequivocal. Brazil stood alone on the issue of the slave trade – a point reiterated by the government to the Brazilian legislature. Abolition of the slave trade was recognized as a value of the "civilized world," backed by British power. Brazil could not hope to resist.[57]

[54] Hudson to Palmerston, August 5, 1848, quoted in Bethell, *Abolition*, 313 (emphasis in the original); and *ibid.*, 309, 313–314.

[55] Jeffrey D. Needell, "The Abolition of the Brazilian Slave Trade in 1850: Historiography, Slave Agency and Statesmanship," *Journal of Latin American Studies*, 33 (2001), 681–711 esp. pp. 705–707.

[56] See Graden, *Slavery to Freedom in Brazil*, ch. 2.

[57] Speech of Paulino José Soares de Soura to the Brazilian Chamber of Deputies, July 15, 1850, summarized in Bethell, *Abolition*, 338.

To preserve consensus without risking a conflict with Britain, the slave-holding planter class, or the political opposition, the Brazilian government isolated the slave traders as the sole cause of Brazil's predicament. Because so many of the traders were Portuguese, nationalist antagonism could be focused on an exogenous source of Brazil's predicament. It was far easier to expel a few unarmed foreign merchants than to challenge the world's most formidable foreign navy. Two points are worth emphasizing. Before the crisis of 1850, there was a generation of continuous discussion of the slave trade. The press, including previously pro-trade newspapers, unleashed a barrage of editorials against the slave trade in July 1850. Many papers were able to reprint a famous antislave trade speech by the Bishop of Bahia in July 1827.[58]

Nevertheless, during the crisis, antislavery never reached the level of an organized movement or a consensual "public opinion" outside the legislature. The birth date of Brazil's first nominal antislavery society is significant. Its first exploratory meeting coincided precisely with the first legislature session on the British naval crisis. Its formation occurred in conjunction with the secret session of September 1850. Its title, the *Sociedade contra o tráfico e promotora da colonização* (*Society against the Slave Trade and for Colonization*) encapsulated the linkage between surrendering an African source of labor and developing a future European one. The Society was ideologically unconnected to slave emancipation and organizationally similar to the small elite societies of continental Europe. Discussions about the immorality or inhumanity of the traffic do not appear to have ranked very high on the Society's agenda. At the very moment when planning began for the Society's organization, a hitherto antiabolitionist newspaper, the *Jornal do Comércio*, editorialized that the evil to be addressed was the slothful and impure civilization imported from Africa.[59]

The shallow roots of antislavery in Brazilian society during the second quarter of the nineteenth century favor assigning a larger role to British action than to Brazil's political elite or public opinion as the catalyst for abolition in 1850. The formation of abolitionist societies followed the trauma of slave trade abolition, and was usually ephemeral. Although one historiographical school allots a dominant role to slave mobilization in the passage of the Brazilian abolition act, the threat of insurrection was never mentioned in the decisive closed meeting of the Imperial Council of State.[60]

---

[58] Bethell, *Abolition*, 337.

[59] *Ibid.*, 334 n. 2.

[60] Compare Dale Torston Graden, *From Slavery to Freedom in Brazil: Bahia, 1835–1900* (Albuquerque: University of New Mexico Press, 2006), 13–04, with Jeffrey D. Needell, "The Abolition of the Brazilian Slave Trade in 1850: Historiography, Slave Agency and Statesmanship," *Journal of Latin American Studies*, 33 (2001), 681–711.

The equally striking feature of Brazilian abolition, however, is the dispatch with which the government acted to enforce the legal termination of the transatlantic slave trade. Within less than a year, and with the overwhelming support of the press, the Justice Ministry could claim that the law of September 1850 "met with the powerful support of public opinion." This, too, occurred without any sustained popular mobilization. British naval captains expressed amazement that Brazilians, who had attacked British seamen during the crisis, were now bringing slave traders to the authorities and welcoming British ships. In the wake of abolition, popular hostility was, as the government had hoped, directed more at the Portuguese than either the Africans or the British. When Brazilians would have acted without British intervention is uncertain, but the very ease of the shutdown makes it appear that, below the mercantile/planter class, active support for the slave trade must have been shallow. Subsequently, rare attempts by slavers to reopen the door to the reentry of slaves were unsuccessful. The few exceptions again demonstrate the efficacy of the rule.[61]

Short-run economic explanations for abolition in 1850 are the least convincing. That the demand for slaves remained strong in Brazil until 1850 is beyond question. The peak year for the arrival of captive Africans in Brazil or to any single region in the history of the transatlantic slave trade was in 1848. The peak biennium was likewise in 1848–1849, and the peak triennium, 1847–1849. Nor did the record numbers signal any "overproduction" of Africans for the Brazilian market. The rapid rise in slave prices immediately after 1849 and the ensuing rise in domestic slave trade prices indicate a robust and sustained market before and after abolition. There appears to be little evidence that, in 1850, contemporaries concluded that the Brazilian slave trade had reached the "natural" turning point to saturation forecast by MP Hutt in Parliament a few months before Brazilian abolition.

As we have noted, the appetite for African slaves in the Americas remained intact at mid-century. During the decade following Brazilian suppression, Cuba doubled its importation of African slaves. This trend persisted despite the fact that British patrols caused slave prices to rise at their steepest rate in the nineteenth century. By the second half of the 1850s, the price of slaves being loaded in Africa dropped by over 40 percent, but in Cuban markets they increased by 75 percent. Although Cuban planters had increasing access to Chinese indentured labor, exploited in conditions almost indistinguishable from slaves, Cubans still purchased two Africans for every indentured Asian during the 1850s. Half a century after British abolition, the balance of economic incentives looked all too familiar. Any sign of weakening in British vigilance, wrote the *Economist* of London, and "Brazil would revert quickly

---

[61] Eltis, *Economic Growth*, 214–217.

to her old and profitable trade," followed by Spain, Portugal, France, with her slave-apprentices, and even the United States.[62]

Indeed, the British government was so impressed by the continuing economic temptation to reopen the Brazilian trade that they refused to repeal the humiliating Aberdeen Act of 1845, which authorized the British seizures of Brazilian ships, until two years after the *last* recorded enslaved Africans had landed in the Americas. Ironically, "the last important stand of humanitarian politics," against the Hutt motion in Britain had triggered the last and most important single victory over the transatlantic slave trade since the Anglo-American slave trade abolition acts of 1807. Whatever the echoes of Algiers three decades earlier, the show of force had been far from deadly on either side. Only one British seaman was killed and two wounded. Whatever the relative roles of the Brazilian and British participants, the crisis of 1850 was for Palmerston the crowning achievement of his life. His death in 1865 coincided almost exactly with the termination of the Atlantic slave trade.[63]

More importantly, the ending of the slave trade to Brazil marked another turning point in the history of abolition. During each generation between 1750 and 1850, between 1.8 and 2 million Africans had been carried in horrible conditions across the oceans. Most had been doomed to a lifetime of toil on the plantations in the Americas. For the slave trade's last decade and a half, the annual toll fell to fewer than 15,000, a rate not seen since the early seventeenth century, and one fifth of the average between 1750 and 1850. Slavery itself now seemed doomed to inexorable decline everywhere in the plantation Americas except Cuba and the U.S. South. Everywhere else, the combination of voluntary migration, manumission, and the annual excess of deaths over births ensured that the Americas would henceforth be dominated by free men and laborers. In the course of the single generation, abolitionism had accelerated the sense of slavery's relative diminution.[64]

Midway through the nineteenth century, British abolitionists looked back with a mixture of pride and frustration. At the close of the eighteenth century, the antiabolitionist Earl of Westmoreland had mocked abolitionists as would be "emperors of the world," for imagining that they could pass a law to prohibit the slave trade along a broad stretch of the African coast. Four decades later, his mockery seemed to have alchemized into prophecy. At the World Antislavery Convention of 1840, the British abolitionists, flush with their series of victories, seemed poised to extend their "great

[62] Quotation in Drescher, *The Mighty Experiment*, 195. Compare the 1850s' importations of slaves in Eltis, *Economic Growth*, p. 245, Table A 2, with figures for arrivals of indentured servants into Cuba in David Northrup, *Indentured Labor in the Age of Imperialism, 1834–1922* (Cambridge: Cambridge University Press, 1992), 156–157, Table A 1. See also Drescher, *Mighty Experiment*, 195.

[63] Christopher Lloyd, *The Navy and the Slave Trade: The Suppression of the African Slave Trade in the Nineteenth Century* (London: Longmans, Green 1949), 145.

[64] Needell, *Party of Order*, 153.

experiment" to every corner of the earth. Just one decade later, British abolitionists recognized that as one door slammed shut on servitude, another opened up. Final closure of the slave trade seemed to be indefinitely stymied by the slaveholding republic of the United States. The world's appetite for slave grown products continued unabated. Not a single slaveholding class in the world believed that they would gain the transformation from slave to wage labor.[65]

Most daunting of all, in 1850, there still remained nearly 6 million slaves in the New World, well over half of them confined within an institution impervious to the ending of the slave trade and chained to the most powerful economic and political entity in the Western Hemisphere. At mid-century, many U.S. citizens could still casually imagine that, whatever the fate of the Atlantic slave trade, their own institution's manifest destiny included unlimited possibilities for expansion. Early in the 1850s, an American naval officer was charged with exploring the tropical valley of the Amazon. His report envisioned the great Latin American river valley divided into large estates and cultivated by slave labor so as "to produce all that they are capable of producing." An enterprising spirit with free trade and black slaves could transform the vast lowland rainforests of South America. There, the "wealth and grandeur of ancient Babylon and modern London must yield to that of the depôts of trade . . . at the mouths of the Orinoco, the Amazon, and the La Plata."[66] In distant London, reviewers read and shuddered. Far beyond the reach of the British naval patrols and British diplomacy, the United States of America cast a long shadow of uncertainty over half a century of victories.

[65] Drescher, *Mighty Experiment*, 157.
[66] William Lewis Herndon, *Exploration of the Valley of the Amazon* (New York: Grove Press, 2000, rept 1854 284).

II

The End of Slavery in Anglo-America

Abolitionism Emerges in U.S. Civil Society

At the beginning of the 1830s, the constitutional pact excluding slavery from the American national agenda still looked ironclad. But, in January 1830, an extended debate in the U.S. Senate pitted Daniel Webster of Massachusetts against Robert Y. Hayne of South Carolina. The Northerner's "Second Reply to Hayne" would be recited for generations as the most eloquent speech ever delivered in Congress: "Liberty *and* Union, now and forever, one and inseparable."[1] The Senator's liberty was quite separable, however, as it applied to the institution of slavery, and faithfully reaffirmed its circumscribed limits. In his speech, the Massachusetts senator repeated, line for line, the very first Congress's resolution renouncing any authority over slaves in any of the states of the Union. Webster reaffirmed its pristine vow: "[F]rom that day to this... No Northern gentleman, to my knowledge, had moved any such question in either House of Congress." None had, ever since 1790, proposed any legislation or resolutions inconsistent with that principle. Nor would Webster himself intrude beyond the line: "It is the original bargain – the compact – let it stand.[2] The American colonies' project of simultaneous liberation and deportation still remained the most advanced articulation of gradual emancipation.

Only four years later, the *cordon sanitaire* that the national legislature had defended for forty years was being threatened by a new wave of

---

[1] Allan Nevins, *Ordeal of the Union* (New York: Scribner, 1947), I, 288; and Henry Mayer, *All On Fire: William Lloyd Garrison and the Abolition of Slavery* (New York: St. Martin's Press, 1998), 106.

[2] *The Webster-Hayne Debate on the Nature of the Union: Selected Documents*, Herman Belz, ed. (Indianapolis: Liberty Fund, 2000), 91. Earlier in the speech, Webster clearly branded "slavery as one of the greatest evils, both morally and political." The cure however, he left "to those whose right and duty it is to inquire and to decide." (That meant the free citizens of the slave states). *Ibid.*, 89.

agitation. Late in 1830, British abolitionists took up Elizabeth Heyrick's call for immediate emancipation with another petition campaign. Five thousand petitions reached Parliament by the following spring. In America, the language of antislavery altered dramatically. Less than a year after he hailed Webster's eloquent speech, Garrison published the first issue of *The Liberator* in Boston. Embracing the Declaration of Independence, demanding the immediate enfranchisement of America's slaves, and recanting his assent to gradual abolition and colonization, *The Liberator* extended the boundaries of American abolitionism.[3]

Two years later, Garrison sailed to England with the dual purpose of combating the American Colonization Society's campaign for funds and appealing for British abolitionist support for his immediatist alternative. Landing in Liverpool late in May 1833, he learned that the British government had just brought an emancipation bill before Parliament. He was equally struck by the size and range of the appeal from out-of-doors that had forced the issue into the legislative arena. He wrote home excitedly about the petitions crowding into Parliament "*by thousands* from every part of the United Kingdom," and ... of one arriving in the House of Lords "signed by EIGHT HUNDRED THOUSAND ladies!!!" ... [and] of one to the House of Commons "containing 187,000 female signatures, which required four members to lay it on the table ... Cheers for the Ladies of Great Britain."[4] This was the characteristic of British abolitionism that Garrison's new perspective contrasted with the earlier American variant. Garrison hailed British slave-trade abolition "as an epochal victory of 'right over wrong, of liberty over oppression,'" achieved through astonishing feats of organization. By contrast, the United States Abolition Act of 1807 was a grudging fulfillment of a twenty-year-old bargain – a "silent abolition" without heroes or popular inspiration.[5]

Garrison's appeal fell on willing ears across the Atlantic. Even before the first stage of British colonial emancipation opened in 1834, British abolitionists had begun to look westward as the first stage in a project to extend their abolitionist impact. Preparations were already underway in the United States to form an abolition society on the British model. Garrison was perfectly situated to witness the successful mass mobilization of British abolitionists and to return home as the bearer of their tactical expertise. Within weeks of the passage of the Emancipation Act in Britain, George Thompson, a British Agency Committee speaker, sparked the rededication of the Edinburgh Emancipation Society to the eradication of slavery throughout the

[3] Mayer, *All on Fire*, 110.
[4] *Letters of William Lloyd Garrison*, I; *I Will Be Heard! 1822–1835*, Walter M. Merrill, ed. (Cambridge, MA: Harvard University Press, 1971), 233; Letter 101, Garrison to *The Liberator*, Liverpool, May 24, 1833; printed in *The Liberator*, July 13, 1833.
[5] Mayer, *All on Fire*, 151–152.

world. Within weeks of the celebration of freedom for slaves, on August 1, 1834, Thompson was on his way to the United States. Funded by Scottish abolitionists, he came as the delegated agent of a British antislavery society. Abolitionists on both sides of the Atlantic hoped to replicate the combination of popular mobilization and legislative action that had terminated the institution of slavery in the British-ruled Caribbean, South Africa, and the Indian Ocean.[6]

The initiative turned out to be a sharp lesson in the limitations of the "British way" to emancipation. The sheer magnitude of the institution of slavery in America had always been the most formidable barrier to envisioning any practical, peaceful means to its rapid end. In 1830, the United States offered the New World's most dynamic challenge to any scenario of a short-term, natural diminution or disappearance of slavery. In the South, slaves had become the region's major source of wealth after the value of land itself. They accounted for a capital worth of 3.5 billion dollars, equal to nearly $70 billion in 2007 dollars, by 1860. In that year, the gross national product of the entire United States was only about 20 percent more than the value of its southern slaves, equivalent, in today's terms, to nearly $10.5 trillion dollars.[7]

Contemporaries were quite aware of the implications of the relative value of human capital in the United States and the British Empire. In February 1836, James Henry Hammond of South Carolina indicated what the potential costs of following the British way to emancipation would be. The British government, he noted, had provided an unprecedented compensation fund of £20 millions or about $100 million to the affected slave owners and their creditors. Hammond estimated that the British slaveholders were receiving about 60 percent of their slaves' market value. He conservatively valued 2.3 million slaves at $400 each. In these terms, they represented 920 million dollars, nine times more than the British compensation fund. Even if slaveholders were willing to settle for 60 cents on the dollar, the American compensation fund would have to be five and a half times greater than its British counterpart. As Hammond noted in 1835, the total yearly public income of the United States federal government was insufficient to pay for the annual natural increase of 60,000 slaves each year. That calculation, he casually added, did not even include the costs of their removal. Full compensation for emancipation of newborn slaves alone at the British rate of compensation would require an annual expenditure of 33 million dollars,

---

[6] See Temperley, *British Antislavery*, 19–27; C. Duncan Rice, *The Scots Abolitionists 1833–1861* (Baton Rouge: Louisiana State University Press, 1981), 35–66; and Iain Whyte, *Scotland and the Abolition of Black Slavery, 1756–1838* (Edinburgh: Edinburgh University Press, 2006), 235–237.

[7] Davis, *Inhuman Bondage*, 298 and 402 n. 5; the figure derives from an estimate by Stanley Engerman.

plus the costs of removal from the United States. That was a sum equal to five times the federal government's annual receipts every two or three years for a century.[8]

The potential bill rose with each subsequent decade. During the generation after 1830,

a continuation of rising demand for slaves in the West, a new surge of demand in the eastern tobacco region, and a slowdown in the rate of natural increase of the slave population all combined to double slave prices between the mid-1840s and the Civil War, which reflected both the high level of immediate profits and the bounding optimism of slave-owners regarding the future prospects.[9]

The capital invested in slaves, who numbered 4 million by 1860, was only one aspect of the economic dimension of the institution. In contrast to most of the other New World plantation economies, cotton, not sugar, was the major crop in the U.S. South. From the beginning of the nineteenth century cotton production expanded rapidly. The United States not only became the leading user of slave labor in the New World by 1830, but also became its major cotton producer. By 1840, America provided more than 60 percent of the Atlantic world's cotton, a proportion that rose to more than 80 percent by 1860. Sixty-four percent of all slaves engaged in plantation labor lived on cotton plantations. The South was also the primary supplier of that product to Britain, the world's leading cotton manufacturer, as well as to continental Europe and New England.[10] The U.S. South was, therefore, another instance

---

[8] William Lee Miller; *Arguing About Slavery: The Great Battle in the United States Congress* (New York: Knopf, 1996), 10.

[9] Fogel, *Without Consent*, 64. See also his "Comparison of the Value of Slave Capital to Total British Wealth and the Share of Total Southern Wealth" in *Evidence and Methods*, 397–398, the companion volume to *Without Consent*. Fogel concludes that British slaves probably accounted for less than 1 percent of British Wealth in 1832. By contrast, the slave share of total U.S. wealth in 1860 was 16 percent. Slaves represented an even larger share of Southern wealth (37 percent), not to mention the potential damage to the value of a slave owner's land in the event of emancipation. More than half the wealth of southern slaveholders' wealth vanished with their slaves after emancipation in 1865. The total potential costs of emancipation under conditions of bargained compensation are examined by Claudia Goldin in "The Economics of Emancipation," in *Without Consent, Technical Papers*, Fogel and Engerman, eds. vol. 2, 614–628.

[10] Fogel, *Without Consent or Contract: The Rise and Fall of American Slavery* (New York: W.W. Norton, 1989), 29–31; 71; Davis, *Inhuman Bondage*, 184–185. On the extended debate over the economic "modernity" of nineteenth-century Southern slavery, see Robert W. Fogel and Stanley L. Engerman, *Time on the Cross: The Economics of American Negro Slavery* (Boston: Little, Brown, 1974; reprinted with a new afterword (New York: W.W. Norton, 1989); Fogel, *The Slavery Debates: 1952–1990* (Baton Rouge: Louisiana State University Press, 2003); Gavin Wright, *Slavery and American Economic Development* (Baton Rouge: Louisiana State University Press, 2006) ch. 2,3. Cotton's domination of the U.S. export trade reached its relative peak at the same moment (1836–1840) when American abolitionists were launching their first mass campaigns. (Douglass C. North, *The Economic Growth of the United States 1790–1860*. New York: Norton, 1966), 75.

in which a major assault on the system of slavery began at the height of its relative value to the global economy in which it was deeply embedded. Cotton remained America's most important export commodity by a wide margin until the Civil War.

Between the 1820s and 1860, the cotton South provided about half the value of U.S. exports within the United States, and the antebellum South grew faster per capita than the north between 1840 and 1860. Most economic historians locate the antebellum South among the less backward economies of the day. By major indicators of dynamism, such as agricultural technology, banks, and even manufacturing, the South of 1860 "was above the world average," well ahead of Brazil, its largest slave counterpart in the Americas. One calculation ranks the South's economy among those of middle-ranking European countries like Spain, Austria, Norway, and Portugal. Others place it much higher – among the most advanced contemporary European economies. With the world's third highest level of per capita income, it ranked above France, the Germanies, or any other geographical region with ten million or more inhabitants. In this respect it placed only behind the antebellum U.S. North and Great Britain.[11]

The South's communications and transportation networks were at the forefront of the world, with more extensive railroad mileage in place by 1860 than any region outside of the northern United States. On the eve of secession, very rich southerners were even more numerous than their northern counterparts. Nearly two of every three American males with estates over $100,000 were citizens of the slave states. The South clearly lagged behind both the U.S. North and Britain in its level of industrial growth. By global standards, however, the South's industrial and commercial sectors were thriving. Slaveholders also challenged antislavery proponents on their laborers' standards of living. James Hammond and other apologists vigorously contrasted the material conditions of their region's slaves with those of free inhabitants of Haiti, Sierra Leone, the British West Indies, and workers in British industrial centers. Some Southerners extended such comparisons to a critique of industrial capitalist society itself.[12]

Not all of the effects of this economic dynamism were regarded as unmitigated gains for slavery. The closing of the transatlantic slave trade in 1807 meant that responses to regionwide demands for labor had to be met from within. Between 1790 and 1860, the internal slave trade produced a remarkable shift in the location of slave populations. In 1790, the future free states contained 10 percent of what the new constitution called "persons in service." The states between Maryland and North Carolina accounted for

---

[11] Compare Gavin Wright, *Slavery and Economic Development*, 124; and Robert W. Fogel and Stanley L. Engerman, *Time on the Cross*, 248–252.

[12] Fogel, *Without Consent*, 83–84; and Eugene D. Genovese, *The Slaveholders' Dilemma: Freedom and Progress in Southern Conservative Thought, 1820–1860* (Columbia, SC: University of South Carolina Press, 1992), passim.

69 percent of the total. The southernmost states contained only 21 percent. By 1860 the lower South's cotton and sugar crops had enabled it to increase its share of slaves to 59 percent, who made up 46.5 percent of the region's total population. The "border South," running from Delaware and Maryland through Missouri, had 20 percent of U.S. slaves in 1790, but only 11 percent by 1860. The "middle South," running from Virginia and North Carolina westward to Arkansas, had 60 percent of U.S. slaves in 1790, but had seen its share reduced to 30 percent by 1860. Anyone who speculated on the future of slavery in the generation before secession paid serious attention to the trends in slavery from one decennial census to the next. Pro-slavery writers and politicians who worried about the erosion of slavery at their region's borders were right to be anxious on this count long before the crisis of 1860–1861.[13]

The British Model

In its transatlantic implications, British emancipation added new dimensions to the attack and defense of the institution of slavery in the United States. Slaveholders as well as abolitionists recognized the implications of the fact that no civil war or bloodbath marred the final contest for or implementation of British emancipation. Even South Carolinian leaders in the national legislatures recognized the subversive potential of a long-term moral crusade on the British model. The "moral power of the world is against us," Francis Pikens warned his fellow Southern representatives during the first British-style assault on slavery at the end of 1835. In the U.S. Senate, John C. Calhoun echoed the cumulative potential of the still small seed of abolitionism. A contest in which slaveholders were incessantly arraigned before the public opinion of the world would be "beyond mortal endurance. We must, in the end, be humbled, degraded, broken down, and worn out."[14]

For free blacks, at the other end of the spectrum of American political influence, the metropolitan network that empowered the Demeraran and Jamaican insurgents in the decade before their emancipation extended to African Americans in the generation afterwards. Olaudah Equiano's progeny were black abolitionists, welcomed into the lecture halls of the United Kingdom to speak to audiences who, in turn, anointed them as the representatives of the civilized world's opinion. That fifty years of British parliamentary debates had produced almost no allusions to black racial inferiority was a constant counterpoint to American legislative discourse. The British Emancipation Bill was crafted to exclude any reference to post-emancipation racial

---

[13] See William W. Freehling, *The Reintegration of American History* (New York: Oxford University Press, 1994), 26–32; and Freehling, *The South vs. The South* (New York: Oxford University Press, 2001), 18–19.

[14] William W. Freehling, *The Road to Disunion: Secessionists at Bay 1776–1854* (New York: Oxford University Press, 1990) ch. 17, 18; quotes on 311, 323.

restrictions on civil or political rights. That no major uprising occurred in the decades before Southern secession may have made the ever-present potential Haitian alternative less threatening.[15]

In America itself, however, the contest over slavery had to work within a different frame of reference. Race was a dimension of political as well as civil rights. It was a national, not a sectional, phenomenon. At the outset of the new abolitionist agitation in the 1830s, racial exclusion and segregation were rigorously maintained even in most northern areas, which had long committed themselves to ending slavery.

Some of the major initiatives against slavery such as the ban on African slave imports in 1807 and the launching of the American Colonization Society a decade later, were premised upon a widely shared hostility toward the presence of blacks in America.

Even before he began his long mission, Garrison's reading of the implications of British immediatism and coalescing free-black urban organization of the kind that had inspired David Walker led him to conclude that a similar policy in America required the open embrace of equal coexistence of blacks and whites in the North as well as the destruction of the institution of slavery in the South. By the same token, the contemplation of race relations in any post-slave society was one of the mainstays of Southern arguments against emancipation. As no European visitor to Jacksonian America could fail to notice, northern emancipation of slaves had not led toward equality, but to the adoption of policies designed to maintain hierarchy and separation. This widespread consensus of inevitable marginalization and potential violence made the prospect of emancipation in the middle and lower South appear to be invitations to racial warfare with echoes of servile insurrection.[16]

---

[15] See Richard Blackett, *Building an Antislavery Wall: Black Americans in the Atlantic Abolitionist Movement 1830–1860* (Ithaca, NY: Cornell University Press, 1989); *The Black Abolitionist Papers*, 5 vols. (Chapel Hill: University of North Carolina Press, 1985), vol. I (*The British Isles, 1830–1865*). On the lack of overtly racist perspectives in British projects for emancipation, see Thomas C. Holt, *The Problem of Freedom: Race, Labor, and Politics in Jamaica and Britain, 1832–1938* (Baltimore: Johns Hopkins University Press, 1992), 32–50. Drescher, *From Slavery*, 285–286; and *Mighty Experiment*, 75–82.

[16] On Garrison's consultation with Boston's black leaders, see Mayer, *All on Fire*, 107–116. In Alexis de Tocqueville's classic analysis *Democracy in America*, Arthur Goldhammer trans. (New York: Library Classics) 404 ff), Tocqueville concluded that the two races would never live anywhere on a footing of equality (*Ibid.*, 411). He was also led to conclude that the lower South would never voluntarily follow either the northern pattern of gradual slave emancipation or the British pattern of centrally managed emancipation:

"If the English of the West Indies had governed themselves, they surely would not have passed the act of emancipation that the mother country has just imposed. . . . The danger more or less remote, but inevitable, of a struggle between Blacks and Whites living in the south, is the distressing nightmare that haunts the American imagination."

During his journey, Tocqueville observed that Northerners fearfully discussed ways to avoid the threat. His Southern respondents remained largely silent. Tocqueville found that silence more foreboding than the northerners' articulated fears. (*Ibid.*, 413–414.)

It was this premise of an unavoidably horrific racial outcome that left the South's political leaders unimpressed by the results of Britain's mighty experiment, even when it appeared as though it might succeed. The studies of Edward Rugemer and Stephen Mitton have recently emphasized the importance of British emancipation in the development of the conflict over American slavery. Stephen Mitton has uncovered a singularly striking demonstration of the racially inflected perspective on the lessons of British emancipation. On the eve of the first World Antislavery Convention in London, a meeting took place at the lodgings of Senator Calhoun in Washington, D.C. The meeting included several other southern legislators.

The featured speaker was the British Quaker abolitionist Joseph Gurney. He had journeyed to the United States en route home from a winter in the British West Indies. Gurney had an access to Washington politicians rarely granted to American abolitionists, certainly not by Southern slaveholders. Two years earlier, Gurney had conducted a service of public worship before a crowded House of Representatives. In May of 1840, his schedule of interviews included President Martin Van Buren, Whig Senators Henry Clay and Daniel Webster, and Massachusetts's Representative and former president John Quincy Adams.[17]

Gurney regarded the meeting with Calhoun's party as his most crucial one. The Quaker crafted his talk to demonstrate conclusively the complete success of Britain's great experiment, whether viewed in terms of morality, security, or economic efficiency. Gurney excluded any reference to his religious principles. He appealed to the free-labor ideology enshrined in Adam Smith's famous verdict.[18] Gurney addressed all of the practical concerns of the representatives of slaveholders. His arguments would soon be reaffirmed in a series of letters addressed to Senator Henry Clay. They were the first full-length account of the British emancipation experiment to be published in the United States.[19] Gurney was pleasantly surprised to find that Calhoun had no difficulty with the presentation of the experiment's success. Indeed, the Senator unreservedly acknowledged the general superiority of freedom over slavery, even from a pecuniary point of view. He also observed Gurney's emphasis of the uniqueness of the British model and Gurney's stress on the care which Britain had taken to control and implement it.

---

[17] The discussion in this paragraph and those later are drawn from Steven H. Mitton's "The Free World Confronted: The Problem of Slavery and Progress in American Foreign Relations 1833–1844," Ph.D. dissertation, Louisiana State University, 2005, chapter 1, "Gurney's Mission."

[18] "It appears, accordingly, from the experience of all ages and nations, I believe, that the work done by freemen comes cheaper in the end than that performed by slaves," Smith, *Wealth of Nations*, 99. For further analysis, see Drescher, *Mighty Experiment*, ch. 2.

[19] Joseph John Gurney, *A Winter in the West Indies: Described in Familiar Letters to Henry Clay of Kentucky* (New York: Press of M. Day, 1840). Multiple editions were published in New York, London, Amsterdam, and Paris.

Finally, Calhoun turned to one fact already emphasized by Tocqueville – Britain's role as an outside, dominant, and "controlling power" in the process. In the decentralized, republican self-governing America federation, there was no such controlling power over slavery. Lacking such exogenous power and lacking any desire to create it, the Senator added a second observation, "Whites and blacks were so distinct as races – so incapable in the nature of things of being amicably mixed" that no peace could be maintained between them on any terms other than "those which already subsisted... that the whites should hold the blacks in slavery."[20]

Actually, Tocqueville's observation about the role of controlling power touched a much more sensitive Southern nerve than did Gurney's argument in favor of the economic success of emancipated labor. Tocqueville himself used the "controlling power" argument when introducing his report to the French Chamber of Deputies in 1839, favoring the abolition of slavery in the French colonies. This same "Report on Abolition" elicited an infuriated southern response. Almost coincidental with Calhoun's polite exchange, the French consul in New Orleans reported to the French foreign minister that "it would be impossible... to describe to you the impact that it [the Tocqueville Report] produced in the United States, which, if it were enacted, would cause a veritable revolution in the colonies, and would not be without effect on the future of the United States...." In the consul's opinion, it was Tocqueville's Report that had so "exalted" American abolitionist passions that it had caused the passage of a cloture resolution on all abolitionist petitions to Congress.[21]

If economic, racial, and constitutional differences between the United States and Great Britain placed enormous obstacles in the way of using the British process to advance emancipation, the two societies converged in ways that encouraged an appeal to analogous means to destroy the institution. Anglo-American civil society and culture had continued to develop

[20] See Mitton, "Free World Confronted," 14. This was more than table talk. John Calhoun had already formulated this argument in the Senate in response to a wave of abolitionist petitions in February 1787. See Edward Rugemer "The Problem of Emancipation: The United States and Britain's Abolition of Slavery," Ph.D. Dissertation, Boston College, 2005, 285. Although Calhoun's coterie enthusiastically agreed with his arguments, it is not at all clear that southerners accepted Calhoun's evaluation of the success of the great experiment, even at this early stage in its implementation. Even southerners who looked forward to eventual emancipation, however, acknowledged that social control of large masses of liberated blacks remaining in America was a fundamental obstacle to emancipation. The most broadly based movement for long-term abolition, the American Colonization Society (ACS), was based upon that premise. The ACS emphasized the climatological exception to Smith's general thesis. (*Ibid.*, 285–288).

[21] *Tocqueville and Beaumont on Social Reform*, Seymour Drescher, ed. and trans. (New York: Harper and Row, 1968), 98–99 n.1. On the necessity for centralized emancipation in the Antilles, see Seymour Drescher, *Dilemmas of Democracy*, (Pittsburgh: University of Pittsburgh Press, 1968), 179–180; and Cheryl B. Welch, "Tocqueville on Fraternity and Fratricide," in *The Cambridge Companion to Tocqueville* (New York: University of Pittsburgh Press, 2006), 303–336.

along similar lines. Both societies prided themselves on providing greater institutional safeguards for the security and activity of free individuals than anywhere else in the world. Their political structures offered fewer barriers for the formation and diffusion of nongovernmental associations than were to be found elsewhere. In some ways, Britain had been outpaced by the United States. In no other society of its time were so many individuals so frequently formulating and reformulating their basic political constitutions. In the United States, Americans were encouraged to associate for purposes pertaining to public security, economic activity, moral reform, and religious organization. There was "nothing the human will despairs of achieving through the free action of the collective power of individuals."[22] Americans of the second quarter of the nineteenth century were encouraged to think of the nation itself as an associative society, organized by autonomous free agents and perpetually engaged in voluntary collective action.

In the United States, the compound principle of free agency and collective association resonated in religious behavior and organization. Few studies of abolitionism in America begin without extensive reference to the "Second Great Awakening" – the spectacular response of American Protestantism during its great westward exodus to the equally spectacular political, economic, and demographic expansion, along with belief in individual ability and moral responsibility, of the United States.[23] The penetration of the free-agency principle was nowhere better displayed than during the famous "Lane Debates" in Cincinnati, Ohio in 1829. Young seminary students discussed their intense conversion to organized immediatism in the United States, in opposition to the alternative of gradual recolonization of blacks to Africa. The clinching point was not only the free agency of the students, but the targets of colonization themselves. The overwhelming refusal of African Americans to depart from the United States required an alternative approach based upon unreserved support of their right to be fully part of America. Abolitionism in the U.S. North would spawn an emotional resonance and identification with black slaves and marginalized free blacks unequaled anywhere in Europe.[24]

It is important to reiterate that the spectacular development of associational creativity and religious fervor in America were no more sufficient

---

[22] *Tocqueville, Democracy in America*, 215–16. In his later journey to England, Tocqueville was surprised to discover an analogous abundance of self-government in Britain. See S. Drescher, *Tocqueville and England* (Cambridge, MA: Harvard University Press, 1964), 88–91. On the interplay between democracy and the abolition of slavery in France, see Cheryl B. Welch, "Tocqueville on Democracy after Abolition: Slaves, Subjects and Citizens," *The Tocqueville Review*, xxvii, no. 2 (2006), 227–254.

[23] Here, I have relied extensively on Davis, *Inhuman Bondage*, ch. 13, and the sources cited in that chapter. See also Fogel, *Without Consent*, 254–264; and Fogel, *The Fourth Great Awakening* and the *Future of Egalitarianism* (Chicago: University of Chicago Press, 2003), ch. 3.

[24] John Stauffer, *The Black Hearts of Men: Radical Abolitionists and the Transformation of Race* (Cambridge, MA: Harvard University Press, 2002).

to convert most Americans to antislavery than were the equally spectacular expansions of economic activity, communications, or political participation. When he wished to illustrate the extraordinary ability of Americans to broaden their local concerns into national movements, Tocqueville cited the temperance and tariff mobilizations, not antislavery, as his empirical examples. The explosion of American abolitionism in the early 1830s was initially and spectacularly illustrative of its inability to mobilize a nationwide constituency and to unite rather than divide religious organizations.

Nevertheless, the perceived analogy with British religious and cultural networks in the early 1830s encouraged and energized abolitionist immediatism in the United States. Northern U.S. abolitionists wished to compress half a century of British abolitionist mobilization into five years. As latecomers, they introduced innovations in targets and tactics that took Britons decades of trial and error to perfect. Simultaneous nationwide propagandizing had been a major weapon in producing a mobilized and united British public opinion.

The American Antislavery Society (AAS), founded within months of the passage of the British Emancipation Act in December 1833, published 122,000 items in 1834, ten times as many the following year, and three million by 1840. This was both a rate of expansion and a volume of publication exceeding anything that the British movement had produced in their early campaigns. The decentralized organization of British abolitionism was quickly replicated and surpassed in the United States. Within five years of its national organization, there were 1,346 local antislavery organizations in the northern states claiming 100,000 members. The British Agency Committee had toured the nation with a roster of six lecturers. As noted the AAS launched its own organized lecture and organizational tour featuring George Thompson, Britain's best professional antislavery speaker. They soon had more than seventy paid agents in service.[25]

The feminization of American organizing and petitioning was equally rapid. The Philadelphia Female Anti-Slavery Society was also founded in December 1833 alongside the formation of the American Antislavery Society. The AAS welcomed already established female antislavery societies and instructed its agents to encourage the formation of both male and female locals. George Thompson himself had a crucial impact on the formation of the latter during his American tour in 1834. In some areas, American abolitionists surpassed their British counterparts in mobilizing nonvoters in the abolitionist process. Of the 183 abolitionist locals in Massachusetts in 1838–1841, 41 were associations of women and 13 were groups of juveniles.[26]

---

[25] Davis, *Inhuman Bondage*, 259–260.
[26] See Julie Roy Jeffrey, *The Great Silent Army of Abolitionism* (Chapel Hill: University of North Carolina Press, 1998), 54; A. Salerno, *Sister Societies: Women's Antislavery Organizations in Antebellum America* (De Kalb: Northern Illinois University Press, 2005), ch. 2;

By the following year, the AAS tapped into the full potential of abolitionist women who had been a crucial weapon during the last decade of Britain's fifty-year mass antislavery movement.

The importance of influencing public opinion was, of course, as fully recognized in the political culture of Jacksonian America as it was in contemporary Britain. In record time, the American barriers to female petitioning were discarded among abolitionists. The outcome for the two branches of abolitionism was starkly different. In Britain, abolitionists were welcomed with respect and crowned by overwhelming success. By the late 1830s, their votes were essential to sustain an administration losing support in Parliament. Abolitionist petitioners were regarded as the voice of the British people, even by the West Indians who saw themselves portrayed as embodying all that was "un-English" in their ownership of human chattel, their treatment of fellow human beings, and their place in the scale of civilization.

Abolitionists in America were, on the contrary, linked to everything that was subversive of their nation and their society. In Britain, Thompson's antislavery lectures were invariable acclaimed by large cheering crowds, particularly when challenged by West Indian lecturers. In America, his tour elicited increasingly hostile mobs, culminating in a large riot in Boston in October 1835. It was one of forty-six riots related to slavery that year, all but eleven directed against abolitionists. All the rest were responses to insurrectionary scares.[27] However, despite the outburst of antiabolitionist mobbing by "gentlemen of property and standing" in the fall of 1835, Southerners soon realized that there was a clear limit to antiabolitionist behavior in the North. Northern mobs might intimidate abolitionists and destroy their property but they were not prepared to extend lynch law to the North or to renounce their position that slavery was an evil.[28]

The abolitionist tactic of inundating the South with abolitionist literature was another matter. It clearly breached the line between free and slave states. The United States Postal Service quickly endorsed the reestablishment of the frontier. After a Charleston mob burned the first abolitionist shipment from the North, the U.S. Postmaster-General allowed each state to

---

and Susan Zaeske, *Signatures of Citizenship: Petitioning, Antislavery and Women's Political Identity* (Chapel Hill: University of North Carolina Press, 2003), 19.

[27] David Grimsted, *American Mobbing, 1828–1861: Toward Civil War* (New York: Oxford University Press, 1998), 4.

[28] *Ibid.*, 25, and Leonard L. Richards, *Gentlemen of Property and Standing: A Study of Northern Anti-Abolition Mobs* (New York: Oxford University Press, 1970). Southerners, of course, also petitioned on matters pertaining to slavery. But, they appear not to have petitioned in any regionally collective manner in a sectional pro-slavery campaign. Southern petitions on slavery were locally reactive to slave resistance or conspiracies. See *The Southern Debate over Slavery: Volume I: Petitions to Southern Legislatures, 1778–1864*, Loren Schweininger, ed. (Urbana: University of Illinois Press, 2001), "Introduction," xxxii, Table 1.

block the publications it deemed to be incitements to disorder. In his annual address to Congress in 1835, President Jackson reaffirmed the policy. The boundary between slave and free states was reaffirmed. The South had to accept the persistence of northern abolitionist agitation. Most Northerners acquiesced in the persistence of the slave states' self-censorship against their subversive intrusions. The boundary was reaffirmed, but the extent of the flare up at the popular level was clearly greater than during the Missouri compromise.[29]

This time, however, the issue of slavery was not allowed to subside. When abolitionists learned that their words could neither breach the sectional line nor convert most Southerners below it they switched to the other major tool of abolitionism. Following British precedent, abolitionists assumed that Congress would have to attend to a broad-based abolitionist appeal on the future of the national capital and on an issue clearly within the complete jurisdiction of the federal government. The abolitionists were correct. Not since the first British petition campaign of 1788 had slaveholders in the Anglo-American world been so shocked by an unexpected intrusion into their familiar world. As William Freehling observes, it was "the Pearl Harbor of the slave controversy" in America.

For forty years after the ratification of the United States Constitution, the slave laws of the District of Columbia had quietly followed the statutory precedents of Virginia and Maryland. These were the states that donated the land to make Washington D.C., the national capital. In the District of Columbia, Congress was primarily concerned with accommodating resident and legislative slaveholders. The legislators dealt with free blacks as noncitizens and with slaves under a black code.[30] In 1828, large-scale petitioning for a gradual abolition of the District's slave trade first reached Congress. The largest document, with more than a thousand signatures, was organized by the Baltimore Quaker, Benjamin Lundy, publisher of *The Genius of Universal Emancipation*. Overwhelming majorities in both Houses rejected motions to investigate the slave trade, condemning this antislavery agitation as a threat to the Union. The only antislavery motion that reached the status of a formal bill would have prohibited the importation of any blacks, when their sale divided families. Even this bill never reached the floor of Congress. Before the mid-1830s, then, slavery and the slave trade in the District remained a minor "political irritant but not a serious national issue."[31]

---

[29] William W. Freehling, *The Road to Disunion: Secessionists at Bay 1776–1854*. (New York: Oxford University Press, 1990), 308–310.
[30] Fehrenbacher, *Slaveholding Republic*, 60–66.
[31] *Ibid.*, 69–73.

The Legislature Reacts

In 1835, coincident with George Thompson's tours, mobbing, blocked mails, and a dramatic increase in northern abolitionist associations, a huge number of petitions were sent to Congress. By the spring of 1836, antislavery petitions were being circulated from Maine to Ohio. The initial wave of American petitions in 1835–1836 deposited 35,000 names at the doors of Congress. The second wave coincided precisely with that of the British antiapprenticeship campaign of 1837–1838. Both accumulated hundreds of thousands of adherents. At the end of the 1830s, an American legislator claimed that the cumulative total of signatures was two million, within hailing distance of their British counterparts for the decade. On both sides of the Atlantic, the petitions were heavily feminized. Of the 400,000 petitioners in the 1837–1838 campaign, 286,000 were female. In a sampling of 67,000 names, Gerda Lerner found that females outnumbered males by a margin of two to one. Another petition showed the same gender ratio. Garrison proffered a still higher ratio claiming that women outnumbered men petitioners by three to one. In any event, antislavery petitioning clearly provided a major opportunity for American women to enter the public sphere at the national level.[32]

There were also some major differences between the Anglo-American mobilizations of the 1830s. Unlike British abolitionists, whose petitions were designed to follow the ancient handwritten tradition and local inspiration, American organizers generated printed petitions for rapid circulation. In Britain, where such a high proportion of even adult males were still disenfranchised, petitioning could claim to be a more accurate measure of popular will. Great care was exercised to prevent children from delegitimizing petitions. Unlike the female petitioners in Great Britain, the intrusion of women into the abolitionist public sphere in the United States came at the beginning, not the end, of the great antislavery mobilization. In Britain, recognition of the legitimacy of women's signatures had followed thirty-five years of massive petitioning on the subject. Precisely because the adult male suffrage was so broad in the Untied States, it was clearly evident from the names of the signatories that a majority of the petitioners were not voting citizens, and sometimes included children. Petitions sometimes contained no signatures, just lists of citizens cut out of newspapers.[33]

In this respect, the American abolitionists helped Southerners to develop the "slippery slope" argument against yielding an inch on the District of

---

[32] Susan Zaeske, *Signatures of Citizenship: Petitioning, Antislavery and Women's Political Identity* (Chapel Hill: University of North Carolina Press, 2003), 43–50; and Gerder Lerner, *The Majority Finds Its Past* (New York: Oxford University Press, 1980, 112–128.

[33] Freehling, *Reintegration*, 198–199.

Columbia's slave trade. For a full generation after 1787, British abolitionist propaganda and petitions had focused narrowly on the slave trade, disclaiming any intention of legislative initiatives against the institution of slavery as already established in the colonies. American abolitionists took the opposite tack. Southerners did not await such a development to initiate massive retaliation against the very first wave of mass abolitionist petitions at the end of 1835.

Most importantly, few northern members of Congress were willing to defend abolition petitions and motions. The petitions of 1835–1838 actually demonstrated that abolitionists did not constitute the northern mainstream of the electorate. Yet, the most extreme Southerners were no longer willing to follow the usual procedure of simply tabling the petitions. Precisely because of prior British emancipation, antislavery petitioning even only at the borders of slavery in the District of Columbia could be construed as an entering wedge of national emancipation. In response to a motion by Congressman James Hammond, abolitionist petitions were to be barred at the door of the national legislature as surely as they had been from the southern post offices.

For the next eight years, Congress enforced a "gag rule" against even acknowledging receipt of antislavery petitions.[34] This motion, offered by radical southerners and acquiesced to by northern politicians, had unforeseen consequences. The increasingly defiant abolitionists flooded Congress with petitions demanding no annexation of Texas, use of the Commerce Clause to outlaw the interstate slave trade, and recognition of Haiti. As the few original defenders of the petitions pointed out, refusal to hear petitions was not just an assault on abolitionism, but on a fundamental Anglo-American link between civil society and the legislature. The right of petition was of far more ancient lineage in that tradition than the more recently acquired rights of free press in newspapers and the U.S. mails. In major centers of abolition, only a minority (8 to 20 percent) of eligible male voters were willing to subscribe to abolitionist petitions. That proportion rose to 37 percent when the petition protested the imposition of the gag rule.[35] Southern lawmakers appeared to be reaching across the sectional divide and attempting to suppress the institutional liberties of free northerners.

The flood of abolitionist petitions in 1835 also accelerated the development of what came to be known as the proslavery ideology. Whether or not many of its components were largely extrapolations of earlier notions, Southerners clearly developed a more comprehensive defense of the institution and a decidedly more intensive effort to gain regional consensus for

---

[34] Edward Magdol, *The Antislavery Rank and File: A Social Profile of the Abolitionist Constituency* (New York: Greenwood, 1986), 101–102.

[35] On the small minority position of northern abolitionists, see William W. Freehling, *The Reintegration of American History: Slavery and the Civil War* (New York: Oxford University Press, 1994), 198; on Hammond's role, see Miller, *Arguing Against Slavery*, 31–35.

upholding slavery as a positive good. A wider range of empirical economic evidence, scientific racial theorizing, and political nationalism was added to the religious, classical, and humanitarian arguments in the apologetic quiver. As the ideas of human progress and the civilizing process deepened their hold on the Western imagination, Southerners sought to fit the development of their own slaveholding societies into the new metanarrative of European development. One of the outstanding characteristics of slavery's defenders in the U.S. South is that their arguments became increasingly unyielding and pervasive. In most other Western societies after the age of revolution, even those who benefited most from an institution of personal bondage tended to become less inclined to defend it as a positive good. They approached their systems of bondage as temporary and inherited problems, focusing on the most orderly, if often the most extended, means of ending the institution. In no other society was the institution of slavery to become as central to the communities self-definition as in some of the writings of U.S. south-erners. Under increasingly systematic attack, they developed an increasingly systematic apologetic.[36]

More immediately, from the abolitionist perspective, the sectional uproar created by mass petitioning and the gag rule may well have postponed the annexation of Texas, but the gag rule also proved to be counterproductive to its originators. It allowed John Quincy Adams to keep protesting the gag rule as a sectional despotism. Displaying an awesome combination of rhetorical power and parliamentary finesse, he converted the gag rule into a southern attack on northern free white rights. In 1844, the controversy finally produced a sectional majority to discard the rule.[37]

---

[36] There appears to be a fairly broad consensus that the mid-1830s were a pivotal moment in the development of pro-slavery, and that the role of the abolitionist offensive was a catalyst in the change. See, inter alia, Larry E. Tise, *Proslavery: A History of the Defense of Slavery in America, 1701–1840* (Athens, GA: University of Georgia Press, 1987), esp. ch. 13, "The South Becomes Ideologized, 1835–1840." Drew Gilpin Faust places the turning point a few years earlier, with Thomas Roderick Dew's meditation on Virginia's debate over emancipation in the wake of Nat Turner's rebellion. Drew Gilpin Faust, *The Ideology of Slavery: Proslavery Thought in the Antebellum South, 1830–1860* (Baton Rouge: Louisiana State University Press, 1981), ch. 1. See also, George M. Fredrickson, *The Black Image in the White Mind: The Debate on Afro-American Character and Destiny, 1817–1914* (Middletown, CT: Wesleyan University Press, 1971), ch. 2. For comparisons with other New World societies, see chapter 12. In the Old World, Russian serfholders followed the general pattern of the Americas. Pro-serfdom sentiment gradually weakened in the generation before emancipation. By the 1840s, few Russians publicly defended the system. See Peter Kolchin, "In Defense of Servitude: American Proslavery and Russian Proserfdom Arguments, 1780–1860," *American Historical Review* 1980 85 (4), 809–827. In many Old World societies, slavery continued to be widely, if not universally, defended as a divinely sanctioned institution. Its defenders did not, however, make its perpetuation so salient an element in their religiously defined communities. See chapter 13.

[37] See Freehling, *Road to Disunion*, ch. 17–19; and Miller, *Arguing About Slavery*, ch. 16–36.

The gag rule controversy also demonstrated the limits of petitioning even regionally in the 1830s. While the U.S. Congress tabled antislavery petitions, the second Anti-Slavery Convention of American Women was being stoned by a mob in Philadelphia. Angela Grimke urged them to look to the English women's antiapprenticeship petition to the young Queen Victoria, measuring two and a quarter miles long. She assured the beleaguered gathering that if a similar great petition reached Congress from the women of America, the nation's legislators would follow.[38] By the end of 1838, the contrast in outcomes was both clear and devastating. Hundreds of thousands of signatures could not do in Washington what they had done in London. In Britain, petitioning had been launched with the intention of demonstrating that the British public was overwhelmingly in favor of discreet policies. In every case, the mobilization had been so overwhelmingly proabolitionist that the government made some move toward implementing the policy. Well before the first mass petition was signed, in the United States, well-organized southerners had demonstrated that the abolitionist propaganda campaign would receive little support from the civic elites in any segment of the country and would incur active repression in more than half the states. Abolitionist activity in the North was met with widespread hostility, even if the antiabolitionist mobs were less deadly and more ephemeral than those further south. American antislavery petitioning also demonstrated that there was no substantial constituency in the South to defend the abolitionist's right to preach or petition against any aspect of the institution.

The U.S. antislavery campaigns of the 1830s also showed that a hostile majority of enfranchised white citizens was quite willing to ignore petitions in which the majority of the signers were disenfranchised women, whose legitimacy as petitioners could be discounted if not denied.[39] In the United States it was the ballot, not the petition, that was the ultimate identifier of the direction of public opinion. Voter turnout in America rose to its extraordinary nineteenth-century heights during the generation after 1836. Between 1840 and 1860, almost every presidential election brought between two-thirds and three-quarters of the eligible electorate to the polls. In many states of the cotton South, the turnout was usually higher. In every off-year election between 1838 and 1858, the South exceeded the North in the percentage of its electorate that cast its vote.[40]

---

[38] Zaeske, *Signatures*, 123.

[39] Freehling, *Road to Disunion*, 311.

[40] *Historical Statistics of the United States*, 5 vols. (New York: Cambridge University Press, 2006), V; *Government and International Relations*, Susan B. Carter, et al. eds., 165–171, Table Eb 62–113: "Voter turnout in presidential elections by state"; and Eb 114–122: "Voter turnout in presidential and congressional elections." For a graphic illustration of the high plateau, see *ibid.*, 5–146, Fig. Eb-B. Pro-slavery mobilization was not limited to the political arena. The churches participated in keeping with the language of the South and split over the issue.

The southern radicals also soon learned that *anti*abolitionism could not be extended into northern abandonment of its own civil liberties. The South would have to live with a permanently organized voice in the Northern states calling for the abolition of their now increasingly "domestic" institution. On both sides of the line between slavery and free soil, the broader aims of national power, political liberty, civil equality, and self-government for the white majority seemed most secure in the hands of national crosssectional parties. Both abolitionists in the North and secessionists in the South were stymied after their clashes in the mid-1830s. Their combined pressures to make the destruction of slavery the highest priority on the national agenda had failed. Neither extreme had been able to solidify each section as a political unit. In the following generation, the issue that precipitated the deepest divisions between the free-and slave states was not the fate of the institution of slavery itself but the degree to which it would be allowed to expand westward during the generation before the outbreak of the Civil War.[41]

America and the Atlantic Slave Trade

The example of British Caribbean slave emancipation clearly changed the tenor of the American debates over slavery but British foreign policy itself was probably more significant as a perceived threat to American slavery in the decade after 1835. The expansion of American slavery within its own territory remained well beyond the power or desire of the British government to effect. The British West Indies and the U.S. South appeared to be heading in opposite directions. In the generation before the American Civil War, British Caribbean sugar production had still not recovered to its preemancipation level. No North American economic crisis matched that of the British West Indies sugar industry at the end of the 1840s. In the United States, cotton production more than doubled in the two decades after the end of British system of slave apprenticeship. Even in the tobacco South, there was never a time "between the American Revolution and the Civil War that slave-holders became so pessimistic about the economic future of their peculiar institution that their demand for slaves went into a period of sustained decline."[42]

The natural increase of the American slave population lay entirely beyond the reach of the British navy and the outcome of its attack on the slave trade. Full British success could only enhance the situation of the U.S. slaveholders. Between the ending of British apprenticeship system in 1839 and the

---

[41] Michael F. Holt, *The Political Crisis of the 1850s* (New York: Norton, 1983), ch. 3.

[42] Robert William Fogel, *Without Consent or Contract: The Rise and Fall of American Slavery* (New York: Norton, 1989), 63, 97; and *Evidence and Methods*, R.W. Fogel, R.A. Galantine, and Richard L. Manning, eds. (New York: Norton, 1992), ch. 20 and 21.

American Civil War, the former British slave colonies imported 140,000 indentured servants. During the same period, American domestic slave traders transferred more than half a million slaves to their own developing territories, or between 3 and 4 slaves for every indentured servant landed in those colonies.[43]

It was only beyond the borders of the United States that Britons could hope to set any further limits to the expansion of the slave trade and slavery. For nearly two decades after 1807, there appeared to be an Anglo-American convergence of interests. In 1819, Congress authorized naval patrolling along the African coast as well as in the Caribbean. By the early 1820s, the smuggling of African slaves into the United States was no longer a serious problem and the American flag on slavers had disappeared along the African coast. In 1824, the United States also seemed on the verge of becoming part of Britain's network of bilateral diplomatic treaties to close down the illegal slave trade and accepting a mutual right of search agreement.[44]

The draft of that Anglo-American agreement was never ratified. Some southern senators became alarmed at the possible implication of the British government's announcement of preliminary steps towards colonial slave emancipation. By the early 1830s, the American government would no longer negotiate anything approaching a mutual right of search for fear of further exacerbating a South already aroused over the growth of the domestic abolitionist movement. Slaveholders' concern with the demoralization of slavery, given voice by John Calhoun's condemnation of abolitionist petitions, became a major factor in United States foreign relations.[45]

Clashes with Britain were exacerbated by the problem of American ships driven by weather into British waters. Ships loaded with slaves for intercoastal transport to ports in the Gulf of Mexico landed in the Bahamas. There, British authorities freed the slaves. A protesting American consul was informed that anyone attempting to carry the former slaves away would be

---

43 For the interregional slave trade of the U.S. South in 1810–1839, see Michael Tadman, "The Interregional Trade in the History and Myth-Making of the U.S. South," in *The Chattel Principle*, Walter Johnson, ed. (New Haven: Yale University Press, 2004), 117–142, esp. 120, Table 6.1. Tadman's figures indicate that 650,000 slaves were moved. By another estimate, relying upon Fogel "Revised Estimates of the U.S. Slave Trade and Native-Born Slaves of Black Population," in *Without Consent or Contract: Evidence and Methods* (New York: W.W. Norton, 1999), 53–58), I estimate a total interregional transfer of 527,000 slaves. The smaller figure gives a ratio of twenty American slaves transferred for every British Caribbean slave laborer moved between colonies from 1808 to 1838. See S. Drescher, "Fragmentation of the Atlantic Slave Trade," in *ibid.*, 234–255, esp. Table 10.1. For a critique of Tadman's figures, see Jonathan B. Pritchet "Quantitative Estimates of the United States Interregional Slave Trade, 1820–1860," delivered at the Social Science History Association meeting (1998). See www.tulane.edu/~pritchet/personal/trade.pdf.

44 Eltis, *Economic Growth*, 249, Table A.8; and Fehrenbacher, *Slaveholding Republic*, 150–156.

45 Fehrenbacher, *Slaveholding Republic*, 162–165.

liable to hanging. Even before the final emancipation of its colonial slaves, the British government attempted to extend its protective Canadian free soil principle into the Caribbean. The British now maintained that U.S. laws enforcing property in persons did not extend to any slaves moving beyond the boundaries of individual slave states under whose jurisdiction they were legally enslaved. The American government refused to accept this encroachment on U.S. intercoastal trade.

As disputes over slave seizures piled up, the American ambassador in London argued that slaves were inextricably considered property in the United States Constitution. As described in the ambassador's extensive brief, in the U.S. constitution there was "no distinction in principle between property in persons and property in things." Slaves "formed 'a basis of representation' in the federal government; it was 'infused' into federal law and mixed itself with 'all the sources' of federal authority."[46]

In 1837, the British agreed to compensate owners of slaves who had been landed in British territory prior to the enactment of the British Emancipation Act. However, no slaves were repatriated and the British government warned that no further claims for slaves entering its jurisdiction would be honored, regardless of the circumstances. Foreign Secretary Palmerston was extending the automatic freedom of slaves to the British waters off the coast of Florida. American Ambassador Stevenson, in turn, adopted a self-imposed gag rule in London. He maintained that the United States government would never consider discussing with a foreign government the question of an American slave's status as property.

In 1840, John Calhoun finally induced the American Senate to go on the record in support of the American diplomatic position. He introduced a series of motions (the *Enterprise Resolutions*) asserting American slaveowners' rights under international law. Once again the *Somerset* decision was the point of departure. Mansfield had rejected a British slaveholder's claims to have colonial slave law extended to England. However, contended Calhoun, the principle could not be extended to non-British citizens as a part of international law. Slavery did not violate the "law of nations." Two decades earlier, American Chief Justice John Marshall had himself affirmed that old Roman Law distinction. Speaking for a divided Supreme Court in a case involving the slave trade, he held that the slave trade was contrary to the law of nature but consistent with the law of nations. Therefore, slaving did not constitute a consensual violation of international law, as did piracy. Slavery could be criminalized only by individual polities and only by statute. And enacted statutes had the force of law only within the jurisdictions of those states which enacted the legislation.

Calhoun asked the Senate to defend the inviolability of American property rights beyond the nation's sovereign limits. Otherwise, its intercoastal trade

[46] Fehrenbacher, *Slaveholding Republic*, 104–106.

would be placed in jeopardy. The Enterprise Resolutions were debated under the shadow of the approaching World Antislavery Convention in London. The senator placed direct responsibility for Britain's assertive policy on its own abolitionists, now at the peak of their power. He emphasized the fact that the weakening British administration was at considerable risk of losing its precarious majority in Parliament. The Senate brushed aside a motion to table the Enterprise Resolutions on the ground that the United States should not demand the right to recover slaves from a foreign jurisdiction. On April 15, 1840, it voted thirty-three to zero in favor of Calhoun's Enterprise Resolutions.

For John Quincy Adams, the most galling aspect of the unanimous vote was the behavior of its potential opponents. Its passage resulted from the collusion of "twenty-two slave-breeders and eleven craven Democrats ... ". The vote did not register the fifteen "more craven spirits *absent*, skulking from the question upon which they dared not vote yea or nay." For Calhoun, however, that same fact was equally dismaying. The fifteen absentees were all northerners. They voted not according to party, but section: eight Whigs and seven Democrats. The cup was more empty than full. More northerners had refused to uphold the sanctity of slave property than had supported it. For Calhoun, antislavery sentiment ran still deeper than he had expected.[47]

The British refusal to return slaves reached a new level a year later. In the autumn of 1841, the brig *Creole*, with 135 slaves aboard, was en route from Virginia to Louisiana. Led by Madison Washington, a slave, nineteen blacks revolted, killing a passenger and wounding several ship's officers and seamen. The nonmutineers were all set free on arrival in Nassau. The nineteen mutineers were also released after a few months. As Don Fehrenbacher observes, this was "the most successful slave rebellion in American history, succeeding with active British collaboration." Lord Aberdeen, the new Foreign Secretary of the Tory government, proved to be as unyielding as Palmerston. Although a general treaty to settle all outstanding Anglo-American differences was under discussion, Aberdeen would offer no guarantee about future indemnification. Public opinion, he stressed, would prohibit any such assurance.[48]

In America, those most invested in the problem of slavery weighed in on both sides. Calhoun called the release of the slaves the "most atrocious outrage ever perpetrated on the American people." The *Creole* mutiny now opened the door to combating Calhoun's Enterprise Resolutions with counterresolutions. Ohio Congressman Joshua Giddings reverted to *Somerset*. He upheld the foreigner's position that slavery was legally a matter of municipal

---

[47] For the above paragraphs, see Mitton, "Free World Confronted," 25–30; Fehrenbacher, *Slaveholding Republic*, 106–107.

[48] Fehrenbacher, *Slaveholding Republic*, 108.

(i.e., limited local) jurisdiction. A ship leaving its nation's territorial waters ceased to be subject to them. For Southerners, Gidding's Resolutions indicated how far American abolitionism had moved toward an alignment with a British–sanctioned servile rebellion at sea and a haven for its murderous perpetrators.

With British colonial sugar production now sinking rapidly, it was not difficult to reframe British antislavery policy as driven by desperate economic stress rather than humanitarian motives. The Giddings Resolutions were rejected and he was censured. Giddings was supported by only 10 percent of the House, a measure of antislavery sentiment in Congress. The subsequent election for his seat demonstrated the potential gap between regional and national opinion. Following Giddings's resignation, his constituency returned him to Washington by a nine to one margin.[49]

The *Creole* affair marked the apex of the clash between Britons and Americans over the limits of slavery at sea. In February 1842, Lord Ashburton, a special British envoy, arrived in Washington to negotiate a bilateral resolution to all outstanding differences between the two countries. Once again, and for all, Americans rejected any mutual "right of search" treaty as the basis for suppression of the Atlantic slave trade. Instead, the United States agreed to "joint patrols," with American and British vessels cruising together in search of suspected slavers flying the American flag. Each navy had a "right of visit." This allowed both fleets to board suspected slavers for the sole purpose of determining its nationality, not to search the vessel. The treaty signaled a détente over inspection. The British did not entirely cease to visit suspected ships but largely abandoned efforts to establish ownership and backed off if there was clear evidence of French or U.S. owners, neither of whose nations would allow a right of search.

Thereafter, the performance of the U.S. patrol varied with the officers in charge. The treaty worked most effectively in favor of American slavers in the 1840s. As the British navy more effectively intercepted Portuguese and Brazilian vessels, the slavers' flag of choice shifted. The American consul in Rio de Janeiro signaled the growing American participation in the Brazilian slave trade as early as 1841. In 1844, the United States Minister to Brazil claimed that the slave trade was being conducted largely under the American flag and on American-built ships. He reported to Washington that all the slave traders had to do was to display American colors when meeting with British patrols, and that they laughed at the American squadron. His successor, Henry A. Wise, future governor of Virginia, wrote that Americans, or at least those who sailed under its flag, were "the only people who can now fetch and carry any and everything for the slave trade, without fear of

[49] Miller, *Arguing About Slavery*, 444–454.

English cruisers.... In fact, without... our flag, it could not be carried on with success at all."⁵⁰

According to some contemporary reports, at least half of the African slaves imported into Brazil in the 1840s were carried with some degree of American participation. This would have made the United States flag accountable for 275,000 captives landed with American aid in Brazil between 1840 and 1849. This was more than all the Africans deposited in British North America between 1727 and 1807. Put another way, in the decade 1840–1849, more African slaves were moved from the Old World to the New under the American flag (509,000 to Brazil; 92,000 to Cuba) than were moved from the old exporting South to the importing South within the United States.⁵¹

Before the Civil War, there was only one final flare-up over British captures of American flagged vessels. It came during the late 1850s when the aggressive Palmerston's return to the Foreign Office caused President Buchanan to protest the consequent rise in seizures of slavers and to dispatch warships to the Gulf of Mexico to prevent further detention of U.S. vessels.⁵² Despite President Buchanan's actions, the importation of African slaves into Cuba reached a higher point in 1859 than at anytime since the mid-1830s. The slavers, of course, sailed mostly under the American flag. By the 1850s, it had been clear for decades that the one nation whose slave system was increasing without recourse to the African slave system was also now also the only remaining obstacle to ending transatlantic slaving. This did not halt American annexationists from claiming that their major rationale for acquiring Cuba from Spain was to prevent the further Africanization of Cuba.

Even as American expansionists used the prospect of ending the Atlantic slave trade as a rationale for annexing Cuba, some slaveholders took the opposite position. To demonstrate southern distinctiveness and its citizens' determination to uphold the institution of slavery, they called for the reopening of the African slave trade to the United States. In 1853, South Carolina's governor "drew national attention to the issue when he devoted much of his annual legislative message to calling for repeal of the federal anti-slave-trade laws."⁵³ His suggestion was abhorrent to the overwhelming majority of citizens, even in the upper and middle South. Those

---

⁵⁰ Quoted in Lawrence F. Hill, *Diplomatic Relations between the United States and Brazil* (Durham, NC: Duke University Press, 1932), 122 and Bethell, *Abolition of the Brazilian Slave Trade*, 128. The American correspondents were, of course, referring to mainly non-Americans sailing under a flag of convenience.

⁵¹ Calculations from Eltis, et al., Slave Trade Database, and Michael Tadman "The Interregional Slave Trade," 120, Table 6.1.

⁵² Fehrenbacher, *Slaveholding Republic*, 180–181.

⁵³ See Ronald T. Takaki, *A Pro-Slavery Crusade: The Agitation to Reopen the African Slave Trade* (New York: Free Press, 1971), 1–22; and Fehrenbacher, *Slaveholder's Republic*, 180.

who supported the principles of the American Colonization Society or who feared further intrusions of any blacks, slave or free, into the United States, found it equally unacceptable. Even for many southerners who had no wish whatsoever to rescind the Slave Trade Abolition Act of 1807, abolitionism remained more intolerable as a moral than as an economic issue. The western world's growing consensus in condemning the slave trade loomed ever larger as a moral threat with each passing decade.

The significance of the moral dimension of the issue was registered in the national legislature. In 1856, Congressman Emerson Etheridge moved a resolution condemning all proposals for a revival of the slave trade as "shocking to the moral sentiment." Any such reversal by the United States he declared, would invite "the reproach and execration of all civilized and Christian people." After a highly emotional debate, the House of Representatives passed a resolution to that effect by a vote of 152 to 57. Three-quarters of the Southern congressmen voted in the negative. A South Carolina Democrat then immediately moved another resolution, minimally declaring that the repeal would be "inexpedient, unwise, and contrary to the settled policy of the United States." This resolution, stripped of the moral dimension of abolition, passed by a vote of 183 to 8. Once again, the margins of victory in 1807 and 1819 were achieved. A majority of southern representatives were opposed to both a repeal of the Abolition Act of 1807 and to any moral inference about the relation of the trade to slavery itself.

The repeal of the slave trade abolition act figured as a minor issue in the disintegration of the Democratic Party. At the 1860 Democratic national convention in Charleston, a draft proposal that favored the protection of "persons and property on *the high seas*" was flatly rejected by the majority. It was denounced as an implicit protection of the African slave trade, which would inflict "incalculable" damage on Northern democrats. The majority's rejection of the phrase that threatened to unravel the Abolition Act of 1807 prompted a partial Southern walkout.

The Continental Divide

For citizens of the United States, the fate of their own institution of slavery would clearly be decided within the great landmass of North America. The question that most profoundly divided the North and South was whether slavery should be allowed to expand westward beyond the boundaries of the states in the generation before the Civil War. By the 1830s, the vast underdeveloped area of northern Mexico remained the most contentious zone between slavery and freedom. Mexico's own struggle for independence had begun there in 1810, and slavery was abolished in 1829.

Beginning with President John Quincy Adams in the 1820s, American administrations had begun to request westward boundary adjustments. While they diplomatically pressured Mexican governments to relinquish all or part of Texas, American settlers began to migrate into the thinly populated area. In 1836, an Anglo-American uprising declared Texas to be an independent republic available for annexation by the United States. President Andrew Jackson and his designated successor, Martin Van Buren, moved with great caution. Sectional feeling was running high.[54] The House of Representatives was invoking its gag rule against abolitionist petitions, which expanded their own agenda to include opposition to allowing Texas into the Union. On the question of the expansion of slavery, the abolitionists did not speak in isolation. In 1838, resolutions favoring annexation of Texas failed in both houses of Congress. In 1840, the election of William Henry Harrison of the Whig party on a platform hostile to American extension into Texas, seemed to foreclose the annexation of Texas for the immediate future.[55]

The Whig president's death soon after his inauguration transferred the presidency to John Tyler, an enthusiastic expansionist. He promptly aligned himself with a group of pro-slavery politicians devoted to the acquisition of Texas. To overcome the sectional tensions that their policy would provoke, they intended to use the accumulated Anglo-American frictions over the slave fugitives, the right of search, and the disputes over Oregon to overcome the obstacles to acquiring Texas. They were aided by the adverse economic developments in the British Caribbean economy. Land values in Jamaica were falling despite protection. Maintaining protection for free-grown colonial sugar meant rising prices for British consumers just as the metropolitan economy was undergoing a severe crisis. Alternatively, opening the market to slave-grown sugar would mean encouraging the very trade that British policy was pledged to suppress and antagonizing the abolitionists. News of the expulsion of abolitionist David Turnbull from Cuba for subversive activities added to the impression that Britain was engaged in activities to subvert slavery beyond their own colonies.

British abolitionists were simultaneously engaged in an attempt to prevent Texas from becoming a new slave frontier. Texas was also the first western area susceptible to development as a slave territory since British emancipation. Indeed, no new area had been organized as a United States slave territory since the early 1820s. With its ill-defined boundaries, American settlers threatened to open up a vast area for slavery, equivalent to five or six new slave states within the federal Union. As an independent slave state after 1835, Texas claimed sovereignty over 375,000 square miles available for expansion, more than all of the emancipated British plantation colonies and the Cape Colony combined. As a free soil territory stretching northward to the Oregon territory, the United States would effectively have closed the

---

[54] *Ibid.*, 76.
[55] Fehrenbacher, *Slaveholding Republic*, 118–121.

expansion of slavery and quarantined the institution within the limits of the Missouri compromise.

When the first World Anti-Slavery Convention met in London in 1840, Texas still contained fewer than 15,000 slaves. In that same year, Palmerston negotiated a mutual right of search with the new nation in exchange for British recognition of Texas's independence from Mexico.[56] At the second London Anti-Slavery Convention in 1843, a Committee on Slavery in Texas portrayed the outcome as a matter of life and death for the institution in America. The Convention voted to request the British government to offer to maintain Texan independence by encouraging British capitalists to underwrite a large portion of the republic's debt in return for slave emancipation.

An Anglo-American delegation from the Convention gained an audience with Palmerston's successor to propose the plan. Lord Aberdeen declined to pursue the proposal, but promised the delegation that the British government would use "all legitimate and honorable means to secure it [abolition]."[57] Aberdeen's cautious refusal of an "emancipationist" loan to the abolitionists was backed up by a cautious but encouraging reminder of British principles to Texas's Minister in London: "The well-known policy and wish of the British Government to abolish slavery everywhere" made "abolition in Texas... very desirable."[58]

The combination of abolitionist access to the British government and Aberdeen's reiterated statement of interest in abolition "everywhere" provided the U.S. administration in Washington with a major selling point in seeking congressional approval for annexation of Texas. Even more serious, from the Tyler administration's perspective, was Aberdeen's suggestion to the Mexican and Texas governments that the former's recognition of Texan independence should be contingent upon slave emancipation. Aberdeen withdrew the proposition when he saw that English-sponsored emancipation became additional grist for a preemptive United States annexation.

Conditions along the Texas-Caribbean axis stimulated a highly publicized pro-slavery argument for the immediate annexation of Texas. The economic difficulties of the new free-labor colonies offered a plausible explanation for Britain's eagerness to extinguish slavery not only in Texas, but throughout the world. John Calhoun, now the U.S. Secretary of State, seized the opportunity to expand the diplomatic exchange into a panoramic overview of the world conflict between slavery and free labor. Calhoun dispatched a communication to William King, the American ambassador to France, to American ministers in the German states, Spain, Austria, Russia, Belgium, the Netherlands, and Brazil. In pamphlet form, it was published in South

---

[56] Lelia M. Rochell "Bonds over Bondage: British Opposition to the Annexation of Texas," *Journal of the Early American Republic*, 19 (1999), 257–278.

[57] *Ibid.*, 272, quoting from the *Anti-Slavery Society Minute Book*, July 28, I f. 94.

[58] Freehling, *Road to Disunion*, 355–452.

Carolina and reprinted in news outlets on both sides of the Atlantic as far as the Cape Verde islands.[59]

Calhoun's primary argument for annexation rested on Texas's natural destiny to be part of the United States. His explanation for British interference in the process was simple. British opposition to annexation was part of a global policy now driven by the failure of its colonial experiment in slave emancipation. The British had made a fatal economic miscalculation. They assumed that the labor of their ex-slaves would be at least as profitable as it had been before and that products could also be produced more cheaply elsewhere in the tropics by free Africans and Indians than by slaves. The result had been costly and ruinous: "Negroes had proved less productive without improved conditions."[60]

Drawing on the British periodical press, Calhoun presented a stark statistical summary: In ten years, the combination of British slave-trade abolition and emancipation policies had so far cost the British people $250 million. On top of this, the experiment had put twice as much wealth in land at risk in the British West Indies. By contrast, Euro-American capital in the *non*-British New World slave zones amounted to $4 billion since 1808, a gain equal to more than five times the British loss. That $4 billion now produced goods totaling $220 million per year, up from $72 million in 1808. Britain's continuously declining share of tropical production was as visible in the production of cotton as it was in coffee and sugar. The disparity in the performance of these two systems now forced the British to press harder for slave-trade abolition and slave emancipations, and for reasons other than humanitarian. It could hope to salvage and recoup its deteriorating position only by reducing its more productive competitors down to its own colonial level. Whatever abolitionism's original moral impulse, it was now greed, power, and political economy that drove British policy against foreign slavery. To his economic argument Calhoun added his familiar racial one, now expanded. In the United States, Cuba, and Brazil, there was no overarching outside power to maintain white supremacy. The only other path was the creation of a new Haiti. One race or the other would be left standing amid the ruined economies of the New World.[61]

Calhoun may have wished to rally the South on behalf of annexation of Texas and install pro-slavery as the official national doctrine of U.S. foreign relations but, further north, the fear of a British halt to American expansion and the prospect of acquiring Oregon as well as Texas dominated the nationalist discourse. The slavery extension issue strained the bonds of

---

[59] Edward Rugemer, "The Problem of Emancipation: The United States and Britain's Abolition of Slavery," Ph.D. Dissertation, Boston College, 2005, esp. 347.

[60] John C. Calhoun's Letter to William R. King August 12, 1844, in *The Papers of John C. Calhoun*, vol. 19 (Columbia: University of South Carolina Press, 1990), 568–578.

[61] Rugemer, *Problem of Emancipation*, 346–351; Drescher, *Mighty Experiment*, 170–173.

party loyalty, but the abolitionist Liberty Party received only 62,300 votes in the presidential election of 1844, less than 3 percent of the total. For the vast majority of voters and politicians in the mid-1840s, Texas was more a party issue than a sectional one.[62] In a series of congressional votes on territorial expansion between 1843 and 1845, between 75 and 96 percent of the Democrats strongly favored expansion, whereas between 88 and 93 percent of the Whigs opposed it. Unintentionally, the Liberty Party votes led to the narrow victory of James K. Polk, the Democratic expansionist candidate, ensuring Texas's entry into the Union.

During the decade after its colonial slave emancipation, British abolitionist policy clearly loomed fairly large in the calculations of American abolitionists, both black and white. It offered a major foil to southern proslavery and pro-expansionist politics. It figured in the strategies of successive administrations from Jackson to Tyler. One might be tempted to ascribe to British abolitionism much of the credit for the increasingly escalating demands of antebellum southern politicians for northern acquiescence in the growth of the institution. John Quincy Adams and others saw the fate of Texas as a major step in a slaveholding conspiracy to dominate the Union.

Yet, in the perspective of the period between 1845 and 1860, it is remarkable how quickly the British presence diminished in the American debates over the future of slavery. Once the acquisitions of Texas and Oregon were concluded, Britain virtually ceased to be a major factor in the fate of the institution of slavery. By the late 1840s, American expansionist projects into Meso-America encountered no major British military or diplomatic deterrent. On the contrary, in 1856, the British returned the Bay Islands to Honduras. The British government wanted the treaty to stipulate that slavery should never be permitted in the returned territory. Responding to congressional pressure, President Buchanan informed the British that the United States could not endorse any treaty between Great Britain and a third nation excluding slavery. The free soil proviso was deleted from the final agreement. The constraints on an American acquisition of Cuba by purchase were clearly more domestic than foreign.[63]

By the early 1850s, neither America nor any other slave power in the tropics had to be concerned about Britain's perceived need to undermine slave systems to save is own failing colonies. In 1846, Britain dramatically switched its political economy toward a policy of free trade. During the 1850s, the primary concern of British manufacturers and policy makers over

---

[62] Holt, *The Political Crisis of the 1850s*, 44.
[63] Fehrenbacher, *Slaveholding Republic*, 126–133. For the slackening of British pressure on Cuba, see Luis Martínez Fernández, "The Havana Anglo-Spanish Mixed Commission for the Suppression of the Slave Trade and Cuba's *Emancipados*," *Slavery and Abolition*, 16:2 (1999), 205–225.

slave-grown produce was not moral in nature, but rather a fear that over-whelming dependency on American cotton could leave them prey to a civil conflict the United States. On the eve of the American Civil War, a 900-page compilation, *Cotton is King*, gleefully quoted British commentaries on the disappointments following British emancipation and the falsified prophecies about India's free-labor power to displace southern slavery. Disillusionment with slave emancipation in the West Indies combined with dependency on cotton helped southerners to imagine that, in the event of secession, they could embargo the English and French into intervention on their behalf. It was time for abolitionists to wonder about flagging zeal in Britain. In 1859, Frederick Douglass worried over disturbing signs of a British retreat from intervention in American affairs.

Slavery and the Crisis of Disunion

The succession of crises in the United States in the fifteen years before southern secession was largely home grown. Texas was only the harbinger of a far greater expansion to the Pacific Ocean. The war with Mexico in 1846–48 opened an enormous new territory for settlement, potentially extending as far as Central America. The war's outcome was the precipitating cause of the erosion of the national party system, climaxing with the dissolution of the Union. The severity of this crisis was exacerbated by enormous economic and social tensions within the United States during the 1840s and 1850s.

At the end of the age of revolution, the Mississippi river system was still the great artery of interior settlement and commerce. Kentucky, Tennessee, Louisiana, and Missouri grew more rapidly before 1820 than most of the states of the Midwest. The flow of their trade went up and down the Mississippi basin via New Orleans. By 1840, the dominant flow of trade shifted east to west across the Great Lakes, and the Erie Canal, opened in 1825. This lateral trend was accelerated by the great wave of railroad building during the next two decades.[64]

The enormous flow of immigrants during the 1840s and 1850s settled primarily in the North. By 1860, more than six out of seven foreign-born inhabitants lived in the free states and western territories.[65] In many ways, the huge influx of immigrants deeply divided the North by religion and culture. This division not only aided the disintegration of the two-party system but deeply compromised the ability of a new free soil party to form a sectional coalition against the "Slave Power" in 1853–1855. These European migrants did not arrive with predominantly abolitionist sentiments. But, the very location of their settlement became an accusation in an increasingly

---

[64] Fogel, *Without Consent*, 302–309.
[65] Drescher, *From Slavery to Freedom*, 128, Table 5.1.

sectionalized and polarized nation. In the mid-1850s, an Alabama newspaper editorialized: "Their aversion to our institutions is manifested by their choice of homes in the nonslaveholding states."[66] The terms of the U.S. Constitution ensured that the electoral balance in the House of Representatives and the electoral college choosing the president inexorably shifted in favor of the North with each passing decade.

The huge expanse of land seized by the United States from Mexico crystallized the question that had lain dormant since the Missouri compromise. What was to be the status of the new territories with regard to slavery? The rough balance of power between the free and slave states quickly emerged as one that would determine the future of the institution and of the United States itself. The status of slavery in the newly occupied area was precisely the opposite of what it had been in the acquisition of Louisiana. Slavery had been a well-established institution in both the settled southern (New Orleans) and northern (St. Louis) areas of Louisiana. In the absence of any major antislavery mobilization around the issue at the time of the purchase, Congress had yielded to the demands of the slaveholding inhabitants of the territory within the purchase.

The Mexican case was clearly different. Mexico remained a free soil zone as a result of laws enacted under Mexican sovereignty in 1829. To allow slavery within the newly acquired area would revert free soil to slave territory. Moreover, the areas best suited for agricultural expansion in the lands acquired from Mexico in 1848, were also located predominantly in its northern and far western sectors.

When, in August 1846, President Polk asked Congress for an appropriation to conduct negotiations with Mexico, a Northern Democrat, David Wilmot of Pennsylvania, moved that slavery, already prohibited in Mexico, continue to be banned in any territory to be acquired. In two sectionally divided votes, the northern-dominated House approved the proviso. The more evenly divided Senate prevented the bill's passage and the question remained unsettled. Wilmot had no sympathy for either the slaves' condition or their color. He only sought to create an exclusive space where "my own race and own color can live without the disgrace" of "association Negro slavery." But, in this case, and, henceforth, even antiblack color prejudice seemed to be working against the establishment of a slave system. The Wilmot proviso threatened southern ambitions to have slavery formally sanctioned as a national institution in the newly acquired territories. Congress seemed to endorse a declaration that southerners deserved "national odium."[67]

---

[66] See Fogel, *Without Consent*, 354–380; (Quote on 375). See also, Davis, *Inhuman Bondage*, 287.
[67] Freehling, *Road to Disunion*, 458–461.

The impulse toward the prohibition of slavery was part of a larger campaign to indict southern institutions and culture as inimical to the future of whites, even in a racially exclusive democracy. Southern insistence on nationalizing slavery quickly demonstrated that the policy's supporters chose to resist even the fundamental premise of majority rule. After the proviso was stalemated, each stage in the settlement of the new territories provoked a more intense confrontation. The rapid influx of Americans into California by 1849 led to the territory's early appeal for entry into the Union with a free-state status.

This created a double crisis. It threatened the all-important sectional balance in the U.S. Senate and it precipitated a demand to settle the general principles of territorial organization in the rest of the Mexican cession. Discussion of implications of a wholesale decision, like the Wilmot proviso, had gone on so long that no one was prepared to allow the territories to be settled incrementally and without implications for the future. Southerners saw that simply following Mexican precedent would doom the institution of slavery to exclusion from the whole of the huge new territory and would subject American slaveholders to the fate of their British West Indian predecessors. They intensified demands for the recognition of slavery as a nationally protected institution. After a deep congressional crisis, a second compromise, really an armistice, was reached in 1850.[68] It admitted California as a free state and defined the boundary of Texas with the New Mexico territory, one of two areas formed out of the rest of the Mexican acquisition.

The organization of the two territories after California's entry into the Union was indicative of the degree to which even symbolic recognition of slavery, even on land unsuited for plantation agriculture, had become vital to the South. Two territorial legislatures provided legal sanction for slavery: Utah in 1852 and New Mexico in 1859. Nevertheless, the 1860 census reported only twenty-nine slaves in the Utah territory and none in New Mexico. It was the legitimacy and national parity of the claims for the institution that were being affirmed, not its economic superiority or its probable salience in the territory. Two other items completed the package of 1850 compromises. The first restricted the open slave trade in Washington, D.C., a prime target for condescending foreign visitors. The second item was a revised Fugitive Slave Law. It was enacted to secure southern slaves as property within free states. Its language was also uncompromising, "as though antislavery noses were being rubbed in the legitimacy of the peculiar institution."[69]

The Fugitive Slave Law was designed as if to demonstrate to northerners just how far their "free soil" was from the world of the *Somerset* decision. It

---

[68] Fehrenbacher, *Road to Disunion*, 487; David Potter, *The Impending Crisis*, 113.
[69] Fehrenbacher, *Slaveholding Republic*, 232.

set up an acid test of northern fidelity to, or at least complicity in, the original constitutional sanction for the recovery of fugitives throughout the Union. The result was a running series of widely publicized confrontations both in the courts and on the streets. Before 1850, fugitive slave riots had largely been led by African Americans, with minimal white support. The distinctive element of such confrontations after 1850 was the prominent presence of that old class of white "gentlemen of property and standing," now, however, often helping runaway slaves instead of intimidating abolitionists. There was no consensual shift in abolitionist or northern civil society towards the use of violence "but there was intensification of extenuation, toleration, and even pride in its use."[70]

The successive controversies of the 1850s came on so rapidly that they began to overlap with one another. In the angry backlash over the repeal of the Missouri compromise, in 1854, a mass meeting in Wisconsin resolved that because all compromises were being repealed, the Fugitive Slave Law should also be repealed. The next day a mob battered down the door of the Milwaukee jail and freed Joshua Glover, a fugitive in federal custody. The state Supreme Court set aside convictions of the ringleaders by the federal court. States rights and popular sovereignty were increasingly being used by Northerners as weapons to nullify an unpopular federal law. For all of the intensification, however, the shakily emerging Republican coalition in the late 1850s made no mention of the Fugitive Slave Law. In 1859, Lincoln himself warned that any proposal advocating its repeal would explode the convention and the party.[71]

Much more damaging to the norms of civil society was the white-on-white confrontation generated by the fight between free soil and pro-slave settlers over the expansion of slavery in the territorial west. The Wilmot proviso had been designed, like the abolition of the U.S. Atlantic slave trade, as much to bar entry to blacks as to prohibit slavery. The Missouri Compromise had closed the Louisiana Purchase territory north of 36° 30' to slavery. By 1850, southerners stood ready to block attempts to organize the region above 36° 30' into free white territories. Senator Stephen Douglas of Illinois attempted to break the logjam to rapidly open the way for the construction of a continental railway line that would accelerate the growth of the region and the western cities of St. Louis and Chicago. Douglas successfully sponsored the Kansas-Nebraska Act of 1854 to rescind the Missouri Compromise. Each territory would henceforth resolve its own status by majority rule and popular sovereignty whenever it drew up its state constitution. Because most westward-moving Americas were northerners, he foresaw no different outcome than the one legally prescribed by the Missouri Compromise.

[70] Grimsted, *American Mobbing*, 73–81.
[71] Fehrenbacher, *Slaveholding Republic*, 245.

The actual outcome of the Kansas-Nebraska Act was two more bursts of sectional outrage. The first occurred in the North against what was regarded as the unraveling of a solemn thirty-year-old pact on the distribution of slave and free territory. Rallies of tens of thousands gathered from Maine to Wisconsin to denounce the Kansas-Nebraska Act as a violation of the nation's trust and a national pact. Even the wall of antiimmigrant hostility was breached, with Irish petitioners accounting for nearly 8 percent of the signatures. German middle-class and radical artisans formed another novel component of the protesters.[72] Mass rallies of laborers now joined the "free soiler" cry that the area set aside for their settlement was being reopened to slavery. Mass meetings drew up mass petitions to Congress. Seventy percent of northern Democratic congressmen who had voted for the Kansas-Nebraska Act lost their seats in the 1854 elections. It reinforced all of the elements exacerbated by southern expansionism: moral antipathy to black slavery, racial antipathy to blacks, fears of a subversion of free labor, and distrust of a slave power conspiracy.[73]

If the Kansas-Nebraska Act transformed the struggle for power in the North, it was the South's turn to be outraged when they discovered that they would not be sharing in the spoils of the Kansas-Nebraska Act. What quickly became evident in Kansas was that the civil and political norms of American society broke down. Two ideologies of liberty that had cohabitated uneasily by virtue of geographical distance or mutual understanding now became ideas in arms. Two mobilized groups of white citizens defied each others' duly constituted deliberative bodies and even federal authority. Violence and terrorism overruled due process and majority rule. Scenes that Europeans and Americans were apt to place in Latin American civil conflicts were enacted in the heart of North America. Opportunities for black slaves followed a pattern to those in similar conflicts. On a small scale, slaves found opportunities to flee their masters to escape from Missouri or to end up incorporated into the armed groups of initially racist "free state" fighters. The 1860 census registered only two slaves in tumultuous Kansas as opposed to fifteen in calmer Nebraska. Free African Americans in Kansas outnumbered those in Nebraska by ten to one (625 to 67). The violence of "bleeding Kansas" was reenacted in the United States Senate, where Charles Sumner of Massachusetts was caned into bloody unconsciousness by Preston Brooks of South Carolina. The nation was traumatized by the pitched battles that accompanied the settlement of Kansas, complete with two rival governments each claiming to be the legitimate authority in the territory.

While the battle over Kansas was raging, another major branch of the government weighed in to resolve the issue of limits to slavery in the United

---

[72] Magdol, *Antislavery Rank and File*, ch. 8; Bruce Levine, *Spirit of '48: German Immigrants, Labor Conflict and the coming of the Civil War* (Urbana: University of Illinois Press, 1992).
[73] Holt, *Political Crisis*, 148–149.

States. The Supreme Court's Dred Scott decision held that the federal constitution was indeed a document that implicitly protected slavery throughout the nation. It definitively ruled that the Constitution prevented congressional interference with southern property rights in the territories. The decision also attempted to define the status of African Americans, ruling that blacks had not been nor could they be citizens of the United States. In response to the ruling that free blacks were incapable of citizenship, New York's legislature considered the possibility of returning to the model of the Virginia and Kentucky nullification proceedings against federal oppression.[74]

The executive branch deepened the rift. President Buchanan suggested that even if Kansas eventually abolished the institution of slavery, all slaves already resident in the territory would have to remain in bondage. Although the antislavery majority in Kansas grew progressively stronger, a rump convention at Lecompton drafted a pro-slavery constitution in 1857. The ratifying referendum on the document offered only a choice between unrestricted slavery and one restricted to those slaves already resident in the territory. Stephen Douglas denounced the attempt to override the principle of popular sovereignty that underpinned the Kansas-Nebraska Act. Given another chance to vote on the Lecompton constitution, the majority defeated it by 11,300 to 1,788. Southern attempts to override popular sovereignty by having Congress provide a slave code for the territories failed, nullifying the implementation of the Dred Scott decision.[75]

The Republican Party, a limited antislavery coalition, entered the elections of 1860 pledged to ban slavery from the territories. By then, it was clear to the South that the northern Democratic model of popular sovereignty could no longer guarantee the extension of slavery into the territories. Northern Democratic popular sovereignty would no more sanction the presence of black slaves than the Republicans' promise of prohibition. Douglas, the northern presidential choice, declared that the courts could not force the people of any territory to support slavery. Kansas dismayed Southern radicals by demonstrating the trajectory of Northern white migration and disposition in favor of free soil. Both republicans and southern extremists agreed that slavery had to expand for political, if not economic, reasons if it were not to face the slow death of its West Indian counterpart. That any legal process might have to stretch out over generations of political and constitutional hurdles was no longer reassuring in the light of violence in Kansas and John Brown's incursion in Virginia. When southern states began to secede in the wake of Lincoln's election, the new president was adamant that whatever compromise measures Congress might consider, they were to "refuse to consider any compromise respecting the *extension* of slavery."

---

[74] Fehrenbacher, *Slaveholding Republic*, 282–284.
[75] *Ibid.*, 282–284.

The turn to military violence, like the civil violence that had preceded it in Kansas, revealed how quickly the fortunes of war could impact the behavior of the combatants in ways that had been unforeseen at its inception. As soon as Lincoln was elected in 1860, a prominent South Carolina secessionist called upon the British Consul in Charleston to sound out the potential for a relationship between the United Kingdom and a new Confederacy, whose economy accounted for the prosperity of one of Britain's important industries. The Consul noted that he had been informed that the traffic in African slaves "was likely to be encouraged" in its new federal assembly. He cautioned that "Great Britain would require from that Body some very distinct assurance . . . on this subject before she could be brought to enter cordially into communications with it." The secessionist proudly replied that

no Southern State of Confederacy would ever be brought to negotiate upon such a subject; that to prohibit the Slave Trade was, virtually, to admit that the Institution of Slavery was an evil and a wrong, instead of, as the South believed it, a blessing to the African Race and a system of labour appointed of God.[76]

Two months later, however, the delegates to the Constitutional Convention of the Confederacy made prohibition of the African slave trade a fundamental article of their constitution. That document further required the prospective national legislature to ensure the effective enforcement of that article. The new state was in no position to provoke "the anathemas of all Europe," and to risk having vessels sailing under an unrecognized flag searched and seized by foreign (i.e., British) warships – "equivalent to a declaration of war."[77] The incipient new state realized that its independence would make its ships as vulnerable to seizures by the British as U.S. ships had been to North African corsairs after 1783. Even more importantly, the seven new confederate states would have increased the risk of losing the adhesion of states of the upper South, whose citizens had already been alienated by the pro-slave trade agitation. Even in the core Gulf states, the prohibition clause was no impediment to confirmation. They all overwhelmingly ratified the Confederate constitution.

The transformation of Northern attitudes towards the British naval patrol after the beginning of the Civil War was equally dramatic. As late as 1857, an increase in British boardings of American vessels off the coasts of Africa and Cuba became a source of Anglo-American verbal conflict. The resistance to British boardings remained as strong as ever in the North as well as the South. Following the attack on Fort Sumter in 1861, however, the American African squadron was recalled and the patrolling was once more exclusively British. Soon after, William Seward, Lincoln's new secretary of state, indicated to the British, a willingness to shift from America's long-standing resistance to

[76] Takaki, *Pro-Slavery*, 203–204.
[77] *Ibid.*, 209.

the mutual right of search. As the British had previously done with many European governments, a charade had to be enacted, implying that the initiative came exclusively from the American side. In 1862, the United States finally adopted a mutual right of search between the actual British African naval patrol and the virtual American one. In the absence of the new Confederate states, the U.S. Senate adopted the treaty. As noted, with America's withdrawal from opposition to British policy, the Atlantic slave trade vanished entirely within five years.

Confederate secession and the long Civil War that followed destroyed slavery in the United States and hastened its ending in the Americas. When the conflict began, it seemed unlikely that the institution of slavery would so quickly come to an end. The willingness of both sides to sustain huge losses of soldiers and at such a high cost also discloses that the Confederacy was not only economically viable, but also ideologically and politically robust. The South's 260,000 military deaths represented a higher per capita loss than the North's 360,000. Not only was the North's reservoir of eligible white males higher than that of the South but it was able to call upon 200,000 African Americans, a potential source of men under arms, rejected until the end by the Confederacy. The per capita toll of death and destruction may have been less than those entailed in the Haitian Revolution but in magnitude it represented the largest military toll in the history of New World conflicts involving the fate of slaves.

As in the Spanish-American wars of independence, the American Civil War only became a struggle against slavery well into the conflict. Lincoln's initial assurances failed to dissuade the lower South from secession and his determination to save the Union by military force added four more slave states to the Confederacy. The president led a divided North and needed to hold the strategic northern tier of slave states within the Union. In those border states, and probably to a considerable extent elsewhere, there were many Unionists who looked "upon slavery as a curse" and looked upon free blacks "as a greater curse."

Also, as in South America, the need to draw deeply on the human reserves over the course of a long war allowed American slaves to play a greater role in the destruction of the institution of slavery than anyone might have imagined in 1860. The long-stalemated North ultimately recruited 200,000 African Americans into the Union army, one-fifth of whom did not survive the war. They constituted the largest military contingent of men of African descent who participated in the New World conflicts for national independence and slave emancipation. The toll of human life during the conflict probably also allowed the normally strong current of antiblack racism in America to be overborne by hostility to the former beneficiaries of the institution who had instituted secession and its bloody aftermath.[78]

[78] Davis, *Inhuman Bondage*, 310.

The sheer destruction of human life and wealth in the American Civil War cost more than any conceivable plan of compensated emancipation. But, it allowed for the temporary occupation of the conquered South and for the passage and enforcement of the Thirteenth, Fourteenth, and Fifteenth Amendments to the Constitution of the United States. Even with the passage of the Thirteenth Amendment abolishing slavery, the immediate reaction of southern state legislatures elected by "unreconstructed" former rebels demonstrated the need for further protective legislation and policing. Southerners enacted Black Codes modeled on the now banned slave codes that had previously served to control the African-American population. Former masters were unable to restore the status of ex-slaves as property, but the codes provided for race-specific restrictions on gun ownership, alcohol, vagrancy, marriage partners, participation in the legal process, and differential criminal penalties.[79]

The Republican-dominated national legislature extended the life and scale of the Freedmen's Bureau in 1866. It was originally conceived as an expedient to provide for the temporary needs of displaced ex-slaves, protect them against abuses in labor relations, and enforce a possible land reform that never materialized. The U.S. Congress enacted a Civil Rights Act along with extending the Freedmen's Bureau, over the vetoes of Andrew Johnson, who had succeeded to the presidency after Lincoln's assassination in April 1865. The passage of the Fourteenth Amendment was intended to constitutionalize prohibitions on racially discriminatory legislation.

By 1870, the Republicans enacted further legislation to ensure African-American suffrage and to sustain the principles under which the Union victory had concluded the struggle.[80] A series of amendments and laws not only prevented the restoration of the institution of slavery, but also made the half-way house of indentured servitude and apprenticeship unavailable as alternatives to contractual labor or share cropping.

The greatest mobilization and conflict in the history of the Americas, therefore, preserved the Union and removed one contradiction – the institution of slavery – in a society whose founding document was dedicated to the creation of free and equal citizens. Yet, it failed to remove the enduring resistance to legislation against political and social equality for blacks in the south. Radical Republican efforts to enforce reconstruction along the lines of land redistribution to blacks failed almost immediately. Over the next decade "the north began to emphasize *reunion* with the southern states rather than the *reconstruction* of their social system."[81]

---

[79] Eric Foner, *Reconstruction: America's Unfinished Revolution 1863–1877* (New York: Perennial Classics, 2002), 199–216.

[80] Fehrenbacher, *Slaveholding Republic*, 328–335; and Foner, *Reconstruction*, ch. 3 and 6.

[81] Roger L. Ransom, *Conflict and Compromise: The Political Economy of Slavery, Emancipation, and the American Civil War* (New York: Cambridge University Press, 1989), 25

The antislavery political impulse gradually subsided after the mid-1870s. The last remaining federal troops left the south in 1877. The centennial of American independence in 1876 ironically marked a retreat from the idea that the federal government would be the principal guarantor of the individual rights of American citizens. In all of the Anglo-American areas with descendants of slave populations, the last third of the nineteenth century saw the withdrawal of many advantages that had initially seemed assured by emancipation. In the British Caribbean, this withdrawal took the form of eliminating the colonial assembly system that had prevailed in most of the preemancipation British slave colonies.[82] In the U.S. South, this withdrawal was at the state, rather than the national, level. It took the more direct form of racial disenfranchisement in the states' representative institutions. Legal freedom was hardly an empty gift, but the combination of poverty and disenfranchisement in which many southern blacks found themselves half a century after the Anglo-American emancipations marked a deceleration of those benefits.

In retrospect, most American economic historians agree that slavery was neither a moribund nor a declining system at the moment that it was mortally attacked. In that respect, it resembled all other major variants of the institution. The histories of slave societies in the century after 1780 show that only overwhelming political or military power could bring to an end New World slavery. In some contexts, fears of post-emancipation race relations were an even greater deterrent to emancipation than fears of economic decline. As the American border slave states graphically demonstrated, there was often no inclination to abolish slavery from within, right down to their rejection of the Thirteenth Amendment to the U.S. Constitution in 1865.

Further north, there was certainly even less inclination to enact any emancipation that would have required fully compensating slave-owners for capital losses amounting to 80 percent of the gross national product of the United States in 1860. Because almost all of the antebellum schemes of emancipation had to address the probability of deportation as well as compensation, the costs of peacefully dismantling the institution of slavery might have had to include enormous transportation costs, even if enslaved African Americans had consented to go. Otherwise, the process would have replicated the devastation of the Middle Passage in reverse.

Ransom argues that land distribution alone would have been insufficient to enable black farmers to escape debt peonage after 1880. African Americans who did hold on to their property in South Carolina's ricelands may well have emerged poorer than laborers in the cotton fields (*ibid.*, 248–249). On the dead end of the peasant-like agriculture in much of the post-emancipation South, see also Eric Foner, *Nothing But Freedom: Emancipation and its Legacy* (Baton Rouge: Louisiana State University Press, 1983), 109.

[82] Green, *British Slave Emancipation*, 396–399. On the public sphere and the rapid decline of abolitionism, see Francesca Gamber, "The Public Sphere and the End of American Abolitionism, 1833–1870, *Slavery and Abolition*, 28:3 (2007), 351–368.

The Civil War entailed the death of six hundred thousand men under arms. It cost the nation more than three times the value of slaves in the United States in 1860. But, without this expenditure of blood and treasure, it is easy to imagine that both U.S. and world slavery would have been far more robust institutions during the last third of the nineteenth century than they had proven to be in the century before.[83] We might imagine any number of counterfactual scenarios built on the survival of American slavery beyond the 1860s. What is certain is that its sudden destruction sent a deep tremor through those slave societies that remained intact. The mid-1860s thus signaled both the ending of the transatlantic slave trade and the intensification of pressure on the institution of slavery itself in its Ibero-American redoubts.

---

[83] Claudia Goldin, "The Economics of Emanciaption," in *Without Consent or Contract, Technical Papers*, vol. II, Robert William Fogel and Stanley L. Engerman, eds. (New York: Norton, 1992), art. 31, 614–628. As the British, French, Spanish, Dutch, and Luso-Brazilian emancipations demonstrate, slavery was rarely terminated with greater per capita violence, more material destruction, more debilitating long-term consequences.

12

Abolishing New World Slavery – Latin America

Cuba and Puerto Rico

On the eve of the disruption of the American Union, the last two dynamic Ibero-American slave systems appeared to be as robust as ever in their potential for future growth. In Cuba, Spain's largest slaveholding colony, planter economic expectations for the future remained high.[1] Cuba, unlike Brazil or the United States, was the last New World system to tap into Africa as its reservoir of slave recruitment, albeit at rising prices because of British naval constraints. By 1856–1860, the price of slaves being loaded in Africa had dropped by more than 40 percent, but slave prices in Cuba had risen by 75 percent.[2] Cuban planters increasingly concentrated their slaves on growing sugar – the most productive crop between 1830 and 1860. In 1827, about a quarter of the Cuban slave population worked on cultivating sugar and a third on coffee. In 1846, 36 percent were working in sugar and 18 percent in coffee. By 1862, the respective percentages were 47 percent to 7 percent. So avid was Cuba's search for labor that the Spanish government opened a market for indentured migrant labor from China. Yet, Cubans still preferred enslaved Africans to indentured Asians as long as they could purchase them. Although slave prices were always higher than indentured contacts during the 1850s, Cuban planters purchased two Africans for every indentured laborer landed from Asia. In this situation, Cuban sugar planters were well able to absorb the increased slave prices because of the rising

---

[1] Eltis, *Economic Growth*, 187–193; For an excellent overview of the economic prospects of the "Big Three," New World slave societies in the 1850s, consult Laird W. Bergad, *The Comparative Histories of Slavery in Brazil, Cuba and the United States* (New York: Cambridge University Press, 2007), ch. 5.

[2] Slave Trade Database, figures for 1841–1860. See also Laird Bergad et al., *The Cuban Slave Market 1790–1880* (New York: Cambridge University Press, 1995), p. 152, fig. 7.6.

physical output per slave.[3] The orientation of Cuban planters shifted ever more intensely toward the production of sugar, and both production levels and values in 1860 stood at their highest point and showed no signs of losing momentum. Cuban slavery was prospering in relation to the world, as well as compared to its own record. The U.S. Civil War disrupted Louisiana's sugar production whereas the value of Cuban sugar production in 1861–1865 was 170 percent higher than in 1841–1845. As final abolition approached in 1877, 77 percent of Cuba's slaves resided in the principal provinces of the sugar economy. Per capita income in Cuba's western sugar zone has been estimated at two to three times the figures for the United States and Great Britain in 1862. And, one must bear in mind David Eltis's assessment that, in per capita output, midcentury Cuba "must have ranked among the top half dozen of the world's nations."[4]

Although the wealth of the newest "Pearl of the Antilles" had become legendary by midcentury, its expanding slave population was recognized as a potential source of peril. The slave population rose by more than 160 percent between 1817 and 1846. Memories of the Escalera conspiracy and its brutal suppression remained vivid. With slaves representing 36 percent of its population in 1846, Cuba was more analogous to Virginia than Jamaica in its share of slave labor. Like the citizens of Virginia, it was possible for Cubans to imagine a politics of "whitening" through immigration as a peaceful pathway to the elimination of the slave trade and the gradual elimination of the institution itself.[5] Throughout the 1840s and 1850s, dissident Cuban elites wrestled with the alternatives of a future within a reformed Spanish imperium or the United States as the solution to the combined problems of autonomy, security, and communal identity. By the beginning of the American Civil War, however, the demographic threat seemed less urgent. Even after the final surge of the African slaves into Cuba in the late 1850s, slaves accounted for only 27 percent of the population, and whites were in the majority.[6]

On the whole, advocates for colonial reform remained largely ineffectual before 1860. Some who desired political liberty could argue that liberty and slavery, if not the slave trade, were reconcilable in Cuba. José Antonio Saco looked to the southern United States where slave owners enjoyed full

---

[3] Compare Eltis, *Economic Growth*, 191–192, and 245, Table A.2 on Cuban slave imports in 1851–1860 with arrivals of indentured servants during the same period, given in David Northrup, *Indentured Labor in the Age of Imperialism, 1834–1922* (Cambridge: Cambridge University Press, 1992), 156–157, Table A.1.

[4] Eltis, "Slave Economies," 123; Eltis, *Economic Growth*, 191–192, 236, and 284; and Bergad, *Cuban Slave Market*, 32–33.

[5] Christopher Schmidt-Nowara, *Empire and Antislavery: Spain, Cuba and Puerto Rico, 1833–1874* (Pittsburgh: University of Pittsburgh Press, 1999), 27–32.

[6] Arthur F. Corwin, *Spain and the Abolition of Slavery in Cuba, 1817–1886* (Austin: University of Texas Press, 1967), 146–147.

control over the future of their property in persons.[7] Cuba, on the contrary, was still a part of a colonial empire in which it had no institutional political power. In the 1830s, the Spanish Cortes had voted overwhelmingly to exclude the colonies from the imperial legislature. The island possessed no autonomous provincial legislature assembly and civil society was tightly controlled. Externally, Cuba had been under continuous British diplomatic pressure for four decades to end the inflow of African slaves and liberate tens of thousands of illegally imported Africans who had been unable to exercise their nominally free status. Cuba was not the sole cause of Spanish economic progress in the thirty years before the American Civil War, but the Spanish government strongly believed that its metropolitan economic development, public revenues, and international standing were enhanced by the possession of Cuba.

As previously noted, during the 1850s it was possible for the Spanish government to play off the annexationist ambitions of the United States against the abolitionist and antiannexationist policies of Great Britain. In 1855, the Spanish Cortes unanimously approved a status quo policy vis-à-vis slavery: "The Government . . . entertains the innermost conviction that slavery is a necessity and an indispensable condition for the maintenance of landed property in the Island of Cuba, and has sought to [give the Creole] property-holders assurances . . . never to meddle with the system in any manner whatsoever."[8] It simultaneously reassured the United States that there was no secret understanding with Britain because the institution of slavery was necessary for Cuban prosperity. Although there was a good deal of discussion of the subject in private circles, the public sphere remained largely devoid of openly abolitionist propositions beyond appeals for the actual enforcement of laws against the slave trade.

Before the American Civil War, Puerto Rico offered a more promising site for the development of antislavery within the Spanish imperial orbit. During the generation after Waterloo, Puerto Rican planters had taken full advantage of the opportunities opened up by the successive closings of the African slave trade under British, Dutch, and (later) French flags. Puerto Rico briefly became one of the dynamic zones of Caribbean staple production. By midcentury, however, slavery's growth leveled off and the colony's slave importations virtually came to an end.[9] The smaller island's planters could not sustain the pace of their Cuban counterparts and Puerto Ricans slowly began to switch from sugar to coffee and tobacco. In producing these crops,

---

[7] See Schmidt-Nowara, *Empire and Antislavery*, 25 and Corwin, *Spain and the Abolition*, 196.

[8] Corwin, *Spain and the Abolition*, 125.

[9] Eltis, *Economic Growth*, 219–220. Joseph C. Dorsey, *Slave Traffic in the Age of Revolution: Puerto Rico, West Africa and the non-Hispanic Caribbean* (Gainesville: University Press of Florida 200), argues for a more extended indirect trade with Africa via other European slave colonies.

they were able to employ the resident free population. Even when the slave share of the island's population reached its peak in 1846, they represented less than one-eighth of the total population, compared to more than one-third in Cuba. Puerto Rico even became an exporter of slaves to Cuba in the 1840s until British pressures reduced the intercolonial transfers to negligible proportions during the following decades.[10]

Nevertheless, with its 42,000 resident slaves, sugar and slavery were still prominent features in Puerto Rico's economy. Rising slave prices in the 1850s induced Puerto Rican sugar planters to scramble for new sources of labor. They called for a revival of their slave trade, expanding the flow of Asian indentured laborers, and regulations to require unemployed free workers to sign labor contracts with employers. In this context of perceived labor shortage, even Puerto Rican reformers refrained from attacking the institution of slavery itself before the 1860s.[11]

In his account of the abolition of slavery in the Spanish Empire, Schmidt-Nowara emphasizes the significance of the transformation of the public sphere between the mid-1850s and mid-1860s as a precondition for the emergence of Spanish abolitionism. Within the metropole itself, the collective support for antislavery among the elite was as feeble as in most other European societies. Abolitionism did not emerge in the industrial and commercial sectors, but among journalists and members of the "free professions" – lawyers, doctors, and engineers. They were people who routinely viewed Spain's economic and political question in terms of a broad and comparative European perspective. They agreed that Spain lagged behind most advanced societies of the West socially, economically, and culturally. Whatever its relative profitability, slavery was clearly not lifting Spain out of underdevelopment nor raising its standing in the civilized world. Those sympathetic to antislavery appeals were less concerned with the short-run economic advantages or disadvantages offered by colonial slavery than with the disadvantages of having Spain's polity tied to authoritarian conservatism at home and an increasingly anomalous institution abroad.[12]

The three decades between the 1830s and 1860s witnessed an efflorescence of civil associations, especially in Madrid. The number of newspapers quintupled between 1837 and 1865. Growing enrollments at the central university were outpaced by an explosion of specialized schools of higher education on the model of the French *grandes écoles*. By the 1850s, new public forums served as platforms for a variety of Spanish and Antillean reforms. The very meaning of the public expanded to incorporate "the totality of

---

[10] Corwin, *Spain and the Abolition*, 156.
[11] See Schmidt-Nowara, *Empire and Antislavery*, 49.
[12] Schmidt-Nowara, *Empire and Antislavery*, ch. 3 and 4.

persons who share the same interests or who choose to gather in a specific place to promote a common interest or concern."[13]

Nevertheless, for all this associational development, neither the slave trade nor slavery appeared on the political agenda of the government, the Cortes, or in the public sphere before the 1860s. As late as 1860, British abolitionists complained that more slave ships were departing for Africa than at any time since slave traffic had been officially outlawed by Spain. The claim was overblown but the fact remained that the number of African slaves landed in Cuba at the end of the 1850s was four times greater than it had been a decade earlier.[14]

The U.S. Civil War transformed a potential future without the slave trade and slavery into an imminent threat. Well into the Civil War, Spanish diplomats could envision the formidable Southern Confederacy as an additional moral and political bulwark for slavery in Cuba. The conflict initially reduced America's annexationist threat. By the spring of 1865, however, the bulwark vanished. The Spanish minister in Washington, D.C. advised his government "to consider in one form or another the means for initiating the abolition of slavery." Suddenly, it appeared that the very existence of slavery in Cuba might be used by a victorious and militarily formidable Union as a pretext for Cuba's annexation.[15] Even before the formation of the Spanish Abolitionist Society in 1865, Spanish civil society began to stir. The Free Society of Political Economy and the Academy of Jurisprudence and Legislation began their first public discussions of abolition in 1864. For the first time in a generation, deputies in the Cortes anxiously suggested that the government should take timely steps toward abolition. In tightly controlled Havana, a new association sanctioned by the Captain-General was formed to campaign for the effective ending of slavery. The already outlawed slave trade was again abolished in 1866, this time more as postmortem than prescription.[16]

Spain's first abolitionist society was an offspring of the new international configuration of power as well as Spain's new public sphere. Three decades

---

[13] *Ibid.*, 51–53. The expansion of associational activity coincided with three decades of exceptional Spanish industrial growth between the 1830s and 1860s. See Nicholas, *The Economic Modernization of Spain 1830–1930*, Sanchez Albernozed ed. (New York: New York University Press, 1987), 83; and J. Vicens Vives, *An Economic History of Spain* (Princeton: 1969), 709–10. Accompanying this growth was the founding of associations dedicated to studying and resisting economic reform: The Free Society of Political Economy (1857); the Association for Tariff Reform (1859); the *Revista Industrial*; the Spanish Economic Circle; and The First International. (see Schmidt-Nowara, *Empire and Antislavery*, 56–88.

[14] Transatlantic Slave Trade Database, comparing disembarkations of African slaves in Cuba 1848–1850 and 1858–1860.

[15] Corwin, *Spain and the Abolition*, 161–162; and See Murray, *Odious Commerce*, 299.

[16] Murray, *Odious Commerce*, 318–319.

earlier, in 1836, a shadowy abolitionist group seems to have briefly flickered in Madrid during a discussion of colonial reform in the Cortes. It had quickly disappeared, leaving no trace. From its founding in 1865, the Spanish Abolitionist Society aspired to model itself on the Anglo-American pattern of a popular movement. The abolitionists adopted the classic icon of a slave on bended knee, his chained hands raised in supplication. The Society established an international presence in correspondence with Victor Hugo.[17] In contrast to previous European emancipationist organizations, the Spanish Abolitionist Society considered itself to be an imperial, rather than merely a metropolitan, association. Its organizational godfather was Puerto Rican Julio Vizcarrondo. With other Puerto Ricans in Madrid, he spearheaded the founding of the Spanish Abolitionist Society in April 1865.

The Spanish abolitionists wanted to deploy the full panoply of Anglo-American techniques to mobilize public opinion. Unlike their continental predecessors, they quickly moved beyond the cautious modes of action that had characterized French abolitionism during most of the constitutional monarchy. The popular press, public rallies, and petitioning were immediately included in the movement's repertoire. Vizcarrondo's Philadelphia-born wife, Harriet Brewster, organized a women's chapter of the Society.[18]

The differences between the Spanish and Anglo-American movements, however, are readily apparent. The founder of the women's branch was triply an outsider in Madrid – she was the North American, Protestant spouse of a Puerto Rican. More significantly, there seems to be no evidence of women's collective activity after 1865. Equally noteworthy is the absence of a popular religious dimension in organized Spanish abolitionism. During the intensification of debates over the future of slavery after 1865, the Catholic clergy "were conspicuous by their absence. With rare exceptions, neither in Spain nor Cuba did they take up the abolition cause." There was a tendency among the secular Spanish abolitionists to deride the potential of religion to accelerate the emancipation process. At the high point of the debate over the Spanish law of emancipation, Emilio Castelar, a great orator and future president of the Spanish Republic, appealed to the legacy of Lincoln, Wilberforce, Wendell Phillips, and Toussaint Louverture. As for Catholicism: "Nineteen centuries of Christianity and there are still slaves among Catholic peoples! One century of revolution and there are no slaves among revolutionary peoples."[19]

The activities of British nonconformity and of the second great awakening in the Northern United States had no organizational counterpart in

---

[17] Jordi, Maluquer de Motes, "Abolicionismo y Resistencia a la abolicion en la España del siglo xix," *Anuario de Estudios Americanos*, 43 (1986), 311–331, esp. 315–316; and Corwin, *Spain*, 158–159.

[18] Schmidt-Nowara, *Empire, and Antislavery* 117; and Corwin, *Spain*, 159.

[19] Quotations from Corwin, *Spain*, 166, 250.

the Spanish movement. Membership in the Spanish antislavery movement appears to have been overwhelmingly secular and usually anticlerical in its affiliations as well as its rhetoric. This had important implications for popular antislavery as well. In the Anglo-American orbit, religious institutions were always an important means of mobilizing a large, cross-class antislavery constituency. In Spain, the movement seemed to be of limited popularity among working-class Spaniards. When one of the largest public abolitionist rallies in Madrid attracted a crowd of between ten and sixteen thousand people, abolitionists noted the absence of workers. They had to be satisfied with a claim to have the "solid support of Madrid's middle classes."[20]

The political economy of the imperial complex also limited the effectiveness of antislavery's popular appeal. In Spain, abolitionism was linked to the movement to dismantle the protectionist structure of the metropolitan political economy. Against the abolitionists were arrayed major groups, public and private, who profited from the neomercantilist strategy of making Cubans pay high prices for both protected Spanish commodities and foreign products. "Full blown free trade" meant the loss of the Cuban market because of the relative weakness of Spanish industry.[21]

Pressures, both foreign and imperial, for abolition were met by a countermobilization led by metropolitan manufacturers, shippers, merchant houses, and bankers with interests in the imperially protected Cuban market. These groups were primarily interested in the slowest possible transition from slavery to freedom, assuring both sustained colonial production and Spain's retention of the island. Against immediate abolition, therefore, ranged a list of figures "that read like a who's who" of Spain's most prominent capitalists and political figures.[22]

Within Spain, this elite was able to organize a metropolitan countermobilization that equaled, if it did not surpass, the abolitionist effort. In 1872, the Spanish Cortes prepared to vote on immediate abolition for Puerto Rico. The dozens of petitions favoring abolition were met by more than one hundred antiabolitionist petitions from all over Spain. They testified to the linked political interests of Cuban slave owners and protectionist metropolitans. In 1872–73 antiabolitionists could attract the signatures of more than a thousand petitioners in Barcelona and organize an insurrection in Madrid. The Catalonian petitioners included artisans as well as merchants, ship owners and industrialists from Barcelona. Abolitionists countered with a national petition drive to demand immediate abolition in Cuba as well as Puerto Rico. They organized public demonstrations in more than half a dozen major cities

---

[20] Schmidt-Nowara, *Empire*, 152.
[21] Robert Whitney, "The Political Economy of Abolition: The Hispano-Cuban Elite and Cuban Slavery, 1868–1873," *Slavery and Abolition*, 13:2 (August 1992), 20–36, quote on 23.
[22] *Ibid.*, 29.

from Barcelona to Cádiz. Filipinos, blacks, and workers joined artists, merchants, and bankers in these public parades. Finally, the abolitionist forces in both Puerto Rico and Spain succeeded in enacting abolition in Puerto Rico in March 1873, along with transitional compulsory labor provisions.[23]

The abolitionist mobilizations in Spain never worked as smoothly as they had in the British colonies or the northern United States. Abolitionist popular contention did not always elicit orderly interactions with governmental authorities or favorable legislative outcomes. A good case, in fact, can be made for the argument that Spanish imperial abolition proceeded according to Blackburn's model of revolutionary emancipation in which the institution's dismemberment emerges out of a convergence of political economic and social crises often tangential to the issue of slavery itself.[24] In the decade after 1865, Spain was beset by a severe economic crisis in 1866, political revolution entailing a change of dynasty and a short-lived republic in 1873, and a monarchical restoration in 1874. The decade was punctuated by working class and peasant rebellions, and radical republican resistance. The elite Liberal and Conservative legislative parties had no mass following and often needed military support to secure power. Instability within the metropole was more than matched by a deeper and more durable conflict in Cuba as a war of independence raged from 1868 to 1878.

Beyond the metropolitan and imperial orbits, lay an Anglo-American world no longer divided over slavery. Both the United States and Great Britain applied persistent, if varying, pressures on the Spanish government in favor of abolition. In the period just before the Cuban revolution of 1868, these extraimperial pressures probably played an important role in accelerating Spain's movement toward abolition. As soon as the U.S. Civil War ended, both the British and American governments pressed for a final end to the Cuban slave trade. As indicated, the final decree in Spain (September 1866) and its proclamation in Cuba (September 1867) were little than more exercises in ritual burial. The Spanish government also initiated an enquiry into possible emancipation. It convened a special commission on its overseas empire the (*Junta de Informacion de Ultramar*). The Junta immediately faced a deep split between the elected Puerto Rican and Cuban commissioners. The majority of the Puerto Rican delegation favored the immediate abolition of slavery for their island, with or without indemnification. The Cuban delegation countered with a proposition for gradual emancipation based upon the principle of immediate freedom for slaves over 60 years, all newborn children of slaves (*vientre libre*), and children under 7 years. The infants and children would be bound as apprentices to their mothers' masters until the age of 18 years. The Cubans wanted a compensation fund to be established for the owners of the approximately 300,000 remaining slaves.

---

[23] Schmidt-Nowara, *Empire and Antislavery*, 153–154.
[24] Blackburn, *The Overthrow of Colonial Slavery 1776–1848* (London: Verso, 1988), ch. 1; and Schmidt-Nowara, *Empire and Antislavery*, 157–160.

It would be raised from Cuban revenues usually destined for the Spanish treasury. The Spanish government accepted the Junta's consensual conclusion that the problem of slavery had to be resolved by emancipation. It remained undecided, however, on a plan for implementation. The mode of indemnification to be borne by the metropolitan treasury was deemed unaffordable and unacceptable. Spain was simply too poor to follow the British abolitionist model. Moreover, in 1867, it was impossible to gauge Cuban public opinion. Public discussion of abolition in Cuba had been under ban for a decade and was largely inoperative during the deliberations. In both of Spain's Caribbean islands, the positions of the Junta's colonial delegations were denounced for having drifted so far in the direction of abolition.

As soon as the Junta disbanded, the government found plausible reasons for delaying even gradual action. The Spanish Abolition Society, temporarily outlawed, found it difficult to publicize its cause.[25] Nevertheless, the brief period of open metropolitan discussion after 1865 appears to have encouraged the free labor vision of Antillean slaves as potential laborers who would respond "naturally" to economic incentives. In this respect, the Spanish abolitionists faithfully adhered to the principles of political economy that the British abolitionists had adopted in their campaigns for colonial slave emancipation.[26]

It is noteworthy that the threat of racial revolution played no major role in the Junta's extended discussions. In this respect, the Junta's deliberations resembled the British rather than the American discourses preceding their respective debates over emancipation. There was no defense of slavery, such as John C. Calhoun's speech before the United States Senate exactly thirty years before, arguing "that in the present state of civilization where two races of different origin . . . and . . . physical differences, as well as intellectual, are brought together, the relation now existing in the slaveholding states between the two, is instead of an evil, a good – a positive good." In the subsequent debates, there was a vision of the white racial and cultural unity of "Spaniards" on both sides of the Atlantic. Racial competition was often framed as a global race between the Latin and Anglo-Saxon races for the occupation of the New World. This could be accomplished by the relative marginalization of the African race through a policy of mass immigration of whites to Cuba.[27]

The next move towards emancipation emerged from the clash of opinions in political and civil society in almost simultaneous uprisings on both

[25] Corwin, *Spain*, 189–215; Schmidt-Nowara, *Empire*, 107–108.

[26] Above all, see Thomas C. Holt, *The Problem of Freedom: Race Labor and Politics in Jamaica and Britain, 1832–1938* (Baltimore: Johns Hopkins University Press, 1992), ch. 1–3; Drescher, *Mighty Experiment*, 138; and Schmidt-Nowara, *Empire and Antislavery*, 120–121.

[27] Fredrickson, *Black Image in the White Mind*: The Debate on Afro-American Character and Destiny, 1817–1914 (New York: Harper and Row, 1972) 47; and Schmidt-Nowara, *Empire and Antislavery*, 105–106; 118–122.

sides of the Spanish Atlantic. In September 1868, a military-led coup proclaimed the "Glorious Revolution," announcing the downfall of the Bourbon monarchy. The new Spanish government, dominated by generals, was
torn over a number of vital issues: choosing between a more constitutional
monarchy under a new dynasty or forming a new republic; shifting Spain's
political economy of protectionism towards free trade; integrating the overseas colonies into a more imperial parliament; and implementing a slave
emancipation project that had already been accepted in principle by the
previous government. Attracted by the British example of orderly transition, the Junta was deterred by the potential compensation costs of emancipation, which might undermine state finances that depended so much on
the slave plantation sector of the empires. However, there was no systematic pro-slavery defense of the institution of slavery either in the deliberations of the Junta or subsequent debates over emancipation in the Cortes
itself. On the contrary, both proponents and opponents of the emancipation
bills focused upon the least disruptive means of terminating the institution. Like its Pennsylvania precedent, the Spanish emancipation law placed
a biological time limit on the institution. By simultaneously freeing both
newborns and those more than 65 (later 60) years of age, it even designated a definitive termination date. All those unlucky enough to be born
before the date of the Glorious Revolution in 1868 would not be free until
1928. In defending the delay, the law appealed to Abraham Lincoln's pre-
presidential prediction of a peaceful termination of American slavery around
1900. Lincoln's forecast was to be repeated many times by conservatives.[28]
The result of emancipation efforts in Spain was the Moret Law of July 4,
1870.[29]

Across the Atlantic, the colonies themselves were deeply divided over the
pace and direction of colonial reform. Puerto Rico, less dependent upon
slavery, encouraged its abolitionists to press for immediate abolition, with
indemnification as a secondary concern. A far more hostile Cuban position,
elaborated by the old planter elite, was suddenly called into question in
October 1868, by a revolution within the island. This major uprising became
known as the Ten Years War (1868–1878). The origins of the war lay in
the divergent development of two different areas of the island. Although
Cuban slavery as a whole had been dramatically expanding during the fifty
years before 1868, it was the western half of the island that had prospered
most through the marriage between sugar and slavery. In the 1860s, slaves
accounted for half the population of the boom areas. Indentured laborers raised the proportion of unfree laborers to 60 percent. The peak years
for imported indentured Chinese laborers came in the four years between
the dramatic drop in African imports in 1864 and the outbreaks of the

[28] Corwin, *Spain*, 250.
[29] *Ibid.*, 246–247.

revolution in 1868. As elsewhere in the Americas, Cuban sugar production reached a thirty-year peak at the same moment.[30] From the perspective of Cuba's slaveholders, the 1868 Cuban uprising for independence came at the very moment when unfree labor was at the peak of its contribution to their prosperity. In those areas where both reliance on slave labor and the potential threat of social disorder were greatest, the vast majority of planters were therefore most unwilling to either endanger the institution of slavery or support an insurgency against Spanish rule. The economy of eastern Cuba had fared less well after 1850. In this part of the island, coffee, tobacco, and cattle farms, standing alongside sugar estates, were a much more significant part of the region's economy. The institution of slavery was correspondingly weaker. In the area where the rebel movement of 1868 gained its first foothold, slaves represented less than 2.5 percent of the population. In none of the jurisdictions where it took root did the slave population account for as much as 9 percent of the inhabitants.[31]

This did not mean that abolition was a higher priority among those who began the Cuban uprising than among the initiators of the earlier wars of Spanish-American independence. It is true that the revolutionary Carlos Céspedes addressed his slaves as "citizens" on the first day of the Cuban uprising. He assured them: "You are as free as I am," and invited them to join the fight for Cuban independence. The first collective revolutionary manifesto, however, proclaimed only the principles of gradual and indemnified abolition, which had been accepted by all delegates to the Madrid Junta the year before. Moreover, the rebels noted that the emancipation was to be implemented only after the successful completion of the war.[32]

As in most of the Spanish Americas, slavery in Cuba was to be ended only gradually and hesitantly over the course of decades. Even in the area dominated by the insurgency, the need to appeal to slaves and reassure masters meant that the path to liberation remained uncertain. It reflected the elite leadership's hesitations about the very people to whom liberation was being offered as an inducement to loyalty. The revolutionaries had deep reservations about the slaves' fitness for immediate civil and political freedom. As with so many combatants before them, they tried to differentiate between the slaves of opponents, whom they could liberate and recruit for action, and slaveholding revolutionaries, whose property rights must be respected. The leadership opportunistically expanded an original decree (April 1869) liberating all inhabitants, then backtracked by requiring all citizens to lend their "services" as required by the new regime.

---

[30] Rebecca J. Scott, *Slave Emancipation in Cuba*, 29, Table 6 and Eltis et al., database on slave arrivals in Cuba.

[31] See Ada Ferrer, *Insurgent Cuba: Race, Nation and Revolution, 1868–1898* (Chapel Hill: University of North Carolina Press, 1999), 17–21, and Table 1.1.

[32] Ferrer, *Insurgent Cuba*, 22.

In effect, Cuban revolutionaries faced the same problem of labor withdrawal that had confronted Victor Hugues, Toussaint Louverture, and others in situations of revolutionary war. It was necessary to keep a sufficient number of people in menial tasks to serve as domestics or provide supplies for the fighting forces.[33] Even when forced labor was officially ended in rebel territory at the end of 1870, no ex-slaves were to be free to remain idle. What occurred, even within insurgent lines, was a constant renegotiation of the boundaries of freedom. Because those boundaries shifted with the fortunes of war and the presence of Spanish or loyalist troops, ex-slaves also had more leeway to desert to loyalists claiming that they had been carried or lured away by rebel forces that they now rejected.

As in previous conflicts, continuous appeals for recruitment clearly eroded the institution of slavery by the ten-year duration of the war and the indeterminacy of its outcome. In 1878, the peace terms worked out in the Pact of Zanjon freed all slaves and indentured servants currently in armed insurrection. In the two rebellious provinces of Puerto Principe and Santiago de Cuba, the revolutionary decade saw slave numbers dramatically diminish from 62,300 to 15,350, a decline of 75 percent. In the heavily enslaved provinces with less impact from the war, the slave population diminished by only one-third. Some of the diminution was due to the operation of the metropolitan Moret Law of 1870. During the turmoil of hostilities, the Moret Law became a more porous institution than had been intended. In addition to free-birth and old-age liberations, all slaves not registered in the previous censuses were automatically freed. This provision also liberated ten thousand *emancipados*. These were the Africans who had been rescued from slave ships and placed under Cuban masters for a limited period of service. For many, their service obligations had turned out to be lifetime bondage.[34]

Because, by 1878, there were no longer any slaves below the age of nine or over sixty most of the diminution of slavery in the prosperous west was a result of the operation of the Moret Law. As in so many previous conflicts, a decade of revolution had accelerated the process of slave labor concentration in the most prosperous agricultural zone. If Cuban slaveholders actually demonstrated "a diminishing emotional attachment to the formal institution of slavery," the emotion seems to have varied according to conditions of comparative profitability. Sugar planters appeared to be the most determined to make maximum use of the diminishing supply of slaves for as long as possible.[35] In the zone of insurgency, the war undoubtedly changed

---

[33] *Ibid.*, 27–35.

[34] See, Scott, *Slave Emancipation*, ch. 4.

[35] For the above paragraph, see Scott, *Slave Emancipation*, ch. 4, quotation on 107. In considering the comparative impact of the insurrection of 1868 and the Moret Law on gradual abolition in 1870, the latter was, of course, less of a shock to Cuban slaveholders than

master-slave social relations. Spanish authorities recognized that ex-slave rebels, if forced to return to their old habitations, were "likely to demoralize the slave forces and become fugitives [*cimarrones*]."[36] For those slaves who fled and survived the conflict, the war clearly accelerated their personal liberation.

The rebellion alone, however, did not force Spain to yield to pressures for emancipation. In imperial perspective, there were other forces besides the eastern Cuban uprising at play in Spain's uneven path towards emancipation. In fact, the metropolitan government responded to the revolutionary challenge by withholding abolition from Cuba. They feared that abolishing slavery under the threat of violence would lead them down the costly economic path of the Franco-Caribbean revolutions and the American Civil War. The Spanish government instead relied upon loyalty of the slaveholders and the military support of mobilized Spanish loyalists ("the Volunteers") in Cuba. These two groups enabled the Spanish authorities to retain control over most of the island.

The loyalist forces remained sufficiently powerful within Cuba to expel a Captain-General in 1869, whom they deemed too conciliatory towards the insurgents. However, the government simultaneously experienced contrary pressures from its other Caribbean colony, ironically one more completely under Spanish control. In the same month as the Cuban uprising, a separatist insurrection broke out in Puerto Rico. It was suppressed within a few days. Puerto Rican abolitionists then pushed for a legal resolution of the emancipation question. They argued that slavery was sufficiently insignificant and free labor sufficiently abundant that neither a racial threat nor a labor problem stood in the way of immediate implementation.[37] The United States government added some exogenous pressure to this intraimperial debate. It offered its "good offices" to help negotiate an end to the Cuban insurrection, in which Spain would recognize Cuban independence, slavery would be abolished, and Cuba would pay an indemnity for all public property belonging to Spain. The American government ominously added that if Cuba remained "unsettled," the United States might recognize the insurgents' status as belligerents with eventual recognition and arms shipments. The threatening terms of the U.S. proposal were leaked to the press by a member of the Spanish government. There was such a popular outcry in Madrid that

was the outbreak of the Ten Years War. The war quickly reduced slave prices by more than 30 percent from 1868 to 1869. (Bergad, *Cuban Slave Market*, 61). As the insurrection was confined within eastern Cuba, slave prices recovered and finally exceeded the peaks previously reached in the 1850s. Only in the late 1870s did prices fall until complete emancipation was achieved in 1880. Even with only a limited horizon, Cuban slaveholders in settled areas continued to purchase slaves at prices that allowed for short-term use. (*Ibid.*, 61).

[36] *Insurgent Cuba*, 68.
[37] Schmidt-Nowara, *Empire and Antislavery*, 132–137.

the Spanish government, aided by French, British, and Prussian diplomatic support, refused the American offer.[38]

Because the United States was claiming reparations from Britain for its recognition of the South's belligerent status during the Civil War, the United States did not follow through on its threat to recognize the Cuban insurgency. The American and British governments and Puerto Rican abolitionists now argued that the insurrection in Cuba offered no reason for delaying action on slavery in Puerto Rico. Disarming an American public that favored the Cuban rebels, the Spanish government enacted emancipation in Puerto Rico, where neither its national honor, imperial authority nor its metropolitan popularity were in question. As noted above, in principle, the Moret Law of 1870 combined the Pennsylvania model of freedom from slavery at birth with a British-style compensation package and a clause postponing Cuban emancipation during the conflict. Because the empire's slave colonies were constitutionally integral parts of the Spanish kingdom, in 1870 Spain became the last European state outside the Ottoman Empire to announce that there would be no more slaves born on Spanish soil. All slaves more than 65 (later 60) years of age, all *emancipados*, and all who served in Spanish forces against Cuban independence were likewise freed.[39]

Passage of the Moret Law gave the Spanish government no respite on the question of slavery. Two problems still remained unresolved – the issue of indemnity and the continuity of labor. As many historians have noted, the tone of the final parliamentary debates of 1879–1880 was far different from those on the Moret Law a decade earlier. There was less heated abolitionist rhetoric within a conservative gathering concerned almost exclusively with problems of post-emancipation labor continuity and damage control to the sugar industry.[40] The Spanish government was still in no fiscal position to compensate Cubans for its 200,000 slaves as it had done in the case of the far smaller cohort of 31,000 Puerto Rican slaves in 1873.

Just ten years after the Moret Law, the Emancipation Law of 1880 combined a declaration of immediate abolition with an eight-year condition of restricted labor. The law created a new institution the *patronato*. Like British apprenticeship, it guaranteed the continued labor of the ex-slaves. This system was to last for eight years as a partial substitute for the promised indemnity. The ex-slaves could shorten their period of constraint by buying out of the *patronato*. The law of 1880 not only ended slavery, but set dates for timed liberations of apprentices, culminating in 1888. In each year, between 1884 and 1887, one quarter of each master's slaves was to be freed.

---

[38] Corwin, *Spain*, 232–234.
[39] *Ibid.*, 24.
[40] Scott, *Slave Emancipation*, 123–124.

Slaves could also purchase their own freedom or reduce the time of service by installments. The Cortes passed the law by a large majority in 1880 and Cuba became the next to last area in the Americas to abolish the institution. On the island, the emancipation act went into force with far less fanfare than had accompanied emancipation in the British Caribbean or even in Puerto Rico only seven years before.

The low level of intensity was paralleled by a high level of acquiescence in Cuba. The postponement of full freedom was accepted without any uprisings. Three years after emancipation, a British Vice-Consul could not recall any Spanish law that was "carried out or executed so near to the letter of the law as this Emancipation Act of 1880." The new system also offered greater leverage at the individual level for determining the course of emancipation. Again, abolitionist pressure, as in the British case, brought the transition system to an end two years before its scheduled expiration. The final denouement of October 7, 1886 was implemented almost without resistance, either in Spain or Cuba.[41]

During the sixteen-year transition from the Moret Law to the end of the *patrocinado*, Cuban slaveholders seem to have managed the transition to freedom with less interruption, if not with less plantation violence, than all of their predecessors. They did so through alternative labor immigration. The new labor supply came in various forms: indentured workers, convicts, soldiers, and free workers.

The slaves' participation in the armed struggles for independence may have eased the struggle for full citizenship in another way. Cuban ex-slaves did not suffer the regression of political and civil rights that afflicted contemporary southern blacks in the United States. From the perspective of the sugar industry, Cuba's production dropped by only three percent in the *patrocinados* years (1881–1886) compared with the prior equivalent period. During the six years following the end of the *patrocinado* in 1886, Cuba's average annual output actually increased by 18 percent.

The process of imperial abolition in the Spanish empire contrasted with those of Britain, France, and the United States. Before the 1860s, neither the virtually slaveless Spanish metropolis nor the Caribbean slave colonies had a geographical or public space in which antislavery could easily move from a diffuse sentiment to political abolitionism. Nor was there an autonomous slave uprising strong enough to call the institution of slavery into question. The Spanish empire had the distinction of being the last large-scale importers of African slaves in the Americas. Extraimperial forces clearly dominated in the timing of the slave trade's termination in the mid-1860s. The institution of slavery itself was placed under new pressure. Deep and violently opposed factions developed in both metropole and the colonies in favor of advancing

---

[41] Corwin, *Spain*, 307–311; Scott, *Slave Emancipation*, 129–140.

or retarding an emancipationist agenda. The foreign threat was often more critical than intraimperial conflicts in forcing decisive action. Abolitionism developed to different degrees among elites in all three zones of the Spanish Atlantic empire.

It was the smallest unit, Puerto Rico, in which the public pressure was first decisively mobilized in favor of immediate emancipation. Puerto Rico also acted as the imperial catalyst for decisive action. In Spain, the forces aligned both for and against abolition seemed evenly balanced. They made any option but the most gradual transition difficult. By contrast, the Cuban independence movement was clearly unable mobilize the bulk of the island's free population into a victorious coalition against slavery.

As in the earlier Spanish wars of independence, slaves escaped and won freedom through the crevices created by conflicts among the nonslaves. They could not mobilize sufficient independent power to force both sides to destroy the institution by reciprocal bidding for slave support alone. The fighting slaves, however, left a fruitful legacy beyond the ending of the institution. As in previous Spanish-American conflicts, they opened a route to post-emancipation political rights that was rescinded or postponed in the Anglo-American post-slave societies. It was an advantage that they would sorely need in a late nineteenth-century Euro-American world that was increasingly tolerant of a racialized view of the human community.

However belatedly, the Caribbean remnant of the Spanish empire followed the pattern laid out by its Latin American predecessors more than half a century earlier. Gradual slave emancipation came partly as a byproduct of a struggle for independence within deeply divided societies and through unstable polities on both sides of the Atlantic.

Brazil

Unlike its counterparts in the Anglo-French Caribbean and North America, Brazil entered the third quarter of the nineteenth century with a dynamic and thriving slave system. Its export economy continued to be heavily dependent upon slave labor into the 1880s, particularly in the coffee sector, which was situated in the central-south of the large nation. The abrupt termination of the slave trade to Brazil required adjustments but seemed to place the institution of slavery itself under no immediate economic or political threat. Brazil's labor requirements for growth of its economy remained but were far less acute than they were to become a generation later. Sugar, coffee, and cotton continued to be major export commodities. In the late 1850s, there was a temporary decline in sugar output but cotton and coffee continued their upward climb in value and volume over previous decades. In response to rising slaves prices, productivity also increased.[42]

---

[42] Eltis, *Economic Growth*, 193–196, 285–286, Tables F.3, F.4, and F.5.

Towards the end of the 1850s, the coffee sector in south-central Brazil was tangibly more buoyant than other zones of the country. In the absence of the African source of labor, this meant that coffee planters began to draw slaves from other economic sectors and regions. Before the end of the American Civil War, however, this did not have major disruptive effects upon the relations between the principal crop sectors or their regions. During most of the 1850s, the slave price differential between the coffee zone of Brazil's South-Center and the markets of the cotton and sugar zone of the northeast was relatively small. The threat of internal shifts in the regional distribution of Brazilian slaves still seemed remote.[43] Into the 1860s, the slave trade *within* the most dynamic coffee-growing sector was probably more important than any intraregional transfers from outside. What was occurring, therefore, in all regions in the 1850s entailed internal transfers of slaves from towns and small slaveholder farms to more prosperous proprietors. The pool of slaves in these marginal or domestic economic activities still constituted a large reservoir of slave labor that could be drawn upon by the plantation economies throughout the nation.[44]

In short, midway through the nineteenth century Brazil, had experienced no major sectional conflict of interest, social movement, or ideological offensive that threatened the immediate future of the institution of slavery in the manner of the crisis in the United States. The institution of slavery was still legally intact in every Spanish republic bordering Brazil except Uruguay. Slavery was still a virtually unchallenged institution from the Amazon to Rio Grande do Sul. The dominant conservative party focused on facilitating economic development so that the merchant and planter elites could do "what they had always done with greater advantages of access, security and capital."[45] In no decade since Brazilian independence had the institution of slavery seemed less threatened. Externally, the abolition of the slave trade

[43] See Robert Conrad, *The Destruction of Brazilian Slavery 1850–1888* (Berkeley: University of California Press, 1972), 54–65; and especially Robert W. Slenes, "The Brazilian Internal Slave Trade, 1850–1888: Regional Economics, Slave Experience and the Politics of Peculiar Market," in *The Chattel Principle*, Walter Johnson, ed. (New Haven: Yale University Press, 2004), 333–339.

[44] Slenes "Brazilian Internal Slave Trade," 331, estimates that about 5,000 slaves a year were transferred to the coffee-producing areas from other regions in the 1850s. This accords with contemporary British estimates. See Bethell, *Abolition*, 373–374; and Eltis, *Economic Growth*, 195. The deurbanization of slaves was analogous to that in the United States in the 1850s. (Ibid., 341–343). It was well into the 1870s before the interregional market became more robust and 10,000 slaves a year were transferred southward. In the 1850s, the main political concern of slaveholders in exporting regions was to slow down the rate of slave transfers because of the rising price of labor. A legislative attempt to prevent interregional trading failed to block the flow of slaves. See Richard Graham, "Another Middle Passage? The Internal Slave Trade in Brazil," in *Chattel Principle*, 291–324.

[45] Jeffrey D. Needell, *The Party of Order: The Conservatives, the State, and Slavery in the Brazilian Monarchy, 1831–1871* (Stanford: Stanford University Press, 2006), 161; Roderick Barman, *Citizen Emperor: Pedro II and the Making of Brazil, 1825–1891* (Stanford:

had been a tacit bargain within the elite to disentangle Brazilian society from the continuous British imperial and abolitionist intrusions that had weighed on Brazil for a generation.

Slave trade abolition was intended to silence further agitation from within as well. During the 1850s, Brazilian governments confidently resisted all attempts by the British governments to resolve residual problems linked to the slave trade. These included the fate of thousands of Africans recaptured by the British navy and brought to Brazil to serve out fixed periods of "apprenticeship." In fact such assignments often amounted to lifetime servitude. Brazil was not only able to fend off British interference with these *emancipados* but to resist all suggestions to establish a registry of slaves. Everyone knew that this had been the abolitionists' first step on the road to British colonial slave emancipation after the Napoleonic wars. The British also made a point of not interfering with the intercoastal traffic transferring slaves from one part of Brazil to the other. The Brazilian government also made it categorically clear that all Africans illegally imported into the country between 1830 and 1850 would remain in slavery. The planters remained confident in the duration of their own institution at the time of American Southern secession.[46]

Despite the ending of its African labor supply, the nation's annual production of coffee tripled between 1850 and the eve of abolition. The demand for slave labor in the dynamic Center-South coffee region of the nation remained so strong that slave prices continued to rise for three more decades.[47] Unlike the situation in the British Empire and the United States, industrial and commercial enterprises also developed within the most dynamic slave regions. The same held for the transportation sector. In the Anglo-American world, railroad building proceeded most rapidly in areas without slave labor. In Brazil, the opposite held true. Again, the coffee region was the pioneer zone. In 1889, the three provinces of Rio de Janeiro, São Paulo, and Minas Gerais had 65 percent of Brazil's total railroad mileage. At the time of the passage of the gradual abolition act in 1871, there were less than 500 miles of track in Brazil. Almost all of it was located in the Center-South area. Even in

Stanford University Press, 1999), 193; and Robert Conrad, *The Destruction of Brazilian Slavery, 1850–1888* (Berkeley: University of California Press, 1972).

[46] Graham, *Britain and the Onset of Modernization in Brazil* (London: Cambridge University Press, 1968), 168, 376, 382. See Robert Wayne Slenes, "The Demography and Economics of Brazilian Slavery 1850–1888," Ph.D. Dissertation, Stanford University, 1975, 358.

[47] Robert W. Slenes, "The Brazilian Internal Slave Trade, 1850–1888. Regional Economies, Slave Experience, and the Politics of a Peculiar Market," in *The Chattel Principle: Internal Slave Trade in the Americas*, Walter Johnson, ed. (New Haven: Yale University Press, 2004), 328, Figure 4.2 "Slave Prices in Relation to Coffee and Sugar Prices: Plantation Regions of the Center-South and Northeast, 1850–1885" and Conrad, *The Destruction of Brazilian Slavery 1850–1888* (Berkeley: University of California Press, 1972), 304, Table 26, Brazilian Coffee Production, 1850–1890.

1880, at the beginning of the intensified pressure for abolition, 78 percent of Brazil's 2,000 miles of track was still located within the Center-South. Railroads were built primarily to serve the flow of slave-grown products for the international market. International capital, too, flowed most abundantly into the zone of dynamic slave production.[48]

Other leading indicators of economic modernization followed the same pattern. Nearly seven out of every eight migrants to the United States settled in the free labor states and western territories. The much smaller migration flow of free persons to Brazil showed precisely the opposite pattern. Nearly seven out of every eight settlers settled in the provinces with the greatest numbers and proportions of slaves.[49] The magnitude of migration to the United States was, of course, much larger. In 1860, there were four million foreigners in the United States. More were located in the U.S. South alone than resided in all of Brazil at the time of its 1871 gradual emancipation law. It is clear, however, that migrants to Brazil moved to those areas where the growth of slave labor also was most evident. Brazilian urbanization followed the same pattern. The largest cities in the nation had proportions of slaves that were equal to or well above the proportion of slaves in Brazil as a whole (16 percent) at the time of the gradual emancipation act of 1871.[50]

Thus, many of the indicators of economic modernization ordinarily invoked to demonstrate nineteenth-century progress under free labor were more characteristic of the most dynamic slave regions of Brazil. Industries were not the main factor in the growth of Brazilian cities as they were in other parts of the world. Urbanization was primarily the product of commercial expansion "resulting from . . . the vitality of the export economy much more than the expansion of the sugar market." Brazil's ports were more closely linked to Europe than they were to their own hinterlands, both economically and culturally. Industrial growth was modest and, until the 1880s, industrialists tended to align themselves both socially and politically with the landed elite. Nor was there any large-scale middle class mobilization against slaveholders during the third quarter of the nineteenth century: "[For] every one

---

[48] See Mircea Buescu, "Regional Inequalities in Brazil During the Second Half of the Nineteenth Century," *Disparities in Economic Development Since the Industrial Revolution*, Paul Bairoch and Maurice Levy-Leboyer, eds. (New York: St. Martin's Press, 1981/85) 349–358; William R. Summerhill, *Order Against Progress: Government, Foreign-Investment, and Railroads in Brazil, 1854–1913* (Stanford: Stanford University Press, 2003), 54–57; and Emilia Viotte da Costa, *The Brazilian Empire: Myths and Histories* (Chicago: Dorsey, 1985), 192.

[49] See Drescher, *From Slavery to Freedom: Comparative Studies in the Rise and Fall of Atlantic Slavery* (New York: New York University Press, 1999), 126–127, Tables 5.1 and 5.2; and Merrick and Graham, *Population and Economic Development*, 73.

[50] Compare Conrad, *Destruction*, 284, Table 2, Free and Slave Populations of Brazil, 1874, and Drescher, "Brazilian Abolition," 127, Table 5.2, Percentage of the labor force in the four largest cities of Brazil.

in the middle classes who supported abolition or who joined the Republican party there was another who sided with the traditional oligarchies."[51]

As indicated earlier, regional stresses developed only very slowly after the closing of the Brazilian transatlantic slave trade. The inexorably diminishing slave population, from small slaveholders to large planters, from cities to the countryside, and from the less dynamic northeast to the more robust Center-South sustained slave prices for three decades after 1850. The major legislation in the dismantling of the institution of slavery, the Rio Branco law, was taken well before the slow regional redistribution of slaves could have decisively affected the political process of abolition. Before the passage of the Rio Branco law, there was no "free labor" area in the empire to act as haven for fugitives or as a base from which to attack the national institution of slavery.

Political power also remained concentrated in the hands of the slaveholders, the monarch, and their allies. Politics was constitutionally designed to be the prerogative of a socially cohesive if geographically dispersed elite. In its seigniorial political culture, the fundamental distinction within free citizenry was between a "class...of well-off citizens" and a "class of those less favored by fortune."[52] In this respect, Brazil's Constitution of 1824 was analogous to that of the French constitutional monarchy during the first half of the nineteenth century. It was designed to be a regime of "notables," with a monarch, a Senate, an elected Chamber of Deputies, and a cabinet-style government. The executive, Emperor Pedro II, was endowed with a "moderative power" including the right to form cabinets and to appoint senators for life from a list of three candidates chosen by the Chamber of Deputies. He also had the power to dissolve parliaments and call for new elections.

Beyond the constitutional division of powers, in which the monarch's role was clearly dominant, every effort was made to ensure the influence of the elite within a larger society dominated by patronage and hierarchical networks of influence. The government chosen by the emperor appointed socially prominent local leaders to extend their clientele and advance their own subordinates within a cascading scale of power and influence. The system aimed to maximize moderation, elite representation, parliamentary government, and legal and social stability.[53] The representative system was equally designed to mute conflict in favor of elite consensus. National

[51] Quotations from Costa, *Brazilian Empire*, 194, 196; see also Conrad, *Destruction*, 145; and Warren Dean, *The Industrialization of São Paolo, 1880–1945* (Austin: University of Texas Press, 1969), 36–38.

[52] Quoted in Roger A. Kittleson, *The Practice of Politics in Postcolonial Brazil* (Pittsburgh: University of Pittsburgh Press, 2006), 22.

[53] Richard Graham, *Patronage and Politics in Nineteenth-Century Brazil* (Stanford: Stanford University Press, 1990), ch. 2; Jeffrey D. Needell, *The Party of Order: The Conservatives, the State, and Slavery in the Brazilian Monarchy* (Stanford: Stanford University Press, 2006), ch. 3.

elections were carried out in two steps. Voters (qualified by gender, age, and financial independence) chose provincial electors. This "electoral college" collectively selected the candidates who would be seated in the Chamber of Deputies. The cabinet, however, chosen by the emperor, appointed the local magistrates and police chiefs, whose main function was to fix the elections and to produce a working majority for the administration.[54]

This outcome was usually achieved through a mixture of reward, fraud, social pressure, and violence. What Richard Graham refers to as the "theater of elections" was designed to dramatically reproduce the layered social system before closely watched individual voters. Varying degrees of rewards and coercion could be applied to reinforce the power of authority and the outcome of local elections. As election by fraud became routinized, the Chamber's role as the representative of the nation's will was subverted. The very success of the system also lessened the utility of elections as indicators of public opinion.

To gauge public sentiment, the emperor and his cabinets had to rely on the political press, collecting summaries filtered up through the provincial executive's private correspondence or gathered from trusted advisors and highly structured encounters with less well-connected commoners.[55] The notion that the Chamber did not truly represent the will of the people actually made the emperor more tolerant and desirous of a free press. Newspapers had remarkable latitude for criticism of the government and the political system. Even after the deep political crisis that culminated with the abolition of the slave trade, civil liberties were maintained. Long before the emergence of any popular movement for abolition, urban newspapers might routinely condemn slavery in Brazil in a manner that would have elicited official reprisals in Cuba or popular violence in the U.S. South.[56]

From the 1840s through the 1870s, however, journalists appear to have had little purchase whatsoever in the Brazilian parliament, even during the intense debates over the gradual emancipation ("free womb") debates of 1871. Nor did they stimulate a durable popular movement before the 1880s. Newspapers were also tainted by well-deserved reputations for being subsidized by different pressure groups and even foreign interests.[57]

There seems to be little evidence that groups or geographical regions active in abolitionist movements elsewhere in the Atlantic world played a prominent role in pressing for abolitionist initiatives during the generation

---

54 Needell, *Party of Order*, 176.
55 Graham, Patronage, ch. 3, 4. On Pedro II's means of sampling the opinion of his subjects, see Roderick J. Barman, *Citizen Emperor, Pedro II and the Making of Brazil, 1825–91* (Stanford: Stanford University Press, 1999), 179–189.
56 Barman, *Citizen Emperor*, 192; and Dale Torston Graden, *From Slavery to Freedom in Brazil: Bahia 1835–1900* (Albuquerque: University of New Mexico Press, 2006).
57 See Eltis, *Economic Growth*, 114–115, on British official bribery of the press, justices of the peace, officers of customs, etc., in matters related to the abolition of the slave trade.

after the closure of the Brazilian slave trade in 1850. As in Spain, the organized Church played no role in the passage of the Rio Branco law in 1871. Reflecting their relatively small role in organizations outside religious and charitable institutions, women appear to have been largely absent from anti-slavery activities in Brazil before the 1880s. Slaves themselves never ceased to attempt to gain individual or group liberation through flights to *quilombos* or maneuvering for individual manumission. There is evidence in the secondary literature of continuous resistance along these very traditional lines but no measurable upsurge in collective resistance or violence during the generation after 1850.[58]

Whatever the activities of those outside the narrow political elite, the first moves to place slavery on the national political agenda in Brazil appear to have been taken by emperor Dom Pedro II himself, and directly against the wishes of the majority of the "party of order." Memory of the traumatic British incursion of 1850 was reinforced by Britain's six-day naval blockade of Rio de Janeiro in January of 1863 on behalf of freedom for the *emancipados*. It was a sharp reminder of Brazil's vulnerability. The hundreds of thousands of slaves illegally transported from Africa after 1830, in violation of Anglo-Brazilian treaties, and their children, were hostages to future interventions. As in Cuba, the turning tide of the American Civil War compounded the emperor's anxieties about the future of the institution of slavery in Brazil. The fate of the United States offered a glimpse of the divisive potential that slavery might produce in Brazil. Brazil's minister in Washington also kept his government as fully informed about the implications of a Northern victory as did his counterpart in the Spanish embassy. In January 1864, the emperor brought the envoy's dispatches to the cabinet's attention: "Events in the American Union require us to think about the future of slavery in Brazil, so that what occurred in respect to the slave trade [in 1850] does not happen again to us."[59]

The Emperor was also concerned with Brazil's standing in the "civilized world" after the sequence of Lincoln's emancipation proclamation, the passage of the Thirteenth Amendment to the U.S. Constitution, and the convening of the Spanish Junta for colonial reform in Madrid. Brazil aspired to be an outpost of European culture and civilization in a nation with the highest proportion of population of African descent on the mainland of the New World. The emperor's whole political position derived from a constitution modeled on the French monarchy. His cultural capital was Paris. He was more sensitive to a strongly worded petition for abolition emanating

[58] See Roger A. Kittleson, *The Practice of Politics in Post-Colonial Brazil*, 46–47, 82–83. Graden surveys a large number of incidents of slave resistance throughout the empire in the late 1860s and early 1870s, concluding that slaves played "an undiminished role." (*From Slavery to Freedom*, 70–72).
[59] Bethell, *Abolition*, 382–383; Borman, *Citizen Emperor*, 195.

from a French abolitionist committee in July 1866 than to the steady stream of denunciations coming from a few Brazilian poets and journalists in the 1860s. Although he did not have to respond to the letter of a foreign private committee, he persuaded his cabinet to reply to the French notables that emancipation was only "a question of means and opportunity."[60]

In Brazil, the political opportunity took longer to evolve than it did in the Spanish empire. Brazil was less vulnerable to immediate external pressure than the Spanish government at the end of the American Civil War. The emperor proceeded cautiously. In his annual speech from the throne in 1867, Dom Pedro II announced that "the servile element cannot fail to merit your consideration at the appropriate time" carefully adding that it could be done only "while respecting existing property and without causing great upset to agriculture, our leading industry." Whereas warfare in the United States and Cuba accelerated moves towards abolition, Brazil's own major conflict in the 1860s actually postponed further legislative initiatives. The Paraguayan War (1864–1870) demanded an unprecedented mobilization of Brazilian human and fiscal resources. In these circumstances the Brazilian cabinet, dominated by conservatives, refused to bring the issue before the legislature pending a final victory in Paraguay.[61]

In other ways, however, the war highlighted the stresses between the slave-holding political elite and the central government. Once beyond an initial phase of enthusiasm, the government experienced increasing difficulties. The prolonged conflict created a series of deepening social tensions in both the cities and the countryside and between the state and the provincial plantation interests. The latter were reluctant to diminish their policing resources against potential slave unrest by depleting the local national guard. When conscription of free Brazilians (denounced as slavery) brought increasing resistance, the emperor's decision to recruit slaves elicited resistance from the master class.

Brazil's anemic political and associational system depleted the government's ability to rally any segment of the nation in favor of slave recruitment. Unlike the situation in the United States, "neither organized social movements nor the pressure of public opinion" supported the government's action. Slaveholders resisted any diminution of their slave labor force. Faced with a negative fertility rate among slaves, the closing of the African slave trade meant that the slave population was inexorably declining. Consequently, private donations of slaves amounted to only 2 percent of Brazil's entire wartime slave recruitment of 4,000. More than half of the recruits came from areas dependent upon imperial domination. Slaveholders regarded any seizure of their own slaves as an imperial wedge toward broader emancipation. No forced levy was instituted, but taking advantage

---

[60] Barman, *Citizen Emperor*, 209–210.
[61] See Needell, *Party of Order*, 233–255.

of the high proportion of colored troops in the Brazilian military, some slaves fled to enlist, posing as free men.[62] Most significantly, the government felt it necessary to discuss the entire question of abolition as a matter of national security behind closed doors. Even parliament was excluded from the discussion, which was limited to the Council of State.

Given the reluctance of the slaveholders to relinquish their slaves, the government decided to concentrate on recruiting slaves owned by the state and church. By law, the slaves would have to be freed before induction into the military. Because state owned slaves were considered to be living in better conditions than those in the private sector, Nabuco de Araujo, father of the future abolitionist, recommended that their "capture" and induction be carried out in secret to prevent any slave refusals of freedom or flights from service. Moreover, among all of the participants in the cabinet favoring slave recruitment, urban dwellers and undesirable slaves were the preferred targets. Nabuco wanted to favor rebellious urban slaves whose location and concentration constituted a permanent danger to public order. Urban recruitment would complete the task already begun, after 1850, by the market-driven redeployment of slaves from cities. Another member considered recruitment as a step towards emancipation via decimation. By consigning blacks to the battlefields, as happened elsewhere in South America, their mortality would improve, that is, whiten Brazil's long-term racial configuration while alleviating the immediate military crisis.[63]

In contrast to their situation in the United States, conscripted freedmen in Brazil were still fighting for a slaveholding state. Taking advantage of the weakening of the policing apparatus, slaves occasionally rebelled in peripheral provinces remote from the main centers of plantation slavery. More frequent were the instances of desertion. Their decisions were part of the larger panorama of desertion from conscription, mutinies, or attacks against police escorts of chained or jailed recruits. The rise in successful flights indicated a breakdown of the traditional constraints on lower class behavior but neither dramatically undermined the institutions of the army or slavery.[64]

During the late 1860s, moves towards deliberate emancipation in Brazil continued to come from above. When the emperor openly raised the question in Parliament for the first time in May 1867, it "was like a bolt of lightning in a cloudless sky." Thereafter, all forward movement was blocked by the cabinet from 1868 to 1870. Only with victory achieved over Paraguay in May 1870 could the emperor move forward without fear of subverting the

---

[62] Victor Izecksohn, "War, Reform and State-Building in Brazil and the United States: Slavery, Emancipation and Decision-Making Processes in the Paraguayan and Civil Wars (1861–1870)," Ph.D. dissertation, University of New Hampshire, 2001, 305, 326–327.

[63] *Ibid.*, 315–318.

[64] *Ibid.*, 188–201.

military effort. The role of the emperor in bringing the issue to a head seems manifest.[65] As further evidence of the emperor's own intentions, his son-in-law, the Count d' Eu who commanded the victorious Brazilian forces, urged the Paraguayan government to abolish slavery in 1869. This is probably the only instance in which a slaveholders' state induced the abolition of slavery in another nation while still sustaining the institution at home.

In Brazil, however, even with the enormous weight of his constitutional prerogatives, it took Dom Pedro II months to assemble a cabinet willing to bring Brazil's first abolition bill to the legislature in May 1871. The heart of the Rio Branco law, named after the leader of the Cabinet, provided for the emancipation of all slaves born after its passage. Its precedents stretched across nine decades, from Pennsylvania's law in 1780 to Spain's Moret Law of 1870. Raising the "free womb" children was the masters' obligation for eight years. The master could then choose to relinquish the responsibility for an indemnification or use the children's labor as compensation until they reached the age of twenty-one. Those who remained slaves were afforded the option of buying out the remaining value of their labor service. As had been the case in one system after another since the Napoleonic wars, all slaves had to be registered under penalty of confiscation and liberation.[66]

In a comparative perspective, popular mobilization before the Rio Branco law appears unimpressive. Setting aside the mass movements of the Anglo-American world, even French abolitionism just before the revolution of 1848 and Spanish abolitionism in the decade after 1865 played larger roles in placing emancipation on their national parliamentary agendas. Some Brazilian antislavery societies appeared briefly after 1871, but then languished. Bahia's Society reappeared only in 1883. The most detailed account of the passage of the Rio Branco law offers evidence that both abolitionists and their opponents in the Chamber of Deputies spoke as though "public opinion" was not in favor of the gradual emancipation bill.[67]

Instead, the mobilization over the bill came primarily from those who vigorously opposed it. During months of legislative debates, opponents of the bill "began to enter into the record something unprecedented in Chamber

---

[65] Joachim Nabuco, *Abolitionism*, 49; and Needell, *Party*, 238 Appropriately, Barman's recent biography entitles the chapter on abolition "Triumphs of the Will, 1864–1871."

[66] Conrad, *Destruction*, 90–91. There has been much dispute over the role of elite, popular, and even slave abolitionism as catalysts of the Rio Branco law (Emilia Viotti da Costa, *Da Senzala à colônia* (São Paulo: Livraria Editora Ciencias Humanas, 1982), 379–80; Conrad, *Destruction*, 80–85; Robert Brent Toplin, *The Abolition of Brazilian Slavery in Brazil* (New York: Athenaeum, 1972) 41–46; Barman, *Citizen Emperor*, 195–196. Graden, *From Slavery*, ch. 3, argues in favor of a large role for slavery. See also Richard Graham, "Causes for the Abolition of Negro Slavery in Brazil: An Interpretive Essay," *Hispanic American Historical Review*, 46:2 (May 1966), 123–137 and especially Needell, *Party of Order*, 233–240, and Ch. 7, who are skeptical about the predominant role of popular mobilizations.

[67] Needell, *Party of Order*, 263, 289, 412, Graden, *From Slavery*, 227.

history." There were petitions from merchants and planters of Rio and its environs. Once the principle of gradual emancipation was decided upon, the planters and merchants launched another round of petitions to foreclose any threat to their hegemonic position in the traditional rural economy.[68] The account of this campaign offers a glimpse at the dimensions of Brazilian civil society at that juncture. For the elite in the Chamber, public opinion in Brazil still meant what it had signified in most of continental Europe a generation before – the opinion of those who still dominated political discourse. In 1870, both pro- and antislavery factions were still part of this self-contained elite. The conservatives opposed to the Rio Branco bill could still depend upon the hostility of most of the landed class and the nonparticipation of the free population at large. Even when slaveholders routinely acknowledged the moral inferiority and doomed destiny of slavery, antislavery sentiment had not yet become politicized public opinion.

In terms of racial ideology, the debate in the Brazilian legislature most closely resembled the discourse that had just occurred in the Spanish Cortes. No one in the Chamber argued that slavery was morally or racially preferable on grounds of race. No one attacked the right of freed or free Afro-Brazilians to participate as citizens because of their racial origins. No one argued that the slaves lacked the civilizational development to enter fully into the larger society. The emerging society of all adult slaves under forty years of age had been nurtured in a Brazilian milieu. To the extent that the fate of those to be emancipated was discussed, it was whether the ranks of the newly freed were to be formed "naturally" by the operation of the free-womb principle or controlled by planters' gradual emancipations of annual cohorts.

In assessing the reason for the passage of Rio Branco through an elite-dominated legislature in the absence of pressure from without, Robert Conrad offers a regional explanation. A regional split among the elite pitted "region against region," setting militant anti-Branco coffee planters against moderate and declining planters.[69] The argument is plausible but it remains unclear just why this split occurred. As indicated above, the interprovincial trade was far lower in the 1850s and 1860s than it was to become in the 1870s. Neither northern fears of losing slaves nor Center-Southern fears of a loss of northern "interest" in slavery were clearly articulated in the course of the Rio Branco debates. There is also an unexplained regional "anomaly" in the voting data. The Center-South legislators in the lower House voted *against* Rio Branco by 2.5 to 1. senators from the same region voted by 2 to 1 (and, including Rio Grande do Sul, by almost 3 to 1) in favor of the law. Conrad's explanation of the anomaly, that the senators were unresponsive to regional considerations, is not compelling. Senators were putative "representatives" of their provinces' elites

---

[68] Needell, *Party of Order*, 289.
[69] Conrad, *Destruction*, 91–93.

no less than members of the Chamber of Deputies. Needell offers a different explanation. The poorer deputies from the poorer northern regions were
more dependent upon government patronage. Those deputies were voting in
response to the ministerial patronage system and not because of a different
ideological position towards slavery or more disinterest in the future of the
institution.[70]

Had the coffee provinces already been seriously alarmed by the erosion
of commitment to slavery within the provinces or the regionalized voting on
Rio Branco, the political movement to close down or constrain the internal
slave trade would have begun at the time of Rio Branco rather than the end
of the 1870s. Equally clear is the minimal presence of Brazil's slaves and
the free poor in the legislative discourse. The euphemistic references to the
"servile element" are noteworthy in their marginality. Even when abolitionists made reference to "servile insurrections," they most often referred to
insurrections long past or of different empires – to the Haitian Revolution
of the 1790s or to the uprisings in Demerara (1823) and Jamaica (1831).
The Mâlé uprising in Bahia, Salvador, in 1835, was the only Brazilian revolt
noted alongside the others. The slaves, of course, remained as a looming
presence but no major surge of collective violence or flights accompanied
debates over emancipation that stretched out over four full months from
May through September of 1871. On the contrary, in Salvador, slave flights
fell to their lowest point in a decade.[71] This was certainly not because the
question of their own emancipation was at issue in the legislative debates. As
far as emancipation was concerned, neither those enslaved nor their living
children were helped by the law. Apart from slaves owned by the state, none
were liberated. The zone of freedom was restricted to the wombs of enslaved
women. Free womb still meant servile body. A national emancipation fund,
created to stimulate and accelerate master-initiated liberation, resulted in
only 11,000 manumissions, or less than 1 percent of the Brazilian slave population during the 1870s. The absence of any wave of revolts or conspiracies
in 1871 may indicate the low expectations of the slaves themselves during
or following the long debates in Rio de Janeiro. Only in one province was
there "a surge of unrest," perhaps in disappointment over the fact that the
Rio Branco law had freed no living slaves at all.[72]

The slaveholders remained sanguine about their future as masters. Robert
Conrad concludes, "an important result of the Rio Branco Law was the
postponement of true abolitionism as the Rio Branco government had
hoped...."[73] After the law's passage, slave prices stabilized and then rose to

[70] Needell, *Party of Order*, 300.
[71] Graden, *From Slavery*, 46; Needell, *Party of Order*, 415–416, finds a deficiency of direct
evidence for large-scale slave agency in 1871 as compared with 1878–1888.
[72] Conrad, *Destruction*, 105.
[73] Although Needell explains why northern deputies voted in favor of Rio Branco he does not
explain why South-Central senators also approved it by a margin of 2 to 1. Presumably they
were less susceptible to the economic pressures exerted on northerners in the lower House.

heights in the coffee region unequalled since the peak years of the late 1850s. The domestic slave trade also increased. The volume of the interprovincial slave trade doubled from its level near the end of the U.S. Civil War. As late as 1880, slaveholders still expected slavery to last another forty years.[74]

Whatever their differences of interpretation regarding Rio Branco, there is widespread agreement among historians of Brazil that the 1880s witnessed a new form of mobilization against the institution of slavery. Before the 1870s, Brazilian planters had never had to worry about the double threat that faced other slaveholders in the Americas at the end of the age of revolution. All of them contained large metropolitan or domestic areas without slaves. Most also contained zones with rapidly diminishing proportions of slaves and slaveholders (e.g., the upper U.S. South, Puerto Rico, and Western Cuba.) There was no area of Brazil where both slaves and the institution of slavery itself were not integral to the social and legal order.[75] Thus, as far as the Brazilian master class was concerned, there appears to have been no deep sectional division of political attitudes toward preserving the institution of slavery or the status of the slave labor force even into the late 1870s. Indeed, the major sugar planters of the northeast bought significant numbers of slaves from within their own regions. In contrast to the U.S. South, it was the cotton growers of Rio Grande do Norte, Ceará, Paraíba, and Piauí who suffered the greatest losses of major staple producers. Under the combined pressures of falling world prices and a severe regional drought between 1877 and 1880, slaveholders in these areas shipped record numbers of their chattels to more remote markets. Rio Grande do Sul's beef-raising zone also increased exports from Brazil's southernmost province to the more prosperous Center-South coffee region in the 1870s.[76]

The interprovincial slave exchange accelerated in the 1870s and was to have important consequences in the following decade. Slaves entering the Center-South provinces for sale surged in the 1870s. During that decade, the annual interregional transfers reached about 10,000 per year, double

---

[74] Pedro C. de Mello, "Expectation of Abolition and Sanguinity of Coffee Planters in Brazil, 1871–1881," in *Without Consent or Contract: Conditions of Slave Life and the Transition to Freedom Technical Papers*, Robert William Fogel and Stanley L. Engerman, eds., 2 vols. (New York: Norton, 1992), ch. 32, 629–646, Table 32.3 "The 'Political Death' of Slavery," 644. Conrad reasonably begins the "era of abolition" only at the end of the 1870s. (Conrad, *Destruction*, Part Two, 1879–1888), and for Needell, the 1871 struggle "is the culmination of a large political history of which abolition itself is a crucial but not the central, issue." (Needell, *Party of Order*, 320).

[75] See William W. Freehling, *The Reintegration of American History* (New York: Oxford University Press, 1994), ch. 9, 10; Ferrer, *Insurgent Cuba*, ch. 1; Nowara, *Empire*, ch. 2; Conrad, *Destruction*, 284–285, Tables 2 and 3; and Slenes, "Brazilian Internal Trade," 340–346.

[76] Slenes, "Brazilian Internal Trade," 337–339; and Peter L. Eisenberg, "A Mentalidad dos Fazendeiros no Congresso Agricola de 1878," in *Modos de Produção e Realidade Brasileirà*, José Roberto do Amaral, ed. (Petrópolis: Vozes, 1980), 167–194.

the average before 1865. When compared with regional transfers in the United States, movements of slaves in Brazil occurred over extremely long distances. Many of these slaves were sent overland under conditions that rivaled the Middle Passage of the Atlantic trade.[77] The impact on slaves in terms of family and community disruption was correspondingly intensified in the late 1870s. Slave transfers from Bahia briefly reached their all time peak in the mid-1870s, as did fugitive slave arrests. The uprooting and separations affected both those deported and those detained. They prepared the way for the slave uprisings that were to occur at the heart of the dynamic coffee sector in the late 1870s and 1880s.[78]

Already, on the eve of popular abolitionism, the flood of slaves to the Center-South coffee region was causing widespread concern in major plantation zones of Brazil. By the late 1870s, some northern planters, blaming the growing labor shortage in their area on the Rio Branco law and the interregional movement of slaves, no longer looked to slavery as the solution for their continuing labor problems. They suggested luring free European laborers with guarantees of military exemption and positive incentives, including public investment in schools. In the Center-South area, suspicion grew that the more distressed provinces were unburdening themselves of their "dreadful merchandise" as quickly as they could. The nightmare of the U.S. cotton South returned to haunt Brazil's Center-South area.

In the coffee zones, the planters watched with rising anxiety as the urban areas, led by the national capital Rio de Janeiro, reduced their slave populations between the 1850s and the beginning of the 1880s. At a time when prices for slaves were at their all time peak, bringing twice as much in real terms as they had in 1850, a bill was introduced into the São Paulo Provincial Assembly to impose a prohibitive tax upon further imports of slaves.[79] Even before the emergence of an abolitionist movement planters sought to stem the potential erosion of a commitment to the national institution in slave-exporting provinces. A similar motion was introduced into the national Chamber in 1880. The bill was defeated by a coalition that included a significant bloc of northerners anxious to keep the interprovincial market open to sustain the maximum value of their human capital. The Center-South was still further alarmed by "the ever-increasing disproportion of the number of slaves in the northern and southern provinces" increasing the necessity to "preserve the uniformity of the interests of the whole country."[80]

---

[77] Conrad, *Children of God's Fire: A Documentary History of Black Slavery in Brazil* (Princeton: Princeton University Press, 1983), 354–355.

[78] Maria Helena Pereira Toledo Machado, *Crime e Escravado* (São Paulo: Brasiliense, 1987), 48–49.

[79] Conrad, *Destruction*, 170 and Mello, "Expectation," 635, Table 32.1 Rio de Janeiro: All Slave Prices, 1835–1887.

[80] *Gazeta de Tarde*, September 17, 1880, quoted in Conrad, *Destruction*, 172.

The Center-South, Rio de Janeiro, São Paulo, and Minas Gerais rapidly passed prohibitive duties on the further importation of slaves from the other provinces. This action had an important ramification in the north. Five days after the passage of the São Paulo restriction, an abolitionist group in one of the most depressed northeastern provinces successfully mobilized to close the port of Ceará. They did so to lower the price of its slaves and accelerate the dispersal of public funds established to purchase manumissions. By mid-1881, liberation societies had emerged in six of Ceará towns. They launched a town-by-town expansion of free-soil zones. Slaves were liberated either voluntarily or by popular subscription. By the spring of 1884, the abolitionists of Ceará notified the world by telegraph that "Ceará is free." Although pockets of slavery actually remained in the province, the Ceará action acted as the model for local liberations all across Brazil. Soon dubbed a "second Canada," Ceará became a refuge for fugitives from neighboring provinces in a Brazilian underground railway that ultimately extended to the heartland of the Center-South.[81]

The new national context of abolitionism remained far more reassuring to the "slaveocracy" for the institution than the sectional division over the interprovincial slave trade. The last stages of Brazilian slave emancipation were to occur within a political system that dramatically reduced the electorate allowed to participate in the voting process. A rapidly expanding urban population began to challenge the traditional power of the planters over their rural dependents. Some planters also feared a diminishing capacity to sustain control as the free-womb law increased the size and electoral weight of the rural masses. As a result, the final stages of abolition coincided with a dramatic reduction in the numbers of those eligible to vote. A new electoral law in 1881 cut against the dominant Western precedent during the late nineteenth century. It established a minimal property qualification combined with rigorous demands for documentary proof of income. The law effectively excluded the great mass of the people who previously had been eligible to vote. The registration list was now reduced to fewer than 150,000 electors in a population of 13 million, or less than 2 percent of Brazil's adult male population. In terms of the formal political process, the final battle of abolition therefore occurred within a dramatically shrunken electoral sphere. At the provincial level, too, legislators sought to evade any discussion of abolitionism well into the 1880s.[82]

---

[81] Conrad, *Destruction*, 176–192; Graden, *From Slavery*, 164.

[82] Graham, *Patronage and Politics*, 196–205. In 1887, a Liberal member of the Chamber of Deputies noted that in some interior counties the number of electors was less than thirty, leaving these areas without enough eligible citizens to fill the necessary political offices. *Ibid.*, 205. In 1886, the last legislative elections before Brazilian slave emancipation, there were 117.7 thousand voters in a national population of 13.2 million, or 0.89% percent exercising the suffrage. In the first presidential election under the new republic in 1898, there were 462.2 thousand voters in a population of 17.1 million, or 2.7 percent. The electoral base

In an equally significant development, the constriction of legislative discussion of abolition was matched by a corresponding expansion of Brazil's
extra-parliamentary public sphere. Historians of Brazil seem to be largely
in accord on this phenomenon. Beginning in 1880, there was enormous
innovation and expansion in urban politics.[83] The impetus for abolition no
longer emanated from an emperor seeking malleable ministers to ensure the
end of the institution over the lifetime of its remaining slaves. The emperor
himself seems to have found popular abolitionism ever more distressing during the 1880s. His anxiety was underlined by his departure for Europe at
the critical climax of the abolitionist campaign in 1887–1888. In contrast
to his earlier voyage in 1871, this journey signified his loss of control over
the political process.

Not since British abolitionist mobilization, ninety years before, had extra-
parliamentary agitation appeared to play so large a role in a relatively nonviolent victory for abolition. In 1879, an initial motion in the Chamber of
Deputies, requesting steps towards full emancipation, fell on deaf ears. The
following year, the motion's reintroduction coincided with the organization
of clubs formed to arouse popular opinion outside the legislature. During
the parliamentary session, an Emancipation Association and Brazilian Anti-
Slavery Society formed in the capital, aiming to nationalize the movement
through propaganda and public meetings. Following North Atlantic models, a movement journal, *O Abolicionista*, called for a crusade against the
institution. Unsure of its base at home, the small movement, like the Spanish
Antislavery Society, sought to internationalize Brazilian antislavery. They
elicited a letter from the United States ambassador that dramatized the
North American exit form slavery. A banquet in America's honor featured
a portrait of Abraham Lincoln reading the Emancipation Proclamation to
his Cabinet.[84]

Brazilians within and beyond the political elite began to understand political action in a new way. Ceará's provincial designation of its territory
as "free soil" transformed the way that slaves, as well as free citizens,

---

expanded under the republic, but because literacy was a prerequisite of voting participation,
the proportion of ex-slaves allowed to vote must have been well below the national average
of accessibility. The national literacy rate was only 14.8 percent in 1890. See Joseph L.
Love, "Political Participation in Brazil, 1881–1969", *Luso-Brazilian Review*, 7:2 (1970),
3–24. On the provincial legislature's reactions to the first wave of popular abolitionist
mobilization in the early 1880s, see Celso Thomas Castilho, "Abolitionism Matters: The
Politics of Antislavery in Pernambuco, Brazil, 1869–1888," Ph.D. Dissertation, University
of California, Berkeley, Fall 2008, 45–48.

[83] See Sandra Lauderdale Graham, "The Vintem Riot and Political Culture: Rio de Janeiro,
1880," *Hispanic American Historical Review*, 60:3 (1980), 431–449. See also Costa, *Brazilian Empire*, 193; Kittleson, *The Practice of Politics in Postcolonial Brazil, 1845–1895* (Pittsburgh: University of Pittsburgh Press, 2006), ch. 4; Graden, *From Slavery*, ch. 7, Liberation
1880–1888; and Castilho, "Abolitionism Matters," 80–146.

[84] Conrad, *Destruction*, 141–143.

understood abolitionism throughout the nation. In neighboring Pernambuco, thousands gathered in the city of Recife to celebrate the declaration. Newspaper support for abolitionism began to accelerate. Two foreign editors in Rio and new radical newspapers like the *Gazeta da Tarde* enthusiastically reported on abolitionist activities.[85] Still more significant were the novel forms of popular contention by which the new abolitionism began to be conveyed. The Brazilian extra-parliamentary movement was, of course, aware of Anglo-American recipes for popular mobilization. The first public meetings in Rio de Janeiro and Pernambuco were held in theaters and concert halls rather than town halls, churches, and chapels, which had formed the sites of Anglo-American gatherings. The latter had mobilized in imitation of their familiar political and religious venues. Solemn meetings followed the rules, procedures and discourse of civic assemblies, always ending in formal resolutions, votes, petitions, or resolutions calling for responses or pledges from legislators.

One of the striking differences between Anglo-American and Brazilian mobilizations was the dearth of national petitions from the Brazilian abolitionist repertoire. It was as though those who mobilized public events in support of emancipation expected no positive response to direct appeals to the formal legislative bodies. The way in which Brazilian mass mobilization differed from its Anglo-American predecessors may be indicative of the gap felt by participants in the civil and political orders in Brazil. The first British national mobilization in 1788 was immediately echoed by the leaders of both political parties in the House of Commons. Both the initial and later popular manifestations of abolitionism in Brazils' hinterland occurred in the teeth of national legislative silence and resistance. The abolitionist movement, into the mid–1880s had to grow province by province, municipality by municipality and block by block across the length and breadth of civil society.

Brazilian popular gatherings had little experience with successful direct legislative responses to pressures from without. Their gatherings flowed more easily from the familiar modes of public entertainment and street protest. The proportion of programs grounded in festivals and commemorations and given over to music, plays, and poetry at rallies would probably have surprised veterans of British or American abolitionist meetings half a century before. Rallies were as much performances as deliberative bodies.[86] As striking as the abolitionists' novel use of public space in Brazil was the expansion of popular participation. Brazilian abolitionists both followed and deviated from the path of British abolitionism in defining emancipation as much in cultural as moral terms. Carnival offered a major opportunity for popular mobilization. "The growth of the free Afro-Brazilian population in

---

[85] Conrad, *Destruction*, 148–149.
[86] Conrad, *Destruction*, 148–149; and Drescher, *From Slavery*, 138.

the latter half of the nineteenth century played a major role in transforming carnival celebrations. . . . from an elite show to a popular spectacle." In Pernambuco, an abolitionist society chose to participate in the celebration with an allegoric representation of a Congolese king. Campaigns to collect money for manumission funds allowed for women's public entry into abolitionism. On a scale not seen since the Anglo-American women's mobilization, abolitionism opened space for women. Already collectively involved in urban charitable causes such as caring for orphans, educating the children of the poor, and administering shelters, Brazilian women participated vigorously in abolitionist public events. They offered musical recitals and inspirational readings. They played prominent roles in organizing fundraising auctions, bazaars, and dances.[87]

Only the strong cultural barriers against women's engagement in more overtly political activity limited this "blurring of the lines of public politics." Because their roles continued to be defined as nonpolitical, the feminized discursive space of abolitionism could be politically effective in the mid-1880s. Women paraded openly in public processions as symbols of liberty but their antislavery contributions in newspapers and journals appeared anonymously. Few rose to leadership positions, but they could serve as members of commissions to liberate slaves. As in Britain eight decades before, women began to participate more directly in politics by going through city streets canvassing for abolition. As in the French and Spanish cultural orbits, the organized Catholic Church hesitated to identify itself with abolitionism, a source of bitterness among some of the movement's Brazilian leaders. Individual priests, however, echoed the new radical message of liberation. In September 1884, at the end of a two-day festival designed to raise ransom money for slaves, the Bishop of Porto Alegre celebrated a mass at the city cathedral.

By the mid–1880s, the institution showed clear signs of disintegration at the local rather than the national level. In the wake of the Rio Branco law of 1871, planters had remained quite optimistic that slavery would be stabilized until the free-womb law had run its slow course sometime in the twentieth century. In the 1870s, slave prices in the Rio de Janeiro slave market remained at levels equal to or exceeding the highs of the 1850s. Only the new abolitionist mobilization of the 1880s, and especially the increasing nationalization and coordination of local popular mobilizations in 1883–1884, seems to have altered the slaveholders' perspectives. Finally, large-scale slave conspiracies and flight sapped the slaveholders' confidence in the governmental apparatus.[88]

---

[87] Castilho, "Abolitionism Matters," 93–106; and Kettleson, *Practice of Politics*, 128–135.

[88] Maria Helena Machado, *O Plano e o Pânico: Os Movimentos Sociais na Década da Abolição* (Rio de Janeiro: UFRJ, EDUSP, 1994), ch. 4; 147–158. Several slave revolts in São Paulo were disrupted or disarmed in 1883 and 1885. *Ibid.*, ch. 2–5; Slenes, "Brazilian

As de facto zones of freedom were established on the Ceará model, the Brazilian Underground Railroad also came into its own. By comparison with the similar phenomenon in the United States, it was far more massive and far less "underground" than its predecessor. Fleeing slaves often used the new Brazilian railways themselves. Far more often than in the United States, flight was undertaken collectively, with slaves sometimes abandoning entire plantations. At critical moments, both the urban police and the armed forces proved unreliable, and even hostile, to attempts to enforce the law.[89]

Violence was not absent from Brazilian abolition. In view of the size of the slave population and the scale of its defiance and evasion of legal constraints, however, the final phase of Brazilian abolition almost certainly lies at the less violent end of the spectrum of resistance and rebellion. In recounting even the bloodiest of its incidents, most historians of abolition explicitly or implicitly note that violence and brutality were regarded as exceptional, not normative. Masters' use of violence shocked the public rather than polarizing it. It seems indicative that one of the worst incidents of vigilante violence involved two veterans of the U.S. Confederacy who had previously taunted Brazilian masters for their lack of manhood and honor. The U.S. southerners taunted their Brazilian fellow-planters with having "the blood of cockroaches" and called for "rivers of blood" against a police official who had refused to capture runaway slaves. In this instance, the government of a major slave-holding province was forced by public opinion to indict the vigilantes when they killed a police official who refused to capture runaway slaves. To a Brazilian witness, the American southerner "seemed taken with a mad fury.... jabbing the lifeless victim with his spurs."[90]

The shift in popular opinion was demonstrated in the public reaction to the mistreatment of slaves. Attempts at violent punishment seem to have increased sympathy for the slaves and further radicalized the movement. The case of four slaves condemned to whipping in Rio de Janeiro province in 1886 is striking. Two died while receiving a punishment of three hundred lashes. The outrage was so widespread that the minister of justice proposed outlawing whipping as a legal punishment. A bill to that effect passed into law within five days. The emperor wholeheartedly supported prohibition of the most crucial tool of daily coercion available to the masters. The rapid passage of the law through a legislature explicitly dedicated to making

Internal Slave Trade," 360. That no massive and successful slave uprising occurred in the climactic moments before emancipation may have resulted from to the combined abundance of alternatives in civil society and the increasing public intolerance of the ordinary forms of coercion.

[89] Robert Brent Toplin, *The Abolition of Slavery in Brazil* (New York: Atheneum, 1972) ch. 8; Conrad, *Destruction*, ch. 16. A slave population that had diminished by less than 20% between 1874 and 1884 dropped by more than an additional 40% in the following three years. (Conrad, *Destruction*, 285, table 3, "Slave Populations," 1864–1887).

[90] Toplin, *Abolition*, 212–213; Conrad, *Destruction*, 256–257.

no further alterations in the law was striking. Its passage may have been hastened by news of Spain's termination of the last constraints on ex-slaves in 1886.

When slaves themselves engaged in violence, they seemed to be testing the shift in public opinion. That many presented themselves to the authorities immediately after committing acts of violence indicates a substantial level of trust in the fairness of judicial authorities. As with the rebels of Demerara and Jamaica, rather than those of Saint Domingue, there were no accounts of slaves collectively extending their vengeance to the families of slaveholders. Public authorities carefully avoided summary executions and the whole arsenal of ritualized torture. After 1885, Brazilian slaves appear to have concluded that neither bloody insurrections nor guerilla warfare was necessary or productive.[91]

As the institution of slavery dissolved before their eyes, the planters tried desperately to hold on to residual aspects of the institution. They tried to elicit either monetary compensation or labor obligations in exchange for dissolving their proprietary legal claims. The planters of Rio Grande do Sul began to liberate their slaves en masse on the condition that they were to labor for between three and five years. In this context, the number of slaves fell 86 percent from 60,000 to fewer than 8,500 between 1885 and 1887. Capitalizing on the public agitation against exploitation of dependent labor, the new status of these "contractees" opened yet another door for legal challenges to masters' conditions as coercive. Thus, the courts became sites of further resistance.[92]

By 1885, planters in the dynamic coffee region collectively estimated that slavery would probably last no longer than the end of the decade.[93] In the wake of the resurgence of popular mobilization in 1883–1884, the Chamber of Deputies considered the first major revision of the Rio Branco law of 1871. The 1885 debate lasted even longer than its Rio Branco predecessor. Designed to halt the abolitionist momentum, this law took its cue from the Rio Grande do Sul model. All slaves over the age of 60 years were to be freed immediately. They were required to provide three more years of unpaid labor to their former masters. A fund was to be created to pay for liberated slaves nearing the age of liberation: The fund was also to be used to free younger slaves in exchange for five more years of forced labor and to subsidize the importation of labor from abroad. Prices on the Rio slave market showed that buyers were indeed estimating full emancipation in 1890.

A conservative victory in the national election of 1886 appeared to confirm the success of the slaveholding elite in stemming the popular tide of emancipation. The results aligned the imperial administration and the

---

[91] Drescher, *From Slavery*, 140.
[92] Conrad, *Destruction*, 209; Kittleson, *Practice*, 135–142.
[93] Mello, "Expectation," 664, Table 32.3.

legislature against further steps towards abolition. The major abolitionists were not returned to the Chamber of Deputies. Once again, however, events in the provinces demonstrated the fragility of the countermobilization at the national level. In the core slaveholding areas of the Center-South, massive slave flights began in 1886 and accelerated in 1887. In view of this dispersion, transition contracts lost their appeal to slaves who were witnessing the collapse of the institution. In June 1886, a Rio province master offered to manumit twelve slaves in exchange for a transitional labor contract. Under its terms, the slaves faced, at most, a contractual obligation of four to six years. One slave needed to work for only one or two more years. Everyone refused the offer. The slave's calculations were correct. The collapse of slavery came sooner than the planters expected, even in São Paulo itself – the hardiest zone the institution.[94]

Equally distinctive was the role played by the large, free-black population in Brazil. Except in Ceará, only a small minority of the population beyond the cities had participated in the earliest phase of the abolitionist movement between 1878 and 1882. Abolitionist leaders initially commented on the absence of ex-slaves and workingmen in their ranks. Nevertheless, there was also in Brazil an absence of the deep racial divide that had helped to make most U.S. Southern whites effective policing agents of the institution before secession and armed defenders of the Confederacy during a four year civil war. The demographics of Brazil's free population came into full play in the final phase of slave emancipation.

By 1886, abolitionists had built an effective organization able to go out to the plantations themselves and enjoin slaves to abandon estates en masse. The first masters to be targeted were those with the worst reputations. Abolitionists under Antônio Bento included blacks, whites, and men of all social classes. Once the slaves were convinced to escape, they were escorted on foot or by train to flee to the port cities. There, they formed part of an ever-increasing urban cohort marching in a redemptive procession, like the liberated Europeans three centuries before, to advertise their past victimization and current liberation.

The decisive failure of the slaves to sign up for transitional "conditional freedom" contracts that would have run to 1890 shifted the planters' concern toward the immediate recruitment of free labor. Some planters reached agreements with the abolitionist leader Antônio Bento to accept slaves who had abandoned other masters as laborers. The exchange of employers would in itself publicly notarize the new employer's acceptance of their liberty.

---

[94] On the election, see Graham, *Patronage and Politics*, 204–205. On slave flight, see Slenes, "Brazilian Internal Slave Trade," 361–362; and Maria Helena Machado, "From Slave Rebels to Strikebreakers: The Quilombo of Jabaquara and the Problem of Citizenship in Late Nineteenth-Century Brazil," *Hispanic American Historical Review*, 86:2 (2006), 247–274.

From the middle of 1886, the volume of mass flights began to cause an acute crisis in the supply of labor. This nonviolent dispersion offered no target for a military response other than guaranteeing that there would be no imminent danger to public order. In October 1887, the army officers asked the government that they be spared the humiliation of hunting down fugitive slaves. The commander of an army unit sent to São Paulo early in 1888 openly refused to capture slaves.[95]

Without legislation, a process that had evolved at the local and regional level was being resolved at the local level. The hemorrhage of its labor force, despite the opposition of both the national and provincial legislatures, finally convinced the coffee planters to accept the imminent demise of the institution. By 1886, coffee planters turned decisively toward importing free labor from outside Brazil. A new immigration society in São Paulo obtained a contract with the provincial government to provide transportation to the plantations. The level of European migration into São Paulo, especially from Italy, rose from 6,500 in 1885, to 32,000 in 1887, and 90,000 in 1888. The combined arrivals almost equaled the 107,000 slaves still registered in the province on the eve of abolition. The planters' successful importation of free labor within a year and a half converted the chief defenders of slave labor into leaders in the final thrust towards legal emancipation.

By the time the Chamber of Deputies began its session in May 1888, its immediate task was to regain legal management of an institution that was in the final stages of disintegration. The degree to which popular mobilization, both free and slave, had overwhelmed the legislative process may be seen in what did not become part of the final law. The conservative party was now willing to acquiesce on immediate emancipation, embedded in a century's traditional conditions. It wanted the bill to include monetary compensation in the mode of all of the European systems, from British colonial slave emancipation in 1833 to Puerto Rico in 1873. Indeed, following the enactment of emancipation, planters claimed an indemnification of about £20,000,000 for the 725,000 slaves who had remained on the registry of Brazilian slaves in 1887. This was, perhaps not coincidentally, exactly the sum that had been given to British colonial slave owners for 750,000 slaves fifty years earlier.

Like their predecessors, from Sonthonax in Saint Domingue to the Cortes in Spain, Brazilian masters wished to extend their ex-slaves' labor obligations. They wanted slaves to be forced to work for their masters through the next harvest, obliged to remain in their local *municípios* for six years, and penalized for vagrancy by compulsory labor. The Liberal majority in the Chamber realistically and successfully insisted that slavery would have to end without any residual obligations. The bill simply declared the immediate and unconditional extinction of the institution. It passed through the

---

[95] Conrad, *Destruction*, 251–252.

legislature in five days instead of the five months allotted to Rio Branco. For speed of passage, it most closely resembled the French Revolutionary session of 16 Pluviôse an II (February 4, 1794), far more than the extended Rio Branco debates. All regulations were swept away. The committee charged with guiding the bill through the legislature dispensed with all procedural requirements, even printing the bill to allow for a vote on the day after the final vote, May 13, 1888. The few supporters of slavery who accepted the unconditional bill noted that they had merely assented to reality. From the perspective of the Conservative party, the legislature's real task was to try to end the "insubordination, turmoil, the disruption of labor *and everything else*" that was required for law and order.[96]

Outside parliament, abolition's passage ended at it had begun, with celebrations. The festivities began as soon as the bill was introduced on May 8, 1888, and continued at every stage through the passage of the "Golden Law." Nevertheless, the enormous popular mobilization that flourished outside the nonslave institutions that had been designed to keep them marginal to decision making did not succeed in dramatically altering the elite-dominated political system. Radical abolitionist leaders' demands for a "democratization of the soil" through a division of large landholdings were not successful. In terms of political rights, the newly liberated were no more successful in gaining access to the suffrage than the overwhelming majority of the old free population. Brazilians did not gain even the temporary access to the vote, which freedmen in the United States enjoyed briefly after the Civil War. Nor were they able to gain such voting rights by their military participation in the Cuban revolutionary movements between the 1870s and national independence during the last third of the nineteenth century. The overthrow of Dom Pedro II by a military *coup d'etat* in 1889 established a conservative republic with only a slightly less restricted suffrage than the last imperial electoral system of 1881.[97]

Economically, blacks were soon marginalized by the huge migration of European labor. Socially, the "new infusion of blood" was designed to integrate a "whitening" Brazil more firmly into European civilization. From the perspective of their more constrained individual and collective lives as slaves, even marginalized newly freed men and women could still imagine their new condition as a real opportunity for greater independence, mobility, and potential advancement. From the perspective of overseas abolitionists, further removed from the day-to-day Brazilian struggle for existence, the most significant aspect of its abolition was seen as the final act of emancipation in the New World and its opening act in the Old one.

In his encyclical congratulating of Brazilians on the abolition of slavery in their country, Pope Leo XIII referred to the "new roads" and "new commercial enterprises undertaken in the lands of Africa," where apostolic men

---

[96] Conrad, *Destruction*, 257, 258, 270–276.
[97] Andrews, *Afro-Latin America*, 113.

could endeavor to find out how they could best secure the safety and liberty of slaves.[98] In Africa itself, David Brion Davis notes, a celebration of Brazilian emancipation took place in the small British colony of Lagos. The island had already become home to more than three thousand Afro-Brazilian *emancipados* who settled in the secure British enclave near Yorubaland, Nigeria. In response to the news of emancipation from across the Atlantic, a six-day commemoration was organized. It began with a high mass at the cathedral and ended with a carnival. The local Brazilian emancipation committee thanked the British government for the privileges enjoyed by the settlers, the endeavors of philanthropists to abolish the foreign slave trade, and for British slave emancipation. The governor of the colony expressed confidence that the repatriates of Lagos, increased by Brazilian emancipation, "would become a 'formidable contingent' in helping to liberate the African mainland."[99] The British governor alluded only selectively to a long British presence on the coast of Africa. But, his observation that a new phase of abolition had already begun in Africa was accurate.

---

[98] *In Plurimus,* Encyclical of Pope Leo XIII, 5 May 1888, To the Bishops of Brazil, art 20.
[99] Davis, *Slavery and Human Progress* (New York: Oxford University Press, 1984), 298–299, and Suzanne Miers, *Britain and the Ending of the Slave Trade,* (London: Longman, 1975) 49–50, 159.

13

Emancipation in the Old World, 1880s–1920s

Exactly a century after the first great stirrings of abolition in Britain, slavery had been legally abolished by Brazil's "Golden Law." In a broad swath of the Old World, however, stretching from the Atlantic coast of Africa through the eastern reaches of the Indian Ocean World, the institution of slavery remained both intact and robust.[1] When the Americas were closed to enslaved Africans in the 1850s and 1860s, the institution was attaining its maximum extension within Africa.[2] As noted in chapter 10, the World Antislavery Convention had been informed that there were 6 to 8 million slaves in India. Another contemporary writer placed the figure as high as 16 million or about one-tenth of the subcontinent's population. At that

---

[1] See, inter alia, *Breaking the Chains: Slavery, Bondage, and Emancipation in Modern Africa and Asia*, Martin A. Klein, ed. (*Madison: University of Wisconsin Press, 1993*) (*Henceforth: Breaking*); *The Structure of Slavery in Indian Ocean Africa and Asia*, Gwyn Campbell, ed. (London: Frank Cass, 2004); *Slavery and Resistance in Africa and Asia*, Edward Alpers, Gwyn Campbell and Michael Salman, eds. (London: Routledge, 2007); *Abolition and its Aftermath in Indian Ocean Africa and Asia*, Gwyn Campbell, ed. (London: Routledge, 2005); and *After Slavery: Emancipation and its Discontents*, Howard Temperley, ed. (London: Frank Cass, 2000). Also very useful is Martin A. Klein, "Slavery, the International Labour Market and the Emancipation of Slaves in the Nineteenth Century," *Slavery and Abolition*, 15:2 (1994), 197–220.

[2] On the declining importance of slavery in Indonesia from the early nineteenth century, see Anthony Reid, "The Decline of Slavery in Nineteenth-Century Indonesia," in Klein, ed. *Breaking*, 64–82; esp. 69–77). On Africa and the Americas, see Patrick Manning, *Slavery and African Life: Occidental, Oriental, and African Slave Trades* (New York: Cambridge University Press, 1990), 23; on India, see Dharma Kumar, "Colonialism, Bondage, and Caste in British India," in Klein, *Breaking*, 112–130; Howard Temperley, "The Delegalization of Slavery in British India," in *After Slavery: Emancipation and its Discontents*, 169–187, esp. 177; and Temperley, *British Antislavery*, 94; on Thailand, see David Feeny, "The Demise of Corvée and Slavery in Thailand, 1782–1913, in Klein ed. *Breaking*, 83–111. See also Martin A. Klein, "The Emancipation of Slaves in the Indian Ocean," in Campbell, *Abolition and its Aftermath*, 198–218, esp. 199–200.

moment, India probably contained more people in servile status than any other political unit in the world.

Old World servitude was not only larger and more widespread than its New World counterpart, but more diverse as well. In India, there was a range of servile statuses, some hereditary, some temporary, that Westerners subsumed under the rubric of slavery. These bondsmen and women occupied a wide range of niches, from those analogous to New World occupations in agriculture, industry, and households to eunuchs, concubines, courtiers, and military officers, without parallels in the Americas. Slaves were still being recruited through interregional slaving and assuring the institution's survival. The employment of slave sailors probably increased during the second third of the nineteenth century. With the exception of seamen on British ships, slaves and freedmen in the northern Indian Ocean "probably formed the majority of the crews on coastal and oceangoing ships, large and small" until the 1880s. Many thereby escaped the worst potential effects of slavery but their combination of mobility and constraint helps to explain their continued use into the last quarter of the nineteenth century.[3]

The transatlantic slave trade was characterized by relative stability in total volume during the first half of the nineteenth century, a sharp drop between 1850 and 1865, and final disappearance by 1870. In the Old World, Olivier Pétré-Grenouilleau estimates that the total long-distance Eastern trade (*"traite orientale"*) across the Sahara desert and Indian Ocean rose from 9,000 per year in the eighteenth century to 43,000 per year in the nineteenth century – a "veritable explosion" in coerced migration. In the Ottoman Empire, the slave trade appears to have reached its peak during the third quarter of the nineteenth century. Ehud Toledano estimates its volume, excluding Egypt's internal traffic, at around 11,000 captives per year. In the 1860s, just as the Atlantic slave trade was closing down, Egypt received 25,000 slaves every year, five times its average during the previous decade. Into the last quarter of the century, the distribution of slaves may have altered between one or another sector but the continuity of the system showed no signs of dramatic decline. The ending of the transatlantic slave trade resulted in transformations within slavery, but did not immediately threaten to eliminate the institution.[4]

---

[3] See Janet J. Ewald, "Crossers of the Sea: Slaves, Freedmen, and other Migrants in the Northwestern Indian Ocean, c. 1750–1914," *American Historical Review*, 105:1 (2002), 69–91, esp. 77, 90.

[4] Olivier Pétré-Grenouilleau, *Les traits négrières: Essai d' histoire globale* (Paris: Gallimard, 2004), 149, and ch. 3. (See also note 86, below) On Africa, see inter alia, Paul Lovejoy, *Transformations in Slavery: A History of Slavery in Africa* (New York: Cambridge University Press, 1983); Trevor R. Getz, *Slavery and Reform in West Africa: Toward Emancipation in Nineteenth-Century Senegal and the Gold Coast* (Athens, OH: Ohio University Press, 2004), ch. 2. On the Ottoman Empire, see Ehud Toledano, *The Ottoman Slave Trade and its Suppression: 1840–1890* (Princeton, NJ: Princeton University Press, 1982), 90.

Deeply embedded in Africa, slavery demonstrated persistence and vigor into and past the fourth quarter of the nineteenth century. For many areas, historians have estimated the slaves at between one-fifth and one-half of the total population – from Madagascar to northwest Africa.[5] On the eve of the era of intensified European imperialism, slavery was expanding in sub-Saharan Africa. Even at the height of the transatlantic slave trade, the majority of enslaved Africans were probably retained in Africa. Given the preponderance of enslaved males among the exported "huge numbers of women and girls must have been absorbed before the departure of the residue."[6] The process of gradual exclusion of the slave trade from specific coastal areas during the first half of the nineteenth century and its relatively abrupt closure during the third quarter reinforced the tendency for the accumulation of slaves within Africa. The example of the Gold Coast after British slave trade abolition was emblematic of a more general development. The sharp drop in slave prices a decade after the Anglo-American abolitions of 1807 made slave owning more affordable to farmers and traders outside the elite. The expansion of palm oil plantations by the late 1830s allowed the use of slaves to play an even larger role in the economy. Despite occasionally rising prices, slave labor was still cheaper and more available than wage labor.

The Anglo-American abolitions, rather than ending slavery, facilitated the commercialization of agriculture and promoted the integration of servile labor into a capitalist production system in Africa, which continued well

---

[5] See, Gwyn Campbell, "Unfree Labour and the Significance of Abolition in Madagascar, c. 1825–97," in Campbell, *Abolition and its Aftermath*, 66–82, and Martin Klein, *Slavery and Colonial Rule in French West Africa* (New York: Cambridge University Press, 1998), David Richardson, "Across the Desert and the Sea: Trans-Saharan and Atlantic Slavery, 1500–1900," *The Historical Journal*, 38:(1) 1995, 195–204. Daniel J. Schroeter, "Slave Markets and Slavery in Moroccan Urban Society," *Slavery and Abolition*, 13:1 (April 1992), 185–213, "conservatively" estimates slave imports into Morocco alone between 1874 and 1894 at 100,000, not including those killed in raids and sold within sub-Sahara. Sterling Joseph Coleman, Jr., "Gradual Abolition or Immediate Abolition of Slavery? The Political, Social and Economic Quandry of Emperor Haile Selassie I," *Slavery and Abolition*, 29:1 (2008), 65–82, estimates the Ethiopian slave population in the early twentieth century at two million out of a total of ten million. Martin Klein observes that slaves often made up over two-thirds of the populations (or near Caribbean proportions) in some zones of West Africa. They were also the most important form of wealth in Guinea (*Slavery and Colonial Rule*, 3, 157). In the Indian Ocean world, slaves accounted for a quarter to a third of the population of Thailand in the mid-nineteenth century. (David Feeny, "The Demise of Corvée and Slavery in Thailand, 1782–1913," in Klein *Breaking*, 83–111, 96, Table 3.8.

[6] Klein, *Slavery and Colonial Rule*, 1, 39–41. During the last six decades of the Atlantic slave trade, adult women constituted one-sixth of the captives compared with more than one-quarter during the eighteenth century. During those same final six decades, two-thirds of the captive were males, slightly higher than their share during the previous century. David Eltis and Stanley L. Engerman, "Was the Slave Trade Dominated by Men?," *Journal of Interdisciplinary History*, 23:2 (1992), 237–257, Table 1, 241.

into the third generation of the twentieth century.[7] In agriculturally developed areas, new products aided the expansion of slavery. In Guinea, peanut production dominated the coastal trade until a rubber boom began about 1880, allowing for a relatively smooth economic transition when imperial intervention closed down the slave trade. As Martin Klein concludes, "the demand for slaves within Africa was high and grew higher during the century."[8]

On the east coast of Africa, the same sequence occurred. By the mid-nineteenth century, Omani migrants to the island of Zanzibar almost completely dominated the world market in cloves, a crop they had never planted before the British abolition of the Atlantic slave trade. The clove plantation system reached its height in the third quarter of the nineteenth century, before further British pressure to close down the slave trade. As with Senegal and the Gold Coast in the west, Zanzibar took advantage of the flexibility of slavery in response to the shifting opportunities of the international capitalist markets. During the 1850s and 1860s, coconut production and other tropical items increased the diversification of the slave economy. Expanding agriculture demanded "a truly enormous number of slaves." By the early 1870s, Zanzibar and its coastal satellites were developing into true plantation societies. Slave productivity had become a major concern of planters. Zanzibar's trajectory of expansion portended further encouragement of the institution of slavery.[9]

Involvement in the capitalist world market also increased the penetration of the long-distance slave trade. The slaving frontier moved further into the interior of Africa: the Zambezi valley, Bechuanaland, Buganda, Angola, the Congo, the Sudan, and Ethiopia. In all of these areas, slave raiding intensified during the third quarter of the nineteenth century.[10] The firearms that were to be the major tools of European imperial domination at the close of the nineteenth century were first instruments of Muslim slaving. Martin Klein describes the third quarter of the nineteenth century as the deadly generation of the "weapons revolution." Between 1848 and 1872, European armies were replacing breech loading rifles with repeating rifles. These newer arms flowed relentlessly into Africa until the Brussels Convention of 1890. In areas

---

[7] Getz, *Slavery and Reform in West Africa: toward emancipation in nineteenth-century Senegal and the Gold Coast*, (Athens, OH: Ohio University Press, 2004), 41: "The internal sale of slaves, previously directed toward domestic and stool slavery, easily expanded to incorporate the dealing of slaves for agricultural use after 1807."

[8] Klein, *Slavery and Colonial Rule*, 53, 144. Patrick Manning's most recent projections show a sharp upward surge in slaving in the mid-nineteenth century (Personal communication, June 5, 2008).

[9] Frederick Cooper, *Plantation Slavery on the East Coast of Africa*, (Portsmouth: Heinemann, 1997), ch. 2.

[10] See especially the essays in *The End of Slavery in Africa*, Suzanne Miers and Richard Roberts, eds. (Madison: University of Wisconsin Press, 1988).

that were otherwise without cheap and easy access to the world market, merchants and state builders could sell slaves to purchase new weapons and accumulate revenue. In the markets of the Sudan, captives often constituted the bulk of the marketable and taxable value of exports.[11]

Appeals to religion added an ideological rationale to the toxic cycle of expanding slavery for deadly weapons. In Muslim frontier areas, the argument for *jihād* was made with greater frequency. The linkage of war and enslavement was opportunistically carried over into early European imperialism. Early European wars of conquest in the Sudan sometimes adopted the traditional distribution of human booty in men and women as a means of rewarding their African recruits. These methods coexisted alongside the founding of "villages of liberty," created as refuges for fugitive slaves. Slaving thus became part of the European mode of warfare in the Sudan until the completion of the conquest in the 1890s.

Many historians of late nineteenth-century Africa detail the peaking of slave raiding and trading in the late nineteenth century.[12] They also note the presence of hundreds of thousands or millions of slaves in various African regions at the beginning of the "Scramble for Africa," including upwards of a million in Buganda in the 1870s, nearly 3 million in French West Africa, and between 1 and 2.5 million in the Sokoto Caliphate, at the time of the colonial conquest. In the early 1900s, caravans could carry forced migrations of up to 50,000 a year through Angola. The hinterlands of the northern Rhodesian and Angolan interior were the reservoirs of enslavable victims.[13] Estimates of enslaved Africans in the nineteenth century seem comparable in magnitude to those in the largest slave economies of the Americas in the 1850s. The proportion of slaves in most African societies where the institution flourished appears to have been as high or higher than it was in preemancipation Brazil, Cuba, or the United States. Whatever the differences between the institutions of slavery on either side of the Atlantic, African slavery appeared far less threatened than its counterparts in the Americas during the century after 1775. As Paul Lovejoy concludes, on the eve of the European imperial assault, the African social order was more firmly rooted in slavery than ever before.[14]

---

[11] Klein, *Slavery and Colonial Rule*, ch. 2, 42–58 and 5; and Richard Roberts, "The End of Slavery in the French Sudan, 1905–1914," in *End of Slavery in Africa*, 282–307, esp. 283–284.

[12] Miers and Roberts, *The End of Slavery in Africa*, 122, 256, 433, 441; and Lovejoy's *Transformations in Slavery* refer to the nineteenth-century African slaving in terms of its "booming," "peaking," "intensification," "unabated massiveness," and even "explosion" in the late pre-colonial era. Lovejoy, *Transformations in Slavery*, 155–162.

[13] Linda M. Heywood, "Slavery and Forced Labor in the Changing Political Economy of Central Angola, 1850–1949," in *End of Slavery in Africa*, 415–436, esp. 420–421.

[14] Lovejoy, *Transformations*, 252.

This is not to say that local struggles against enslavement were not continuous and frequent in Africa. Resistance continued throughout the eighteenth and nineteenth centuries.[15] As in the preabolitionist Americas, the cumulative outcome of these events is further evidence that slave resistance alone did not undermine the institution of slavery before European domination in Africa. Indeed, limited European intrusion did not significantly encourage slave trading to expand during the generation following the ending of the Atlantic slave trade.

Without the exogenous pressure of abolitionism, one can imagine only a much more drawn out path to the decline of slavery. Muslim state consolidation might have ultimately reduced the zone of populations vulnerable to enslavement, but it is worth recalling that professing of Islam did not protect individuals and groups at the turbulent slaving frontier. It is also possible to imagine that the continued growth of slaving would have been halted by crises of genocidal depopulation, analogous to the overhunting that diminished the volume of the ivory trade in East Africa toward the end of the nineteenth century.

The century of European and Anglo-American emancipations put the problem of slavery on the agenda of European imperialism. This is not to imply that antislavery or humanitarian ideology in Europe played a major role in stimulating European political intrusion into Africa, either north or south of the Sahara. If anything, the responsibility for eliminating the institution of slavery in those parts of the African continent under European sovereignty often made the British and French governments hesitate to expand their sovereignty and moral responsibility. If anything, the outstanding characteristic of Euro-African relations for more than half a century after abolition of the British slave trade was the reluctance of the northern European colonial bureaucracies to erode the line between the European and African social orders. British concentration on the slave trade involved the high costs of reducing the flow of Africans to the New World and distributing those recaptives to Africa and the Americas. During the second half of the nineteenth century, planters in the former British and Dutch slave colonies looked primarily to Asian indentured servants. Imperial France and Portugal sponsored the purchase of African slaves, converting them into "free" indentured laborers for specified periods. During the second half of the nineteenth century, these involuntarily "apprenticed" Africans no longer represented a major transcontinental migration flow. About 150,000 bound servants left the African continent between 1850 and 1900. During the same

---

[15] See Ismail Rashid, "A Devotion to the Idea of Liberty at Any Price: Rebellion and Antislavery in the Upper Guinea Coast in the Eighteenth and Nineteenth Century," in *Fighting the Slave Trade: West African Strategies*, Sylviane A. Diouf, ed. (Athens, OH: Ohio University Press, 2003), 132–151.

period, almost ten times that number of African slaves were shipped to areas dominated by non-Europeans.[16]

Until the late nineteenth century, Europeans tended to avoid complicating their relations with African rulers and slave owners by avoiding direct involvement with slavery or slave-master relations. After their brief flurry of activism at the peak of antislavery agitation in the early 1840s, the British government generally enforced the distinction between areas directly under British sovereignty and those with the status of protectorates or independent polities. Before the last quarter of the nineteenth century, therefore, the major European powers had little inclination to expand their jurisdictions far beyond the tropical areas they had already acquired by the end of the Napoleonic wars.[17] Even in South Africa, the British showed no inclination to stamp out the slaving and trading in Natal at the frontier of their Cape Colony. Boer Voortrekkers who fled British sovereignty and entered Transorangia, Natal, and the Transvaal, took part in raids for cattle and slaves to accelerate settlement. They sometimes acknowledged that they waged war against the Zulus for the purpose of capturing slaves. Although the Sand River Convention (1852) between the British government and the Transvaal Boers prohibited slavery north of the Vaal, raids on African communities thereafter increased dramatically. Colonial appeals to the Cape officials received no response. The British apprenticeship system had been instituted primarily to bridge the transition from slavery to freedom in the plantation colonies. It was retained in the Boer republics down to the end of the nineteenth century, subjecting Africans to military abduction, sales, and distribution. Thus, the booty system practice by France in northwestern Africa was preceded by Boer practices in the southeast.[18]

On the West African coast, colonial bureaucratic rules limited sovereignty to the British and French enclaves of the Gold Coast, Sierra Leone, and Senegal. They also curtailed interference with the slave trade or slavery. Even during Britain's most activist abolitionist phase, around 1840, the prime minister authorized a campaign to expand antislave trade treaties only with the strict understanding that they called for no territorial annexation.[19] British coastal magistrates sometimes acquired informal jurisdiction to arbitrate disputes over slaves between neighboring African States, but they were continually reminded of their limits. They could not use English law to abolish the institution. In Britain, MPs made periodic motions to withdraw from

---

[16] Lovejoy, *Transformations*, 151–156; and Petre-Grenouilleau, *Traites négrières*, 148–156.

[17] Christopher Fyfe, *A History of Sierra Leone* (London: Oxford University Press, 1962).

[18] *Slavery in South Africa: Captive Labor on the Dutch Frontier*, Elizabeth A. Eldredge and Fred Morton, eds. (Boulder: Westview Press, 1994), ch. 7–9. From Fred Morton's estimate of captives between 1731 and 1869 (255, Table 10.2), it would appear that in the period after 1840, the number of captives doubled before coming to an end around 1870.

[19] Fyfe, *History of Sierra Leone*, 217.

some or all of the settlements. Interest in West Africa probably reached its nineteenth-century nadir with a Parliamentary Select Committee on West Africa in 1865. It recommended withdrawal from the West African coast, retaining only Sierra Leone, the main debarkation point for captives rescued from the slave trade.

All French governments practiced similar constraint after abolishing slavery for the second time in 1848. The colony of Senegal was composed of two island bases, St. Louis and Gorée, plus some forts along the coast and the Senegal River. Half of the colony's population consisted of slaves at the time of France's emancipation in 1848. In the wake of that decree, French colonial officers feared a massive flight of slaves from the environs of their colony and a disruption of relations with both Muslim traders and warrior elites. The Minister of Colonies in Paris immediately moved to foreclose this possibility by refusing refuge to outside slaves. Thereafter, the incorporation of neighboring villages was accompanied by a refusal to extend the "free soil" line to all their inhabitants. Slaveholding was prohibited only to French citizens. Violations were to be enforced only against citizens. Slaveholding "subjects" retained their property rights as slaveholders. Children of ex-slaves or outsiders were assigned to families – a traffic that continued until 1904. In newly acquired contiguous settlements, such as Dakar, the enforcement of antislavery legislation had to await the stabilization of the Third Republic in the late 1870s.

Local bureaucrats also developed practices allowing discreet evasion of metropolitan policies that might disrupt colonial regimes manned by overburdened officials and minimal police forces. Colonial agents considered themselves to be a buffer against "unrealistic" demands in Europe that were periodically aroused by surges of embarrassing information about the persistence of slavery in the colonies. Into the 1880s, "the ability of Europeans in Africa to sustain an imperial agenda was based on their skill at deception." The French government, in a Napoleonic retreat from emancipation, was even willing to "disannex" territory on the outskirts of the French West African colonies to preempt metropolitan pressure to act more rigorously against slavery or the slave trade. Just across the border from Senegal, in British-controlled Gambia, slaves were "still debited and credited" to traders' accounts "under the head of cattle."[20] Up to the late 1870s, on the French side, expanding commerce led to the greatest importation of slave labor in the history of Senegal.

In the absence of pressure from without, Euro-African capitalism and African slavery expanded together. For six decades after 1815, the French territorial ambitions on the continent were limited to northern Africa. It was always easy for colonial agents to respond to metropolitan pressures for social change. They noted that political necessity, the interests of the

---

[20] Klein, *Slavery and Colonial Rule*, 35–36.

native populations, and negotiated treaties all obliged the French to abide by status-quo agreements with slave owners.

As with the major slave systems in the Americas, the major assault against slavery in Africa was launched at the height of the institution's economic vibrancy and social power. The major initiatives for dismantling the system in Africa in the last quarter of the nineteenth century, as in the eighteenth century Atlantic, initially depended upon the continuing development of European civil society and public opinion. Left to their own devices, European bureaucracies favored colonial paradigms of action that precluded direct or radical assaults on the institution, as discussed below. Before the 1870s, then, the caution displayed by both metropolitan governments and their overseas agents was a forecast that colonial agents would not usually be at the cutting edge of the liberation process either in Africa or the Indian Ocean world. Nor did free non-European inhabitants of those areas usually constitute the catalytic agents of antislavery or political abolitionism.

The British government and its colonial agents acknowledged a major aspect of slavery in the East that distinguished it from the New World variant. In Afro-Asian countries characterized by deep poverty and no state welfare network, the institution of slavery often had a voluntary dimension. Self-sale, child sale, and complexities of family ties were formidable obstacles to emancipation well into the period of European domination. Slavery was sure to die more slowly when physical death through starvation might follow from the separation of masters and their bondsmen or concubines. Already, on the eve of Indian quasi-abolition in the 1840s, one British law commissioner described slavery in the subcontinent as the "Indian Poor Law." In Africa, especially during places and times of instability or famine, some forms of slavery could also be a refuge from other forms of hardship. The fact that concubinage continued long after legal support for the status ended, showed its power to endure as an alternative to flight or abandonment.[21]

Eastern Slavery

Europeans also encountered formidable ideological barriers to policies that implied the abolition of an institution that some believed was cosmically or divinely ordained. Late nineteenth-century Muslims certainly developed some theories that paralleled those developed in European discourse during the previous century of abolition acts. One of the most fruitful lines of argument was the interpretation of statements and commentaries in the

[21] For further discussions, see Stanley L. Engerman, "Slavery, Freedom and Sen," in K. Anthony Appiah and Martin Bunzl, eds., *Buying Freedom: The Ethics and Economics of Slave Redemption* (Princeton: Princeton University Press, 2007); and Engerman, *Slavery, Emancipation and Freedom: Comparative Perspectives* (Baton Rouge: Louisiana State University Press, 2007), 23–25.

Qur'an to the effect that Muhammad's statements and the "Spirit of Islam," like that of Christianity, always intended the gradual withering away of slavery. As with earlier Christian apologetics for slavery's duration among believers, the words of Muhammad encouraged at least an amelioration of the condition of slaves within Islam and the ultimate demise of the institution with the triumph of the faith. Early responses to novel European antislavery policies quickly established a faith-saving distinction. Whatever happened to preserve slavery in Muslim lands was the fault of Muslims and not of the *Qur'an*.[22]

Further Muslim critiques of slavery began to appear in the last third of the nineteenth century. Some of the most vigorous rejoinders emerged in direct response to the mounting criticism by Europeans of Islam's sanctioning of slavery. When these Muslims addressed their British audiences in the early 1870s, the legal status of slavery within the Raj had already been severely undermined. As noted in chapter 10, the World Antislavery Convention of 1840 had publicized estimates of 6 to 8 million slaves living in India. Another contemporary estimated the combined number in the British protectorates and princely territories at nearly 16 million. Either way, these figures made India's institution of slavery larger than the entire New World combined. By the time Muslims began to respond to British antislavery discourses, the Indian Penal Code of 1860, building upon Act V of 1843, made it illegal to abduct or trade in slaves in British-ruled India. There was no urgent need for Muslims within the Raj to take a stance for or against antislavery. Nevertheless, the legal system was beginning to convict individuals for violation of the antislavery statute. Slaving raids were still reported beyond the borders of British control and domestic slavery continued within the princely states into the 1870s and 1880s, despite "delegalization."[23]

The initial purpose of the Muslims entering the Western discourse on slavery was to rebut charges that Islamic societies were rendered incapable of participating in modern antislavery. The Muslims in London rebutted the charge that Islamic societies were inherently incapable of an antislavery variant of modernity. Saiyid Ahmad Khan and Sayyid Ameer Ali, two Indian Muslim residents in Britain and trained in the law, began to gingerly address the question. Significantly, in their initial forays, neither writer mentioned India. Their writings were apologetic defenses of Qu'uranic exegesis rather than overtly abolitionist arguments. They both drew upon Western sources

[22] William Gervase Clarence-Smith, "Islam and the Abolition of the Slave Trade and Slavery in the Indian Ocean," in Campbell, ed, *Abolition*, 137–149, and *idem, Islam and the Abolition of Slavery* (New York: Oxford University Press, 2006), ch. 10, "Rationalism."

[23] Dharma Kumar, "Colonialism, Bondage and Caste in British India," in Klein, ed. *Breaking*, 121–123; and Howard Temperley, "The Delegalization of Slavery in British India," in Temperley, ed. *After Slavery*, 169–187.

to demonstrate medieval Islam's relatively progressive attitude toward slavery compared with those of Greco-Roman or early Christian writings. They also avoided responding to Western characterizations of female slavery and concubinage among Muslims. Like their contemporaries in the Ottoman Empire and many in British India, most Muslim writers avoided entering into details of domestic slavery representing it as a benign form of servitude. Nevertheless, one of the writers, Saiyid Ahmad, addressed the issue of violent recruitment and maintained that the *Qur'an* prohibited slavery and that the enslavement of war captives was inherently unIslamic. He also looked beyond India, expressing shame at the fact that female slaves were sold "like cows" in Arabia.[24]

In the Ottoman Empire, serious Muslim engagement with the Western abolitionist ideas also intensified in the last quarter of the nineteenth century. As with many of the Indian modernists, noted above, the issue was usually addressed in highly hermeneutic or literary genres. Even the politically oriented "Young Ottomans" considered the issue of abolition to be marginal.[25] What seems clear is that, even into the 1870s, the discussion of antislavery within Muslim-dominated lands was at the prepolitical level of the Atlantic world a century before. The associational component that formed the political mobilization of antislavery sentiment in the Anglo-American world a century before was still lacking. When Saiyid Ahmad published his condemnation in Urdu, rather than less accessible English, it was greeted by an outpouring of tracts, *fatwas*, and newspaper articles virulently contesting his assertion that the *Qur'an* does not support enslavement in legitimate war. A Meccan *'ulama* issued a *fatwa* of infidelity against Ahmad. None of the *'ulama* of the Ottoman Empire responded to his challenge to discuss the meaning of the "freedom verses" in the *Qu'ran*.[26]

The absence of a concrete focus on contemporary slaving and slavery in Muslim discourse is still more striking. For the most part, discussants offered a plethora of arguments based upon exegesis of sacred or legal texts. These writings tended to be defenses of the faith rather than calls for action against slavery itself.[27] There was no literary equivalent to the outpouring of harrowing images of brutal capture: no detailed accounts of the Arab slave trade; no major attempt to marshal statistical accounts of its toll in lives and family separation; no detailed descriptions of females sold in Saiyid Ahmad's words "like cows in bazaars"; no Caravan manifests

24 Avril A. Powell, "Indian Muslim Modernists and the Issue of Slavery in Islam," in *Slavery and South Asian History*, Indrani Chatterjee and Richard M. Eaton, eds. (Bloomington: Indiana University Press, 2006), 262–286, quotation on 275–276; and Ehud R. Toledano, "Ottoman Concepts of Slavery in the Period of Reform," 1830s–1880s, in Klein, ed. *Breaking*, 37–63.
25 See Toledano, "Ottoman Concepts," 46–53.
26 Powell, *Muslim*, 273–280.
27 Clarence-Smith, *Islam and the Abolition*.

of lists of prices obtained for various categories of human beings, broken down by age, race, gender, or states of health; and no detailed descriptions of the killings of the disabled or the mutilation and death entailed in the production of eunuchs. There was no outpouring of poetry dedicated to individualizing the experiences of slaves who had survived the ordeal of raiding and transportation across desert or ocean and "seasoning" in their new environment. There were no highly publicized autobiographies of slaves who successfully escaped the institution nor any visual equivalent to the slave ship Brooks. There was no equivalent popular press to publicize court cases involving masters' cruelty or illegal enslavement.

One could elaborate the differences at greater length. Above all, the norms of civil society do not seem to have encouraged the formation of collective localized antislavery organizations, much less a broader social movement. The same *jihads* that provoked massive slave uprisings usually ended by continuing the practice of enslavement by the new victors over the newly vanquished.[28] The only antislavery association mentioned by Clarence-Smith in his exhaustive study of Islam and abolition alludes to an implicit "club of 'the more advanced Mohammedan princes.'" The very existence of this informal organization dated from the mid-1920s after half a century of European diplomatic pressure on the slave trade and slavery in the Muslim and Indian Ocean worlds. Given the exclusiveness and elusiveness of the club's membership and the paucity of other associational formations, Clarence-Smith aptly concludes that "it remains unclear when Muslim secular elites really turned against bondage."[29]

The relatively barren page of collective antislavery activity is probably not because of the constraints of authoritarian Muslim rulers. Once he had determined to implement abolition in the 1840s, Tunisia's ruler employed a mixture of traditional religious and modern European rhetoric to outlaw the institution of slavery. The Bey's edict of 1846 stressed the "inhumane treatment" of the oppressed as contrary to the spirit of the *shari'a*, the necessity of affording justice to the weak, and the multiple avenues to manumission that Islamic law sanctioned. The edict also included a distinctive appeal to the imperatives of the "public good." The frequent flights of slaves to foreign consulates in response to previous preparatory decrees posed a challenge to Tunisian authority and sovereignty. Thus, the first major abolitionist legislation in the Muslim world echoed the abolitionist rationale for emancipation on principles of humanity, religion, justice, and policy.

Beyond the sphere of the rulers, there was clearly a relative dearth of collective activity against the institution of slavery.[30] Associational activity was

---

[28] Klein, *Slavery and Colonial Rule*, 51, on the interconnected logic of slave raiding, trading, and use.

[29] Clarence-Smith, *Islam*, 128.

[30] Montana, "Transaharan Slave Trade," 166–170.

legally permitted in Muslim areas of British India and within a polity where slavery itself had already been legally proscribed. It is highly unlikely that the British Raj would have hindered the formation of abolitionist organizations, whether Muslim, Hindu, or Christian, that wished to stimulate antislavery in areas beyond British jurisdiction. The ideological elements were there. The organizational ones were not.

Saiyid Ahmad's arguments against slavery spread rapidly from northwest India into western Asia. Mecca issued a *fatwa* against him. Even in India's northwestern Muslim provinces, the discussion of slavery remained highly scholastic defenses of Islam. Saiyid Ahmed's attempt to stimulate a broad debate over slavery in Istanbul through a radical Arabic newspaper was equally unsuccessful. The "ulama of the Ottoman empire did not take up his invitation to respond," much less organize an antislavery group in Istanbul. Istanbul intellectuals criticized slavery in novels, plays, and poems but a campaign to abolish the predominant and most painful varieties of Ottoman slavery "was never contemplated by Western proponents of abolition."[31]

As significant as the absence of collective antislavery activity among Muslim elites was the dearth of evidence for antislavery mobilizations within the ranks of the free Muslim population as a whole. Innumerable conflicts were generated by European initiatives and the reactions of slaves themselves to the openings to action afforded by these initiatives, both of which will be treated below. There was, of course, a dearth of political possibilities for free men, not to mention women.

A major contrast between the New World and Old World slave trades was that most victims remaining in the Old World orbit were young women and girls. The proportion of female slaves traded rose in the modern period, and accounted for as much as three-quarters of the nineteenth-century human exports into the Muslim world. The expansion of long distance trades, migrations, and conquests in the late nineteenth century also enlarged the demand for service, along with other obligations. A few writers criticized concubinage and its connection with slavery. However, these discussions about altering the status of women offered few openings to women themselves.[32]

The difference in opportunities for popular antislavery mobilization was most strikingly evident in the antislavery crusade launched by Cardinal Lavigerie, the Archbishop of Algiers and founder of the White Fathers mission in Africa. Before 1888, the Catholic hierarchies of Europe had never

---

[31] Powell, "Indian Muslim Modernists," 273–74; and Toledano, "Ottoman Concepts," 58. For the influence of South Asian radicals in the Russian-dominated parts of the Muslim world, see Clarence-Smith, *Islam*, 210–211. Most reformers in the Czar's dominions did not confront slavery directly.

[32] Clarence-Smith, *Islam*, 197, 198, 209. For other assaults on concubinage, see Powell, "Indian Muslim Modernists," 274, and Campbell, "Introduction," 16–18.

encouraged either clerical or mass mobilization against slavery. Only a few months after the abolition of slavery in Brazil, the institution's last redoubt in the western world, Lavigerie launched his campaign for support in Europe. Characteristically, he appealed to public opinion, "the true queen of the world today."[33] He quickly gained the support of Pope Leo XIII and lectured to packed crowds in London and Brussels. Supporting organizations were founded in countries with large or predominantly Catholic populations: France, Belgium, Germany, Switzerland, Spain, Portugal, Austria, Italy, and Haiti.

The emergence of this broad band of continental antislavery associations seemed to echo the formation of British abolitionism exactly a century after its organization. Antislavery, it appeared, had ceased to be the preserve of Protestant nonconformists and secular radicals. As a pan-European movement, this antislavery revival was a disappointment. It remained divided along national and sectarian lines and by the Cardinal's attempt to keep the movement's leadership firmly in Catholic hands. After 1888 antislavery initiatives in France were usually initiated by conservative Catholics, not radical anticlericals. Lavigerie envisioned the movement as a crusade to win Africa for Christianity, although he did not identify Islam with the intransigent defense of slavery. In 1888, he declared that the "Qur'an" did not "enjoin slavery but merely permits it" ... [placing] "the liberation of captives at the top of the list of merciful deeds."[34] Nevertheless, the attack on an institution still legally and ideologically defended within the Muslim world portended a sharp new boundary between the two faiths at the peak of the European partition of Africa, including its predominantly Muslim north.

Lavigerie's campaign culminated in an international conference in Brussels on African slavery in 1889. The Brussels Convention of 1890 minted antislavery as the gold standard of Western civilization. Slavery's continued toleration under any European flag had now become both an embarrassment and an opportunity. Antislavery quickly and retroactively became a moral rationale for European domination of the African continent. Every signatory power at Brussels pledged to initiate immediate steps to eliminate slave trading within their imperial jurisdictions. They also agreed to bring the institution itself to a gradual end. The Muslim rulers of Zanzibar, Persia, and the Ottoman Empire were also invited to attend. Since the institution was still legal in their realms, all were pressured into signing the final protocol. The Ottoman ambassador defended the Empire's "mild slavery." The Persian representative absented himself to avoid "troublesome engagements," especially over the supply of eunuchs.

---

33 Miers, *Britain and the Ending*, 202.
34 Clarence-Smith, *Islam*, 17; and François Renault, *Le Cardinal Lavigerie* (Paris: Fayard 1992), 566.

Outside Brussels, too, Lavigerie's crusade stimulated a vigorous defense of Islam's variant of slavery. The mobilization of European states increased uneasiness among some intellectuals but Muslim antislavery sentiment was not transformed into a movement to undermine the institution. Shafik Ahmad, a French-educated Egyptian, stimulated a long debate in the Egyptian and foreign press with *L'esclavage au point de vue musulman* (*Slavery From the Muslim Perspective*).[35] It was quickly translated into Arabic, Turkish, and Urdu. Ahmad remained loyal to the belief in *jihād* against unbelievers as a lawful means of enslavement. In response to Lavigerie's antislavery campaign and the Brussels Convention, no Muslim group took the opposite tack and attempted to launch a *jihād* in favor of terminating the institution. In this respect, again, it would appear that Muslim civil society was not easily mobilized against slavery as a legitimate institution. Nor was the Islamic world unique in this regard. As of the late nineteenth century, the situation of Afro-Asian societies outside of Islam was much the same as that within its orbit of power. There was little evidence yet of any indigenous antislavery movement among those affiliated with Hinduism, Buddhism, or any of the sub-Saharan religions. It is the novel pressure of European intrusions and their reverberations, then, to which we must first look to account for the eastward sweep of abolitionist and liberationist movements in the half century between 1875 and 1925, when Western imperialism was reaching its apogee.[36]

---

[35] (Cairo, 1890.)

[36] See Toledano, "Ottoman Concepts," 49–53. It is noteworthy that Toledano (49) "underscores" the "Young Ottomans' pregnant whisper on slavery," not unlike Marques's "Sounds of Silence" as applied to earlier Portuguese attitudes, compared with the ever-present pressure of their British interlocutors. David Feeny's account of "The Demise of Corvée and Slavery in Thailand, 1782–1913," in Klein, ed. *Breaking*, 83–111, emphasizes the agency of the monarch (above all, King Chulalongkorn) in a process undertaken for other purposes, including the preservation of national independence. The conversion of enslaved war captives into common subjects was necessary to prevent the loss of sovereignty to foreign claims of jurisdiction over people residing in Thailand. Feeny makes no mention of internal collective activity in the process. Antislaveholder mobilizations usually emerged within other responses to European or anti-European initiatives. From a global perspective, focusing upon the religious roots of abolitionism or antiabolitionism in the late nineteenth century may be as misleading for slavery in Muslim societies as it is for Christian ones. Besides repeating the temptation to import hidden dualisms of condemnation or religious apologetics into the analysis, it turns attention away from historically conditioned stimuli to collective behavior and from political action to millennial texts that had never before engendered attacks on slavery per se. We risk attempting to explain a variable (antislavery) by a constant – a fundamental text. The same caveat, of course, applies to early nineteenth-century New World abolitionism. Different Christian groups and polities developed different attitudes toward abolitionist agendas. This alerts us to the datum that mobilizations against slavery did not automatically emerge from the agendas of religious thought or preaching. Protestant nonconformist denominations, like Methodists and Baptists, were pioneers in collective abolitionist mobilization in Anglo-America. In another part of

Black Africa

What then of European antislavery initiatives, usually recognized as the most disorienting exogenous force in the attack on slavery in the Afro-Asian world in the late nineteenth century? We have already noted that Europeans between 1825 and 1875 were remarkably reticent to expand their domination over slave societies or to dramatically terminate the institution of slavery in Afro-Asia. In the 1840s, the intensity of the attack on Indian slavery in particular had to be lowered for two additional reasons. The abolitionists hoped that East Indian free labor would undercut American slave-grown cotton. They were also acutely aware that U.S. southerners quickly saw the advantages of adopting the abolitionist slogan that Indian indentured migrants to the British colonies were undergoing "a new form of slavery." At that peak moment of abolitionist influence in 1838–1845, the British antislavery movement's highest priority was to suppress the Atlantic slave trade.

Fifty years later, in the heyday of European imperialism, other issues concerned European governments when considering pursuing antislavery. The dismantling of the Atlantic slave trade and emancipating colonial slaves had required economic and public financial sacrifices. During the six decades in which Britain led Europe in the suppression of the slave trade and in slave emancipation (1807–1867), abolitionism had cost its metropolitan citizens 1.8 percent of their national income. Disbursing sums like those in Britain's "mighty experiment" were burdens beyond the wildest dreams of

Anglo-America, the antebellum South, they became scriptural defenders of slavery in the New World. Within the Catholic tradition, Las Casas's searing assault on Amerindian slavery was not followed by a movement anywhere within Latin Christianity against either Old or New World slavery for centuries. In a broader sense, the most significant detail about the ending of slavery in the Old World is the dearth of evidence that the traditional religious and political formations do not appear to have developed collective antislavery formations only late in the assault on chattel slavery, and then largely in response to European pressures. Non-European political formations began to insist upon servitude as a fundamental affront to the dignity of their people when their claims to world respect could be recast as antiimperial or anti-Western nationalist movements demanding change or independence on universalist grounds. Ghandi's mobilization in South Africa against racial discrimination after 1875 was begun by an Indian trained in British law. The initial campaign for the liberation of women in China also emerged within the Western imperial enclaves of Hong Kong and Shanghai. As earlier in Europe gendered practices in most Afro-Asian societies hindered the emergence of popular abolitionist societies before the early twentieth century. (See, inter alia, *Women and Chinese Patriarchy: Submission, Servitude, and Escape*, Maria Jaschok and Suzanne Miers, eds. (Hong Kong/London: Kong University Press 1994); Indrani Chatterju, *Gender, Slavery and Law in Colonial India* (New Delhi: Oxford University Press, 1999); Chaterjie, "Abolition by Denial: the South Asian Example," in Campbell, *Abolition*, 150–168; Ehud R. Toledano, "Ottoman Concepts of Slavery in the Period of Reform, 1803–1880s," in Klein, *Breaking*, 37–63; and Miers and Roberts, *End of Slavery*.

societies such as Spain, Portugal, or Brazil. They were equally beyond consideration for antebellum United States Legislators, taxpayers, and voters, even if they ultimately paid more to end the institution in a Civil War. For European governments contemplating a scramble for the maximum imperial possessions during the last quarter of the nineteenth century, a British scenario was unthinkable. In Africa and Asia, Europeans assumed dominion over slave populations many times the size of those liberated in the Americas. Historically, Old World slaves had been created by institutions Europeans had not sponsored or sanctioned. Finally, in economic terms, the cumulative lessons of colonial liberations during the half century between British emancipation in the 1830s and the Ibero-American abolitions in the 1880s had hardly been encouraging.

Much has been made of a fundamental link between capitalist industrialization in Europe and the transformation of European labor into a free-wage labor system. Capitalist imperialism supposedly premised the universal moral superiority and economic efficiency of wage labor. At the same time, inefficient Old World slaves "could be converted into sober self-disciplined workers."[37] In actuality, half a century of New and Old World experiments, great and small, convinced Europeans that some coercion was necessary

---

[37] See David Brion Davis, inter alia, *Problem of Slavery in the Age of Revolution*, 242. On the hegemony of the "free labor ideology" and applicability to the African and Indian Ocean worlds, see Cooper, *From Squatters*, 26; Campbell, "Introduction," in Campbell, ed. *Abolition and its Aftermath*, 2. Before British emancipation, abolitionists, although not planters or economists, assured planters that immediate emancipation meant lower labor costs and higher profits. Davis, *Human Progress*, 222. There were various components to the ideology. Free labor was supposedly more efficient because it was more highly motivated than slaves; slaves were a fixed cost and largely immobilized. The most important aspect of the "free-labor ideology," however, was that it was not regarded as immediately superior to coerced labor. Adam Smith's famous pronouncement on free labor superiority had come with a temporal caveat: "I believe," he wrote, "that the work done by freemen comes cheaper *in the end* than that performed by slaves." (Adam Smith, *Wealth of Nations* (Indianapolis: Liberty Fund, 1979), I, 70 (my emphasis). Robert Fogel and Gavin Wright have identified this as an axiom that was far more deeply embedded in the minds of later historians than was in the minds of masters and rulers. Fogel points to the widespread "assumption that productivity is necessarily virtuous." Wright has analyzed the abolitionist assumption that "slave labor was unproductive because the lash was an ineffective incentive." Both assumptions alternatively, or in combination, undergirded this historiographical premise of the superiority of free labor. See Seymour Drescher, *The Mighty Experiment: Free Labor versus Slavery in British Emancipation* (New York: Oxford University Press, 2002), ch. 2–12; Fogel, *Without Consent or Contract*, 409–411; Fogel, *The Slavery Debates 1952–1990: A Retrospective* (Baton Rouge: Louisiana State University Press, 2003), 29–44; and Gavin Wright, *Slavery and American Economic Development* (Baton Rouge: Louisiana State University Press, 2006), 2–6. In fact, in Britain itself, during the age of New World emancipation, employers made frequent use of Masters and Servants Laws to enforce penally coercive labor contracts and incarcerate farm workers for breach of service. This endured until the eve of the scramble for Africa. (Robert J. Steinfeld, *Coercion, Contract, and Free Labor in the Nineteenth Century* (New York: Cambridge University Press, 2001).

for the recruitment and maintenance of a labor force in underdeveloped tropical areas. Whether they framed their arguments in terms of backward peoples or negative labor-supply curves, the logic of their arguments was identical. The English Masters and Servants Acts were the model for post-emancipation labor relations in British India, South Africa, the Caribbean, and parts of Asia in the wake of slave emancipations between the 1830s and 1870s.

As a universal economic principle, the free-labor ideology was not consensual in British society among planters, economists, parliamentarians, and capitalists. Deep disappointment with the rapid transition from slavery to freedom in the British colonies had added a persistent racial dimension to the difficulties of terminating coerced-labor systems.[38] However, whether elucidated in racial or economic terms, by the end of the nineteenth century both pro- and antiimperialists stressed the great difficulties and potential costs of any transition to freedom. For the antiimperialist, J. A. Hobson, at the end of the century there were only two genuinely economic forces which could bring labor to do "steady and continuous work" – the pressure of population on the land or the pressure of "new needs" and a rising standard of consumption. Unfortunately, as Smith had hinted, these "natural forces" operated very slowly.[39]

The impetus to end slavery in Africa did not stem from the eagerness of either businessmen or bureaucrats to utilize abolition to enhance productivity of labor. In the generation before 1880, economic growth in sub-Saharan Africa often occurred in comfortable tandem with an increasing supply of slaves. The ending of the transatlantic slave trade to the Americas after 1850 ensured a greater potential supply of labor in Africa. Before French expansion into the African interior in the 1880s, French colonial officials remained hostile to free or freed labor. Few expected any change in productivity from emancipations. As late as the 1880s, the French colonial agents turned a blind eye toward the importation of slave children into their colonies.[40]

British expansion in the Gold Coast in the early 1870s became the harbinger and model for the Scramble for Africa a decade later. On the Gold Coast, the British government did not undertake emancipation for the purpose of accelerating economic development, either before or after the first serious expansion into the interior of Africa in 1873. In Britain, the free-labor ideology was at its nadir with regard to West Africa. "European managers of enterprises in the tropics remained convinced that some kind of forced labor was still a necessity." They could no longer advocate retrogression to slavery, but they were no less prone than before to envision development within the framework of some form of coerced enforcement under long-term

---

[38] Drescher, *Mighty Experiment*, 217–223.
[39] J. A. Hobson, *Imperialism*, (London: Allen & Unwin, 1938), 255.
[40] Roberts and Miers, *End of Slavery*, "Introduction," 14, quoting a 1986 paper by Martin Klein.

labor contracts. Above all, the British government was dead set against linking any plan for economic development to British territorial expansion. Any extension of British sovereignty now implied an extension of the free soil principle. Among the local commercial and industrial interests on the coast, the weight of evidence indicates a prevailing indifference or opposition to any interference with existing master-slave relations beyond the zone of British jurisdiction.[41]

In many respects, therefore, the power of antislavery was at a low ebb in Britain at the end of the third quarter of the nineteenth century. Britain's most forceful abolitionist activity after 1807 derived from its maritime hegemony, unchallenged for seven decades after the battle of Trafalgar. Its imperial mission for the first three quarters of the nineteenth century was to close down the seaborne slave trade, primarily in the Atlantic and, secondarily, the Mediterranean and Indian Ocean networks.

By 1870, the transatlantic trade had ended and the Atlantic naval patrol terminated. In the Mediterranean and the Indian Ocean, Britain continued to negotiate a series of treaties with Muslim rulers progressively inhibiting or prohibiting their participation in the Eastern slave trade. In 1822, a limiting boundary to the seaborne slave trade was drawn in the Indian Ocean. A new "Moresby line" was negotiated with the Sultan of Muscat (later Zanzibar). He agreed to restrict exports of African slaves to the "Muslim" zone of the ocean. Like many subsequent Muslim rulers, the Sultan considered such demands to be intrusions into the legitimate activities of his Muslim subjects. He even had his subjects pray that Westerners "would come to their senses."[42] Under the threat of a British blockade, the Sultan prohibited further exports of slaves from the mainland and closed the public slave markets on the island of Zanzibar. He agreed to provide judicial protection for freed slaves. British naval vessels obtained the right to search all vessels flying his flag. Slaveholding was prohibited to all British Indian subjects residing in his realm. In return for these concessions, Egypt, less forthcoming about limiting the slave trade, was forced to surrender forts they had seized from the Sultan. Britain thus became an arbitrator for non-European powers with imperial ambitions on the East African coast.[43]

---

[41] Raymond Dumett and Marion Johnson, "Britain and the Suppression of Slavery in the Gold Coast Colony, Ashanti, and the Northern Territories," in *ibid.*, 71–116, esp. 107; and Philip D. Curtin, *The Image of Africa: British Ideas and Action, 1780–1850* (Madison: University of Wisconsin Press, 1964), 450–454. Quotation on 451. As an alternative to penal coercion, direct taxation to be paid out of wages from labor (originally suggested by emancipation plans for the West Indies), was applied in Natal, Sierra Leone, and the Gold Coast. The tax was so difficult to collect in the Gold Coast that it was abandoned more than a decade before the second Anglo-Ashanti war in 1873–1874.

[42] Clarence-Smith, *Islam*, 123.

[43] Miers, *Britain and the Ending*, 91–92.

The Iranian Shah's anti-slave-trade *farmān* of 1848 offers the most strik-ing evidence of how small a role the internal popular or elite pressures played in these initial abolitionist initiatives in Middle Eastern lands. The Shah's decree finessed the issue of religious or moral legitimacy. He couched the decree as a token of personal gratitude to the British *chargé d'affaires*, Colonel Francis Farrant. The policy was a reward for the officer's service as an instructor to the Iranian army: "Let them [his subjects] no longer bring Negroes by sea, only by land. Purely for the sake of Farrant, with whom I am much pleased, I have consented to this."[44] The British govern-ment, too, had been pressured by the Antislavery Society through publicity and parliamentary questioning on the Indian Ocean slave trade. Britain's world seafaring supremacy continued to render it both the prime agent and arbiter of activity against the slave trade. France alone objected to this extension of British oversight of Indian Ocean vessels sailing under European flags.

In other respects, the momentum of British activity visibly decelerated a few years after the heady days of the Antislavery Convention. Abolitionists were certainly no longer in a position to summon record numbers for public meetings and petitions for broadening the definition of the slave trade to include indentured servitude. Contract labor from India was officially desig-nated as voluntary, not a "new kind of slave trade." The flow of indentured migrants to Britain's ex-slave colonies peaked in the 1860s and 1870s. It served to limit the antislavery movement's power in two respects. The flow of new labor gradually reversed the decline of sugar exports in most of the British Caribbean. In global terms, abolitionists were reduced to repeating the "vaguest of pieties about the greater efficiency of free labor," without being able to specify how a wage labor economy would function or where it had so far done so.[45]

The difficult transition from slavery to free labor in the Western Hemi-sphere had a deep impact upon projects for analogous institutional change in the East. The outcome of Britain's "Mighty Experiment" dramatically reversed earlier casual linkages between free labor and free trade. The open-ing of the British market to all sugar producers toward the end of the 1840s caused a deep economic crisis in the British colonies and a boom in the Cuban and Brazilian plantations, both still operating under slave labor. In 1833, Britain had added £20 million to its national debt in compensation to

---

44 Behnay A. Mirzai, "The 1848 Abolitionist *Farmān*. A step towards ending the slave trade in Iran," in Campbell, *Abolition*, 94–102, esp. 99.

45 See Cooper, *From Slaves to Squatters*, 39. Drescher, *The Mighty Experiment*, 172–173 and David Northrup, *Indentured Labor in the Age of Imperialism, 1834–1922* (New York: Cambridge University Press, 1985), 159–160, Table A.2. In global terms, the 1860s also marked the peak of indentured servants in the French and Spanish colonies as well as Peru. Dutch Surinam, Africa, and the Pacific Ocean world added to the demand for indentured labor in the 1870s.

British slave owners in its colonies. No one in Britain, thereafter, dreamt of requesting its legislators and taxpayers to add incalculably greater sums to pay African or Asian slaveholders in the Old World. In a formulation that was endlessly repeated by British colonial agents for three generations after 1833, the costs in bloodshed and chaos that would follow an immediate and total emancipation of myriads of slaves under British sovereignty might irreparably shake imperial authority in the affected colonies. Invading the homes and harems of oriental domestic slavery, built upon ancient laws, traditions, and religions, was likened to political insanity.[46]

In the East, the incremental delegalization of the institution of slavery in India became the generic model for Old World emancipation or what historians have come to call the "Indian Model of Abolition."[47] Despite the fact that some contemporary Indian slaveholders viewed Act V of 1843 as a "glimpse of apocalypse," the transition in India went off even more smoothly than the widely heralded and more dramatic emancipation of the British West Indian slaves.[48] Mansfield and the Indian imperial bureaucracy could not have asked for more. There were not even the scattered incidents of collective strike resistance that greeted slave emancipation on the night of August 1, 1834. The structure of India's civil society accounted for the non-event as much as the stealth of its implementation. In the subcontinent, the elite consensus about hierarchy and deference extended across the Muslim-Hindu divide. No collective conflict over the transformation occurred either within the slaveholders' ranks or between them and the social groups lying along the spectrum of bondage and mastery. Open violations of either *Shari'a* or Hindu laws on bondage were certain to provoke a widespread collective backlash. Delegalization also meant that the ambiguities of servile statuses still remained embedded within the range of customary law. As noted above, enforcement was strengthened, in 1860, when the Indian Penal Code made trading and abducting slaves for sale punishable by imprisonment. Like Act 5, this legislation engendered no disruption. The laws made it difficult for officials to favor masters, but both the courts and colonial agents left the balance of power in the hands of employers. The Indian version of the Masters and Servants Acts, in the form of a Workman's Breach of Contract Act, was introduced the year before the criminalization of slaveholding. This left the door open to the penal enforcement of debt bondage. India followed the incremental judicial road to gradual emancipation.[49]

---

[46] Drescher, *Mighty Experiment*, ch. 11–12.

[47] Temperley, *British Antislavery*, ch. 5; Miers and Roberts, "Introduction," in *End of Slavery*, 12–13; Klein, "Introduction," in *Breaking the Chains*, 19–20; Miers, "Slavery to Freedom in Sub-Saharan Africa: Expectations and Realities," in Temperley, *After Slavery*, 237–264; esp. 239–240; and Paul E. Lovejoy and Jan S. Hogendorn, *Slow Death for Slavery: The Course of Abolition in Northern Nigeria, 1897–1936* (Cambridge University Press, 1993), 64.

[48] Chatterjee, *Gender*, 213–214.

[49] Kumar, "Colonialism, Bondage, and Caste in British India," in Klein, *Breaking*, 112–130.

Almost all Old World imperial agents adhered to this putative distinction between Western plantation slavery and Eastern domestic servitude. It played an especially important role in limiting the intrusion of the imperial state into gender relations within the household. The widespread acceptance of concubinage affected policy making towards women and girls within family relationships. In the aftermath of the uprising against British rule in 1857–1858, colonial agents became particularly cautious about intruding on activities within the household. Thus, even after the passage of penal sanctions in 1860, a high British official referred to the trade in young girls as something *"like slavery though not perhaps actually so."*[50]

Even in the longer run, magistrates were reluctant to enforce separations of young people from their families even when poverty or famine drove families to sell their children into prostitution and concubinage. Most of the non-European parts of the British Empire lacked the network of English "poor laws" institutions that provided basic welfare and shelter to the indigent. As Gyan Prakash concludes, although "British rule installed the discourse of freedom and made free labor appear as a natural human condition, freedom remained haunted by unfreedom," debt-bondage, and child prostitution.[51]

As striking as the discourse of denial and ambiguity is, the relative absence of a story of visible collective action by metropolitan groups within India or in the metropolis to diminish the zones of servitude. A tacit acceptance of India's differences in poverty, religion, laws, and social structure fortified the premise that "domestic" slavery in the East demanded more patience and discretion than it had in the West. The question of antislavery policy was reopened on the western coast of Africa in 1873–1874. When Britain annexed its first sizeable interior territory on the Gold Coast, the memory of the recent Western and Eastern imperial "experiments" both weighed heavily on policy makers' minds.

The government immediately had to address the concerns of the metropolitan antislavery lobby about the fate of slaves within the new boundaries of British colonial jurisdiction. For a generation, colonial office archives had reflected the opinion that "[d]omestic slavery has existed from time immemorial as a social institution on the Gold Coast, as well as in other parts of Africa." The colonial agents described West African slavery as the mildest form of the institution that had ever existed. No quarter could be given to the inhuman slave trade. Slavery itself, however, was a different matter. The cautionary testimony of abolitionist Richard Madden was invoked as evidence of the institution's function as a shelter from the destitution of the free unattached laborer in Africa. "Economically," concluded Madden, "the condition of a Gold Coast slave may be, under some circumstances, even an advantageous one as compared with that of a free labourer." Before 1874,

[50] Chatterjee, "Abolition by Denial," 154.
[51] Gyan Prakash, "Terms of Servitude: The Colonial Discourse on Slavery and Bondage in India," in Klein, *Breaking*, 131–149.

the British agents closely followed the Mansfield precedent as formalized by
Lord Stowell in 1827. Ex-slave residents on free soil were to be reattached
to their slave status if they returned to slave territory beyond the bounds of
British jurisdiction.

The initial British expansion into the West African interior was the result
of a conflict arising from an Ashanti invasion of the coastal region in 1873–
1874. It was not the consequence of policies advocated by economic or
political interests either in Africa or in the metropolis.[52] British annexations
were designed as much to block the sources of Ashanti arms as to preempt
the French from extending their own sphere of influence along the coast.
Once annexation occurred, the colonial office realized that it would have
to align policy with the controversial presence of slavery now under formal British jurisdiction. The West Indian model of immediate emancipation
and compensation was quickly ruled out of consideration. Parliamentary
pressure forced the immediate issuance of ordinances against the slave trade
and in favor of gradual emancipation. Once more, "delegalization" was the
obvious alternative: There was "no disturbance of labor relations." Contracts were not required. Slaves who silently went on serving were deemed
"contented." "There was no excitement and no compensation," but emancipation in the official view "was far more complete than in any country
and affected more millions of men than in the West Indies and America put
together."[53] As Mansfield had said a century before, "for I would have all
masters think they were free and all negroes think they were not, because
they would both behave better." Exit from the institution of slavery would
occur person by person.

One must not overlook the fact that African civil society had been
responding to British imperial development for decades before the Asante
war. The initial decree of abolition, unaccompanied by procedural and
defined limits, produced panic among many slaveholders. Significantly, they
responded with petitions both to local officials and to London. The antiabo-
lition campaign was, among other things, an effort to safeguard the servile
labor of which they were beneficiaries, and to stake claims for compensation for possible losses. Whatever the colonial office might have decided,
the West Indian process of compensated emancipation was familiar to West
African elites. The elites were also quite clear about the role that petitioning
played in the transformation of the British public sphere in general and of the
institution of British slavery in particular. Significantly, one of the African
documents submitted to colonial authorities was a ladies' petition.[54]

---

[52] Dumett and Johnson, "The Gold Coast," in *End of Slavery*, 78–79.
[53] *Ibid.*, fol. 376.
[54] See the important article by K. O. Akurang-Parry, "'A Smattering of Education' and Petitions
as Sources: A Study of African Slaveholders' Responses to Abolition in the Gold Coast
Colony, 1874–75," in *History in Africa*, 27 (2000), 39–60. He demonstrates how the Gold

Nor was Gold Coast civil society confined to antiabolitionists. As in Latin American societies, many among the Gold Coast elite had become convinced that abolition was inevitable. They were incensed precisely because the British government was adopting the ambiguous and quasi-deceptive route of the Indian model. Not only did the emancipation package provide no compensation to ease the transition, but it also provided no network of places of refuge to which slaves might flee. The British government offered slaves neither economic alternatives nor social support to take advantage of the liberating ordinances. This helps to explain the failure of slaves to react in large numbers to abolition.[55]

On slave raiding and trading, the British quickly reaffirmed their policy. They attacked the overland slave markets in 1874. By the late 1880s, magistrates claimed to have eliminated public sales of slaves and prosecuted dealers whenever they were discovered. Driven from public sites, the slave trade fragmented into small-scale clandestine operations.

As in India, the Gold Coast emancipation ordinance of 1874 was not consistently enforced. There were wide variations from one district to another. Slavery was no longer legal but officials were not given blanket authorization to interfere in master-servant relations. Slaves had to initiate legal intervention or lodge complaints against forcible constraint or cruelty. When the ordinance was given some publicity, slaves were often reluctant to file complaints against their masters because of their economic vulnerability in the event of separation. A few months before the ordinance was promulgated, a Foreign Office official declared that if the slave population did not emancipate itself under liberal rules of liberation "we would not be at fault."[56] Given the strong dependency/welfare element in Akan servitude and the powerful threats of ostracism and retaliation against those already integrated into the community, slaves infrequently brought cases to the courts. The culture of collective disapproval of informing against neighbors was apparently more powerful than hostility to coercive dependency.

As in India, the majority of slaves who felt able to choose freedom achieved it without judicial or legal intervention. They took advantage of delegalization to return home if they had been recently enslaved or to remain tenant cultivators in the vicinity of their former masters. Free villages of ex-slaves ultimately appeared but they amounted to only a small fraction of

Coast intelligentsia deployed petitioning as part of the repertoire of British constitutional methods to submit antiabolitionist petitions to British officials. Their methods included the petitioning by women. Their demands for compensated abolition may have encouraged the British government's decision to avoid any use of the West Indian precedent of 1833 in Africa.

55 Kwabena O. Akurang-Parry, "We Shall Rejoice to see the Day when Slavery shall cease to exist: *The Gold Coast Times*, The African Intelligentsia, and Abolition in the Gold Coast," in *History in Africa* 31 (2004), 19–42.

56 PRO CO 879/6, fol. 206v, E. Fairfield, Downing Street, 19 March 1874.

the slave population. The range of economic opportunities remained small, and new European capital investment was of modest proportions. As late as 1900, a full generation after Gold Coast emancipation, wage laborers working for Europeans constituted only 5 percent of the adult male workforce.[57] In the Gold Coast, then, as in India, there was no mass flight towards freedom, probably reflecting the modest flow of enslaved outsiders into the region prior to British annexation. In 1874, Britain's main innovations in Ghana on the Indian model were to outlaw debt bondage and pawning, and to add a "free womb" clause to the ordinance. After January 1, 1875, anyone born in, or entering, the Gold Coast was legally free.

When multinational expansion European into Africa escalated in the 1880s, the adoption of the low-cost, low-risk Indian precedent was already the unquestioned policy of choice. The sequence of events in the Scramble for Africa makes it abundantly clear that attention to African slavery was an unintended consequence, not a cause, of the European divisions of the territorial spoils. The first international conference on Africa met in Berlin in 1884–85. Its primary purpose was to formalize the process of determining the boundaries of domination not emancipation. The creation of a new German overseas empire and the simultaneous acceleration of French military ambitions in Africa were clear signs that the era of undisputed British paramountcy beyond Europe was over. France and Germany launched new initiatives in West and East Africa. Belgium's King Leopold made a successful bid for jurisdiction over the Congo. Offshore, the movement of continental European warships through the Suez Canal made it apparent to non-European rulers that the British navy was no longer the only presence in the Indian Ocean. British abolitionist initiatives ceased to be a matter for leisurely negotiations between British pressure groups, government ministries, colonial agents, and commercial interests.

With the convening of the Berlin conference, the British press noted that the terms of power had clearly shifted towards a multipolar rather than a British hegemonic context.[58] On the eve of the meeting, the British government decided to push for an antislave trade clause in the final agreement. This would reaffirm Britain's standing as the guardian of African welfare. With long experience of the complications that could arise at home from commitments to immediate emancipation, the British sought to confine their obligations to their own core commitment against the slave trade.

The final document, ratified in Berlin, clearly prohibited the maritime slave trade. It more vaguely condemned the overland traffic. The British diplomats and, of course, all other signatories, consciously avoided any

---

[57] Dumett and Johnson, "Gold Coast," 84–92.

[58] William Roger Louis, "The Berlin Congo Conference and the (non-) Partition of Africa, 1884–1885," in Louis, *Ends of British Imperialism: The Scramble for Empire, Suez and Decolonization: Collected Essays* (London: I. B. Tauris, 2006), 75–126; esp. 78–79.

open-ended commitment to the abolition of slavery. Until the scramble raised the stakes by threatening to extend to Africa the European barriers to free trade, the problem of slave emancipation was more of a reason for resisting than initiating territorial expansion. If Britain annexed any territory, "warned Lord Selborne, Britain's chief judicial officer slavery must cease to exist."[59]

Only after the Brussels Conference of 1889–1890, launched after the Lavigerie mobilization, was the elimination of the entire slave trade formalized as imperialist obligation. The Brussels' Act of 1890 left procedures against the institution of slavery itself to the discretion of each imperial power. The British government stuck to its Old World formula. Soon the British antislavery lobby itself formally sanctioned the gradualist transition, coupling antislavery initiatives to what would cause "the least disturbance to the Arab and slave populations." The slave trade was henceforth prohibited, and any rights derived from claims to property in persons were no longer enforceable in courts.

The status of concubines was shifted into the category of wives. Provisions were made for their release from ex-masters by the courts in cases of cruelty. As the first European-wide pronouncement on capitalist attitudes toward non-European labor, the document showed little confidence in what has come to be called the free-labor ideology. Nothing was done to prohibit barriers to the mobility of workers. Colonial legislation was free to discourage the idleness and independence of workers through vagrancy laws and penal enforcement of contracts.[60]

In the late 1890s, the almost simultaneous slave emancipations in Zanzibar on East Africa's coast and in northern Nigeria to the west showed the confluence of assumptions and ideas. Frederick Lugard, the architect of emancipation in northern Nigeria, had already served in East Africa. He agreed firmly with his counterparts in Zanzibar that the Indian model should prevail. The West Indian experiment was rejected as despotic and disruptive. To the abolition of the slave status in northern Nigeria in 1897, Lugard added a free-womb proviso in 1901.

To ensure continuity of labor, Lugard ordered resident agents to make every effort to discourage a "wholesale assertion of 'freedom'," or departures of farm workmen from agriculture. The ideal, again, was to have slaves individually obtain their freedom, over time, in Islamic courts and through self-purchase or ransom by third parties. Meanwhile the mobility of West Africans, like those in the east, could be restrained by vagrancy laws, master and servant laws, and restricted access to land. As in the Indian Ocean emancipations, the issue of concubines and slave women was carefully separated from other aspects of emancipation. Women's separations

[59] Louis, "Berlin Congo Conference," 116.
[60] Cooper, *From Slaves*, 41, 235–248.

from their masters/spouses were treated as movements between families, "a desire to leave one husband or man. . . . in order to live with another".[61]

Among the other colonial powers, the French had the strongest tradition of extending the principle of freedom to their overseas colonies. Although the Second Empire (1852–1870) did not rescind the second French emancipation in 1848, it cut back its benefits. Lacking recaptive Africans and Indian indentured labor for their ex-slave colonies, French governments authorized the purchase-cum-redemption of slaves in Africa as contracted servants (*engagés*) in the colonies. Although French legal experts drew a careful distinction between these bound laborers who could refuse deportation and slaves who could not, the policy encouraged African slavers to enslave captives and deliver them to the coast.

The French terminated the practice only after an Anglo-French convention allowed the French planters to acquire indentured servants in British Indian ports under the same rules as those governing British recruitment. The supply of Indian labor continued to flow into the French tropics under the Third Republic into the 1880s. Within Africa, slavery continued with official French acquiescence. The Governor of Senegal established a Parisian-approved legal distinction that allowed non-French "subjects" to retain their slaves on French "free soil." French authorities expelled runaway slaves of friendly African masters and sanctioned the apprenticeship of children brought into the colonies by their masters. French officials made every effort to keep these dubious practices from attracting metropolitan public notice.[62] The pattern was disrupted only when prominent metropolitans exposed individual violations of French principles. Hampered by a less active abolitionist lobby, antislavery initiatives remained more sporadic. With the advent of the Third Republic in 1870, the former French slave colonies were again represented in the metropolitan legislature. Black deputies who visited French Africa could stimulate parliamentary embarrassment over the tolerance of slavery in Senegal. In the French senate, Victor Schoelcher continually exposed the contradictions between metropolitan principles and bureaucratic practices. These contradictions continued the pattern of routine violations punctuated by episodes of parliamentary and press exposure. Even Schoelcher felt constrained by the argument that justice required honoring Franco-African treaties limiting interference with slavery.[63]

---

[61] Paul E. Lovejoy and Jan S. Hogendorn, *Slow Death for Slavery: The Course of Abolition in Northern Nigeria, 1897–1936* (Cambridge: Cambridge University Press, 1993), ch. 3.

[62] Klein, *Slavery and Colonial Rule*, ch. 2. David Northrup, "Freedom and Indentured Labor in the French Caribbean, 1848–1900" in *Coerced and Free Migration: Global Perspectives*, David Eltis, ed. (Stanford: Stanford University Press, 2002), 204–228.

[63] Klein, *Slavery and Colonial Rule*, ch. 8, and Alice L. Conklin, *A Mission to Civilize: The Republican Idea of Empire in France and West Africa, 1895–1930* (Stanford: Stanford University Press, 1997), 96.

As in the case of the United States, a dramatic surge of territorial expansion upset the political equilibrium between ideology and slavery in French West Africa. The sudden expansion of French domination in Africa during the 1880s and 1890s deepened the gap between metropolitan antislavery commitments and colonial governance. The French conquest of the western Sudan was achieved by a small number of French officers leading largely African fighting forces. Commanders functioned with small operating funds and stretched supply lines. Africans were recruited largely by promises of booty, and the principal form of transferable wealth consisted of slaves. Like Muslim rulers before them, the French quickly learned the advantages of reversing the relationship between conquerors and the vanquished. Commanders recruited captives and paid them with other captives. Women could be liberated or redistributed as the occasion allowed. Thus, the conquest itself was analogous to a last great precolonial surge of slave raiding that was already endemic in the region. An African army recruited and organized according to African methods and European weapons created "a bloodier and more horrible period than the Sudan had ever known." As in the Haitian revolution, both sides acted with ruthless brutality. Only with the conquest of the region and the removal of rivals to French domination could slave raiding be dramatically diminished.[64]

As long as France was being awed by the successive tales of quick and easy victories in Africa in the 1880s and early 1890s, antislavery concerns were given much lower priority than military success. By 1900, the French state ruled more territory in northwest and central Africa than Napoleon had acquired at the beginning of the century. It is obvious why French tolerance of slavery was most marked during the conquest. Even in the heat of their campaigns, however, French generals were always conscious of the antislavery potential entailed in their own success. In 1886, to resolve logistical supply problems, the military began to create villages near military posts, even over the opposition of allied chiefs. Slaves fleeing enemy rulers could be given refuge in these "liberty villages" in exchange for their services as workers or fighters. The French military allotted them a few months of rations and a day or two a week to support themselves. For most fleeing slaves, these were areas of temporary refuge until restored security enabled them to move on. As workers for the French, their wages could be used to obtain the purchase price for their freedom.[65]

In France itself, the legislature never debated a formal motion to abolish slavery in its new colonial realms. However, a parliamentary debate over Madagascar, in 1896, heralded a more active post-conquest metropolitan policy. All legislators agreed that French acquisition of a region entailed the termination of slavery. All agreed that France had to proceed cautiously.

[64] Klein, *Slavery and Colonial Rule*, ch. 5.
[65] Klein, *Slavery and Colonial Rule*, 84–88; and Conklin, *A Mission*, 96.

There was no widespread support for a revolutionary decree of immediate emancipation under the auspices of the Third Republic. Deputies from
the Left and Center, however, denounced the government's one attempt to
postpone any immediate initiative. The achievement of personal liberty was
inseparable from the French imperial mission. The government was directed
to undertake action leading toward emancipation. As in India, however, it
was argued that widespread poverty left the mass of the estimated 400,000
slaves (a fifth of the island's population) without economic resources.
They were obliged either to stay with their ex-masters or become share-
croppers.[66]

Almost every area of Africa acquired by European states followed a
sequence from suppression of slave raiding to more tempered suppression
of slave trading to a more drawn out delegalization of the institution itself.
Suppression of slave raiding was in every case the most urgent prerequisite of further economic activity and was itself a prima facie justification
of invasion and conquest. Germany, the newest entrant into the imperialist
venture, behaved no differently than its predecessor. Effective German conquest in East Africa began around 1890. The intervention against slave raiding and trading was swift and brutal. Within a decade, large-scale raiding,
kidnapping, and wholesale slave trading were on the wane.[67] In northern
Cameroon, where occupation remained incomplete, the German government was unprepared to accelerate development, as local rulers continued
to accumulate slaves by raiding and trading.[68]

In the proscription of slave raiding, international standing and humanitarian motives most clearly coincided. Neither security nor state power could
coexist with the levels of violence created by predatory conflict. Security of
property and mobility were prerequisites for economic development. In the
broader transition from slavery to freedom, however, short- and long-term
economic incentives parted company. The only mention of conditions of
contract laborers in the Brussels International Conference Act of 1890, was
the injunction that the signatories should ensure the legality of contracts
for labor service. The door was left wide open for state-sponsored levies of
labor. In the notorious case of the Congo Free State, King Leopold of Belgium
used the directives of the Brussels Act to establish posts for labor recruitment. All "vacant" land was expropriated. Without the financial resources
of an established European state treasury, the king quickly established a
forced labor system. Appealing to the Brussels Act, he defended this policy

---

[66] Campbell, "Unfree Labour," 76–77; and Klein, "Emancipation," 207; both in Campbell,
Abolition and its Aftermath in Indian Ocean Africa and Asia. For French policy in Indo-
China between 1877 and 1897, see *ibid.,* 207.

[67] Jan-Georg Deutsch, *Emancipation without Abolition in German East Africa c. 1884–1914*
(Athens OH: Ohio University Press, 2006), 170.

[68] Miers, *Slavery in the Twentieth Century,* 41.

as a humanitarian measure designed to develop African incentives for steady labor. Businesses were authorized to launch punitive expeditions to recruit workers. African rulers and communities were forced to provide administrators and concessionaires with food, fuel, porterage, and *corvée* labor without wages. A terrorist system of hostage taking, beatings, and mutilation ensured that the recruited laborers met their state-defined quotas in the production of exportable commodities. The shift from slave raiding to labor recruitment was here a distinction without a difference. In the case of the Congo Free State, the mode of forced conscription seemed to flow seamlessly from the Old Zanzibari slave traders to the new regime. Chiefs filled their quotas for conscription from among the weak, kinless, and friendless, including their own pool of slaves and prisoners of war. The boundary between freedman and militiaman disappeared. Children too young to work were rounded up, sent to "school camps," and trained for the militia or labor force. Large government projects like railroad construction also employed conscription.

The system was so ruthless and brutal that exogenous pressures were necessary to bring the atrocities to light. Initially, missionaries supported the establishment of the Congo Free State to enhance the extension of their own organizations into central Africa. Moreover, they did not unite in opposition to state authorities even after the condition of the state's subjects became clear. Instead, the largest mobilization against the Congo labor system slowly developed out of a British missionary lecture campaign reminiscent of the emancipation rallies seven decades earlier. British nonconformists again formed the organizational nexus of a popular Congo Reform Association. Parliamentary debates over mounting reports of atrocities culminated in a British electoral campaign in 1906. The Congo Reform Association's campaign fortunately coincided with a wave of popular mobilization in Britain over religious issues. It was the last hurrah of the old popular antislavery base. In November 1908, King Leopold bowed to international and domestic pressure. He transferred the Congo Free State to Belgium.[69]

Although the scale of atrocities in the Congo diminished, the mechanisms of taxation and compulsory labor still verged on a brutal forced-labor system. Public works projects and private enterprises using conscripted labor expanded in other areas as well as notably in French equatorial Africa, the Portuguese Atlantic islands, and Mozambique.[70] In the Portuguese colonies, metropolitan pressures and oversight were less effective than in the French

---

[69] See Kevin Grant, *A Civilized Savagery: Britain* (N. Y. Routledge, 2005), ch. 2. The transfer of the Congo to Belgian national rule in 1908 produced slow changes under international pressure. The enforcement of abolition decrees was uneven because of the fear of producing serious dislocations in the labor market. Northrup, "The Ending of Slavery in the Eastern Belgian Congo," in *End of Slavery*, 462–489.

[70] See Miers, *Slavery in the Twentieth Century*, 51–53, 135–141.

and British zones. In tandem with the abolition of slavery in Portuguese Africa in 1878, new forms of post-emancipation bondage flourished down to the end of the nineteenth century. Central Angola became a labor reservoir for both the Congo Free State and the venerable Portuguese plantation system on the Atlantic islands in the Gulf of Guinea. The Ovimbundu inhabitants, who had participated as purchasers and traders before Portuguese conquest, now found themselves obliged to sell their own pawns and slaves to recruiters. The Portuguese simply created a new forced-labor pool by blurring the line between free and dependent populations.

By 1920, the Portuguese government no longer distinguished between enslaved and free Ovimbundus. Working conditions, treatment, remuneration, and immobility deteriorated from those that had prevailed in the earlier slave system. Debt labor expanded to draw further recruits into the labor pool. A state-sponsored system of forced labor was fully institutionalized in the first third of the twentieth century. By the end of World War II, the Ovimbundu had lower life expectancies and greater family disruption than they had enjoyed in the pre-Portuguese social system. The groundwork was laid for desperate and devastating uprisings between the 1960s and 1980s.[71]

At the beginning of the twentieth century, Britain and France were the two imperial nations with the most powerful metropolitan antislavery pressure groups. They had also accrued the largest numbers of overseas slaves within their domains. And, the slaves in their jurisdictions were able to act most decisively and rapidly in altering their status. As indicated earlier, on the eve of the British invasion of the Sokoto Caliphate, the area contained one of the largest slave populations in the world. British conquest of the area began in 1897 and was effectively completed with the creation of a Protectorate of Northern Nigeria in 1900. High Commissioner Lugard immediately put the region on notice that both the slave trade and slavery would be brought under state control. By 1903, Lugard declared that large-scale slave raiding had ended and slave markets closed. Slave dealing was confined to frontier areas that were less easily brought under colonial control. They were not terminated until 1920.

Regarding slavery as an institution, official policy in northern Nigeria followed the Indian model. The legal status of slavery was abolished. Slaves were not prevented from leaving their masters but were discouraged and even obstructed from departing to prevent massive disruption in the social

---

[71] See Linda M. Heywood, "Slavery and Forced Labor in the Changing Political Economy of Central Angola, 1850–1949," in *End of Slavery*, 415–436. In both the Congo and Angola, the abolition process bore a striking similarity to M. I. Finley's description of the ending of slavery in the Roman Empire. It was driven by the deterioration of the peasants' status rather than the amelioration of the slaves. See M. I. Finley, *Ancient Slavery and Modern Ideology* (New York: Veheng Press, 1980), ch. 4.

and economic systems. The colonial administration found it necessary to admonish resident British missionaries "not to encourage, far less initiate, any slave initiative to depart from their masters."[72] Abolitionist expectations seem to have been stimulated in the British sphere of operations even during the process of military conquest. The appearance of the British Royal Niger Company in an area signaled to the slaves that they were free to flee. The Company's subsequent announcement that it was providing sanctuary for fugitives provided a precedent that Lugard could certainly not publicly disown. Slaves took full advantage of the opportunity of a proclaimed policy of conquest under the banner of liberation.[73]

When Lugard assumed office in West Africa in 1900, he was already faced with the crisis of slave flight. One British agent had gone around his district telling its residents that they were free, and that individuals would no longer be enslaved. Communities of fugitives resisted attempts to convince them to return them to their former masters or even their communities of captivity. Some British authorities hurriedly tried to draw some boundary line of limitations. They allowed masters to hold "domestic" slaves in custody and to sanction the slave status, if the slave markets were closed. In one Mahdi-led rebellion (1905–1906), the British were willing to force those allied with the Mahdi rebels back into slavery as a terror tactic against future resistance. As with Cromwell's similar strategy, more than two centuries earlier, the action was effective. Incidents of administrative massacre and reenslavement, of course, had to be deleted from reports designed for metropolitan consumption.

Hogendorn and Lovejoy estimate that at least 200,000 slaves, approximately one tenth of the slave population, participated in a great exodus during the decade after British conquest. Most seem to have been recent captives and were more likely to be welcomed by their families and communities of origin, if they still existed. The size of the exodus is probably testimony to the scale of the slave raiding/trading environment of the Sokoto Caliphate in the years prior to the European invasion. It is also evidence of one of the possibilities for slave agency opened up by the European intrusions. One needs to compare the tens of thousands of slaves in annual flight from their conditions in northern Nigeria with the tens of thousands of slaves still being enslaved in the borderlands between Angola and northern Rhodesia during the same decade.[74]

An even more dramatic exodus occurred in the French-occupied Sudan. It did not, as in British Nigeria, begin with the disorder of the conquest. Initially, the French, like their African enemies, regarded the redistribution of human beings as integral to their battle plans: "The French army was as

[72] Lovejoy and Hogendorn, *Slow Death for Slavery*, 33–34.
[73] *Ibid.*, 33–38.
[74] *Ibid.*, 61–62; and Heywood, "Central Angola," in *End of Slavery*, 421.

much a part of this savagery as any other, and their African agents often exploited French power to accumulate wealth and slaves."[75] The French attack on the institution of slavery began only after the end of the conquest with the imposition of a civil government and metropolitan priorities in 1900. A left-wing coalition, composed of radicals, socialists, and moderate Republicans, welded together by the Dreyfus affair, came to power in 1899. For a few years, it offered France a unique experience in stability and policy continuity. Its radical Republican orientation had an impact on colonial policy. It was committed to a systematic attack on slavery.[76]

In 1903, a new governor-general of French West Africa, Ernest Roume, took measures to develop a coherent policy on emancipation in the Sudan. As in British Afro-Asia, his plan offered no compensation funds to masters and no welfare funds to slaves. Roume rejected beginning with a "free womb" law. That would recognize the existence of slavery in a territory already under the sovereignty of the French republic. Slavery had now become such an embarrassment in the Western lexicon that it presented obstacles to gradual legislative elimination. Delegalization seemed the safest, cheapest, and least disruptive strategy. All further sales of persons were to be prohibited. As elsewhere, some aspects of servitude would be exempted from legal interference. These included the "customary authority of husbands over wives and minors, and any voluntary service exchanged for relief from destitution." This would continue the private welfare dimension of the old institution while avoiding massive new financial obligations for the state.[77]

The 1905 decree on slavery once more replicated the Mansfield strategy. It abolished only the sale, gift, or exchange of persons. Once again, of course, the actual impact of the decree extended much further than its guarded language. The colonial state would neither recognize the institution of slavery nor return runaway slaves to their masters. Contracts would constitute the new nexus for buyers, borrowers, and bosses. As with all previous delegalizations, slavery could no longer be buttressed by legally sanctioned recruitment or enforcement.

The slaves of the Sudan themselves began to implement the new policy on a scale that neither Mansfield or Granville Sharp nor any of their judicial and abolitionist descendants probably could have imagined. In the spring of 1905, an exodus began in the western Sudan at Banamba, a town founded in the 1840s. For half a century, it had become the most important slave market in the Sudan and the region's major distribution center for salt and horses.[78] The hub of slavery in Sudan, the city also held the region's most

---

[75] Klein, *Slavery and Colonial Rule*, 125; and ch. 8 generally.

[76] Conklin, *Mission*, 94–106.

[77] Klein, *Slavery and Colonial Rule*, 136. On the normative status of slavery as an embarrassment to civilized status, see Michael Salman, *The Embarrassment of Slavery: Controversies over Bondage and Nationalism in the American Colonial Philippines* (Berkeley: University of California Press, 2001), 14–17.

[78] Klein, *Slavery and Colonial Rule*, 55.

uprooted population. For the next five years, slaves all across the Sudan streamed back to their homes. Hundreds of thousands began to rebuild ravaged communities. The result, as Martin Klein relates, was the collapse of much of the preconquest labor system in French West Africa.

Fearing a total collapse of public order, the governor-general ordered troops in Banamba to detain runaways and mediate with the leaders of the desertion movement. Masters used the opportunity to seize children and personal goods. William Merlaud-Ponty, the principal official on site in the Sudan, decided to support the slaves. He ordered the authorities to protect domestics who wanted to leave their masters. Passes were issued to all who wished to leave. The mass flight continued with remarkable order. As word spread of the new policy, the movement surged and spread. People in regions still vulnerable to raids joined the migration of those already enslaved. The large-scale movements continued for a decade, until a series of famines intervened on the eve of World War I.

The authorized departures were a remarkable reversal of the consensus of three generations of colonial officialdom that a mass departure of slaves would bring chaos or revolution. French troops were too thinly spread to prevent some instances of master-initiated violence, but the collective action was too broad to stanch. Slaves previously accumulated by allied chiefs, colonial agents, and African soldiers, absconded. Even the usual gender differentiation that gave master/husbands authority over their wives was threatened. Faced with one crisis after another the French colonial government also attempted to draw some new boundary lines. It was decided that "liberty papers" given to a female slave had no effect on her matrimonial obligations and entailed no diminution of male spousal rights. In the same spirit as the *Somerset* decision, the French allowed, but gave almost no help to "liberty villages," collectives of runaways that temporarily sprang up during the exodus. Despite the fear of social disintegration, Ponty persisted in reminding his local commandants that their obligation was to ensure personal liberty for the former slaves. To the government, he stressed the orderliness of the migration and the eagerness of the ex-slaves to work for themselves.

Ponty's final summary of the great migration was a vindication of the result in economic as well as in humanitarian terms. The institution of slavery, he emphasized, was neither abolished nor tolerated in fact: "There are no longer either servants or slaves.... Often [the slave] has remained, but under the conditions of a contract. Liberty suddenly given or refound has in no way embarrassed him. He returned quietly to his homeland or has gone to offer his labor in our cities or in our workshops."[79]

There were difficulties in many areas but, in general, the negative economic reverberations appear to have been temporary, even where they were

---

[79] Quoted in *ibid.*, 167, written by Governor-General Ponty, 13 January 1913. This account is drawn largely from Klein.

recorded. One widespread European civil institution in the Sudan was ironically immobilized during the exodus. The separation of the French state and the Catholic Church reached its climax in 1905. The consequent withdrawal of public funding from the missionaries meant that they lacked resources to feed the migrants just when it was most needed. The convergence of secular and religious antislavery movements foundered on metropolitan struggles.

Economically, the exodus of former slaves was neither encouraged nor sustained for reasons of capitalist development. The colonial administration was often quite distrustful of industrial capitalism and supportive of both native property rights and treaty obligations. For domestic, political, and international reasons, the metropolitan state wanted to remove the stigma of state support of slavery. The French government hoped for as few changes as possible in Africa as were commensurate with this goal. Those who ultimately praised the creation of a free-labor market did so after the fact, when the predicted total disaster did not occur.

In the Sudan, more than anywhere else, it was the slaves who collectively provided the catalyst for the breakthrough to that labor market.[80] In French West Africa, as elsewhere, slavery underwent a slow death. By the outbreak of the Great War in 1914, only a fraction of the population had abandoned their situations. All of the other brakes to full freedom – gender, famine, poverty, limited ownership of or access to fertile land, and elite resistance – hindered the pace of transformation. Increased reliance on the chiefs after the World War I was followed by increasing distrust of the labor market. An important segment of the European elite continued to believe that, in West Africa, economic development required coercing Africans to work. They remained much closer to the perspective of the policy makers in Portuguese and Belgian Africa. In French West Africa, forced labor continued to be used to develop the infrastructure and commercial agriculture of the region's, railways, canals, roads, and plantations.

Eventually, elites did loosen controls of former slaves everywhere but the dramatic exodus of up to 900,000 slaves in early twentieth-century French West Africa did not bring the complete ending of slavery in that area any sooner than the rest of the continent. Into the twenty-first century, the Islamic Republic of Mauritania continued to report that chattel slavery still persisted within its borders.[81] The arduous path to Mauritanian emancipation highlights the general contrast between slavery in the Old World and New World, first illustrated by the case of India. Slave-like systems of labor and domestic relations persisted in India long after delegalization or prohibition of property rights in persons. In some areas, the institution was embedded in a thicket of other forms of constraint. Destitution, communal

---

[80] *Ibid.*, 176–177.
[81] *Ibid.*, p. 173 and Miers, *Slavery in the Twentieth Century*, 418.

identity, economic poverty, conjugal dependency, gender roles, and rights over offspring all constrained departure from masters and spouses.[82]

Slavery and the League of Nations

Generally, the slow death of slavery in sub-Saharan Africa was followed by an equally slow death of alternative systems of forced labor and the diminution of constraints on women in the family. The European conquests and European-directed forced-labor systems, which succeeded the raiding and slaving era before the 1880s, postponed the benefits of slave-trade abolition in certain areas well beyond the first quarter of the twentieth century. In other areas, however, the increased security provided by imperial rule opened the door to both the massive recorded exoduses in British and French West Africa and the less dramatic movement of slaves out of both their legal status as slaves and local confinement.[83]

From the perspective of the world market, it still seems impossible to calculate the composite impact of slave-trade abolition and emancipation on labor productivity and the production of cash crops in Africa during the half century between 1880 and 1930. The more pervasive institution of domestic slavery probably eroded most slowly and with the least measurable impact on the world market. Even areas of commercial slavery in Africa probably had not offered masters the productivity advantages of gang laborers in the plantations in Americas. Only in a few places along main trade routes had slavery been transformed in response to the world market before abolition.[84] Indeed, in some parts of the continent, such as South Central Africa, the formal emancipation of the slaves combined with levies degraded former masters into conscripted labor. Forced labor for public works remained a prerogative that many colonial states were long reluctant to surrender.

---

[82] R. R. Madden was the abolitionist who vituperously criticized Jamaican slaveholders for their ill-treatment of apprentices. He was virulently accused of spreading revolutionary doctrines in Cuba. He behaved more cautiously when dispatched to the Gold Coast by Prime Minister Russell in 1841. There, he was beset with the same problem that confronted offers of freedom thirty years later. When he told the slaves of Accra on the Gold Coast that they were free by the Queen's Law, they asked him whether "the Queen would give them anything to eat, otherwise they would prefer to remain slaves." The slaves' reply echoed through bureaucratic reports for generations (See PRO#CO 879/6 *Gold Coast, History of Settlement*, printed for the Colonial Office, March 1874: fols. 196–198).

[83] See, for example, Cooper, *From Slaves*, esp. ch. 6, regarding Zanzibar and coastal Kenya; Deutch, *Emancipation Without Abolition*, ch. 7, on German East Africa; Lee V. Cassanelli, "The Ending of Slavery in Italian Somalia: Liberty and the Control of Slavery," in *End of Slavery*, ch. 10, on Italian Somalia. For Indians, indentured servitude also constituted a means of social and geographical mobility, accounting for up to 28 million migrants mainly to the tropics, between 1846 and 1932. See Kingsley Davis, *The Population of India and Pakistan* (Princeton, NJ: Princeton University Press, 1951), 98–99.

[84] Lovejoy, *Transformations*, 285.

By the end of the first quarter of the twentieth century the new League of Nations was prepared to enshrine a collective consensus to "progressively" secure the disappearance of "the status or condition of a person over whom any or all of the powers attaching to the right of ownership are exercised."[85] The Covenant of the League of Nations itself did not include a declaration of human rights or a condemnation of slavery. It only bound members to "secure fair and humane condition for the labor of men, women and children" and the "just treatment" of natives under colonial powers. The Treaty of Versailles also pledged those powers to move toward a convergence of European and colonial conditions of labor.

By 1925, the League of Nations was ready to formulate a formal agreement on the abolition of slavery. Outside Britain, nongovernmental pressure was generally weak. Extending the proposed convention to include forced labor was out of the question. The opposition of governments with extensive forced-labor systems, such as in the Belgian Congo and Portuguese Africa, made it clear that it would be difficult to obtain compliance even with weaker clauses in the draft Convention. The United States also acceded to the Convention only with reservations. Some of its southern states continued to practice forced convict labor. Once again, in deference to the "complexities" of authority and dependency in many societies, concubinage was not included as an issue to be resolved in the Convention. Any imperial signatory was permitted to exempt portions of its colonial territories from some obligations.[86]

After preliminary discussions, the decision was made to begin reforming the institution by refusing to recognize slavery's legal status, eliminating the institution on a case by case basis. Thus, the "Indian model" of delegalization reached its culmination in the League of Nations' Slavery Convention. The consensus that complete abolition was not possible "at the stroke of a pen" for fear of worsening the condition of the natives was balanced by the observation that slave raiding and the maritime slave trade had been dramatically reduced in a single generation. From the tens of thousands of slaves traded annually beyond sub-Saharan Africa during the fourth quarter of the nineteenth century, the volume of the slave trade had fallen precipitously by 1925. With Ethiopia's formal prohibition in 1923, the entire world had been closed as a legal source for the slave trade.[87]

---

[85] Miers, *Slavery in the Twentieth Century*, 123.

[86] Miers, *Slavery in the Twentieth Century*, 122–128. The French remained faithful to their century-old tradition by refusing, in principle, either to designate the seaborne slave trade as piracy or to permit a full mutual right of search. The British were also hesitant. Forced labor was used in India and Burma.

[87] See C. W. W. Greenidge, *Slavery* (London: Allen and Unwin, 1958), 49. Censuses of the slave trade to the Muslim lands seem to go no further than the first decade of the twentieth century. See inter alia, Pété-Grenouillean, *Traites Negrières*, 144–156, and Ralph Austen's two censuses of the Islamic slave trade in *Slavery and Abolition*, 9:3 (1988), 21–44; and

The League of Nations' reports on slavery itself tended to focus (more narrowly) on the Sahara, the Sudan, Ethiopia, the neighboring Arabian peninsula, the Persian Gulf, and areas of South and Southeast Asia. The signatories adhered to the Convention in a frame of mind that considered the document as one more great landmark in the progressive and gradual disappearance of all forms of involuntary servitude. Earlier in the twentieth century, British abolitionists recognized that consensual agreement on dismantling the institution of slavery created opportunities to turn international attention toward other forms of coercion and exploitation simply by identifying them as forms of slavery in disguise. In a sense, this marked another broadening of the definition of bondage, as when Arthur Young or Adam Smith counted nineteen of twenty of the world's inhabitants as slaves. The door had never been closed to metaphorical extensions of the slave trade or slavery. "Wage" slavery, the "white" slave trade of prostitution, and the "sexual" slavery of Asian concubines were all early candidates for inclusion. However, as antislavery became the international gold standard of civilization in the early twentieth century, the tropes of slavery and the slave trade became more widely employed than ever before.[88]

An equally powerful vision of slavery in the world perspective emerged in the 1920s. The Western-led consensus on the institution's delegalization designated slavery as a "remnant," confined to non-Westernized areas of the world. The history of abolition could now be made perfectly congruent with the Western-led march of human and moral progress. The separation of slavery as a distinctively non-Western phenomenon was reinforced by the creation and mission of the International Labor Organization (ILO). Article 421 of the Treaty of Versailles bound all signatories to adhere to all conventions protecting labor in their non–self-governing dominions. The pledge was immediately institutionalized in 1919, with the founding of the ILO. In discussions leading up to the slavery convention, however, governments could not agree on the inclusion of all forms of colonial forced labor within its purview. The assumption of a backward bending labor supply curve among "backward peoples" informed all discussions of the transition from slave labor to free-wage labor. The preliminary report for the

Slavery and Abolition, 13:1 (1992), 214–248). Of the four to five million, nearly half were considered to reside in the realm of the Ethiopian Emperor Haile Selassie. See Sterling Joseph Coleman, Jr., "Gradual Abolition or Immediate Abolition of Slavery? The Political, Social and Economic Quandry of Emperor Haile Selassie I," *Slavery and Abolition*, 29:1 (2008), 65–82. For the list of twentieth-century antislavery laws, see Ziskind, *Emancipation Acts*.

88 For the early twentieth century, see Kevin Grant, *A Civilised Savagery: Britain and the New Slaveries in Africa, 1884–1926* (New York: Routledge, 2005; for the late twentieth and early twenty-first centuries, see Kevin Bales *Disposable People: New Slavery in the Global Economy* (Berkeley, CA: University of California Press, 1999/2004).

convention significantly limited itself to recommending the promotion of private property and peasant production.

That sense of spatial separation and temporal distance preserved the deeply embedded notion that the estimated four to five million slaves left in the world were still "beyond the line" of civilization. The notion had real impact upon those deemed to be isolated in a dark, if shrinking, world extending from the Persian Gulf through Ethiopia. Britain's push for an extension of protection for a forced-labor convention as a practice analogous to slavery in the 1920s ran into united opposition from France, Belgium, Italy, and Portugal, the other major colonial powers in Africa. They all had various practices which might come under attack under such a convention. The conceptual boundaries between labor in the noncolonial world and the colonial world remained intact. The ILO itself treated forced labor as, primarily, a colonial phenomenon and an extension of the international struggle against slavery. During the economic recovery of the 1920s, the demand for labor was not being met by wage-labor markets. The international labor standards developed by the ILO were framed with reference to industrialized Western societies, and its "colonial clause" granted the governments of these societies the right to exclude some or all of these labor standards in their overseas territories. The ILO sought to expose coercive abuses as a disincentive to educating the natives to "the advantages of work." At the same time, its director accepted the view that the "habits of free labor" were more lacking among the farmers of Africa than those of the self-governing world. Only the British government supported the immediate abolition of forced labor, at least for private enterprises. The "overseas exception" remained largely in place between the world wars. The resultant Forced Labor Convention of 1930 bound governments only to ending public forced labor within "the shortest possible period," with no actual termination date. It also reinforced the distinction between forced labor and slavery, and looked forward to protecting the workers of the "industrial world" from the competition of unorganized colonial workforces.[89]

In one sense, the normative stature of antislavery was reaffirmed more globally than ever before in the League of Nation's Committee of Experts on Slavery. By the late 1920s, there was also a pervasive assumption that the path of slavery was already set toward rapid extinction. National receptions of the convention of 1926 were, therefore, both commemorative and anticipatory. The French harkened back to their slave emancipation decree of 1848, burying the great Saint Domingue uprising of 1791, the radical revolutionary emancipation of 1794, and the Napoleonic restoration of slavery in 1802, in a common grave. The Portuguese, as the pioneers of Europe's

[89] Miers, *Slavery in the Twentieth Century*, 103, 115, 145–148; and Roger Daniel Maul, "The International Labour Organization and the Struggle against Forced Labour from 1919 to the Present," *Labor History*, 48:4 (2007), 477–500.

overseas empires, converted their five-hundred-year record of slaving into a five-hundred-year-old "civilizing policy" of "Christian brotherhood with native peoples." Portugal's centuries of contributions to the Atlantic slave trade and overseas slavery, on the other hand, were treated as incidental, limited, and "fortuitous." Portugal's reconstruction of imperial history as an antislavery narrative appeared particularly self-exculpatory because it was offered in the midst of another scandal over Portuguese use of African forced labor.

In a larger sense, however, Portugal's reconstruction was only the most striking version of a more generic moral realignment of Europe's relationship to the institution of slavery. All of Europe's imperial nations, in one way or another, burnished their imperial histories as civilizing missions. If Portugal now claimed to have worked for half a millennium for what it had agreed to only yesterday, there was biblical precedent here too: "And the last shall be first." What diplomat at Geneva would deny the prodigal's return when slavery itself was already almost history?

PART FOUR

REVERSION

14

Reversion in Europe

The centenary of British colonial slave emancipation in 1933, was celebrated as a national and imperial triumph. The city of Hull, the home town of Wilberforce, was the designated site of celebration. A great civic procession led by Hull's Lord Mayor and a host of dignitaries and descendants of the liberator filed past his birthplace, his grammar school, and its assembled students. The Archbishop of York consecrated the proceedings, accompanied by the hymns and spirituals of black and white choruses. The flags of fifty nations were simultaneous unfurled before tens of thousands of spectators. The *Times* headlined the events at Hull as the "Centenary of Wilberforce."[1]

For the reigning historians of England, emancipation had raised all of mankind to a higher moral plane. Antislavery's expansion to global proportions was the purest evidence of human progress. The historians never wearied of repeating William Lecky's designation of the fight against slavery as "among the three or four virtuous pages in the history of nations." The beneficiaries were also evoked: West Indian slaves who had devoutly assembled on the hilltop during the night before liberation awaiting the sunrise of freedom and the natives of Africa, as yet unaware in 1833 that British imperial expansion would entail the slow death of the institution in their own "heart of darkness."[2] Here, if anywhere, in the historiography of slavery lay the watershed event in the progressive interpretation of history. However, had the eye of a casual reader drifted from the columns reporting on the festivities at Hull, the same newspapers were reporting accounts of Jews being driven into the streets of Germany to perform symbolically degrading tasks. At the same moment, when tens of thousands gathered in Hull,

---

[1] See *The Times* (London), 25 and 29 May 1833, and 2, 4, 5, 9 August 1933.
[2] Lecky, W. E. H. *A History of European Morals*, 2 vols. (London 1869; 6th ed. 1884), I, 153; S. Drescher, "The Historical Context of British Abolition," in *Abolition and its Aftermath: The Historical Context, 1790–1916*, David Richardson, ed. (London: Frank Cass, 1985), 3–24.

tens of thousands of others were preparing to march under other banners at Nuremberg to enact the first Nazi party rally since Hitler's ascension to power.

The Soviet Gulag

Elsewhere in Europe, a retreat from free labor had already been systematically and massively launched in a country that had nominally brought the working class to supreme power – the Soviet Union. The European campaign against slavery, which enjoyed a supreme moment of triumph with the ratification of the League of Nations Slavery Convention in 1926, was undergoing a severe setback. Whereas the League of Nations had defined slavery as the status or condition of a person over whom the rights of ownership are exercised, the Soviets appeared to be reopening the issue of forced labor on a massive scale through the still universally permitted legal pathway of penal labor. In February 1931, the British House of Lords debated the reappearance of "slave labor" in the remote timberlands of the Soviet Union.[3]

The early 1930s opened a new chapter in the history of coercion. In 1926, the Soviet Union was not a member of the League of Nations and refused to associate itself with the antislavery convention. Nevertheless, its self-identification as the state founded on working-class supremacy was institutionalized in its penology. Among penologists, there was a broad international consensus by the early twentieth century that prison systems should reform and rehabilitate inmates, especially through work. Soviet penal literature emphasized the goal was to accustom criminals to "communal life" through compulsory labor and educational enlightenment. Disciplinary punishment was to be administered under strict rules and without physical coercion or torture. Members of the "toiling class" were to be accorded additional consideration. They were to be sent to agricultural colonies with the least restrictive regimen and offered accelerated processes of liberation. Colonies were to become learning centers for peasants in their regions. In the difficult economic situation of the decade after the revolution, however, the system was unable to fulfill the most basic tasks of its progressive penal mission.[4]

Alongside this normative penal system, a second system was created as early as the Russian Civil War. It was under secret police authority (successively Cheka, 1918; OGPU, 1922; NKVD, 1934; and MVD, 1946). Its camps were placed in the remotest and most inhospitable areas of Russia. It was this institution that evolved into the Main or State Administration

---

[3] See David Brion Davis, *Slavery and Human Progress*, 313–314, citing *Parliamentary Debates* (Lords), 5th series, vol. 39, cols. 842–867.

[4] Mary Ellen Wimberg, "Replacing the shackles: Soviet penal theory, policy and practice, 1917–1930," Ph.D. Dissertation, University of Pittsburgh 1996, ch. 1.

Camps, or the Gulag. Forced labor was meant to be punitive. In an ironic inversion of the old problem of inducing habits of free labor, force would reform the work habits of the congenitally idle upper class. The Soviet government had earlier adopted the principle that prisons were to be "schools of labor," for the idle class of gentlemen used to living "without occupation." In a society plagued by scarce capital and scarce public revenue, there were also heavy fiscal pressures to create a correctional system that would do more to pay for itself. The use of forced labor was initially limited to forestry and fisheries in the northern Slovetsky Camp of Special Destination (SLON), specifically designed to isolate counterrevolutionaries.

The Gulag's first major surge of growth came in the wake of Stalin's first Five Year Plan (1928–1932). Victorious within the party by 1928, Stalin consolidated an administrative-command economy to manage "the most important social and economic experiment of the twentieth century."[5] It entailed a variant of Karl Marx's concept of "primitive capital accumulation," that is, the shifting of agricultural "surpluses" to provide the capital to finance industrialization. It meant that the peasants had to be prepared to tolerate lower living standards without a loss of agricultural output. State procurements, not agricultural marketing, would be the supreme priority. Whether the original hopes that a dramatic restructuring of agriculture (collectivization) would enable the surplus to be procured easily, Stalin was convinced from the outset that force and punishment would be necessary to accomplish the procurement. Forced collectivization set off a rural war against Soviet policy. The outcome was an enormous destruction of assets. Stalin's decision that kulaks – the "class enemy" – would not be admitted to the new collective farms ensured that there would also be a massive uprooting and displacement of agricultural workers. The waves of arrests and deportations came to include village notables, bourgeois specialists, and communist party members designated as enemies of the revolution.[6]

The sudden appearance of hundreds of thousands of legally criminalized and uprooted peasants opened new vistas for their use. Like most other nineteenth-century political economists, Karl Marx had subscribed to the

[5] Paul R. Gregory, *The Political Economy of Stalinism: Evidence from the Soviet Secret Archives* (New York: Cambridge University Press, 2004), 1.

[6] "When the head is cut off, you do not weep about the hair.... Can kulaks be admitted to the collective farms? Of course it is wrong to admit the kulak into the collective farms. It is wrong because he is the accursed enemy of the kolkhoz movement." Stalin's speech to the Communist Academy, published in *Pravda*, Dec. 29, 1929 (quoted in R. W. Davies, *The Socialist Offensive: The Collectivization of Agriculture*, vol. 1 (Cambridge, MA: Harvard University Press, 1980), 197–98; and Paul R. Gregory, *The Political Economy of Stalinism*, 43). On the economic rationale for Stalin's establishment of camps for massive use of coerced labor, see also Peter H. Solomon, Jr. "Soviet Penal Policy, 1917–1934: A Reinterpretation," *Slavic Review*, 39:2 (1980), 195–217.

axiom of the generic superiority of wage labor over forced labor. He also, however, made room for an exception in frontier colonial zones.[7]

For many Western economists, the problem of abundant land and inhospitable climate made the potential of free labor superiority irrelevant in many areas of the world. The post-revolutionary Soviet government faced the same problem in the arctic zone that colonizing governments had previously faced in the tropics. Both free European migrants and resident populations were often unwilling to enter into the sustained production of exportable cash commodities. A Soviet labor force, successively fueled by state strategies of collectivization, party purges, ethnic displacement, and returned prisoners of war, was subjected to forced displacement and hard labor. This politically induced "reserve army of labor" offered an unanticipated economic opportunity. As an internal bureaucratic document noted, "the history of the Gulag is the history of the colonization and industrial exploitation of the remote regions of the state." In the context of the early 1930s, the industrial exploitation of remote and inhospitable, but resource-rich, regions could be based upon this labor windfall. Members of society whose presence would otherwise constitute security risks could now be converted to disciplined and profitable labor "beyond the (new) line."[8]

There were certain important differences between the older forms of the institution of slavery and the status of Soviet prisoners. Private individuals had no access to property in the persons of Soviet inmates. Their closest analogy was to the slaves of rulers of the state. Nor were Soviets incorporated

---

[7] Oleg V. Khlevniuk, *History of the Gulag: From Collectivization to the Great Terror* (New Haven: Yale University Press, 2004), 9–12; Karl Marx, *Capital*, 3 vols. (Moscow: Foreign Languages Publishing, 1961/1962), I, ch. 14. In *Capital*, Marx chose Australia to illustrate the capitalist's need for coerced labor in the early development of distant and sparsely populated areas. A century before the establishment of the Soviet Gulag, Australia was dependent upon a convict labor force in the British Empire. Marx used Edward Wakefield's account of "Mr. Peel's" disastrous experiment in transporting 3,000 free working-class men, women, and children to Swan River, Australia. Once arrived, "Mr. Peel was left without a servant to make his bed or fetch him water from the river." (Marx, *ibid.*, I, 766 citing E. G. Wakefield, *England and America: A Comparison of the Social and Political State of Both Nations* (London, 1833), vol. 2, p. 33) Marx further followed Wakefield's generic conclusion: "In civilized countries the labourer, though free, is by nature dependent upon capitalists; in colonies this dependence must be created by artificial means (*ibid.*, 779). Australia was to develop a sugar plantation system with indentured labor from the Pacific Ocean islands in Queensland in the second half of the nineteenth century and was the first British colony to prohibit non-European immigration at the beginning of the twentieth century. See Adrian Graves, "Colonialism, Indentured Labour Migration in the Western Pacific, 1840–1915," in *Colonialism and Migration: Indentured Labour before and after Slavery.* (Dordrecht: M. Nijhoff, 1986), 237–259; and Stanley L. Engerman, "Servants to Slaves to Servants: Contract Labour and European Expansion," in *ibid.*, 263–294.

[8] See inter alia, Paul Gregory, "An Introduction to the Economics of the Gulag", in *The Economics of Forced Labor: The Soviet Gulag*, Paul R. Gregory and Valery Lazarev, eds. (Stanford: Hooves Institution Press, 2003), 4.

into the nexus of family relationships in formally recognized relations of concubinage or secondary wives. One could not be classified as a member of the Gulag from "the very day of his birth," at least until the age of twelve. The requisite for an individual sentence for criminal acts meant that the status was not inherited as it was with the lifetime bondage of a serf. The degree to which due process was afforded in the case of the convicted was a separate matter. Nor, of course, did the Soviet Union ever create institutions like those created by the Nazis, where premeditated mass murder was one of its principal activities.[9]

The colonies of the Gulag archipelago initially offered the same carceral advantages as had the isolated Caribbean islands of the seventeenth century. They ensured the isolation of captives in zones of high risk for escapees. In economic terms, the concentration of labor in remote regions offered benefits by remunerating laborers at rates closer to subsistence than to the prevailing cost of free labor elsewhere in the Soviet Union. As with earlier convict labor systems in the Atlantic, penal servitude was initially a mobile source of coerced labor. In one major respect, however, Soviet forced labor was more analogous to sub-Saharan Africa. The "primitive accumulation" of its labor force was cheaper than in America. It was the by-product of legal activities that were directed against large numbers of politically targeted enemies.

As in Africa, the process entailed an enormous destruction or misapplication of human capital. The uprooting of some of the society's most successful farmers rendered their skills less effective in the harsh new environment. It may also have cost the society far more in depleted human capital than could possibly have been gained by procuring marketable metals or lumber

---

[9] S. Swianiewicz, in *Forced Labour and Economic Development: An Enquiry into the Experience of Soviet Industrialization* (London: Oxford University Press, 1965), outlined four ways in which the Soviet system differed from the status of individuals in previous institutions of slavery. The status of Soviet forced laborers was not a lifetime status. It was time bound by specific individual sentences. The laborer was never subject to private ownership because private ownership of the means of production had been abolished, although their hiring out and allocation to specific industries was widely practiced. The offspring of forced laborers were not allocated to the status by birth although their "social origin" attached certain challenges to their life chances. Finally, and most importantly for the long-term fate of the institution, slavery was officially rejected as a pre-communist social formation, regressive even by the standards of the preceding bourgeois capitalist system. This was clearly a key reason why the concepts of reeducation for socialist reintegration always remained a formal goal of the system. It was also clearly a reason why great effort was expended in keeping secret both the systems of recruitment and treatment of forced laborers. The dismantling of the Gulag required no reversal of the public principles upon which the Soviet Union was founded. Aleksandr I. Solzhenitsyn, *The Gulag Archipelago, 1918–1958*, 3 vols. (Boulder, CO: Westview Press, 1998) II (Part III), 154 and ch. 17, "The Kids." For the crucial difference in magnitude between that part of Nazi facilities set aside for mass murder and the Soviet Gulag, see Stephen Wheatcroft, "The Scale and Nature of German and Soviet Repression and Mass Killings, 1930–1945," *Europe-Asia Studies*, 48:8 (1996), 1319–1353.

for national or international markets. In treating the Gulag populations as an undifferentiated windfall of surplus human capital, the state made no effort to assess the opportunity costs to both the economy and the civil society accessible by less arbitrary and coercive terror.

The administrative-command economy was less tempted to calculate the potential alternative value to its labor force. The private slaveholder in the Americas, "nested in a market economy," had to apply market-based calculations in deploying his slaves. Given the political parameters of the Soviet regime as well as its internal mechanisms of control, time was the overriding consideration:

To slow down the tempo [of industrialization] means to lag behind.... Old Russia ... because of her backwardness, ... was constantly being defeated by the Mongol Khans, by the Turkish beys ... by the British and French capitalists. Beaten because of backwardness.... We are fifty or a hundred years behind the advanced countries. We must make good this lag in ten years. Either we do it or they crush us.[10]

At its initial emergence as a mass labor system in the early 1930s, the Soviet leadership was still acutely sensitive to Western economic and political power. The "advanced" world power was centered in those areas of western Europe and the United States that had led in the expansion of free individual labor. The reaction to western European pressure was still apparent at the launching of the Gulag. Information about the camp system stimulated a British parliamentary debate in 1931. News of the mass arrest and transfer of peasants into the timber industry was a particular target of Western diplomacy. In the summer of 1930, the United States limited Soviet imports and banned timber in particular. Other countries imposed similar sanctions.

The first Soviet reaction was to limit the flow of information while denying that convict labor was used in export industries. It withdrew prisoners from loading foreign ships. All contacts with inspectors' representatives from foreign countries and captains of foreign vessels were discontinued. All indicators of prisoner employment in the timber industry were removed or concealed. A counter-bourgeois campaign was organized to emphasize the general superiority of the socialist organization for labor. The Soviet government effectively targeted growing unemployment in capitalist countries and the continued existence of slavery in some western European empires. Stalin was sufficiently concerned about the foreign campaign against forced labor to personally annotate V.M. Molotov's official rebuttal of "Forced Labor" at the Sixth Congress of Soviets in March 1931. That report insisted that all of the 1.1 million laborers in the lumber industry were free. The 60,000 convicts in other regional enterprises "would only envy the work and

---

[10] Alan Bullock, *Hitler and Stalin: Parallel Lives* (New York: Random House, 1991), 276.

living conditions of prisoners in our northern regions." In 1932, the Soviet labor code was amended to prohibit the employment of prisoners and others sentenced to obligatory work from participating in goods intended for export.[11]

Thereafter, the shifting balance of power in a world moving toward global conflict diminished international criticism of forced labor in the Soviet Union. In 1941, the German invasion of Russia and Hitler's declaration of war against the United States almost silenced Western criticism of Soviet labor policies. United States Vice President Henry Wallace was invited to a major Gulag facility on the Arctic Circle. In visiting Kolyma, a major arctic gold mining camp in May 1944, he was unaware that he was touring a prison complex. At the height of the Russo-American alliance, he condemned any radical critique of the Soviet way of life as a criminal attempt to incite conflict between the two allies.[12] After the Wehrmacht's invasion of Russia, the Soviet industrial revolution demonstrated that Stalin's dictatorship outmatched the German military-industrial complex. By the end of World War II, the Soviets could not, like earlier Afro-Asian societies, be pressured from without to alter their policies towards coerced labor. Coerced labor was now conceived as a bulwark against the pressures of the societies who had pioneered in constricting extra-European slave labor. To preempt a bourgeois threat, the Soviet state imposed a vast constrictive system on its own citizens. By 1939, labor contracts of free laborers outside the Gulag were increased to five-year terms. The following year a law not only tied workers to their enterprises, but introduced criminal punishments for laziness, poor discipline, absenteeism, and drunkenness. More than in the indentured servant regimes of the nineteenth century, workers were liable to pay with their bodies for a variety of infractions of their (no longer consensual) contracts. Only in 1956 did the post-Stalinist leadership turn decisively away from "sticks" in favor of "carrots" for their non-Gulag workforce.[13]

The outstanding feature of the coerced-labor system was its expansion despite all of the destabilizing events of the generation between 1930 and the early 1950s. It constituted a continuous revolutionary process in the direction of coerced labor. Once the reserve army of labor had been created by the drive for collectivization, the system was adjusted to fit the further tumultuous surges caused by the Great Terror of 1937–1938, Soviet westward expansion in 1939–1940, the German offensives of 1941–1943, the second westward expansion of 1944–1945, and the reconstruction era between 1946 and the death of Stalin.

[11] Oleg V. Khlevniuk, *The History of the Gulag*, 28–30.
[12] Anne Applebaum, *Gulag: A History* (New York: Random House, 2003), 444.
[13] Andrei Sokolov, "Forced Labor in Soviet Industry: The End of the 1930s to the Mid-1950s: An Overview," in P.R. Gregory and V. Lazarev, *The Economics of Forced Labor* (Stanford: Stanford University Press, 2003), 24–38.

Apart from forced labor in general, in the Gulag complex the numbers of prisoners fluctuated from 200,000 at the beginning of the 1930s to more than ten times that number in the early 1950s.[14] Partially in response to the German threat, the populations targeted for the Gulag became more identified by ethnicity, and more dramatically so after the German invasion of 1941. From the moment that the Soviet Union began to expand its western borders into Poland, the Baltic States, and Romania in 1939–1940, an increasing proportion of foreigners was interned the Gulag. Its composition changed even more rapidly after the German invasion. Numbers of prisoners dropped during the war years, but new camps were created for prisoners of war and for more than two million deported citizens from ethnic groups suspected of potential sympathy for the invaders.[15] Labor, identified more than ever as a central dimension of human activity, was intensified in the Gulag. Strict regime camps for disciplinary punishment functioned as analogues to the punishment camps in Germany. Food rations were likewise linked to productivity in a nutritional hierarchy based upon performance. By 1944, beyond its own industrial organizations, the Gulag administration "rented" the labor of over 900,000 prisoners to other commissariats.[16]

The Gulag, however, was less significant to the Soviet war economy than was the coerced labor system of Nazi Germany. The Gulag produced an average of only 1.9 percent of the Soviet GNP for 1941–1943, well below its share of the workforce. It was, therefore, a lagging rather than a leading sector of the "Soviet armaments miracle" in war production in the decisive years 1942–1943. The miracle came at enormous sacrifice on the home front, without as well as within the Gulag, "where hundreds of thousands, if not millions of people starved to death as a result of the war effort."[17]

[14] Applebaum, *Gulag*, Appendix: "How Many?", 578–586. One of the most exemplary sectors of forced labor illustrates the dynamism of the system. In the whole Perm *oblast*, a forestry center, the forced-labor population was less than 7,500 in the early 1930s. The labor camp populations deposited there reached almost 34,500 by 1938 and, on the eve of the war, there were 44,000 in the *oblast*. By the end of World War II, 80,000 prisoners were held in the camps of the newly renamed Molotov *oblast*. Just before the time of the 1956 Kruschev amnesty, the figure had risen to 112,000. See Judith Pallot, "Forced Labour for Forestry: The Twentieth Century History of Colonisation and Settlement in the North of Perm *oblast*," *Europe-Asia Studies*, 54:7 (2002), 1055–1063, esp. 1061.

[15] Pavel Polian, *Against Their Will: The History and Geography of Forced Migrations in the USSR* (New York: Central European University Press, 2004), 313, Table 19.

[16] Steven A. Barnes, "All for the Front, All for Victory!: The Mobilization of Forced Labor in the Soviet Union during World War Two," *International Labor and Working Class History*, 58 (2000), 245.

[17] Compare *ibid.*, 245, and Adam Tooze, *Wages of Destruction: The Making and Breaking of the Nazi Economy* (New York: Viking Press, 2007), 588–589. It was truly "All for the Front, all for Victory!" According to Povel Polian, 5.9 million people were subjected to internal forced migrations and another 6 million were affected by international forced migrations. See *Against Their Will: The History and Geography of Forced Migrations in the USSR* (New York: Central European Press, 2004), 312–313.

During the generation after 1930, the number of forced internal migrations under Soviet control matched the number of transatlantic forced migrants over a period ten times as long.

Although the initial rationales for creating forced labor were political and punitive, the enormous number of uprooted people quickly suggested their application to economic needs. They eased the opening of remote regions unattractive to uncoerced workers. These workers could be exploited to the point of extreme hunger, cold, and exhaustion. They served as a deterrent to dissident action or speech. They relieved pressure on sparse supplies of consumption and housing among the nonprisoner population. Failures could be abandoned without accountability to the larger society. Moreover, the initiators of the system were encouraged by a number of apparent successes in the early 1930s, when the pace of industrialization had priority over other economic considerations.[18]

On the eve of the German invasion in 1941, there were about 2.3 million people in all Gulag divisions, not counting millions of ex-inmates, and millions more who had been indicted and convicted, but were not placed within the system. In some areas, the system appeared to score successes. In 1941, the NKVD provided 12–13 percent of all Soviet timber. Forced labor in some extraction industries proved to be cheaper than noncoerced labor, especially in inhospitable areas. At various times during its existence, the Gulag accounted for up to 20 percent of construction labor, 35 to 45 percent of nickel and copper, 70 percent of the Soviet Union's tin, 60 to 80 percent of its gold, and virtually all of its diamonds and platinum.[19]

Enormous amounts of labor, however, were expended upon remote construction and infrastructure projects that never produced any appreciable sustained development. The planners and administrators of the forced labor system were concerned about the aggregate human costs and profits of their operations. If they attached little value to the freedom lost by individuals, they had to be concerned with mortality and morbidity except when, as during the Great Terror, surges of convicts encouraged a perception of unlimited pools of costless and overabundant recruits. As with the Caribbean three centuries earlier, high concentrations of forced labor seemed secure where the natural environment prohibitively increased the risks of escape. Infrastructural development sometimes had the unintended effect of raising security costs.[20]

---

[18] Oleg Khelevnyuk, "The Economy of the OGPU, NKVD, and MVD of the USSR, 1930–1953," in *Economics of Forced Labor, The Soviet Gulag,* Paul R. Gregory and Valery Lazarev, eds. (Stanford: Hoover Institution Press, 2003) 43–66.

[19] Paul Gregory, "An Introduction to the Economics of the Gulag," in *The Economics of Forced Labor,* 8, Figure 1.2: "Gulag Labor, Investment and Production as Percentages of the Total Economy;" and Klevnuik, *History of the Gulag,* 328–338.

[20] Valery Lazarev, "Conclusions," in *Economics of Forced Labor,* ch. 10.

In some ways, the Gulag approached a corporative form of slaveholding. In a regime that strictly prohibited the private sale of human labor, Gulag laborers were hired to outside employers. The administration secured the right to contract out labor even in an economy generally hostile toward any form of leasing. The revenue produced by these workers increased from 11 percent in 1941 to 25 percent in 1950. There is little evidence that this contradiction provoked any widespread pressure against the Gulag from the larger society. The Gulag was nested within the larger coercive apparatus of the Stalinist regime. Terror itself exacerbated divisions between the convicted and the unconvicted, especially when aimed at targeted classes, nationalities, or religious groups. During the Stalinist period, no movement emerged outside the Gulag to agitate for its contraction.

Concerning the abolition of the institution of forced labor itself, the balance of numbers is telling. The turn towards dismantling the system of Soviet forced labor came at its demographic and economic zenith. Stalin's personal investment in the mechanisms of repression and the economics of slave labor ensured that, at the end of his life, the prison population officially stood at ten times the level it was at the end of the first Five Year Plan in 1932. In 1952, the Ministry of Internal Affairs, which ran the Gulag, controlled 9 percent of the economy's capital investment. The Soviet ruler's dedication to the organization and economics of forced labor meant that his last Five Year Plan called for the doubling of Gulag-based investment between 1951 and 1955.[21]

The decision to begin dismantling the Gulag system came from the top. Stalin died on March 5, 1953. One day after the consolidation of a successor government, the head of the MVD, Lavrenty Beria, sent the Central Committee a draft decree on amnesty. It called for the release of about one million Gulag inmates and further proposed to reduce the terms of those remaining in camps by half. Within three months, 1.5 million prisoners, or 60 percent of the Gulag's population, were released.

The turnabout was not initiated from without nor in response to agitation from major portions of the nonprison sectors of society. Nor was it made under the impact of international threat such as those that had spurred the French legislature to decree colonial emancipation in 1794. Policy discussion was carefully kept within the walls of the MVD bureaucracy. From the late 1940s, the administration had been trying to convert the Gulag's prisoners into an "exile" labor force. Bureaucratic plans were developed for transitional regimes. Like the "apprentices" of the nineteenth century, "the new exiles" were to have a juridical status halfway between Gulag inmates and free workers.[22] Moral issues were never offered as a motive for the proposed

---

[21] Applebaum, *Gulag*, 570.
[22] See Alexsei Tikhonov, "The End of the Gulag," in *Economics of Forced Labor*, 67–73.

changes. The Gulag administration was primarily groping for a more efficient means of securing prisoners while meeting its ordinary production goals. The prevailing bureaucratic rationale for considering contraction was that the system was costing more than it produced.

Outside of the bureaucratic apparatus, it was from within the Gulag rather than the larger Soviet society that the greatest popular pressure emerged for a major contraction of the system. Before the early 1950s, collective resistance within the Gulag archipelago was extremely rare. As in many other systems of forced labor, the Gulag had its emblematic uprising at a militarily opportune moment. At the beginning of 1942, the Soviet Union had just stopped the Nazi advance on Moscow. Three million Red Army soldiers had been starving to death in Nazi camps. At this moment, a mass uprising broke out in the far north, in the Vorkuta "corrective labor" camp. It took the NKVD more than a month of armed conflict to suppress the uprising. Thereafter, the authorities successfully reinforced their surveillance and carried out "operative-prophylactic measures" of prevention. As with most other systems of coercion the ("Ust-Usa") uprising in Vorkuta was a rarity in the annals of the Gulag.[23] Only in retrospect did such an isolated instance figure as a harbinger of the system's decline.

It was in the wake of Stalin's death and the grant of amnesty that the internal discipline of the Gulag began to be massively challenged throughout the camp system. As Tocqueville observed, "it is not always in going from bad to worse that one falls into revolution. It more often happens that a people who have borne without complaint the most burdensome laws, reject them violently once their weight is lightened."[24] The dramatic release of 60 percent of the camp's population exacerbated resentments among those who remained incarcerated. Major strikes broke out. The government responded with both military suppression and better treatment. This certainly curtailed the growth of the Gulag. The death knell itself awaited Nikita Khuschev's secret speech to the Twentieth Party Congress of the Communist Party in February 1956. In the ten months that followed Khuschev's intervention, 617,000 convicts were rehabilitated. There was never again an attempt to revive the camps on a Stalinist scale. The Soviet government finally took steps to again align its penal system with those of other Western states. By the mid-1970s, Amnesty International reported that no more than 10,000 convicts were still incarcerated in the two remaining Soviet "political" camps.[25]

---

[23] Applebaum, *Gulag*, 404–407; and Smith, "All for the Front," 250–251.
[24] Tocqueville, *The Old Regime and the Revolution*, Alan S. Kahan, trans. (Chicago: University of Chicago Press, 1998), 222.
[25] Applebaum, *Gulag*, 528. A decade later, in 1986, Michael Gorbachev granted a general pardon to all Soviet political prisoners. For references to the wave of uprisings in 1953–1954, see L. Latkoviskis, "Baltic Prisoners in the Gulag Revolts of 1953," *Lituanus*, 51:3

Germany's Racial Slavery

The Nazi German empire, rather than the Soviet Union, demonstrated how quickly and how massively the nineteenth-century trajectory toward free labor could be reversed. In Western Europe, the incorporation of civilians into a legally coerced workforce had largely disappeared, centuries before the beginnings of the rise of organized abolitionism. By the mid-nineteenth century, coerced labor was rare even with regard to the temporary labor of prisoners of war. The United States committed only 10,000 captured confederate soldiers to work during the Civil War. A decade later, Prussian military plans to force French prisoners of war (POWs) to work were applied to only a small fraction of the captives.

World War I, with its enormous military mobilizations and its long duration, dramatically expanded recourse to captive forced labor. Between 7 and 8.5 million POWs accumulated in Germany and Austria-Hungary from 1914 to 1918 were put to work. Russia acted similarly with more than 2 million captured Austro-Hungarians and Germans. France and Britain, with far fewer captives, also put tens of thousands of POWs to work. Most of the belligerents remained largely within the permissible guidelines of the 1907 Hague Convention on warfare signed by the warring nations.[26] The German government, however, in violation of the Hague Convention, began to make massive use of enemy civilian coerced labor almost from the onset of the war. Controlling large swaths of enemy territory and beset by shortages of labor, the German government invoked the doctrine of military necessity to conscript civilians first on the eastern and then on the western front.

At the outbreak of hostilities in 1914, German authorities prohibited Polish agricultural laborers from returning home after the harvest. They gradually extended restrictions on other laborers. Pressure to open a similar mobilization of western labor intensified when Polish agricultural laborers in Germany were prohibited from switching to the industrial sector for the duration of the war. By 1916, civilians in occupied territories were being deported into Germany. Occupation forces transported at least 34,000 Poles, including 5,000 Jewish workers from the Lodz area. The German authorities discovered that of all the economic hardships imposed upon the population in the eastern areas, deportations for forced labor aroused the most intense

---

(2005), 4–39 and Steven A. Barnes, "In a Manner Befitting Soviet Citizens: An Uprising in the Post-Stalin Gulag," *Slavic Review*, 64:4 (2005), 823–850. The Kengir's remarkable aspect was the moderation of the prisoners' demands, voiced by a former Red Army officer, under banners reading "Long Live the Soviet Constitution!" The uprising was ended with a negotiated settlement, which did not secure the lives of a half-dozen leaders, but did result in substantial reforms over the next few years.

[26] Mark Spoerer and Jochen Fleischhacker, "Forced Laborers in Nazi Germany: Categories, Numbers and Survivors," *Journal of Interdisciplinary History*, 33:2 (2002), 169–204.

hatred and the greatest resistance. Thousands of escaped Russian POWs and partisans made large occupied areas insecure.[27]

The need for labor stemming from the mobilization of more than three million German men for military service produced the same pressure for substitute laborers from the West. By mid-1916, the German military and industrialists were insisting that seven hundred thousand workers in Belgium be made available to "the home market." The government was aware that action in Belgium would create more difficulties abroad than the eastern mobilizations. Americans were helping to transport food supplies to the Belgian civilian population through the Allied blockade. Moritz von Bissing, the German Governor-General of occupied Belgium, protested that compelling intransigent foreign laborers to work in Germany was an unprecedented violation of international law "in a civilized state." The Governor-General was overruled. Both civilian and military officials advocated deportation as a military necessity that overrode German obligations to international law. Even after the war, German Chancellor Bethmann-Hollweg, who acknowledged the violation, never regretted it.[28]

Nevertheless, the German deportation of Belgians encountered far more obstacles than their treatment of Polish workers. International relief assistance had reduced the desire of unemployed Belgians to seek work in Germany. From beginning to end, the implementation was regarded, even by its initiators, as a disaster. In February 1917, when further deportations were halted, 70 percent of the 55,000 deported Belgians were still gathered in assembly camps. Malnutrition, ill treatment, poor hygiene, and inadequate food rations produced high rates of mortality and permanent disabilities. Negative public opinion and the reaction among German workers constituted the greatest obstacle to effective continuation of the program. In the words of German historian Gerhard Ritter, "The whole scheme offered the appearance of regular slave transports and slave markets, which mitigation by well-intentioned local commanders could not alter."[29]

The international repercussions were equally costly. The uproar extended beyond the Allied powers to neutral states, the papacy, and private citizens. No issue did more to increase German diplomatic isolation or to turn American opinion against Germany at a crucial moment when the German chancellor had launched a peace initiative and the German military was on the brink of adopting a policy of unrestricted submarine warfare against U.S.

---

[27] Ulrich Herbert, *Hitler's Foreign Workers: Enforced Foreign Labor in Germany Under the Third Reich*, William Templer, trans. (Cambridge: Cambridge University Press, 1997), 18–19, 170; and Isabel V. Holt, *Absolute Destruction: Military Culture and the Practices of War in Imperial Germany* (Ithaca: Cornell University Press, 2005), 243–248.

[28] Hull, *Absolute*, 236, 241.

[29] Quotations from Herbert, *Foreign Workers*, 25; and Gerhard Ritter, *The Sword and the Scepter: The Problem of Militarism in Germany*, 4 vols. Heinz Norden, trans. (Coral Gables, FL: University of Miami Press, 1969), III, 369.

shipping. German public opinion and protests in the Reichstag combined to put the government under enormous, and successful, pressure to reverse its forced migration policy. The German government shifted to an alternative strategy. Wages in Belgium were lowered and material incentives for voluntary movement of Belgians to Germany were increased until the end of the war.[30] Despite the halt in forced migration, hundreds of thousands of Belgian and French civilians were conscripted for forced labor in German-occupied territories. These further breaches of international law were added to the Franco-Belgian reparations bill at war's end.

On the whole, the German experience with civilian forced labor was viewed as a tactical disaster. It was clear that the complex of administrative, police, and logistical requirements could only have succeeded if more ruthless methods were systematically implemented on a vast scale. When the National Socialists came to power in Germany, in 1933, they appeared to have no inclination to repeat experiments in large-scale coerced labor. Nazi ideology did, of course, ascribe a natural superiority and propensity for rule to its own Aryan race. Other groups, especially Slavs, were deemed naturally servile. They were "*Untermenschen,*" destined by "nature" for unskilled physical labor. In the early 1930s, Hitler reiterated his ideological indifference to the normative identification between antislavery and civilization. At the beginning of the 1930s he declared, "Human culture cannot be developed any further without creating a certain modern form of bondage or, if you like, slavery."[31]

As noted, this did not mean that the Nazi-dominated government aimed to create a slave class from the outset. Despite the hierarchical premises of its ideology and the symbolic degradation of Jews cleaning the streets of Germany, the creation of a coerced labor force was not on the Nazi political agenda as they consolidated power. Hitler's immediate aim was rather to "safeguard the right to work of our German compatriots (*Volksgenossen*)" and to prevent migrant foreigners from taking jobs. With German unemployment at its all time Depression peak of 6 million idle workers, Hitler's first recorded speech promised a four-year program to deliver the peasants from poverty and to overcome the German workers three-year nightmare of unemployment. For the moment, the focus was on work for the workers: "Every Worker his Work." Only privately, to the military leadership and the Cabinet, did Hitler reaffirm his longer-term objective for the acquisition of new *Lebensraum* (living space) in the East and the priority of rearmament as the means to do so. Thereafter, in cases of future conflict between all other economic demands and those of the military, the latter in every instance had priority. In "macro-economic terms the Third Reich shifted a larger percentage of national resources into rearmament than any other capitalist

---

[30] Herbert, *Foreign Workers*, 21–22; Holt, *Absolute Destruction*, 240–241.
[31] Herbert, *Forced Labor*, 45.

regime in history. Its only rival in this respect was the Stalinist Soviet Union."[32]

A combination of concern with unemployment and "alien blood pollution" meant that there were no more legal foreign workers (230,000) in Germany in 1936 than there had been on the eve of the Depression five years before. The long-term presence of Polish seasonal agricultural laborers had been halted first by the Depression and then by the Nazi government. Once the immediate crisis of unemployment was resolved, Hitler's longer-term priorities began to emerge. Two years later, the unemployment rates dipped as low as the most prosperous period in the Weimar Republic. However, Germany still enjoyed a standard of living only half that of the United States and two-thirds that of Great Britain. For Hitler, the only way out of relative poverty lay in expansion – in the creation of a Germany as large as the North American continent. Only within such living space (*Lebensraum*) could Germans achieve farmer-land ratios equal to those of the United States or Canada. Only in the East could Germany find sufficient contiguous territory for its expansive needs. And only German military forces could acquire this prerequisite to prosperity and power.

Between January 1933 and the eve of the Munich crisis, the regime's allocation of resources to the military increased from less than 1 to almost 20 percent of national output. The ultimate result was the emergence of an unanticipated, coerced foreign labor force in Germany. In 1938, Germany crossed the boundary into a new situation. A fully employed economy was suffering from an acute shortage of labor and unemployment stood at only 1 percent of the workforce. In response, the regime issued a decree providing itself with general powers of labor conscription. Workers could be deployed at specific jobs for any length of time. By 1939, more than 1.3 million had been subjected to compulsory work. The military was also exponentially expanding. Before 1945, more than 12 million men would be conscripted into the armed forces.[33]

Already, in 1938, the leadership also believed itself to be threatened by a national food crisis. Attributing the collapse of the German home-front morale in World War I to hunger, the government was willing to take ever more radical steps to avert the possibility of another food crisis. One obvious solution to the shortage of agricultural labor was to expand the traditional recruitment of Polish workers in German agriculture. Countering this option were two fears. There was the perennial concern with internal security. To this was added the new ideological threat to the "purity of the race" entailed in an inundation of foreigners and inevitable sexual relations

---

[32] See Adam Tooze, "The Economic History of the Nazi Regime," in *Nazi History*, Jane Caplan, ed. (Oxford: Oxford University Press, 2008), 180 and Table 2: "The Arms Race – 1933–1945," ibid. 181. See also, Tooze, *Wages of Destruction*, ch. 2, and p. 48, Figure 1.

[33] Spoerer, "Forced Laborers in Nazi Germany," 184.

between undesirables and Aryans. By definition, Poles were regarded as undesirable additions to the German racial stock.

The resolution of these systemic concerns came through a combination of ruthlessly coerced importation and increased hierarchical subordination of foreign labor. The decisive development occurred following the rapid conquest of Poland in September 1939. A general obligation to labor was proscribed for Poles in the months following the occupation. A package of decrees regulating working and living conditions for Poles sent to Germany was to be the prototype for civilian workers deployed from the East. Workers in Germany were to be rigorously differentiated by nationality and subject to a system of surveillance and repression. The system mediated between the institutional demands of the Schutzstaffel (Protective Squadron) and its affiliated organizations, guaranteeing racial purity and subservience, and the state's escalating demands for massive deployment of foreign labor. Appropriate degrees of treatment would be ensured by a badge. This anticipated subsequent markers – the "Jewish Star" and other stigmatic forms. Poles were denied access to public transportation, as well as German religious and cultural sites. Interracial sexual acts were capital offenses. Polish workers' wages were fixed at rates lower than those for German workers. In Poland itself, voluntary work for Polish employers was estimated as a dead loss to the imperial economy since Poles "under German management could achieve three to four times the output level they might attain in Poland."[34] Initially, the government preferred voluntary recruitment to lower the security costs of gathering and surveillance. By the spring of 1940, however, German targets for transferring half a million Poles to the Reich were 60 percent under target. The new Government General of Poland then ordered compulsory labor for all age groups between 25 and 35, followed by assigned quotas to each locality. The process then degenerated into "exemplary" measures of terrorism and roundup. The pattern was to continue and intensify.

During the five years between 1939 and 1944, approximately 13.5 million foreigners worked in Germany, 12 million of them involuntarily. The closest analogy to German slave labor may lie, however, in ancient Roman slavery. Rome made heavy and continuous military demands on its citizens in ever-expanding wars of conquest. This process offered both abundant opportunities for the enslavement of defeated enemies and for profitably in hiring them out. This same combination of enslavability and profitability reemerged full-blown in the heart of twentieth century Europe.[35] Comparatively, as many European workers were forcibly imported into Germany in five years as were Africans loaded for the New World for the Atlantic slave

[34] Herbert, *Foreign Labor*, 82.
[35] Spoerer, "*Forced Laborers*," 200. On Rome, see Walter Sheidel, "The Comparative Economics of Slavery in the Greco-Roman World," in *Slave Systems Ancient and Modern*, Enrico Dal Lago and Constantina Katsari eds. (New York: Cambridge University Press, 2008), 105–126.

trade between the mid-fifteenth and the mid-nineteenth centuries. The system's rate of growth was unprecedented. On the eve of the German invasion of the Soviet Union in 1941, Germany already employed 1.2 million mainly French prisoners of war and 1.3 million "civilian" workers, mainly Poles. By the autumn of 1944 the number of foreign workers reached 8.1 million, including 2 million POWs (nearly half Soviets) and 6 million civilians.

Increasingly, German desperation eroded the line between "privileged" military captives and racialized enemies. During the course of the war, 885,000 French, Italian, and Polish workers were shifted into civilian status. In the final year of the war, foreign workers accounted for more than 20 percent of the total German workforce, including more than a third of its armaments workers and almost half of its agricultural workforce. Thus, the 11 million Germans in arms, dispersed from Norway to the Maghreb and from the Atlantic to the Volga, had to be counterbalanced by a labor army of more than 13 million foreigners. The Wehrmacht was dipping ever deeper into teenage cohorts and factory labor while losing 60,000 lives in conflict every month between June 1941 and May 1944.[36]

In establishing this massive turn to coerced labor, the Nazi leadership explicitly rejected the antislavery ethos that had seemed so secure less than two decades earlier. Their ideology denied that either human progress or civilization required the abolition of slavery and the constriction of coerced labor. On the contrary, Hitler had affirmed that a superior culture must be built on the slavery and servile labor of poorly endowed races. When it became clear, in 1942, that Germany would have to rely on the long-term use of forced labor to have any hope of ultimate victory, Himmler minced no words at a meeting of senior SS leaders:

If we do not fill our camps with slaves – in this room I mean to say things very firmly and very clearly – with worker slaves, who will build our cities, our villages, our farms without regard to any losses, then even after years of war we will not have enough money to be able to equip the [new German] settlements in such a manner that real Germanic people can live there [in the East] and take root in the first generation.

Slaves were clearly an asset, even if a wasting one, and a substitute for other forms of investment capital.[37]

Long before coming to power, Hitler had outlined a vision in which German Aryan settlement would entail a demographic rearrangement in which any Eastern populations left in place would serve as slave labor on German settler farms. Between the conquest of Poland and preparations for the invasion of the Soviet Union, 180,000 Germans had been settled on Polish farms. Expelled Jews were concentrated in urban ghettoes. Poles were evicted from farms and millions conscripted for work in Germany or

[36] See Tooze, *Wages of Destruction*, p. 517; and Spoerer, "Forced Laborers," Tables 4 and 5.
[37] *Ibid.*, 473.

forced labor on formerly Polish soil.[38] By the end of 1941, anticipation of
a long and deadly struggle in the Soviet Union made use of Russian labor
imperative. But, the very possibility had to be envisioned in terms of a seg-
regated workforce degraded even beyond the Polish labor decrees of 1940.
Russians were to be badged, housed behind barbed wire, worked in gangs,
fed below the level of already constricted rations of other captives, reserved
for the lowest labor tasks, and brutally treated. Whatever concessions were
made in practice to meet the requirements of the economy were balanced by
compensatory brutality and degradation deemed appropriate to *untermenschen* – the dull, slavish, and inert segment of humanity.

The final institutional dispersion of foreign workers covered a broad
range of statuses marked by ethnic, racial, and other criteria. About one
worker in twelve had access to a limited contract, social insurance, workplace safety, leisure allotments and fringe benefits on a par with German
workers. A second tier had less mobility but retained access to legal protections concerning living and working conditions. A third level had no avenue
to complain about conditions of treatment and were subject to terroristic
and arbitrary treatment on the job or in special disciplinary institutions
and SS camps.[39] Differences of status and treatment were based upon racial
affinity as defined by the Nazis: Western or Eastern origin, prisoners of
war or civilians, or as citizens of friendly or enemy states. Himmler again
most clearly articulated the ideological disdain that informed the status of
the lowest laborers. When Goebbels, after Stalingrad, attempted to mitigate
some of the counterproductive effects of the anti-Russian image dispersed
through propaganda, Himmler continued to insist on treating Russians as
"a dull unfeeling mass." As far as he was concerned, whether or not 10,000
Russian women collapsed with exhaustion or died in droves on construction
gangs was relevant only in its impact on the task being performed. That theoretical perspective was to become empirical reality before the war ended.[40]

Political context thus played an important role in the degrees of treatment. Slavs whose governments had engaged in active military resistance
to Germany (Poles and Russians) were assigned to the lowest rung of slavery. Slavic Croats and Slovaks, aligned with the Reich, were placed in the
most privileged tier. Italians found themselves transferred from the highest
to the least privileged categories overnight following Mussolini's temporary
overthrow and his successors' attempt to withdraw from the Axis alliance.
German discipline quickly made up for the "privileged" treatment that Italian workers had enjoyed in Germany. Other groups began and ended at
the bottom of the Nazi hierarchy of contempt. Western POWs continued
to be treated according to International conventions, acceding to the same

[38] *Ibid.*, 180, 464.
[39] Benjamin B. Ferencz, *Less than Slaves: Jewish Forced Labor and the Quest for Compensation*
  (Cambridge, MA 1979).
[40] Herbert, *Foreign Workers*, 279.

retaliatory threat that had earlier helped to dissuade European monarchs from enslaving each others' subjects on either side of the Atlantic. Two ethnic groups, Jews and Gypsies, were "less than slaves." Their potential labor value could be overridden by ideological consignment to mass annihilation even after the need for labor became acute. Jews and Gypsies were groups without a state. Their case demonstrated how difficult it was to avoid the most degraded status and brutal treatment when one had no national state to intervene for them.

Slaves were not, of course, only sent back to the Reich. Many Soviet POWs were converted into "Hiwis" (*Hilfswillege*, or auxiliaries) of the German military, especially after 1942. The chief of the Quartermaster 2 section in the Staff of Army Group Center, Lieutenant Colonel Schettler, affirmed that half of the slaves were then used by the troops themselves. A portion was kept as *leibsklaven*, that is, personal slaves. Others were used in the construction of roads, military quarters, supply networks and on the railways. It is likely that as many Belarusians were transformed into coerced laborers in Belarus as were deported to Germany. The claims of field troops and army groups to laborers diminished the flow of forced laborers to Germany itself.[41]

On the other hand, female workers sent from the East to be German household domestics might make a good "racial" impression and be looked upon as salvageable candidates for incorporation into the Volk. Many soldiers returned to the Reich with a Russian house servant on their own account. Hitler decided that Germans would have to reconsider "our school knowledge," because there were so many blond, blue-eyed Ukrainians who "might be the peasant descendants of German tribes who had never migrated." Nevertheless the official decree of September 1942, stressed the security and Volk-risks posed by employing Soviet domestics. Although they had to look as "German" as possible, they were to be kept in separate quarters and kept subordinate to German domestics to prevent the emergence of a "sense of solidarity." Many German housewives preferred Russian girls because they were less arrogant, lazy, and promiscuous. Above all, they were more affordable – they could be kept working without vacation, given only a few hours off each week, and ordered to do the dirtiest and heaviest tasks.[42]

The fact that foreign workers within Germany were divided by a broad range of privileges and disabilities offers us a model of servile statuses that was in some respects more akin to the complexities of Old World rather than New World slavery. In any event, there are significant analogies between the Nazi institution of forced labor and the classic slave systems. The first lies

---

[41] The information in this paragraph was brought to my attention by my colleague Christopher Gerlach. Further details may be found in his study of White Russia under German occupation. *Kalkulierte Morde: Die deutsche Wirtschafts-und vernichtungspolitik in Weissrussland 1941–1944* (Hamburg: Hamburger Edition, 1999), 480–501 and 831.

[42] Herbert, *Foreign Workers*, 188–189.

in the recruitment and distribution processes. In the East, the ordinance of compulsory labor for all Polish workers made it possible to conscript all Polish workers by placing quotas on local governments or by direct raids on individual targets. A survey of defense plant workers in May 1942 showed that only 42 of the 27,000 workers had reported voluntarily for employment. Large swoops to obtain workers were then underway as the cumulative pressures of German military losses and new recruitment intensified.

This clearly reflected the conditions of German military recruitment: already in the autumn of 1941, the Wehrmacht had reached the "bottom of the barrel" in its traditional reservoir of cohorts. In 1942, military recruitment reached down to teenage cohorts and even those adolescents could barely replace military losses of that magnitude. Previously exempt armaments workers were then drafted. Women, not fully mobilized before 1942, were insufficient to compensate for the combination of accelerating casualties and increasing production demands. Germany needed millions of new workers. By the end of 1942, large-scale raids were becoming a regular feature of police action in the general government of Poland. A Polish state commercial school was surrounded while classes were in session: "The young men and women were indiscriminately loaded into freight cars and transported without warm clothing or food to a mass camp in Cracow." In some raids, youngsters below the age of 17 "weak and completely unfitted for heavy labor" were included in the transports. Nevertheless, they were redesignated for transportation to other sites. Governor-General Hans Frank of Poland complained that the brutality of the deployment of Poles for labor in the Reich was regarded as ruthless captivity, with its badge brandings, constraints on movement, bans on marriage and all sexual contact with Germans, bad food, poor clothing, high death rates, and penal labor camps.[43]

Further East, the situation repeated itself often in even more draconian fashion. Even before the Wehrmacht's disastrous defeat at Stalingrad in the winter of 1943, able-bodied Soviet inhabitants were deported. From some regions, they often included both young and old, pregnant women, and the disabled. Schools and villages were surrounded and depopulated; hostages were taken in reprisal for attempted flights or partisan attacks. These soon ceased to be isolated terroristic measures designed to boost the number of reluctant voluntary recruits. They became "the *rule*, and were often the only way to obtain any workers whatever."[44] In some areas, it was made official policy to burn the farms of those who refused to work, and family members could be placed in labor camps to induce compliance of runaways.

The Europeanwide search induced Gauleiter Fritz Sauckel, appointed general plenipotentiary for labor mobilization (GBA) in 1942, to expand

[43] Tooze, *Wages of Destruction*, 513–515; and Herbert, *Forced Labor*, 200 and 321.
[44] Herbert, *Forced Labor*, 280.

the age-range of eligible workers. For the first time in centuries, European children were uprooted in tens of thousands for deployment as servile labor. "Operation Hay" had the double aim of labor and welfare. Fifty thousand children, as young as the age of ten, were conscripted for employment in armaments factories. Their seizure by the Wehrmacht prevented the reinforcement of the enemy and reduced his "biological strength over the long term."[45]

Although Sauckel's press gangs were pan-European, the Wehrmacht enforced massive evacuations of civilians as it retreated from Russia in 1943 and 1944. The analogy with past slaving practices struck both perpetrators and their targets. Those conducting such trolling raids routinely spoke of them as "razzias," the term used by Muslim slave raiders in Africa. Razzias of Polish Jews for forced labor also offered occasions for German amusement. They began in the first weeks of the occupation of Poland in 1939 and were extended throughout Europe over the next five years.[46]

Analogies with previous forms of slavery sprang effortlessly to mind. A German official described the raids in the East as employing "the whole bag of tricks" previously used by Arab slave hunters in Africa. Anne Frank viewed the Amsterdam round-up of Jews in Amsterdam as analogous to the treatment of "slaves in the olden days." At the loading platforms of railway cars to Auschwitz, Primo Levi recalled the officer in charge asking "*Wieviel Stück*" ("How many pieces")? The corporal replyed smartly, "six hundred and fifty 'pieces.'" The nomenclature echoed the term assigned by Portuguese traders to the enslaved Africans over four centuries. Non-Jewish victims made similar analogies to the slave trade.[47]

After Stalingrad, German propaganda increasingly sought to improve worker performance by pan-European slogans against the Bolshevik menace.

---

[45] *Ibid.*, 281.

[46] See especially, Christopher Browning, *Nazi Policy, Jewish Workers, German Killers* (Cambridge: Canbridge University Press, 2000), 60, 133. On manhunts and razzias in Belorrussia, see Christian Gerlach, *Kalkulierte Morde*, 469–473. For razzias and other forms of recruitment in the occupied Italian areas after the Italian capitulation to the Allies, see "Herrenmenschen und Badoglioschweine, Italienische Militaerinternerte in deutcher Kriegsgefangenschaft 1943–1945: Erinnerungen von Attilio Buldini und Gigina Querzé aufgezeichnet von C. V. Schminck-Gustavus." The Germans also alternated between razzias and quota requisitions in Poland. Recruitment for labor in Germany amounted to upwards of 1.6 million Polish citizens, and hundreds of thousands more were set to work within the Government-General itself. More than three million people were imported from the Soviet Union to the Reich. For a numerical breakdown by nationality/ethnicity, see the article by Mark Spoerer, cited above.

[47] See Norman Rich, *Hitler's War Aims: The Establishment of the New Order*, 2 vols. (New York: Norton, 1974), 326–332; 342–343; *The Diary of Anne Frank: The Critical Edition* (New York: Doubleday, 1987), 265, 273, 316; and Primo Levi, *Survival in Auschwitz: The Nazi Assault on Humanity*, Stuart Wolf, trans. (New York: Macmillan, 1993), 16; and *Hitler's Secret Conversations, 1941–1944* (New York: Farrar, Strauss and Young, 1953), esp. June-December 1941, 4, and 57.

Some industrialists promoted a variety of positive incentives in improved working and living conditions. From 1943 onward, Nazi authorities, now under enormous pressure to increase output, placed a higher value on foreign labor. Toward the war's end, there were discussions about whether it was more productive to allow French workers to remain in France or to redeploy them to the Reich. Different agencies often worked at cross-purposes. Even in western Europe, Sauckel continued to assemble agents, French and Italian men and women who, for a good wage, would go out to hunt for people, like the old practice of shanghaiing. Of the five million workers brought to Germany, Sauckel concluded, fewer than 200,000 (4 percent) had entered voluntarily.[48] The radicalism and brutality of the recruitment process intensified as the military situation deteriorated.

There was one fundamental difference between the earlier Atlantic and Nazi Germany's systems of coerced labor recruitment. European rulers developing the Atlantic slave system viewed much of the tropical and subtropical lowland Americas as land rich and underpopulated. Europeans developing the New Order in Nazi Europe viewed much of the land eastward of Germany as both over- and ill-populated. Hitler always viewed the presence of the Jewish population within the boundaries of Germany as an intolerable and dangerous racial situation. The successive occupations of Austria, Bohemia, Moravia, and Poland, increased the problems of racial pollution more than a hundredfold by incorporating huge numbers of Jews and Poles. It also invited increasingly expansive plans for its solution. The most fundamental assumption of Nazi territorial planning from 1939 onward was that the incorporation of the territory to Germany's east required the removal of the vast majority of its inhabitants. As early as 1940, German planners developed an unprecedented demographic program for Poland, requiring the medium-term expulsion of 7.5 million Poles.[49]

Their vision expanded exponentially in planning for "Operation Barbarossa" against the Soviet Union in 1940–41. The drafts of General Plan East, and its variants, focused as much on the elimination as on the enslavement of its native population. The plans reflected Hitler's view of Russia as the equivalent of the North American frontier. Its abundant fertile soil and natural resources would provide the basis for the German domination of the Eurasian landmass and the permanent expansion of the Aryan race. German invasion plans also assumed that all Russians who remained alive after the conquest would work only under compulsion. The Slavic idea of freedom was deemed to encompass only to the right to wash on feast days. Their New World analogue for Russians was North America's vanishing "redskins."[50]

---

[48] Herbert, *Foreign Workers*, 277.

[49] See Browning, *Nazi Policy*, 12–13.

[50] *Hitler's Secret Conversations, 1941–1944* (New York: Farrar, Strauss and Young, 1953), esp. June-December 1941, 4, and 57.

Well before the invasion of Russia, the Germans devised a two-fold process of deportations. Initially the resettlement of hundreds of thousands of ethno-racial Germans on the eastern borderlands beyond Germany would accompany the deportation of a million people from those Polish territories immediately incorporated into the Reich. All planners, both military and nonmilitary, assumed the rapid and total defeat of the Soviet Union in another Blitzkrieg offensive. They casually envisioned the removal of between two-thirds and seven-eighths of the Poles, Russians, and Ukrainians, as well as the entire Jewish population. Many of these people were not to be expelled or enslaved but to be annihilated through starvation – what Christian Gerlach has called the "Hunger Plan."[51]

The population currently inhabiting that territory was thus in double deficit. Its racial inferiority threatened the purity of Aryan settlement. Its "useless mouths" threatened the nutritional health of German consumers. Both problems could be solved in two genocidal plans: the expulsion and subsequent destruction of European Jewry and upwards of 30 million Slavs. Altogether eleven million Jews were targeted, including, as Hitler told the grand mufti of Jerusalem in November 1941, "the destruction of the Jewish element residing in the Arab sphere under the protection of British power."[52] The most "realistic" German projections estimated the number of designated victims at 45 million people. Although there was ample need for servile Jewish workers as well, their fate was nested within an overall frame of reference that entailed deportation, starvation, sterilization, and mass murder, alongside coercion and exploitation. At moments of mass "selections" of Jews, the most skilled or able-bodied were at least temporarily preserved. The unprecedented rate of mortality in their ranks revealed a primary aim of destruction rather than economic exploitation. Of the more than 3 million Jews in Poland at the end of 1941, 90 percent were gone by the end of the following year. Ninety percent of those survivors were gone by the end of 1943.

During the initial invasion of the Soviet Union, Russians, too, were viewed through the lenses of extraneous consumption and racial excrescence. Of the 3.35 million prisoners of war captured by the Germans between June of 1941 and the opening of the second German offensive in 1942, only 167,000 captives, or 5 percent of the original cohort, were ever deployed as laborers.[53]

---

[51] Christian Gerlach, *Krieg, Ernährung, Völkermord: Forschungen zur deutschen Vernichtungspolitik im Zweiten Weltkrieg* (Berlin: 1998), 13–30.

[52] Browning, *Nazi Policy*, 23–24, 49–50; Tooze, *Wages of Destruction*, ch. 14; and Gerhard Weinberg, "The Allies and the Holocaust," in *The Holocaust and History: The Known, The Disputed, the Re-examined*," Michael Berenbaum and Abraham J. Peck, eds. (Bloomington, IN: Indiana University Press, 1998), 480–491, esp. 489. Even the increasing crisis of the labor supply in 1942–1944 never more than briefly interrupted the high priority of a total annihilation of European Jewry. (Ulrich Herbert, "Labour and Extermination: Economic Interest and the Primacy of *Weltanschauung* in National Socialism," *Past and Present*, 138 (1993), 144–195.

[53] Browning, *Nazi Policy*, 86, 257.

Even when German priorities shifted in favor of slave labor mobilization in the spring of 1942, the annihilation of the Jews accelerated. As Adam Tooze notes, whatever menial labor Jews might have been assigned to was overborne by racial aims: "The Holocaust must have claimed the lives of at least 2.4 million potential workers." The concentration camps added another 1.1 million wasted potential workers to the mortality rates, 800,000 of whom were non-Jews. All in all, adding the 2.4 million deaths of non-Jewish captives to the 2.4 million potential Jewish workers and Soviet POWs initially allowed to starve meant that nearly 7 million potential workers were lost to the German war economy. A state with a greater appetite for forced labor than all previous colonial systems in the Americas combined destroyed far more potential workers in four years than were lost in the Atlantic transit of Africans over the course of four centuries. The Nazi war machine deprived itself of more potential workers than were landed by transatlantic slavers during the peak century of the slave trade (1750–1850).[54] In addition to the tale told by mortality figures, every individual entrapped within this deadly vortex of racial and labor policies had to confront the regime's daily indifference to the value of their individual lives and well-being. A substantial proportion of Europe's population (Jews, Gypsies, and Poles) had no chance of altering their status. The same held true for most Russians, unless they were permitted to enter into military service under General Vlasov or other military formations. As laborers, they lacked any claim to legal protection concerning conditions of work and were unable to appeal to any public or private authority about their treatment. Their bodies were at the disposal of others. Jews and Gypsies have appropriately been characterized as less than slaves, because their SS holders had no interest whatsoever in their individual survival.[55]

In the last stages of the war, new work plans were developed to use servile labor to maximize weapons production. The combination of labor and mass killing reached its apogee during the final year of the war. In the spring of 1944, hundreds of thousands of Hungarian Jews were rounded up and consigned to the gas chambers and crematoria at Auschwitz. At the same time, the desperate labor shortage required a partial reversal of the policy of the previous two years. Jewish captives were once again imported

---

[54] Compare Tooze, *Wages of Destruction*, 522–523 and the Transatlantic Slave Database, second edition.

[55] See Spoerer "Forced Laborers," 173–74; and Benjamin B. Ferencz, *Less Than Slaves: Jewish Forced Labor and the Quest for Compensation* (Cambridge, MA: Harvard University Press, 1970). Beginning in 1942, Jews within the Reich were displaced by other groups of foreign laborers as soon as possible. (Michael Thad Allen, *The Business of Genocide: The SS, Slave Labor and the Concentration Camps* (Chapel Hill: University of North Carolina Press, 2002), 150–152). Just beyond the boundaries of the Reich itself, SS planners drew up plans for a permanent slave-labor complex at Auschwitz-Birkenau, surrounded by a complex of satellite plants for various production and agricultural projects.

as slave laborers into the Reich itself. Tens of thousands were shipped to high-priority armaments projects in Germany.

Within this ebb and flow of deportations, annihilations and enslavements Germany's coerced foreign labor, like its predecessors in the Atlantic system, conformed to some elementary principles of classical economics.[56] Forced-labor productivity remained far higher within the Reich than anywhere else in occupied Europe. To the very end, no leading member of the regime ever questioned the need for the ruthless recruitment of eastern workers. Nor was any doubt expressed about the Wehrmacht's evacuation of hundreds of thousands of Europeans during the course of their retreat from the East into the rapidly shrinking area of the Reich. Given the overwhelming recourse to coerced labor after 1941, questions were frequently raised as to how imported workers should be treated. Initially, the predominant consideration followed the assigned racial hierarchies predicated on Nazi ideology, modified for western POWs and the alignment of nationalities in favor or against the Nazi empire.

Initial orders reserving corporal punishment of foreign workers in German industry to the police and SS had to be modified by the need for on-site discipline and to prevent interruptions in the flow of production. A conference with Krupp managers assured them that no degree of coercion was too much and any German worker could act to enforce discipline, "when a Russian pig has to be beaten."[57] Coalminers were explicitly authorized to punish foreign laborers. Procedures still had to be negotiated between the SS and industrial managers. If the brutality of flogging demoralized the workers, the employer might request that the punishments be delivered off-site to prevent diminished productivity. As in other slave regimes, sexual exploitation was rampant. Eastern female workers had to service German camp commanders or their superiors to obtain bread on the black market in rations. Punishments included face-beating with nail-studded boards. Hosing down captives in cold weather before the assembled inmates could be used to enhance discipline.

Degrees of coercion varied with the task or tempo of the project. Toward the end of the war, an underground armaments installation was constructed at both record speed and human cost. The V-2 rocket factory was probably the only modern weapons system to inflict more death in its construction than in its use. Construction required 50,000 prisoners running in 72 hour shifts. Daily selections for work capability were made by a guard going up and down along rows of prisoners. He would slug each one before role call. Those able to remain standing were usable; "those who fell over were as good as dead." Absolute terror was added to discourage any hint of slackening pace. As project director Kammler put it, when prisoners were thought to be

---

[56] Tooze, *Wages of Destruction*, 518–528.
[57] Herbert, *Foreign Workers*, 322–323; Tooze, *Wages of Destruction*, 530.

malingering, I "let 30 hang in special treatment [*Sonderbhandlung*]. Since the hanging things proceed in a little better order."[58]

The division of labor reinforced the production interests of management and separated the desperate, "privileged" skilled laborers from the desperate, unprotected unskilled ones. For special projects, the division of labor combined efficient production and extermination through work. Prisoners doing skilled jobs were treated as valuable factors of production. They received extra rations and fewer beatings. Those forming the larger cohorts of unskilled bucket brigades or dirt movers by wheelbarrow were worked to exhaustion, dispatched without ceremony, and immediately replaced.[59]

In this sector of the economy and at this stage of the war, the most extreme propensities of the Nazi slave system moved to the fore. The principal advantage of the SS was that they were able to provide both industrial clients and their own camp facilities with a continuous flow of new inmates. SS supervisors carried out regular "selections," culling workers whose productive capacity fell below desired levels. Neither employers nor the political command structure had cause for complaint. A concentration camp labor force was not a stock of individuals slowly replenished at the margins but a rapid flow of interchangeable human beings. The task of the SS was not to supply individuals, but to maintain their aggregate flow.[60] In the desperate construction of "miracle weapons" factories that might "turn the tide" of the war, the scarcest variable was neither land, capital, nor labor, but time. As economic overlord Albert Speer observed, the crucial factor in building the underground V-2 installations was that the SS managers brought them to "completion out of their raw condition in the almost impossibly short period of two months." You have transformed them, he told the SS managers, "into a factory which has no European comparison and remains unsurpassed even in American conceptions."[61]

Among the larger mass of foreign laborers not working for "miracle" weapons, however, a Pavlovian compromise between ideology and pragmatism was necessary. Some managers instituted a system called "performance feeding." They divided Eastern laborers into a hierarchy of productivity. Those achieving an average level of performance received their meager full rations. Underperformers had deductions made from normal levels. The available food was divided in favor of workers calculated to provide the best return per calorie consumed. This form of selection through labor was a slower form of deterioration through labor.

---

[58] Hans Kammler, a manager, quoted in Allen, *Business of Genocide*, 225.

[59] Browning, *Nazi Policy*, 102.

[60] Tooze, *Wages of Destruction*, 533.

[61] Allen, *Business*, 223. This was just the "beautiful" outcome that Speer promised to "communicate to the Reichsführer SS Himmler" himself. (Speer to Hans Kammler, Dec. 17, 1943.)

However indifferent they were to the lives of individuals, the SS never considered them to be valueless. Negotiations between the SS and the I.G. Farben manager worked out arrangements at Auschwitz that placed members of the new workforce within the orbit of the League of Nation's 1926 Convention on Slavery – "a person over whom any of the powers attaching to the right of ownership are exercised." The right to rent bodies at fixed prices was implied in agreements both in Berlin and on site from the spring of 1941. The financial aspects were easily worked out: "a payment of RM 3 [marks] per day for unskilled workers and RM 4 per day for skilled workers is to be made for each inmate. This includes everything, such as transportation, food, etc., and we [I. G. Farben] will have no other expenses for the inmates, except if a small bonus (cigarettes, etc.) is given as an incentive." In the same agreement package, Himmler's SS-owned DESt Corporation, operating the Auschwitz sand and gravel pits, also set rates of delivery for bricks from SS-controlled factories. The bodies of the laborers were as completely at the disposal of the SS as were the sand and gravel and pits.[62]

Once the contract was in hand, the SS began to expand. Quarters designed for inmates, initially Soviet POWs, uncannily resembled those of a slave ship. Each "roost" was equal to the "space of a large coffin or the volume of a shallow grave." One latrine was provided for every 7,000 inmates, who, therefore, often waded through pools of feces. A durable pool of labor itself was built into the eastern invasion plan. Its author, geographer Konrad Meyer, emphasized that Germanization absolutely depended on capital projects requiring "labor gangs of prisoners of war and comparable foreign workers." Their abundance was to be fully utilized for a generation after victory. In the initial decade, it was envisioned that this slave labor force would number 450,000. A third Five Year Plan would use 300,000; a fourth, 150,000; a fifth, 90,000. Himmler foresaw a system in which most of the foundational work of reorganization would be borne by slaves assembled in large cantonments.[63]

The SS set a rental price of 5 Zloty per head for all leased workers. In industrial manufacturing, the balance between the fees paid to the SS by managers was apparently favorable to the employer. Even with all of the overhead costs of security and of replacing the disabled inmates by fresh stock, the captives apparently remained more profitable or accessible to use than noninmate labor – so profitable, in fact, that the government

---

[62] See Debórah Dwork and Robert Jan van Pelt, *Auschwitz 1270 to the Present* (New York: W. W. Norton, 1996), 208, 265–268.

[63] *Ibid.*, 308–309. For a summary of the Siemens' group use of coerced foreign labor and its notion that this would be durable institution, see Karl Heinz Roth, "Zwangsarbeit in Siemens-Konzern (1938–1945)," in Hermann Kainenburg, ed. *Konzentrationslager und deutsche Wirtschaft 1939–1945* (Opladen: Leske and Bushich, 1996) pp. 149–168. For conditions aboard slave ships see, inter alia, Marcus Rediker, *The Slave Ship: A Human History* (New York: Viking Press, 2007), ch. 9.

attempted to draw back some of the "surplus" profit. The Eastern worker system quickly expanded.

Overall, Eastern workers' productivity ranged between 60 and 100 percent of German norms. In worksites, where the threat of imminent execution was added to the usual incentives, slave labor output could even exceed German free-labor norms. Despite reductions in rations, Jewish laborers at one location fulfilled every German request by more than 100 percent. At times of extermination sweeps, Jews made extraordinary efforts to diminish their selection for death through intensified labor. How deeply this labor-life linkage was internalized was related by an observer in 1943. When an SS officer seized a three-year-old Jewish girl to deport her to a killing center, she pleaded for her life "by showing him her hands and explaining that she could work. In vain."[64]

As the rest of the foreign and forced-labor force expanded, its average productivity increased. As usual, the ending of the coerced foreign labor system did not flow from a diminishing productivity of labor either at the industrial workplace or on the farms of Germany. Whatever the overhead costs imposed upon managers by racial labor laws or by rapid turnover, the performance of captive Soviet workers also increased sharply in 1943 and remained high until the devastation by bombers in the summer of 1944.[65]

The collapse of the Nazi labor system in 1945 most obviously resulted from the convergence of the Allied military forces and the devastation of Germany's infrastructure. When the signs of collapse first appeared in the summer of 1944, the German government's response was to give highest priority to the armaments industry. To meet production requirements, discipline was, as we have seen, intensified. Even the great campaign to eliminate the Jewish presence in the Reich was reversed in the final year of the war. Of the 500,000 Jews deported from Hungary beginning in the spring of 1944, more than a quarter were not immediately destroyed in the selections at Auschwitz and elsewhere. The highest priority for their deployment was given to Kammler's underground building sites. Toward the war's end, slave labor became more crucial than ever to the military supply sector of the economy. By 1944, one third of the workforce in Wehrmacht armaments was foreign.[66]

The intensification of discipline and recruitment was in vain. From mid-1944, Allied bombing ensured a fall in armaments production. The decline in this most favored sector was reflected in the progressive collapse of Germany's economic structure. The system's end was primarily determined by external force. The system of forced labor endured until the Allied forces

[64] Raoul Hilberg, *The Destruction of the European Jews*, definitive edition, 3 vols. (New York: Holmes and Meier, 1985), vol. 2, 529; and Browning, *Nazi Policy*, 134.
[65] Herbert, *Foreign Workers*, 323; Tooze, *Wages of Destruction*, 537–538.
[66] Tooze, *Wages of Destruction*, 640.

met in Germany in April 1945. Until then, coerced European workers in Germany conformed very much to the pattern set by slaves in the Atlantic system. As in both the New and Old Worlds, most resistance took the form of individual action: malingering, stealing, trafficking, self-mutilation, and absconding. These individual acts of resistance were not usually interlinked and did not constitute a systemic threat to the Nazi system of deployment or discipline. Absenteeism and flight took the form of individual or small group actions against the constraints and brutality of the authorities.[67]

As the number of foreign workers in Germany increased, reports of missing workers were sufficient to create a new challenge to internal security. Toward the end of 1943, the number of missing workers reached a monthly plateau of about 45,000. The official tabulation of absentees, however, included "Western" voluntary workers who overstayed their entitled vacation period at home or failed to return to Germany. Herbert estimates that five out of every six of those departing workers were counted as fugitives. Eastern workers did not generally have the privilege of leaving their jobs for any purpose. For those from the distant Soviet Union, chances of successful flight and return home were especially slim. The greatest source of absentees was workers seeking to join other family members deployed elsewhere in the Reich, those attempting to flee air-raid zones, or those seeking to escape punishment by torture in the disciplinary "Labor Education Camps." The 500,000 recorded absentees per year impeded the smooth functioning of enterprises and, in the case of armaments, even slowed output. But they did not pose either a serious political threat to the Nazi regime or an economic threat to its organization of coerced labor.[68]

Because the system was formed in the context of a simultaneous assault on so many ethnic groups in Europe, the Nazis always feared that there might be politically organized uprisings by civilians or POWs. The menace of "Bolshevized" Soviet citizens in particular was cited to justify routinely brutal treatment of that group. The surrounding civilian population was also apparently concerned about a mass uprising. Until 1944, however, actual cases of organized foreign resistance were rare. The debilitating conditions of daily life and the apparatus of terror were apparently sufficient to discourage attempts at large-scale armed resistance. As with their African counterparts, ethnic differences and camp-structured racial hierarchies of nutrition and discipline also helped to discourage collective solidarity. No major wave of resistance, violent or passive, disrupted the growth of the coerced-labor system as it moved towards its numerical apogee. As late as the spring of 1944, groups identified as threats remained localized in their contacts.[69]

---

[67] Herbert, *Foreign Workers*, 326–328.
[68] *Ibid.*, 341–344.
[69] *Ibid.*, 351.

At the extreme, in the SS run camps, the slow starvation regimen served to reduce daily life to a question of elemental survival. As Primo Levi noted of Auschwitz, in the Lager each man was alone, and the struggle for life was "reduced to its primordial mechanism." The "saved" were those who found niches assuring a "normal ration." One avoided contact with the "drowned." The latter "had no secret method of organizing," even to remain alive, much less for collective action. Linkage with the powerful was more important than linkage with the powerless. Within the Reich, organized labor resistance remained on a very small scale and highly decentralized almost to the end. As David Geggus observed of earlier slave uprisings in the Caribbean, the principal determinant of modes and frequency of collective resistance was the political and military context. In the German camps, the "all-pervasive police apparatus of informers and terror" functioned best within a context in which few foreigners believed in the imminence of a German defeat.[70]

With the combined assaults of the Soviet Union in the East and the success of the Western powers in Italy and France in mid-1944, the Gestapo began to report the existence of organized resistance in most large cities of the Reich. Even after the reported rise of resistance organizations in the spring of 1944, only 2,700 activists out of millions of workers were identified and arrested. It is not clear whether or not the Gestapo underestimated collective threats by non-Slavic workers. Although Gestapo reports generally attributed a greater degree of politicization to Soviet workers, however, they never recommended curtailing their importation on security grounds. Foreign workers were also aware that small local uprisings did not and would not alter Nazi policy. As Christopher Browning notes, the Jewish uprising in the Warsaw Ghetto in April 1943, did shake Himmler. Its effect, however it was to reinforce his notion that a Jewish presence was the deadliest cause of subversion.[71] Their radical elimination, therefore, had to be accelerated. Eastern workers in Germany were probably generally aware of the deadly fate suffered by 200,000 Warsaw residents as a result of their uprising in August 1944. In the wake of its suppression, 600,000 deportees passed through a German selection before the end of the year.

Allied propaganda explicitly encouraged a policy of passive resistance and flight rather than armed challenge and revolution. Any attempts at mass collective action were deemed to be hazardous and futile. As the Allies closed in on Germany in September 1944, General Eisenhower addressed foreign workers in Germany by radio. He made no call for armed revolt. Instead, he advised foreign workers to escape their jobs as soon as possible, to boycott informers, and not to allow the Gestapo to "provoke you to unorganized action."[72] The threat of foreign workers may have had some destabilizing

[70] Primo Levi, *Survival in Auschwitz*, ch. 9, "The Drowned and the Saved," esp. 87–92.
[71] Browning, *Nazi Policy*, 82–83.
[72] Herbert, *Foreign Workers*, 351–357.

impact upon the slave labor system, but it also had a well-documented effect on the increasingly desperate security forces. They apparently decided to exact a heavy price upon those who still lay within their grasp. Death March redeployments and roadside executions produced no widespread sympathy or protest from the surrounding civilian Germany population. In the closing months of the war, there were no large-scale attempted uprisings by the Reich's foreign workers. German officials who regarded their Soviet workers both as primitives and innate revolutionaries saw their role as preempting uprisings among a population at once servile and politicized.

When a mass dispersion of workers did begin in the autumn of 1944, it resulted more from Allied bombings than Allied exhortations. Increasing numbers of homeless foreign workers, with no provisions or jobs, tried desperately to find refuge in the rubble of former cities. They hunted for sustenance in the face of an ever-diminishing food supply. In turn, the Gestapo hunted for escapees. Becoming as decentralized as their targets, German security forces dispensed summary executions on deserters and foreigners alike. It is impossible to estimate the number of executions during the final weeks of the war among the seven million non-German "aliens" on the move within the borders of a collapsing Germany.[73]

By May 1945, one of the largest and deadliest systems of annihilation, forced migration, and domination ever created by a Western state disintegrated along with the state itself. It had developed in the absence of any public sphere able to mitigate, much less challenge, a labor system that expanded at a blitzkrieg tempo between 1939 and 1944. The fact that there were no abolitionist voices in Nazi Germany is hardly surprising given the relation of its civil society to the state. Ameliorationist arguments for better nutrition or treatment within officialdom were invariably cast in productionist terms. They had to promise more efficient ways of contributing to higher productivity or to extracting more output per calorie or per person. Productionist rationales, even from Speer's office, always encountered strong countercurrents of resentment. Grass roots administrators resisted improving conditions for racial aliens. Gestapo reports recorded civilian hostility to on-site ameliorations that evolved in some workplaces. The more some managers attempted to increase the output of foreign workers based upon food-per-performance, the more intensely the security networks of guards, agents, and informers worked to uphold the principles of racial hierarchy.[74]

Gestapo summaries of German public sentiment noted that popular acceptance of the Eastern workers as subhuman *Untermenchen* was well entrenched in both the military and civilian sectors before the invasion of the Soviet Union. Thereafter, German security assessments noted widespread

---

[73] *Ibid.*, 381.
[74] Herbert, *Foreign Workers*, 205–231; Browning, *Nazi Policy*, 88; Allen, *Business of Genocide*, 15–16.

fear among Germans about the deployment of alien peoples within the Reich. Resentment increased in proportion to the hardships incurred from bombing raids in 1943 and 1944. Summary executions were deemed appropriate for "swamp dwellers from the East." Pressures to link better nutrition to performance were countered at the local level by camp personnel. They were supported by "a widespread opinion" that such pilfering of food was not a crime "since it is preferable for 'subhumans' to go hungry rather than Germans."[75]

The regime's leaders had not overestimated the memory of the hunger of the First World War. Security reports recorded public demands that any reduction in German rations be matched by further reductions in the already low rations for foreign workers. The slogan "Before Germany starved it would be the turn of other peoples," attributed to Hitler, was repeated throughout Germany. The same perspective induced Germans to exclude foreign laborers from air raid shelters and to allow them to go homeless in the wake of the ever-diminishing supply of shelter.[76]

Some comparisons may serve to place the role of German attitudes in perspective. Nazi policy towards foreign workers differed from some other large-scale racial programs because of its greater public impact upon the German population as a whole. For most of the war, the Reich tried to keep details of the mass murder of Europe's Jews semisecret from the German population. The official euphemisms for physical extermination bespoke an extreme reluctance to offer any public acknowledgement of the annihilation. Degrees of "knowing" and "not knowing" allowed Germans to filter out rumors according to individual conscience and taste.

Only during the final phase, during the long death marches of Jews inside Germany, did civilian indifference to the fate of victims fully reveal itself. Despite occasional acts of individual pity, Germans who witnessed the transits of the starving marchers more often jeered, threw stones, and participated in the slaughter of collapsing captives. Their guards had no difficulty in maintaining the prescribed racial distance. By that time, German indifference to Jewish suffering and death reinforced the general hostility and indifference to the fate of foreigners held responsible for German suffering. Non-Jewish foreign workers in Germany were not deported to isolated Gulag Camps. Imported into the Reich and ubiquitous in the everyday life of the population, these foreigners were deployed in every major city and throughout the countryside. They were housed in German neighborhoods and set to work in farms and factories alongside German farmers and workers. Long before the final encroachment of Allied armies, "it was the attitude of the German population which was decisive in determining whether the

---

[75] Herbert, *Foreign Workers*, 156, 320–326.
[76] Tooze, *Wages of Destruction*, 542–544.

program of foreign deployment would be a success in accordance with the wishes of the leadership."[77]

This was not just a matter of ancient hatreds. In many cases, the transformation of public attitudes was stark. In 1939, the *Sicherheitsdienst* (Security Service) saw its mission as reversing a "too favorable" attitude towards Polish laborers by the Roman Catholic clergy and a segment of the population. As early as 1940, the regime believed that it had succeeded in establishing a firm master-servant divide between German and Polish workers and among the German population in general. There were no serious protests against this racialization policy. The accelerated movement of Germans into the military and foreign civilians and POWs into the workforce reinforced the racial hierarchy by a functional assignment of unpleasant and menial jobs to foreigners. The influx of Soviet POWs in the early months of operation Barbarossa reinforced the trend toward racial contempt well before the Red Army turned the military tide decisively against the Wehrmacht. On the whole, Germans displayed little concern with the fate of foreigners and accepted the Reich's general allocation of lower status to the *Ostarbeiter* (*Eastern Workers*). Their designation as a group without rights became an accepted fact of everyday life. The accounts of police assessments of private sentiment registered a tacit German acceptance of national and racial inequality.[78]

The virtual absence of public protest against the prewar segregation and degradation of German Jewry, prior to the "Final Solution" was, in this respect at least, analogous to the statutory reduction of millions of foreign workers into slaves and "less-than-slaves." Within the various institutions of the German state, there was no extended discussion of the implications of the legislation that authorized the imposition of forced labor on entire national populations. The legal implicitly violated some of the international agreements governing slavery and forced labor. The implicit rejection of half a century's international conventions against slavery after the Brussels Act of 1890 is noteworthy. During World War I, the German government had debated the implications of its violation of international law when it undertook to deploy Belgian civilians in the Reich. Their deportation to Germany during the winter of 1916–1917 mobilized enough internal and international protest to force the policy's termination. When confronted by German public protest alone, however, the German military successfully maintained its

---

[77] Herbert, *Foreign* Workers, 394 (my emphasis). See also Daniel Goldhagen, *Hitler's Willing Executioners: Ordinary Germans and the Holocaust* (New York: Knopf, 1996), ch. 13 and 14.

[78] Herbert, *Foreign Workers*, 394–396. The systematic study of the gradual and then accelerated disenfranchisement of laborers was begun by Karl-Heinz Roth, "I. G. Auschwitz, Normalität oder Anomalie eines kapitalistischen Entwicklungssprunges?" in *Hamberger Stiftung zür Förderung von Wissenschaft und Kultur* (Hamburg: VSA – Verlag, 1991). My thanks to Karsten Voss for his historiographic research on this subject.

policies of coerced importation and forced labor in the East. It did so over both protests in the Reichstag and substantial resistance from the targeted population in Poland. It would appear that the widespread protest from neutral states (and a potentially belligerent United States) induced the Imperial government to discontinue the western European deportations. In the East, there was no western neutral mobilization on behalf of the Polish population before or after the Belgian agitation, despite the fact that roundups in Poland occasioned more violent resistance than they had in Belgium. Just as Europeans considered forced labor more appropriate to Africans than themselves in the early twentieth century, widespread German opinion considered forced labor more appropriate for eastern than western Europeans at the outbreak of the Great War in 1914.[79]

Even this boundary of relative immunity could shift quickly under the pressure of circumstances. During World War I, forced labor was less dramatically implemented in German-occupied France. So, it may well be that total military control, in the absence of a mobilized public or external pressure, was enough to ensure a successful imposition of coerced labor. As in the settlement of the Americas, it was ultimately the presence of external retaliatory power that prevented the reduction of some fellow Europeans to servitude. Without the mechanisms of public mobilization and oversight, moral condemnation of a system alone could not achieve the termination of new systems of bondage for European civilians.

A generation later, institutional agencies of internal public discussion no longer existed in Germany. Even among nonbelligerent states in Europe, the press, parliaments, and diplomatic corps of Sweden, Switzerland, Spain, and even the Vatican remained virtually silent about the development of the massive projects of deportation, coercion, and annihilation before the successful Soviet and Western offensives during the summer of 1944. The "tipping point" was best illustrated in the deportations, annihilations, and enslavement of Hungarian Jews. Reaction to the initial deportations of Jews from rural Hungary during the spring of 1944 was still silence.

Suddenly, protest burst forth against the second stage, intended to extend the "Final Solution" to the Hungarian capital in the summer and fall of 1944. Between these two reactions lay the stunning series of Soviet victories in the East and the successful Allied landing in France. Continental press campaigns against "phase two" began in late June 1944. By July, there were diplomatic protests by the Swiss, Swedish, Spanish, and Vatican legations in Budapest, reinforced by a threat of airborne retaliation from the United States. The interrupted final phase was never fully implemented before the Red Army seized the Hungarian capital in January 1945.

The development of Germany's coerced-labor system also allows us to reconsider the relation of race to slavery in comparative perspective. In

---

[79] Hull, *Absolute Destruction*, 236–242; Herbert, *Foreign Workers*, 20–24.

the creation of New World slavery codes, inherited civil law codes constituted the primary basis for defining relationships. Slavery was racialized and Africanized only slowly over the course of three centuries after 1450. In the case of Nazi Germany, racial differentiation defined potentially enslavable populations prior to successive German expansions. In two short years, between 1939 and 1941, the Nazi-German leadership designated groups potentially amounting to nearly half the population of Europe as eligible for coercion, deportation, and elimination. The recourse to coercion was often a pragmatic concession to the other two options.

In both hemispheres, from the late eighteenth to the early twentieth century, abolitionists, revolutionaries, and imperialists alike attacked slave systems in the face of a rising acceptance of color-coded racist ideologies. By contrast, the creators of Germany's European labor system did not operate in the context of expanding traditional customary practices. Nor did they assume that the world beyond their immediate power accepted their standards of enslavability. The Nazi leadership was quite revolutionary in this regard. They were self-defined innovators and managers of a policy that they alone had the will to create. They understood that their institutions of coerced labor and mass annihilation might cost them their lives.[80] In the eyes of their enemies, their vast labor complex had so little legitimacy that no Allied declaration or edict was deemed necessary to end it. Most of the former managers did their best to vanish. Most of the workers returned to their homes or entered displaced persons camps as soon as Allied troops appeared.

The immediate legacy of the German forced-labor system was its designation as a crime against humanity, a phrase already employed by abolitionists. Its longer-term legacy was to set a precedent for forced-labor reparations. At the Nuremberg war crimes trial of Fritz Sauckel, Hitler's "labor czar," the tribunal had no doubt that the majority of foreign workers brought to Germany had been treated as slaves. American Associate Justice Robert Jackson considered the mode of their deportation to be perhaps "the most horrible and expansive slavery operation in history." One of Sauckel's principal claims for exoneration was his claim that he had called Hitler's attention to the fact that civilian labor conscription violated international law. Sauckel's own directive on the status of the laborers followed the cost-benefit reasoning adopted by most German officials. It referred to the poor productivity of "underfed slaves, diseased, resentful, despairing and filled with hate."[81]

[80] Seymour Drescher, "The Atlantic Slave Trade and the Holocaust: A Comparative Analysis," in *From Slavery to Freedom: Comparative Studies in the Rise and Fall of Atlantic Slavery* (York: New York University Press, 1999), ch. 10.

[81] See Drexel A. Sprecher, *Inside the Nuremberg Trial: A Prosecutor's Comprehensive Account*, 2 vols. (Lanham, MD: University Press of America, 1999), I, 162; and Joseph E. Persico, *Nuremberg: Infamy on Trial*, (New York: Viking Press, 1994), 164. In the aftermath of the Nuremberg trials, German defenders of those convicted of "economic crimes" casually referred to "the slave labor program" and "alien slave workers." (See Dr. Helmuth

Asia and Africa

If the German coerced-labor system constituted one of the most dramatic instances of resurgent coerced labor in the second third of the twentieth century, it was far from alone. World War II produced analogous pressures for conscripted labor mobilization among other major combatants. In Asia and the islands of the Pacific Ocean, the Japanese government impressed millions of foreigners into labor service for indefinite periods of times. One of the most distinctive features of wartime coerced labor in Asia was the systematic conscription of women for sexual services. Under the rubric of "comfort women," the Japanese military extended the system throughout its burgeoning "East Asian Co-prosperity Sphere."

The comfort-station system expanded rapidly after the "rape" of Nanjing. Army commanders were less concerned about the violent degradation of the victims than by the potential impetus to resistance created by mass rape of the Chinese civilian population. Estimated numbers of women recruited for prostitution range from 80,000 to 200,000, of which perhaps 80 percent were Koreans. The remainder consisted of Taiwanese, Chinese, Filipinos, Indonesians, and Malaysians. Both recruitment and treatment appear to have been tiered by nationality. Koreans and Taiwanese, long under Japanese rule, were more proficient in Japanese language and culture. They were procured by the least violent means and reserved for higher military ranks. In occupied zones designated as hostile, women between the ages of 15 to 18 years were usually detained in military compounds for periods up to six months. Their condition most closely approached slave-like status, if only for limited periods.[82] A similar pattern was followed in the guerilla-disputed zones of the Philippines. The Japanese military resorted to abduction and captivity in garrisons for varying periods. The attitude of their liberators was generally less hostile to those coerced for sexual, rather than labor, services, and refracted by their prevailing racial perspectives. The United States occupation government rarely showed interest in pursuing the comfort-women system as a criminal activity. It did prosecute the operators of a military brothel that had forced Dutch women into sexual service in Indonesia and the Japanese who had run brothels on U.S. territory on Guam. In Japan itself, the United States government showed little inclination to prosecute any Japanese beyond the supreme military leadership.

Dix, *"The Judgments of the Nuremberg: German Views of the War Trials*, ed. Wilbourn E. Benton and Georg Grimm, eds. (Dallas: Southern Methodist University Press, 1955), 160–176, esp. 167. None of the contributors were concerned with distinguishing German foreign labor from slavery).

[82] Yuki Tavaka, *Japan's Comfort Women: Sexual Slavery and Prostitution during World War II and the U.S. Occupation* (London: Routledge, 2002).

Japanese forced labor projects, while less notorious, encompassed far more inhabitants of occupied areas throughout East and Southeast Asia. One survey of Japan's occupations places the total number of forced-labor survivors from China, the East Indies, Korea, Burma, and Thailand at 18 million. China alone accounted for two-thirds of that estimate. Hundreds of thousands of Koreans and Chinese were deported to Japanese coal mines. Similar numbers were deployed outside Japan, in Sakhalin and the South Pacific. Well over 100,000 people, including children, were conscripted for construction on railways in Burma and Java.[83]

Whereas the United States entered World War II with vast unused labor capacity as a legacy of the Great Depression, the demands for coerced labor that afflicted Germany, Japan, and the Soviet Union also had reverberations within the British Empire. Africa became a reservoir for both military and civilian mobilization on a large scale. Much of the new British army in Africa consisted of noncombatants drafted specifically for general military labor or related tasks. In Africa, the transition was less dramatic than elsewhere. Forced labor was still widely practiced throughout colonial Africa on the eve of the conflict, although in the British colonies it operated largely through customary law. Each colonial administration was, therefore, allowed leeway in maintaining its own employment practices. Although emergency legislation was passed at the outbreak of war, substantial sections of their domestic economy initially continued to operate on free-market lines.

Large-scale civil conscription for war-time production, however, especially for private enterprises, was a new departure. Civil conscription was first used in East Africa in 1940–1941, and spread to southern, western, and offshore colonies as the war intensified. Countervailing pressures often limited its implementation. The imperial decisions to allow forced labor in East Africa were severely criticized in the House of Commons in March 1942, especially the deployment of such workers on private European farms. Both Parliament and the colonial office continued to receive critical reports and insisted upon additional assurances of protection for this coerced labor force. In the tin mines in Nigeria, severe conditions for workers caused by poor housing, inadequate food, and medical services and, especially, evidence of high mortality, resulted in massive desertion and parliamentary demands for the termination of coercion. The government was obliged to respond to such demands by attempting to improving welfare and working conditions.

---

[83] Werner Gruhl, *Imperial Japan's World War Two 1931–1945* (New Brunswick, NJ: Transaction Publishers, 2007), 107–112 and 144, Table 9.2, "Allied Asian-Pacific War Severely Affected Casualties" and W. Donald Smith, *"Beyond The Bridge on the River Kwai: Labor Mobilization in the Greater East Asia Co-Prosperity Sphere,"* *International Labor and Working Class History*, 58 (2000), 219–238.

A second source of constraint was the potential of locally recruited workers to engage in community-supported evasion, desertion, or flight to other colonies or South Africa. On the other hand, fear of antagonizing European mine owners of vital military material sometimes ensured state capitulation to their requests for perpetuating compulsory labor beyond the emergency circumstances that had rationalized its introduction.[84]

In other imperial zones, the tradition of forced labor was already more widespread before the war. During the war, the practice was sanctioned by the Italian, Belgian, Portuguese, and French colonial regimes. It was French West Africa, however, that became the site of the most dramatic termination of West African forced labor at the end of the war. After the collapse of the Third Republic in 1940, the Vichy regime pursued forced colonial labor to unprecedented heights. The Gaullists, in turn, sustained the system when they assumed control of West Africa. The reconstitution of the metropolitan government in 1944–1945, offered a new opportunity for fundamental change. In October 1945, Africans, under a limited franchise, were invited to elect representatives to participate in drafting a new French constitution. In February 1946, a group of African delegates, led by Felix Houphët-Boigny from the Ivory Coast, seized the initiative in a resolution demanding the definitive end of the forced-labor system in Africa: "Millions of men (sic) have sent us here giving us a precise mandate to struggle with all our might to abolish the slavery which is still practiced in Black Africa by men, civil servants and civilians, who are traitors to France and to her noble civilizing mission." The antislavery rhetoric was followed shortly by a formal bill stating that "forced or obligatory labor is forbidden in the most absolute fashion in the overseas territories." The law was passed without debate by the metropolitan deputies.[85]

Behind the small African delegation that sponsored the motion was a large and vigorous overseas civil society. Before the resolution was moved, a two-month strike began in Dakar, French West Africa's leading port. French officials could only resolve the stoppage by treating the strikers as modern industrial workers. African planters themselves had formed a new network for recruiting labor outside the colonial planters' system, still dependent upon state-supported forced labor. African rural mobilization was the counterpart to the urban labor organization in Dakar. The emerging organization of African civil society helped dissipate the metropolitan rationale for

---

[84] David Killingray, "Labour Mobilisation in British Colonial Africa for the War Effort, 1939–46," in *Africa and the Second World War*, ed. David Killingray and Richard Rathbone, eds. (New York: St. Martin's Press, 1986), 68–96; and David Johnson, "Settler Farmers and Coerced African Labour in Southern Rhodesia, 1936–1946," *Journal of African History*, 13 (1) (1992), 111–128.

[85] Frederick Cooper, et al., *Beyond Slavery: Explorations of Race, Labor, and Citizenship in Post-emancipation Societies* (Chapel Hill: University of North Carolina Press, 2000) 137–138.

maintaining a different system of West African labor relations based upon the implicit hierarchy of civilization.[86]

The demand for equality in citizenship as members of the French empire, now renamed the French Union, came at a moment of deep change in the balance of "great powers." The Europe that emerged from the defeat of the Axis powers also affected western Europe's role in postwar antislavery. Like the restored French monarchy after the defeat of Napoleon, France's independence and its imperium were reinstituted by foreign armies. In a world whose balance of military power had moved to the bipolar domination of the Soviet Union and the United States, France desperately needed its overseas empire to give it standing as global player. Britain, too, long the principal supporter of international antislavery, emerged a weakened player on the international scene. The diminution of Britain's power at the onset of the Cold War with the Soviet Union, along with the extra-European mobilization of anti-colonialism, altered the parameters of the discussion of slavery.

In 1948, the Soviet Union's delegation was the first in the United Nations to move the condemnation of slavery, "in all its aspects," in the new Universal Declaration of Human Rights. The Soviets were suspected of taking the lead on the issue in retaliation for Western declarations against Russia's forced-labor system, now reaching its demographic apogee, and to discredit the moral position of the Arab governments allied with a British government just extricating itself from its Palestinian mandate. Both sides in the Cold War therefore had an interest in reaffirming the international antislavery consensus. In article 4, slavery became the first human condition to be specifically condemned as a violation of human rights. In the heavily politicized atmosphere of the United Nations, discussions of slavery easily spilled over into attacks on colonialism, racism, and apartheid. These could rationalize opposition from countries in which other forms of "slave-like conditions," as well as the communist Gulag, persisted.[87]

In its traditional mode the British government continued its pressure tactics but on a far lower key. Its worldwide influence was rapidly waning. Pockets of slavery in South Asian colonies made Britain vulnerable to the same charge of hypocrisy that had persisted against its antislavery posture for more than a century and a half. The traditional core targets of antislavery, the African slave trade and slavery in North Africa and the Middle East, were slowly eliminated or reduced in piecemeal fashion during the generation

---

[86] See Cooper, *Beyond Slavery*, 134–143 and Frederick Cooper, "The Senegalese General Strike of 1946 and the Labor Question in French Africa," *Canadian Journal of African Studies*, 24 (1990), 165–215. On the broader context of the convergence of African labor and independence movements, see Cooper, *Decolonization and African Society: The Labor Question in French and British Africa* (New York: Cambridge University Press, 1996), 65.

[87] Suzanne Miers, *Slavery in the Twentieth Century: The Evolution of a Global Problem* (New York: Rowman and Littlefield, 2003), ch. 18–21.

following World War II. Other changes in the Middle East also helped to impede antislavery action. The rush of oil wealth made for a brief revival of the slave trade and slavery both within and beyond the traditional British sphere of influence in the Arabian peninsula. It was only in the 1960s and 1970s that the "embarrassment of slavery" induced Saudi Arabia and the British protectorates in Yemen, Aden, Muscat, and Oman to promulgate decrees to abolish the institution without directly confronting issues of the *Shari'a* sanction of the institution. Oil wealth also made it far more feasible than ever before to substitute alternative forms of foreign labor for African slaves. By the 1970s, slavery had disappeared from the spectrum of legally sanctioned forms of service in Arabia.[88]

If postwar wealth briefly sustained slavery in Arabia, poverty and war sustained it far longer in Africa. The ultimate case was Mauritania, where slavery had been legally prohibited by the general French West African decree of 1905. In 1974, the world was jolted by the Mauritanian government's decree abolishing slavery, with a provision for future compensation. In 1980, the now Islamic Republic of Mauritania again outlawed chattel slavery, but the now skeptical Anti-Slavery Society identified its persistence four years later, when a new Mauritanian government requested economic assistance to complete the transition. Although Mauritania's constitution guaranteed all human rights, its courts, using *Shari'a* law, continued to recognize a master's rights to his former slave's service. Elsewhere in some Muslim-dominated states, the practices of marriage and concubinage, which had absorbed the energies of European colonial administrators for a century and a half, continued to preoccupy human rights groups, now more responsive than before to gender discrimination. In eastern and southern Africa, the increase of postcolonial armed conflicts triggered resurgences of chattel slavery in Sudan and southern Africa.[89]

For the most part, however, the diminution of the older forms of the intercontinental slave trade and the delegalization, if not abandonment, of chattel slavery in every part of the world stimulated increased attention to conditions of labor or gender relations that could be analogized to slavery or slave-like conditions. This was a phenomenon that emerged wherever the slave trade and slavery had already long since become objects of popular and legal condemnation. By the last quarter of the twentieth century, antislavery had become the gold standard of civilization throughout the planet. Almost two centuries before, the exploitation of children, labor, and women in early industrial Britain had begun to be linked to the popularization of the plight of overseas slaves. By the late twentieth century, institutionalized human rights groups, both governmental and nongovernmental organizations (NGO) wrestled over the implications of extending the term slavery to

[88] Miers, *Slavery*, ch. 20.
[89] *Ibid.*, 418–423.

analogous conditions: the exploitation of children for labor, pornographic and military service; coerced female marriage and commercial sexual service; female genital mutilation; debt bondage; trafficking in illegal migrants; and abuse of refugees; all slave-like practices already enumerated in the Slavery Conventions of 1926 and 1956.[90]

In this respect, the NGOs continued the extension of the concept of slavery to practices beyond the boundary of an institution once defined as the capture, sale, or use of individuals and their descendants legally placed at the disposition of other individuals, institutions, or rulers. If the ascription of slaves to the situation of these victims of coercion did not always alleviate them, it did lead to more attempts to locate them, count them, and come to their aid. As a consequence, newly designated forms of slavery have led to new global estimates of ten to thirty million exploited men, women, and children still entrapped in servile conditions for part or all of their lives. Incorporating all of these variants of exploitation, one might conclude that the cycles of slave-like coercion continue unabated after more than two centuries of popular mobilization, revolution, international legislation, and media exposure. One might draw solace, however, from the perspective that even by the expanded contemporary standards, there has been a massive shift in the proportion of humanity entrapped in servile institutions. Recall that on the eve of the age of revolution, writers routinely reckoned that nineteen of twenty inhabitants on the planet were unfree. One might take some solace from the estimates that those in slave-like bondage now account for less than one in a hundred. Against coercion, success is never final, but, at the beginning of the twenty-first century, slavery is, by millennial reckoning, again in retreat.

[90] Fact Sheet No. 14, *Contemporary Forms of Slavery*, (first published by the Office of the High Commissioner for Human Rights, Geneva, June 1991).

Cycles Actual and Counterfactual

During the past five centuries, slavery helped to transform the world while the world transformed slavery. When Europeans launched their seafaring explorations in the mid-fifteenth century, slavery existed in highly stratified societies on every continent. Most of its variants were separated from each other by great geographic and cultural differences. The two great landmasses of the earth, separated by oceans, were largely sealed off from large-scale exchanges with each other. The earliest reports of intercontinental travelers between them only reinforced the notion that there were large groups everywhere living in conditions of extreme vulnerability and domination. As late as the end of the eighteenth century, European geographers unfailingly identified people as enslaved in every great subdivision of the planet. Their enslavement flowed from varying proportions of war and captivity, birth, destitution, and criminal punishment. The institution's rationale also lay in this sense of universality.

By the late fifteenth century, some northwestern Europeans persistently noted the absence of such an institution in their own small corner of the earth. They identified this situation as an exceptional phenomenon, without immediate implications for the institution of slavery beyond their own realms. Individuals wandering outside of their zone of security understood all too well that they, too, were vulnerable to enslavement. Their own society's "freedom principle" appeared to be the result of a process rarely marked by great upheavals. Their peculiar "revolution" remained in the words of Adam Smith, "one of the most obscure points in modern history."

Europeans' sense of exceptionality in this regard was reinforced by massive intercontinental movements of human populations during three centuries after 1450. As the states bordering the Atlantic formed seafaring empires and accumulated extra-European dependencies, their imperial extensions became deeply enmeshed in the expansion of slave systems. European-sponsored colonies in the Atlantic and Indian Ocean worlds transformed slavery into one of the wealthiest economies on earth. Nowhere else were archipelagos of coerced migration converted into such efficient organizations of production. Nowhere else was such an abundance of commodities delivered over such long distances to such rapidly growing numbers of consumers. After two centuries of bitter rivalry, slaves were axiomatically deemed integral to the wealth and power of all the empires stretching across the Atlantic and into the Indian Ocean. Into the nineteenth century, Europeans and their rulers attempted to establish or develop new zones of slavery. European economic incentives to expand New World slavery were reinforced by their experiences in the Old World. Everywhere from West Africa to Japan and southward to the East Indies, Europeans encountered forms of slavery. They seamlessly integrated their own settlements, trading posts, and seafaring empires into these older slavery systems. Nowhere to the South or the East did Europeans encounter networks of labor or social systems that led them to question the sense that they had formed in their sixteenth-century explorations of the institution's ubiquity.

During the last quarter of the eighteenth century, slavery came under sustained collective attack for the first time. Europeans with the most acute sense of difference between their settlements at home and those "beyond the line" became pioneers in questioning one or another facet of the system. The very dichotomous structure of transoceanic European empires ultimately made the challenge a transcontinental one. Antislavery discourses and movements developed as countermovements, questioning both the expansion and morality of the institution. Those areas most closely linked to the economically dynamic and successful systems of slavery came under the earliest and most sustained ideological, social, and political assault. Moreover, as antislavery spread from one area to another, the institution showed no sign of faltering as a system, which could successfully compete with any alternative labor system that replaced it. Indeed, in one empire after another, the first sustained attack on slavery came at a point when the system was at the peak of its historic performance.

Therefore, the challenge of antislavery, whether violent or nonviolent, had to be formidable. The challengers ranged from Euro-American statesmen and intellectuals to affluent and poor individuals, men and women, free persons and slaves, descendants of Africans, Europeans, and the progeny of both groups. The development of antislavery was very uneven. Civil mobilizations were extensive in some areas, small in others, minuscule in most. Political mobilizations in different empires were rarely coordinated. The resistance to antislavery initiatives was also extensive. One of the nineteenth-century abolitionist's most cherished beliefs, slavery's natural inefficiency, was sadly misplaced. Agreements based upon the inherent economic inefficiency of slave labor were deeply flawed. A persistent pessimism among most slaveholders was reinforced by observations of the performance of post-emancipation economies for nearly a century.

The advances and setbacks of antislavery were rarely coordinated from one imperial zone to the next. Nevertheless, the first great cycle of challenge and response (the "age of revolution") redrew and more sharply defined the boundaries between slave and free soil. The first imperial orbits to experience the shock of antislavery challenges were the first to embed the principal of freedom in their regional and national myths – the English common law, the United States Declaration of Independence, the French Declaration of the Rights of Man and Citizen, and the constitutions of Spanish America. Memories of centuries of economic and political investment in slavery could be buried in stories of later political, military, or economic disinvestment.

The challenges entailed uneven mixtures of violence and nonviolence, and the outcomes were equally uneven. In Europe, Britain became the nation and the state most invested in sustained action against slavery beyond the formal boundaries of its own empire. Britain's abolitionist mobilizations against the slave trade affected every continent as early as the 1810s. Thereafter, British economic and naval power enabled it to successfully tighten international constraints against the Atlantic slave trade until the policy's successful conclusion in the 1860s. By then, the long campaign against the Indian Ocean trade was well underway.

On land in the Americas, the new Spanish and Anglo-American independent states successively began to prohibit the further importation of African slaves between 1807 and the 1860s. Because most New World plantation systems required continuous imports from Africa to sustain and increase their slave populations, the ending of that source doomed these systems to relative stagnation or decline. Terminations of the institution between the 1770s and the 1880s often occurred within the context of violent mobilizations for other purposes: wars between empires and nations or within empires and nations. In Latin America, only in Brazil did emancipation come without concomitant revolutionary, civil, or international violence. By coincidence, that last great abolitionist mobilization for emancipation in the Americas occurred exactly a century after the first great abolitionist mobilization in Europe.

The normative victory of antislavery was evidenced at the pinnacle of European overseas political domination. This surge of European imperialism unleashed in the 1880s was formally grounded in antislavery by international agreement. Slavery beyond the line of sovereign nations became the moral gateway to dominion, and antislavery became the gold standard of civilization. In their Eastern Hemispheric dominions, the imperial powers preferred to act against slavery outside the public sphere that had driven antislavery in Europe and the New World. When they moved to dismantle this form of slavery, however, they tended to move quickly only against the most disruptive aspects of the institution, such as slave raiding and public marketing. They approached the institution more cautiously and indirectly. In African and Asian societies, slaves were located at the centers of elite wealth and power, and within its intimate family spaces. Slaves were eunuchs and concubines as well as soldiers, officials and domestic servants as well as farmers and artisans. The institution of slavery was nested in societies with fewer networks of civil associations and political assemblies. The imperial powers displayed little desire to speed the growth of the autonomous civil and political organizations that had driven the most powerful antislavery movements in the Atlantic world. They certainly had no desire whatsoever to replicate the social risks of Western emancipations from below or the financial costs of compensated emancipations from above.

On the heels of the last great redistribution of European imperial territory following World War I came the League of Nations Slavery Convention in 1926. By the mid-1920s, slavery was relegated to ever-diminishing regions of Africa and Asia and to the list of ancient but vanishing scourges. The second quarter of the twentieth century, however, offered traumatic reminders that devastating forms of mass coerced labor could still reemerge anywhere, even on the continent that had first identified itself as the heartland of the freedom principle. It could be reinstitutionalized in contexts of both abundant and sparse populations. The creation of the Gulag demonstrated that extreme degradation and labor coercion could occur within a society pledged to the supremacy of labor and the empowerment of the working class. In Nazi Europe, of course, antislavery was held in contempt by a political system ideologically grounded in a radical repudiation of human equality. Europe's new rulers proclaimed slavery to be necessary for the achievement of their higher culture. For a brief moment, almost all of Europe was forced to supply bodies to the most rapidly developed slave empire in human history. Outside Europe, World War II also stimulated the expansion of coerced labor in large swaths of Afro-Asia.

Beyond the actual cycles of slavery one must also be mindful of the critical significance of antislavery and its achievements. In the absence of a globalizing agenda, the most successful assaults against slaving and slavery in any one place would have continued to be offset by compensatory expansions elsewhere. Indentured and free-wage laborers were usually a second or third best alternatives for those who wished to recruit labor for plantation economies. As David Eltis cogently argues with regard to the slave trade, an unrestricted transatlantic flow of coerced African migrants would have exceeded that of free Europeans for most of the nineteenth century. Millions more would have been added to the uprooted, traumatized, and lost in transit to the millions of Africans whose fate is already inscribed in the Transatlantic Slave Trade Database.

To the potential toll of an unrestricted Atlantic trade must be added still millions more had the closure of the "Eastern" slave trade also been postponed. Moreover, whatever the actual human costs of the Scramble for

Africa, imagine a world in which the floodgates of late nineteenth-century imperialism were thrown open before antislavery had become a hegemonic European norm. Then add what the "weapons revolution" and the cheap new means of transportation of the late nineteenth century would have wrought in that continent well into the twentieth century.

We can hardly ignore the potential toll of an intact institution in late nineteenth-century colonized Africa. Half a century's delay in the timing of New World slave emancipations would have had devastating global consequences in the twentieth century. Had the Southern Confederacy in the United States succeeded in departing from the Union, the probable costs to its own chattels would have compounded those enslaved elsewhere. The perpetuation of the largest slaveholding polity in the world would certainly have lessened pressures for rapid emancipation beyond North America. Even without an expansionist slave Confederacy, the remaining Latin American economies based upon racial slavery might easily have endured until well into the next century.

Only three generations after the abolitions of the transatlantic slave trade and U.S. slavery, Europe itself was reorganized on the basis of an institutionalized racial hierarchy. The program of its rulers axiomatically included the elimination and enslavability of inferior races. As it was, Germany was able to make a strong bid for the dominion of Eurasia. What impact might two major New World slave powers have had on the history of the twentieth century after the rise and expansion of a European state institutionally organized for mass enslavement and annihilation?

Estimating the possible impact of robust New World slaveholding societies on resurgent slavery in the Old World may allow for too many contingent outcomes to be counterfactually compelling. We can, however, at the very least hypothesize that the existence of major twentieth-century slave societies in the Americas, and perhaps in the Afro-Asian world as well, would hardly have diminished the growth of European racism during the half century of "high imperialism" between the 1880s and the 1930s. Any authoritarian hierarchical state that appeared in the Old World, whether in Europe, Africa, or the Far East, would certainly have attracted the attention and gained at least the benevolent neutrality of its counterparts in the Americas. There would have been far less of a free New World to call into existence to redress the wrongs of the Old World.

In this sense, the global achievements of antislavery a century ago left two indelible legacies. In the course of a century and a half (1770s–1920s), it destroyed or sharply restricted an institution, which had devastated and abbreviated the lives of tens of million of human beings in two hemispheres. By the mid-twentieth century, it succeeded in reasserting slavery's position at the top of the list of practices condemned in the Universal Declaration of Human Rights. For more than sixty years, reviving slavery has remained beyond the bounds of any contemporary movement's dreams or any state's ambition. Slavery rhetorically remains the evil of choice for any movement or government that seeks to mobilize sentiment against exploitative practices and coercive domination anywhere in the world. And, the story of slavery's reduction remains a model of comparative achievement for all who seek to expand the range of of human rights.

Index